Historical Linguistics

An Introduction

Historical Linguistics

An Introduction

SECOND EDITION

Lyle Campbell

The MIT Press
Cambridge, Massachusetts

First MIT Press edition, 1999.
Originally published in 1998 by Edinburgh University Press.

Library of Congress Cataloging-in-Publication Data

Campbell, Lyle.
    Historical linguistics : an introduction / Lyle Campbell.—2nd ed.
        p. cm.
    Includes bibliographical references and indexes.
    ISBN 0–262–53267–0 (alk. paper)
    1. Historical linguistics. I. Title
P140.C36 2004
417′.7—dc22
                                                2004042637

Typeset in Times by Pioneer Associates, Perthshire, and
printed and bound in Great Britain.

10 9 8 7 6 5 4 3 2 1

Contents

List of Tables ix
List of Figures and Maps xii
Preface xiii
Acknowledgements xvii
Phonetic Symbols and Conventions xix
Phonetic Symbols Chart xxi

1 Introduction 1
  1.1 Introduction 1
  1.2 What is Historical Linguistics About? 4
  1.3 Kinds of Linguistic Changes: An English Example 6
  1.4 Exercises 10

2 Sound Change 16
  2.1 Introduction 16
  2.2 Kinds of Sound Change 17
  2.3 Non-phonemic (Allophonic) Changes 19
  2.4 Phonemic Changes 20
  2.5 Sporadic Changes 27
  2.6 General Kinds of Sound Changes 27
  2.7 Kinds of Common Sound Changes 33
  2.8 Relative Chronology 46
  2.9 Chain Shifts 47
  2.10 Exercises 52

3 Borrowing 62
  3.1 Introduction 62
  3.2 What is a Loanword? 63
  3.3 Why do Languages Borrow from One Another? 64
  3.4 How do Words get Borrowed? 65

3.5	How do we Identify Loanwords and Determine the Direction of Borrowing?	69
3.6	Loans as Clues to Linguistic Changes in the Past	74
3.7	What Can Be Borrowed?	77
3.8	Cultural Inferences	82
3.9	Exercises	84

4 Analogical Change — 103
4.1	Introduction	103
4.2	Proportional Analogy	104
4.3	Analogical Levelling	106
4.4	Analogical Extension	108
4.5	The Relationship between Analogy and Sound Change	109
4.6	Analogical Models	111
4.7	Other Kinds of Analogy	113
4.8	Exercises	120

5 The Comparative Method and Linguistic Reconstruction — 122
5.1	Introduction	122
5.2	The Comparative Method Up Close and Personal	125
5.3	A Case Study	147
5.4	Indo-European and the Regularity of Sound Change	155
5.5	Basic Assumptions of the Comparative Method	164
5.6	How Realistic are Reconstructed Proto-languages?	166
5.7	Exercises	167

6 Linguistic Classification — 184
6.1	Introduction	184
6.2	The World's Language Families	184
6.3	Terminology	186
6.4	How to Draw Family Trees: Subgrouping	188
6.5	Glottochronology (Lexicostatistics)	200
6.6	Exercises	210

7 Models of Linguistic Change — 211
7.1	Introduction	211
7.2	The Family-tree Model	211
7.3	The Challenge from Dialectology and the 'Wave Theory'	212
7.4	Dialectology (Linguistic Geography, Dialect Geography)	215

7.5	A Framework for Investigating the Causes of Linguistic Change	218
7.6	Sociolinguistics and Language Change	219
7.7	The Issue of Lexical Diffusion	222
8	**Internal Reconstruction**	**225**
8.1	Introduction	225
8.2	Internal Reconstruction Illustrated	225
8.3	Relative Chronology	229
8.4	The Limitations of Internal Reconstruction	238
8.5	Internal Reconstruction and the Comparative Method	240
8.6	Exercises	242
9	**Semantic Change and Lexical Change**	**252**
9.1	Introduction	252
9.2	Traditional Considerations	254
9.3	Attempts to Explain Semantic Change	266
9.4	Other Kinds of Lexical Change – New Words	272
9.5	Exercises	280
10	**Syntactic Change**	**283**
10.1	Introduction	283
10.2	Mechanisms of Syntactic Change	283
10.3	Generative Approaches	289
10.4	Grammaticalization	292
10.5	Syntactic Reconstruction	297
10.6	Exercises	306
11	**Explaining Linguistic Change**	**312**
11.1	Introduction	312
11.2	Early Theories	313
11.3	Internal and External Causes	316
11.4	Interaction of Causal Factors	317
11.5	Explanation and Prediction	326
12	**Areal Linguistics**	**330**
12.1	Introduction	330
12.2	Defining the Concept	330
12.3	Examples of Linguistic Areas	331
12.4	How to Determine Linguistic Areas	338
12.5	Implications of Areal Linguistics for Linguistic Reconstruction and Subgrouping	340

Contents

12.6   Areal Linguistics and Proposals of Distant
Genetic Relationship   342

13 Distant Genetic Relationship   344
13.1   Introduction   344
13.2   Lexical Comparison   347
13.3   Sound Correspondences   348
13.4   Grammatical Evidence   350
13.5   Borrowing   352
13.6   Semantic Constraints   353
13.7   Onomatopoeia   353
13.8   Nursery Forms   354
13.9   Short Forms and Unmatched Segments   355
13.10 Chance Similarities   355
13.11 Sound–Meaning Isomorphism   356
13.12 Only Linguistic Evidence   356
13.13 Erroneous Morphological Analysis   357
13.14 Non-cognates   357
13.15 Spurious Forms   359
13.16 Methodological Wrap-up   359

14 Philology: The Role of Written Records   361
14.1   Introduction   361
14.2   Philology   361
14.3   Examples of What Philology Can Contribute   362
14.4   The Role of Writing   367
14.5   Getting Historical Linguistic Information for
Written Sources   369
14.6   Exercises   373

15 Linguistic Prehistory   378
15.1   Introduction   378
15.2   Indo-European Linguistic Prehistory   379
15.3   The Methods of Linguistic Prehistory   393
15.4   Limitations and Cautions   418

Bibliography   421
Language Index   436
Name Index   442
Subject Index   444

List of Tables

—

Table 2.1   Sanskrit–Latin cognates showing Sanskrit merger
 of *e, o, a > a*   21

Table 2.2   Historical derivation of 'mouse', 'mice', 'foot', 'feet'   23

Table 2.3   Grassmann's Law and its interaction with other
 Greek changes   31

Table 2.4   Grimm's Law in English, Spanish and French
 comparisons   50

Table 4.1   Latin rhotacism and the interaction of analogy with
 sound change   110

Table 5.1   Some Romance cognate sets   125

Table 5.2   Kaqchikel–English comparisons   128

Table 5.3   Some additional Romance cognate sets   136

Table 5.4   Further Romance cognate sets   138

Table 5.5   Some Mayan cognate sets   139

Table 5.6   Central Algonquian sound correspondences and
 Bloomfield's reconstruction   141

Table 5.7   Nootkan correspondences involving nasals   146

Table 5.8   Some Finno-Ugric cognate sets   148

Table 5.9   Indo-European cognates reflecting Grimm's Law   156

Table 5.10   Exceptions to Grimm's Law in consonant clusters   160

Table 5.11   Examples illustrating Verner's Law   162

Table 5.12   Examples contrasting the effects of Grimm's Law
 and Verner's Law on medial consonants   163

Table 5.13   Verner's Law in grammatical alternations   163

List of Tables

Table 6.1   Distribution of language families in the world   184
Table 6.2   Some of the better-known language families   185
Table 6.3   Some Nootkan sound correspondences   199

Table 8.1   Internal reconstruction and derivation of Tojolabal *k-*   228
Table 8.2   Internal reconstruction and derivation of Nahuatl
      roots with initial *i*   229
Table 8.3   Finnish internal reconstruction   230
Table 8.4   Derivation showing Finnish relative chronology   231
Table 8.5   Hypothetical derivation of Finnish with the
      wrong relative chronology   231
Table 8.6   Derivation showing loss of intervocalic *s* in
      Classical Greek   232
Table 8.7   Derivation showing *t* to *s* before *i* in Classical Greek   233
Table 8.8   Hypothetical derivation showing wrong
      chronological order in Classical Greek   233
Table 8.9   Derivation showing the correct chronological order
      in Classical Greek   233
Table 8.10   Derivation for Hypothesis I for Classical Greek
      'vein'   235
Table 8.11   Derivation for Hypothesis II for Classical Greek
      'vein'   235
Table 8.12   Derivation of *$*ait^h iop$-* 'Ethiopian' in Hypothesis II   236
Table 8.13   Internal reconstruction of Classical Greek
      'nominative singular' forms   237
Table 8.14   Historical derivation of 'mouse', 'mice', 'goose',
      'geese'   240
Table 8.15   Comparison of Balto-Finnic 'leg' forms after
      internal reconstruction   242
Table 8.16   Comparison of Balto-Finnic 'leg' forms before
      internal reconstruction   242

Table 10.1   Derivation of *whom* in Grammar$_1$ 289
Table 10.2   Derivation of *who(m)* in Grammar$_{1'}$ 290
Table 10.3   Derivation of *who* in Grammar$_2$ 290
Table 10.4   Balto-Finnic comparative verbal morphology   302
Table 10.5   Comparison of Balto-Finnic 'with' forms   303

Table 11.1   Estonian verb forms after certain sound changes   319

Table 12.1   Nootkan sound correspondences   341

List of Tables

Table 13.1 Forms of the verb 'to be' in some Indo-European
           languages   351

Table 14.1 Contrastive *h* and *x* in Classical Yucatec Maya   363
Table 14.2 The origin of Huastec labialized velars   364

List of Figures and Maps

—

Figure 2.1 The Great Vowel Shift in English   52

Figure 5.1 Proto-Romance family tree (and genealogy of
            Spanish)   124

Figure 6.1 The Indo-European family tree   190
Figure 6.2 The Uralic family tree   192
Figure 6.3 The Austronesian family tree   193
Figure 6.4 Mayan Subgrouping   194

Map 3.1   Diffusion of the velar palatalization rule in   80
            K'ichean languages

Map 7.1   Geographical distribution of words which retained
            /k/ in areas of Normandy   214
Map 7.2   Some major dialect areas in the USA   216

Map 11.1   Distribution of the names for 'rooster' in the
            southwest of France   323

Map 15.1   The Uralic languages   395
Map 15.2   The Uto-Aztecan homeland   403
Map 15.3   Distribution of place names of Scandinavian origin
            in England   416

Preface

—

A number of historical linguistics textbooks exist, but this one is different. Most others talk *about* historical linguistics; they may illustrate concepts and describe methods, and perhaps discuss theoretical issues, but they do not focus on how *to do* historical linguistics. A major goal of this book is to present an accessible, hands-on introduction to historical linguistics which does not just talk about the topics, but shows how to apply the procedures, how to think about the issues and, in general, how to do what historical linguists do. To this end, this text contains abundant examples and exercises to which students can apply the principles and procedures in order to learn for themselves how to 'do' historical linguistics. This text differs also by integrating topics now generally considered important to the field but which are often lacking in other historical linguistics textbooks; these include syntactic change, grammaticalization, sociolinguistic contributions to linguistic change, distant genetic relationships (how to show that languages are related), areal linguistics and linguistic prehistory. Also, the range of examples is greater and the number of languages from which examples are presented is much broader. Many examples are selected from the history of English, French, German and Spanish to make the concepts which they illustrate more accessible, since these are languages with which more students have some acquaintance, but examples from many non-Indo-European languages are also presented; these show the depth and richness of the various concepts and methods, and sometimes provide clearer cases than those available in the better-known Indo-European languages. In short, this text differs in its emphasis on accessibility, its 'how-to' orientation, its range of languages and examples, and its inclusion of certain essential but neglected topics.

Preface

This book is intended as an introductory textbook for historical linguistics courses, and assumes only that readers will have had an introduction to linguistics. It is hoped that linguists in general and others interested in language-related matters will also find things of interest to them in this book, though it is primarily intended for students of historical linguistics who have little background.

Historical linguistic practice today is linked with theories of general linguistics, particularly with regard to attempts to explain 'why' language changes. In this book, an attempt is made to keep to a minimum the complications for understanding and applying historical linguistics that diverse current theories often occasion. At the same time, however, basic linguistic terminology is employed with little explanation. Readers who have had some prior introduction to linguistics will fare better; in particular, some familiarity with phonetic symbols may be useful. (The symbols of the International Phonetic Alphabet are used in this text; see Chart 1 for a list of these and other symbols utilized in this book.) However, even without getting bogged down in theoretical details, phonetic notation or the mass of general linguistic terms utilised in talking about language, one can understand much of historical linguistics. For more detail on the topics covered here, the references cited throughout the book and the sources given in the general bibliography at the end, which contains references to most of the general works on historical linguistics, can be consulted.

Readers will perhaps notice a recurring struggle in the text. I believe it is important for students to have some sense of the general thinking concerning the various topics discussed, and to this end I occasionally mention how matters are typically presented in other textbooks or how they are generally seen by practising historical linguists. At the same time, I personally do not necessarily accept everything that is talked about and so feel some obligation to argue for what (I hope) is a better understanding of some topics. In such instances, I have attempted to present a reasonably unbiased account of opposing opinions. It is important for students to understand how historical linguists think and the sorts of arguments and evidence that would be necessary to resolve such issues. Ultimately, most of these involve areas where the differences of opinion can be decided only on the basis of substantive evidence which is not currently available but is hoped for from future research. Seeing the various sides of these issues should provide a basis for students to reach their own conclusions when the evidence becomes available, although it is not appropriate or possible in an introductory text to go into intricate detail concerning controversies and unresolved issues of the field.

A second struggle concerns the question of how to present complex notions. Definition and description without examples is usually not clear, but examples with no prior understanding of the concepts involved are also not clear. So, what should be presented first, context-less definitions or contextless examples? I have chosen to present first the concepts and then the examples to illustrate them. In several cases in the text, it will prove most valuable for clarity's sake to read the definitions, description and discussion, then the examples, and then to reread the general description and discussion – this may be true of anything, but is especially relevant in some contexts here.

Acknowledgements

I thank Alice C. Harris, Brian Joseph and Roger Lass for extremely helpful comments on a manuscript version of this book, and Raimo Anttila, William Bright, Una Canger, Antony Deverson, Adrienne Lehrer, Heidi Quinn, Seija Tiisala and Sarah Thomason for their help and answers to questions pertaining to specific sections. I also thank the several scholars who answered questions or offered helpful information, comments or corrections which helped in the preparation of this second edition, especially Rich Alderson, Cynthia Allen, Andrew Carstairs-McCarthy, Tony Deverson, Jaan Terje Faarlund, Andrew Garrett, Russell Gray, Verónica Grondona, Laszlo Honti, Jay Jasanoff, Johanna Laakso, Yaron Matras, Elisabeth Norcliffe, Victor Parker, Heidi Quinn, Don Ringe, Malcolm Ross, Tapani Salminen, Pekka Sammallahti, Brent Vine and Michael Weiss, among several others. It goes without saying that none of these friends and scholars is responsible for any misuse or disregard of some of their comments and information. (Not all their recommendations could be implemented, due in part to limitations of space, sometimes to competing recommendations they made, and at times to my own difference of opinion.) I am extremely grateful to these scholars for their input.

I thank Tim Nolan, of Black Ant Productions, for making the maps.

Also, two basic references have been employed extensively in examples cited in this book. For Indo-European forms, I have relied primarily on Calvert Watkins' *The American Heritage Dictionary of Indo-European Roots* (2000). This has the advantage of being consistent and a readily available basic reference, for comparison. It does not, however, represent the Indo-European laryngeals directly in the main entries. (Mallory and Adams *Encyclopedia of Indo-European* (1997) can be consulted to see the forms with the laryngeals present.) For the history of words in English, I have used the *Oxford English Dictionary* (Oxford University Press, 1989) extensively.

Phonetic Symbols and Conventions

———

The conventions for presenting examples used in this book are widely utilized in linguistics, but it will be helpful to state the more important of these for readers unfamiliar with them.

Most linguistic examples are given in italics and their glosses (translations into English) are presented in single quotes, for example: Finnish *rengas* 'ring'.

In instances where it is necessary to make the phonetic form clear, the phonetic representation is presented in square brackets ([ ]), for example: [sĩŋ] 'sing'. In instances where it is relevant to specify the phonemic representation, this is given between slashed lines (//), for example: German *Bett* /bɛt/ 'bed'.

Double slashes (// //) are used for dictionary forms (or underlying representations).

The convention of angled brackets (< >) is utilised to show that the form is given just as it was written in the original source from which it is cited, for example: German <Bett> 'bed'.

A hyphen (-) is used to show the separation of morphemes in a word, as in *jump-ing* for English *jumping*. Occasionally, a plus sign (+) is used to show a morpheme boundary in a context where it is necessary to show more explicitly the pieces which some example is composed of.

It is standard practice to use an asterisk (*) to represent reconstructed forms, as for example Proto-Indo-European **pətér* or **ph₂tér* 'father'.

A convention in this text (not a general one in linguistics) is the use of ✗ to represent ungrammatical or non-occurring forms. Outside of historical linguistics, an asterisk is used to indicate ungrammatical and non-occurring forms; but since in historical linguistic contexts an asterisk signals reconstructed forms, to avoid confusion ✗ is used here for ungrammatical or non-occurring forms.

It is standard in historical linguistics to use > to mean 'changed into', for example: *p > b (original p changed into b), and < to mean 'changed from, comes from', for example: b < *p (b comes from original p).

To show an environment where something occurs, the notation of / __ is used, where __ indicates the location of the material that changes, much as in the idea of 'fill in the blank'. Thus, a change in which p became b between vowels is represented as: p > b / V__V. A change conditioned by something in the context before the segment which changes is represented as, for example, in: k > č / __ i (meaning k became č [IPA [tʃ]] in the environment before i). A change conditioned by something in the environment after the segment which changes is represented as, for example, in: k > č / i __ (meaning k became č in the environment after i). The symbol # means 'word boundary', so that / __ # means 'word-finally' and / # __ means 'word-initially'.

To avoid notational (and theoretical) complications, when whole classes of sounds change or when only a single phonetic feature of a sound or class of sounds changes, sometimes just individual phonetic attributes are mentioned, for example: *stops > voiced*, meaning 'all the stop consonants change by becoming voiced'. Distinctive feature notation and other theoretical apparatus are not used in this text in order to make the examples more accessible to readers who have less background.

Finally, there are traditions of scholarship in the study of different languages and language families which differ significantly from one another with respect to the phonetic notation that they use. For example, vowel length is represented by a 'macron' over the vowel in some (as for example, [ā]), as a colon (or raised dot) after the vowel in others (as [a:]), and as a repetition of the vowel in still others (as [aa]). In this book, for the presentation of some of the examples cited, some of these different notational conventions commonly used for the various languages involved have been kept, though in cases where difficulty of interpretation might result, forms are also given in IPA symbols.

Phonetic Symbols Chart

	Bilabial	Labiodental	Dental	Alveolar	Palato-alveolar	Retroflex	Palatal	Velar	Uvular	Pharyngeal	Glottal
Voiceless stops	p			t		ʈ		k	q		ʔ
Voiced stops	b			d				g	ɢ		
Voiceless affricates				ts	č						
Voiced affricates				dz	ǰ						
Voiceless fricatives	ɸ	f	θ	s	ʃ	ʂ	ç	x	χ	ħ	h
Voiced fricatives	β	v	ð	z	ʒ	ʐ		ɣ	ʁ	ʕ	
Nasals	m			n		ɳ	ɲ	ŋ	ɴ		
Approximants	w			ɹ			j		ʀ		
Laterals				l							

	Front		Central		Back
High					
close (tense)	i	y	ɨ	ʉ	u
open (lax)	ɪ	ʏ			ʊ
Mid					
close (tense)	e	ø	ə		o
open (lax)	ɛ	œ			ɔ
Low	æ		a		ɑ

Phonetic Symbols Chart

Cʰ	aspirated consonant
C̤	dental consonant
C'	glottalized consonant
Cʷ	labialized consonant
Cʲ	palatalized consonant
V̥, C̥	voiceless sound
tl	voiceless lateral affricate
ɫ	velarised or pharyngealized lateral approximant
l̥	voiceless lateral approximant (sometimes symbolised as ɫ)
ɓ	voiced imploded bilabial stop
s̩	voiceless apical alveolar fricative
š̬	voiceless laminal retroflex fricative
č	voiceless laminal retroflex affricate
ć	voiceless prepalatal affricate (IPA [tɕ])
r (or r̃)	voiced alveolar trill
ſ	voiced alveolar flap (tap)
lʲ, lʸ	voiced palatalized alveolar lateral approximant, palatal "l" (IPA [ʎ])
ḥ	voiceless pharyngeal fricative (used in Arabic sources)
ḍ, ṭ, ṣ	pharyngealized consonants (as in Arabic)
C̣	retroflex consonants as represented in Sanskrit, South Asian and Native American sources
i̯	voiced high front semivowel (second vowel in some diphthongs, not the nucleus of the syllable)
ʍ	voiceless rounded labiovelar approximant or fricative (devoiced w)
Ṽ, V̨	nasalized vowel
V:, V̄	long vowel (vowel length)
C:	long consonant (geminate consonant)
ñ, nʲ	palatalized alveolar nasal, palatal nasal (IPA [ɲ])
x̟	fronted velar fricative
ṇ	symbol for retroflex nasal used in Sanskrit sources
ń	palato-alveolar nasal (Sanskrit)
ś	voiceless palato-alveolar fricative (used in Sanskrit sources) (IPA [ʃ])
ś	voiceless prepalatal fricative (IPA [ɕ])
ç	voiceless alveo-palatal fricative
ʐ	voiced alveo-palatal fricative
*k̂, *ĝ, *ĝh	"palatal" stops in Indo-European

Note that usually no distinction is made between [a] and [ɑ], and *a* is used to symbolize both.

1

Introduction

3e [ye] knowe ek [also] that in [the] fourme [form] of speche
    [speech] is chaunge [change],
With-inne [within] a thousand 3eer [years], and wordes tho [then]
That hadden [had] pris [value], now wonder [wonderfully]
    nyce [stupid] and straunge [strange, foreign]
Us thenketh hem [we think them/they seem to us]; and 3et [yet] thei
    [they] spake [spoke] hem [them] so,
And spedde [succeeded] as wel [well] in loue [love] as men now do.

(Geoffrey Chaucer [1340–1400],
Troilus and Criseyde, book II, lines 22–6)

1.1 Introduction

What is historical linguistics? Historical linguists study language
change. If you were to ask practising historical linguists why they study
change in language, they would give you lots of different reasons, but
certainly included in their answers would be that it is fun, exciting and
intellectually engaging, that it involves some of the hottest topics in
linguistics, and that it has important contributions to make to linguistic
theory and to the understanding of human nature. There are many reasons
why historical linguists feel this way about their field. For one, a grasp
of the ways in which languages can change provides the student with a
much better understanding of language in general, of how languages
work, how their pieces fit together, and in general what makes them
tick. For another, historical linguistic methods have been looked to for
models of rigor and excellence in other fields. Historical linguistic
findings have been utilized to solve historical problems of concern to
society which extend far beyond linguistics (see Chapter 15). Those

1

dedicated to the humanistic study of individual languages would find their fields much impoverished without the richness provided by historical insights into the development of these languages – just imagine the study of any area of non-modern literature in French, German, Italian, Spanish or other languages without insights into how these languages have changed. A very important reason why historical linguists study language change and are excited about their field is because historical linguistics contributes significantly to other sub-areas of linguistics and to linguistic theory. For example, human cognition and the human capacity for language learning are central research interests in linguistics, and historical linguistics contributes significantly to this goal. As we determine more accurately what can change and what cannot change in a language, and what the permitted versus impossible ways are in which languages can change, we contribute significantly to the understanding of universal grammar, language typology and human cognition in general – fundamental to understanding our very humanity.

More linguists list historical linguistics as one of their areas of specialization (not necessarily their first or primary area of expertise) than any other subfield of linguistics (with the possible exception of sociolinguistics). That is, it is clear that there are many practising historical linguists, though this may seem to be in contrast to the perception one might get from a look at the lists of required courses in linguistics programmes, from the titles of papers at many professional linguistic conferences, and from the tables of contents of most linguistics journals; nevertheless, historical linguistics is a major, thriving area of linguistics, as well it should be, given the role it has played and continues to play in contributing towards the primary goals of linguistics in general.

1.1.1   What historical linguistics isn't

Let's begin by clearing away some possible misconceptions, by considering a few things that historical linguistics is *not* about, though sometimes some non-linguists think it is. Historical linguistics is not concerned with the *history of linguistics*, though historical linguistics has played an important role in the development of linguistics – being the main kind of linguistics practised in the nineteenth century – and indeed historical linguistic notions had a monumental impact in the humanities and social sciences, far beyond just linguistics. For example, the development of the comparative method (see Chapter 5) is heralded as one of the major intellectual achievements of the nineteenth century.

Another topic not generally considered to be properly part of historical linguistics is the ultimate *origin of human language* and how it may have evolved from non-human primate call systems, gestures, or whatever, to have the properties we now associate with human languages in general. Many hypotheses abound, but it is very difficult to gain solid footing in this area. Historical linguistic theory and methods are very relevant for research here, and can provide checks and balances in this field where speculation often far exceeds substantive findings, but this is not a primary concern of historical linguistics itself.

Finally, historical linguistics is also not about determining or preserving pure, 'correct' forms of language or attempting to prevent change. The popular attitude towards change in language is resoundingly negative. The changes are often seen as corruption, decay, degeneration, deterioration, as due to laziness or slovenliness, as a threat to education, morality and even to national security. We read laments in letters to newspapers stating that our language is being destroyed, deformed and reduced to an almost unrecognizable remnant of its former and rightful glory. These are of course not new sentiments; laments like this are found throughout history. For example, even from Jakob and Wilhelm Grimm (1854: iii), of fairytale fame and founding figures in historical linguistics, we read:

> The farther back in time one can climb, the more beautiful and more perfect he finds the form of language, [while] the closer he comes to its present form, the more painful it is to him to find the power and adroitness of the language in decline and decay.

The complaint has even spawned poetry:

> Coin brassy words at will, debase the coinage;
> We're in an if-you-cannot-lick-them-join age,
> A slovenliness provides its own excuse age,
> Where usage overnight condones misusage,
> Farewell, farewell to my beloved language,
> Once English, now a vile orangutanguage.
>
> (Ogden Nash,
> *Laments for a Dying Language*, 1962)

However, change in language is inevitable, and this makes complaints against language change both futile and silly. All languages change all the time (except dead ones). Language change is just a fact of life; it cannot be prevented or avoided. All the worries and fears notwithstanding, life always goes on with no obvious ill-effects in spite of linguistic change. Indeed, the changes going on today which so distress some in our society are exactly the same in kind and character as many past changes about which there was much complaint and worry as they were taking place but the results of which today are considered enriching aspects of the modern language. The beauty (or lack thereof) that comes from linguistic change may be in the eye (better said, in the ear) of the beholder, but language change is not really good or bad; mostly it just is. Since it is always taking place, those who oppose ongoing changes would do their stress-levels well just to make peace with the inevitability of language change. Of course, society can assign negative or positive value to things in language (be they new changing ones or old ones), and this can have an impact on how or whether these things change. This sociolinguistic conditioning of change is an important part of historical linguistics (see Chapters 7 and 11).

1.2   What is Historical Linguistics About?

As already mentioned, historical linguistics deals with language change. Historical linguistics is sometimes called *diachronic* linguistics (from Greek *dia-* 'through' + *chronos* 'time'+ -*ic*), since historical linguists are concerned with change in language or languages over time. This is contrasted with *synchronic* linguistics, which deals with a language at a single point in time; for example, linguists may attempt to write a grammar of present-day English as spoken in some particular speech community, and that would be a synchronic grammar. Similarly, a grammar written of Old English intended to represent a single point in time would also be a synchronic grammar. There are various ways to study language *diachronically*. For example, historical linguists may study changes in the history of a single language, for instance the changes from Old English to Modern English, or between Old French and Modern French, to mention just two examples. Modern English is very different from Old English, as is Modern French from Old French. Often the study of the history of a single language is called *philology*, for example English philology, French philology, Hispanic philology and so on. (The term *philology* has several other senses as well; see Chapter 14.)

The historical linguist may also study changes revealed in the comparison of related languages, often called *comparative* linguistics. We say that languages are related to one another when they descend from (are derived from) a single original language, a common ancestor: for example, the modern Romance languages (which include Italian, French, Spanish, Portuguese and others) descend from earlier Latin (see Chapters 5 and 6).

In the past, many had thought that the principal domain of historical linguistics was the study of 'how' languages change, believing that answers to the question of 'why' they change were too inaccessible. However, since the 1960s or so, great strides have been achieved also in understanding 'why' languages change (see Chapter 11). Today, we can say that historical linguistics is dedicated to the study of 'how' and 'why' languages change, both to the methods of investigating linguistic change and to the theories designed to explain these changes.

Some people imagine that historical linguists mostly just study the history of individual words – and many people are fascinated by word histories, as shown by the number of popular books, newspaper columns and radio broadcasts dedicated to the topic, more properly called *etymology* (derived from Greek *etumon* 'true' [neuter form], that is, 'true or original meaning of a word'). The primary goal of historical linguistics is *not* etymologies, but accurate etymology is an important product of historical linguistic work. Let us, for illustration's sake, consider a couple of examples and then see what the real role of etymology in historical linguistics is. Since word histories have a certain glamour about them for many people, let's check out the history of the word *glamour* itself. Surprisingly, it connects with a main concern of modern linguistics, namely *grammar*. (The example of *glamour* is also considered in Hock and Joseph 1996 and by Pinker 1994.)

Glamour is a changed form of the word *grammar*, originally in use in Scots English; it meant 'magic, enchantment, spell', found especially in the phrase 'to cast the glamour over one'. It did not acquire its sense of 'a magical or fictitious beauty or alluring charm' until the mid-1800s. *Grammar* has its own interesting history. It was borrowed from Old French *grammaire*, itself from Latin *grammatica*, ultimately derived from Greek *gramma* 'letter, written mark'. In Classical Latin, *grammatica* meant the methodical study of literature broadly. In the Middle Ages, it came to mean chiefly the study of or knowledge of Latin and hence came also to be synonymous with learning in general, the knowledge peculiar to the learned class. Since this was popularly believed to include also magic and astrology, French *grammaire* came to be used sometimes for the name of these occult 'sciences'. It is in this sense that it survived in *glamour*, and also in English *gramarye*, as well as in French *grimoire* 'conjuring book, unintelligible book or writing'. English *gramarye*, *grammary* means 'grammar, learning in general, occult learning, magic, necromancy', a word revived in literary usage by later writers; it is clearly archaic and related to the cases of vocabulary loss discussed in Chapter 9.

What is of greater concern to historical linguists is not the etymology

5

of these words per se, but the kinds of changes they have undergone and the techniques or methods we have at our disposal to recover this history. Thus, in the history of the words *glamour* and *grammar* we notice various kinds of change: borrowing from Greek to Latin and ultimately from French (a descendant of Latin) to English, shifts in meaning, and the sporadic change in sound (*r* to *l*) in the derived word *glamour*. Changes of this sort are what historical linguistics is about, not just the individual word histories. These kinds of changes that languages can and do undergo and the techniques that have been developed in historical linguistics to recover them are what the chapters of this book are concerned with.

Let's take *goodbye* as a second example. This everyday word has undergone several changes in its history. It began life in the late 1500s as *god be with you* (or *ye*), spelled variously as *god be wy ye*, *god b'uy*, and so on. The first part changed to *good* either on analogy with such other greetings as *good day*, *good morning* and *good night*, or as a euphemistic deformation to avoid the blasphemy of saying *god* (taboo avoidance) – or due to a combination of the two. The various independent words in *god be with you* were amalgamated into one, *goodbye*, and ultimately even this was shortened (clipped) to *bye*.

In large part, then, a word's etymology is the history of the linguistic changes it has undergone. Therefore, when we understand the various kinds of linguistic change dealt with in the chapters of this book, the stuff that etymologies are made of and based on becomes clear. Historical linguists are concerned with all these things broadly and not merely with the history behind individual words. For that reason, etymology is not the primary purpose of historical linguistics, but rather the goal is to understand language change in general; and when we understand this, then etymology, one area of historical linguistics, is a by-product of that understanding. For an explanation of the notions of borrowing, analogy, amalgamation, clipping and sound change mentioned in these examples, see Chapters 2, 3, 4 and 9.

1.3 Kinds of Linguistic Changes: An English Example

As seen in these sample etymologies, there are many kinds of linguistic change. A glance at the chapter titles of this book reveals the major ones. In effect, any aspect of a language's structure can change, and therefore we are concerned with learning to apply accurately the techniques that have been developed for dealing with these kinds of changes, with sound change, grammatical change, semantic change, borrowing, analogy and so on, and with understanding and evaluating the basic assumptions upon which these historical linguistic methods are based.

We can begin to get an appreciation for the various sorts of changes that are possible in language by comparing a small sample from various stages of English. This exercise compares *Matthew* 27:73 from translations of the Bible at different time periods, starting with the present and working back to Old English. This particular example was selected in part because it talks about language and in part because in translations of the Bible we have comparable texts from the various time periods which can reveal changes that have taken place:

1. Modern English (*The New English Bible*, 1961):
   Shortly afterwards the bystanders came up and said to Peter, 'Surely you are another of them; your accent gives you away!'
2. Early Modern English (*The King James Bible*, 1611):
   And after a while came vnto him they that stood by, and saide to Peter, Surely thou also art one of them, for thy speech bewrayeth thee.
3. Middle English (*The Wycliff Bible*, fourteenth century):
   And a litil aftir, thei that stooden camen, and seiden to Petir, treuli thou art of hem; for thi speche makith thee knowun.
4. Old English (*The West-Saxon Gospels*, c. 1050):
   þa æfter lytlum fyrste genēalǣton þa ðe þær stodon, cwædon to petre. Soðlice þu eart of hym, þyn spræc þe gesweotolað.
   [Literally: then after little first approached they that there stood, said to Peter. Truly thou art of them, thy speech thee makes clear.]

In comparing the Modern English with the Early Modern English (1476–1700) versions, we note several kinds of changes. (1) *Lexical*: in Early Modern English *bewrayeth* we have an example of lexical replacement. This word was archaic already in the seventeenth century and has been replaced by other words. It meant 'to malign, speak evil of, to expose (a deception)'. In this context, it means that Peter's way of speaking, his accent, gives him away. (2) *Grammatical* (syntactic and morphological) change: from *came vnto* [unto] *him they* to the Modern English equivalent, *they came to him*, there has been a syntactic change. In earlier times, English, like other Germanic languages, had a rule which essentially inverted the subject and verb when preceded by other material (though this rule was not obligatory in English as it is in German), so that because *and after a while* comes first in the sentence, *they came* is inverted to *came they*. This rule has for the most part been lost in Modern English. Another grammatical change (syntactic and morphological) is seen in the difference between *thou . . . art* and *you are*. Formerly, *thou* was 'you (singular familiar)' and contrasted with *ye/you* 'you (plural or singular formal)', but this distinction was lost. The *-eth* of *bewrayeth* was the 'third person singular' verb agreement suffix; it was replaced in time by *-(e)s* (*giveth* > *gives*). (3) *Sound change*: early Modern English was not pronounced in exactly the same way as Modern English, but it will be easier to show examples of sound changes in the later texts (below). (4) *Borrowing*: the word *accent* in Modern English is a loanword from Old French *accent* 'accent, pronunciation' (see Chapter 3 on borrowing). (5) *Changes in orthography* (spelling conventions): while mostly differences in orthography (spelling conventions) are not of central concern in historical linguistics, we do have to be able to interpret what the texts represent phonetically in order to utilize them successfully (this is part of philology; see Chapter 14). In *vnto* for modern *unto* we see a minor change in orthographic convention. Earlier in many European languages, there was in effect no distinction between the letters *v* and *u* (the Latin alphabet, upon which most European writing systems are based, had no such difference); both could be used to represent either the vowel /u/ or the consonant /v/ or in other cases /w/, though for both /v/ and /u/ usually *v* was used initially (<vnder> 'under') and *u* medially (<haue> 'have'). One could tell whether the vowel or consonant value was intended only in context – a *v* between consonants, for example, would most likely represent /u/. More revealing examples of changes in orthography are seen (below) in the Old English text. In *thou* (formerly pronounced /θuː/) we see the influence of the French scribes – French had a monumental influence on English after the Norman French conquest of England in 1066. The *ou* was the French way of spelling /u/, as in French *nous* /nu/ 'we'; later, English underwent the Great Vowel Shift (a sound change, mentioned below) in which /uː/ became /au/, which explains why words such as *thou*, *house* and *loud* (formerly /θuː/, /huːs/ and /luːd/ respectively) no longer have the sound /uː/ that the French orthographic *ou* originally represented.

Examples of kinds of changes seen in the comparison of the Middle English (1066–1476) text with later versions include, among others, (1) *Sound change*: final *-n* was lost by regular sound change under certain conditions, as seen in the comparison of Middle English *stooden*, *camen* and *seiden* with their modern equivalents *stood*, *came* and *said*. (2) *Grammatical change* (morphological and syntactic): the forms *stooden*, *camen* and *seiden* ('stood', 'came' and 'said') each contain the final *-n* which marked agreement with the third person plural subject ('they', spelled *thei*). When final -*n* was lost by sound change, the grammatical change was brought about that verbs no longer had this agreement marker (-*n*) for the plural persons. (3) *Borrowing*: the *hem* is the original third person plural object pronoun, which was replaced by *them*, a borrowing from Scandinavian, which had great influence on English.

Between Old English (c. 450–1066) and Modern English we see many changes. Some of the kinds of change represented in this text include (1) *Lexical change*: there are instances of loss of vocabulary items represented by the words in this short verse, namely *genēalǣton* 'approached', *cwǣdon* 'said' (compare archaic *quoth*), *soðlice* 'truly' (*soothly*, compare *soothsayer* 'one who speaks the truth') and *gesweotolað* 'shows, reveals'. (2) *Sound change*: English has undergone many changes in pronunciation since Old English times. For example, the loss of final -*n* in certain circumstances mentioned above is also illustrated in *þyn* 'thy' (modern 'your') (in *þyn sprǣc* 'thy speech' [modern 'your accent']). A sporadic change is seen in the loss of *r* from *sprǣc* 'speech' (compare German *Sprache* 'language, speech', where the *r* is retained). English vowels underwent a number of changes. One is called the Great Vowel Shift (mentioned above), in which essentially long vowels raised (and long high vowels /i:/ and /u:/ became diphthongs, /ai/ and /au/, respectively). This is seen in the comparison of some of the Old English words with their Modern English equivalents:

Soðlice /so:θ-/	soothly /suθ-/ ('soothly, truly')
þu /θu:/	thou /ðau/
þyn /θi:n/	thy /ðai/
þe /θe:/	thee /ði/

(3) *Grammatical*: the change mentioned above, the loss of the subject–verb inversion when other material preceded in the clause, is seen in a comparison of *genēalǣton þa* 'approached they' with the modern counterpart for 'they approached'. The loss of case endings is seen in *æfter lytlum*, where the -*um* 'dative plural' is lost and no longer required after prepositions such as *after*. The same change which was already mentioned above in the Middle English text is seen again in the loss of the -*n* 'third person plural' verbal agreement marker, in *genēalǣton* '(they) approached', *stodon* '(they) stood' and *cwǣdon* '(they) said'. Another change is the loss of the prefix *ge*- of *genēalǣton* 'approached' and *gesweotolað* 'shows'. This was reduced in time from [je] to [j] to [i] and finally lost, so that many perfect forms ('has done', 'had done') were no longer distinct from the simple past ('did'); that is, in the case

of *sing/sang/have sung*, these remain distinct, but in the case of *bring/ brought/have brought* they are not distinct, though formerly the *have brought* form would have borne the *ge-* prefix, distinguishing it from the *brought* ('past') without the prefix, which is now lost from the language. (4) *Orthographic*: there are many differences in how sounds are represented. Old English *þ* 'thorn' and *ð* 'eth' have been dropped and are spelled today with *th* for both the voiceless (θ) and voiced (ð) dental fricatives. The *æ* (called 'ash', from Old English *æsc*, its name in the runic alphabet) is also no longer used.

The various sorts of changes illustrated in this short text are the subject matter of the chapters of this book.

1.4 Exercises

Exercise 1.1

This exercise is about attitudes towards language change.

1. Try to find letters to newspapers or columns in newspapers or magazines which express opinions on the quality of English in use today and about changes that are taking place. What do you think they reveal about attitudes towards language change?
2. Ask your friends, family and associates what they think about language today; do they think it is changing, and if so, is it getting better or worse?
3. Find books or articles on 'proper' English (prescriptive grammar); do they reveal any attitude towards changes that are going on in today's language?
4. Consider the many things that schoolteachers or school grammar books warn you against as being 'wrong' or 'bad grammar'. Do any of these involve changes in the language?
5. Compare books on etiquette written recently with some written thirty years ago or more; find the sections which deal with appropriate ways of speaking and use of the language. What changes have taken place in the recommendations made then and now? Do these reveal anything about change in the language or in language use?

Exercise 1.2

Observe the language you hear about you, and think about any changes that are going on now or have taken place in your lifetime. For example, if you are old enough, you might observe that *gay* has changed its basic meaning: today it mostly means 'homosexual' although until recently it did not have this meaning, but rather meant only 'happy, cheerful'. Slang changes at a rather fast rate; what observations might you make about recent slang versus earlier slang? Can you find examples of ongoing change in other areas of the language besides just vocabulary?

Exercise 1.3

Changes in spelling and occasional misspellings have been used to make inferences about changes in pronunciation. This can, of course, be misleading, since spelling conventions are sometimes used for other purposes than just to represent pronunciation. Try to find examples of recent differences in spelling or of misspellings and then try to imagine what they might mean, say, to future linguists looking back trying to determine what changed and when it changed. For example, you might compare the spelling *lite* with *light*, *gonna* with *going to*, *wannabee* with *want to be*, or *alright* and *alot* with *all right* and *a lot* respectively. In particular, variations in spellings can be very revealing; see if you can find examples which may suggest something about language change.

Exercise 1.4

A number of examples from Shakespeare's plays, written in the Early Modern English period, are presented here which illustrate differences from how the same thing would be said today. Think about each example and attempt to state what changes have taken place in the language that would account for the differences you see in the constructions mentioned in the headings, the negatives, auxiliary verbs and so on. For example, in the first one we see: *Saw you the weird sisters?* The modern English equivalent would be *Did you see the weird sisters?* Had the heading directed your attention to yes–no questions, you would attempt to state what change had taken place, from former *saw you* (with inversion from *you saw*) to the modern version which no longer involves inversion but requires a form of *do* (*did you see*) which was not utilized in Shakespeare's version.

Treatment of negatives:

1. Saw you the weird sisters? . . . Came they not by you? (*Macbeth* IV, i)
2. I love thee not, therefore pursue me not (*A Midsummer Night's Dream* II, 1, 188)
3. I know thee not, old man: fall to thy prayers (*Henry V* V, v)

11

4. Let not thy mother lose her prayers, Hamlet: I pray thee, stay with us; go not to Wittenberg (*Hamlet* I, ii)
5. But yet you draw not iron (*A Midsummer Night's Dream* II, i, 196)
6. Tempt not too much the hatred of my spirit (*A Midsummer Night's Dream* II, i, 211)
7. And I am sick when I look not on you (*A Midsummer Night's Dream* II, i, 213)
8. I will not budge for no man's pleasure (*Romeo and Juliet* III, i)
9. I cannot weep, nor answer have I none (*Othello* IV, ii)
10. I am not sorry neither (*Othello* V, ii)

Treatment of auxiliary verbs:

1. Macduff is fled to England (*Macbeth* IV, i) = 'has fled'
2. The king himself is rode to view their battle (*Henry V* IV, iii) = 'has ridden'
3. Thou told'st me they were stolen into this wood (*A Midsummer Night's Dream* II, i, 191) = 'had stolen away/hidden'

Treatment of comparatives and superlatives:

1. She comes more nearer earth than she was wont (*Othello* 5, 2)
2. This was the most unkindest cut of all (*Julius Caesar* 3, 2)
3. What worser place can I beg in your love (*A Midsummer Night's Dream* II, i, 208)

Differences in verb agreement inflections (endings on the verbs which agree with the subject):

1. The quality of mercy is not strain'd
   It droppeth as the gentle rain from heaven
   Upon the place beneath: it is twice blessed;
   It blesseth him that gives and him that takes
   (*The Merchant of Venice* IV, i)
2. The one I'll slay, the other slayeth me
   (*A Midsummer Night's Dream* II, i, 190)
3. O, it offends me to the soul to
   Hear a robostious periwig-pated fellow tear
   A passion to tatters
   (*Hamlet* III, i, 9–11)
4. And could of men distinguish, her election
   Hath seal'd thee for herself: for thou hast been
   As one, in suffering all, that suffers nothing
   (*Hamlet* III, i, 68–71)

Exercise 1.5

The following is a sample text of Middle English, from Chaucer c. 1380. It is presented three lines at a time: the first is from Chaucer's text; the second is a word-by-word translation, with some of the relevant grammatical morphemes indicated; the third is a modern translation. Compare these lines and report the main changes you observe in morphology, syntax, semantics and lexical items. (Do not concern yourself with the changes in spelling or pronunciation.)

The Tale of Melibee, Geoffrey Chaucer (c. 1380)

Upon a day bifel that he for his desport is went into the feeldes
    hym to pleye.
on one day befell that he for his pleasure is gone to the fields
    him to play.
'One day it happened that for his pleasure he went to the fields
    to amuse himself.'
    [NOTE: *is went* = Modern English 'has gone'; with verbs of motion
    the auxiliary used was a form of the verb 'to be', where today it is
    with 'to have']

His wif and eek his doghter hath he laft inwith his hous,
his wife and also his daughter has he left within his house,
'His wife and his daughter also he left inside his house,'
    [NOTE: *wif* = 'wife, woman']

of which the dores wer-en faste y-shette.
of which the doors were-Plural fast Past.Participle-shut
'whose doors were shut fast.'

Thre of his old foos ha-n it espied, and setten laddres to the walles
    of his hous,
three of his old foes have-Plural it spied, and set-Plural ladders to
    the walls of his house,
'Three of his old enemies saw this, and set ladders to the walls of
    his house,'

and by wyndowes ben entred, and betten his wyf,
and by windows had entered, and beaten his wife,
'and entered by the windows, and beat his wife,'
    [NOTE: *ben entred* = 'have entered', a verb of motion taking 'to be' as
    the auxiliary]

and wounded his doghter with fyve mortal woundes in fyve sondry
    places –
and wounded his daughter with five mortal wounds in five sundry
    places –
'and wounded his daughter with five mortal wounds in five
    different places –'

this is to sey-n, in hir feet, in hir handes, in hir erys, in hir nose,
    and in hir mouth, –
this is to say-Infinitive, in her feet, in her hands, in her ears, in her
    nose, and in her mouth, –
'that is to say, in her feet, in her hands, in her ears, in her nose,
    and in her mouth –'

and left-en hir for deed, and went-en awey.
and left-Plural her for dead, and went-Plural away.
'and left her for dead, and went away.'

(Lass 1992: 25–6)

Exercise 1.6

The text in this exercise is a sample of Early Modern English, from
William Caxton, *Eneydos* (c. 1491). As in Exercise 1.5, three lines are
presented: the first is from Caxton's text; the second is a word-by-word
translation, with some of the relevant grammatical morphemes indicated;
the third is a more colloquial modern translation. Compare these lines
and report the main changes you observe in morphology, syntax, semantics and lexical items. (Again, do not concern yourself with the changes
in spelling or pronunciation beyond the most obvious ones.)

And that commyn englysshe that is spoken in one shyre varyeth
    from a nother. In so moche
and that common English that is spoken in one shire varies from
    another. In so much
'And the common English that is spoken in one county varies so
    much from [that spoken in] another. In so much'

that in my days happened that certayn marchauntes were in a ship
    in tamyse
that in my days happened that certain merchants were in a ship in
    Thames
'that in my time it happened that some merchants were in a ship on
    the Thames'

for to haue sayled ouer the see to zelande/ and for lacke of wynde
  thei taryed atte forlond;
for to have sailed over the sea to Zeeland. And for lack of wind
  they tarried at.the coast;
'to sail over the sea to Zeeland. And because there was no wind,
  they stayed at the coast'
  [NOTE: Zeeland = a province in the Netherlands]

and wente to land for to refreshe them And one of theym, named
  sheffelde a mercer
and went to land for to refresh them. And one of them, named
  Sheffield, a mercer,
'and they went on land to refresh themselves. And one of them,
  named Sheffield, a fabric-dealer,'

cam in to an hows and axed [aksed] for mete, and specyally he
  axyd after eggys.
came into a house and asked for meat, and especially he asked
  after eggs.
'came into a house and asked for food, and specifically he asked
  for "eggs".'

And the goode wyf answerede. that she coude no frenshe.
and the good woman answered that she could no French.
'And the good woman answered that she knew no French.'

And the marchaunt was angry. for he also coude speke no frenshe.
and the merchant was angry, for he also could speak no French,
'And the merchant was angry, because he couldn't speak any
  French either.'
  [NOTE: *coude* = 'was able to, knew (how to)']

but wolde haue hadde egges/ and she vnderstode hym not/
but would have had eggs; and she understood him not.
'but he wanted to have eggs; and she did not understand him.'
  [NOTE: *wolde* = 'wanted', the source of Modern English *would*]

And thenne at laste a nother sayd that he wolde haue eyren/
and then at last an other said that he would have eggs.
'and then finally somebody else said that he wanted to have eggs.'

then the good wyf said that she understod him wel/
then the good woman said that she understood him well.
'Then the good woman said that she understood him well.'
                    (Source of Caxton's text: Fisher and Bornstein 1974: 186–7)

2

—

Sound Change

—

From one point of view the sound shift seems to me to be a barbarous aberration from which other quieter nations refrained, but which has to do with the violent progress and yearning for liberty as found in Germany in the early Middle Ages, and which started the transformation of Europe.

(Jakob Grimm, 1848)

2.1 Introduction

Perhaps the most thoroughly studied area of historical linguistics is sound change. Over time, the sounds of languages tend to change. The study of sound change has yielded very significant results, and important assumptions that underlie historical linguistic methods, especially the comparative method, are based on these findings. An understanding of sound change is truly important for historical linguistics in general, and this needs to be stressed – it plays an extremely important role in the comparative method and hence also in linguistic reconstruction, in internal reconstruction, in detecting loanwords, and in determining whether languages are related to one another. These topics and the methods for dealing with them are the subject of later chapters. This chapter is about how sounds change.

Sound change is a major concern of historical linguistics; it is often the main feature of books on the history of individual languages. Typically, sound changes are classified, often in long lists of many different kinds of sound changes, each with its own traditional name (some with more than one name). To be at home with sound change, it is necessary to know the most frequently used of these names. The most commonly recurring kinds of sound changes in the world's languages are listed and exemplified in this chapter. They are organized in a representative classification of sound changes, but there is nothing special about this particular arrangement, and different textbooks present a variety of other classifications.

2.2   Kinds of Sound Change

Regular sound changes are accorded far more attention in historical linguistics, and rightly so – they are extremely important to the methods and theories about language change. In fact, the most important basic assumption in historical linguistics is that sound change is regular, a fundamental principle with far-reaching implications for the methods that will be considered in later chapters. *Regular* changes recur generally and take place uniformly wherever the phonetic circumstances in which the change happens are encountered. To say that a sound change is regular means that the change takes place whenever the sound or sounds which undergo the change are found in the circumstances or environments that condition the change. For example, original *p* regularly became *b* between vowels in Spanish (p > b/V__V); this means that in this context between vowels, every original *p* became a *b*; it is not the case that some original intervocalic *p*'s became *b* in some words, but became, say, *ʃ* in some other words and *ø* in still other words, in unpredictable ways. If a sound could change in such arbitrary and unpredictable ways, the change would not be regular; but sound change is regular (though as we will see in other chapters, some other kinds of change can also affect sounds, so that the results do not appear regular but are subject to other kinds of explanations).

This is called 'the *regularity principle*' or 'the *Neogrammarian hypothesis*'. The Neogrammarians, beginning in about 1876 in Germany, became extremely influential in general thinking about language change, and about sound change in particular. The Neogrammarians were a group of younger scholars who antagonized the leaders of the field at that time by attacking older thinking and loudly proclaiming their own views. The early Neogrammarians included Karl Brugmann, Berthold Delbrück, August Leskien, Hermann Osthoff, Hermann Paul and others. They were called *Junggrammatiker* 'young grammarians' in German, where *jung-* 'young' had the sense of 'young Turks', originally intended as a humorous nickname for the rebellious circle of young scholars, although they adopted the term as their own name. English *Neogrammarian* is not a very precise translation. Their slogan was:

sound laws suffer no exceptions (Osthoff and Brugmann 1878). The notion of the 'regularity of the sound laws' became fundamental to the comparative method (see Chapter 5). By 'sound laws' they meant merely 'sound changes', but they referred to them as 'laws' because they linked linguistics with the rigorous sciences which dealt in laws and law-like statements. We will return to the regularity principle in more detail in Chapter 5.

Sound changes are also typically classified according to whether they are *unconditioned* or *conditioned*. To understand these categories, it will be helpful to read the description of them here, then look at the examples, and then reread these definitions again. When a sound change occurs generally and is not dependent on the phonetic context in which it occurs, that is, not dependent on or restricted in any way by neighbouring sounds, it is *unconditioned*. Unconditioned sound changes modify the sound in all contexts in which it occurs, regardless of what other sounds may be found in words containing the changing sound: that is, the change happens irrespective of the phonological context in which the sound that changes may be found. When a change takes place only in certain contexts (when it is dependent upon neighbouring sounds, upon the sound's position within words, or on other aspects of the grammar), it is *conditioned*. Conditioned changes are more restricted and affect only some of the sound's occurrences, those in particular contexts, but not other occurrences which happen to be found in environments outside the restricted situations in which the change takes effect. For example, the Spanish change of *p* to *b* intervocalically (mentioned above) is conditioned; only those *p*'s which are between vowels become *b*, while *p*'s in other positions (for example, at the beginning of words) do not change. On the other hand, most varieties of Latin American Spanish have changed palatalized *l* to *y* (IPA *l^j* (or [ʎ]) to *j*) unconditionally (as for example in *calle* > *"caye"* [/kal^{j}e/ > /kaje/]) – every instance of an original *l^j* has changed to *y* (IPA [j]) regardless of the context in which the *l^j* occurred.

The distinction between *phonemic* and *non-phonemic* changes is present in some fashion in most treatments of sound change. It has to do with the recognition of distinct levels of phonological analysis in linguistic theory – the phonetic level and the phonemic level. There is sometimes disagreement about how the second level is to be understood, that is, about how abstract phonemes may be (how different or distant they can be from the phonetic form) and how they are to be represented. Naturally, if there were full agreement in phonological theory about the 'phonemic' level, there would be more of a consensus in historical linguistics on how to talk about the aspects of sound change which relate to it. However, for our purposes, a definitive characterization is not crucial, so long as we recognize that talk about sound change makes reference to two distinct levels. In general, it is helpful to think of phonetics as representing the actually occurring physical sounds, and of phonemes as representing the speakers' knowledge or mental organization of the sounds of their language. A non-phonemic change (also called *allophonic* change) does not alter the total number of phonemes in the language. Some call the non-phonemic changes *shifts*, referring to the shift in pronunciation (at the phonetic level), with no change in the number of distinctive sounds. A *phonemic* change is defined as one which does affect the inventory of phonemes (the basic sounds that native speakers hold to be distinct) by adding to or deleting from the number of phonemes/basic sounds of the language.

2.3 Non-phonemic (Allophonic) Changes

Non-phonemic changes have not been considered as important as phonemic changes (below), perhaps because they do not change the structural organization of the inventory of sounds.

2.3.1 Non-phonemic unconditioned changes

(1) In varieties of English, $u > ʉ$ (central rounded vowel), and in some dialects even on to *y*, as in 'shoe' [ʃu] > [ʃʉ], and in some even [ʃy].

(2) Pipil (a Uto-Aztecan language of El Salvador): $o > u$. Proto-Nahua, Pipil's immediate ancestor, had the vowel inventory /i, e, a, o/. When Pipil changed *o* to *u*, this did not change the number of distinctive vowels, and therefore it is a non-phonemic change. Since the change affected all instances of *o*, turning them all into *u* regardless of other sounds in the context, it is an unconditioned change.

(3) Guatemalan Spanish: $r > s$. The 'trilled' *r* found in most Spanish dialects has become the so-called 'assibilated' *r* (phonetically a voiceless laminal retroflex fricative) in rural Guatemalan Spanish. Since *r* becomes *s* in all contexts, without restrictions which depend upon neighbouring šounds, this is an unconditioned change. In this change, one sound, orginal *s*, is switched for another, for *r*, but the number of distinctive sounds (phonemes) in the language is not changed; therefore, it is a non-phonemic change.

2.3.2 Non-phonemic conditioned changes

(1) Many English dialects have undergone a change in which a vowel

is phonetically lengthened before voiced stops, for example, /bɛd/ > [bɛ·d] 'bed'.

(2) Spanish dialects: n > ŋ /__ #. In many dialects of Spanish, final *n* has changed so that it is no longer pronounced as [n], but rather as a velar nasal [ŋ], as in *son* 'they are' [son] > [soŋ], *bien* 'well, very' [bjen] > [bjeŋ]. This is a conditioned change, since *n* did not change in all its occurrences, but only where it was at the end of words. It is non-phonemic, since the change results in no change at the phonemic level. Before the change, the phoneme /n/ had one phonetic form (allophone), [n]; after the change, /n/ came to have two non-contrastive variants (allophones), predictable from context, with [ŋ] word-finally and [n] when not in final position.

2.4 Phonemic Changes

Two principal kinds of phonemic changes are *mergers* and *splits*.

2.4.1 Merger (A, B > B, or A, B > C)

Mergers are changes in which, as the name suggests, two (or more) distinct sounds merge into one, leaving fewer distinct sounds (fewer phonemes) in the phonological inventory than there were before the change.

(1) Most varieties of Latin American Spanish: *ll* (IPA [l^j] or [ʎ]) and *y* (IPA [j]) merged (l^j, *j* > *j*). Spanish used to contrast the two sounds *ll* ([l^j]) and *y* ([j]), and the contrast is still maintained in some dialects of Spain and in the Andes and adjacent regions of South America; however, in most of Latin America and in many dialects of Peninsular Spanish (as the Spanish of Spain is called), these two sounds have merged into one, to *y* (IPA [j]), as in *calle* > *"caye"* (/kal^je/ > /kaje/) 'street', *llamar* > *"yamar"* (/l^jamar/ > /jamar/) 'to call'. As a consequence, for example, both *halla* 'find' and *haya* 'have (subjunctive)' have merged (/al^ja/ and /aja/ > /aja/), resulting in the two words being homophonous.

(2) Latin American Spanish: *θ*, *s* > *s̪*. Peninsular Spanish contrasts the two sounds, dental fricative *θ* and apical alveolar fricative *s*, which merged to *s̪* in Latin American and some Peninsular dialects. For example, *caza* /kaθa/ 'hunt, chase' and *casa* /kasa/ 'house' are both /kas̪a/ throughout Latin America. This change illustrates the rarer kind of merger where the two original sounds merge into some third sound which was not formerly present in the language (symbolized above as A, B > C).

(3) Sanskrit: *e, o, a > a* (in most contexts, the *o > a* part is conditioned in some instances) (*e, o > a*; that is, *e* and *o* merging with existing *a*). Some words which illustrate this merger are seen in Table 2.1 where the Sanskrit examples (which have undergone the merger) are compared with Latin cognates (which preserve the original vowel); the original vowel before the Sanskrit change is also seen in the Proto-Indo-European forms listed, from which both the Sanskrit and Latin words derive.

TABLE 2.1: Sanskrit–Latin cognates showing Sanskrit merger of *e, o, a > a*

Sanskrit	Latin	Proto-Indo-European	
ad-	ed-	*ed-	'to eat'
danta	dent-	*dent-	'tooth'
avi-	ovi-	*owi-	'sheep'
dva-	duo	*dwo-	'two'
ajra-	ager	*aĝro-	'field' (compare *acre*)
apa	ab	*apo	'away, from'

(NOTE: the asterisk (*) is used to symbolize forms that are unattested but reconstructed by linguists; see Chapter 5.)

(4) Proto-Indo-European (PIE) *o, *ə, *a > Proto-Germanic *a. Some examples which illustrate this change in Germanic but not in other branches of Indo-European are as follows (only the first syllable is relevant here).

	PIE	Greek	Latin	Gothic	OHG	English
*o	*oĥtố(u)-	oktố	octo	ahtau [axtau]	ahto	'eight'
*ə	*pəter-	patḗr	pater	fadar	fater	'father'
*a	*aĝro-	agrós	ager	akrs	ackar	'field' (acre)

(5) Proto-Indo-European (PIE) *ō, *ā > Proto-Germanic *ō. For example: PIE *plō-tu- > Proto-Germanic *flōduz 'flowing water, deluge' (Old English *flōd* 'flood'); PIE *bhrāter- > Proto-Germanic *brōþar- 'brother' (Old English *brōðor* 'brother'; compare Sanskrit *bhrātar*, Latin *frāter*).

An important *axiom* concerning mergers is: *mergers are irreversible*. This means that when sounds have completely merged, a subsequent change, say some generations later, will not be able to restore the original distinctions. Thus, for example, in the Sanskrit case in paragraph

(3) above, after the merger, children would learn all the words in Table 2.1 with the vowel *a*, and there would be no basis left in the language for determining which of these words with *a* may have originally had *e* or which had *o* which became *a*, or which had retained original *a* unchanged. A language learner arriving upon the scene long after the merger was completed would find no evidence in these words which would permit him or her successfully to change the vowel back to *e* where it had once been an *e* in *danta* 'tooth', and not to *e* but rather back to *o* in *dva-* 'two'.

Occasionally we encounter examples of what at first might appear to be instances of reversal of merger, but these never turn out to be real instances of complete mergers in the speech of all the speakers involved. An example which illustrates this is the merger of /v/ and /w/ in dialects of southern England, especially in Cockney, East Anglia and the southeast, with *walley* for *valley*, *willage* for *village*, also with hypercorrection, *voif* for *wife* – Sam Weller in Charles Dickens' *Pickwick Papers* calls himself *Veller*. This merger disappeared towards the end of the nineteenth century. It was stigmatized in local speech, and the greater prestige of the non-merged pronunciations in the broader speech community – where the merger had not taken place – won out, making it appear that the merger was reversed, when in fact no such reversal took place. Rather, the merger was simply lost with the adoption of the more prestigious non-merged pronunciation that had always been extant in the speech community. (Cf. Ihalainen 1994: 227.)

2.4.2 Split (A > B, C)

To comprehend splits, we need to understand another axiom: *splits follow mergers*. That is, in splits, the sounds in question do not themselves change in any physical way, but phonetically they stay as they were; rather it is the merger of other sounds in their environment which causes the phonemic status of the sounds involved in the splits to change from being predictable conditioned variants of sounds (allophonic) to unpredictable, contrastive, distinctive sounds (phonemic). This is illustrated well by the history of 'umlaut' in English.

(1) Split in English connected with umlaut. 'Umlaut' is a kind of sound change in which a back vowel is fronted when followed by a front vowel (or *j*) (usually in the next syllable). Umlaut initially created front-vowel allophones of back vowels, which became phonemic when the following front vowel of the umlaut environment was lost. Note that for the purposes of splits and mergers, loss is considered to be merger

with 'zero'. We'll trace this in stages to see the developments and the split as a consequence of the merger.

STAGE 1 (Proto-Germanic), just phonemic /u/ and /o/, each with only one variant (allophone):

mūs- 'mouse', *mūs-iz* 'mice'; *fōt-* 'foot', *fōt-iz* 'feet'

STAGE 2 (umlaut), /u/ and /o/ develop allophones, [ȳ] and [ø̄], respectively, when followed by /i, j/ in the next syllable:

mūs-i > *mȳsi* 'mice'; *fōt-i* > *fø̄ti* 'feet'; *mūs* 'mouse', *fōt* 'foot'

STAGE 3 (loss of final *i*):

mȳsi > *mȳs* 'mice'; *fø̄ti* > *fø̄t* 'feet'; *mūs* 'mouse', *fōt-* 'foot'

At this stage, since the final -*i* which had conditioned the variants (allophones) was no longer present, but had been lost (merged with 'zero'), the result was that *ū* contrasted with *ȳ* and *ō* contrasted with *ø̄*, all four now as distinct phonemes. At this stage, we see the split as a consequence of the merger, but let's complete the story. Next, the front rounded vowels lost their rounding (*ȳ* > *ī*; *ø̄* > *ē*), an unconditioned change in which the rounded front vowels merged with their unrounded counterparts: *mȳs* > *mīs* 'mice'; *fø̄t* > *fēt* 'feet'. Finally, these underwent the Great Vowel Shift, in which long vowels raised (for example, *ē* > *ī*) and long high vowels diphthongized (for example, *ī* > *ai*), with Modern English as a result: *mīs* > /mais/ 'mice' and *fēt* > /fit/ 'feet'. This series of changes is shown graphically in Table 2.2, where // represents the phonemic status of these forms, and [ ] shows the phonetic status.

TABLE 2.2: Historical derivation of 'mouse', 'mice', 'foot', 'feet'

	mouse	*mice*	*foot*	*feet*
Stage 1 (no changes)	/mu:s/	/mu:s-i/	/fo:t/	/fo:t-i/
	[mu:s]	[mu:s-i]	[fo:t]	[fo:t-i]
Umlaut	/mu:s/	/mu:s-i/	/fo:t/	/fo:t-i/
	[mu:s]	[my:s-i]	[fo:t]	[fø̄:t-i]
Loss of -*i*	/mu:s/	/my:s/	/fo:t/	/fø̄:t/
(= split after merger)	[mu:s]	[my:s]	[fo:t]	[fø̄:t]
Unrounding	/mu:s/	/mi:s/	/fo:t/	/fe:t/
	[mu:s]	[mi:s]	[fo:t]	[fe:t]
Great Vowel Shift	/maus/	/mais/	/fu:t/	/fi:t/

(2) Palatalization in Russian. In Old Russian, palatalization of consonants was predictable (allophonic), conditioned by a following front vowel, as in *krovĭ* [krov^{j}ĭ] 'blood' in comparison with *krovŏ* [krovŏ] 'shelter'. Later, however, the short/lax final vowels *ĭ* and *ŏ* were lost (ĭ, ŏ > Ø / __#), a merger with Ø ('zero'). So, *ĭ* and *ŏ* merged with Ø ('zero'), leaving /v^j/ and /v/ in contrast and therefore as distinct phonemes, as shown by new minimal pairs such as *krov^j* 'blood' and *krov* 'shelter' which come about as a result of the merger with Ø (actually loss) of the final vowels, one of which (the front one) had originally conditioned the allophonic palatalization so that the palatalized and non-palatalized versions of the sound were merely variants of a single basic sound (that is, they were allophones of the same phoneme). Thus, in this example, *v^j* and *v* split as a result of the merger with Ø which affected these final vowels.

(3) English /n/ had the predictable (allophonic) variant [ŋ] which occurred only before *k* and *g*. Later, final *g* was lost in these forms (g > Ø / ŋ__#); that is, final *g* merged with Ø in this context, leaving /n/ and /ŋ/ in contrast, since now both nasals came to occur at the end of words where formerly the *ŋ* had depended on the presence of the following *g* which is no longer there, as in /sɪn/ 'sin' and /sɪŋ/ 'sing' (from earlier [sɪŋg] before the *g* was lost). Thus /n/ split into /n/ and /ŋ/ when the merger of another sound (*g* with Ø in this case) left the two in contrast.

(4) Split and merger in Nahuatl. The axiom that splits follow mergers is illustrated well by a merger in Nahuatl that caused the split which resulted in /ʃ/ contrasting phonemically with /s/. In Nahuatl (Uto-Aztecan family), *s* originally had two variants (allophones), [ʃ] before *i* and [s] everywhere else, as in:

Phonemic:	/sima/ 'to shave'	/sɨma/ 'to prepare plant leaves for extracting fibres'
Phonetic:	[ʃima]	[sɨma]

Then Nahuatl underwent the merger, *i, ɨ > i* (that is, *ɨ > i*, resulting in former *ɨ* being merged with *i*): *sɨma* > [sima] 'to prepare leaves . . .' ([ʃima] 'to shave' remained [ʃima]). However, as a result of the merger of *i* and *ɨ*, the *s* and *ʃ* split into separate phonemes, since the different conditioning sounds in their environment (*i* and *ɨ*) which had originally made them predictable variants (allophones) of the single original phoneme /s/, were no longer distinguished (both now *i*), and hence they could no longer serve as the basis for determining when the phoneme /s/ would be pronounced [ʃ] (formerly before *i*) and where it would be [s] (before former *ɨ*). This left these consonants in contrast, thus changing their status from that of variants (allophones) of one distinctive sound (one phoneme, /s/) to being distinctive, contrastive sounds (separate phonemes, /s/ and /ʃ/):

/ʃima/ 'to shave'   /sima/ 'to prepare plant leaves for extracting fibres'

In the case of the split, the two sounds, *ʃ* and *s*, did not themselves change at all (phonetically); they were both present before the change and are still present in the same phonetic form after the change; however, they now contrast with one another and can serve to distinguish words of different meaning, and so their phonemic status has changed; they have, as a result of the merger, now split into separate phonemes.

Actually historical linguists often distinguish two kinds of splits. The examples discussed so far illustrate what is know as *secondary split* (sometimes also called *phonologization*). In secondary splits, the total number of phonemes in the language increases – new phonological contrasts in the language are produced. As seen in the examples above, in this kind of split the environment for understanding the formerly non-contrastive distribution of the sounds (former allophones) changes in such a way that the complementary distribution of the sounds is no longer visible after the mergers which cause the secondary splits, but was visible in an earlier stage of the language, before the merger took place. The other kind of split is known as *primary split* (also sometimes called *conditioned merger*, which is actually a more representative name, given what happens in this kind of change). Primary splits are often considered more complex and thus more difficult to understand than secondary splits, though the idea is reasonably simple: some variant (allophone) of a sound (a phoneme) abandons that original phoneme and joins some other phoneme instead, leaving a gap in the environments in the language where the phoneme can occur. That is, it could originally occur in certain contexts in which after the change it is no longer found. In this type of split, a variant of a phoneme (an allophone) merges with some other already existing phoneme, but only in certain specific environments. In such changes, the number of phonemes in the language remains unaltered. One of the most cited examples of primary split is rhotacism in Latin (see 2.7.4 below). In rhotacism, intervocalic *s* changes to *r* (*s* > *r* /V_V), illustrated in such English loans from Latin as *rural* (< *rūs-al*, having undergone rhotacism) but *rustic* (Latin *rūs-ticus*, with no rhotacism, since the *s* of *rūs-* is not intervocalic here), based on the Latin root *rūs* 'country, countryside'. Some other instance of English loans from Latin which illustrate the *r/s* alternation of Latin resulting from rhotacism between vowels are: *opus/opera* (Latin *opus* 'work'), *onus/onerous* (Latin *onus* 'burden'), *corpus/corpora/corpo-ral/corporeal* (Latin *corpus* 'body'), and the less obvious *pus/purulent* (Latin *pūs* 'pus'). Since Latin already had *r* as a distinct phoneme, and since only some instances of *s* (just those intervocalic ones) shifted to *r* and thus joined the already existing *r* phoneme of Latin, this is an instance of primary split. Primary splits can be illustrated as in the following diagram:

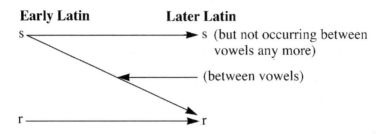

Early Latin   **Later Latin**

s ⟶ s (but not occurring between vowels any more)

(between vowels)

r ⟶ r

Another example illustrating primary split is seen in the change of Latin *k* to French *s*, *ʃ* and *k* in different contexts: *k > s* before *i*, *e* (*centum* [kentum] > *cent* [sã] 'hundred'; *k > ʃ* before *a* (*cantāre* [kanta:re] > *chanter* [ʃãte] 'to sing'); and *k* remaining *k* in other contexts (*clārus* [kla:rus] > *claire* [klɛ:ʀ] 'clear', *cor* [kor] > *coeur* [kœ:ʀ] 'heart'). For example, since *s* already existed as a distinct phoneme, the transfer of some instances of original *k* to *s* (but not others) represents a primary (conditioned) merger.

2.4.3 Unconditioned phonemic changes

We have already seen several examples which fit this category; for example the merger of Spanish palatalized *l* and *y* to *y* (IPA /lʲ/, /j/ > /j/) in most of Latin America was unconditioned – it happened in every environment in the language – and it resulted in fewer contrasting phonemes in the language. In South Island Māori, *ŋ > k* (that is, *ŋ, k > k*); that is, *ŋ* became *k* everywhere, with no limits on where, and the merger of *ŋ* with former *k* resulted in fewer contrastive sounds. Examples of this sort are quite common in languages of the world.

2.4.4 Conditioned phonemic changes

Examples are also abundant of changes in which a sound's phonemic status changes but only in certain circumstances. For example, the well-known 'ruki' rule of Sanskrit is a conditioned change in which original *s* becomes retroflex *ṣ* after the sounds *r*, *u*, *k*, and *i* or *j* (s > ṣ / i, j, u, k, r__), for example *agni-* 'fire' + *-su* 'locative plural' > *agniṣu* 'among the fires'; *vāk* 'word' + *-su* > *vākṣu* 'among the words'. There is a version of this rule also in Avestan and Lithuanian in which *s* > *ʃ* and in Old Church Slavonic in which *s* > *x* in contexts similar to that of the Sanskrit rule.

2.5 Sporadic Changes

Sound changes are also sometimes classified according to whether they are *regular* or *sporadic*. *Sporadic* changes affect only one or a few words, and do not apply generally throughout the language; that is, a change is considered sporadic if we cannot predict which words in a language it will affect. A couple of examples of sporadic changes were seen in Chapter 1: Modern English *speech* has lost the *r* of Old English *spræc* 'language, speech', but *r* is not generally lost in this context, as shown by the fact that *spring, sprig, spree* and so on retain the *r*. *Glamour* comes from *grammar* through the sporadic change of *r* to *l*, but this change is not found regularly in other words; *graft, grain, grasp* and so forth did not change their *r* to *l*.

2.6 General Kinds of Sound Changes

Ultimately, the two distinctions, conditioned/unconditioned and phonemic/non-phonemic, while generally present in the treatments of sound change, are often ignored in discussions of specific sound changes. If a change takes place in all environments, then it is clearly unconditioned whether this is pointed out directly or not; similarly, changes which are limited to particular phonetic contexts are obviously conditioned changes. As for phonemic versus non-phonemic changes, in a great many actual sound changes it is possible to talk about how one sound changes into another without concern for the phonemic status of the sounds in question, or better said, the resulting phonemic status is often clear even if not pointed out specifically. On the other hand, virtually all treatments present a classification (often just a list) of the kinds of sound changes most often encountered in the languages of the world. These are defined and exemplified in what follows, with some indication of which ones are more important and which terms are used less commonly. Historical linguists often do not bother with the more recondite of these.

2.6.1 Assimilation

Assimilation means that one sound becomes more similar to another, a change in a sound brought about by the influence of a neighbouring, usually adjacent, sound. Assimilatory changes are very common, the most frequent and most important category of sound changes. Assimilatory changes are classified in terms of the three intersecting dichotomies *total–partial*, *contact–distant* and *regressive–progressive*. A change is *total* assimilation if a sound becomes identical to another by taking on all of its phonetic features. The change is *partial* if the assimilating sound acquires some traits of another, but does not become fully identical to it. A *regressive* (*anticipatory*) change is one in which the sound that undergoes the change comes earlier in the word (nearer the beginning, more to the left) than the sound which causes or conditions the assimilation. *Progressive* changes affect sounds which come later in the word than (closer to the end than, to the right of) the conditioning environment. These three parameters of classification interact with one another to give the following combinations of named changes.

2.6.1.1 *Total contact regressive assimilation*

(1) Latin *octo* > Italian *otto* 'eight', *noctem* > *notte* 'night', *factum* > *fatto* 'done'. The *k* (spelled *c*) is before/to the left of the *t* which conditions it to change; thus the change is *regressive*. The *k* is immediately adjacent to the *t*, meaning that this is a *contact* change. And, the *k* assumes all the features of the conditioning *t*, becoming itself a *t*, meaning that the assimilation is *total*. In *septem* > *sette* 'seven', *aptum* > *atto* 'apt, fit for', we see the same sort of assimilation but with *p*.

(2) Latin *somnus* > Italian *sonno* 'sleep, dream'.

(3) In Caribbean dialects of Spanish, preconsonantal *s* typically becomes *h*, which frequently assimilates totally to the following consonant (in casual speech): *hasta* /asta/ > [ahta] > [atta] 'until'; *mismo* > [mihmo] > [mimmo] 'same'.

(4) Swedish *ŋk* > *kk*: **drinka* > *drikka* 'to drink' (compare English *drink*), **tanka* > *takka* 'to thank' (compare English *thank*) (where the spelling *nk* represents [ŋk]) (Wessén 1969: 39).

2.6.1.2 *Total contact progressive assimilation*

(1) Proto-Indo-European **kolnis* > Latin *collis* 'hill'. The *n* is after/to the right of the *l* which conditions the change; thus the change is *progressive*. The *n* is immediately adjacent to the *l*, thus a *contact* change. The *n* takes on all the features of *l* which conditions the change, a *total* assimilation. The same change is seen in Proto-Germanic **hulnis*

(from Proto-Indo-European **kolnis*) > Old English *hyll* > Modern English *hill* 'hill', Old English *myln* > Modern English *mill* 'mill' (ultimately a loan in English from Vulgar Latin *mulina* 'mill'; compare French *moulin* and Spanish *molina* 'mill').

(2) In Finnish, earlier *ln* assimilated to *ll*, as in **ʃalna* > *halla* 'frost'.

2.6.1.3   *Partial contact regressive assimilation*

(1) Proto-Indo-European **swep-no-* > Latin *somnus* 'sleep'. This change is *partial* because *p* only takes on some of the features of the conditioning *n*, namely, it becomes more like the *n* by taking on its feature of nasality, becoming *m*. Because the *p* is next to the *n*, this is a *contact* change; it is regressive because the *p* is before the *n* which conditions the change.

(2) In Spanish (in the non-careful pronunciations of most dialects), *s* > *z* / __ voiced C, as in: *mismo* > [mizmo] 'same', *desde* > [dezde] 'since'.

(3) The assimilation of nasals in point of articulation to that of following stops, extremely frequent in the world's languages, is illustrated in English by the changes in the morpheme /ɪn-/ 'not', as in *in-possible* > *impossible; in-tolerant* > *intolerant; in-compatible* > *iŋcompatible* (in the last case, the change of *n to ŋ* is optional for many speakers).

2.6.1.4   *Partial contact progressive assimilation*

(1) The English suffixes spelled *-ed* formerly had a vowel, but after the change which eliminated the vowel, the *d* came to be adjacent to a preceding consonant, and it became voiceless if that preceding consonant was voiceless (and a non-alveolar stop), as in /wɔkt/ 'walked', /træpt/ 'trapped' (d > t / voiceless C__).

(2) English suffixes spelled with *-s* also assimilated, becoming voiced after a preceding voiced (non-sibilant) consonant, as in /dɔgz/ 'dogs', /rɪbz/ 'ribs'.

2.6.1.5   *Distant (non-adjacent) assimilation*

Assimilation at a distance (non-adjacent or non-contact) is not nearly as common as contact assimilation, though some changes having to do with vowels or consonants in the next syllable are quite common. Distant assimilations can be partial or total, and regressive or progressive. These are illustrated in the following examples.

(1) Proto-Indo-European **penkʷe* > Latin *kʷinkʷe* (spelled *quinque*) 'five' (*total distant regressive assimilation*); Proto-Indo-European **pekʷ-* > Italic **kʷekʷ-* 'to cook, ripen' (compare Latin /kokʷ-/ in *coquere* 'to cook').

(2) Proto-Indo-European **penkʷe* > pre-Germanic **penpe* 'five' (compare German *fünf*) (*total distant progressive assimilation*)

(3) Umlaut (see the example above illustrating phonemic split in English) is a well-known kind of change which involves distant assimilation in which a vowel is fronted under the influence of a following front vowel (or a *j*), usually in the next syllable. Umlaut has been particularly important in the history of Germanic languages.

2.6.2 Dissimilation

Dissimilation, the opposite of assimilation, is change in which sounds become less similar to one another. Assimilation is far more common than dissimilation; assimilation is usually regular, general throughout the language, though sometimes it can be sporadic. Dissimilation is much rarer and is usually not regular (is sporadic), though dissimilation can be regular. Dissimilation often happens at a distance (is non-adjacent), though contact dissimilations are not uncommon. The following examples illustrate these various sorts of dissimilatory changes.

(1) English dialects dissimilate the sequence of two nasals in the word *chimney* > *chim(b)ley*.

(2) Instances of multiple occurrences of *r* within a word are often sporadically dissimilated in Romance languages; for example, sequences of /r . . . r/ often become /l . . . r/, sometimes /r . . . l/: Latin *peregrīnus* 'foreigner, alien' > Italian *pellegrino* 'foreigner, pilgrim, traveller'; French *pèlerin* (compare Spanish *peregrino* which retained the two *r*'s; (English *pilgrim* is a loanword from Old French *pelegrin*); Latin *arbor* > Spanish *árbol*. This is distant progressive dissimilation. In a more regular dissimilation involving these sounds, the Latin ending -*al* dissimilated to -*ar* when attached to a root ending in *l*; this is illustrated in the following Latin loans in English, *alveolar, velar, uvular*, which have dissimilated due to the preceding *l*; these can be contrasted with forms in which -*al* remains unchanged because there is no preceding *l*, for example, *labial, dental, palatal*. Some examples from Mexican Spanish which illustrate this suffix (though with a different meaning) in both its original and dissimilated form are: *pinal* 'pine grove' (based on *pino* 'pine'), *encinal* 'oak grove' (compare *encino* 'oak'), but *frijolar* 'bean patch' (compare *frijol* 'bean'), *tular* 'stand of reeds' (see *tule* 'reed, cattail'), *chilar* 'chile patch' (based on *chile* 'chili pepper').

(3) *Grassmann's Law*, a famous sound change in Indo-European linguistics, is a case of regular dissimilation in Greek and Sanskrit where in roots with two aspirated stops the first dissimilates to an unaspirated

stop. These are voiced aspirated stops in Sanskrit and voiceless aspirated stops in Greek:

Sanskrit *bhabhūva* > *babhūva* 'became' (reduplication of root *bhū-*)

Greek *phéphūka* > *péphūka* 'converted' (reduplication of *phū̄- '*to engender').

Frequently cited Greek examples which show Grassmann's Law in action are:

trikh-ós 'hair'(genitive singular) / *thrík-s* (nominative singular)
tréph-ō 'I rear (nourish, cause to grow)' / *thrép-s-ō* 'I will rear'
trekh-ō 'I walk'/ *threk-s-ō* 'I will walk'

Greek *trikhós* 'hair' (genitive singular) comes from earlier **thrikh-ós*, to which Grassmann's Law has applied to dissimilate the *th* because of the following aspirated *kh* (**th . . . kh > t . . . kh*); similarly, *tréphō* 'I rear' is from **thréph-ō*, where **th . . . ph > t . . . ph*. In *thríks* 'hair (nominative singular)', from **thrikh-s*, the *kh* lost its aspiration before the immediately following *s* (the nominative singular ending) (**khs > ks*), and thus Grassmann's Law did not apply in this form. This left initial *th* still aspirated, since there was no longer a sequence of two aspirates in the same root which would cause the first to dissimilate and lose its aspiration. Similarly, in *thrépsō* 'I will rear' (from **thréph-s-ō*) **phs > ps*, and with no second aspirated consonant (no longer a *ph* but now only *p*), the *th* remained aspirated in this word. These changes are seen more clearly in Table 2.3 (nom = nominative, gen = genitive, sg = singular).

TABLE 2.3: Grassmann's Law and its interaction with other Greek changes

	'hair' nom sg	'hair' gen sg	'I will rear'	'I rear'
Pre-Greek	*thrikh-s	*thrikh-os	*threph-s-ō̄	*threph-ō̄
deaspiration before *s*	thriks	—	threpsō̄	—
Grassmann's Law	—	trikhos	—	trephō̄
Greek forms	thriks	trikhos	threpsō̄	trephō̄

Most of the examples presented so far have been cases of distant dissimilations; some additional examples of contact and distant dissimilation are as follows.

(4) Finnish k > h/__ t, d, as in, for example, /tek-dæ/ > *tehdæ* 'to do' (spelled *tehdä*) (compare *teke-e* 'he/she does'); /kakte-na/ > *kahtena* 'as two' (compare *kaksi* 'two') from /kakte-/ to which other changes

31

applied, e > i/__# (*kakte* > *kakti*) and t > s/__i (*kakti* > *kaksi*); since as a result of these changes the *k* no longer appeared before a *t* or *d* in *kaksi*, it remained *k* and so it did not change to *h* (as it did, for example, in *kahtena* 'as two'). This is a regular change; all *kt* and *kd* clusters in native words changed to *ht* and *hd* respectively.

(5) In K'iche' (Mayan), the velar stops (*k, k'*) were palatalized when the next consonant after an intervening non-round vowel was a uvular (*q, q', χ*): *kaq* > *kʲaq* 'red'; *iʃk'aq* > *iʃkʲ'aq* 'fingernail, claw'; *k'aq* > *kʲ'aq* 'flea'; *ke:χ* > *kʲe:χ* 'horse'. The difference between a velar and a uvular stop in the same word is difficult both to produce and to perceive, and for this reason words with *k(')Vq(')* have palatalized the velar (*k, k'*) in order to make them more distinguishable from the uvular (*q, q'*) in these words. This is a regular change (Campbell 1977).

(6) In the history of Finnish, an /a/ before an /i/ of a following morpheme in non-initial syllables regularly changed to /o/ or /e/, depending on the nature of the vowel in the preceding syllable. If the preceding vowel was non-round, /a+i/ became /oi/, and if it was round, /a+i/ became /ei/, thus dissimilating by taking the opposite value of rounding from that of the vowel of the preceding syllable, as in:

sadoilla 'by hundreds' (< *sata* 'hundred' +*i* 'plural' +*lla* 'by')
sodeissa 'in the wars' (< *sota* 'war' +*i* 'plural' +*ssa* 'in') (later, in a
   further change, the *ei*, as in *sodeissa*, monophthongized to give
   modern Finnish *sodissa*).

(7) Dahl's Law is a sound change which took place in a number of East African Bantu languages in which two voiceless consonants in a word dissimilate so that the first becomes voiced. For example, in Kikuyu the change affects only /k/, as in: *gikuyu* 'Kikuyu' < *kikuyu*; *githaka* 'bush' < **kithaka*; *gukua* 'die' < **kukua* (Newman 2000: 268). The change is commonly stated as involving the dissimilation of aspiration, where the first aspirated stop if there is more than one loses its aspiration and becomes voiced, as in Nyamwezi: *-kʰatʰi* 'in the middle' > *gatʰi*, *-pʰitʰ-* 'to pass' > *-bitʰa*, etc. (Mutaka 2000: 253; see also Collinge 1985: 280.)

While several of the examples just presented involve dissimilation in regular sound changes, sporadic dissimilations are more frequent on the whole. Another example of sporadic dissimilation is:

(8) In Old French *livel* (from which English borrowed *level*), the sequence of two *l*'s dissimilated, giving *nivel*, which became Modern French *niveau* 'level' through subsequent sound changes which affected the final *l*.

2.7 Kinds of Common Sound Changes

The following is a list of the names for various kinds of sound changes that are used in the literature on language change. In parentheses after each name is a visual representation based on nonsense forms which shows what happens in the change. A number of real examples of each kind of change is presented.

2.7.1 Deletions

2.7.1.1 Syncope *(atata > atta)*
The loss (deletion) of a vowel from the interior of a word (not initially or finally) is called *syncope* (from Greek *sunkopé* 'a cutting away', *sun-* 'with' + *kopé* 'cut, beat'); such deleted vowels are said to be 'syncopated'. Syncope is a frequently used term.

(1) The change in many varieties of English which omits the medial vowel of words such as *fam(i)ly* and *mem(o)ry* illustrates syncope.

(2) Starting in Vulgar Latin and continuing in the Western Romance languages, the unstressed vowels other than *a* were lost in the interior of words three syllables long or longer, as in *pópulu-* 'people' (*pópulu- > poplV-*), reflected by French *peuple* 'people' and Spanish *pueblo* 'people, town' (English *people* is borrowed from French); *fābulare* 'to talk' became *hablar* 'to speak' in Spanish (*fābulare > fablar(e) > hablar* /ablar/).

While syncope is normally reserved for loss of vowels, some people sometimes speak of 'syncopated' consonants. It is more common in the case of consonants just to speak of *loss* or *deletion*.

(3) For an example of 'syncopation' of consonants, in Swedish (and Scandinavian languages generally), in consonant clusters with three consonants, the middle consonant was lost, as in *norðman > norman* (seen, for example, in *Normandy*, and *Norman French*, for the area of northern France where Vikings settled); **norðr-vegi > *norwegi* (which gives English *Norway*, German *Norwegen*), which went on in Swedish to *Noregi > Norge* [norjɛ] 'Norway, Norwegian'; *Västby* 'a town name' [*Väst* 'west' *+by* 'town'] > *Väsby* (Wessén 1969: 68).

2.7.1.2 Apocope *(tata > tat)*
Apocope (from Greek *apokopé* 'a cutting off', *apo-* 'away' + *kopé* 'cut, beat') refers to the loss (apocopation, deletion) of a sound, usually a vowel, at the end of a word, said to be 'apocopated'. Apocope is a frequently used term.

(1) In words which had final *e* in Latin, this *e* was regularly deleted

in Spanish in the environment VC__# if the consonant was a dental (*l*, *r, n, s, θ*) or *y* [j], as in *pane > pan* 'bread', *sōle > sol* 'sun', *sūdāre > sudar* 'to sweat'.

(2) A comparison of the following Old English nouns with their modern counterparts shows the apocope of the final vowels in these words:

Old English	Modern English
sticca	stick
sunu	son
mōna	moon

(3) Estonian (a Finno-Ugric language) lost final vowels in words where this vowel was preceded either by a long vowel and a single consonant or by two consonants:

*jalka > jalg [jalk] 'foot, leg'
*härkä [hærkæ] > härg [hærk] 'bull'
*hooli > hool 'care, worry'
*leemi > leem 'broth'

However, the vowel was not lost when preceded by a short vowel and a single consonant, as in *kala > kala* 'fish', *lumi > lumi* 'snow'.

2.7.1.3 Aphaeresis (or apheresis) *(atata > tata)*

Aphaeresis (from Greek *aphairesis* 'a taking away') refers to changes which delete the initial sound (usually a vowel) of a word. Aphaeresis can be regular or sporadic. The sporadic change where the initial vowel which was present in Latin *apotēca* 'storehouse, wine-store' is lost in Spanish *bodega* 'wine cellar, storeroom, warehouse' illustrates aphaeresis. (In this instance, intervocalic *-p- > -b-* in Spanish, but initial *p-* remains *p-*; the *b* of *bodega* shows that the initial *a-* was still present when *p > b* and was deleted after this change, *apotēka > abodega > bodega*.) Spanish dialects show many cases of sporadic aphaeresis: *caso < acaso* 'perhaps, by chance'; *piscopal < episcopal* 'episcopal', 'of the bishop'; *ahora > hora* 'now' (especially frequent in *horita < ahorita* 'right now'). The Sapaliga dialect of Tulu (Dravidian) provides an example of regular aphaeresis, where the loss can be seen in comparison with the Shivalli dialect, which has not lost the original vowel. (Here, <c> = [č], IPA [tʃ]; the consonants with dots under them are retroflexed, according to the convention in the Indian linguistic tradition: <d> = IPA [ɖ], <l> = IPA [ɭ]):

Sapaliga Tulu	*Shivalli Tulu*	
dakki	aḍakki	'throw'
lappu	aḷappu	'plough'
latti	eḷatti	'tender'
laccilɨ	olaccilɨ	'stumble'
dattɨ	eḍattɨ	'left'

(Bhat 2001: 66)

Aphaeresis is a rarely used term; many prefer just to speak of initial vowel loss.

2.7.2 Epentheses or insertions (asta > asata)

Epenthesis inserts a sound into a word. (*Epenthesis* is from Greek *epi-* 'in addition' + *en* 'in' + *thesis* 'placing'.) In sound change, sounds can be inserted in several different ways; several of these have their own names and are considered in the sections that follow, though it is common to refer to them all simply as kinds of epenthesis or insertions.

2.7.2.1 Prothesis (tata > atata)

Prothesis (from Greek *pro-* 'before' + *thesis* 'placing') is a kind of epenthesis in which a sound is inserted at the beginning of a word. This is not a particularly frequent term, and such changes are also referred to as word-initial epentheses.

(1) Starting in the second century, Latin words beginning with *s* + Stop (*sp, st, sk*) took on a prothetic short *i*. The following examples trace the development to modern French and Spanish. The prothetic *i* became *e*, and later in French the *s* was lost when it occurred before other consonants. (a) Latin *scola* [skóla] 'school' > *iskola* > *eskola* > Old French *escole* [eskole] > Modern French *école* [ekol]; for Spanish: *scola* [skóla] > *iskola* > *escuela* [eskuéla]. (b) Latin *scūtum* [skū́tum] 'shield' > *iskutu* > *eskutu* > Old French *escu* > Modern French *écu* [eky] 'shield, money'; the sequence in Spanish was from Latin *scūtum* [skū́tum] > *iskutu* > *eskutu* > *escudo* 'shield'. (c) Latin *stabula* [stábula] 'stable' > *istabula* > *estabula* > Old French *estable* > Modern French *étable* [etábl]; for Spanish: *stabula* [stábula] > *istabula* > *estabula* > Spanish *estable* 'stable'.

(2) In Nahuatl, forms which came to have initial consonant clusters, due to the loss of a vowel in the first syllable, later changed to take on an epenthetic (prothetic) *i*: **kasi* > *kʃi* > *ikʃi* "foot' (compare *no-kʃi* 'my foot', where no epenthetic *i* occurs because there is no word-initial consonant cluster).

2.7.2.2 Anaptyxis (anaptyctic) *(VCCV > VCV̆CV)*

Anaptyxis (from Greek *ana-ptussō* 'unfold, open up, expand') is a kind of epenthesis in which an extra vowel is inserted between two consonants (also called a '*parasitic*' vowel or '*svarabhakti*' vowel). This term is used very infrequently, since epenthesis covers this sort of change.

(1) Examples of sporadic anaptyxis are the pronunciation in some dialects of English of *athlete* as ['æθəlit] with the extra vowel and of *film* as ['fɪləm]; in varieties of Spanish, Standard Spanish *Inglaterra* 'England' > *Ingalaterra*, *crónica* 'chronicle' > *corónica*. In the process of borrowing German *Landsknecht* 'mercenary', French inserted an anaptyctic vowel, *lansquenet* (from which English borrowed its less well-known *lansquenet* 'mercenary soldier', 'a card game').

(2) In Finnish dialects of eastern Finland, after the first syllable (which bears the stress), a short copy of the preceding vowel is added regularly between consonants of a consonant cluster which begins with *l* or *r*. (The *ä* of Finnish spelling represents [æ].) For example:

Eastern dialects	Standard	Finnish
nelejä	neljä	'four'
kolome	kolme	'three'
pilikku	pilkku	'comma, dot'
jalaka	jalka	'foot, leg'
kylymä	kylmä	'cold'
silimä	silmä	'eye'

(Kettunen 1930: 120; Kettunen 1969: map 199)

2.7.2.3 Excrescence *(amra > ambra; anra > andra; ansa > antsa)*

Excrescence (from Latin *ex* 'out' + *crēscentia* 'growth') is a type of epenthesis which refers to a consonant being inserted between other consonants; usually the change results in phonetic sequences which are somewhat easier to pronounce than the original clusters would be without the excrescent consonant.

(1) Old English *θy:mel* > Modern English *thimble* (compare *humble/ humility*); Old English *θunrian* > Modern English *thunder* (compare the German cognate *Donner* 'thunder'). The example of *chimney* > *chimbley* in English dialects was already mentioned above.

(2) Proto-Indo-European ** n̥-mr̥t-os* > Greek *ambrotos* 'immortal' (seen in English in *ambrosia* 'food of the gods' (what makes you immortal), a loan with its origin ultimately in Greek).

(3) Spanish *hombre* [ombre] 'man' is from Latin *hominem*, which became *homne* through regular sound changes: syncope, *hominem* > *homne(m)*, then *homre* through dissimilation of the adjacent nasals (*mn*

> *mr*), and then *b* was inserted – an example of excrescence – to make the transition from *m* to *r* easier to pronounce ([omre] > [ombre]). Contrast French *homme* 'man', which shows a different history, where at the *homne* stage, the *n* assimilated to the preceding *m* (*homne* > *homme*). Latin *fēmina* 'woman' became *femna* through syncope of the middle vowel; Old French assimilated the *n* to the adjacent *m*, ultimately giving *femme* 'woman'; Spanish, however, dissimilated the two nasals (*femna* > *femra*), and this then underwent excrescence, inserting a *b* between the *m* and *r*, giving modern Spanish *hembra* /embra/ 'female' (in Spanish, *f*- > *h*- > Ø, though *h* remains in the orthography). Another example is Latin *nomināre* 'to name' > *nomnar* > *nomrar* > *nombrar* in Spanish; French assimilated *mn* to *mm* in this word, giving *nommer* 'to name'. In a similar example: Latin *numerus* 'number' > Old French *numere* > *numbre*, borrowed into English as *number*.

(4) French *chambre* 'room' comes from Latin *camera* 'arched roof'; when the *mr* cluster was created because of the regular syncope of the medial *e* (*camera* > *camra*) the *b* was added between the two (this is the source of the loanword *chamber* in English, from French *chambre* 'room').

(5) Greek *andros* 'man (genitive singular)' comes from earlier *anr-os* (compare Greek *anēr* 'man (nominative singular)').

2.7.2.4 Paragoge *(tat > tata)*

Paragoge (from Greek *paragōgé* 'a leading past') adds a sound (usually a vowel) to the end of a word.

(1) Dialects of Spanish sometimes add a final -*e* (sporadically) to some words that end in -*d*: *huéspede* < *huésped* 'guest'; *rede* < *red* 'net'.

(2) Arandic languages (a branch of Pama-Nyungan, in Australia) regularly added a final ə at the end of words that end in a consonant (Ø > ə / C __#), as in **nuŋkarn* > *ŋkwərnə* 'bone' (Koch 1997: 281–2). This is a rarely used term; examples of this kind of change are rare, and many linguists are quite hostile to the use of this term. It is probably best not to have to be bothered with it, since mention of the insertion of a final vowel covers the examples.

2.7.3 Compensatory lengthening (tast > ta:t)

In changes of compensatory lengthening, something is lost and another segment, usually a vowel, is lengthened, as the name implies, to compensate for the loss.

(1) In the history of English, a nasal was lost before a fricative with the simultaneous compensatory lengthening of the preceding vowel, as in the following from Proto-Germanic to English: *tonθ > tōθ (> Modern English /tuθ/) 'tooth'; *fimf > fíf (> Modern English /faiv/) 'five'; *gans > gōs (> Modern English /gus/) 'goose' (compare the German cognates, which retain the *n*: *Zahn* [tsa:n] 'tooth', *fünf* 'five' and *Gans* 'goose').

(2) An often-cited example is that of the compensatory lengthening which took place in the transition from Proto-Celtic to Old Irish, as in:

Proto-Celtic	Old Irish	
*magl	ma:l	'prince'
*kenetl	cene:l	'kindred', 'gender'
*etn	e:n	'bird'
*datl	da:l	'assembly'

(Arlotto 1972: 89)

(3) Old Norse compensatorily lengthened vowels together with the loss of *n* before *s* or *r* (n > Ø / __s, r), as in Proto-Scandinavian *gans > gōs 'goose', *ons > ōs 'us', *þunra- 'thunder' > þōr 'thunder, Thor' (the latter is the name of the Scandinavian god *Thor* and the source of *Thursday*, literally 'Thor's day'; compare English *thunder* and German *Donner* 'thunder', cognates of these Scandinavian forms). (Compare Wessén 1969: 48.)

(4) Middle Indo-Aryan sequences of vowel-nasal-consonant changed to a long nasalized vowel-consonant (VNC >Ṽ:C) in modern Indo-Aryan language, as seen in the following examples:

Middle-Indo-Aryan	Hindi	Bengali	Gujarati	
kampa-	kã:p-	kã:p-	kã:p-	'tongue'
ganthi	gã:ṭh	gã:ṭh	gã:ṭh	'knot'
bandha	bã:dh	bã:dh	bã:dh	'bond, dam'
sañjha	sã:jh	sã:jh	sã:jh	'twilight'

(Masica 1991: 188)

2.7.4 Rhotacism (VsV > VrV)

Rhotacism (from Greek *rhotakismos* 'use of *r*') refers to a change in which *s* (or *z*) becomes *r*; usually this takes place between vowels or glides; some assume that often cases of rhotacism go through an intermediate stage of -s- > -z- > -r-, where *s* is first voiced and then turned into *r*. The best-known examples of rhotacism come from Latin and Germanic languages.

(1) In older Latin, *s* > *r* / V__V, as seen in *honōr-is* 'honour (genitive singular)' and *honōr-i* 'honour (dative singular)'; *honōs* 'honour (nominative singular)' retains *s*, since it is not between vowels in this form. (In later Latin, *honōs* 'nominative singular' became *honor*, due to analogy with the other forms which contain the intervocalic *r* due to rhotacism; see Chapter 4.)

(2) In West Germanic and North Germanic, **z* > *r*: Proto-Germanic **hauzjan* 'hear' > Old High German *hôren* (Modern German *hören*), Old English *hieran* (Modern English *hear*); contrast the Gothic cognate *hausjan* 'hear' which did not undergo the change (Gothic is East Germanic). Proto-Germanic **maizōn* 'greater' (from Proto-Indo-European **mē-is*, comparative of **mē-* 'big') underwent rhotacism to become Old English *māra* 'greater', modern English *more*. (*Most* is from Old English *mæst*, Germanic **maista-* 'most', from Proto-Indo-European **mē-isto-*, the superlative of 'big'.)

While changes involving rhotacism are rare, the term is a frequent one in linguistic textbooks, due no doubt to the examples of rhotacism known from Latin and Germanic.

2.7.5 Metathesis (asta > atsa; asata > atasa)

Metathesis (from Greek *metathesis* 'transposition, change of sides') is the transposition of sounds; it is a change in which sounds exchange positions with one another within a word. Most instances of metathesis are sporadic changes, but metathesis can also be a regular change.

(1) Sporadic examples of metathesis occur in the history of English: Old English *brid* > Modern English *bird*; Old English *hros* > *horse* (rV > Vr).

(2) Spanish has sporadic cases of *l/r* metathesis, as in *palabra* 'word' < Latin *parabola* 'explanatory illustration, comparison' (r . . . l > l . . . r).

(3) Spanish has undergone a reasonably regular change of metathesis in which sequences of *dl*, which were created by vowel loss, shifted to *ld*, as in *tilde* 'tilde, tittle' (the 'swung dash' on ñ) < Latin *titulus* 'label, title' (through a series of regular changes: *titulus* > *tidulo* > *tidlo* > *tildo* [metathesis *dl* > *ld*] > *tilde*); *molde* 'mould, pattern' < Latin *modulus* 'small measure' (*modulus* > *modlo* > *moldo* > *molde*) (Cf. English 'module', borrowing from the same Latin source.)

(4) Some examples of sporadic metatheses in various Spanish dialects are: *probe* < *pobre* 'poor'; *sequina* < *esquina* 'corner'; *naide* < *nadie* 'nobody'; *Grabiel* < *Gabriel* 'Gabriel'.

2.7.6 Haplology (tatəsa >tasa)

Haplology (from Greek *haplo-* 'simple, single') is the name given to the change in which a repeated sequence of sounds is simplified to a single occurrence. For example, if the word *haplology* were to undergo hap- lology (were to be haplologized), it would reduce the sequence *lolo* to *lo*, *haplology > haplogy*. Some real examples are:

(1) Some varieties of English reduce *library* to '*libry*' [laibri] and *probably* to '*probly*' [prɔbli].

(2) *pacifism < pacificism* (contrast this with *mysticism < mysticism*, where the repeated sequence is not reduced and does not end up as *mystism*).

(3) English *humbly* was *humblely* in Chaucer's time, pronounced with three syllables, but has been reduced to two syllables (only one *l*) in modern standard English.

(4) Modern German *zauberin* 'sorceress, female magician' < *zaubererin* (*zauber* 'magic, enchantment, charm' + *-er* 'one who does' (like *-er* in English) + *-in* 'female agent' (like *-ess* in English).

2.7.7 Breaking

Breaking refers to the diphthongization of a short vowel in particular contexts. While changes which diphthongize vowels are common (see below), the term 'breaking' is most commonly encountered in Germanic linguistics, used for example in discussions of the history of Afrikaans, English, Frisian and Scandinavian.

(1) For example, Old English underwent the breaking of **i > io*, **e > eo*, **a > ea* before *l* or *r* followed by a consonant, or before *h*, as in **kald- > ceald* 'cold', **erθe > eorþe* 'earth', **næh > nēah* 'near', **sæh > seah* 'saw' (compare Beekes 1995: 275; Hogg 1992: 102–3). (The history of breaking in English is very complex and the phonetic inter- pretation is disputed; the spelling <ea> probably represented [æa].)

(2) Old Norse *e > ea* (then later *> ia*) before *a* of the next syllable, which is then syncopated, as in **heldaz > hialdr* 'battle', and *e > eo > io > iɔ̄* before *u* of the next syllable (which also later underwent syncope), as in **erþu > iɔ̄rþ* 'earth' (Beekes 1995: 67).

2.7.8 Other frequent sound changes

There are several other kinds of sound change which are frequently found in discussions of the history of various languages, even though they are usually not included in typical lists of kinds of sound changes. Some of the most common of these follow, described in less detail and with fewer examples. This is by no means an exhaustive listing.

Sound Change

2.7.8.1 Final-devoicing

A very common change is the devoicing of stops or obstruents word-finally; some languages devoice sonorants (*l*, *r*, *w*, *j*, nasals) and some devoice final vowels. In some languages, the devoicing takes place both word-finally and syllable-finally (as in German). In Kaqchikel (Mayan), l, r, w, y > voiceless / __ #. The sonorants *l*, *r*, *w*, *y* (*y* = IPA [j]) underwent the sound change in which they became voiceless at the end of words, for example, *a:l* 'child' [a:l] > [a:l̥], *kar* 'fish' [kar] > [kar̥], *kow* 'hard' [kow] > [kow̥], *xa:y* 'house' [xa:j] > [xa:j̥].

2.7.8.2 Intervocalic voicing (and voicing generally)

It is also very common for various sounds to become voiced between vowels. This affects just stops in some languages, fricatives in others, all obstruents in others. Often the voicing is not just between vowels, but also occurs with the glides *w* and *j*. Many languages also voice stops (some also voice other consonants) after nasals or after any voiced sound; some also voice other sounds when they come before voiced sounds. For example, in the transition from Latin to Spanish (and this includes other Western Romance languages as well), the voiceless stops become voiced between vowels, as illustrated in *lupu* > *lobo* 'wolf' (*p* > *b*), *vīta* > *vida* 'life' (*t* > *d*) and *fīcu* > *higo* 'fig' (*k* > *g*).

2.7.8.3 Nasal assimilation

It is extremely common for nasals to change to agree with the point of articulation of following stops (in some languages with any following consonant): *np* > *mp*, *mt* > *nt*, *nk* > *ŋk*, and so on.

2.7.8.4 Palatalization

Palatalization often takes place before or after *i* and *j* or before other front vowels, depending on the language, although unconditioned palatalization can also take place. Two common kinds of changes are called 'palatalization'. One is the typical change of a velar or alveolar sound to a palato-alveolar sound, as in *k* > *č*, *t* > *č*, *s* > *ʃ* and so on. For example, in colloquial English, sequences of *t* + *y* [j] > *č* [tʃ] and *d* + *y* [j] > *ǰ* [dʒ], as in examples such as *"whatcha doin'"* ['what are you doing?'], *"I betcha"* ['I bet you'], *"didja go"* ['did you go?'], seen also in English varieties where *ty* [tj] word-internal sequences have changed to *č* [tʃ], as in *nature, picture, literature, lecture, fortune*, and *dy* [dj] sequences changed to *ǰ* [dʒ], in *module, grandeur.* English has undergone many changes involving palatalizations throughout its history. For example, Old English *cinn* [kɪn:] > *"chin"* [čɪn] ([tʃɪn]) illustrates the palatalization of *k* before front unrounded vowels (compare the German cognate *Kinn* 'chin, jaw'). In another example, in the history of Spanish the sequence *kt* became *it* (where *i* was the second element of a diphthong), and then the *t* further became palatalized because of the *i*, producing *č*, as in *lakte* > *laite* > *leite* > *leiče* > *leče* 'milk' (spelled *leche*) and *okto* > *oito* > *oičo* > *očo* 'eight' (spelled *ocho*). In a second kind of change called palatalization, a consonant becomes palatalized by taking palatalization as a secondary manner of articulation, as in eastern dialects of Finnish, where consonants are palatalized before *i*, *susi* > *sus^ji* (*sus^j*) 'wolf', *tuli* > *tul^ji* (*tul^j*) 'fire'. Slavic languages are well known for a number of palatalization changes. Changes of the first sort of palatalization not conditioned by front vowels are not uncommon. For example, the change of *k* > *č* spread among several languages of the Northwest Coast linguistic area (see Chapter 12); in Cholan as well as in a few other Mayan languages, **k* > *č* in general.

2.7.8.5 Diphthongization

Diphthongization refers to any change in which an original single vowel changes into a sequence of two vowel segments which together occupy the nucleus of a single syllable. For example, earlier (in the discussion of splits) we saw the change in English in which original long high vowels /ī/ and /ū/ became /ai/ and /au/ respectively, in /mīs/ > /mais/ 'mice' and /mūs/ > /maus/ 'mouse' (a part of the Great Vowel Shift; see section 2.8, p. 48 below). In Spanish, the Proto-Romance vowels **ɛ* and **ɔ* diphthongized to *ie* and *ue* respectively when in stressed position, as in **pɛtra* > *piedra* 'stone', **bɔno* > *bueno* 'good'. In French, by the ninth century, e > ei, and o > ou. These later changed further; ou > eu > ø (dolor > dolour > doleur > dolør <doleur> 'pain'); ei > oi > oe > we > wa (me > mei > moi > moe > mwe > mwa <moi> 'me', lei > [lwa] <loi> 'law', rei > [rwa] <roi> 'king') (Darmsteter 1922: 96–7, 142–3). The *ī* and *ū* of Middle High German became *ai* and *au* respectively in Modern German, as in *īs* > *Eis* /ais/ 'ice' and *hūs* > *haus* /haus/ 'house'. In Finnish, original long mid vowels diphthongised by raising the first portion of the vowel: *e:* > *ie* (long vowels in Finnish are spelled orthographically with a double vowel, *tee* > *tie* 'road'); *o:* > *uo* (*too* > *tuo* 'bring'); *ø:* > *yø* (*tøø* > *tyø* [spelled *työ*] 'work'). *Breaking* (above) is a kind of diphthongization.

2.7.8.6 Monophthongization

In monophthongization, a former diphthong changes into a single vowel, as in the change from Classical Latin to Vulgar Latin of *au* to *o* which shows up as *o* in the modern Romance languages, as in *auru-* >

Spanish *oro*, French *or* 'gold'; *tauru-* > Spanish *toro* 'bull'; *causa-*
'cause, case, thing' > Italian *cosa*, Spanish *cosa* 'thing', French *chose*
[ʃoz] 'thing'. An example from English is the monophthongization of
/ai/ to /a:/ before *r* in some dialects, as in [fa:(r)] 'fire', [ta:(r)] 'tire' (cf.
Wells 1982: 239). Another case is the Sanskrit change of **ai* > *e* and **au*
> *o*, as in the first syllable of *kekara* 'squinting' < Proto-Indo-European
*kaiko- 'one-eyed, squinting' (compare Latin *caecus* 'blind'). An instance
of monophthongization found in the history of French is somewhat
complicated by other changes and by the orthographic conventions with
which it is represented. At the end of the twelfth century, French
changed *al* > *au* before consonants, as in *altre* > *autre* 'other'; then later
au monophthongized to *o*, [otR] (still spelled *autre*) 'other'. Thus,
cheval [ʃəvál] 'horse' retained *al*, since no consonant follows it, but
chevals > *chevaux* [ʃəvó] 'horses' (*als* > *aus* > *os* > *o* in this case)
because a consonant (*s*) did follow. Such forms are spelled in Modern
French with *x*, which stems from the practice in the Middle Ages of
using *x* to abbreviate *-us* (for example, <nox> for *nous* 'we, us'); this
gave the spelling <chevax> for 'horses,' which ended in [aus], and
when the use of the abbreviation ceased, <x> came to be understood as
a substitute for <s>, and so the *u* heard at that time in the *au* diphthong
was reinstated in the writing of such words, hence the modern spelling
chevaux (Darmesteter 1922: 151–2).

2.7.8.7 *Vowel raising*

Changes in which low vowels change to mid (or high) vowels, or mid
vowels move up to high vowels, are quite common. In particular, long
or tense vowels frequently rise. Sometimes these changes can involve
rather wholesale changes in much of the vowel system, known as vowel
shifts, as in the Great Vowel Shift in English (see pp. 51–2 below). One
environment in which raising is not uncommon is at the ends of words,
such as the Finnish change of *e* to *i* word-finally (for example, *vere-* >
veri 'blood'). William Labov (1994, 2001) argues that in vowel shifts,
long (or tense, or peripheral) vowels tend to rise, as in the Great Vowel
Shift in English (considered in section 2.9 below).

2.7.8.8 *Vowel lowering*

Vowel lowering, the opposite of raising, results in high vowels becoming
mid or low vowels, or mid vowels becoming low. For example, vowels
are often lowered before uvular and pharyngeal consonants, and when a
lower vowel occurs in the next syllable, to mention a few common environments. Also, nasalized vowels are lowered very frequently. For

example, Proto-Dravidian *i and *u were lowered before *a in the next syllable in South Dravidian languages, as in *ilay > elay 'leaf', *pukay > pokay 'smoke' (y = [j]) (Zvelebil 1990: 5–6). However, vowel lowering does not necessarily need to be conditioned.

2.7.8.9 Nasalization

In nasalization, vowels often become nasalized in the environment of nasal consonants. The typical scenario is for the nasalized vowels to become phonemic (contrastive) when later in time the nasal consonant is lost, as in French *bon* > [bõn] > [bõ] 'good' (spelled *bon*).

2.7.8.10 Lenition (weakening)

Lenition is a reasonably loose notion applied to a variety of kinds of changes in which the resulting sound after the change is conceived of as somehow weaker in articulation than the original sound. Lenitions thus typically include changes of stops or affricates to fricatives, of two consonants to one, of full consonants to glides (*j* or *w*), sometimes of voiceless consonants to voiced in various environments, and so on. Lenition can also include the complete loss of sounds. An example of lenition is the change of the intervocalic stops which were voiceless in Latin (*p*, *t*, *k*) to voiced stops (*b*, *d*, *g*) in Spanish, as in *skōpa* > *eskoba* (spelled *escoba*) 'broom', *natāre* > *nadar* 'to swim', *amīka* > *amiga* 'female friend'.

2.7.8.11 Strengthening

The variety of changes which are sometimes referred to as 'strengthening' share a loosely defined notion that, after the change, the resulting sound is somehow 'stronger' in articulation than the original sound was. For example, in the change in Q'eqchi' (Mayan) of *w* > *kw* (*winq* > *kwi:nq* 'person') and *y* > *ty* (IPA [j] > [tj]) (*iyax* > *ityax* 'seed'), the *kw* and *tj* are perceived as being stronger than the original *w* and *j*.

2.7.8.12 Gemination

Gemination (from Latin *gemināti̅ō̄n-em* 'doubling', related to *geminus* 'twin', seen in the astrological sign *Gemini*) means, as the name suggests, the doubling of consonants, that is, the change which produces a sequence of two identical consonants from a single starting consonant, as in *t* > *tt*. For example, in certain Finnish dialects in a sequence of short vowel–short consonant–long vowel (VCV:) the consonant is regularly geminated (long vowels and long or geminate consonants are written double: /aa/ = [a:], /ss/ = [s:]), as in *osaa > ossaa* 'he/she knows', *pakoon > pakkoon* 'into flight (fleeing)'.

2.7.8.13 Degemination

When a sequence of two identical consonants is reduced to a single occurrence, the change is often called *degemination*. An example is the change from Latin *pp*, *tt*, *kk* to Spanish *p*, *t*, *k* respectively, as in: *mittere > meter* 'to put', *pekkātu- > pekado* (spelled *pecado*) 'sin, misfortune'.

2.7.8.14 Affrication

Affrication refers to changes in which a sound, usually a stop, sometimes a fricative, becomes an affricate; for example, *t > ts /__i*, and *k > č /__i, e* (*č* = IPA [tʃ]) are quite common.

2.7.8.15 Spirantization (fricativization)

Not uncommonly, an affricate will be weakened (lenited) to a fricative, or a stop will become a fricative. In Cuzco Quechua, syllable-final stops become fricatives, as for example in *rapra > raɸra* 'leaf, wing'; **suqta > soχta* 'six'. A common change is the spirantization of stops between vowels, well known in Dravidian languages (for example, Proto-Dravidian **tapu* 'to perish' > Kannada *tavu* 'to decrease') (Zvelebil 1990: 8). Balto-Finnic languages underwent a similar change in closed syllables (that is, in /__CC or /__C#, as in Finnish *tava-n* 'custom-Accusative Singular' < **tapa-n*).

2.7.8.16 Deaffrication

When an affricate becomes a fricative (not an uncommon change), it is sometimes called deaffrication. For example, *č > ʃ* in Spanish in areas of Chile, and in Panama (in the speech of younger people, varying according to sociolinguistic conditions) (Canfield 1982: 33, 69). In another example, in Chiltiupán Pipil (a Uto-Aztecan language of El Salvador), *ts > s*, as in *tsutsukul > susukul* 'water jug'.

2.7.8.17 Lengthening

Lengthening refers to the change in which some sound, usually a vowel, is lengthened in some context. For example, in Q'eqchi' (Mayan), vowels are lengthened before a consonant cluster which begins with a sonorant (*l, r, m* or *n*): *kenq' > ke:nq'* 'bean', *ɓalk > ɓa:lk* 'brother-in-law'.

2.7.8.18 Shortening

Sounds, particularly vowels, often undergo changes which shorten them in a variety of contexts, such as word-finally, before consonant clusters, when unstressed, and so on. Long vowels also often merge with short vowels generally in a language. For example, in Middle English, long vowels were shortened before a consonant cluster, as in Old English *cēpte* > Middle English *kepte* 'kept' (compare modern *keep/kept*), and in trisyllabic forms when followed by two or more syllables, as in *hōliday* > *holiday* 'holiday' (contrast modern *holy* with *holiday*).

2.8 Relative Chronology

A sound change pertains to a particular period of time in the history of the language in which it takes place. This means that some sound changes may take place in the language at some earlier stage and then cease to be active, whereas others may take place at some later stage in the language's history. Often in the case of different changes from different times, evidence is left behind which provides us with the clues with which to determine their relative chronology, that is, the temporal order in which they took place. (For those who are familiar with rule ordering in synchronic phonology, it may be helpful to point out that relative chronology is very similar, but in historical linguistics refers to the historical sequence in which different changes took place.) Part of working out the phonological history of a language is determining the relative chronology of the changes which have affected the language. A couple of straightforward examples show what is involved.

(1) In the history of Swedish, the change of umlaut took place before syncope, in the sequence:

> Umlaut: a > e / __(C)Ci
> Syncope: i > Ø / V(C)C__r after a root syllable (approximate form of the changes; they are more general, but only the portions affecting this example are presented here).

From Proto-Germanic to Modern Swedish: **gasti-z* > Proto-Scandinavian *gastiz* > *gestir* > Old Norse *gestr* > Modern Swedish *gäst* 'guest' (*gastiz* > *gestir* > *gestr* > *gest* (spelled *gäst*)) (Wessén 1969: 10–11). We can be reasonably certain that these changes took place in this chronological order, since if syncope had taken place first (*gastir* > *gastr*), then there would have been no remaining *i* to condition the umlaut and the form would have come out as the non-existent ✗*gastr*. (Note that ✗ is the symbol used in this book to signal ungrammatical and incorrect forms, distinguished from * which signals reconstructed forms).

(2) Finnish underwent the two changes:

> (1) e > i / __ #
> (2) t > s / __ i

In words such as Proto-Finno-Ugric *wete* 'water' which became *vesi* in
Finnish, clearly (1) (e > i / __ #) had to change final *e* into *i* before (2)
(t > s / __ i) could take place, since (2) only applied with *i*, and the *i* of
vesi would not have been present in this word unless (1) had applied. In
vete-nä (ä = [æ]) 'water (essive singular case)', the root *vete-* retained
its *e* because it is not in word-final position, but rather is followed by the
case ending *-nä*; since there is no final *i* in *vete-nä*, the *t* did not become
s by sound change (2). (Examples involving relative chronology come
up again in several places in this text, especially in Chapters 3, 5 and 8.)

2.9 Chain Shifts

Sometimes several sound changes seem to be interrelated, with more
far-reaching impact on the overall phonological system of the language.
These changes do not happen in isolation from one another, but appear
to be connected, dependent upon one another in some way. Such interconnected changes are called *chain shifts*. Several reasons have been put
forward for why chain shifts should occur, and the final word about this
is surely yet to come, though the connectedness of the changes involved
has often been attributed to notions such as 'symmetry in phonemic
inventories', 'naturalness' or 'markedness', 'maximum differentiation'
and 'a tendency for holes in phonological patterns to be filled'.

Let's begin to clarify what this means with a brief characterization of
what is involved. It is believed that the sounds of a sound system are
integrated into a whole whose parts are so interconnected that a change
in any one part of the system can have implications for other parts of the
system. The general idea behind the chain shifts is that sound systems
tend to be symmetrical or natural, and those that are not, that is, those
which have a 'gap' in the inventory, tend to change to make them
symmetrical or natural (to fill in the gap). However, a change which fills
one gap may create other gaps elsewhere in the system which then
precipitate other changes towards symmetry/naturalness to rectify its
effects, thus setting off a chain reaction.

Chain shifts are classified into two types, *pull chains* (often called
drag chains) and *push chains*. In a *pull chain*, one change may create a
hole in the phonemic pattern (an asymmetry, a gap) which is followed
by another change which fills the hole (gap) by 'pulling' some sound

from somewhere else in the system and changing that sound to fit the needs of symmetry/naturalness so that it fills the gap, and, if the sound which shifted to fill the original hole in the pattern leaves a new hole elsewhere in the pattern, then some other change may 'pull' some other sound in to fill that gap.

Behind a *push chain* is the notion that languages (or their speakers) want to maintain differences between sounds in the system in order to facilitate understanding, the processing of what is heard. If a sound starts changing by moving into the articulatory space of another sound, in the push-chain view, this can precipitate a change where the sound moves away from the encroaching one in order to maintain distinctions important to meaning. If the fleeing sound is pushed towards the artic- ulatory space of some other sound, then it too may shift to avoid the encroachment, thus setting off a chain reaction called a push chain. Sometimes the notion of 'maximum differentiation' is called upon in these instances. The idea behind maximum differentiation is that the sounds in a sound system tend to be distributed so as to allow as much perception difference between them as the articulatory space can pro- vide. Thus, if a language has only three vowels, we expect them to be spread out, with *i* (high front unrounded), *u* (high back rounded) and *a* (low central or back unrounded); we do not expect them to be bunched up, for example, all in the high front area (say, *i, ɪ* and *y*), and these intu- itions are confirmed by the languages of the world, where most of the three-vowel systems have /i, u, a/ or /i, o, a/. If a language has four stops, we do not expect them to be bunched at one point of articulation, say all labials (*p, b, p', pʰ*) with none at other points of articulation; rather, we expect them to be spread across alveolar, velar and perhaps other points of articulation (see Martinet 1970).

Let's now look at some specific examples to give these abstract notions some substance.

(1) Classical Latin had three series of stops intervocalically, the gem- inates (*pp, tt, kk*), the single voiceless (*p, t, k*), and the voiced (*b, d, g*). These three original series of stops changed from Latin to Spanish in an interrelated fashion:

1. Geminate (double) stops became single voiceless stops: *pp > p, tt > t, kk > k*, as in Latin *cuppa* [kuppa] > Spanish *copa* [kopa] 'cup'; *gutta > gota* 'drop'; *bucca* [bukka] 'puffed-out cheek' > *boca* [boka] 'mouth'.
2. Plain voiceless stops became voiced stops: *p > b, t > d, k > g*, as in Latin *sapere* > Spanish *saber* 'to know'; *wīta > vida* 'life'; *amīka > amiga* 'female friend'.

3. Voiced stops (except *b*, which remained) were lost: $d > \emptyset$, $g > \emptyset$ ($b > b$), as in Latin *cadere* > *caer* 'to fall', *crēdere* > *creer* 'to believe'; *rēgīna* > *reina* 'queen'.

The series of changes in the stops in the development from Latin to Spanish has been interpreted as a push chain (let *tt*, *t* and *d* represent all the stops in the three respective series), having taken place in the order:

(1) tt > t, (2) t > d, (3) d > $\emptyset$.

In this view, as the geminates began to simplify, (1) *tt* > *t*, this put pressure on the plain voiceless series to get out of the way, (2) *t* > *d*, which in turn put pressure on the voiced series, causing it to be lost (except for *b*), (3) *d* > $\emptyset$. It would also be possible to interpret this series of changes as a pull chain, applying in the temporal sequence:

(3) d > $\emptyset$, (2) t > d, (1) tt > t.

In this possible scenario, the loss of the voiced stops, (3) *d* > $\emptyset$, left a gap in the inventory, which was filled by the shift of the plain voiceless stops to voiced, (2) *t* > *d*; but this then left a gap for the voiceless stops, and a language with voiceless geminates but no plain voiceless stops would be unexpected, so (1) *tt* > *t* took place.

(2) Grimm's Law is an extremely important set of sound changes in historical linguistics; it is intimately involved in the history of the comparative method and the regularity hypothesis (and so we come back to it in more detail again in Chapter 5). Grimm's Law covers three interrelated changes in the series of stops from Proto-Indo-European to Proto-Germanic:

voiceless stops > voiceless fricatives:

$$*p \quad > \quad f$$
$$*t \quad > \quad \theta$$
$$*k, *\hat{k} > h (x)$$
$$*k^w \quad > hw$$

voiced stops > voiceless stops

$$*b \quad > \quad p$$
$$*d \quad > \quad t$$
$$*g, *\hat{g} > k$$
$$*g^w \quad > kw$$

voiced aspirated (murmured) stops > plain voiced stops

$$*bh \quad > \quad b$$
$$*dh \quad > \quad d$$

*gh, *ĝh > g

*gʷh   > gw, w

(The sounds *k̂ *ĝ and *ĝh represent the 'palatal' series in Indo-European. See also section 5.4.1 in Chapter 5.)

This means that words in modern Germanic languages, because they inherit the results of these changes from Proto-Germanic, show the effects of the changes, but when cognate words from other Indo-European languages (not from the Germanic branch) are compared with those from Germanic languages, they do not show the results of these changes. Some examples which illustrate the effects of Grimm's Law are given in Table 2.4, which compares words from English (Germanic) with cognates from Spanish and French (Romance languages, not Germanic). In some cases, Spanish and French have undergone other changes of their own, making the correspondences expected from Grimm's Law not so obvious today, though the connections are clear when we take the full history of these languages into account – this is particularly true of the voiced aspirated sounds, for which examples from Sanskrit and Latin are substituted instead.

TABLE 2.4: Grimm's Law in English, Spanish and French comparisons

	Spanish	*French*	*English*
*p > f	pie	pied (Old French pié)	foot
	padre	père	father
	por	per	for
*t > θ	tres	trois	three
	tu	tu	thou
*k > h	(can)	chien (< kani-)	hound (< hūnd)
	ciento	~~cien~~ (< kent-) *cent*	hundred
	corazón	cœur	heart
*b > p	[NOTE: *b was rare in Proto-Indo-European; some say it was missing]		
*d > t	diente	dent	tooth (< tanθ)
	dos	deux	two
*g > k	—	genou	knee
	grano	grain	corn

	Sanskrit	*Latin*	*English*
*bh > b	bhrā́tar	frāter	brother
	bhára-	fer-	bear
		(f < *bh)	
*dh > d	dhā-	facere	do, did, deed
		(f < dh)	
*gh > g	haṃsa (<*gh)	(h)anser	goose
	[hə̃sə]		

Grimm's Law can be interpreted as either a pull chain or a push chain (where *t, d* and *dh* represent all the stops of these series). If the temporal sequence were

(1) t > θ, (2) d > t, (3) dh > d,

then it would be assumed that (1) $t > \theta$ took place first, leaving the language with the three series, voiceless fricatives (*f, θ, h*), voiced stops (*b, d, g*) and voiced aspirates (*bh, dh, gh*), but no plain voiceless stops (no *p, t, k*). This would be an unnatural situation which would pull in the voiced stops to fill the gap ((2) $d > t$); however, this would leave the language with voiced aspirates but no plain voiced stops, also an unnatural arrangement, and so the voiced aspirates would be pulled in to fill the slot of the plain voiced stops ((3) $dh > d$), making a more symmetrical system.

In the push-chain scenario, the voiced aspirates first started to move towards the plain voiced stops, a natural change towards easier articulation ((3) $dh > d$), but the approach of *dh* into the space of *d* forced original **d* to move towards *t* ((2) $d > t$), which in turn pushed original **t* out in order to maintain a distinction between these series of sounds ((1) $t > \theta$).

(3) The English Great Vowel Shift, mentioned in examples above, is one of the best-known of all chain shifts. Between Chaucer (c. 1400) and Shakespeare (born 1564), English underwent a series of interrelated vowel changes known as the Great Vowel Shift, in which long vowels systematically raised, and the highest long vowels diphthongised, as seen in Figure 2.1.

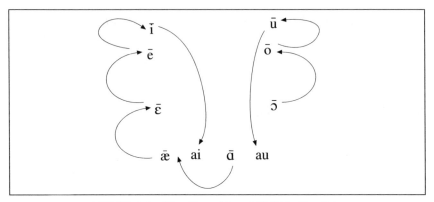

FIGURE 2.1: The Great Vowel Shift in English

These changes are seen in the following words:

Middle English	Chaucer	Shakespeare	Modern English	
bite(n)	/bītə/	/bəit/	/bait/	'bite' (ī > ai)
tide	/tīd/	/təid/	/taid/	'tide'
bete	/bētə/	/bīt/	/bi(:)t/	'beet' (ē > i)
mete	/mēt/	/mēt/	/mi(:)t/	'meat'(ɛ̄ > ē > i)
bete 'strike'	/bǣt/	/bēt/	/bit/	'beat' (ǣ > i)
name	/nāmə/	/nǣm/	/neim/	'name'
hous	/hūs/	/həus/	/haus/	'house' (ū > au)
boote	/bōt/	/būt/	/bu(:)t/	'boot' (ō > u)
boat	/bɔt/	/bōt/	/bout/	'boat' (ɔ̄ > ou)

(4) *Mamean shift.* Chain shifts of various sorts, some more complex, some involving only a couple of changes, are known from many languages, not just Indo-European. One example is the chain shift in Mamean languages (a branch of the Mayan family) in which:

*r > t (for example, Mam *ti:x* < **ri:x* 'old man', the prefix *t-* < **r-* 'his, hers, its')

*t > č (*čap* < **tap* 'crab', *čeʔw* < **teʔw* 'cold')

*č > ç̌ [a laminal retroflex grooved affricate] (*ç̌'o:ç̌'* < **ç̌'ohč* 'earth', *ç̌'am* < **ç̌'am* 'sour').

2.10 Exercises

Exercise 2.1 Sound change – Proto-Germanic to Old English
Compare the Proto-Germanic forms with their descendants in Old English

and determine what sound changes involving vowels have taken place. Write out the sound change involved, and identify (by name) the kind of change found. (Note that *ī, ō, ū* and *ā* are long vowels.)

Proto-Germanic   Old English

1.	*fimf	fīf	'five'
2.	*gans-	gōs	'goose'
3.	*grinst	grīst 'a grinding'	'grist'
4.	*hanh-	hōh	'heel, hock'
5.	*linθj(az)-	līθe	'mild, lithe'
6.	*munθ-	mūθ	'mouth'
7.	*tanθ-	tōθ	'tooth'
8.	*gang-	gang	'a going'
9.	*grind-	grind	'grind'
10.	*hlink-	hlink	'ridge, links'
11.	*hund-	hund	'dog, hound'
12.	*land-	land	'land'
13.	*sing-	sing-	'sing'
14.	*slink-	slink-	'slink'
15.	*sundan	sund-	'swimming, sea, sound'
16.	*swing-	swing-	'swing'
17.	*θingam	θing-	'assembly, (legal) case, thing'
18.	*wund-	wund	'a wound'

Exercise 2.2   Sound change – Sanskrit to Pali

Compare the Sanskrit forms with their descendants in later Pali; determine what sound changes have taken place. Write out the changes, and identify (by name) the kind of changes where possible.

NOTE: Sanskrit *s* = [s], *ś* = [ʃ], *ṣ* [ʂ]. Each set is in effect a separate sound change exercise, though some changes may be illustrated in the examples of more than one set.

Set I

	Sanskrit	*Pali*	
1.	śaśa	sasa	'hare'
2.	kēśa	kesa	'hair'
3.	dēśa	desa	'country'
4.	dōsa	dosa	'fault'
5.	dāśa	dasa	'slave'
6.	śiṣya	sissa	'pupil'
7.	saṡya	sassa	'grain'

Set II

	Sanskrit	Pali	
8.	sna:na	sina:na	'bathing'
9.	sneha	sineha	'friendship'
10.	snihyati	sinihyati	'is fond of'
11.	snigdha	siniddha	'oily'

Set III

	Sanskrit	Pali	
12.	āuṣadha	ōsadha	'herbs, medicine'
13.	gāura	gōra	'white, light yellow'
14.	kāuśika	kōsika	'owl'
15.	gaura	gōra	'pale'
16.	mauna	mōna	'silence'
17.	augha	ōgha	'flood'
18.	tāila	tēla	'oil'
19.	vāira	vēra	'enmity'
20.	śaila	sēla	'rocky'
21.	aikya	ekka	'oneness'

Set IV

	Sanskrit	Pali	
22.	pariṣat	parisā	'assembly'
23.	matimant	matimā	'wise'
24.	ārakāt	ārakā	'from afar'
25.	dharmāt	dhammā	'merit (ablative)'
26.	arthāt	atthā	'that is'
27.	bhagavant	bhagavā	'venerable'
28.	mitravant	mittavā	'having friends'

(Bhat 2001: 67, 68, 70, Masica 1991: 168)

Exercise 2.3   Sound change – Sanskrit to Prakrit

Compare the Sanskrit forms with their descendants in later Prakrit; determine what sound changes have taken place. Write out the changes, and identify (by name) the kind of changes where possible.

NOTE: consonants with subscript dots are retroflex; Sanskrit *s* = [s], *ś* = [ʃ], *ṣ* = [ʂ]. Each set is in effect a separate sound change exercise, though some changes may be illustrated in the examples of more than one set.

Set I

	Sanskrit	Prakrit	
1.	sapta	satta	'seven'
2.	dugdha	duddha	'milk'
3.	udgāra	uggāla	'spit out'
4.	tikta	titta	'pungent'
5.	mudga	mugga	'mung bean'
6.	ardha	addha	'half'
7.	karpaṭa	kappaḍa	'rag, cloth'
8.	kurkura	kukkura	'dog'
9.	darpa	dappa	'arrogance'
10.	parṇa	paṇṇa	'leaf'
11.	karma	kamma	'work'

Set II

	Sanskrit	Prakrit	
12.	saras	sara	'lake'
13.	šara	sara	'arrow'
14.	sapta	satta	'seven'
15.	šakta	satta	'able'
16.	sarva	savva	'all'
17.	šava	savva	'corpse'
19.	si:sa	sīsa	'lead'
20.	ši:la	sīla	'conduct'

Set III

	Sanskrit	Prakrit	
21.	kāšmīra	kamhīra	'Kashmir'
22.	gri:ṣma	grimha	'summer'
23.	vismaya	vimhaya	'surprise'
24.	ūṣman	umhā	'heat'
25.	viṣṇu	viṇhu	'Visnu'
26.	prašna	paṇha	'question'
27.	snāna	ṇhāṇa	'bath'

(Bhat 2001: 6–7, 32, 83)

Exercise 2.4   Sound change – Proto-Slavic to Russian

What sound changes that have taken place in Russian since Proto-Slavic times are illustrated in the following data? Write rules to account for the palatalization of consonants, the change in the stem vowels, loss of vowels, and change in voicing of consonants. Do not attempt to write sound change rules for the changes in the consonant clusters (*bl*, *tl*, *dl*) in examples 1, 2, and 3. More than one change has applied to some forms; for these, state the relative chronology of these changes (the order, temporal sequence) in which the different changes took place. (The breve /˘/ over vowels means 'short'.)

	Proto-Slavic	*Russian*	
1.	*greblŭ	grʲop	'rowed'
2.	*metlŭ	mʲol	'swept'
3.	*vedlŭ	vʲol	'led'
4.	*nesŭ	nʲos	'carried'
5.	*pĭsŭ	pʲos	'dog'
6.	*domŭ	dom	'house'
7.	*grobŭ	grop	'coffin'
8.	*nosŭ	nos	'nose'
9.	*rodŭ	rot	'gender'
10.	*volŭ	vol	'bull'
11.	*dĭnĭ	dʲenʲ	'day'
12.	*konĭ	konʲ	'horse'
13.	*vĭsĭ	vʲesʲ	'all'

(Verb forms in these data = 'third person masculine past tense')

Exercise 2.5 Sound change in dialects of Tulu (Dravidian)

The forms in the Sapaliga dialect correspond to those of the oldest stage of the language; therefore, compare the forms in the other dialects to those of Sapaliga and determine what sound changes have taken place in each of the other dialects of Tulu. Write out and list the sound changes for each dialect, and identify (name) the kind of change involved in each instance, wherever this is possible. Do you imagine that some of the dialects went through more than one change in intermediate stages to arrive at some of the individual sounds they now have? If so, what might the intermediate stages have been?

NOTE: <c> = [č] (IPA [tʃ]); consonants with dots beneath = retroflex.

	Sapaliga	*Holeya*	*Setti*	*Jain 1*	*Jain 2*	
1.	tare	care	sare	hare	are	'wear off'
2.	tali	caḷi	sali	hali	ali	'sprinkle'
3.	tavḍu	cavḍu	savḍu	havḍu	avḍu	'bran'
4.	tōjɨ	cōjɨ	sōjɨ	hōjɨ	ōjɨ	'appear'

	Sapaliga	*Holeya*	*Setti*	*Jain 1*	*Jain 2*	
5.	tinɨ	cinɨ	sinɨ	hinɨ	inɨ	'eat'
6.	tudɛ	cudɛ	sudɛ	hudɛ	–	'river'
7.	tōḍu	cōḍu	sōḍu	hōḍu	ōḍu	'stream'
8.	tanɛ	canɛ	sanɛ	hanɛ	anɛ	'conceiving (of cattle)'
9.	tappu	cappu	sappu	happu	appu	'leaf'
10.	tay	cay	say	hay	ay	'die'
11.	tavtɛ	cavtɛ	savtɛ	havtɛ	avtɛ	'cucumber'
12.	tuttu	cuttu	suttu	huttu	uttu	'wear'
13.	tumbu	cimbu	sumbu	humbu	umbu	'carry on head'
14.	tū	cū	sū	hū	ū	'see'

(Bhat 2001: 51)

Exercise 2.6   *Sound change – Brule Spanish*

Brule Spanish is the dialect of Ascension Parish, Louisiana. Spanish speakers from the Canary Islands settled there in the late 1700s. Compare the Brule Spanish forms in the following data with the corresponding forms in Standard (American) Spanish, written in phonemic notation (standard spelling given in parentheses). Assume Standard Spanish is the older stage from which Brule Spanish has derived. That is, look for changes only in Brule Spanish – find these changes by comparing Brule Spanish with Standard Spanish. Determine what sound changes have taken place in Brule Spanish and write rules to represent them. Do not attempt to determine what happened in cases involving differences in *o/u*, *e/i*, *s/z* or *v/b*. (Based on data from Holloway 1997.) NOTE: in these data, intervocalic /r̃/ is [r] (voiced alveolar trill) and /r/ is [ɾ] (voiced alveolar flap/tap); there is no contrast between these sounds initially and finally, and though initial /r/ is trilled, it is represented as <r> in these data. *y* represents IPA [j].

	Brule Spanish		*Standard (American) Spanish*
1.	'lalgo	'long'	'largo (largo)
2.	mal'tiyo	'hammer'	mar'tiyo (martillo)
3.	'valba	'Spanish moss'	'barba (barba) 'beard'
4.	'syemple	'always'	'syempre (siempre)
5.	tem'plano	'early'	tem'prano (temprano)
6.	'kwælpo	'body'	'kwerpo (cuerpo)
7.	sæl'vyeta	'table napkin'	ser'byeta (servieta)
8.	'kwælvo	'crow'	'kwerbo (cuervo)
9.	pæl'sona	'person'	per'sona (persona)

Brule Spanish			Standard (American) Spanish
10. æl'mano	'brother'		er'mano (hermano)
11. 'mwælto	'dead'		'mwerto (muerto)
12. 'naa	'nothing'		'nada (nada)
13. 'too	'all'		'todo (todo)
14. ve'nao	'deer'		be'nado (venado)
15. ru'iya	'knee'		ro'diya (rodilla)
16. pa're	'wall'		pa'red (pared)
17. 'pare	'father'		'padre (padre)
18. 'mare	'mother'		'madre (madre)
19. 'pyera	'stone, rock'		'pyedra (piedra)
20. ko'myeno	'eating'		ko'myendo (comiendo)
21. 'kwano	'when'		'kwando (cuando)
22. 'one	'where'		a'donde (adonde)
23. kul'tinah	'curtains'		kor'tinas (cortinas)
24. 'gatoh	'cats'		'gatos (gatos)
25. dyoh	'God'		dyos (Diós)
26. 'nočeh	'nights'		'nočes (noches)
27. rah'kano	'scratching'		ras'kando (rascando)
28. ehko'peta	'shotgun'		esko'peta (escopeta)
29. 'kohta	'coast'		'kosta (costa)
30. peh'kao	'fish'		pes'kado (pescado)
31. ko'zyeno	'sewing'		ko'syendo (cosiendo)
32. u'za	'to use'		u'sar (usar)
33. ka'miza	'shirt'		ka'misa (camisa)
34. be'zer̃o	'calf'		be'ser̃o (becerro)
35. ka'za	'to marry'		ka'sar (casar(se))
36. di'sir	'to say'		de'sir (decir)
37. vih'tir	'to dress'		bes'tir (vestir)
38. pi'aso	'piece'		pe'daso (pedazo)
39. ru'iya	'knee'		ro'diya (rodilla)
40. u'yir	'to hear'		o'ir (oir)
41. yu'vyeno	'raining'		yo'byendo (lloviendo)
42. vih'pero	'beehive'		abis'pero (avispero)
43. ma'riyo	'yellow'		ama'riyo (amarillo)
44. ma'r̃a	'to tie up'		ama'r̃ar (amarrar)
45. 'one	'where'		a'donde (adonde)
46. 'legle	'happy'		a'legre (alegre)

Brule Spanish			Standard (American) Spanish
47. bi'hon	'bumblebee'		abe'xon (abejón)
48. fei'ta	'to shave'		afei'tar (afeitar)
49. 'viya	'city'		'biya (villa) 'town'

Exercise 2.7 Sound change – Balto-Finnic

Determine what sound changes affecting the vowels have taken place in Finnish and Estonian. Write the rules which specify these changes and under what conditions they took place. Identify (name) the changes, where possible.

NOTE: ä = [æ], ö = [ø], ü = [y], õ = [ɨ]. Double vowels (for example *aa*, *oo*, and so on) are long vowels. Orthographic <b, d, g> in Estonian are represented here phonetically as [p, t, k] respectively, although these sounds are between voiced and voiceless, described sometimes as 'semi-voiceless' or 'half-voiced'.

Proto-Balto-Finnic	Finnish	Estonian	gloss
1. *maa	maa	maa	'land'
2. *noori	nuori	noor	'young'
3. *koori	kuori	koor	'bark, peel'
4. *hooli	huoli	hool	'care, worry'
5. *jooni	juoni	joon	'line, direction'
6. *leemi	liemi	leem	'broth'
7. *mees	mies	mees	'man'
8. *meeli	mieli	meel	'mind'
9. *keeli	kieli	keel	'tongue, language'
10. *reemu	riemu	rõõm [rɨːm]	'joy'
11. *meekka	miekka	mõõk [mɨːk]	'sword'
12. *peena	piena	põõn [pɨːn]	'slat, rail, cross-piece'
13. *veeras	vieras	võõras [vɨːras]	'foreign'
14. *luu	luu	luu	'bone'
15. *hiiri	hiiri	hiir	'mouse'
16. *kyynärä	kyynärä	küünar	'ell (measure)'
17. *töö	työ	töö	'work'
18. *möö-	myö-	möö-	'along, by'
19. *kala	kala	kala	'fish'
20. *lapa	lapa	laba [lapa]	'blade'
21. *kylä	kylä	küla	'village'

Proto-Balto-Finnic	Finnish	Estonian	gloss
22. *ikä	ikä	iga [ika]	'age'
23. *isä	isä	isa	'father'
24. *joki	joki	jõgi [jɨki]	'river'
25. *kivi	kivi	kivi	'stone'
26. *lumi	lumi	lumi	'snow'
27. *läpi	läpi	läbi [læpi]	'through, hole'
28. *suku	suku	sugu [suku]	'family'
29. *ilma	ilma	ilm 'world'	'weather, world'
30. *jalka	jalka	jalg [jalk]	'foot, leg'
31. *kalma	kalma	kalm	'grave (mound)'
32. *nälkä	nälkä	nälg [nælk]	'hunger'
33. *härkä	härkä	härg [hærk]	'ox, bull'
34. *silmä	silmä	silm	'eye'
35. *marja	marja	mari	'berry'
36. *karja	karja	kari	'cattle'
37. *orja	orja	ori	'slave'
38. *lintu	lintu	lind [lint]	'bird'
39. *hullu	hullu	hull	'crazy'
40. *mänty	mänty	mänd [mænʲtʲ]	'pine'
41. *synty	synty	sünd [synʲtʲ]	'birth'
42. *hanki	hanki	hang [haŋk]	'crust of snow'
43. *kurki	kurki	kurg [kurk]	'crane'
44. *nahka	nahka	nahk	'leather'
45. *lehmä	lehmä	lehm	'cow'
46. *lehti	lehti	leht	'leaf, sheet'
47. *hauta	hauta	haud [haut]	'grave'
48. *lauta	lauta	laud [laut]	'board'
49. *lava	lava	lava	'platform, frame'
50. *haava	haava	haav	'wound'
51. *hinta	hinta	hind [hint]	'price'
52. *into	into	ind [int]	'passion'
53. *halko	halko	halg [halk]	'piece/block of wood'
54. *kylmä	kylmä	külm	'cold'

Proto-Balto-Finnic	Finnish	Estonian	gloss
55. *hullu	hullu	hull	'crazy'
56. *hiki	hiki	higi [hiki]	'sweat'
57. *kylki	kylki	külg [kylk]	'side'
58. *kirppu	kirppu	kirp [kirp:]	'flea'
59. *verkko	verkko	võrk [vɨrk:]	'net'
60. *onsi	onsi	õõs [ɨ:s]	'a hollow place'
61. *kansi	kansi	kaas	'cover'
62. *kynsi	kynsi	küüs	'fingernail, claw'
63. *mesi	mesi	mesi	'honey'
64. *kuusi	kuusi	kuus	'six'
65. *kusi	kusi	kusi	'urine'
66. *mato	mato 'worm'	madu [matu]	'snake'
67. *elo	elo	elu	'life/building'
68. *hako	hako	hagu [haku]	'evergreen sprig, brushwood'
69. *ilo	ilo 'joy'	ilu	'beauty'
70. *himo	himo	himu	'lust, desire'
71. *iho	iho	ihu	'skin, hide'
72. *vesa	vesa	võsa [vɨsa]	'sprout, brush, weed'
73. *helma	helma	hõlm [hɨlm]	'skirt, frock'
74. *terva	terva	tõrv [tɨrv]	'tar'
75. *velka	velka	võlg [vɨlk]	'debt'
76. *perna	perna	põrn [pɨrn]	'spleen'
77. *leuka	leuka	lõug [lɨuk]	'jaw, chin'
78. *tosi	tosi	tõsi [tɨsi]	'true'
79. *solki	solki	sõlg [sɨlk]	'buckle, brooch'
80. *sormi	sormi	sõrm [sɨrm]	'finger'
81. *pohja	pohja	põhi [pɨhi]	'bottom, base'
82. *poski	poski	põsk [pɨsk]	'cheek'
83. *korpi	korpi	kõrb [kɨrp]	'dark woods, wilderness'
84. *metsä	metsä	mets	'woods'
85. *leppä	leppä	lepp [lep:]	'alder'

3

Borrowing

When a foreign word falls by accident into the fountain of a language,
it will get driven around in there until it takes on that language's
colour.

(Jakob Grimm)

3.1 Introduction

It is common for one language (actually speakers of the language) to
take words from another language and make them part of its own vocabulary: these are called *loanwords* and the process is called linguistic
borrowing. Borrowing, however, is not restricted to just lexical items
taken from one language into another; any linguistic material – sounds,
phonological rules, grammatical morphemes, syntactic patterns, semantic
associations, discourse strategies or whatever – can be borrowed, that
is, can be taken over from a foreign language so that it becomes part of
the borrowing language. Borrowing normally implies a certain degree
of bilingualism for at least some people in both the language which
borrows (sometimes called the *recipient* language) and the language
which is borrowed from (often called the *donor* language). In this
chapter, we are concerned with answering the questions: (1) what are
loanwords?; (2) why are words borrowed?; (3) what aspects of language
can be borrowed and how are they borrowed?; (4) what are the methods
for determining that something is a loanword and for identifying the
source languages from which words are borrowed?; and (5) what
happens to borrowed forms when they are taken into another language?
(Other aspects of linguistic borrowing are treated in Chapter 10 on
syntactic change and in Chapter 12 on areal linguistics.)

3.2 What is a Loanword?

A loanword is a lexical item (a word) which has been 'borrowed' from another language, a word which originally was not part of the vocabulary of the recipient language but was adopted from some other language and made part of the borrowing language's vocabulary. For example, Old English did not have the word *pork*; this became an English word only after it was adopted from French *porc* 'pig, pork', borrowed in the late Middle English period – so we say, as a consequence, that *pork* is a French loanword in English. French has also borrowed words from English, for example *bifteck* 'beefsteak', among many others. Loanwords are extremely common; some languages have many. There are extensive studies of the many Scandinavian and French loans in English; Germanic and Baltic loans in Finnish; Basque, German and Arabic loans in Spanish; Native American loanwords in Spanish and Spanish loans in various Native American languages (called *hispanisms*); Turkic in Hungarian; English in Japanese; Sanskrit in Malay and other languages of Indonesia; Arabic in various languages of Africa and Asia; and so on, to mention just a few cases which have been studied intensively.

A quick glance at the contents of our kitchen pantry will begin to give us an appreciation for the impact of loanwords on English vocabulary:

catsup, ketchup < apparently originally from the Amoy dialect of Chinese *kôe-chiap, kè-tsiap* 'brine of pickled fish or shellfish', borrowed into Malay as *kēchap*, taken by Dutch as *ketjap*, the probable source from which English acquired the term.

chocolate < Nahuatl (Mexico, the language of the Aztecs) *čokolātl* 'a drink made from the seeds of the cacao tree', borrowed as Spanish *chocolate* from which other languages of the world obtained the term.

coffee < Arabic *qahwa* 'infusion, beverage', originally said to have meant some kind of 'wine', borrowed through the Turkish pronunciation *kahveh* from which European languages get their terms.

Coca-Cola < *coca* < Quechua *kuka* 'coca leaves, coca bush', borrowed via Spanish *coca*, and *cola* < languages of west Africa *kola* 'cola nut' (for example Temne *kola*, Mandingo *kolo* 'cola (tree species)').

flour < Old French *flour* 'flower' (compare French *fleur de farine* 'flower of meal/flour', that is, the 'best or finest of the ground meal').

juice < French *jus* 'broth, sauce, juice of plant or animal'.

pantry < Old French *paneterie* 'bread-room, bread-closet', based on Latin *pānis* 'bread'.

pepper < ultimately of ancient oriental origin (compare Sanskrit *pippalī* long pepper'); it came early to Germanic peoples via Latin *piper.*

potato < Taino (Cariban language of Haiti) *patata*, borrowed through Spanish *batata, patata* to many other languages.

rice < ultimately from Dravidian *aril/*ariki* 'rice, paddy' (compare Tamil *ari/ari-ci*), via Latin *oriza* and Greek *orúza*.

spaghetti < Italian *spaghetti*, plural of *spaghetto* 'small thread', the diminutive of *spago* 'string, twine'.

sugar < ultimately from Arabic *sukkar*, through Old French *çucre*.

tea < ultimately from Chinese (compare Amoy dialect *te*), probably borrowed through Malay *te/teh* into Dutch and from Dutch to English.

tomato < Nahuatl *tomatl*, through Spanish *tomate*.

These are but a few of the borrowed forms among English foodstuffs.

3.3 Why do Languages Borrow from One Another?

Languages borrow words from other languages primarily because of *need* and *prestige*. When speakers of a language acquire some new item or concept from abroad, they *need* a new term to go along with the new acquisition; often a foreign name is borrowed along with the new concept. This explains, for example, why so many languages have similar words for 'automobile' (as in Russian *avtomobil^j*, Finnish *auto*, Swedish *bil* – from the last syllable of *automobil*); 'coffee' (Russian *kofe*, Finnish *kahvi*, Japanese *kōhii*); 'tobacco' (Finnish *tupakka*, Indonesian *tembakau* [təmbakau], Japanese *tabako* 'cigarette, tobacco', ultimately from Arabic *ṭabāq, ṭubāq* 'a herb which produced euphoria' via Spanish *tabaco*); and *Coca-Cola*, for example, since languages presumably needed new names for these new concepts when they were acquired. Of course, most examples of loanwords are more local, not so widespread as these.

The other main reason why words are taken over from another language is for *prestige*, because the foreign term for some reason is highly esteemed. Borrowings for prestige are sometimes called 'luxury' loans. For example, English could have done perfectly well with only native terms for 'pig flesh/pig meat' and 'cow flesh/cow meat', but for reasons of prestige, *pork* (from French *porc*) and *beef* (from French *bœuf*) were borrowed, as well as many other terms of 'cuisine' from French – *cuisine* itself is from French *cuisine* 'kitchen' – because French had more social status and was considered more prestigious than English during the period of Norman French dominance in England (1066–1300). For example, Udmurt (Votyak, a Finno-Ugric language) borrowed from Tatar (a Turkic language) words for such things as 'mother', 'father', 'grand-mother', 'grandfather', 'husband', 'older brother', 'older sister', 'uncle', 'human', among other things. Since Votyak had native terms for 'father' and 'mother' and these other kin before contact with Tatar, need was not the motivation for these borrowings, rather prestige was. Similarly, Finnish borrowed words for 'mother' (*äiti*, from Germanic; compare Gothic *aipei* [ɛθī], Old High German *eidī*, Proto-Germanic **aiθī*) 'daughter' (*tytär*, from Baltic; compare Lithuanian *dukteř̃s* (genitive form)); 'sister' (*sisar*, from Baltic; compare Lithuanian *seser̃s* (genitive form)); and 'bride', 'navel', 'neck', 'thigh' and 'tooth', among many others from Baltic and Germanic (compare Anttila 1989: 155). Clearly, Finnish had previously had terms for close female kin and for these body parts before borrowing these terms from neighbouring Indo-European languages, and thus it is prestige which accounts for these borrowings and not need.

Some loans involve a third, much rarer (and much less important) reason for borrowing, the opposite of prestige: borrowing due to negative evaluation, the adoption of the foreign word to be *derogatory*. Here are a few examples, all borrowed presumably for derogatory reasons. French *hâbler* 'to brag, to boast' is borrowed from Spanish *hablar* 'to speak'. Finnish *koni* 'nag' [old horse], with negative connotations, is borrowed from Russian *koń*, a neutral term for 'horse', with no negative connotations in the donor language. English *assassin* and the similar words with the same meaning in a number of other European languages (see French *assassin*, Italian *assassino*, Spanish *asesino* 'assassin') may be another example; *assassin* is ultimately from Arabic *ḥaʃʃaʃīn* 'hashish-eater' (for the name of an eleventh-century Muslim sect who would intoxicate themselves with hashish or cannabis when preparing to kill someone of public standing; they had a reputation for butchering opponents, hence the later sense of 'murderer for hire or for fanatical reasons'). Korean *hɔstis*, borrowed from English *hostess*, has a negative connotation, meaning the women who work at nightclubs and bars which serve mainly male customers. It is possible, of course, that some examples of this sort were not borrowed with derogatory purposes in mind at all, but rather merely involve things which have low status.

3.4 How do Words get Borrowed?

Borrowed words are usually remodelled to fit the phonological and morphological structure of the borrowing language, at least in early stages of language contact. The traditional view of how words get borrowed and what happens to them as they are assimilated into the borrowing language holds that loanwords which are introduced to the borrowing language by bilinguals may contain sounds which are foreign to the receiving language, but due to *phonetic interference* the foreign sounds are changed to conform to native sounds and phonetic constraints. This is frequently called *adaptation* (or *phoneme substitution*). In adaptation, a foreign sound in borrowed words which does not exist in the receiving language will be replaced by the nearest phonetic equivalent to it in the borrowing language. For example, formerly Finnish had no voiced stops *b*, *d*, *g*; in loans borrowed into Finnish from Germanic languages which contained *b*, *d*, *g*, voiceless stops (*p*, *t*, *k*), the closest phonetic counterparts in Finnish, replaced these sounds, as seen in, for example, *parta* 'beard' (from Germanic **bardaz*) and *humpuuki* 'humbug' (from English *humbug*). Similarly, in Sayula Popoluca (a Mixe-Zoquean language of southern Mexico), which had no native *l* or *r*, the foreign *l* and *r* of borrowed words were replaced by native *n*, as in Sayula Popoluca *kúnu:ʃ* 'cross', borrowed from Spanish *cruz* [krus], *mu:na* 'mule' from Spanish *mula*, and *puná:tu* 'plate, dish' from Spanish *plato*. Occasionally in borrowings, substitutions may spread the phonetic features of a single sound of the donor language across two segments in the borrowing language; for example, Finnish had no *f*, so intervocalic *f* in loanwords was replaced by the sequence *hv*, as in *kahvi* 'coffee' (from Swedish *kaffe*) and *pihvi* 'beef' (from English *beef*). In this instance, some of the features of foreign *f* are represented on the first segment – *h* conveys 'voiceless' – and other features on the second segment – *v* conveys 'labiodental' – and both *h* and *v* signal 'fricative'.

Non-native phonological patterns are also subject to *accommodation*, where loanwords which do not conform to native phonological patterns are modified to fit the phonological combinations which are permitted in the borrowing language. This is usually accomplished by deletion, addition or recombination of certain sounds to fit the structure of the borrowing language. For example, Mayan languages do not permit initial consonant clusters, and consequently Spanish *cruz* /krus/ 'cross' was borrowed as *rus* in Chol (Mayan), where the initial consonant of the donor form was simply left out, and as *kurus* in Tzotzil (another Mayan language), where the consonant cluster has been broken up by the insertion of a vowel between *k* and *r*. Similarly, in the Sayula Popoluca example above, since the language did not have initial consonant clusters, the *kr* and *pl* of Spanish were broken up by the insertion of *u* in, for example, *kunu:ʃ* 'cross' (< Spanish *cruz*, just mentioned) and *puná:tu* 'plate' (< Spanish *plato*). Similarly, Finnish, with no initial consonant clusters in native words, eliminated all but the last consonant of initial consonant clusters in loanwords, for example *Ranska* 'French' (< Swedish *Franska* 'French'), *risti* 'cross' (< Old Russian *kristĭ*), *ruuvi* 'screw' (< Swedish *skruv* 'screw').

However, there are many different kinds of language-contact situations, and the outcome of borrowing can vary according to the length and intensity of the contact, the kind of interaction, and the degree of bilingualism in the populations. In situations of more extensive, long-term or intimate contact, new phonemes can be introduced into the borrowing language together with borrowed words which contain these new sounds, resulting in changes in the phonemic inventory of the borrowing language; this is sometimes called *direct phonological diffusion*. For example, before intensive contact with French, English had no phonemic /ʒ/. This sound became an English phoneme through the many French loans that contained it which came into English, such as *rouge* /ruʒ/ (< French *rouge* 'red') (and added to by the palatalization in the eighteenth century of /zj/ > /ʒ/, as in *vision*, *Asia* and so on). In the case of *v*, formerly English had an allophonic [v] but no phonemic /v/. It became phonemic due in part to French loans containing *v* in environments not formerly permitted by English. The sound [v] occurred in native English words only as the intervocalic variant (allophone) of /f/; a remnant of this situation is still seen in alternations such as *leaf–leaves*, *wife–wives* and so on, where the suffix *-es* used to have a vowel in the spoken language. Words with initial *v* of French origin – such as *very* from French *vrai* 'true' and *valley* < Old French *valée* – caused /v/ to become a separate phoneme in its own right, no longer just the allophonic variant of /f/ that occurred between vowels. The phonological patterns (phonotactics, syllable or morpheme structure) of a language can also be altered by the acceptance in more intimate language contact of loans which do not conform to native patterns. For example, while native Finnish words permit no initial consonant clusters, now through intimate contact and the introduction of many borrowings from other languages, especially from Swedish and later from English, Finnish phonology permits loans with initial clusters, as seen in, for example, *krokotiili* 'crocodile', *kruunu* 'crown' (compare Swedish *krona*), *presidentti* 'president' and *smaragdi* 'emerald' (from Swedish *smaragd*), and so on.

While there may be typical patterns of substitution for foreign sounds and phonological patterns, substitutions in borrowed words in a language are not always uniform. The same foreign sound or pattern can be borrowed in one loanword in one way and in another loanword in a different way. This happens for the following reasons. (1) Sometimes different words are borrowed at different times, so that older loans reflect sound substitutions before intimate contact brought new sounds and patterns into the borrowing language, while more recent borrowings may exhibit the newer segments or patterns acquired after more intensive contact. (The extent to which the source language is known by speakers of the borrowing language is relevant here.) An example is Sayula Popoluca *turu* 'bull' (recently from Spanish *toro*), with *r*, where earlier loans would have substituted *n* for this foreign sound (mentioned above). Another example is seen in the comparison of Tzotzil (Mayan) *pulatu* 'dishes' (from Spanish *plato* 'plate, dish'), borrowed earlier when Tzotzil permitted no initial consonant clusters, and Tzotzil *platu* 'plate', borrowed later from the same Spanish source, now containing the initial consonant cluster which was formerly prohibited. (2) In most cases, borrowings are based on pronunciation, as illustrated in the case of Finnish *meikkaa-* 'to make up (apply cosmetics)', based on English pronunciation of *make* /meik/. However, in some cases, loans can be based on orthography ('spelling pronunciations'), as seen in the case of Finnish *jeeppi* [jɛːpːi] 'jeep', which can only be based on a spelling pronunciation of English 'jeep', not on the English pronunciation (/ʤip/) – borrowed nouns that end in a consonant add *i* in Finnish.

Loanwords are not only remodelled to accommodate aspects of the phonology of the borrowing language, they are also usually adapted to fit the morphological patterns of the borrowing language. For example, Spanish and French borrowings into some varieties of Arabic have been made to fit Arabic morphological paradigms, which involve alternations in the vowels of the root to signal different morphemes, such as 'singular' and 'plural' difference, as in:

> *resibo* 'receipt' (singular), but *ruāseb* (plural) < Spanish *recibo*
> *bābor* 'a steamship, steamer', but plural *buāber* < Spanish *vapor* /bapor/ 'steam, steamship' (see Vendryes 1968: 95). (Compare Modern Arabic *bābūr* 'steamship, locomotive' (singular), *bwābīr* (plural).)

Chiricahua Apache often has verbs where European languages have adjectives, and as a consequence the Spanish adjectives *loco* 'crazy' and *rico* 'rich' were borrowed but adapted to the verb paradigm, as in:

lô:gò	'he/she is crazy'	*ʒî:gò*	'he/she is rich'
lô:ʃgò	'I am crazy'	*ʒî:ʃgò*	'I am rich'
lóngò	'you are crazy'	*ʒíngò*	'you are rich'

Here, as might be expected, it is the third person verb form ('he is crazy/rich') which phonetically matches the form of the original Spanish adjectives most closely (where *ʒ* is the closest substitution for Spanish *r*, which Apache lacked; the diacritics on the vowels indicate tones and are required by Chiricahua Apache for verbs such as these. (See Anttila 1989: 158.)

3.5 How do we Identify Loanwords and Determine the Direction of Borrowing?

An important question is: how can we tell (beyond the truly obvious cases) if something is a loanword or not? In dealing with borrowings, we want to ascertain which language is the source (donor) and which the recipient (borrower). The following criteria (perhaps better called rough rules of thumb) address these questions (compare Haas 1969a: 79; Sapir 1949).

3.5.1 Phonological clues

The strongest evidence for loanword identification and the direction of borrowing comes from phonological criteria.

(1) Phonological patterns of the language. Words containing sounds which are not normally expected in native words are candidates for loans. For example, in the Chiricahua Apache example just mentioned, the fact that *ʒîːgò* 'he is rich' has an initial *ʒ* and that *lôːgò* 'he is crazy' has an initial *l* makes these strong candidates for loans, since neither *ʒ* nor *l* occurs word-initially in native words. In another example, native Nahuatl words are not expected to begin with *p*, since Proto-Uto-Aztecan initial **p-* was lost through regular sound change in Nahuatl (**p > h > Ø*, for example Proto-Uto-Aztecan **paː* > Nahuatl *aː-* 'water'). For this reason, Nahuatl roots such as *petla-* 'woven mat', *poːčoː-* 'silk-cotton tree (ceiba)' and *pak-* 'to cure'/*paʔ-* 'medicine' violate expectations for sounds in native forms, making them candidates for possible loans. On further investigation, the sources of these borrowings are found in neighbouring languages: *petla-* comes from Mixe-Zoquean **pata* 'woven mat' (in other words of Nahuatl, *a > e* in this environment, and *t > tl* before *a*); *poːčoː-* is from Totonac *puːčuːt* 'silk-cotton tree (ceiba)'; *pak-/paʔ-* is from Totonac *paʔk* 'to cure, get well'. It is the aberrant initial *p-* of these forms which suggests that they may be loans and which prods us to look for their sources in neighbouring languages.

Words which violate the typical phonological patterns (canonical forms, morpheme structure, syllable structure, phonotactics) of a language are likely to be loans. For example, Mayan languages typically have monosyllabic roots (of the form CVC); the polysyllabic morphemes found in Mayan languages, which violate the typical monosyllabic pattern, turn out mostly to be loanwords or compounds. For example, the polysyllabic monomorphemic *tinamit* 'town' of Kaqchikel (Mayan) is a loanword from Nahuatl (Uto-Aztecan). Since this polysyllabic form violates the typical monosyllabic structure of Mayan roots, the inference is that it is probably a loan, and indeed its source is found in Nahuatl *tena:mi-tl* 'fence or wall of a town/city', 'fortified town'.

(2) Phonological history. In some cases where the phonological history of the languages of a family is known, information concerning the sound changes that they have undergone can be helpful for determining loans, the direction of borrowing, and what the donor language was. For example, in the Mayan family, a number of languages have borrowed from Cholan (Mayan), since Cholan speakers were the principal bearers of Classic Maya civilization. Cholan, however, has undergone a number of sound changes which languages of the other branches of the family did not, and this makes it fairly easy to identify many of these Cholan loans. For example, Cholan underwent the sound change *o: > u*. Yucatec did not undergo this sound change, although some borrowings from Cholan into Yucatec show the results of this Cholan change; for example, Yucatec *kùts* 'turkey'< Cholan *kuts* (from *ko:ts*); Yucatec *tù:n* 'stone, year, stela (monument)' < Chol *tun* 'stone' (compare Proto-Mayan *to:ŋ* 'stone'). Since these words in Yucatec show the results of a sound change that took place in Cholan but which native Yucatec words did not undergo (compare Cholan *suts'*, Yucatec *sò:ts'* < Proto-Mayan *so:ts'* 'bat'), it is clear in these cases that Yucatec borrowed the words and Cholan is the donor language (Justeson et al. 1985: 14).

3.5.2 Morphological complexity

The morphological make-up of words can help determine the direction of borrowing. In cases of borrowing, when the form in question in one language is morphologically complex (composed of two or more morphemes) or has an etymology which is morphologically complex, but the form in the other languages has no morphological analysis, then usually the donor language is the one with the morphologically complex form and the borrower is the one with the monomorphemic form. For example, English *alligator* is borrowed from Spanish *el lagarto* 'the alligator'; since it is monomorphemic in English, but based on two morphemes in Spanish, *el* 'the' + *lagarto* 'alligator', the direction of borrowing must be from Spanish to English. *Vinegar* in English is a loan from French *vinaigre*, which is from *vin* 'wine' + *aigre* 'sour'; since its etymology is polymorphemic in French but monomorphemic in English, the direction of borrowing is clearly from French to English. English *aardvark* turns out to be borrowed from Afrikaans *aardvark* (composed of *aard* 'earth + *vark* 'pig'), since the Afrikaans form has a morphologically complex etymology while the English form is monomorphemic. American English *hoosegow* 'jail' is borrowed from Spanish *juzg-ado* 'courtroom, panel of judges' (literally 'judged'), which is composed of two morphemes (*juzga-* 'judge' + *-(a)do* 'past participle', pronounced without *-d-* in many Spanish dialects, [xusgao]), whereas the English form is a single morpheme. French *vasistas* [vazistas] 'fan-light, ventilator' is a loan based on German *was ist das* 'what is that?'; given that the German source has three morphemes (words) but the French word only one, German is the donor.

Spanish borrowed many words from Arabic during the period that the Moors dominated Spain (901–1492). Many Arabic loans in Spanish include what was originally the Arabic definite article *al-* but are monomorphemic in Spanish. A few examples of this are: *albañil* 'mason' (Arabic *bannā* 'builder, mason'), *albaricoque* 'apricot' (Arabic *barqūq* 'plum'), *albóndiga* 'meat ball' (Arabic *bunduq* 'bullet, hazelnut'), *alcalde* 'mayor' (compare Arabic *qādī* 'judge'), *alcoba* 'bedroom, alcove' (Arabic *qubba* 'dome, cupola'), *alcohol* 'alcohol' (Arabic *kul* 'collyrium, fine powder used to stain the eyelids'), *alfalfa* 'alfalfa' (from Hispano-Arabic *faṣfaṣa* 'the best sort of fodder', Arabic *fiṣfiṣa* itself a loan from Persian *aspest*), *algodón* 'cotton' (Arabic *quṭn, quṭun* 'cotton'; English *cotton* is also ultimately from Arabic), *alguacil* 'constable, bailiff, peace officer' (Arabic *wazīr* 'minister, vizier', also the source of English *vizier*), *almacén* 'storehouse' (Arabic *maxzan* singular [plural' *maxazīn*]'storeroom, depository, magazine'; English *magazine* is ultimately from the same source), *almohada* 'pillow' (Arabic *mixadda* 'pillow, cushion', derived from *xadda* 'cheek, side'). Since these are polymorphemic in Arabic, composed of the article *al-* + root, but each is monomorphemic in Spanish, the direction of borrowing is seen to be from Arabic to Spanish.

Frequently, the early loans from Spanish into Native American languages (called *hispanisms*) were based on the Spanish plural forms. A few examples from Mayan languages are: Jakalteko *kaplaʃ* 'goat' (< Spanish *cabras* 'goats'); Huastec *pa:tuʃ*, Tzotzil *patoʃ* (< *patos* 'ducks'),

K'iche' *pataʃ* (< Spanish *patas* 'female ducks') 'duck'; Motocintlec *ko:liʃ* 'cabbage' (< *coles* 'cabbages', compare *col* 'cabbage'); Chol *wakaʃ* 'bull, cow', Tojolabal *wakaʃ* 'cattle, beef'(< *vacas* 'cows'). In sixteenth-century Spanish, the sound represented orthographically as *s* was phonetically [s], an apico-alveolar fricative; it was taken by speakers of these languages as being phonetically closer to their /ʃ/ than to their /s/, which accounts for the /ʃ/ seen in these (monomorphemic) borrowings which corresponds to the (polymorphemic) Spanish plural forms with *-(e)s*.

The Sanskrit word **kana* 'one-eyed' appears to be borrowed from Proto-Dravidian **kan* 'eye' + **-a* 'negative suffix' (Zvelebil 1990: 79), and it is the morphological complexity of the Dravidian form which shows the direction of the borrowing.

This is a very strong criterion, but not foolproof. It can be complicated by cases of folk etymology (see Chapter 4), where a monomorphemic loanword comes to be interpreted as containing more than one morpheme, though originally this was not the case. For example, Old French monomorphemic *crevice* 'crayfish' was borrowed into English and then later this was replaced by folk etymology with *crayfish*, on analogy with *fish*. Now it appears to have a complex morphological analysis, but this is not original.

3.5.3 Clues from cognates

When a word in two (or more) languages is suspected of being borrowed, if it has legitimate cognates (with regular sound correspondences, see Chapter 5) across sister languages of one family, but is found in only one language (or a few languages) of another family, then the donor language is usually one of the languages for which the form in question has cognates in the related languages. For example, Finnish *tytär* 'daughter' has no cognates in the other branches of the Finno-Ugric family, while cognates of Proto-Indo-European **dhugǝter* (**dhughₐter*) 'daughter' are known from most Indo-European languages, including ones as geographically far apart as Sanskrit and English. Therefore, the direction of borrowing is from one of these Indo-European languages (actually from Baltic) to Finnish. Spanish *ganso* 'goose' is borrowed from Germanic **gans*; Germanic has cognates, for example German *Gans*, English *goose*, and so on, but this Spanish word has no true cognate in other Romance languages. Rather, they have such things as French *oie*, Italian *oca*, and others reflecting Latin *ānser* 'goose'. Thus, the direction of borrowing is from Germanic to Spanish. (Ultimately,

Germanic **gans* and Latin *ānser* are cognates (from Proto-Indo-European **ghans-*), but that does not affect the example of Spanish *ganso* as a loan from German.) In another example, the Proto-Mixe-Zoquean word **tsiku* 'coati-mundi' has cognates throughout the languages of the family; in the Mixe branch of the family, due to sound changes, the cognates reflect **čik*. On the other hand, in the Mayan family (of thirty-one languages in Mexico and Guatemala), essentially only Yucatecan has the form *či?k* for 'coati-mundi'; the other Mayan languages have native words **ts'uts'*, **si:s* or **kohtom* for 'coati-mundi'. From the general distribution of cognate forms in Mixe-Zoquean, it is concluded that Yucatecan borrowed the word from Mixe-Zoquean, and from its phonological shape, it appears that Yucatecan took the word more directly from the Mixean branch of that family (Justeson et al. 1985: 24).

3.5.4 Geographical and ecological clues

The geographical and ecological associations of words suspected of being loans can often provide clues helpful to determining whether they are borrowed and what the identity of the donor language is. For example, the geographical and ecological remoteness from earlier English-speaking territory of *zebra*, *gnu*, *impala* and *aardvark* – animals originally found only in Africa – makes these words likely candidates for loanwords in English. Indeed, they were borrowed from local languages in Africa with which speakers of European languages came into contact when they entered the habitats where these animals are found – *zebra* is from a Congo language (borrowed through French), *gnu* from a Khoe language, *impala* from Zulu, and *aardvark* from Afrikaans.

It is known that Nahuatl (the language of the Aztecs and Toltecs) started out in the region of northwestern Mexico and the southwestern USA and migrated from there into central Mexico and on to Central America. Since cacao (the source of chocolate, cocoa) did not grow in the original Nahuatl desert homeland, the Nahuatl word *kakawa-* 'cacao' is likely to be a loan. Indeed, it was borrowed from Mixe-Zoquean (Proto-Mixe-Zoquean **kakawa* 'cacao'). Several other loans in Nahuatl reflect the adoption of names for plants and animals not encountered before the migration into lower Mexico, where heretofore unknown items indigenous to the more tropical climate were encountered. In Nez Perce (a Sahaptian language of the north-western USA), *lapatá:t* 'potato' is borrowed from Canadian French *la patate*; it is clearly a loan and clearly from French, not only because it is morphologically analysable in French but not in Nez Perce, but also because we know that potatoes were introduced to this area after European contact (Callaghan and Gamble 1997: 111). Knowledge of this history suggests that the term for them could be a borrowing. Further investigation shows this to be the case, a borrowing from French into Nez Perce in this case.

Inferences from geography and ecology are not as strong as those from the phonological and morphological criteria mentioned above; however, when coupled with other information, the inferences which they provide can be useful.

3.5.5 Other semantic clues

A still weaker kind of inference, related to the last criterion, can some-times be obtained from the semantic domain of a suspected loan. For example, English words such as *squaw, papoose, powwow, tomahawk, wickiup* and so on have paraphrases involving 'Indian'/'Native American', that is, 'Indian woman', 'Indian baby', 'Indian house' and so on; this suggests possible borrowing from American Indian languages. Upon further investigation, this supposition proves true; these are bor-rowed from Algonquian languages into English. In another example, in Xinkan (a small family of four languages in Guatemala) most terms for cultivated plants are known to be borrowed from Mayan; this being the case, any additional terms in this semantic domain that we encounter may be suspected of being possible borrowings. This criterion is only a rough indication of possibilities. Sources for the borrowing must still be sought, and it is necessary to try to determine the exact nature of the loans, if indeed borrowings are involved.

3.6 Loans as Clues to Linguistic Changes in the Past

Evidence preserved in loanwords may help to document older stages of a language before later changes took place. An often-cited example is that of early Germanic loans in Finnish which document older stages in the development of Germanic. These loans bear evidence of things in Germanic which can be reconstructed only with difficulty from the evidence retained in the Germanic languages themselves – some of these reconstructed things are confirmed only through comparisons of Germanic with other branches of Indo-European. For example, Finnish *rengas* 'ring' (borrowed; see Proto-Germanic **hreng-az*) reveals two things about Germanic. First, it documents Germanic at the stage before the sound change of *e* to *i* before *n* (*e* > *i* /__*n*) – all attested Germanic languages show only the forms with *i*, the result after the change, as in English *ring*. A comparison of Finnish *rengas* and *kuningas* 'king' (also borrowed from Germanic, Proto-Germanic **kuning-az*) shows that Germanic originally contrasted *i* and *e* in the position before *n*, which is not seen in Germanic after the two sounds merged before *n*. Second, both these loans document the Proto-Germanic ending **-az*, suggested by comparative Germanic evidence (but lost in most Germanic languages, seen as -*s* in Gothic). It is only by confirming **-az* through comparisons from other branches of Indo-European (compare the cognates, Latin -*us* and Greek -*os* 'nominative singular') and from borrowings such as these from earlier Germanic into Finnish that we can be certain of the reconstruction. In another case, some loans in Finnish document Germanic before the umlaut change took place. For example, Finnish *patja* 'mattress' (borrowed from Germanic; see Proto-Germanic **badja* 'bed') documents Germanic before umlaut in which *a* > *e* when followed in the next syllable by *j* or *i* (as seen in English *bed*, German *Bett* – later the **-ja* was lost through a series of changes, **badja* > *bedja* > *bed*). The pre-umlaut stage can be reconstructed from other considerations, in particular in comparisons with cognate words from related languages outside of the Germanic branch of Indo-European. In the umlaut context, modern Germanic languages preserve only words which have undergone the change; Gothic is the only Germanic language which did not undergo umlaut. Another loanword in Finnish, *airo* 'oar', preserves evidence of another suffix which is difficult to reconstruct, the Proto-Germanic feminine ending **-ō* (compare Gothic -*a*, Proto-Scandinavian **-u*) (Krause 1968: 53). The loans which bear evidence of the earlier forms before the changes took place, such as these examples from Finnish, help to confirm the accuracy of the reconstructions.

In another example, Spanish used to contrast bilabial stop *b* and fricative *v*, although these are fully merged in modern Spanish (though still spelled differently, <b> and <v>, which are no longer distinct phonemes). The stop *b* came from Latin initial *b* and intervocalic *p*, whereas fricative *v* came from late Latin initial *v* and from intervocalic *v* and *b*; these two phonemes, /b/ and /v/, merged in Spanish to the single /b/ of modern Spanish. However, early loanwords from Spanish into American Indian languages (hispanisms) show clearly that the contrast persisted at least long enough to arrive in America, although soon afterwards the merger took place and later hispanisms reflect only the merged sound. In the early hispanisms, /v/ was borrowed typically as *w*, since most Native American languages lacked *v* (*w* being their sound which is nearest phonetically to *v*), whereas the /b/ of earlier Spanish was borrowed as /b/, /ɓ/ or /p/, depending on the sounds available in the particular borrowing language which could be considered the closest phonetic equivalent to Spanish *b* in each recipient language. The following are a few early hispanisms in Mayan languages which show the earlier contrast in Spanish before these sounds later merged. Forms 1–3 show original intervocalic /b/ (borrowed as *p*, *b* or *ɓ*):

1. Spanish *jabón* 'soap' (phonetically [ʃabón] in the sixteenth century), borrowed as: Chol *ʃapum*, Huastec *ʃabu:n*, Q'anjobal *sapon*, Motocintlec *ʃa:puh*, K'iche' *ʃɓon*, Tzeltal *ʃapon*.
2. Spanish *nabo* 'turnip': K'iche' *napuʃ*, Tzotzil *napuʃ* (< *nabos* 'turnips', borrowed from the Spanish plural form).
3. Spanish *sebo* 'tallow, grease': Q'anjobal *ʃepuʔ*, K'iche' *ʃepu*, Tzotzil *ʃepu*.

Forms 4–6 show original intervocalic /v/ (borrowed as *w* or *v*):

4. *navaja* 'knife, razor': Akateko *nawas*, Chol *ñawaʃaʃ*, Q'anjobal *nawus*, Tzotzil *navaʃaʃ* (< *navajas*, 'plural' form).
5. *clavo* 'nail': Akateko *lawuʃ*, Chol *lawuʃ*, K'iche' *klawuʃ*, Tzeltal *lawuʃ*, Tojolabal *lawuʃ* ('nail', 'spur'), Tzotzil *lavuʃ* (< *clavos*, borrowed from the plural form).
6. Old Spanish *cavallo* < Latin *cavallus* 'work horse'): Akateko *kawayú* 'horse, beast of burden', Chol *kawayu*, Q'anjobal *kawayo*, Q'eqchi' *kawa:y*, Motocintlec *kwa:yuh* 'horse, mule', Tzeltal *kawu*, Tzotzil *kawayú* 'beast of burden'. (Cf. Modern Spanish *caballo* 'horse'.)

These loans demonstrate (1) the phonetic nature of original sounds, (2) the time when the sounds merged, and (3) the fact that this merger of /b/ and /v/ had not yet taken place in the mid-sixteenth century when these languages began to borrow from Spanish.

Evidence from loanwords can also sometimes contribute to understanding the *relative chronology* of changes in a language (introduced in Chapter 2, and discussed again in Chapters 5 and 8). For example, Motocintlec (Mayan, of the Q'anjobalan branch) *čo:ŋ* 'to sell' is borrowed from Cholan (a different branch of Mayan) *čon* (compare Proto-Mayan **ko:ŋ*). (Recall that Cholan was the principal language of Classic Maya civilization, and as such contributed numerous loans to languages of the region.) We know that Cholan underwent two changes:

k > *č* and *ŋ* > *n*, though both *k* and *ŋ* remain unchanged in
Motocintlec (as seen, for example, in *koŋoɓ* 'market', which retains the
native form, from **ko:ŋ* 'to sell' + *-oɓ* 'place of, instrumental suffix').
Therefore, loanwords of Cholan origin such as Motocintlec *čo:ŋ* reveal
that in Cholan the change of **k* > *č* took place earlier than the change
of **ŋ* > *n*, since from the form of the loan in Motocintlec we conclude
that Motocintlec borrowed *čo:ŋ* at the stage when **k* > *č* had already
taken place in Cholan, but before Cholan had undergone the change of
*ŋ > *n*. Thus loans such as this one reveal the relative chronology of
Cholan changes, first **k* > *č*, followed later by **ŋ* > *n*.

3.7 What Can Be Borrowed?

Not only can words be borrowed, but sounds, phonological features,
morphology, syntactic constructions and in fact virtually any aspect of
language can be borrowed, given enough time and the appropriate sorts of
contact situations. Let's look at a few examples of non-lexical borrowings.
(See also Chapter 12.)

3.7.1 Borrowed sounds or features used in native lexical items

Foreign sounds can be borrowed – that is, speakers of one language can
borrow sounds from another language with which they are familiar.
There are two main ways in which non-native sounds can end up in
native words: through areal diffusion (see Chapter 12) and through onomatopoeia and expressive symbolism.

Through intense long-term contact, foreign sounds can be borrowed
and come to occur in native words. A few examples are: the clicks borrowed from so-called Khoisan languages (Khoe and San languages) of
southern Africa into some neighbouring Bantu languages (for example,
Xhosa, Zulu, Sotho; Proto-Bantu had no clicks); glottalized consonants
borrowed into Ossetic and Eastern Armenian from neighbouring languages of the Caucasus linguistic area; and the retroflex consonants of
Indo-Aryan languages, which owe their origin, at least in part, to contact
with Dravidian languages in the South Asian (Indian) linguistic area
(see Chapter 12; Campbell 1976).

Expressive symbolism is the use of certain phonetic traits to symbolize affectations, heightened expressive value, or the speaker's attitude.
An example of a foreign sound which has been extended into native
words through onomatopoeia and affective symbolism is the *r* of Chol

and Tzotzil (two Mayan languages). Before contact with Spanish, these languages had no *r*; this sound was introduced through Spanish loan-words which contained it, for example Chol *arus* 'rice' < Spanish *arroz* /aros/, and Tzotzil *martoma* 'custodian' < Spanish *mayordomo*. After *r* was introduced in loanwords, this new sound – which apparently seemed exotic to the speakers of these Mayan languages – came to be employed in certain native words for onomatopoetic or expressive purposes, for example, Chol *buruk-ña* 'buzzing, humming', *burbur-ña* 'noisily', *porok-ña* 'breathing when there is an obstruction', *sorok-ña* 'bubbling'. Some of the expressive Tzotzil words which now have the *r*, which was first introduced through loanwords from Spanish, are native words which formerly had only *l*, for example, *ner-iʃ* 'cross-eyed', where Colonial Tzotzil had only *nel-iʃ* (compare *nel-* 'crooked, twisted, slanted'). The word **kelem* 'strong young man, male' has split into two in modern Tzotzil: *kerem* 'boy (affective)' and *kelem* 'rooster' – Colonial Tzotzil had only *kelem* 'boy, bachelor, servant' (Campbell 1996).

3.7.2 Elimination of sounds through language contact

Not only can foreign sounds be acquired through diffusion, but language contact can also lead to the elimination of sounds (or features of sounds). For example, Proto-Nootkan had nasals, as Nootka still does, but closely related Nitinat and Makah lost nasality – former nasals became corresponding voiced oral stops (**m > b, *n > d, *ṁ > b', *ṅ > d'*) – due to diffusion within the linguistic area. Nitinat and Makah are found in a region of the Northwest Coast of North America, where languages of several different families lack nasal consonants. The lack of nasals in Nitinat and Makah is due to the influence of other nasalless languages in the linguistic area (see Chapter 12). Some other examples of loss of this sort due to language contact are the merger of /l/ and /lʲ/ in Czech to /l/, attributed to German influence in the fashionable speech of the cities (Weinreich 1953: 25); and loss of the emphatic (pharyngealised) consonants and of vowel length in Cypriotic Arabic under the influence of Cypriotic Greek (Campbell 1976).

3.7.3 Retention of native sounds due to language contact

In addition to the loss of sounds, language contact can also contribute to the retention of sounds, even if that sound is lost in other areas where the language is spoken which are not in contact with languages which influence the retention. For example, /l^j/ [spelled <ll>] persists in the Spanish of the Andes region, even though in nearly all other areas of Latin America *l^j* has merged with *j* [spelled <y>] (mentioned above). The area where Spanish has maintained this contrast coincides closely with the region where Quechua and Aymara, languages which have /l^j/, are also widely spoken. Thus, it is due to contact with languages which have the *l^j* that the Spanish of this region preserves /l^j/ in contrast with /j/, a contrast lost elsewhere in Latin American Spanish.

3.7.4 Shifts in native sounds

Another kind of change that can take place in language contact situations is the shift in native sounds to approximate more closely to phonetic traits of sounds in the neighbouring languages. For example, Finnish *ð* shifted to *d* under influence from Swedish, due in part to the Swedish reading model with *d* which was imposed in the Finnish schools. The Nattavaara Finnish dialect shifted native *jj* to *d^{j}d^j*, medial *h* to *ʔ*, and the geminate (long) stops *pp, tt, kk* to *hp, ht, hk* respectively, under influence from Saami. Creek (a Muskogean language of the southern USA) shifted its *ɸ* (bilabial fricative) to *f* (labiodental) under English influence (Campbell 1976).

3.7.5 Borrowed rules

Not only can foreign sounds be borrowed, but foreign phonological rules may also be borrowed. For example, borrowed stress rules are not uncommon, such as first syllable stress of many of the languages in the Baltic linguistic area (see Chapter 12), or the rule which places stress on the vowel before the last consonant (V →V́/__C(V)#), shared by several unrelated American Indian languages of southern Mexico and Guatemala. The rule which palatalizes velar stops when followed by a uvular consonant in the same root (for example, *k'aq* → *k^j'aq* 'flea'; *ke:χ* → *k^{j}e:χ* 'deer') was borrowed from Mamean languages into the adjacent dialects of several K'ichean languages (two distinct sub-branches of the Mayan family), as shown in Map 3.1. Several Greek dialects of Asia Minor have incorporated a vowel-harmony rule under influence from Turkish. The French spoken in Quimper borrowed a rule of final consonant devoicing from Breton, spoken in that region (see Campbell 1976, 1977). Borrowed phonological rules are not uncommon.

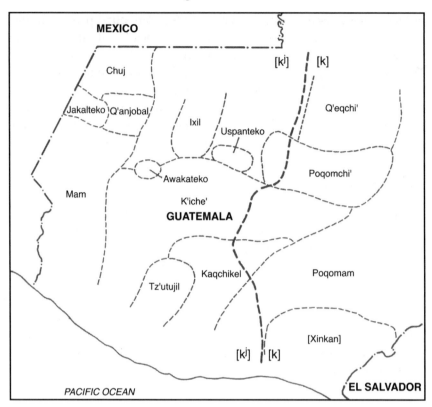

MAP 3.1: Diffusion of the velar palatalization rule in K'ichean
languages (redrawn after Campbell 1977: Map 1)

3.7.6 Diffused sound changes

Related to borrowed phonological rules is the borrowing of sound
changes from one language to another. For example, the change of *k* to
č has diffused throughout the languages of a continuous area of the
Northwest Coast of North America from Vancouver Island to the
Columbia River, affecting languages of different families. A similar
change of *k* to *č* (a laminal palato-alveolar affricate) before front vowels
diffused through Telugu, Tamil, Malayalam and some dialects of Tulu
(Dravidian languages), and Marathi (Indo-Aryan) (in several of these
languages, *č* before front vowels is in complementary distribution with
ts before back vowels). The sound change of *ts* to *s* diffused after European contact among neighbouring Q'eqchi', Poqomchi' and Poqomam
(Mayan languages) (Campbell 1977).

3.7.7 Calques (loan translations, semantic loans)

In loanwords, something of both the phonetic form and meaning of the word in the donor language is transferred to the borrowing language, but it is also possible to borrow, in effect, just the meaning, and instances of this are called *calques* or *loan translations*, as illustrated by the often-repeated example of *black market*, which owes its origin in English to a loan translation of German *Schwarzmarkt*, composed of *schwarz* 'black' and *Markt* 'market'. Other examples follow.

(1) The word for 'railway' ('railroad') is a calque based on a translation of 'iron' + 'road/way' in a number of languages: Finnish *rautatie* (*rauta* 'iron' + *tie* 'road'); French *chemin de fer* (literally 'road of iron'); German *Eisenbahn* (*Eisen* 'iron' + *Bahn* 'path, road'); Spanish *ferrocarril* (*ferro-* 'iron' in compound words + *carril* 'lane, way'); and Swedish *järnväg* (*järn* 'iron' + *väg* 'road').

(2) English has a number of early calques based on loan translations from Latin, for example: *almighty* < Old English *ælmihtig*, based on Latin *omnipotens* (*omni-* 'all' + *potēns* 'powerful, strong'), and *gospel* < *gōdspell* (*gōd* 'good' + *spel* 'news, tidings'), based on Latin *evangelium* which is from Greek *eu-aggelion* 'good-news/message' (<gg> is the normal transliteration of Greek [ŋg]).

(3) A number of languages have calques based on English *skyscraper*, as for example: German *Wolkenkratzer* (*Wolken* 'clouds' + *kratzer* 'scratcher, scraper'); French *gratte-ciel* (*gratte* 'grate, scrape' + *ciel* 'sky'); and Spanish *rascacielos* (*rasca* 'scratch, scrape' + *cielos* 'skies, heavens').

(4) Some Spanish examples include: (1) varieties of American Spanish have *manzana de Adán* 'Adam's apple', a loan translation from the English name (compare Peninsular Spanish *nuez (de la garganta)*, literally 'nut (of the throat)'). (2) Spanish *plata* 'silver' comes from Latin *platta* 'flat' and is thought to have acquired its sense of 'silver' through loan translation from Arabic where the same term meant both 'thin plate' and 'silver'. (3) More modern loan translations in Spanish from English include *cadena* 'chain' and now also 'chain of stores', *estrella* 'star' and now also 'movie star', *canal* 'canal' and now also 'channel (for television)', *guerra fría* 'cold war', *tercer mundo* 'Third World', *aire acondicionado* 'air conditioning', *desempleo* 'unemployment', *supermercado* 'supermarket'.

(5) A number of calques are shared widely among the languages of the Mesoamerican linguistic area (see Chapter 12); these translate the semantic equations illustrated in the following: 'boa' = 'deer-snake', 'door' = 'mouth of house', 'egg' = 'bird-stone', 'knee' = 'leg-head',

'lime' = 'stone(-ash)', 'wrist' = 'hand-neck' (Campbell, Kaufman and Smith-Stark 1986).

3.7.8 Emphatic foreignization

Sometimes, speakers go out of their way to make borrowed forms sound even more foreign by substituting sounds which seem to them more foreign than the sounds which the word in the donor language actually has. These examples of further 'foreignization' are usually found in loans involving slang or high registers; it is somewhat akin to hypercorrection (see Chapter 4). The phenomenon is illustrated in examples such as the frequent news media pronunciations of *Azerbaijan* and *Beijing* with the somewhat more foreign-sounding ʒ, [azerbaiˈʒan] and [beiˈʒɪŋ], rather than the less exotic but more traditional pronunciation with ǰ (IPA [dʒ]), [beiˈǰɪŋ] and [azerˈbaiǰan] (with penultimate stress in the latter). The English borrowing from French *coup de grace* (literally, 'blow/hit of grace') is more often rendered without the final *s*, as /ku de gra/, than as /ku de gras/, where many English speakers expect French words spelled with *s* to lack *s* in the pronunciation and have extended this to eliminate also the /s/ of *grace*, though in French the *s* of *grace* is pronounced, [gʀas]. In borrowings in Finnish slang, sounds which match native Finnish sounds are often replaced with less native-sounding segments; for example, in *bonja-ta* 'to understand', from Russian *ponjat^j*, and in *bunga-ta* 'to pay for, to come up with the money for', from Swedish *punga*, the *p* – a sound which native Finnish has – was further 'foreignized' by the substitution of more foreign-sounding *b*, a sound not found in native Finnish words. (Compare Hock and Joseph 1996: 261, 271.)

3.8 Cultural Inferences

It is not difficult to see how loanwords can have an important historical impact on a culture – just consider what the evening news in English might be like without *money* and *dollars*, or *sex*, or *religion*, *politicians* and *crime*. These words are all loans:

(1) *money*: borrowed in Middle English times from French (see Old French *moneie*; compare Modern French *monnaie* 'money, coin'), ultimately from Latin *monēta*, from the name of *Juno monēta* 'Juno the admonisher' in whose temple in Rome money was coined (ultimately *admonish* and *money* are related, both involving borrowed forms which hark back to Latin *monēre* 'to admonish') (Anttila 1989: 137).

(2) *dollar*: borrowed into English in the sixteenth century from Low German and Dutch *daler*, ultimately from High German *thaler*, in its full form *Joachimsthaler*, a place in Bohemia, literally 'of Joachim's valley', from where the German *thaler*, a large silver coin of the 1600s, came, from a silver mine opened there in 1516. (Cf. German *Tal* 'valley', English *dale*.)

(3) *sex*: first attested in English in 1382, ultimately from Latin *sexus* 'either of the two divisions of organic beings distinguished as male and female respectively', derived from the verb *secāre* 'to cut, divide'. (English *sect, section, dissect* and *insect* are borrowings based on the same Latin root.)

(4) *religion*: borrowed from French *religion*, first attested in English in 1200 (ultimately from Latin *religiōn-em*, of contested etymology, said to be from either *relegere* 'to read over again' or *religāre* 'to bind, religate', reflecting the state of life bound by monastic vows).

(5) *politician*: borrowed from French *politicien*, first attested in English in 1588, 'a political person, chiefly in the sinister sense, a shrewd schemer, a crafty plotter or intriguer'.

(6) *crime*: borrowed from French *crime*, first attested in English in 1382; ultimately from Latin *crīmen* 'judgement, accusation, offence'.

A simple example which illustrates the sort of cultural information that can be derived from loanwords comes from the 'Western American' or 'cowboy' vocabulary in English, a large portion of which is borrowed from Spanish: *adobe* 'sun-dried bricks, a structure made of adobe bricks' < *adobe*; *arroyo* 'a water-carved gully in a dry region' < *arroyo* 'brook, small stream'; *bronco* < *bronco* 'rough, rude'; *buckaroo* < *vaquero* 'cowhand'; *burro* < *burro* 'burro', 'donkey'; *calaboose* 'jail, prison' < *calabozo* 'prison cell, dungeon'; *canyon* < *cañón* 'ravine, gorge, canyon'; *cayuse* 'an Indian pony' < *caballo(s)* 'horse(s)' (perhaps first borrowed from Spanish into Chinook Jargon and from there into English); *chaps* [ʃæps] < *chaparreras* 'open leather garment worn by riders over their trousers to protect them'; *cinch* 'saddle-girth' < *cincha* 'belt, sash, cinch'; *corral* < *corral*; *coyote* < Spanish *coyote* (ultimately from Nahuatl *koyōtl* 'coyote'); *desperado* 'a man ready for deeds of lawlessness or violence' < Older Spanish *desperado* 'without hope, desperate' (compare Modern Spanish *desesperado* 'without hope'); *lariat* < Spanish *la reata* 'the rope, lasso'; *lasso* < *lazo* 'knot, bow, lasso'; *mesa* 'flat-topped hill with steep sides' < *mesa* 'table', 'plateau'; *mustang* < *mestenco* 'lacking an owner'; *palomino* 'horse with pale cream-coloured or golden coat and cream-coloured to white mane and tail' < *palomino* 'dove-like', see Mexican Spanish *palomo* 'pale cream-coloured horse'; *pinto* 'a paint (horse), a mottled horse' < *pinto* 'painted, mottled'; *ranch* < *rancho* 'hut or house in the country', *rancher* < *ranchero* 'farmer, rancher'; *rodeo* < *rodeo* 'a round-up (from *rodear* 'to go round'); *stampede* < Mexican Spanish *estampida* 'crash, uproar'; *vigilante* < *vigilante* '(one who is) vigilant' (from *vigilar* 'to watch, keep an eye on'). Given the large number of loanwords in this semantic domain, we infer that culture and economy of the Old American West were highly influenced by contact with Spanish speakers there.

More extensive examples of this sort are found in Chapter 15, which deals with the information that loanwords can provide for the interpretation of prehistory.

3.9 Exercises

Exercise 3.1

Find ten examples of loanwords (not already mentioned in this chapter) into any language you like, including English. You can consult dictionaries which give historical sources of lexical items or books on the history of particular languages, if you wish. Try to identify the form and meaning of the word in the donor language.

Exercise 3.2 Twentieth-century loans into English

In the history of English, relatively few words were borrowed during the twentieth century when seen in comparison with the large number of loans from earlier times. Still, many did come into the language; here are a few of them. Look up twenty of these (or more if you like) either in a good dictionary of English which indicates the sources from which words come or in a dictionary of the language from which they were borrowed. Try to determine the original meaning and form in the donor language and note any changes (in meaning or form) that the word has undergone as it was adopted into English. The original meanings of many of these may surprise you.

Afrikaans:	apartheid
Chinese:	chow mein, kung fu
Czech:	robot
French:	avant-garde, boutique, camouflage, chassis, cinema, discotheque, fuselage, garage, limousine, sabotage
German:	angst, blitz, ersatz, flak, Nazi, snorkel, strafe, wienerschnitzel
Hawai'ian:	aloha, lei, ukulele
Hebrew:	kibbutz

Italian:	fascism, partisan, pasta, pizza
Japanese:	bonsai, kamikaze, karaoke, karate, origami
Russian:	bolshevik, cosmonaut, glasnost, intelligentsia, perestroika, sputnik
Spanish:	aficionado, macho, marijuana, paella, tango
Swedish	(or Scandinavian generally): moped, ombudsman, slalom, smorgasbord
Yiddish:	schmaltz, schlock, klutz

Exercise 3.3 *Māori and English loanwords*

(1) Based on the criteria for establishing loanwords and the direction of borrowing, determine from the following lists of words which are borrowed into Māori from English and which are borrowed into English from Māori. Note that Māori has the following inventory of sounds: /p, t, k, ɸ, h, r, m, n, ŋ, r, i, e, a, o, u/. In the traditional orthography, /ɸ/ (voiceless bilabial fricative) is spelled *wh*; /ŋ/ is spelled *ng*. Also, native Māori words permit no consonant clusters, rather only syllables of the shape CV (a single consonant followed by a single vowel). (2) Can you say anything about the pronunciation of the variety of English from which Māori took its English loans? (3) What can you say about the social or cultural nature of the contact between speakers of Māori and English? Can you identify semantic domains (areas of meaning) most susceptible to borrowing in either of the languages? (4) How were words from one language modified to fit the structure of the other?

hāhi	'church'
haina	'China; sign'
haka	'haka, Māori dance'
haki	'flag' (< Union *Jack*)
hāma	'hammer'
hānara	'sandal'
hāngi	'hangi, oven' (hole in the ground with wrapped food placed on heated stones in the pit with fire)
hānihi	'harness'
hāpa	'harp'
hāte	'shirt'
hēmana	'chairman'
hereni	'shilling'
heti	'shed'
hipi	'sheep'
hiraka	'silk'

85

hiriwa	'silver'
hoeha	'saucer'
hohipere	'hospital'
hopa	'job'
hōro	'hall'
hū	'shoe'
hui	'meeting for discussion'
huka	'sugar'
hūka	'hook'
hupa	'soup'
hūri	'jury'
iāri	'yard'
ihipa	'Egypt'
ingarangi	'England'
ingarihi	'English'
inihi	'inch'
iota	'yacht'
iwi	'iwi, Māori tribe'
kāka	'cork'
kānara	'colonel'
kapa	'copper, penny'
kāpara	'corporal'
kāpata	'cupboard'
kara	'collar'
karaehe	'grass; glassware, tumbler; class'
karāhi	'glass'
karahipi	'scholarship'
karaka	'clock; clerk'
karauna	'crown'
kāreti	'college; carrot; carriage'
kāta	'cart'
kātaroera	'castor oil'
kātipa	'constable'
kaumātua	'kaumatua, Māori elder'
kauri	'kauri tree'
kāwana	'governor'
kea	'kea' (mountain parrot)
kihi	'kiss'
kirihimete	'Christmas'
kiwi	'kiwi bird'

kōmihana	'commission'
kōti	'court (of law); goat'
kuihipere	'gooseberry'
kūmara	'kumara, sweet potato'
kura	'school'
māhi	'mast'
mana	'mana, influence, prestige'
māori	'Māori, native people' (in Māori *māori* means 'clear, ordinary, native New Zealander')
marae	'marae, enclosed meeting area'
marahihi	'molasses'
moa	'moa' (very large extinct flightless bird)
mokopuna	'mokopuna, grandchild'
motokā	'car, automobile' (< motor car)
nēhi	'nurse'
ngaio	'ngaio, coastal shrub'
ōkiha	'ox'
ōriwa	'olive'
otimira	'oatmeal'
pā	'pa, stockaded village'
pahi	'bus'
paihikara	'bicycle'
paitini	'poison'
pāka	'box'
pākehā	'pakeha, European, non-Māori'
pāmu	'farm'
pāoka	'fork'
parakuihi	'breakfast'
parama	'plumber'
pāua	'paua, abalone shell'
pāuna	'pound'
perakēhi	'pillowcase'
pereti	'plate'
pī	'bee'
pirihi	'priest'
pirihimana	'police(man)'
piriniha	'prince'
piriti	'bridge'
pōkiha	'fox'
pōro	'ball'

pukapuka   'book'
pūkeko   'pukeko, swamp hen'
pune   'spoon'
purū   'blue'
pūru   'bull'
rare   'lolly, sweets'
rata   'doctor'
reme   'lamb'
rērewē   'railroad, railway'
rēwera   'devil'
rīhi   'dish; lease'
rimu   'rimu, red pine'
rōre   'lord' (title)
rori   'road'
takahē   'takahe, bird species' (*Notoris mantelli*)
tana   'ton'
tangi   'tangi, Māori mourning or lamentation'
                  (associated with funerals)
tāone   'town'
taonga   'taonga, heritage, Māori treasure, possessions'
tāra   'dollar'
taraiki   'strike'
tauiwi   'tauiwi, non-Māori'
tēpu   'table'
tiā   'jar'
tiaka   'jug'
tiamana   'chairman; German' (cf. hēmana)
tiāti   'judge'
tīhi   'cheese'
tōtara   'totara' (tree species, *Podocarpus totara*)
tui   'tui, parson bird'
waka   'waka, canoe'
wātene   'warden'
weka   'weka, woodhen'
wētā   'weta, large insect species' (*Hemideina megacephala*)
whakapapa   'whakapapa, genealogy'
whānau   'whanau, extended family' (community of
                  close fellows)
whatura   'vulture'
whira   'violin, fiddle'

whīra	'field'
whurū	''flu'
whurutu	'fruit'
whutupaoro	'football' (rugby)
wihara	'whistle'
wīra	'wheel'
wōro	'wall'
wuruhi	'wolf'

Exercise 3.4 Spanish loanwords

The following is a list of borrowings in Spanish from different languages. What historical and cultural inferences might you suggest about the nature of the contact between speakers of Spanish and each of these other languages based on these? Concentrate on the Germanic and Arabic contacts. Which of the non-Germanic words do you think were further borrowed later from Spanish to English (or from Spanish to French and then on to English)?

From Celtic loans, already in Latin (from Gaul), inherited in Spanish: *abedul* 'birch tree', *bragas* 'breeches, trousers', *camisa* 'shirt', *carro* 'cart', *cerveza* 'beer'.

From Germanic (Swabians in Galicia; Vandals, Alans; Franks – Visigoths entered Spain in AD 412). Loans: *eslabón* 'link', *ganar* 'to gain, win, earn', *ganso* 'goose'; *bandera* 'flag', *botín* 'booty', *dardo* 'dart', *espiar* 'to spy', *espuela* 'spur', *guardar* 'guard', *guerra* 'war', *guía* 'guide', *hacha* 'axe', *robar* 'to rob', *yelmo* 'helmet'; *arpa* 'harp', *banco* 'bench', *barón* 'baron', *blanco* 'white', *brasa* 'live coal', *estaca* 'stake', *falda* 'skirt', *gris* 'grey', *guante* 'glove', *rico* 'rich', *ropa* 'clothing', *sopa* 'soup', *tacaño* 'stingy', *toalla* 'towel'; *norte* 'north', *sur* 'south', *este* 'east', *oeste* 'west'; personal names: *Anfonso, Elvira, Federico, Fernando, Francisco, Gonzalo, Matilde, Ricardo, Rodrigo*; and so on.

From Arabic (Moors landed in Spain in AD 711; by 718 they had spread over most of the Peninsula, where they remained until the recapture of Granada in 1492). Loans: *Guad-* 'river' (in place names, for example, *Guadalajara* 'river of stones', *Guadarrama* 'river of sand'); *alcázar* 'castle' (corruption of Latin *castrum* with Arabic article *al-*), *alférez* 'ensign', *alcalde* 'mayor', *atalaya* 'watchtower', *aldea* 'village', *almacén* 'storehouse', *barrio* 'district of city', *adobe* (sun-dried brick), *albañil* 'mason', *alcoba* 'bedroom' (alcove), *alfarero* 'potter', *bazar* 'bazaar', *alfiler* 'pin', *alfombra* 'rug', *almohada* 'pillow', *ataúd* 'coffin', *aceite* 'oil', *aceituna* 'olive', *albaricoque* 'apricot', *alcachofa* 'artichoke', *alfalfa* 'alfalfa', *algodón* 'cotton', *arroz* 'rice', *azúcar* 'sugar', *limón* 'lemon', *naranja* 'orange', *jazmín* 'jasmine', *alcohol* 'alcohol', *cero* 'zero', *cifra* 'cipher', *cenit* 'zenith', *albóndiga* 'meat ball', *azul* 'blue', *matar* 'to kill' (Arabic *mat* 'dead, checkmate'), *mono* 'monkey', *ojalá* 'if Allah will (oh I wish)', *res* 'cattle'.

From Arawak-Taino: *canoa* 'canoe', *iguana* 'iguana', *nigua* 'nit', *maíz* 'maize, corn', *ají* 'chili pepper', *yuca* 'sweet manioc', *tuna* 'fruit of prickly pear cactus', *barbacoa* 'barbecue', *batata* 'sweet potato', *enagua* 'petticoat, skirt, native skirt', *huracán* 'hurricane', *sabana* 'savanna', *macana* 'club', *cacique* 'chief'; *bejuco* 'vine', *maní* 'peanut'.

From Carib: *caníbal* 'cannibal', *manatí* 'manatee (sea cow)', *loro* 'parrot', *colibrí* 'hummingbird', *caimán* 'cayman, alligator species', *caribe* 'Carib', 'Caribbean'.

From Nahuatl: *hule* 'rubber', *tiza* 'chalk', *petaca* 'covered hamper, trunk, suitcase', *coyote* 'coyote', *ocelote* 'ocelot', *sinsonte* 'mocking bird', *guajolote* 'turkey', *chocolate* 'chocolate', *cacao* 'cacao, cocoa', *chicle* 'gum, chicle', *tomate* 'tomato', *aguacate* 'avocado', *cacahuete* 'peanut', *tamal* 'tamale', *jícara* 'gourd cup, small gourd bowl', *metate* 'quern, grinding-stone', *mecate* 'string, twine', *pulque* 'pulque (drink from century plant juice)', *achiote* 'bixa (food dye)', *camote* 'sweet potato', *ayote* 'pumpkin', *chayote* 'chayote (a vegetable)', *elote* 'ear of corn', *nopal* 'prickly pear cactus', *guacamole* 'guacamole', *cuate* 'buddy, twin', *caite* 'sandal'.

From Quechua: *pampa* 'pampa', *papa* 'potato', *coca* 'coca', *quino* 'quinine', *mate* 'mate (a strong tea)', *guano* 'guano (bird fertilizer)', *llama* 'llama', *vicuña* 'vicuña' (llama species), *alpaca* 'alpaca' (llama species), *cóndor* 'condor', *inca* 'Inca', *gaucho* 'gaucho' (cowboy/ horseman).

From Tupi-Guarani: *jaguar* 'jaguar', *piraña* 'piranha' (violent fish), *tapioca* 'tapioca', *ananás* 'pineapple'.

From English: *bistec* 'beefsteak', *ron* 'rum', huisqui/whisky 'whisky', *orange crush* 'Orange Crush (a soft drink)', *sandwich/sanduche/sanguich* 'sand-wich', *panqueque* 'pancake', *lonche* 'lunch', *boicot/boicotear* 'boycott', *clip* 'paperclip', *piqueteo* 'picketing'/*piquetear* 'to picket', *yate* 'yacht', *parquear* 'to park', *parqueo* 'parking place', *bumper/bómper* 'car bumper', *jet* 'jet', *stop* 'stop', *jeep* 'jeep'; *clóset* 'water closet, toilet', *plywood/plaiwud* 'plywood', *álbum* 'album', *bar* 'bar', *film(e)/filmar* 'film'/'to film', *show* 'show', *ticket/tiquete* 'ticket', *sex appeal/sexapil* 'sex appeal', *stress/estrés* 'stress', *spray/espréi* 'spray', *chequear/checar* 'to check'.

(For some of these and for further examples, see Campbell 1997a; Corominas 1974; Lapesa 1981; Resnik 1981; Spaulding 1965.)

Exercise 3.5   *Loanwords in Japanese*

The following is a list of some of the loanwords into Japanese, primarily
from English (though some other European languages may be involved
in a few of these). How has Japanese modified the foreign sounds to fit
its phonology? What arguments can you make to show that the direction
of borrowing is indeed from English into Japanese? State your evidence.
NOTE: Japanese permits no syllable-final consonants other than -*n*; it
does not tolerate consonant clusters other than -*nC*, though geminates
[double consonants] are allowed, and the only word-final consonant is
-*n*. In Japanese, /t/ is [ts] before *u*, [č] ([tʃ]) before *i*, and [t] elsewhere;
similarly, /s/ is [š] ([ʃ]) before *i*. Japanese has no *l* or *v*, and no *h* before
u (only *f*), and no ə.

aidea	'idea'
aidoru	'idol' (celebrity)
airon	'iron' (appliance)
aisukurīmu	'ice cream'
amachua	'amateur'
ampaia	'umpire'
asuterisuku	'asterisk'
bā	'bar'
baffarō	'buffalo'
bāgen	'bargain, sale'
baiburu	'Bible'
baiorin	'violin'
baitaritī	'vitality'
bajji	'badge'
baketsu	'bucket'
ban	'van'
bando	'band, belt'
baraddo	'ballad'
barē-bōru	'volleyball'
basuketto	'basket'
basu-tāminaru	'bus terminal'
batā	'butter'
batterī	'battery'
batto	'(baseball) bat'
bēju	'beige'
bēkon	'bacon'
benchi	'bench'
beruto	'belt'
bifuteki	'beefsteak'

bīru	'beer'
bīrusu	'virus' (cf. uirusu)
bitamin	'vitamin'
bōi sukauto	'Boy Scout'
borantia	'volunteer'
bōru	'ball'
boru	'bowl' (stadium)
borutto	'bolt' (headed metal pin)
bosu	'boss'
botan	'button'
būmu	'boom' (in prosperity)
burāji	'bra' (< brassiere)
burausu	'blouse'
buresuretto	'bracelet'
burijji	'bridge' (card game)
burondo	'blond'
buronzu	'bronze'
chātā	'charter'
chāto	'chart'
channeru	'channel'
chansu	'chance'
chīfu	'chief'
chīmuwāku	'teamwork'
chizu	'cheese'
chokoreto	'chocolate'
chūbu	'tube'
daietto	'diet'
daiyamondo	'diamond'
dansu	'dance'
depāto	'department store'
dezāto	'dessert'
doa	'door'
doraggu sutoa	'drugstore'
doresu	'dress'
doru	'dollar'
epuron	'apron'
erebētā	'elevator, lift'
fan	'fan' (admirer)
firumu	'film'
fōku	'fork'
fūdo	'hood'

furaipan	'frying pan'
furokku-kōto	'frock-coat'
furūtsu jūsu	'fruit juice'
gādoru	'girdle'
garasu	'glass, pane'
garēji	'garage'
garon	'gallon'
gāru sukauto	'Girl Scout'
gasorin	'gasoline'
gātā	'garter'
gēmu	'game'
gōru	'goal'
gorufu	'golf'
goshippu	'gossip'
gureibī	'gravy'
gurōbu	'glove'
gyamburu	'gamble'
gyaroppu	'gallop'
hābu	'herb'
hādo-weā	'hardware' (computer)
hambāgā	'hamburger'
hammā	'hammer'
hamu	'ham'
hamueggu	'ham and eggs'
handoru	'handle, steering wheel'
hankachi	'handkerchief'
herumetto	'helmet'
hinto	'hint'
hitto	'hit'
hotto doggu	'hotdog'
hyūzu	'fuse'
inchi	'inch'
indekkusu	'index'
infuruenza	'flu'
īsuto	'yeast'
jāji	'jersey'
jakketto	'jacket'
jamu	'jam'
jampā	'jumper'
jazu	'jazz'
jigu-zagu	'zigzag'

jīnzu	'jeans'
jippā	'zipper'
kādo	'card'
kāru	'curl'
kāten	'curtain'
kāton	'carton'
kan	'can, tin'
kareji	'college'
katarogu	'catalogue'
kauntā	'counter'
kēki	'cake'
kisu	'caress, kiss'
kōchi	'coach' (trainer)
kōhī	'café, coffee'
kokku	'cook'
komāsharu	'commercial'
komedī	'comedy'
kompakuto disuku	'compact disk'
kompyūta	'computer'
komyunikēshon	'communication'
konkurīto	'concrete' (building material)
kopī	'copy'
koppu	'cup'
kurabu	'club'
kuraimakkusu	'climax'
kuriketto	'cricket' (game)
kyabetsu	'cabbage'
kyabia	'caviar'
kyampasu	'campus'
kyampēn	'campaign'
kyampu	'camp'
kyandī	'candy'
kyaputen	'captain' (chief, leader)
māchi	'march'
māketto	'market'
māmarēdo	'marmalade'
manējā	'manager'
maton	'mutton'
membā	'member'
merodī	'melody'
meron	'melon'

mineraru uōtā	'mineral water'
miruku	'milk'
mishin	'sewing machine'
morutaru	'mortar'
myūjikaru	'musical' (play)
naifu	'knife'
nambā	'number'
napukin	'napkin'
nattsu	'nut'
nekutai	'necktie'
nettowāku	'network'
nikkeru	'nickel'
nūdoru	'noodle'
nyūsu	'news'
ōba	'overcoat'
ōbun	'oven'
ōkē	'O.K.'
ōkesutora	'orchestra'
ofisu	'office'
omuretsu	'omelette'
orenji	'orange'
oribu	'olive(s)'
pai	'pie'
painappuru	'pineapple'
painto	'pint'
paionia	'pioneer'
paipu	'pipe'
paipu-orugan	'organ' (musical instrument)
panchi	'punch' (fruit punch) (cf. also ponchi, ponsu)
paneru	'panel'
panfuretto	'pamphlet'
panikku	'panic'
pantī	'panties'
pantsu	'underpants, shorts, drawers'
parēdo	'parade'
parupu	'pulp (wood-pulp)'
pāsento	'percent'
pasupōto	'passport'
pātī	'party'
patoron	'patron'
paturōru	'patrol'

pējento	'pageant'
pedaru	'pedal'
pen	'pen'
pēsuto	'paste'
perikan	'pelican'
pikunikku	'picnic'
pin	'pin'
pīnatsu	'peanut'
pinku	'pink'
piru	'pill'
pisutoru	'pistol'
poketto	'pocket'
pondo	'pound'
ponsu	'punch' (fruit punch) (cf. also panchi, ponchi)
posutā	'poster'
posuto	'mailbox, postbox'
puragu	'plug' (electric)
puramu	'plum'
purasuchikku	'plastic'
purin	'pudding' (cf. also pudingu)
pūru	'pool'
rādo	'lard'
raberu	'label'
raifuru-	'rifle'
raimu	'lime'
rain	'line'
rajiētā	'radiator'
rajio	'radio'
ramu	'rum'
rampu	'lamp'
rantan	'lantern'
raunji	'lounge'
rejisutā	'register'
rekōdo	'record'
repōto	'report'
renji	'stove' (cooking stove, < 'range')
rēsu	'lace'
renzu	'lens'
resuringu	'wrestling'
retasu	'lettuce'
ribon	'ribbon'

rinen	'linen'
risuto	'list'
rizōto	'resort'
rizumu	'rhythm'
romansu	'romance'
rosuto chikin	'roast chicken'
sākasu	'circus'
sain	'sign, signal, signature'
sararī	'salary'
sāroin	'sirloin'
sekkusu	'sex'
serori	'celery'
sētā	'sweater'
shaberu	'shovel'
shatsu	'shirt' (cf. waishatsu 'dress shirt' < 'white shirt')
sherutā	'shelter'
shiringu	'shilling'
shiroppu	'syrup'
shisutā	'sister'
shīzun	'season'
shō	'show' (entertainment)
shokku	'shock'
shōru	'shawl'
sokkusu	'socks'
sōda	'soda'
sōsēji	'sausage'
suchimu	'steam'
suchuwādo	'steward' (aeroplane)
suchuwādesu	'stewardess'
sukejūru	'schedule'
sukurīn	'screen' (movie screen)
sukuryū	'screw'
sukyandaru	'scandal'
sukāto	'skirt'
sumāto	'smart' (fashionable)
supaisu	'spice'
superu	'spelling'
supīkā	'speaker' (loudspeaker)
suponji	'sponge'
supōtsu	'sport'
sūpu	'soup'

supūn	'spoon'
supurē	'spray'
supurinkurā	'sprinkler'
surakkusu	'slacks'
surangu	'slang'
surippā	'slipper(s)'
surōgan	'slogan'
sutā	'star' (film star)
sutairu	'style'
sutajio	'studio'
sutēki	'steak'
sutenresu	'stainless steel'
sutōbu	'stove' (heating stove)
sutoraiki	'strike' (by employees)
sutoraiku	'strike' (in baseball)
sūtsukēsu	'suitcase'
sutsūru	'stool'
taipuraitā	'typewriter'
tairu	'tile'
taiya	'tyre'
takkuru	'tackle' (in football)
takushi	'cab, taxi'
tamburā	'tumbler' (drinking glass)
tatorunekku	'turtleneck'
tēburu	'table'
tenisu	'tennis'
terebi(jon)	'television'
tīn-eijā	'teenager'
toire	'toilet' (lavatory)
ton	'ton'
torakku	'truck'
torikku	'trick'
tōsuto	'toast'
tsuīdo	'tweed'
ueitā	'waiter'
ueitoresu	'waitress'
uesuto	'waist'
uīkuendo	'weekend'
uinku	'wink'
uirusu	'virus' (cf. bīrusu)
wain	'wine'

wakuchin	'vaccine'
wanisu	'varnish'
yādo	'yard (measure)'
yotto	'yacht'
yunifōmu	'uniform'

Exercise 3.6 Hispanisms in Mayan languages

The following is a list of some of the 'hispanisms' (loanwords from Spanish) found in some of the Mayan languages (of Mexico and Guatemala). The Spanish forms are presented both in current pronunciation and as pronounced in the sixteenth century. Based on these, what evidence can you derive from these loans in the Mayan languages relevant to changes which have taken place in Spanish since these forms were borrowed? By way of illustration, consider the following example involving Sayula Popoluca (a Mixe-Zoquean language):

Spanish *caja* 'box' (modern [kaxa], colonial [kaʃa]: Sayula Popoluca *kaʃa* 'coffin' ('box for the dead').

From this, you would tentatively conclude that Spanish has undergone the change of ʃ > x after this word was borrowed. Of course, it is necessary to keep in mind that the borrowing language will make substitutions, replacing the Spanish sounds with the closest phonetic counterpart available in the recipient language, so that not all differences in the borrowing language will be due to changes which Spanish has subsequently undergone; to determine this, it will be necessary to compare the sixteenth-century and the modern Spanish forms. In regard to this particular example, it is interesting that Sayula Popoluca later borrowed the Spanish word for 'box' again, after the change, as *kaha* 'cardboard box' (note that Sayula Popoluca has no [x], so that [h] is the language's closest approximation to Modern Spanish [x]).

Note the following phonetic symbols found in these examples:
[s̪] dental (fronted) *s*
[s] apical alveolar *s*
[ṣ̌] laminal retroflex ʃ

Focus on /lʲ/ and /j/:

1. *llave* 'key' (modern [jaβe], colonial [lʲaβe, lʲave]): Akateko *laweh*, Q'anjobal *lawe*, K'iche' *lawe*.
2. *cebolla* 'onion' (modern [seβoja], colonial [seboˌlʲa]): Akateko *sewolya*, Q'anjobal *sewolia*, Tzeltal *sebolia* (none of the Mayan languages has /lʲ/, but they do have /l/ and /j/).

3. *cuchillo* 'knife' (modern [kučijo], colonial [kučiⁱo]): Chol *kučilu*, Huastec *kuči:l*, Q'anjobal *kučiilu* 'knife, razor', K'iche' *kučiʔl*.
4. *silla* 'chair' (modern [sija], colonial ṣilʲa]): Akateko *ʃilah*, Huastec *ʃi:laʔ* 'saddle, chair', Q'anjobal *ʃila*, K'iche' *ʃila*, Tzotzil *ʃila*.
5. *castellano* 'Castilian, Spanish' (modern [kastejano], colonial [kastelʲano]): Choltí *kaʃtilan čaɓ* 'sugar' (literally 'Castilian honey'), *kaʃtilan wa* 'bread' (literally 'Castilian tortilla'); K'iche' *kaʃtilan*, *kaʃlan* 'Castilian, Spanish, pure, correct'.

Focus on /ṣ, /ṣ/, and /ʃ/:

6. *sartén* 'frying pan' (modern [saɾtén], colonial [ṣaɾtén]): Q'anjobal *ʃalten*, *ʃaltin*, Motocintlec *ʃalten*, Tzotzil *ʃalten*.
7. *sebo* 'tallow, fat' (modern [seβo], colonial [ṣebo]): Q'anjobal *ʃepuʔ*, K'iche' *ʃepu*, *ʃepo*, Tzotzil *ʃepu*.
8. *seda* 'silk' (modern [seða], colonial [ṣeða]): Chol *ʃelah-* 'ribbon', Tzotzil *ʃela* 'silk, ribbon'. (Mayan languages have no [ð].)
9. *semana* 'week' (modern [semana], colonial [ṣemana]): Q'eqchi' *ʃama:n*, *ʃema:n*, K'iche' *ʃemano*, Tzotzil *ʃemana*.
10. *señora* 'lady, madam, Mrs' (modern [senʲora], colonial [ṣenʲora]): Chol *ʃinolah* 'non-Indian woman', Mam *ʃnu:l* 'non-Indian woman', Motocintlec *ʃnu:la:n* 'non-Indian woman', Tzeltal *ʃinola* 'non-Indian woman'.
11. *mesa* 'table' (modern [mesa], colonial [meṣa]): Akateko *meʃah*, Huastec *me:ʃa*, Q'eqchi' *me:ʃa*, Motocintlec *me:ʃah*, K'iche' *meʃa*.
12. *patos* 'ducks' (modern [patos], colonial [patoṣ]): Huastec *pa:tuʃ*, Q'eqchi' *patuʃ*, K'iche' *pataʃ*, Tzotzil *patoʃ*, all 'duck'. (Note that several plant and animal terms, though singular, were borrowed from the Spanish plural form, as in this example and the next.)
13. *vacas* 'cows' (modern [bakas], colonial [βakaṣ, vakaṣ]): Akateko *wakaʂ* 'cattle', Chol *wakaʃ* 'bull, cow', Itzá *wakaʃ* 'cattle', Q'anjobal *wakaʂ* 'cow, cattle', Q'eqchi' *kwakaʃ* 'cow, cattle', Mopan *wakaʃ* 'cow, bull, cattle', Tzeltal *wakaʃ* 'beef'. (See also 4 and 5 above.)
14. *cidra* 'a grapefruit-like fruit' (modern [siðra], colonial ṣiðra]): Chol *silah*, Tzotzil *sila*. (Note that these languages have no *d*, *ð* or *r*).
15. *cocina* 'kitchen' (modern [kosina], colonial [koṣina]): Motocintlec *kusi:nah*, Tzotzil *kusina*.
16. *cruz* 'cross' (modern [krus], colonial [kruṣ]): Chol *rus*, Q'anjobal *kurus*, Q'eqchi' *kurus*, Mam *lu:s*, Motocintlec *kuru:s*, Tzotzil *kurus*.

17. *lazo* 'lasso, rope' (modern [laso], colonial [laṣo]): Akateko *lasuh*, Chol *lasoh*, Tzeltal *laso*, Tzotzil *lasu*.

18. *taza* 'cup' (modern [tasa], colonial [taṣa]): Chol *tasa* 'piece of glass', Huastec *ta:sa*, Q'eqchi' *ta:s*.

19. *jabón* 'soap' (modern [xaβón], colonial [ʃabón]): Chol *ʃapum*, *ʃapom*, Huastec *ʃabu:n*, Jakalteko *sapun*, Q'anjobal *sapon*, Motocintlec *ʃa:puh*, K'iche' *ʃɓon*, Tzeltal *ʃapon*.

20. *jarro* 'jug, jar' (modern [xaro], colonial [ʃaro]): Jakalteko *ʃalu*, Q'anjobal *ʃalu*, Mam *sar*, Motocintlec *ʃa:ruh*, K'iche' *ʃaruʔ*, Tzeltal *ʃalu*, Tzotzil *ʃalŭ*.

21. *aguja* 'needle' (modern [aguxa], colonial [aguʃa]): Akateko *akuʃah*, Chol *akuʃan*, Q'anjobal *akuʃa*, Q'eqchi' *aku:ʃ*, *ku:ʃ*, Motocintlec *aku:ʃah*, Tzeltal *akuʃa*, Tzotzil *akuʃa*.

22. *caja* 'box' (modern [kaxa], colonial [kaʃa]): Chol *kaʃa-teʔ* 'chest' (*teʔ* = 'wood'), Q'anjobal *kaʃa* 'box, chest', Q'eqchi' *ka:ʃ* 'chest', Mam *ka:s* 'box', Motocintlec *ka:ʃah* 'box, chest', K'iche' *kaʃa* 'box, čhest, trunk', Tzeltal *kaʃa*.

Focus on /v/ and /b/:

23. *ventana* 'window' (modern [bentana], colonial [βentana, ventana]): Chol *wentana*, Q'anjobal *wentena*, Motocintlec *wanta:nah*.

24. (= 13 above) *vacas* 'cows' (modern [bakas], colonial [βakas, vakas]): Akateko *wakas* 'cattle', Chol *wakaʃ* 'bull, cow', Itzá *wakáʃ* 'cattle', Q'anjobal *wăkas* 'cow, cattle', Q'eqchi' *kwakaʃ* 'cow, cattle', Mopan *wakaʃ* 'cŏw, bull, cattle', Tzeltal *wakaʃ* 'beef'.

25. *calvario* 'Calvary' (modern [kalβaɾio], colonial [kalβaɾio, kalvario]): Q'anjobal *karwal* 'cemetery, graveyard', K'iche' *kalwar*.

26. *clavos* 'nails' (modern [klaβos], colonial [klaβos, klavos]): Akateko *lawuʃ*, Chol *lawuʃ*, Tzeltal *lawuʃ*, Tojolabal *lawuʃ*. (Note that these forms mean 'nail', but are borrowed from the Spanish plural form.)

27. *rábanos* 'radishes' (modern [ráβanos], colonial [ráβanos, rávanos]): Tojolabal *lawuniʃ*, Motocintlec *luwaʔnʃa* 'rábano', Tzotzil *alavanuʃ*. (Note that these all mean 'radish', though borrowed from the Spanish plural form. Tzotzil has a phonemic contrast between /v/ and /b/, but has no /w/; the other languages have no /v/, but do have /w/.) (See also 1 above.)

28. *botón(es)* 'button(s)' (modern [botón], colonial [botón]): Q'eqchi' *ɓoto:nʃ*, K'iche' *ɓotona*, *ɓotoniʃ*, Tojolabal *ɓoton* 'button, knot in wood', Tzotzil *ɓoton*.

29. *bolsa* 'bag, pocket' (modern [bolsa], colonial [bolsa, borsa]):

Chol *borʃa*, Q'eqchi' *ɓoːʃ* 'pocket', K'iche' *ɓorʃa*, Tzeltal *ɓolsa*.
30. *nabos* 'turnips' (modern [naβos], colonial [nabos]): K'iche'
    napuʃ, Tzotzil *napuʃ*, Motocintlec *kolinaʔwa*. (See álso 2 and 7
    above.)

4

—

Analogical Change

—

They have been at a great feast of languages, and stolen the scraps.
(William Shakespeare [1564–1616],
Love's Labour's Lost, V, 1, 39)

4.1 Introduction

Sound change, borrowing and analogy have traditionally been considered
the three most important (most basic) types of linguistic change. In spite
of the importance of analogy, linguistics textbooks seem to struggle
when it comes to offering a definition. Many do not even bother, but just
begin straight away by presenting examples of analogical change. Some
of the definitions of analogy that have been offered run along the following lines: analogy is a linguistic process involving generalization of
a relationship from one set of conditions to another set of conditions;
analogy is change modelled on the example of other words or forms;
and analogy is a historical process which projects a generalization from
one set of expressions to another. Arlotto (1972: 130), recognizing the
problem of offering an adequate definition, gives what he calls 'a pur-
posely vague and general definition': '[analogy] is a process whereby
one form of a language becomes more like another with which it is
somehow associated'. The essential element in all these definitions,
vague and inadequate though this may sound, is that *analogical change
involves a relation of similarity* (compare Anttila 1989: 88).

For the Neogrammarians, sound change was considered regular, borrowings needed to be identified, and analogy was, in effect, everything
else that was left over. That is, almost everything that was not sound
change or borrowing was analogy. Analogy became the default (or

wastebasket) category of changes. In analogical change, one piece of the language changes to become more like another pattern in the language where speakers perceive the changing part as similar to the pattern that it changes to be more like. Analogy is sometimes described as 'internal borrowing', the idea being that in analogical change a language may 'borrow' from some of its own patterns to change other patterns.

By way of getting started, let us consider some examples of analogy. Originally, *sorry* and *sorrow* were quite distinct, but in its history *sorry* has changed under influence from *sorrow* to become more similar to *sorrow*. *Sorry* is from the adjective form of 'sore', Old English *sārig* 'sore, pained, sensitive' (derived from the Old English noun *sār* 'sore'), which has cognates in other Germanic languages. The original *ā* of *sārig* changed to *ō* and then was shortened to *o* under influence from *sorrow* (Old English *sorh* 'grief, deep sadness or regret'), which had no historical connection to *sorry*. This is an analogical change, where the form of *sorry* changed on analogy with that of *sorrow*.

There are many kinds of analogical change. In this chapter, we explore the different types of analogy and the role of analogy in traditional treatments of linguistic change, and we see how it interacts with sound change (and to a more limited extent with grammatical change, looking forward to Chapter 10 on syntactic change).

Some equate analogical change with morphological change, though this can be misleading. While it is true that many analogical changes involve changes in morphology, not all do, and many changes in morphology are not analogical. In this book, aspects of morphological change are treated not only in this chapter, but also in Chapters 2, 3, 10 and 12.

4.2 Proportional Analogy

Traditionally, two major kinds of analogical changes have been distinguished, *proportional* and *non-proportional*, although the distinction is not always clear or relevant. Proportional analogical changes are those which can be represented in an equation of the form, $a : b = c : x$, where one solves for 'x' – a is to b as c is to what? (x = 'what?'). For example: *ride : rode = dive : x*, where in this instance x is solved with *dove*. In this analogical change, the original past tense of *dive* was *dived*, but it changed to *dove* under analogy with the class of verbs which behave like *drive : drove, ride : rode, write : wrote, strive : strove*, and so on. (Today, both *dived* and *dove* are considered acceptable in Standard English, though the use of these forms does vary regionally.) The four-term analogy of the form a : b = c : x is also sometimes presented in other forms, for example as: *a : b :: c : x*; or as:

$$\frac{a}{c} = \frac{b}{x}$$

Not all cases considered proportional analogy can be represented easily in this proportional formula, and some cases not normally thought to be proportional analogical changes can be fitted into such a formula. In the end, the distinction may not be especially important, so long as you understand the general notion of analogy. Let us turn to examples of four-part proportional analogy, which will make the concept clearer.

(1) A famous example comes from Otto Jespersen's observation of a Danish child 'who was corrected for saying *nak* instead of *nikkede* ('nodded'), [and] immediately retorted "stikker, stak, nikker, nak," thus showing on what analogy he had formed the new preterit' (Jesperson 1964: 131). That is, the child produced the proportional formula: *stikker* 'sticks' : *stak* 'stuck' = *nikker* 'nods' : *nak* 'nodded'.

(2) In English, the pattern of the verb *speak/spoke/spoken* ('present tense'/'past tense'/'past participle') developed through remodelling on analogy with verbs of the pattern *break/broke/broken*. In Old English, it was *sprec/spræc/gesprecen* (compare the *spake* 'past tense' of Early Modern English with present-day *spoke*).

(3) Finnish formerly had *laksi* 'bay (nominative singular)'; its possessive form ('genitive singular') was *lahde-n*, just as words such as *kaksi* (nominative singular) : *kahde-n* (genitive singular) 'two'. However, under the weight of Finnish words with the different nominative–genitive pattern as in *lehti* : *lehde-n* 'leaf', *tähti* : *tähde-n* 'star', the *laksi* nominative singular of 'bay' changed to *lahti*, as in the proportional fomula: *lehden : lehti :: lahden : lahti* (< *laksi*). The past tense form of the verb 'to leave' had the same fate: originally the pattern was *lähte-* 'leave' : *läksi* 'left', but this alternation was shifted by the same analogical pattern to give *lähti* 'left' (past tense) in Standard Finnish.

(4) A more grammatical example of proportional analogical change is found in some Spanish dialects in the non-standard pronoun pattern called *laísmo*. Standard Spanish has distinct masculine and feminine third person pronominal direct object forms, but the indirect object pronominal forms do not distinguish gender, as in:

lo ví 'I saw him' [him I.saw], *la ví* 'I saw her' [her I.saw]
le di 'I gave him/her (something)' [him/her I.gave].

In the dialects with *laísmo*, the change created a gender distinction also in the indirect object pronoun forms:

le di 'I gave him (something)', *la di* 'I gave her (something)'.

The proportional analogy in the formula would be:

lo ví 'I saw him' : *la ví* 'I saw her' :: *le di* 'I gave him (something) : *x*
where *x* is solved for *la di* 'I gave her (something)'.

(5) Proto-Nahua had a single verbal prefix to signal reflexives, **mo-*, still the basic pattern in a majority of the modern varieties of Nahua, as in Pipil *ni-**mu**-miktia* 'I kill myself', *ti-**mu**-miktiat* 'we kill ourselves', and ***mu**-miktia* 'he/she kills himself/herself'. However, on analogy with the subject pronominal verbal prefixes (*ni-* 'I', *ti-* 'we'), Classical Nahuatl has created distinct reflexive pronouns, *-no-* 'myself', *-to-* 'ourselves' and *(-)mo-* 'yourself/himself/herself', as in: *ni-**no**-miktia* 'I kill myself', *ti-**to**-miktia?* 'we kill ourselves' and ***mo**-miktia* 'he/she kills himself/herself'.

4.3 Analogical Levelling

Many of the proportional analogical changes are instances of analogical levelling. (Others are extensions; see below.) Analogical levelling reduces the number of allomorphs a form has; it makes paradigms more uniform. In analogical levelling, forms which formerly underwent alternations no longer do so after the change.

(1) For example, some English 'strong' verbs have been levelled to the 'weak' verb pattern, as for instance in dialects where *throw/threw/thrown* has become *throw/throwed/throwed*. There are numerous cases throughout the history of English in which strong verbs (with stem alternations, as in *sing/sang/sung* or *write/wrote/written*) have been levelled to weak verbs (with a single stem form and *-ed* or its equivalent for 'past' and 'past participle', as in *bake/baked/baked* or *live/lived/lived*). Thus *cleave/clove/cloven* (or *cleft*) 'to part, divide, split' has become *cleave/cleaved/cleaved* for most, while *strive/strove/striven* for many speakers has changed to *strive/strived/strived*. (*Strive* is a borrowing from Old French *estriver* 'to quarrel, contend', but came to be a strong verb very early in English, now widely levelled to a weak verb pattern.)

(2) Some English strong verbs have shifted from one strong verb pattern to another, with the result of a partial levelling. For example, in earlier English the 'present'/'past'/'past participle' of the verb *to bear* was

equivalent to *bear/bare/born(e)*, and *break* was *break/brake/broke(n)*. They have shifted to the *fight/fought/fought*, *spin/spun/spun* pattern, where the root of the 'past' and 'past participle' forms is now the same (*bear/bore/born(e)*, *break/broke/broken*).

(3) In a rather large class of verbs in Standard Spanish, *o* (unstressed) alternates with *ue* (when stressed), as in *volár* 'to fly', *vuéla* 'it flies'. Some speakers of Chicano Spanish have levelled the alternation in favour of *ue* alone in these verbs: *vuelár* 'to fly', *vuéla* 'it flies'.

(4) In English, the former 'comparative' and 'superlative' forms of *old* have been levelled from the pattern *old/elder/eldest* to the non-alternating pattern *old/older/oldest*. Here, *o* had been fronted by umlaut due to the former presence of front vowels in the second syllable of *elder* and *eldest*, but the effects of umlaut were levelled out, and now the words *elder* and *eldest* remain only in restricted contexts, not as the regular 'comparative' and 'superlative' of *old*.

(5a) *Near* was originally a 'comparative' form, meaning 'nearer', but it became the basic form meaning 'near'. If the original state of affairs had persisted for the pattern 'near'/'nearer'/'nearest', we should have had *nigh/near/next*, from Old English *nēah* 'near'/*nēarra* 'nearer'/*nēahsta* 'nearest'. However, this pattern was levelled out; *nearer* was created in the sixteenth century, then *nearest* substituted for *next*. Both *nigh* and *next* remained in the language, but with more limited, shifted meanings.
(5b) Similarly, *far* was also comparative in origin (originally meaning 'farther'), but this became the basic form meaning 'far', which then gave rise to the new comparative *farrer*, which was replaced by *farther* under the influence of *further* 'more forward, more onward, before in position'.
(5c) The pattern *late/later/latest* is also the result of an analogical levelling without which we would have had instead the equivalent of *late/latter/last*, with the 'comparative' from Old English *lætra* and the 'superlative' from Old English *latost*. (In this case, *later* replaced *latter*, which now remains only in restricted meaning; and *last*, though still in the language, is no longer the 'superlative' of *late*.)

(6) In Greek, *k^w* became *t* before *i* and *e*, but became *p* in most other environments. By regular sound change, then, the verb 'to follow' in Greek should have resulted in forms such as: *hépomai* 'I follow', *hétēi* 'you follow', *hétetai* 'he/she/it follows'. However, by analogy, the *p* (from original *k^w* before *o* in this case) spread throughout the paradigm, levelling all the forms of 'to follow': *hépomai* 'I follow', *hépēi* 'you follow', *hépetai* 'he/she/it follows' (Beekes 1995: 73).

(7) Many verbs which have the same form in the singular and plural in Modern German once had different vowels, which were levelled by

analogy. Thus, for example, Martin Luther (1483–1546) still wrote *er bleyb* 'he stayed'/*sie blieben* 'they stayed' and *er fand* 'he found'/*sie funden* 'they found', where Modern German has *er blieb/sie blieben* and *er fand/sie fanden* (Polenz 1977: 84).

4.4 Analogical Extension

Analogical extension (somewhat rarer than analogical levelling) extends the already existing alternation of some pattern to new forms which did not formerly undergo the alternation. An example of analogical extension is seen in the case mentioned above of *dived* being replaced by *dove* on analogy with the 'strong' verb pattern as in *drive/drove*, *ride/rode* and so on, an extension of the alternating pattern of the strong verbs. Other examples follow.

(1) Modern English *wear/wore*, which is now in the strong verb pattern, was historically a weak verb which changed by extension of the strong verb pattern, as seen in earlier English *werede* 'wore', which would have become modern *weared* if it had survived.

(2) Other examples in English include the development of the non-standard past tense forms which show extension to the strong verb pattern which creates alternations that formerly were not there, as in: *arrive/arrove* (Standard English *arrive/arrived*), and *squeeze/squoze* (Standard *squeeze/squeezed*).

(3) In some Spanish verbs, *e* (unstressed) alternates with *ie* (when in stressed positions), as in *pensár* 'to think', *piénso* 'I think'. In some rural dialects, this pattern of alternation is sometimes extended to verbs which formerly had no such alternating pairs, for example: *aprendér* 'to learn'/*apriéndo* 'I learn', where Standard Spanish has *aprendér* 'to learn'/*apréndo* 'I learn'. Others include *compriendo* 'I understand' for *comprendo*, *aprieto* 'I tighten' for *apreto*; this also extends to such forms as *diferiencia* for *diferencia* 'difference'.

(4) Where Standard Spanish has no alternation in the vowels in forms such as *créa* 'he/she creates'/*creár* 'to create', many Spanish dialects undergo a change which neutralizes the distinctions between *e* and *i* in unstressed syllables, resulting in alternating forms as seen in *créa* 'he/she creates'/*criár* 'to create'. This alternation has been extended in some dialects to forms which would not originally have been subject to the neutralization. Thus, for example, on analogy with forms of the *créa/criár* type, illustrated again in *menéa* 'he/she stirs'/*meniár* 'to stir', some verbs which originally did not have the stress pattern have shifted to this pattern, as seen in dialect *cambéa* 'he/she changes'/

cambiár 'to change', replacing Standard Spanish *cámbia* 'he/she changes'/*cambiár* 'to change'; *vacéo* 'I empty'/*vaciár* 'to empty', replacing Standard Spanish *vácio* 'I empty'/*vaciár* 'to empty'.

From the point of view of the speaker, analogical levelling and extension may not be different, since in both the speaker is making different patterns in the language more like other patterns that exist in the language.

4.5 The Relationship between Analogy and Sound Change

The relationship between sound change and analogy is captured reasonably well by the slogan (sometimes called 'Sturtevant's paradox'): *sound change is regular and causes irregularity; analogy is irregular and causes regularity* (Anttila 1989: 94). That is, a regular sound change can create alternations, or variant allomorphs. For example, umlaut was a regular sound change in which back vowels were fronted due to the presence of a front vowel in a later syllable, as in *brother* + *-en* > *brethren*; as a result of this regular sound change, the root for 'brother' came to have two variants, *brother* and *brethr-*. Earlier English had many alternations of this sort. However, an irregular analogical change later created *brothers* as the plural form, on analogy with the non-alternating singular/plural pattern in such nouns as *sister/sisters*. This analogical change is irregular in that it applied only now and then, here and there, to individual alternating forms, not across the board to all such alternations at the same time. This analogical change in the case of *brethren* in effect resulted in undoing the irregularity created by the sound change, leaving only a single form, *brother*, as the root in both the singular and plural forms; that is, analogy levelled out the alternation left behind by the sound change (*brethren* survives only in a restricted context with specialized meaning). Here, we should be careful to note that although analogical changes are usually not regular processes (which would occur whenever their conditions are found), they can sometimes be regular.

The history of the verb *to choose* in English shows the interaction of analogy and sound change well. Old English had the forms *cēosan* [čēozan] 'infinitive', *cēas* [čǣas] 'past singular', *curon* [kuron] 'past plural' and *coren* [koren] 'past participle'. These come from the Proto-Indo-European root **geus-* 'to choose, to taste' (which had vowel alternations in different grammatical contexts which gave also **gous-* and **gus-* – the latter is the root behind Latin *gustus* 'taste' and the loanword *gusto* in English). From this Indo-European root came

Proto-Germanic **keus-an* (and its alternates in different grammatical contexts, **kaus-* and **kuz-*). The differences in the consonants among the Old English forms of 'to choose' come from two sound changes. The past plural and past participle forms had undergone Verner's law (see Chapter 5), which changed the **s* to **z* when the stress followed (as it did in the 'past plural' and 'past participle' in Pre-Germanic times), and then intervocalic *z* changed to *r* by rhotacism. The other change was the palatalization in English of *k* to *č* before the front vowels. Together, these changes resulted in different allomorphs with different consonants in the paradigm, *čVs-* and *kVr-*. Analogical levelling later eliminated these consonant differences, leaving Modern English *choose/chose/chosen* uniformly with the same consonants. (In dialects, even the difference in vowels of the strong verb pattern was sometimes levelled, to *choose/ choosed/choosed* or similar forms, though these have not survived well in the face of competition from Standard English.) In this example, clearly the regular sound changes, rhotacism (after Verner's law) and palatalization, created different allomorphs (irregularity in the paradigm for 'choose' in Old English), and subsequent analogical changes restored uniformity to the consonants of this paradigm.

A somewhat more complicated but more informative example is seen in Table 4.1. (See also section 2.7.4 in Chapter 2.)

TABLE 4.1: Latin rhotacism and the interaction of analogy with sound change

Stage 1: Latin before 400 BC		
honōs 'honour'	labōs 'labour'	nominative singular
honōsem	labōsem	accusative singular
honōsis	labōsis	genitive singular
Stage 2: rhotacism: s > r /V__V		
honōs	labōs	nominative singular
honōrem	labōrem	accusative singular
honōris	labōris	genitive singular
Stage 3: after 200 BC, analogical reformation of nominative singular		
honor	labor	nominative singular
honōrem	labōrem	accusative singular
honōris	labōris	genitive singular

In this example, the regular sound change in Stage 2, rhotacism (s > r / V__V), created allomorphy (*honos/honōr-*), that is, irregularity in the paradigm. Later, irregular analogy changed *honōs* and *labōs* (nominative singular forms) to *honor* and *labor*, both now ending in *r*, matching the *r* of the rest of the forms in the paradigm. Thus irregular analogy has regularized the form of the root, eliminating the allomorphic alternations involving the final consonant of the root.

4.6   Analogical Models

In discussions of different sorts of analogical change, it is common to distinguish between *immediate models* and *non-immediate models*. These have to do with the place in the language where we find the 'relation of similarity' which is behind the analogical change. Cases involving *non-immediate models* are, like those of the Latin *labōs > labor* of Table 4.1, due to the influence of whole classes of words or paradigms which do not normally occur in discourse in the near vicinity of the form that changes. In a case such as *honōs > honor* under analogy from other forms in the paradigm, such as *honōrem*, *honōris* and so on, in normal discourse these forms would not occur adjacent to (or nearby) one another. For the majority of analogical changes no immediate model exists, but rather the model is a class of related forms.

An *immediate model* refers to a situation in which the 'relation of similarity' upon which the analogical change is based is found in the same speech context as the thing that changes. This refers to instances where the thing that changes and the thing that influences it to change are immediately juxtaposed to one another or are located very near each other in frequently repeated pieces of speech. Thus, analogical changes based on an immediate model are typically found in frequently recited routines, such as sequences of basic numbers, days of the week, months of the year, or in phrases used so frequently they can almost be taken as a unit. For example, month names are frequently said together in sequence; as a result, for many English speakers, because of the immediate model of *January*, *February* has changed to *Febuary* [fɛbjuwɛɹi], becoming more like *January* [ǰænjuwɛɹi].

(1) In English, *female* ['fimeil] was earlier *femelle* [fɛ'mɛl]; however, in the immediate model of *male and female*, frequently uttered together, the earlier *femelle* (the Middle English form) changed to be more similar to *male*.

(2) Modern Spanish has the following days of the week which end in *s*: *lunes* 'Monday', *martes* 'Tuesday', *miercoles* 'Wednesday', *jueves* 'Thursday', *viernes* 'Friday'; however, *lunes* and *miercoles* come from forms which originally lacked this final *s*, but took it by analogy to other day names which ended in *s* in this immediate context, where the days of the week are commonly recited as a list. The day names are derived

111

from shortened versions of the Latin names which originally contained *dies* 'day', as in the following, where the last sound in these compounds reveals which forms contained the original final *s* and which lacked it: Spanish *lunes* < Latin *dies lunae* 'moon's day' [no final -*s*], *martes* < *dies martis* 'Mars' day', *miercoles* < *dies mercurī* 'Mercury's day' [no final-*s*], *jueves* < *dies jovis* 'Jupiter's day', *viernes* < *dies veneris* 'Venus' day'.

(3) Many examples of analogical changes based on an immediate model are found in numbers. For example, (1) Proto-Indo-European had *k^wetwor-* 'four', *$penk^we$-* 'five'; *p became Germanic *f by Grimm's law, and *k^w should have become *h^w, but we get *four* (with *f*, not expected *whour*) by influence from the *f* of following *five*. (2) Latin *quinque* /k^{w}ink^{w}e/ 'five' (from *$penk^we$-) may be due in part to influence from preceding *quattuor* 'four' (from *k^wetwor-*). (3) In some Greek dialects, the sequence *hepta* 'seven', *oktō* 'eight' has become *hepta, hoktō*; in others, *oktō* has become *optō* 'eight', becoming more like the preceding *hepta* 'seven'. (4) In Slavic, originally 'nine' began with *n*- and 'ten' with *d*-, but they shifted so that 'nine' now begins with *d*-, making it more similar to following 'ten', as in Russian *d^{j}ev^{j}at^j* 'nine' (< Proto-Indo-European *$newn$) *d^{j}es^{j}at^j* 'ten'(< Proto-Indo-European *$dekm$).

The numbers in several Mayan languages illustrate this tendency for numbers counted in sequence to influence each other, as immediate models for analogical change. For example, Poqomchi' numbers have come to have the same vowel in *kiʔi:ɓ* 'two', *iʃi:ɓ* 'three', *kixi:ɓ* 'four', from earlier forms with distinct vowels: Proto-K'ichean *kaʔi:ɓ* 'two', *oʃi:ɓ* 'three', *kaxi:ɓ* 'four'. In Q'eqchi', 'ten' has been influenced by 'nine': *ɓeleɓeɓ* 'nine', *laxe:ɓ* 'ten', from Proto-K'ichean *ɓe:lexeɓ* 'nine', *laxux* 'ten'. The Proto-Mayan forms *waq-* 'six' and *huq-* 'seven' have influenced each other in several Mayan languages: for example, the *w* of 'six' has influenced 'seven' to take *w* instead of its original *h*, as seen in Teco *wu:q* 'seven' and Tzotzil *wuk* 'seven'.

(4) An often-repeated example is Cicero's *senātī populīque Romanī* 'of the Roman senate and people', where *senātūs* 'senate (genitive singular)' is expected. In this case, different noun classes are involved, which had different 'genitive singular' forms:

'nominative singular':	animus 'soul, heart'	senatus 'senate'
'genitive singular':	animī	senātūs

The *senātus* class was small, and only a few nouns belonged to it. The class to which *animus* belonged was much larger. A frequent phrase, in the nominative case, was *senātus populusque romanus* 'the Roman senate and people' (the clitic *-que* means 'and'). Cicero gave it in the genitive case, not with expected *senātūs* 'senate (genitive singular)', but *senatī* based on the immediate model of *populī* 'people (genitive singular)' in this phrase (compare Paul 1920: 106).

4.7 Other Kinds of Analogy

Many different kinds of change are typically called analogy; some of these have little in common with one other. It is important to have a general grasp of these various kinds of changes which are all lumped together under the general heading of analogy, for these terms are used very frequently in historical linguistic works. As pointed out above, the proportional analogical changes which involve levelling and extension, though often irregular, can in some instances be quite regular and systematic. Most of the other kinds of analogy, normally considered non-proportional, are mostly irregular and sporadic (and many of these can be interpreted as proportional, too). There is nothing particularly compelling about this classification of kinds of analogical changes. The names are standard, but one type is not necessarily fully distinct from another, so that some examples of analogical changes may fit more than one of these kinds of change.

4.7.1 Hypercorrection

Hypercorrection involves awareness of different varieties of speech which are attributed different social status. An attempt to change a form in a less prestigious variety to make it conform with how it would be pronounced in a more prestigious variety sometimes results in over-shooting the target and coming up with what is an erroneous outcome from the point of view of the prestige variety being mimicked. That is, hypercorrection is the attempt to correct things which are in fact already correct and which already match the form in the variety being copied, resulting in overcorrection and getting the form wrong.

(1) Some dialects in the western United States have: *lawnd* < *lawn*; *pawnd (shop)* < *pawn*; *drownd* (present tense)/*drownded* (past tense) < *drown/drowned*; and *acrost* (or *acrossed*) < *across*. These changes came about by hypercorrection in an overzealous attempt to undo the effects of final consonant cluster simplification found to one extent or another in most varieties of English, for example the loss of final *d* after *n*, *han'* for *hand* (common, for example, in *han(d)made*), *fin'* for *find*, *roun'* for

round, and of *t* after *s*, *firs'* for *first* (for example, in *firs(t) thing*), and so on.

(2) The frequently heard instances in English of things like *for you and I* for what in Standard English is *for you and me* involve hypercorrection; schoolteachers have waged war on the non-standard use of *me* in subject positions, in instances such as *me and Jimmy watched 'Star Trek'* and *me and him ate popcorn* and so on. Speakers, in attempting to correct these to *I* when it is part of the subject of the clause, sometimes go too far and hypercorrect instances of *me* in direct or indirect objects to *I*, as in *Maggie gave it to Kerry and I*.

(3) Some English dialects in the southern United States have *umbrellow* for 'umbrella' and *pillow* for 'pillar', a hypercorrection based on the less prestigious pronunciations of words such as *fella* and *yella*, changing to match to more formal (more prestigious) *fellow* and *yellow*.

(4) In many rural Spanish dialects, *d* before *r* has changed to *g* (d > g /__ r), as in: *magre* 'mother' (< *madre*), *pagre* 'father' (< *padre*), *piegra* 'stone' (< *piedra*), *Pegro* 'Pedro'. Sometimes speakers of these dialects attempt to change these *gr* pronunciations to match the standard and prestigious *dr* counterpart; however, in doing this, they sometimes hypercorrect by changing instances of *gr* to *dr* where the standard language in fact does have *gr*, as for example *suedros* 'parents-in-law', where Standard Spanish has *suegros*, and *sadrado* 'sacred' instead of Standard *sagrado*.

(5) Standard Finnish has /d/, but many regional dialects do not; several have /r/ instead. An attempt to correct dialectal *suren* 'wolf (accusative singular)' to Standard Finnish *suden* would work out well through the replacement of dialect *r* by *d*. However, this sort of substitution leads to hypercorrections such as *suuden* 'big' (accusative singular) where Standard Finnish actually does have /r/, *suuren* (Ravila 1966: 57).

(6) In regional dialects of Spanish, *f* has become *x* before *u*, and this leads to the following sorts of hypercorrections, since the standard language preserves *f* in these cases, but also has other legitimate instances of *xu* as well (where [x] is spelled in Spanish with *j*): *fugo* < *jugo* 'juice', *fueves* < *jueves* 'Thursday', *fuicioso* < *juicioso* 'judicious'.

4.7.2 Folk etymology (popular etymology)

We might think of folk etymologies as cases where linguistic imagination finds meaningful associations in the linguistic forms which were not originally there and, on the basis of these new associations, either the original form ends up being changed somewhat or new forms based on it are created.

(1) An often-cited example is that of English *hamburger*, whose true etymology is from German *Hamburg* + *-er*, 'someone or something from the city of Hamburg'; while hamburgers are not made of 'ham', speakers have folk-etymologized *hamburger* as having something to do with *ham* and on this basis have created such new forms as *cheeseburger*, *chilliburger*, *fishburger*, *vegiburger* or *vegie burger*, *Gainsburgers* (a brand of dog food in North America), just *burger*, and so on.

(2) In Spanish, *vagabundo* 'vagabond, tramp' has given rise also to *vagamundo* (same meaning), associated by speakers in some way with *mundo* 'world' and *vagar* 'to wander, roam, loaf', since a tramp wanders about in the world, or so it may seem.

(3) Jocular Spanish has created *indiosingracia* 'idiosyncrasy' (for *idiosincrasia*), based on *indio* 'Indian' + *sin* 'without' + *gracia* 'grace'.

(4) The original name of the city of *Cuernavaca* in Mexico was *kwāwnawak* in Nahuatl, but it was folk-etymologized by the Spanish as *cuernavaca*, based on *cuerno* 'horn' + *vaca* 'cow', though the place had no connection with either 'horns' or 'cows'. Its true etymology is Nahuatl *kwaw-* 'trees' + *nāwak* 'near, adjacent to', that is, 'near the trees'.

(5) *(Beef) jerky, jerked beef* in English comes from Spanish *charqui*, which Spanish borrowed from Quechua *č'arqi* – nothing is 'jerked' in the preparation of this dried meat, as the folk etymology seems to assume.

(6) *Handiwork* comes from Old English *handġeweorc*, composed of *hand* 'hand' + *ġeweorc* 'work (collective formation)', where *ġe* > *y* [j] or *i* in Middle English, and then was lost elsewhere. The word was reformulated by folk etymology in the sixteenth century on the basis of *handy* + *work* (compare Palmer 1972: 240).

(7) Many today (mis)spell *harebrained* as *hairbrained*, apparently having shifted the original etymology from 'one having a brain like a hare (rabbit)' to a new folk etymology based on *hair*, 'one having a brain associated in some in way with hair'.

(8) Some dialects of English have *wheelbarrel* for *wheelbarrow*, folk-etymologizing it as having some association with *barrel*.

(9) Some speakers have changed *cappuccino* to *cuppacino*, influenced analogically by the word *cuppa* 'cup of tea', unknown in American English but widely used elsewhere, from *cup of* (*tea* or *coffee*); a seven-year-old boy called it *caffeccino* (based on *coffee*).

(10) Old Spanish *tiniebras* 'darkness' changed to Modern Spanish *tinieblas* through the folk-etymological assumption that it had something

to do with *niebla* 'fog' (cf. Spanish *tenebroso* 'dark, gloomy' < Latin tenebrōsus).

(11) The true etymology of English *outrage* has nothing to do with *out* or *rage*, which are due to folk etymology. Rather, *outrage* is in origin a borrowing from French *outrage* 'outrage, insult', which is based on Latin *ultrā* 'beyond' + the nominalizing suffix *-agium* (cf. *-age*).

(12) The English *country-dance* was borrowed in France between 1715 and 1723, and in the process was folk-etymologized as *contre danse* (*contre* 'counter, against' + *danse* 'dance'). From France it passed to Italian, Spanish and Portuguese (cf. Spanish *contradanza*, Portuguese *contradança*). Later it was borrowed back into English from French as *contre-dance, contra-dance*.

(13) One of the glosses of the *Appendix Probi*, which warns against what the author considered improper pronunciations in Latin (see Exercise 14.1 in Chapter 14), says it should be *effeminatus* 'effeminate' (derived form *femina* 'woman') rather than the folk-etymologized version *infiminatus* (derived from *infimus* 'low, below').

4.7.3 Back formation

In back formation (*retrograde* formation, a type of *folk etymology*), a word is assumed to have a morphological composition which it did not originally have, usually a root plus affixes, so that when the affixes are removed, a new modified root is created, as when children, confronted with a plate of pieces of cheese, often say 'can I have a chee?', assuming that *cheese* is the plural form, and therefore creating the logical singular root, *chee*, by removing the final *s*, which they associate with the *s* of plural. Examples which result in permanent changes in languages are quite common.

(1) *Cherry* entered English as a loan from Old French *cherise* (Modern French *cerise*) where the *s* was part of the original root, but was interpreted as representing the English 'plural', and so in back formation this *s* was removed, giving *cherry*.

(2) English *pea* is from Old English *pise* 'singular'/*pisan* 'plural'; later the final *s* of the singular was reinterpreted as 'plural' and the form was backformed to *pea*. Compare *pease-pudding* and *pease porridge* (preserved in the nursery rhyme, 'Pease porridge hot, pease porridge cold, . . .'), which retain the *s* of the earlier singular form.

(3) A number of new English verb roots have been created by back formations based on associations of some sounds in the original word

with a variant of *-er* 'someone who does the action expressed in the verb': *to burgle* based on *burglar*; *to chauf* 'to drive someone around, to chauffeur', based on *chauffeur* (*-eur* reinterpreted as English *-er* 'agent'), *to edit* from *editor*; *to escalate* based on *escalator*; *to letch* from *lecher*; *to orate* backformed from *orator*; *to peddle* based on *pedlar*; *to sculpt* from *sculptor*.

(4) Some varieties of English have a verb *to orientate*, backformed from *orientation* (competing with or replacing Standard English *to orient*). *Disorientated* is less established, but is sometimes said, derived analogically from *orientated*.

(5) Swahili *kitabu* 'book' is originally a loanword from Arabic *kitāb* 'book'. However, on analogy with native nouns such as *ki-su* 'knife'/*vi-su* 'knives' (where *ki-* and *vi-* represent the noun-class prefixes for which Bantu languages are well known), Swahili has backformed *kitabu* by assuming that its first syllable represents the *ki-* singular noun-class prefix and thus creating a new plural in *vitabu* 'books'. Setswana, another Bantu language (in Botswana and northern South Africa), has *sekole* 'school', borrowed from English (Setswana does not permit initial *sk-* consonant clusters); however, since *se-* is also a noun-class prefix for 'singular', this word has undergone back formation, as seen in *dikole* 'schools', where *di-* is the 'plural' prefix for this class of nouns (cf. Janson 2002: 48).

4.7.4 Metanalysis (reanalysis)

Traditionally two things are treated under the title of metanalysis, *amalgamation* and *metanalysis proper* (today more often called *reanalysis*). Since amalgamation is also a kind of lexical change, it is not treated here, but rather in Chapter 9. *Metanalysis* is from Greek *meta* 'change' + *analysis* 'analysis', and as the name suggests, metanalysis involves a change in the structural analysis, in the interpretation of which phonological material goes with which morpheme in a word or construction.

(1) English provides several examples: *adder* is from Old English *nǣddre*; the change came about through a reinterpretation (reanalysis) of the article–noun sequence *a + nǣddre* as *an + adder* (compare the German cognate *Natter* 'adder, viper'). English has several examples of this sort. *Auger* is from Middle English *nauger*, *naugur*, Old English *nafo-gār* (*nafo-* 'nave [of a wheel]' + *gār* 'piercer, borer, spear', literally 'nave-borer'). *Apron* is from Middle English *napron*, originally a loan from Old French *naperon*, a diminutive form of *nape*, *nappe* 'tablecloth'. The related form *napkin* (from the French *nape* 'tablecloth' + *-kin* 'a

diminutive suffix', apparently ultimately from Dutch) still preserves the original initial *n-*. *Umpire* < *noumpere* (originally a loanword from Old French *nonper* 'umpire, arbiter', *non* 'not' + *per* 'peer'). Finally, *newt* is from Middle English *ewt* (*an* + *ewt* > *a* + *newt*).

(2) Shakespeare (in *King Lear* I, iv, 170) had *nuncle* 'uncle', a form which survives in dialects today. It is derived from a metanalysis based on the final *-n* of the possessive pronouns *mine* and *thine*. In earlier English the form with the final nasal was required when the following word began in a vowel (*mine eyes*) but the nasalless form was employed before words beginning in a consonant (*my lips*). In *nuncle* the original *mine uncle* was reanalysed so that the *-n* was no longer seen as the end of the possessive pronoun *mine* but as the beginning of the following word, hence *mine + uncle > my nuncle*.

(3) Latin *argent-um* 'silver' and *argent-arius* 'silversmith' became in French *argent* [aʁʒɑ̃] 'silver, money' and *argentier* [aʁʒɑ̃tje] (with the analysis *argent + ier*); however, a reanalysis of this form as *argen+tier* is the basis of the *-tier* of newer forms such as *bijoutier* 'jeweller', based on *bijou* 'jewel'; another example is the addition of *-tier* to *café* to create *cafetier* 'coffee house keeper', based on *cabaretier* 'cabaret owner, publican, innkeeper', which bears what was originally the *-ier* suffix, construed as *-tier* from comparison with *cabaret* [kabaʁe] 'cabaret, tavern, restaurant'.

(4) Swedish *ni* 'you' (plural, formal) comes from Old Swedish *I* 'you', where it often came after verbs which ended in *-n* 'plural agreement' and the *-n + I* combination was reinterpreted as together being the pronoun *ni*, as in *veten I > veten ni > vet ni* 'you know', *vissten I > visten ni > visste ni* 'you knew' (Wessén 1969: 219).

Reanalysis is one of the most important mechanisms of syntactic change, and is treated in more detail in Chapter 10.

4.7.5 Blending (or contamination)

In *blends*, pieces of two (or more) different words are combined to create new words. Usually the words which contribute the pieces that go into the make-up of the new word are semantically related in some way, sometimes as synonyms for things which have the same or a very similar meaning. Some blends are purposefully humorous or sarcastic in their origin; others are more accidental, sometimes thought to originate as something like slips of the tongue which combine aspects of two related forms which then catch on. Examples of blending and contamination are sometimes treated as lexical change (see Chapter 9). The following English examples illustrate these various origins and outcomes.

(1) Often-cited examples include: *smog < smoke + fog*; *brunch < breakfast + lunch*; *motel < motor + hotel*, *splatter < splash + spatter*; *flush < flash + blush.*

(2) *(computer) bit < binary digit.*

(3) It is popular to create blends based on *cappuccino*, for example *mochaccino/mocaccino, muggaccino, frappaccino, cyberccino* (involving an internet coffeeshop), *skinniccino/skinnyccino* (small black coffee), *skimmuccino* (cappuccino made with skim milk), *decaphaccino* (cappuccino made of decaffeinated coffee), *soyaccino, kiddiccino*, and others.

(4) Based on a portion of *magazine*: *fanzine* (fan group newsletter-magazine), *videozine* (videotape featuring items comparable to print magazines), *webzine* (Internet sites in magazine format), *e-zine/ezine.*

(5) A suffix-like element was created on the basis of a portion of *marathon*: *telethon, walkathon, bik(e)athon, danceathon*, and so on.

(6) *newscast < news + broadcast*; also *sportscast, sportscaster.*

(7) Based on part of *alcoholic*: *workaholic, chocaholic, foodaholic, gumaholic, shoppaholic*, and so on.

(8) *infomercial < information + commercial*; *infotainment < information + entertainment.*

(9) From combinations based on *hijack*: *skyjack(ing)* and *carjack(ing).*

(10) *neither <* earlier *no(u)ther* through influence from *either.*

(11) *-gate* (a new suffix-like element created on the basis of *Watergate* of the Richard Nixon Watergate scandal): *Contragate, Koreagate, Irangate, Camillagate* (involving Prince Charles's close friend, Camilla Parker Bowles).

Some non-English examples are:

(12) An often-cited case: Latin *reddere* 'to give back' and *pre(he)ndere* 'to take hold of, seize' influenced one another and resulted in the blend in Romance languages illustrated by Spanish *rendir* 'to yield, produce, render', Italian *rendere* 'to render, yield', French *rendre* 'to render' (English *render* is a borrowing from French).

(13) Spanish jocular *indioma* 'language' (from Cantinflas' films) is a blend of *indio* 'Indian' and *idioma* 'language'.

(14) Names of languages which borrow extensively from others or are highly influenced by others are the sources of such blends as *Spanglish < Spanish + English, Finnglish < Finnish + English*; *manglish* was created in feminist discourse to reflect male biases in English, < *man + English*; *Franglais < français* 'French' + *anglais* 'English'.

There are also syntactic blends. Neogrammarians presented many examples (for example, Paul 1920: 165). Some are:

(1) *I'm friends with him*, from a contamination based on *I'm a friend with him* and *we are friends* (Paul 1920: 150).

(2) Non-standard German *mich freut deines Mutes*, from a contamination of the two perfectly normal constructions *ich freu-e mich dein-es Mut-es* [I please-first.person me.Reflexive your-Genitive courage-Genitive], roughly 'I'm pleased over your courage', and *mich freu-t dein Mut* [me.Accusative please-third.person your spirit], roughly 'your spirit pleases me' (Paul 1920: 149).

(3) Finnish has two alternative constructions for verbs meaning 'to command, order', as in 'she told/commanded the boy to come':

> *hän käski poikaa tulemaan* (*poika-a* 'boy-Partitive.Singular' *tule-ma-an* 'come-third.Infinitive-Illative.case')
> *hän käski pojan tulla* (*poja-n* 'boy-Genitive.Singular' *tul-la* 'come-first.Infinitive').

These two have blended for some dialects to give a third construction:

> *hän käski pojan tulemaan* (*poja-n* 'boy-Genitive.Singular' *tule-ma-an* 'come-third.Infinitive-Illative') – not accepted in Standard Finnish.

4.8 Exercises

Exercise 4.1

Observe the language of your friends and of newspapers, television and so on, and attempt to find examples of your own of the various sorts of analogy.

Exercise 4.2 Identifying analogical changes

Determine what kind of analogical change is involved in the following examples. Name the kind of change, and attempt to explain how it came about, if you can.

(1) In some dialects of English, the pattern *bring/brought/brought* has become *bring/brang/brung*.

(2) Where Standard English has *drag/dragged*, some varieties of English have *drag/drug*. It appears in this case that the Standard English pattern is older.

(3) Old Spanish *siniestro* 'left' changed from Latin *sinister* 'on the left' to take on *ie* under the influence of the antonym *diestro* 'right', since *diestro* and *siniestro* frequently occurred together.

(4) In many Spanish dialects, an intervocalic *d* is regularly lost, as in

mercado > *mercao* 'market'; in some instances, however, there are changes of the following sort: dialect *bacalado* < Standard *bacalao* 'codfish'; dialect *Bilbado* < Standard *Bilbao* (a place name).

(5) In the Dominican Republic, forms such as Standard Spanish *atras* 'behind' become *astras*; in this variety of Spanish, preconsonantal *s* is often lost, as in *ata* < *asta* (spelled *hasta*) 'until'.

(6) English *Jerusalem artichoke* (a kind of sunflower, with some similarities to an artichoke) is in origin from Italian *girasóle articiocco*, where Italian *girasole* / ǰirasóle/ contains *gira-* 'turn around, revolve, rotate' + *sole* 'sun', and *articiocco* 'artichoke', with nothing associated with *Jerusalem*; originally.

(7) In English, *Key West* (in Florida) comes from the Spanish name *cayo hueso*, where *cayo* is 'key, small island' and *hueso* is 'bone'.

(8) English *heliport* < *helicopter* + *airport*; *snazzy* < *snappy* + *jazzy*; *jumble* < *jump* +*tumble*.

(9) Colloquial and regional varieties of Spanish have *haiga* where Standard Spanish has *haya* (subjunctive, 'there may be') and *vaiga* where Standard Spanish has *vaya* (subjunctive, 'may go'). These have been influenced by Standard Spanish verb forms such as *traiga* (subjunctive of *traer* 'to bring', 'may bring') and *caiga* (subjunctive of *caer* 'to fall', 'may fall').

(10) Middle English had *help-* 'present tense', *holp* 'past tense'; Modern English has *help*, *helped* for these.

(11) English to *emote* is derived from *emotion*; to *enthuse* is derived from *enthusiastic*.

(12) Many varieties of English have a new verb *to liaise* based on *liaison*.

(13) English *to diagnose* is derived from *diagnosis*.

(14) Finnish *rohtia* 'to dare' resulted from both *rohjeta* 'to be bold enough, to dare' and *tohtia* 'to dare'.

(15) English *hangnail* is derived from Old English *angnægl* 'painful corn (on foot)'. When *ang* 'pain' as an independent word was lost (though later reborrowed in *anguish*), the *angnægl* form was reinterpreted as having something to do with 'hanging', with painful detached skin of toes and then also hands.

5

The Comparative Method and
Linguistic Reconstruction

Linguistic history is basically the darkest of the dark arts, the only
means to conjure up the ghosts of vanished centuries. With linguistic
history we reach furthest back into the mystery: humankind.

(Cola Minis 1952: 107 [Euphorion 46])

5.1 Introduction

The comparative method is central to historical linguistics, the most
important of the various methods and techniques we use to recover linguistic history. In this chapter the comparative method is explained, its
basic assumptions and its limitations are considered, and its various
uses are demonstrated. The primary emphasis is on learning how to
apply the method, that is, on how to reconstruct. The comparative
method is also important in language classification, in linguistic prehistory, in research on distant genetic relationships, and in other areas;
these topics are treated in later chapters.

We say that languages which belong to the same language family are
genetically related to one another: this means that these related languages derive from (that is, 'descend' from) a single original language,
called a *proto-language*. In time, dialects of the proto-language develop
through linguistic changes in different regions where the language was
spoken – all languages (and varieties of language) are constantly changing – and then later through further changes the dialects become distinct
languages.

The aim of reconstruction by the comparative method is to recover as
much as possible of the ancestor language (the proto-language) from a

comparison of the related languages, the descendants of the original language, and to determine what changes have taken place in the various languages that developed from the proto-language. The work of reconstruction usually begins with phonology, with an attempt to reconstruct the sound system; this leads in turn to reconstruction of the vocabulary and grammar of the proto-language. As can be seen from the way languages are classified, we speak of linguistic relationships in terms of kinship; we talk about 'sister languages', 'daughter languages', 'parent language' and 'language families'. If reconstruction is successful, it shows that the assumption that the languages are related is warranted. (See Chapter 6 for family-tree classification and Chapter 13 for methods of determining whether languages are related.)

With the genealogical analogy of your family tree in mind, we can see how modern Romance languages have descended from spoken Latin (better said, from Proto-Romance, which is reconstructed via the comparative method), illustrated in the family tree for the Romance languages in Figure 5.1. (The biological kinship terms added here under the language names in Figure 5.1 are just a trick to reveal the pedigree of the languages; in this case the focus is on Spanish. This is certainly not conventionally done in linguistic family trees.)

By comparing what these sister languages inherited from their ancestor, we attempt to reconstruct the linguistic traits which Proto-Romance possessed. (Proto-Romance is equivalent to the spoken language at the time when Latin began to diversify and split up into its descendant branches, essentially the same as Vulgar Latin at the time. The 'Vulgar' of Vulgar Latin means 'of the people'.) If we are successful, what we reconstruct for Proto-Romance by the comparative method should be similar to the Proto-Romance which was actually spoken at the time before it split up into its daughter languages. Of course, our success is dependent upon the extent to which evidence of the original traits is preserved in the descendant languages (daughter languages) which we compare and upon how astute we are at applying the techniques of the comparative method, among other things. In this case, since Latin is abundantly documented, we can check to see whether what we reconstruct by the comparative method accurately approximates the spoken Latin we know about from written sources. However, the possibility of checking our reconstructions in this way is not available for most language families, for whose proto-languages we have no written records. For example, for Proto-Germanic (from which English descends), there are no written attestations at all, and the language is known only from comparative reconstruction.

Currently existing languages which have relatives all have a history which classifies them into language families. By applying the comparative method to related languages, we can postulate what that common earlier ancestor was like – we can reconstruct that language. Thus, comparing English with its relatives, Dutch, Frisian, German, Danish, Swedish, Icelandic and so on, we attempt to understand what the proto-language, in this case called 'Proto-Germanic', was like. Thus, English is, in effect, a much-changed 'dialect' of Proto-Germanic, having undergone successive linguistic changes to make it what it is today, a different language from Swedish and German and its other sisters, which underwent different changes of their own. Therefore, every proto-language was once a real language, regardless of whether we are successful at reconstructing it or not.

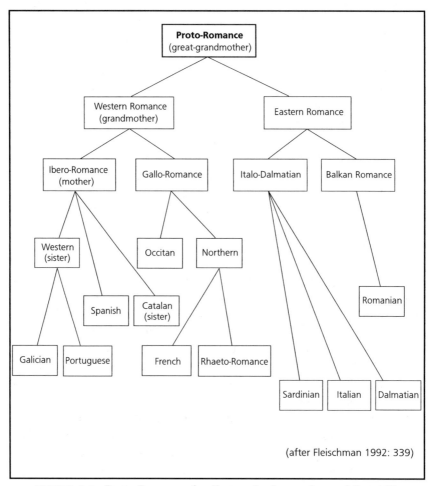

(after Fleischman 1992: 339)

FIGURE 5.1: Proto-Romance family tree (and genealogy of Spanish)

5.2 The Comparative Method Up Close and Personal

To illustrate the application of the comparative method, let's begin by applying it briefly in a simplified fashion to some Romance languages. (There are many more Romance languages, but for illustration's sake, this miniature introduction is limited to just a few of the better-known of these.) First, consider some data, the words compared among Romance languages given in Table 5.1. (The first line represents conventional spelling; the second is phonemic.)

TABLE 5.1: Some Romance cognate sets

Italian	Spanish	Portuguese	French	(Latin)	English gloss
1. capra	cabra	cabra	chèvre	capra	'goat'
/kapra/	/kabra/	/kabra/	/ʃɛvr(ə)/		
2. caro	caro	caro	cher	caru	'dear'
/karo/	/karo/	/karu/	/ʃɛr/		
3. capo	cabo	cabo	chef	caput	'head, top'
/kapo/	/kabo/	/kabu/	/ʃɛf/		
'main, chief'	'extremity'	'extremity'	'main, chief'		
4. carne	carne	carne	chair	carō/carn-	'meat, flesh'
/karne/	/karne/	/karne/	/ʃɛr/		
			(cf. Old French charn/čarn/		
5. cane	can	cão	chien	canis	'dog'
	(archaic)				
/kane/	/kan/	/kãw̃/	/ʃjɛ̃/		

Latin is *not* a Romance language; the Latin forms in Table 5.1 are presented only so that ultimately we can check the reconstructions which we postulate for Proto-Romance to see how close they come to the forms in the actual spoken proto-language, which was essentially the same as Latin in this case.

To understand the comparative method and to be able to apply it, we need to control some concepts and technical terms:

Proto-language: (1) the once spoken ancestral language from which daughter languages descend; (2) the language reconstructed by the comparative method which represents the ancestral language from which the compared languages descend. (To the extent that the reconstruction by the comparative method is accurate and complete, (1) and (2) should coincide.)

Sister language: languages which are related to one another by virtue of having descended from the same common ancestor (proto-language) are sisters; that is, languages which belong to the same family are sisters to one another.

Cognate: a word (or morpheme) which is related to a word (morpheme) in sister languages by reason of these forms having been inherited by these sister languages from a common word (morpheme) of the proto-language from which the sister languages descend.

Cognate set: the set of words (morphemes) which are related to one another across the sister languages because they are inherited and descend from a single word (morpheme) of the proto-language.

Comparative method: a method (or set of procedures) which compares forms from related languages, *cognates*, which have descended from a common ancestral language (the *proto-language*), in order to postulate, that is *to reconstruct*, the form in the ancestral language.

Sound correspondence (also called *correspondence set*): in effect, a set of 'cognate' sounds; the sounds found in the related words of cognate sets which correspond from one related language to the next because they descend from a common ancestral sound. (A sound correspondence is assumed to recur in various cognate sets.)

Reflex: the descendant in a daughter language of a sound of the proto-language is said to be a *reflex* of that original sound; the original sound of the proto-language is said to be reflected by the sound which descends from it in a daughter language.

For ease of description, we will talk about 'steps' in the application of the comparative method. Strictly speaking though, it is not always necessary to follow all these steps in precisely the sequence described here. In practice, the comparative linguist typically jumps back and forth among these steps.

Step 1: Assemble cognates

To begin to apply the comparative method, we look for potential cognates among related languages (or among languages for which there is reason to suspect relatedness) and list them in some orderly arrangement (in rows or columns). In Table 5.1, this step has already been done for you for the few Romance cognates considered in this exercise. In general, it is convenient to begin with cognates from 'basic vocabulary' (body parts, close kinship terms, low numbers, common geographical terms), since these resist borrowing more than other sorts of vocabulary, and for the comparative method we want to compare only true cognates, words which are related in the daughter languages by virtue of being inherited from the proto-language. For successful reconstruction, we must eliminate all other sets of similar words which are not due to inheritance from a common ancestor, such as those which exhibit similarities among the languages because of borrowing, chance (coincidence) and so on (for details, see Chapter 13). Ultimately, it is the systematic correspondences which we discover in the comparative method (in the following steps) which demonstrate true cognates.

Step 2: Establish sound correspondences

Next, we attempt to determine the sound correspondences. For example, in the words for 'goat' in cognate set 1 in Table 5.1, the first sound in each language corresponds in the way as indicated in SOUND CORRE-SPONDENCE 1 (here now we concentrate on the phonemic representation of the sound and not on the conventional spelling):

Sound correspondence 1:
Italian *k-* : Spanish *k-* : Portuguese *k-* : French *ʃ-*

Note that historical linguists often use the convention of a hyphen after a sound to indicate initial position, as *k-* here signals initial *k*; a preceding hyphen indicates that the sound is word-final (for example, *-k*); and a hyphen both before and after refers to a medial sound, one found somewhere in the middle of a word but neither initially nor finally (for example, *-k-*).

It is important to attempt to avoid potential sound correspondences which are due merely to chance. For example, languages may have words which are similar only by accident, by sheer coincidence, as the case of Kaqchikel (Mayan) *mes* 'mess, disorder, garbage' : English *mess* ('disorder, untidiness'). To determine whether a sound correspondence such as that of SOUND CORRESPONDENCE 1 is real (reflecting sounds inherited in words from the proto-language) rather than perhaps just an accidental similarity, we need to determine whether the correspondence recurs in other cognate sets. In looking for further examples of this particular Romance sound correspondence, we find that it recurs in the other cognate sets (2–5) of Table 5.1, all of which illustrate SOUND CORRESPONDENCE 1 for their first sound. If we were to attempt to find recurrences of the seeming *m-* : *m-* correspondence between Kaqchikel and English (seen in the comparison of their words meaning 'mess'), we would soon discover that there are no other instances of it, that it does not recur, as illustrated by the compared words of Table 5.2, where the

English forms begin with *m*, but the Kaqchikel forms begin with various sounds.

TABLE 5.2: Kaqchikel–English comparisons

English	Kaqchikel
man	ači
mouse	č'oy
moon	qatiʔt
mother	nan

Of course, in principle in a situation such as this, it is possible that the compared languages could be related but that we accidentally chose the few words to compare in Table 5.2 where one or the other of the related languages has not retained the cognate due to borrowing or lexical replacement. To be certain that this is not the case, we would need to look at many comparisons (not just the handful presented in Table 5.2 for illustration's sake). However, in the case of English and Kaqchikel lexical comparisons, we will never find more than one or two which exhibit what initially might have been suspected of being an *m-* : *m-* correspondence based on the words meaning 'mess' in the two languages, and this is precisely because these two languages are not genetically related and therefore the *m* : *m* matching does not recur and is not a true correspondence. Similarly, we need to attempt to eliminate similarities found in borrowings which can seem to suggest sound correspondences. Usually (though not always), loanwords do not exhibit the sort of systematic sound correspondences found in the comparison of native words among related languages, and loans involving basic vocabulary are much rarer than borrowings in other kinds of vocabulary (see Chapter 13 for details).

Given that SOUND CORRESPONDENCE 1 recurs frequently among the Romance languages, as seen in the forms compared in Table 5.1, we assume that this sound correspondence is genuine. It is highly unlikely that a set of systematically corresponding sounds such as this one could come about by sheer accident in a large number of words so similar in sound and meaning across these languages.

Step 3: Reconstruct the proto-sound

There is no fixed rule about what should be done next. We could go on and set up other sound correspondence sets and check to see that they recur; that is, we could repeat step 2 over and over until we have found all the sound correspondences in the languages being compared. Or, we could go on to step 3 and attempt to reconstruct the proto-sound from which the sound in each of the daughter languages (represented in SOUND CORRESPONDENCE 1) descended. In the end, to complete the task, we must establish all the correspondences and reconstruct the proto-sound from which each descends, regardless of whether we do all of step 2 for each set first and then step 3 for all the sets, or whether we do step 2 followed by step 3 for each set and then move on to the next set, repeating step 2, then step 3. In either case, as we shall soon see, the initial reconstructions which we postulate based on these sound correspondences must be assessed in steps 5 and 6, when we check the fit of the individual reconstructed sounds which we initially postulate in step 3 against the overall phonological inventory of the proto-language and its general typological fit; it is often the case that some of the reconstructions for sounds postulated in step 3 need to be modified in steps 5 and 6.

The different sounds (one for each language compared) in the sound correspondence set reflect a single sound of the proto-language which is inherited in the different daughter languages; sometimes the sound is reflected unchanged in some daughters, though often it will have undergone sound changes in some (or even all) of the daughter languages which make it different from the original proto-sound. We reconstruct the proto-sound by postulating what the sound in the proto-language most likely was on the basis of the phonetic properties of the descendant sounds in the various languages in the correspondence set. The following are the general guidelines that linguists rely on to help them in the task of devising the best, most realistic reconstruction.

Directionality

The known directionality of certain sound changes is a valuable clue to reconstruction (see Chapter 2). By 'directionality' we mean that some sound changes which recur in independent languages typically go in one direction ($A > B$) but usually are not (sometimes are never) found in the other direction ($B > A$). Some speak of this as 'naturalness', some changes 'naturally' taking place with greater ease and frequency cross-linguistically than others. For example, many languages have changed $s > h$, but change in the other direction, $h > s$, is extremely rare. In cases such as this, we speak of 'directionality'. If we find in two sister languages the sound correspondence s in Language$_1$: h in Language$_2$, we reconstruct *s and postulate that in Language$_2$ *$s > h$. The alternative with *h and the change *$h > s$ in Language$_1$ is highly unlikely,

since it goes against the known direction of change. Usually, the directionality has some phonetic motivation. Some idea of the typical direction
of many of the more commonly recurring sound changes can be gath-
ered from a look at the examples considered in Chapter 2.

In the case of SOUND CORRESPONDENCE 1, we know that the direction of change from *k* to *ʃ* is quite plausible and has been observed to
occur in other languages, but that *ʃ* essentially never changes to *k*.
Actually, even more typical would be for *k* to change to *ʃ* by first going
through the intermediate stage of *č*, that is, *k* > *č* > *ʃ*; documentary
evidence shows that the sound change in French did go through this
intermediate *č* stage. Old French documents had for the words in Table
5.1: *čjɛvr(ə)*'goat', *čjɛr* 'dear', *čjɛf* 'head', *čarn* 'meat' and *čjɛŋ* 'dog'.
This intermediate stage is preserved in many English loans from French
from that time, for example, *chief* and *Charles* with [č], where more
recent loans from the same French sources have [ʃ], the result of the
later French change of *č* > *ʃ*, as in *chef* and *Charlene*, with [ʃ].

In another example of the way in which directionality aids in reconstruction, we know that very often voiceless stops (*p, t, k*) are voiced (*b,
d, g*) between vowels. If we compare two related languages, Language$_1$
and Language$_2$, and we find intervocalic -*b*- in Language$_1$ corresponding
to intervocalic -*p*- in Language$_2$, then we reconstruct *-*p*- and assume
that Language$_1$ underwent the common sound change of intervocalic
voicing of stops (*p* > *b* /V__V, in this case). If we tried to reconstruct
*-*b*- in this situation, we would have to assume that Language$_2$ had
changed -*b*- to -*p*-, but this goes against the direction most commonly
taken in changes involving these sounds between vowels. This example
comes up in SOUND CORRESPONDENCE 2 (below).

The phonetic motivation for the directionality in this case is clear. It
is easy to voice stops between vowels, since vowels are inherently
voiced, and therefore the change (1) *p* > *b*/V__V is very common, while
it is not so easy to make stops voiceless between vowels, which makes
the change (2) *b* > *p*/V__V very rare indeed – for (2) the vocal cords
would be vibrating for the first vowel, then we would need to stop them
from vibrating in order to produce the voiceless [p], and then start the
vocal-cord vibration up again for the second vowel; for (1) we merely
leave them vibrating for all three segments, the two vowels and the
intervening [b]. The known directionality, then, with (1) encountered
frequently across languages and (2) hardly at all, is natural and phonetically motivated. As a beginning linguist's experience with language
changes and phonological systems increases, a stronger understanding
of the directionality of changes develops.

Majority wins

Another guiding principle is that, all else being equal, we let the majority win – that is, unless there is evidence to the contrary, we tend to pick for our reconstructed proto-sound the particular sound in the correspondence set which shows up in the greatest number of daughter languages. Since in SOUND CORRESPONDENCE 1, Italian, Spanish and Portuguese all have k, and only French diverges from this, with f, we would postulate $*k$ for the Proto-Romance sound, under the assumption that the majority wins, since the majority of the languages have k in this correspondence set. This reconstruction assumes that French underwent the sound change $*k > f$, but that the other languages did not change at all, $*k$ remaining k. The underlying rationale for following the majority-wins principle is that it is more likely that one language would have undergone a sound change (in this case, French $*k > f$) than that several languages would independently have undergone the sound change. In this case, if $*f$ were postulated as the proto-sound, it would be necessary to assume that Italian, Spanish and Portuguese had each independently undergone the change of $*f > k$.

Caution is necessary, however, in the use of the majority-wins guideline to reconstruction. Some sound changes are so common (and languages undergo them so easily) that several languages might undergo one of these kind of changes independently of one another (for example, loss of vowel length, nasalization of vowels before nasal consonants, and so on). It is also possible that only one of the daughter languages might have preserved the original sound unchanged while the others all changed it in some way. It is also possible that all the daughter languages may undergo various changes so that none reflects the proto-sound unchanged. Clearly, in these situations there is no majority to do the winning. Moreover, majority rule may not work if some of the languages are more closely related to one another. If some of the languages belong to the same branch (subgroup) of the family (see Chapter 6), then they have a more immediate ancestor which itself is a daughter of the proto-language. This intermediate language (a parent of its immediate descendants but itself a daughter of the proto-language) could have undergone a change and then later split up into its daughters, the members of the subgroup, and each of these would then inherit the changed sound that their immediate common ancestor (once a single daughter of the proto-language) had undergone. For example, French, Spanish and Portuguese all share some sounds which are the results of sound changes that took place in Western Romance before it split up further into French, Spanish and Portuguese. Italian does not share these because it comes from a separate branch of Romance. For example, Western Romance changed syllable-final *k* to *i*, seen in Spanish, Portuguese and French, which separated from one another only after this Western Romance change had taken place, as in **lakte > laite* 'milk', which gives us French *lait*, Portuguese *leite* and Spanish *leche* (where later changes were *ai > ei > e* in these languages, and *it > č* in Spanish); Italian (not a Western Romance language) underwent a different change, *kt > tt*, giving *latte* 'milk' – we see the results of these changes in choices of kinds of coffee on menus, with *cafe au lait* (French), *cafe latte* (Italian) and *cafe con leche* (Spanish). Now if we compare Italian *tt* with the *it* of Portuguese, French and formerly also of Spanish, 'majority wins' would seem to suggest **it* as the reconstruction with *i > t / __t* in Italian; but knowing that Portuguese, Spanish and French are closely related, all members of the Western Romance branch, we no longer need to compare three separate instances of *it* to one of *tt*, but only one *it* case (the result of the single change, **kt > it*, in Western Romance) to one *tt* case (in Italian). It is only with the aid of other information that we discover that the best reconstruction is **kt*, from which both the Italian and Western Romance languages departed due to their separate sound changes. As will be seen in Chapter 6, it is the results of the comparative method which provide the basis for arriving at the classification which tells us which of the related languages belong to the same branches of the family.

So, 'majority wins' is an important principle, but it is easily overridden by other considerations. Still, it would seem to work in the case of SOUND CORRESPONDENCE 1 above, suggesting **k* as the best reconstruction, since it is found in a majority of the languages compared.

Factoring in features held in common

We attempt to reconstruct the proto-sound with as much phonetic precision as possible; that is, we want our reconstruction to be as close as possible to the actual phonetic form of the sound as it was pronounced when the proto-language was spoken. We can never know for sure how accurately our reconstructed sound matches the actual sound of the formerly spoken proto-language, but in general, the more information available upon which to base the reconstruction, the more likely it is that we may be able to achieve a reasonably accurate reconstruction. We attempt to achieve as much phonetic realism as possible by observing what phonetic features are shared among the reflexes seen in each of the daughter languages in the sound correspondence. We determine which phonetic features are common to the reflexes in the daughter languages (and features which can be derived from others by the known direction of sound changes, in Step 2), and then we attempt to reconstruct the proto-sound by building into it these shared phonetic features. To illustrate this, let us consider another sound correspondence from Table 5.1, seen to recur here in the words for (1) 'goat' and (2) 'head' (and in many other cognates not given in Table 5.1):

Sound correspondence 2:
Spanish *b* : Portuguese *b* : French *v* : Italian *p*

The reflexes in all four languages share the feature 'labial'; the Spanish, Portuguese and Italian reflexes share the feature 'stop' (phonemically). Factoring the features together, we would expect the proto-sound to have been a 'labial stop' of some sort, a *p* or *b*. Given that the reflex in Spanish, Portuguese and French is 'voiced', under the principle of 'majority wins' we might expect to reconstruct a 'voiced bilabial stop' (**b*). In this case, however, other considerations – especially directionality – override the majority-wins principle. The directionality is that it is easy for *p* to become voiced between voiced sounds (between vowels in cognate set 3, and between a vowel and *r* in cognate set 1 in Table 5.1), but the reverse is very rare. Therefore, by directionality, **p* is a better choice for the reconstruction, phonetically more plausible; Italian maintained *p* while the others underwent the change to voicing (**p > b* in Spanish and Portuguese; **p > v* in French, actually **p > b > v*). From directionality, we also know that stops frequently become fricatives between vowels (or between continuant sounds), but that fricatives rarely ever become stops in this environment. Thus, it is very likely that the French reflex *v* is the result of this sort of change. Taking these considerations into account, for correspondence set 2, we reconstruct **p* and postulate that in Spanish and Portuguese **p > b*, and French **p > v* (or **p > b > v*). SOUND CORRESPONDENCE 2, then, illustrates how the comparative linguist must balance the various rules of thumb for reconstruction, majority wins, directionality, and factoring in the features shared among the reflexes. (Ultimately, we find out that Western Romance underwent the change of **p > b* in this position, and then after Western Romance split up, the change of *b > v* in French took place. That is, taking the degree of relatedness (the subgrouping; see Chapter 6) into account, there is no longer a majority with the reflex *b*, but rather only Western Romance *b* as opposed to Italian *p*.)

Economy

What is meant by the criterion of economy is that when multiple alternatives are available, the one which requires the fewest independent changes is most likely to be right. For example, if for SOUND CORRESPONDENCE

1 we were to postulate *∫, this would necessitate three independent changes from *∫ > k, one each for Italian, Spanish and Portuguese; however, if we postulate *k for the Proto-Romance sound, we need assume only one sound change, *k > ∫ in French. The criterion of economy rests on the assumption that the odds are greater that a single change took place than that three independent changes took place. Of course, sometimes independent changes do take place, so that the criterion does not always guarantee correct results; but all else being equal, the chances of a reconstruction which embodies more economical assumptions being correct are greater than for a reconstruction which assumes less economical developments. (See below for other examples of the use of the economy criterion.)

The other two general considerations (rules of thumb) which linguists use in reconstructing sounds involve checking to see whether the individual sounds postulated to represent the various sound correspondences fit the overall phonological pattern of the proto-language and to see whether this reconstructed pattern is consistent with linguistic universals and typological expectations. These are *phonological fit* and *typological fit* respectively (steps 5 and 6, below). These two considerations come into play mostly after the full set of sound correspondences has been dealt with and the overall inventory of reconstructed sounds that are being postulated can be considered. For this reason, let's deal first with the other correspondences of Table 5.1, and then come back to these two considerations later.

Let us continue steps 2 and 3, then, for the forms in Table 5.1, and establish the remaining sound correspondences illustrated in these forms and set up reconstructions for them. It does not matter in which order we investigate the sound correspondences. We could first look only at initial consonants for all of the cognate sets, then medial consonants, then final consonants, and finally the various vowels; or, we could proceed by investigating the sound correspondence representing the next sound (the second) in the first cognate set, then go on to the third sound in that set, and so on until all the sounds of that cognate set have been addressed, and then proceed to the next cognate set, dealing with each of the sound correspondences for each of the sounds found in that set in sequence (though some of these may recur in other cognate sets and thus may already have been established in the consideration of the previous cognate sets already dealt with). We continue in this way until all the recurring sound correspondences have been examined and proto-sounds to represent them have been postulated. In this way, we will eventually come to reconstruct the full inventory of sounds in the proto-language.

In the example in Table 5.1, let us continue with the corresponding sounds in cognate set 1, for 'goat'. The first vowel in the forms in cognate set 1 shows SOUND CORRESPONDENCE 3:

Sound correspondence 3:
Italian *a* : Spanish *a* : Portuguese *a* : French *ε*.

We check this to see if it recurs, and we see that it is also found in the other cognate sets of Table 5.1, for 'dear', 'head' and 'meat'. (It is also found again, in effect, in the last vowel of cognate set 1 for 'goat', though we must deal with the later change in French of final *ε* to *ə*/*Ø*.) Under the majority-wins principle, for this sound correspondence we reconstruct **a* for the Proto-Romance sound, assuming that French has undergone the sound change **a > ε*.

The third sound in cognate set 1 'goat' has, in fact, already been dealt with in SOUND CORRESPONDENCE 2 (where we reconstructed **p* for the correspondence set Spanish *b* : Portuguese *b* : French *v* : Italian *p*).

The next sound in the sequence of sounds in the 'goat' cognates gives correspondence set 4:

Sound correspondence 4:
Italian *r* : Spanish *r* : Portuguese *r* : French *r*

SOUND CORRESPONDENCE 4 also recurs, in 'goat', 'dear' and 'meat' (in Table 5.1). For it, we would postulate Proto-Romance **r*, under 'majority wins', since all the languages have this reflex. (To be absolutely accurate, we would have to deal with the fact that in Standard French the *r* became a uvular, but for now we ignore this detail.)

The last sound in 'goat' in effect repeats SOUND CORRESPONDENCE 3, although French later changed final *ε* further (to *ə* or *Ø*). Though technically this must be considered a separate sound correspondence, to make it easier we will just assume here that we would easily discover that the two correspondence sets, for the first and last vowel in the 'goat' cognate set, belong together due to a later conditioned change in French.

To complete the task, we would need to establish the sound correspondences for all the cognate sets and reconstruct sounds to represent them. For example, we would find:

Sound correspondence 5:
Italian *o* : Spanish *o* : Portuguese *u* : French *Ø*.

This recurs, as in 'dear', 'head'. For SOUND CORRESPONDENCE 5, we would reconstruct **o* (majority wins), assuming that Portuguese changed final **o* to *u*, and that French lost final **o*.

With more extensive data (many more cognate sets than presented in Table 5.1), we would confirm these reconstructions, with their attendant sound changes and the conditions under which they took place, and we would eventually find all the sound correspondences and postulate reconstructions for all the sounds of the proto-language and work out its phonemic inventory and phonological patterns.

Step 4: Determine the status of similar (partially overlapping) correspondence sets

Some sound changes, particularly conditioned sound changes, can result in a proto-sound being associated with more than one correspondence set. These must be dealt with to achieve an accurate reconstruction. To see how this is done, we will work through an example. For this, let us consider some additional cognate sets in Romance languages, those of Table 5.3 (numbered to follow those of Table 5.1).

TABLE 5.3: Some additional Romance cognate sets

Italian	Spanish	Portuguese	French	(Latin)	English gloss
6. colore	color	côr	couleur	colōre	'colour'
/kolore/	/kolor/	/kor/	/kulœr/		
7. correre	correr	correr	courir	currere	'to run'
/korere/	/kor̃er/	/korer/	/kuri(r)/		
8. costare	costar	costar	coûter	co(n)stāre	'to cost'
/kostare/	/kostar/	/kostar/	/kuter/	['stand firm']	
9. cura	cura	cura	cure	cūra	'cure'
/kura/	/kura/	/kura/	/kyr/	['care']	

Based on the forms of Table 5.3, we set up a sound correspondence for the initial sound in these forms:

Sound correspondence 6:
Italian *k* : Spanish *k* : Portuguese *k* : French *k*

For SOUND CORRESPONDENCE 6, since all the languages have the same sound, *k*, we would naturally reconstruct **k*. However, SOUND CORRESPONDENCE 6 is quite similar to SOUND CORRESPONDENCE 1 (in Table 5.1), for which we also tentatively reconstructed **k*, repeated here for comparison with SOUND CORRESPONDENCE 6:

Sound correspondence 1:
Italian *k* : Spanish *k* : Portuguese *k* : French *ʃ*

The two sets overlap partially, since both sets share some of the same sounds. In fact, the only difference between the two is in French, which has *k* in SOUND CORRESPONDENCE 6 but *f* in SOUND CORRESPONDENCE 1. In cases such as this of similar (partially overlapping) correspondence sets, we must determine whether they reflect two separate proto-sounds or only one which split into more than one sound in one or more of the languages. In the case of SOUND CORRESPONDENCEs 1 and 6, we must determine whether both sets reflect **k*, or whether we must reconstruct something distinct for each of the two. Because we assume that sound change is regular, the options for possible solutions here are restricted to essentially only two. One possible solution would be for us to find evidence to show that the two correspondence sets are different today but represent only a single proto-sound. To show this, it would be necessary to explain away the difference between the two sets, that is, to show how a single original sound could change in ways that would result in the two different correspondence sets. For this, we would need to show that a single original sound ended up as *f* in certain specific environments in French but as *k* in other circumstances – since the other languages all have only the single reflex, *k*, the most likely candidate is a **k* assumed not to have changed in these languages, but, under this hypothesis, changed to *f* in French only in specific instances. If we cannot succeed in showing this – in being able to predict where the postulated original **k* became *f* and where it remained *k* in French – then we cannot reconstruct a single sound for the two sets and we are forced to consider the other possible solution. In this other possible solution, the two correspondence sets represent two distinct sounds in the proto-language which merged to *k* in all contexts in Italian, Spanish and Portuguese, but remained distinct in French.

In this case, we are able to determine the context in which French sometimes but not always changed **k* to *f*. We notice that in the cognate sets of Table 5.1 which exhibit SOUND CORRESPONDENCE 1, this sound comes before *ɛ* in French and *a* in the other languages (SOUND CORRESPONDENCE 3), while in SOUND CORRESPONDENCE 6, illustrated by the cognate sets in Table 5.3, the initial sound is not before *a* or *ɛ* (as in SOUND CORRESPONDENCE 1), but before *o* or *u* (French *u* or *y*). Therefore, we determine that French underwent a conditioned sound change, that **k > f* before the vowel of correspondence set 3 (**a* which became *ɛ* in French), but retained **k* unchanged before the round vowels seen in the cognates of Table 5.3 (essentially **u* and **o*, though we need to go through the steps to reconstruct these). So, in spite of two distinct sound correspondences (1 and 6), we reconstruct a single proto-sound and show that one of these (SOUND CORRESPONDENCE 1) is the result of a conditioned change which affected only some of the instances of original *k in French (those before original *a) but not the other cases of *k (those before *u and *o).

In some cases, however, we are forced to reconstruct separate proto-sounds in instances of similar, partially overlapping correspondence sets. Consider for example the two sound correspondences illustrated by the initial sounds in additional cognates in Table 5.4.

TABLE 5.4: Further Romance cognate sets

Italian	Spanish	Portuguese	French	(Latin)	English gloss
10. battere	batir	bater	battre	battuere	'to beat'
/battere/	/batir/	/bater/	/batr/		
11. bolla	bola	bola	boule	bulla	'ball, bubble'
/bolla/	/bola/	/bola/	/bul/		
12. bontà	bondad	bondade	bonté	bonitāte	'goodness'
/bonta/	/bondad/	/bõdaǰi/	/bõte/		
13. bev-	beber	beber	boire	bibere	'to drink'
/bev-/	/beber/	/beber/	Old French beivre		
14. venire	venir	vir	venir	venīre	'to come'
/venire/	/benir/	/vir/	/vənir/		
15. valle	valle	vale	val	valle	'valley'
/valle/	/balʲe/	/vale/	/val/		
16. vestire	vestir	vestir	vêtir	vestīre	'to dress'
/vestire/	/bestir/	/vestir/	/vetir/		

Cognate sets 10 to 13 show the sound correspondence in (7):

Sound correspondence 7:
Italian *b* : Spanish *b* : Portuguese *b* : French *b*

Cognate sets 14 to 16 show the sound correspondence in (8):

Sound correspondence 8:
Italian *v* : Spanish *b* : Portuguese *v* : French *v*

Clearly the best reconstruction for SOUND CORRESPONDENCE 7 would be *b, since all the languages have *b* as their reflex. SOUND CORRESPONDENCE 8 partially overlaps with this in that Spanish has *b* for its reflex in this set as well, corresponding to *v* of the other languages. As in the case of Proto-Romance *k (above), either we must be able to explain the difference in these two sets by showing that those languages with *v* changed an original *b to *v* under some clearly defined circumstances, or we must reconstruct two separate sounds in the proto-language, presumably *b and *v, where Spanish would then be assumed to have merged its original *v* with *b*. In this case, to make a long story short, if we look for factors which could be the basis of a conditioned change in Italian, Portuguese and French, which could explain how a single original *b could become *v* in certain circumstances but remain *b* in others in these languages, we are unable to find any. We find both *b* and *v* at the beginnings of words before all sorts of vowels, and with more extensive data we would find that both sounds occur quite freely in the same environments in these languages. Since no conditioning factor can be found, we reconstruct *b for the cognates in correspondence set 7 and *v for those in correspondence set 8, two distinct proto-sounds. From this, it follows that *v merged with *b in Spanish, accounting for why *b* is the Spanish reflex in both cognate sets 14–16 and 10–13 of Table 5.4.

A somewhat more revealing example of the problem of overlapping correspondence sets which prove to contrast and thus require separate sounds to be reconstructed is seen in the example in Table 5.5, from Mayan languages (of which only a few, each representing a major branch of the family, are represented).

TABLE 5.5: Some Mayan cognate sets

K'iche'	Tzeltal	Yucatec	Huastec	Proto-Mayan	English gloss
1. ra:h	ya	yah	yah-	*ra:h	'hot, spicy'
2. riʔx	yix	yiʔih	yeh-	*riʔix	'old (old man)'
3. r-	y-	y-	—	*r-	'his/her/its'
4. raš	yaš	yaʔaš	yaš-	*raʔaš	'green'
5. war	way	way	way	*war	'to sleep'
6. ya:x	yah	yah	yaʔ	*ya:h	'sick'
7. yaš	yaš	—	—	*yaš	'crab, pincers'
8. k'ay-	k'ay-	k'ay-	č'ay-	*k'ay	'to sell'
	['sing']	['sing, sell']	['buy']		

(NOTE: y = IPA [j], š = [ʃ], č = [tʃ], C' = glottalized (ejective) consonants.)

Note that the 'dash' (–) is the convention used by linguists to mean that either no cognate is known or the data are unavailable. In such instances, we must rely on information from the other cognate sets in order to determine features of those languages where the forms are missing. (In the examples that follow from Mayan, *y* = IPA [j].)

Cognate sets 1–5 show SOUND CORRESPONDENCE 1:

Sound correspondence 1:
K'iche' *r* : Tzeltal *y* : Yucatec *y* : Huastec *y*

Cognate sets 6–8 show SOUND CORRESPONDENCE 2:

Sound correspondence 2:
K'iche' *y* : Tzeltal *y* : Yucatec *y* : Huastec *y*

Clearly, by our standard criteria, the best Proto-Mayan reconstruction for SOUND CORRESPONDENCE 2 would be **y* (preserved unchanged in all the languages). However, all the languages except K'iche' also have *y* as their reflex in SOUND CORRESPONDENCE 1, whereas K'iche' has *r* in this case. As in the discussion of the Proto-Romance **k* case (above), we must either explain how the difference in these two sets arose by showing that K'iche' had changed original **y* to *r* in some clear set of phonetic circumstances, or we must reconstruct two separate sounds in the proto-language. In this case, to make a long story short, if we look for factors which could be the basis of a conditioned change in K'iche', we are unable to find any. We find both *r* and *y* at the beginning and end of words, before all sorts of vowels, and so on, and basically either sound can occur in any context without restrictions. Since no conditioning factor can be found, we reconstruct **r* for the SOUND CORRE-SPONDENCE 1 and **y* for SOUND CORRESPONDENCE 2, two distinct proto-sounds. From this, it follows that **r* merged with *y* in Tzeltal, Yucatec and Huastec, accounting for why they have *y* as the reflex also in cognate sets 6–8 of Table 5.5. When we look at still other Mayan languages, we find this distinction further supported, since, for example, Mam has *t* and Motocintlec has *č* where K'iche' has *r* in the cognates that illustrate SOUND CORRESPONDENCE 1, but they both have *y* in cognates where K'iche' has *y* in SOUND CORRESPONDENCE 2. That is, K'iche' turns out not to be the only witness of the distinction between the two sounds of these correspondence sets (Campbell 1977).

There is a famous case which confirms this way of treating partially overlapping sound correspondence sets. Leonard Bloomfield's (1925, 1928) famous proof of the applicability of the comparative method in unwritten ('exotic') languages was based on the correspondence sets from Central Algonquian languages presented with his reconstructions in Table 5.6 (PCA = Proto-Central Algonquian). Bloomfield (1925) postulated the reconstruction of *çk for set 5 as distinct from the others on the basis of scant evidence, but under the assumption that sound change is regular and the difference in this correspondence set (though exhibiting only sounds that occur in different combinations in the other sets) could not plausibly be explained away. Later, his decision to reconstruct something different for set 5 was confirmed when Swampy Cree was discovered, which contained the correspondence *htk* in the morpheme upon which set 5 was based, distinct in Swampy Cree from the reflexes of the other four reconstructions. Based on this discovery, Bloomfield (1928: 100) concluded:

> As an assumption, however, the postulate [of sound-change without exception] yields, as a matter of mere routine, predictions which otherwise would be impossible. In other words, the statement that *phonemes change* (sound-changes have no exceptions) is a tested hypothesis: in so far as one may speak of such a thing, it is a proved truth.

TABLE 5.6: Central Algonquian sound correspondences and Bloomfield's reconstruction

	Fox	*Ojibwa*	*Plains Cree*	*Menomini*	*PCA*
1.	hk	sk	sk	čk	*čk
2.	ʃk	ʃk	sk	sk	*ʃk
3.	hk	hk	sk	hk	*xk
4.	hk	hk	hk	hk	*hk
5.	ʃk	ʃk	hk	hk	*çk

Mayan languages provide a somewhat clearer and more compelling case of the need to reconstruct distinct proto-sounds if the difference between two partially overlapping correspondence sets cannot be explained away. Consider the following two K'ichean (a subgroup of Mayan) sound correspondences:

	Tz'utujil	*Kaqchikel*	*K'iche'*	*Poqomam*	*Uspanteko*	*Q'eqchi'*
(1)	x	x	x	x	x	x
(2)	x	x	x	x	x-/-(V̀)x	h

For example, the correspondence set in (1) is illustrated by:

Kaqchikel	*K'iche'*	*Poqomam*	*Uspanteko*	*Q'eqchi'*	*gloss*
čax	čax	čax	čax	čax	'pine'
k'ax	k'áx	k'ax	k'ax	k'ax	'flour'
k'o:x	k'o:x	k'o:x	k'o:x	k'o:x	'mask'

The correspondence set in (2) is seen in:

Kaqchikel	K'iche'	Poqomam	Uspanteko	Q'eqchi'	gloss
ča:x	ča:x	ča:x	čà:x	čah	'ashes'
ka:x	ka:x	ka:x	kà:x	—	'sky'
o:x	o:x	o:x	ò:x	o:h	'avocado'
q'i:x	q'i:x	q'i:x	q'ì:x	-q'ih	'day, sun'
					(in compounds)

In (1), all the languages have *x* as the reflex, and we would naturally expect to reconstruct **x* for the Proto-K'ichean sound. However, (2) overlaps considerably with (1), where each language also has *x* except Q'eqchi', which has *h*; Uspanteko has *x* too; however, if there is a vowel preceding this *x*, it has falling tone (V̀), which is not the case for vowels preceding the *x* of correspondence set (1). Since no conditioning factor can be found to explain away the difference between the two sets in Q'eqchi' and Uspanteko, separate proto-sounds must be reconstructed. It has been proposed that correspondence set (2) represents a sound which is further forward than *x*, the sound of correspondence set (1), and thus **x̂* (a somewhat fronted velar fricative) has been proposed to represent correspondence set (2). While the reconstruction with **x* and **x̂* for these two sets is not phonetically ideal, nevertheless the decision tô reconstruct something different for the two is confirmed when cognates are compared from other branches of Mayan beyond K'ichean, which exhibit the following corresponding sounds:

	Yucatec	Chol	Chuj	Jakalteko	Mam	K'ichean
(3)	x	h	x	x	x	*x
(4)	n	n	ŋ	ŋ	x	*x̂

The correspondence set in (3) (which matches the K'ichean set (1)) is exemplified by:

Yucatec	Chol	Chuj	Jakalteko	Mam	K'ichean	gloss
tax	tah	tax	tah	tsax	*čax	'pine'
k'ax	č'ah	k'ax	k'ah	k'ax	*k'ax	'flour, pinole'
k'o:x	k'o:h	k'o:x	k'oh	k'o:x	*k'o:x	'mask'

In Proto-Mayan these have **x*; they are, respectively: **ṭax* 'pine', **k'ax* 'flour, pinole', and **k'o:x* 'mask' (where *ṭ* represents a fronted dental or palatalized 't').

The correspondence set in (4) (which matches K'ichean set (2)) is seen in:

Yucatec	Chol	Chuj	Jakalteko	Mam	K'ichean	gloss
taʔan	tan-	taʔaŋ	taŋ	tsaʔx	*čax̭	'ashes'
kaʔan	čan	čaʔaŋ	kaŋ	kyaʔx	*kax̭	'sky'
ò:n	un	oŋ	oŋ	o:x	*o:x̭	'avocado'
k'ì:n	k'in	q'iŋ-	q'iŋ-	q'i:x	*q'i:x̭	'sun, day'

In Proto-Mayan these all have *ŋ; they are, respectively: *ṭaʔŋ 'ashes', *kaʔŋ 'sky', *o:ŋ 'avocado', and *q'i:ŋ 'sun, day'.

That is, the sounds of correspondence set (3) reflect Proto-Mayan *x, whereas those of set (4) reflect Proto-Mayan *ŋ. Since the two sounds are clearly distinguished in the other branches of the family and descend from distinct sounds in Proto-Mayan, the validity of the decision to reconstruct different sounds for Proto-K'ichean, one branch of Mayan, is confirmed. (Perhaps also the phonetics of this reconstruction could be refined. Since the x of K'ichean (and several other Mayan) languages is phonetically [χ] (voiceless uvular fricative), it may seem appealing to reconstruct *χ for set (3) in K'ichean and then let *x (velar) represent set (4). Since K'ichean languages contrast uvular and velar stops, a similar contrast in the fricative series may make some sense (see step 5).)

Step 5: Check the plausibility of the reconstructed sound from the perspective of the overall phonological inventory of the proto-language

Steps 5 and 6 are related. The rule of thumb in step 5 takes advantage of the fact that languages tend to be well behaved, that is, they tend to have symmetrical sound systems with congruent patterns. For example, in the reconstruction of sounds for the individual sound correspondences in step 3, we can reconstruct each sound of the proto-language with little regard for how these sounds may relate to one another or how they may fit together to form a coherent system. Often in step 5 when we consider the broader view of these sounds in the context of the overall inventory, we refine and correct our earlier proposals. For example, if two related languages have the correspondence set Language$_1$ *d* : Language$_2$ *r*, we might initially reconstruct *r and assume *r > d in Language$_1$, since *r* > *d* is known to take place in languages, though the alternative of *d with the assumption that Language$_2$ underwent the change *d > r is just as plausible, since the change *d* > *r* is also found in languages. Suppose, however, that in step 5 we discover that we have reconstructed sounds based on other sound correspondences which would give the following phonological inventory for the proto-language:

*p   *t   *k
*b   *g
      *r
      *l

There is a gap in this inventory where *d would be expected to complete the stop series, where the voiceless stops (*p, *t, *k) would each be matched by a voiced counterpart (*b, *d, *g), if a *d existed, which would make the stop series symmetrical, the pattern congruent. The proto-language as tentatively reconstructed so far, with both *r and *l and *b and *g, but no *d, would be unusual and unexpected. However, by revising our earlier tentative reconstruction of *r for the d : r sound correspondence to the equally plausible *d (assuming *d > r in Language$_2$), we arrive at a much more coherent and likely set of sounds for the proto-inventory, where the two stop series are congruent:

*p   *t   *k
*b   *d   *g
      *l

While this instance is presented as a hypothetical possibility, it is in fact encountered in a number of real language families, for example in branches of Austronesian. It is important, however, to keep in mind that while languages tend to be symmetrical and have pattern congruity, this is by no means always the case.

Let's consider one other hypothetical instance, also actually found in real language families. If in a family of two languages we encounter the correspondence set Language$_1$ s : Language$_2$ ʃ, either we could reconstruct *s (assuming *s > ʃ in Language$_2$) or we could postulate *ʃ (and assume *ʃ > s in Language$_1$). Both of these changes (*s > ʃ and *ʃ > s) are frequently found in other languages. Suppose, however, that in step 5 we discover that the other sound correspondences justify the reconstruction of several proto-sounds in the alveolar series, including *ts, but no other palato-alveolar sound. This would give a proto-language with alveolar *ts but palato-alveolar *ʃ and no *s, but this system would be asymmetrical and odd. However, a proto-language with *ts and *s but lacking *ʃ would be normal and not at all unusual. Therefore, in step 5 we would revise the preliminary reconstruction of Step 3 to make sure that we reconstructed *s for the s : ʃ correspondence set (assuming *s > ʃ in Language$_2$) to ensure a more plausible overall phonological inventory for the proto-language which we reconstruct. A real example which fits precisely this situation comes from Mixe-Zoquean (a family of languages from southern Mexico), where the languages of the Zoquean branch have *s* corresponding to *ʃ* of the Mixean languages, and neither has *č*, only *ts*. So, for Proto-Mixe-Zoquean, **s* is a better reconstruction for the *s* : *ʃ* correspondence set.

Of course, languages do not have to be symmetrical or fully natural, though they tend to be. Also, it is conceivable that a proto-language might have gaps (such as the missing **d* in the first example) and asymmetries (**ts* and **ʃ* rather than **ts* and **s* in the second example); however, unless there is strong evidence to compel us to accept a less expected reconstruction, we are obliged to accept the ones motivated by pattern congruity, symmetry and naturalness. That is, languages in general have symmetrical (natural) systems much more often than not. Therefore, in the case of two possibilities, one with a more expected inventory and the other with a less expected, less normal inventory, the probability that the reconstruction with the symmetrical, natural system accurately reflects the structure of the formerly spoken proto-language is much higher than that the asymmetrical one does. Given the greater odds of the first being right, we choose it, not the second, which is less likely to have existed.

Step 6: Check the plausibility of the reconstructed sound from the perspective of linguistic universals and typological expectations

Certain inventories of sounds are found with frequency among the world's languages while some are not found at all and others only very rarely. When we check our postulated reconstructions for the sounds of a proto-language, we must make sure that we are not proposing a set of sounds which is never or only very rarely found in human languages. For example, we do not find any languages which have no vowels whatsoever. Therefore, a proposed reconstructed language lacking vowels would be ruled out by step 6. There are no languages with only glottalized consonants and no plain counterparts, and therefore a reconstruction which claimed that some proto-language had only glottalized consonants and no non-glottalized counterparts would be false. Languages do not have only nasalized vowels with no non-nasalized vowels, and so we never propose a reconstruction which would result in a proto-language in which there are only nasalized vowels.

Let us look at an actual case. The Nootkan family has the sound correspondences seen in Table 5.7. Since no other guidelines help here, we

TABLE 5.7: Nootkan correspondences involving nasals

	Makah	Nitinat	Nootka
1.	b	b	m
2.	d	d	n
3.	b'	b'	ṁ
4.	d'	d'	ṅ

might be tempted, based on the majority-wins principle, to reconstruct voiced stops for Proto-Nootkan for these four correspondence sets and postulate that these changed to the nasal counterparts in Nootka. However, only a very few languages of the world lack nasal consonants; therefore, we do not expect a nasalless proto-language, and any postulated proto-language which lacks nasals altogether must be supported by very compelling evidence. In this case, Nitinat and Makah belong to the area of the Northwest Coast of North America where languages of several different families lack nasal consonants. The lack of nasals in these languages is due to the influence of other nasalless languages in the linguistic area (see Chapter 12); Proto-Nootkan had nasals, as Nootka still does, but Makah and Nitinat lost nasality – their former nasals became corresponding voiced oral stops (*$m > b$, *$n > d$, *$ṁ > b'$, *$ṅ > d'$). The knowledge of universals and typological expectations in this case would direct us to reconstruct the proto-language with nasals and to assume a subsequent change in Makah and Nitinat.

Of course, in step 5, we also relied on general typological patterns in language and evaluated proposed proto-inventories on this basis; that is, steps 5 and 6 are not really distinct.

Step 7: Reconstruct individual morphemes

When we have reconstructed the proto-sounds from which we assume that the sounds in the sound correspondences descend, it is possible to reconstruct lexical items and grammatical morphemes. For example, from the cognate set for 'goat' in Table 5.1, the first sound (in SOUND CORRESPONDENCE 1) was reconstructed as *k (based on the $k : k : k : ʃ$ correspondence set); for the second sound in the cognates for 'goat', we reconstructed *a, as in SOUND CORRESPONDENCE 3 (with $a : a : a : ɛ$); the third sound is represented by SOUND CORRESPONDENCE 2 ($p : b : b : v$), for which we reconstructed *p; the next sound in cognate set 1, as represented by SOUND CORRESPONDENCE 4, reflects Proto-Romance *r (based on the $r : r : r : r$ correspondence set); and the last sound in the 'goat' cognates reflects SOUND CORRESPONDENCE 2 (or actually a modification of it involving final vowels in French) which was reconstructed as *a. Putting these reconstructed sounds together following the order in which they appear in the cognates for 'goat' in set 1, we arrive at *kapra. That is, we have reconstructed a word in Proto-Romance, *kapra 'goat'. For cognate set 2 'dear' in Table 5.1, we would put together *k (SOUND CORRESPONDENCE 1), *a (SOUND CORRESPON-DENCE 3), *r (SOUND CORRESPONDENCE 4) – all seen already in the reconstruction of 'goat' – and *o (SOUND CORRESPONDENCE 5, with o : o : u : Ø), giving us the Proto-Romance word *karo 'dear'. For cognate set 3 'head', we have combinations of the same correspondence sets already seen in the reconstructions for 'goat' and 'dear', SOUND COR-RESPONDENCES 1, 3, 2 and 5, giving the Proto-Romance reconstructed word *kapo 'head'. In this way, we can continue reconstructing Proto-Romance words for all the cognate sets based on the sequence of sound correspondences that they reflect, building a Proto-Romance lexicon.

The reconstruction of a sound, a word or large portions of a proto-language is, in effect, a hypothesis (or better said, a set of interconnected hypotheses) concerning what those aspects of the proto-language must have been like. Aspects of the hypothesized reconstruction can be tested and proven wrong, or can be modified, based on new insights. These insights may involve new interpretations of the data already on hand, or new information that may come to light. The discovery of a heretofore unknown member of the family may provide new evidence, a different testimony of the historical events which transpired between the proto-language and its descendants, which could change how we view the structure and content of the proto-language. There are a number of well-known cases where this has happened which illustrate this point. Bloomfield's Swampy Cree case has already been mentioned. With the discovery and decipherment of Hittite (or better said, the languages of the Anatolian branch of Indo-European), the whole picture of Proto-Indo-European phonology changed; this included clearer evidence of several new proto-sounds (the laryngeals).

5.3   A Case Study

Let us apply the comparative method in a somewhat more complex example (though still simplified) which illustrates what we have until now been considering mainly through a simplified comparison of Romance languages. The forms in Table 5.8 are cognates found in Finnish, Hungarian and Udmurt (Votyak). These languages belong to the Finno-Ugric family, but since there are many other languages also in this family (see Figure 6.2 in Chapter 6), the data in this example are far from complete enough to offer a full perspective on the proto language – these three are compared here only for illustration's sake. These languages separated from one another a very long time ago, which explains why some of these cognates are not as immediately apparent based on mere superficial similarity. The languages have undergone many changes and are now quite different, and we would need much more information than presented here to reconstruct all the sounds of Proto-Finno-Ugric. Therefore, here we will be concerned only with the initial sounds in these data.

TABLE 5.8: Some Finno-Ugric cognate sets

Finnish	*Hungarian*	*Udmurt (Votyak)*	*gloss*
Set I			
1. pää [pæ:]	fej [fej]	pum, puŋ	'head, end'
2. pata [pata]	fazék [fɔze:k]	—	'pot'
3. pato 'dam, wall'	fal [fɔl] 'wall'	—	
4. pääsky- [pæ:sky]	fecske [fečke]	poçkɨ-	'swallow' (bird)
5. pelkää- [pelkæ:-]	fél [fe:l]	pulɨ-	'to fear'
6. pesä [pesæ]	fészek [fe:sek]	puz-	'nest'
7. pii [pi:] 'tooth of rake'	fog [fog]	pinʲ	'tooth'
8. pilvi [pilvi]	felhő [felhø:]	piˡʲem	'cloud'
9. poika [poika]	fiú [fiu:]	pi	'boy'
10. puno- [puno-]	fon [fon]	pun-	'spin, braid'
11. puu [pu:]	fa [fɔ]	pu	'tree'
Set II			
12. tä- [tæ-]	té- [te:-] (cf. tétova 'here and there')	ta	'this'
13. täi [tæi]	tetű [tety:]	tei	'louse'
14. talvi [talvi]	tél [te:l]	tol	'winter'
15. täyte- [tæyte-]	tel- [tel-] (in derived forms)	—	'full'
16. tunte- [tunte-]	tud [tud]	tod	'to know, sense'

Finnish	Hungarian	Udmurt (Votyak)	gloss
17. tyvi [tyvi]	tő [tø:]	[din^j]	'base'

Set III

18. kala [kala]	hal [hɔl]	—	'fish'
19. kalime- [kalime-]	háló [ha:lo:]	[Komi *kulem*]	'fishnet'
20. kamara [kamara]	hám- [ha:m-]	kəm	'peel'
21. koi [koi]	haj- [hɔj-]	[Komi *kɨa*]	'dawn'
22. kolme [kolme]	három [ha:rom]	kuin^{j}m-	'three'
23. kota [kota]	ház [ha:z]	kwa-/-ko/-ka 'summer hut'/ 'house'	'hut'
24. kunta [kunta] 'community, group, society'	had [hɔd] 'army'	—	
25. kuole- [kuole-]	hal [hɔl]	kul-	'to die'
26. kusi [kusi]	húgy [hu:d^j]	kɨẓ	'urine'

Set IV

27. käte- [kæte-]	kéz [ke:z]	ki	'hand'
28. keri [keri]	kér [ke:r]	kur	'(tree-)bark'
29. kerjää- [kerjæ:]	kér [ke:r]	kur-	'to beg'
30. kii- [ki:-] 'rut, mating'	kéj [ke:j] '(carnal) pleasure'	[*Komi* koj-] 'to make mating call'	
31. kivi [kivi]	kő [kø:]	kə 'mill stone'	'stone'
32. kyynel [ky:nek]	könny [kønnj]	-kɨl^{j}i- (in ¢in-kɨl^{j}i; ¢in(m)- 'eye')	'tear' (noun)
33. kytke- [kytke-]	köt [køt]	kɨtk-ɨ 'to harness'	'to tie'
34. kyy [ky:] 'adder'	kígyó [ki:d^{j}o:]	kɨj	'snake'
35. kyynär [ky:nær]	könyök [køn^{j}øk]	[gɨr-]	'elbow'

Set V

36. salava [salava] 'willow'	szil [sil] 'elm'	—	
37. sarvi [sarvi]	szarv [sɔrv]	¢ur, ¢ɨr	'horn'
38. sata [sata]	száz [sa:z]	¢u	'hundred'

Finnish	Hungarian	Udmurt (Votyak)	gloss
39. silmä [silmæ]	szem [sem]	çinm-	'eye'
40. suu [su:]	szá(j) [sa:j]	çu- (?) (in compounds)	'mouth'
41. sydäme- [sydæme-]	szív [si:v]	çulem	'heart'

Set VI

42. sappi [sappi]	epe [epe]	sep	'gall'
43. sää [sæ:] 'weather'	ég [e:g] 'sky' <'weather'	[*Komi* sinəd] 'sunshine haze, mist'	
44. säynä- [sæynæ-]	őn [ø:n]	son- (son-tçorɨg, tçorɨg 'fish')	'fish (*Leuciscus idus*)'
45. sula- [sula]	olva- [olvɔ-]	sɨlm-	'to melt'
46. suoni [suoni]	ín [i:n]	sɨn	'sinew'
47. syksy [syksy]	ősz [ø:s]	siẑɨl	'autumn'
48. syli [syli]	öl [øl]	sul, sɨl	'lap, bosom'

(Note that in a few cases where Udmurt has no cognate or the cognate is unknown, cognate forms from closely related Komi have been included for comparison.)

Step 1 is already done; the cognates have been assembled in Table 5.8. In step 2, we compare these cognates and set up sound correspondences. It is helpful to keep a good record of what we have looked at, either by noting with each sound correspondence the numbers which identify the cognate sets in which it is found, or if we do not use numbers, then the glosses. This is just a matter of bookkeeping – a means of being able to go back and check things without having to search back through all the data to find the cognates which exhibit the correspondence in question, particularly useful, for example, in steps 5 and 6.

Sound correspondences found in the cognates of Table 5.8 are:

(1) Finnish *p-* : Hungarian *f-* : Udmurt *p-* (in Set I, nos 1–11)
(2) Finnish *t-* : Hungarian *t-* : Udmurt *t-* (in Set II, nos 12–17)
(3) Finnish *k-* : Hungarian *h-* : Udmurt *k-* (in Set III, nos 18–26)
(4) Finnish *k-* : Hungarian *k-* : Udmurt *k-* (in Set IV, nos 27–35)
(5) Finnish *s-* : Hungarian *s-* : Udmurt *ç-* (in Set V, nos 36–41)
(6) Finnish *s-* : Hungarian *Ø-* : Udmurt *s-* (in Set VI, nos 42–48)

In Step 3 we attempt to reconstruct the proto sound which we believe is reflected in each of these correspondence sets. For SOUND CORRE-SPONDENCE (1) (p : f : p) our choices are: [1] reconstruct $*p$ and assume Hungarian changed to f; [2] reconstruct $*f$ and assume Finnish and Udmurt changed this to p; or [3] reconstruct some third thing (say $*p^h$) and assume that it changed in all three languages, that Hungarian changed in one way to give f while Finnish and Udmurt changed in another to give p. From directionality of change as a guideline, we conclude that possibilities [1] ($*p$) and [3] (some third thing, like $*p^h$) are plausible, but not [2] ($*f$), since in sound changes familiar from languages around the world we see that voiceless bilabial stops (p, p^h) frequently become f, but extremely rarely do we find instances of f changing to p or p^h. In the majority-wins guideline, since Finnish and Udmurt both have p, against Hungarian alone with f, majority wins suggests $*p$ as a more likely reconstruction than $*f$. In the guideline of factoring in features held in common, we may conclude from the sounds p and f in the sound correspondence that the proto-sound was voiceless and a labial of some kind, but this is consistent with all three of the possibilities [1]–[3]. In this case, then, factoring in the common features provides no basis for choosing among the alternatives. The guideline of economy also urges us towards [1] ($*p$). With $*p$ (as in [1]), we would need to postulate only a single change, $*p > f$ in Hungarian; in choice [2] ($*f$) we would have to assume the change of $*f > p$ twice, in Finnish and again in Udmurt. Choice [3] ($*p^h$) would require us to postulate the change $*p^h > p$ twice, in Finnish and Udmurt, and another change, $*p^h > f$, in Hungarian. Steps 4 and 5 can help us resolve which of these possibilities is the best reconstruction; however, we have sufficient reason now for selecting [1], with $*p$, based on these considerations from directionality of change, majority wins, and economy.

SOUND CORRESPONDENCE (2) (t- : t- : t-) appears to reflect $*t$- (where none of the language has changed).

SOUND CORRESPONDENCES (3) (k- : h- : k-) and (4) (k- : k- : k-) could present more of a challenge. In (4) we reconstruct $*k$-, since all three languages have k- and thus none of them appears to have changed. However, if (4) were not present to complicate the picture, then (3) would also seem to be best reconstructed as $*k$-. Directionality of change would support this possibility, since the change $k > h$ (as would be required for Hungarian in this hypothesis) is very common and not unexpected, whereas a change h- $> k$- is all but unknown. Also the majority-wins criterion supports $*k$-, with k- in two languages but h- in only one. We move to Step 4 to attempt to resolve the difficulty of the partially overlapping sound correspondences (3) and (4). If we can show that both sound correspondence sets reflect the same original sound because one of the languages has undergone a conditioned change where that sound changed in some environments but not in others, then we can reconstruct just a single sound, the same one for both correspondence sets. We would explain the difference between the two correspondences by pointing out the conditions under which one of the languages changed and thus resulted in two different outcomes from the single original sound. If we cannot explain the difference in this way, then we are obligated to reconstruct two distinct proto sounds, one to represent each of the two sound correspondences, with the assumption that these two originally distinct sounds merged to *k-* in Finnish and Udmurt. This, then, requires us to take a closer look at the cognates in question (those of Sets III and IV). We notice that in the cognates of Set III the *h* of Hungarian appears only before back vowels (*u, o, a*), whereas in the cognates of Set IV Hungarian's *k* occurs only before front vowels. We conclude that Hungarian had a single original sound which changed to *h* before back vowels (as in Set III) but remained *k* before front vowels (as in Set IV). We reconstruct **k*. Someone might wonder whether the proto-language could not have had an **h* which then changed to *k* before front vowels in Hungarian and to *k* in all environments in Finnish and Udmurt. First, directionality argues against this possibility (since the change *h > k* is essentially unknown anywhere). Second, the criterion of economy also go against this alternative; it is more likely that only one change took place, **k > h* before back vowels in Hungarian, than that several independent changes occurred, one of **h > k* before front vowels in Hungarian and independently of the Hungarian development the changes of **h > k* in all contexts in Finnish and in Udmurt.

The SOUND CORRESPONDENCES (5) (*s-* : *s-* : *ç-*) and (6) (*s-* : *Ø-* : *s-*) present a similar problem of partially overlapping correspondence sets. However, the partial overlap in this instance is not like that seen in the sound correspondences (3) and (4), both of which come from a single original sound in different positions due to conditioned sound change. Both sound correspondences (5) and (6) in the cognates of Sets V and VI occur essentially in the same environments: both before the various vowels, front and back, and both before the same sorts of consonants in the following syllable (for example, *l*, of 36, 45, and 48), which would be clearer if we had more cognates in the data presented here. Careful scrutiny in this case eventually shows that it is not possible to explain the difference between the two sound correspondence sets as conditioned phonetic change in some environment, given that both occur in essentially the same environments. This being the case, we have no choice but to reconstruct a different proto-sound to represent each of these two sound correspondences. Let us see how the general guidelines for reconstruction fare in these partially overlapping but ultimately contrastive cases, first applied to (5), then to (6), with the results then compared.

By *directionality*, for (5) (*s-* : *s-* : *ç-*) we might assume either **s* which became *ç* in Udmurt, or **ç* which became *s* in Finnish and Hungarian. Both are known changes, though *s* > *ç* is not common without some conditioning environment, say before front vowels. Thus, while not compellingly strong, the directionality in this instance gives a slightly stronger vote for **ç* than for **s*, that is, for the change **ç* > *s* being the most likely. On the other hand, *majority wins* clearly votes for **s*, since two languages have *s* (Finnish and Hungarian) and only one has *ç* (Udmurt). The criterion of examining the *features held in common* avails little in this instance, since *s-* and *ç-* share all their features except palatalization, meaning the proto-sound presumably had all these same shared features – some kind of *s*-like sound. *Economy* would clearly favor **s*, since this would require only one change, **s* > *ç* in Udmurt; the postulation of **ç* would require the change of **ç* > *s* in Finnish and again in Hungarian. In sum, the guidelines do not all unanimously point in one direction, but appear to favor **s* for (5), which presumes the change **s* > *ç* in Udmurt.

However, the existence of sound correspondence (6) (*s-* : *Ø-* : *s-*) complicates this picture, since it, too, appears to point to **s* as the best probable reconstruction, and yet we were unable to combine the two as possibly coming from the same original sound with some conditioned changes in particular contexts. *Directionality* clearly favors **s* for (6), since *s* > *Ø* is a relatively frequent change (often through the intermediate stage of *s* > *h* > *Ø*), but *Ø* > *s* is unknown and there is no phonetic motivation for why such a change should take place. *Majority wins* also clearly favors **s*, given the two cases with *s* (Finnish and Udmurt) but only one with *Ø* (Hungarian). Similarly, the *features held in common* suggest **s*, since *s* is the sound in two of the languages, and the features of *Ø* do not contribute insight here. Finally, *economy* also supports **s* for (6), since this would require only the single change of **s* > *Ø* in Hungarian. Postulation of **Ø* , for example, because that is the reflex in Hungarian, would require the change of *Ø* to *s* in Finnish and again in Udmurt. Postulation of some third alternative, say **ʃ*, would require even more changes, **ʃ* > s in Finnish and in Udmurt, and , **ʃ* > *Ø* in

Hungarian. In sum, then, the guidelines support *s for (6), with the presumed change *s > Ø in Hungarian.

However, this cannot be right. As already indicated, the two correspondences (5) and (6) occur in contrastive environments and apparently cannot be combined as separate outcomes from the same original sound due to conditioned change. This means that we cannot, then, reconstruct *s both for (5) and for (6), since sound change is regular and such a reconstruction would afford no means of explaining why the proposed single original *s behaves differently in the two different correspondence sets, why in Hungarian it is sometimes s (in Set V cognates) and sometimes Ø (in Set VI cognates), why in Udmurt sometimes ҫ, sometimes s, and so on. We must reconstruct a separate sound for each of these distinct correspondence sets. While the decision about what to reconstruct for each is not as straightforward as we might like, all the guidelines clearly suggest *s for (6) (s- : Ø : s), where for (5) (s- : s- : ҫ-) there was not such agreement – directionality appeared to favour *ҫ. Let us then propose these reconstructions: *ҫ for (5) (postulating the sound changes *ҫ > s in Finnish and in Hungarian), and *s for (6) (with the changes *s > Ø in Hungarian). In fact, with the aid of much additional evidence from other Finno-Ugric languages, specialists reconstruct *ś (IPA [sʲ] or aveolo-palatal [ҫ]) for the sound correspondence of (5) and *s for that of (6) (Sammallahti 1988).

Let us return to SOUND CORRESPONDENCES (1), (2), (3) and (4) and apply Steps 5 and 6. Not enough cognate sets are given in the data here to reconstruct the full phonological inventory of Proto-Finno-Ugric, so that we are unable to apply Steps 5 and 6 fully. However, for now let us assume that we at least have available in the cognates of Table 5.8 the evidence for the voiceless stops and apply these steps to these to illustrate the procedures. Our tentative reconstructions to this point based on the sound correspondences were:

*p (1) Finnish p- : Hungarian f- : Udmurt p- (in Set I, nos 1–11)
*t (2) Finnish t- : Hungarian t- : Udmurt t- (in Set II, nos 12–17)
*k (before back vowels) (3) Finnish k- : Hungarian h- : Udmurt k- (in Set III, nos 18–26)
*k (before front vowels) (4) Finnish k- : Hungarian k- : Udmurt k- (in Set IV, nos 27–35).

We check these in Step 5 to see how plausible the resulting inventory of voiceless stops would be with these sounds in the proto-language. A language with the stops *p, t, k* would be quite normal, with an internally consistent pattern of voiceless stops. If we did attempt to reconstruct possibility [3] (some third thing from which to derive p and f plausibly, say $*p^h$) for sound correspondence (1), we would no longer have a natural, symmetrical phonemic inventory of voiceless stops ($*p$, $*t$, $*k$), but rather the unlikely $*p^h$, $*t$, $*k$. In Step 5, we would see that this would result in a series of stops which is not internally consistent, where the presence of aspirated p^h (with no plain p) is incongruent with t and k (with no t^h and k^h). In Step 6, we would check this pattern to see how well it fits typologically with what we know of the sound systems of the world's languages. Here we would find that languages with only the stops p^h, t, k (but no p and no other aspirated stops) are very rare, while a large majority of languages have a stop series with p, t, k. For possibility [2] (which would reconstruct $*f$), Step 5 tells us a language with f, t, k (but no p) is also internally not as consistent as one with p, t, k, and therefore not as good a reconstruction. Step 6 tells us the same thing; in looking at the sound systems of the world's languages, we find few with f, t, k (and no p), but hundreds with p, t, k. Putting these considerations of directionality, economy, internal consistency and typological realism together, we conclude that the reconstruction of $*p$ is the best of the alternatives for SOUND CORRESPONDENCE (1). In turn, we apply steps 5 and 6 to the reconstructions with $*t$ and $*k$ and we find these to be supported in similar fashion in these steps. We find that the possible alternative with $*h$ for SOUND CORRESPONDENCES (3) and (4) which might have been considered, would be inconsistent internally and typologically (leaving a system with p, t, h, but no k) not to mention being against economy, the known directionality of change, and the majority-wins guidelines.

5.4 Indo-European and the Regularity of Sound Change

The development of historical linguistics is closely associated with the study of Indo-European. *Grimm's Law*, *Grassmann's Law* and *Verner's Law* are major milestones in the history of Indo-European and thus also in historical linguistics, and traditionally all linguists have had to learn these laws – indeed, knowledge of them is helpful (some might say essential) for understanding the comparative method and the regularity hypothesis. (These laws have been considered in preliminary form in Chapter 2.) In this section, each is taken up individually and the development of the claim that sound change is regular based on these laws is considered.

5.4.1 Grimm's Law

The forms of Table 5.9 illustrate Grimm's Law, a series of changes in the stops from Proto-Indo-European to Proto-Germanic:

voiceless stops > voiceless fricatives:

*p	>	f
*t	>	θ
*k, *k̂	>	h (x)
*kʷ	>	hw

voiced stops > voiceless stops

*b	>	p
*d	>	t
*g, *ĝ	>	k
*gʷ	>	kw

voiced aspirated (murmured) stops > plain voiced stops

*bh	>	b
*dh	>	d
*gh, *ĝh	>	g
*gʷh	>	gw, w

(The sounds *k̂, *ĝ and *ĝh represent the 'palatal' series in Indo-European.)

In Table 5.9, the Gothic and English forms show the results of these changes in Germanic, while the Sanskrit, Greek and Latin forms for the most part reflect the Indo-European stops unchanged; that is, they did not undergo Grimm's Law as the Germanic forms did.

TABLE 5.9: Indo-European cognates reflecting Grimm's Law

Sanskrit	Greek	Latin	Gothic	English
Set Ia: *p > f				
pad-	pod-	ped-	fōtus	foot
páńča [páɲča]	pénte	[quinque] [kʷinkʷe]	fimf	five
pra-	pro-	pro-	fra-	fro
pū- 'make clear, bright'	pur	pūrus 'pure'	[OE fȳr]	fire
pitár-	patḗr	pater	fadar [faðar]	father [OE fæder]

Sanskrit	Greek	Latin	Gothic	English

Set Ia: *p > f (*continued*)

Sanskrit	Greek	Latin	Gothic	English
nápāt- 'descendant'		nepōs 'nephew, grandson'	[OHG nefo]	nephew [OE nefa]

Set Ib: *t > θ

Sanskrit	Greek	Latin	Gothic	English
trī-/tráyas	treīs/tría	trēs	þrija	three
tv-am	tū (Doric)	tu	þu	thou
-ti- gátis 'gait'	-ti- básis 'going'	-tis/-sis mor-tis 'death'		-th 'nominaliser' [health, birth, death]

Set Ic: *k, *k̂ > h (or [x])

Sanskrit	Greek	Latin	Gothic	English
śván- [ʃvən-]	kúōn	canis [kanis]	hunds	hound 'dog'
śatám [ʃətə́m]	(he-)katón	centum [kentum]	hunda (pl.)	hundred
kravís 'raw flesh'	kré(w)as 'flesh, meat'	cruor 'raw, blood, thick'		raw [OE hrāw] 'corpse'
dáśa [dáʃə]	déka	decem [dekem]	taíhun [tɛxun]	ten

Set IIa: *b > p (*b* was very rare in Proto-Indo-European, and many doubt that it was part of the sound system; some Lithuanian forms are given in the absence of cognates in the other languages)

Sanskrit	Greek	Latin	Gothic	English
		(*Lithuanian*) dubùs	diups	deep [OE dēop]
	kánnabis	(*Lithuanian*) kanapēs]		hemp (borrowing?)
		Latin lūbricus	sliupan	slip

Sanskrit	Greek	Latin	Gothic	English

Set IIb: *d > t

Sanskrit	Greek	Latin	Gothic	English
d(u)vā́-	dúo/dúō	duo	twái [twɛ]	two
dánt-	odónt-	dent-	tunþus	tooth
dáśa [də́ʃə]	déka	decem [dekem]	taíhun [tɛxun]	ten
pad-	pod-	ped-	fōtus	foot
ad- 'eat'	édō 'I eat'	edō 'I eat'		eat [OE etan]
véda 'I know'	woĩda 'I know'	videō 'I know'	wáit [wɛ̃t] 'I know'	wit 'to know'

Set IIb: *g, *ĝ > k

Sanskrit	Greek	Latin	Gothic	English
janás	génos	genus	kun-i 'race, tribe'	kin
jánu-	gónu	genū	kniu	knee
jnātá	gnōtós	(g)nōtus	kunnan 'to know'	known
áĵra- 'country'	agrós	ager	akrs	acre 'field'
mrj- 'to milk'	(a-)mélgō 'to squeeze out'	mulgeō 'I milk'	miluk-s 'milk'	milk

Set IIIa: *bh > b

Sanskrit	Greek	Latin	Gothic	English
bhar-	phér-	fer-	baír-an [bɛran] 'to bear'	bear
bhrā́tar	phrā́tēr	frā́ter	brōþar	brother
a-bhū́-t 'he was'	é-phū 'he grew, sprang up'	fu-it 'he was'	bau-an [bō-an] to dwell'	be

Sanskrit	Greek	Latin	Gothic	English

Set IIIb: *dh > d

dhā-	ti-thē-mi	fē-cī		do [OE dō-n]
'put'	'I put'	'I made'		
dhrsnóti	thrasús	(fest-)	(ga-)dars	dare [OE dear(r)]
'he dares'	'bold'		'he dares'	'he dares'
dvār-	thúr-a	for-ēs	daúr-	door
			[dor-]	
vidhávā	ē-wíthewos	vidua	widuwo	widow
	'unmarried			
	youth'			
mádhu	méthu			mead
madhya-	mésos	medius	midjis	mid

Set IIIc: *gh, *ĝh > g

haṁs-á-	khēn	āns-er	Gans [*German*] goose	
[hə̃sə́]				
'swan, goose'				
stigh-	steíkhō		steigan	
'stride'	'I pace'		[stīgan]	
			'to climb'	
vah-	wókh-os	veh-ō	ga-wig-an	weigh/wain
'carry'	'chariot'	'I carry'	'to move, shake'	

Grimm's Law embodies systematic correspondences between Germanic and non-Germanic languages, the results of regular sound changes in Germanic. So, for example, as a result of the change *p > f in the examples in Set Ia of Table 5.9, Gothic and English (the Germanic languages) have the reflex f corresponding to p in Sanskrit, Greek and Latin (the non-Germanic languages), all from Proto-Indo-European *p. While Grimm's Law accounts for the systematic correspondences seen in Table 5.9, nevertheless these are not entirely without exceptions. However, as we will see, these exceptions all have satisfactory explanations. One set of forms which seem to be exceptions to Grimm's Law involves stops in consonant clusters, and examples of these are given in Table 5.10. (An Old High German (OHG) form is sometimes substituted when no Gothic cognate is available; OE = Old English.)

TABLE 5.10: Exceptions to Grimm's Law in consonant clusters

Sanskrit	Greek	Latin	Gothic	English
1. páś-	[skep-]	spec-	[OHG speh-]	spy (?) 'to see'
2. (sthiv-) ..	pū	spu-	speiw-an [spīw-an]	spew 'to spit'
3. astáu [əṣtáu] .	oktō	octō [oktō]	ahtau [axtau]	eight
4. nákt-	nukt-	noct- [nokt-]	nahts [naxts]	night
5.		capt(īvus)	(haft)	[OE hæft] 'prisoner'
6. -ti- gátis 'gait'	-ti- básis 'going'	-tis/-sis mor-tis 'death'		-t 'nominaliser' thrift, draught, thirst, flight, drift
7.		piscis [piskis]	fisks	[OE fisc] 'fish'

In these forms, by Grimm's Law, corresponding to the *p* in (1) and (2) of Sanskrit, Greek and Latin we should expect to find *f* in Gothic and English, not the *p* seen in these forms. (And given the *p* of Gothic and English, the Germanic languages, we expect the correspondence in Sanskrit, Greek and Latin to be *b*, not the *p* that actually occurs.) In (3–6) we expect Gothic and English to have /θ/ (not the actually occurring *t*) corresponding to the *t* of Sanskrit, Greek and Latin. And in (7), we would expect Latin *k* to correspond to Germanic *x*, not to the *k* of the Gothic and English words in this cognate set. These exceptions are explained by the fact that Grimm's Law was actually a conditioned change; it did not take place after fricatives (**sp* > *sp*, not ✗*sf*) or after stops (**kt* > *xt*, not ✗*xθ*; the **k*, the first member of the cluster, does change to *x* as expected by Grimm's Law, but the **t*, the second member, does not change). In the case of (6), the difference between *thrift, draught, thirst, flight, drift* of Table 5.10 and the *health, birth, death* of Table 5.9 is explained in the same way. The /θ/ forms (as in Table 5.10) underwent Grimm's Law (**t* > *θ*); the forms with -*t* (in Table 5.9) are exempt from Grimm's Law because this **t* comes after a fricative in English (the <gh> of *draught* and *fight* was formerly [x], which was later lost; see Chapter 14). Thus, when Grimm's Law is correctly formulated – written to exclude stops after fricatives and other stops in consonant clusters, since that environment did not enter the change – the stops in clusters are not, in fact, exceptions to the sound change.

5.4.2 Grassmann's Law

Another set of forms which earlier had seemed to be exceptions to Grimm's Law is explained by Grassmann's Law (seen already in Chapter 2). In Greek and Sanskrit, Grassmann's Law regularly dissimilated the first of two aspirated stops within a word so that the first lost its aspiration, as in the change from Proto-Indo-European *dhi-dhē-mi (*dhi-dheh₁-mi)'I put, place' (with reduplication of root *dhē- (*dheh₁-)) to Sanskrit *da-dhā-mi* and Greek *ti-thē-mi*. As a result of Grassmann's Law, some sound correspondences between Sanskrit, Greek and Germanic languages do not match the expectations from Grimm's Law, as, for example, in the following cognates:

Sanskrit	Greek	Gothic	English	
bōdha	peutha	biudan	bid	'to wake, become aware'
bandha		bindan	bind	'to bind'.

The first is from Proto-Indo-European *bheudha-, the second from *bhendh-; both have undergone dissimilation of the first *bh due to the presence of a second aspirated stop in the word (*dh in this case). This gives the SOUND CORRESPONDENCE in (1):

(1) Sanskrit *b* : Greek *p* : Gothic *b* : English *b*.

By Grimm's Law, we expect the *b* of Sanskrit to correspond to *p* in Germanic (Gothic and English in this case), and we expect Germanic *b* to correspond to Sanskrit *bh* and Greek *ph*. So SOUND CORRESPONDENCE (1) in these cognate sets appears to be an exception to Grimm's Law. The cognate sets with correspondence (1) (and others for the originally aspirated stops at other points of articulation), then, are not real exceptions to Grimm's Law; rather, their reflexes in Germanic are correct for Grimm's Law, and the Sanskrit and Greek reflexes are not those expected by Grimm's Law only because Grassmann's Law regularly deaspirated the first aspirated stop when it occurred before another aspirated stop in the word in these languages. That is, SOUND CORRESPONDENCE (1) (and the others like it at other points of articulation) is the result of regular changes, Grimm's Law in Germanic, and Grassmann's Law in Sanskrit and Greek.

5.4.3 Verner's Law

A final set of what earlier had seemed to be exceptions to Grimm's Law is explained by Verner's Law (called *grammatical alternation* in older sources; see Chapter 2). Some forms which illustrate Verner's Law are seen in the cognate sets of Table 5.11 (OE = Old English; OHG = Old High German).

TABLE 5.11: Examples illustrating Verner's Law

	Sanskrit	Greek	Latin	Gothic	English
(1)	saptá	heptá	septem	sibun [siβun]	seven
(2)	pitár-	patḗr	pater	fadar [faðar]	OE fæder 'father'
(3)	śatám [ʃatəm]	(he-)katón	centum [kentum]	hunda (pl.)	hundred
(4)	śrutás 'heard'	klutós 'heard'			OE hlud 'loud'
(5)		makrós 'long, slender'	macer [maker]	[OHG magar]	meagre

In cognate set (1), by Grimm's Law we expect the *p* of Sanskrit, Greek and Latin to correspond to *f* in Germanic (Gothic and English), but instead we have Gothic *b* ([β]) and English *v*; given Gothic *b*, we expect the correspondence in Sanskrit to be *bh* and in Greek to be *ph*. Similarly, in cognate sets (2–4) we have the correspondence of Sanskrit, Greek and Latin *t* to Germanic *d*, not the θ expected by Grimm's Law in Germanic (and not the Sanskrit *dh* and Greek *th* we would expect, given Germanic *d*). These apparent exceptions to Grimm's Law are explained by Verner's Law. Verner's Law affects medial consonants; when the Proto-Indo-European accent followed, medial (plain) voiceless stops and fricatives in a root became voiced in Germanic; otherwise (when the accent preceded the sound or when the sound was root-initial) Grimm's Law applied. Since later in Proto-Germanic the accent shifted to the root-initial syllable, the earlier placement of the accent can only be seen when the cognates from the non-Germanic languages are compared. Thus, in the cognate sets of Table 5.11, we see in the Sanskrit and Greek cognates that the accent is not on the initial syllable but is on a later syllable, after the sound that changed, and that the Germanic forms do not match expectations from Grimm's Law in these instances. In (1), we would not expect Gothic *sibun*, but rather something like *sifun*, given the *p* of Sanskrit *saptá* and Greek *heptá*; however, since the accent is on the last syllable in the Sanskrit and Greek forms, Verner's Law gives Gothic *b* in this case. The forms of Table 5.12 show how the forms with the accent later in the word (which undergo Verner's Law, symbolised as . . . C . . . ´) contrast with forms with the accent before the sound in question (indicated as ´ . . . C . . ., cases which undergo Grimm's Law).

TABLE 5.12: Examples contrasting the effects of Grimm's Law and Verner's Law on medial consonants

Grimm's Law	*Verner's Law*
´...C...	...C...´
*p > f	*p > b [β]
(1a) OE hēafod 'head'	(1b) Gothic sibun [siβun] 'seven'
Latin cáput [káput]	Sanskrit saptá-
*t > θ	*t > d [ð]
(2a) Gothic brōþar [brōθar] 'brother'	(2b) OE fæder 'father'
Sanskrit bhrătar-	Sanskrit pitár-
*k > x	*k > g [ɣ]
(3a) Gothic taíhun 'ten'	(3b) Gothic tigus 'decade'
Greek déka	Greek dekás

It is easy to see why Verner's Law was also often called 'grammatical alternation' (*grammatischer Wechsel* in German). The accent in Proto-Indo-European fell on different syllables in certain grammatically related forms, as seen in the forms compared in Table 5.13 (PIE = Proto-Indo-European; P-Germ = Proto-Germanic). As a result, Germanic languages have different allomorphs in grammatical paradigms which depend upon whether or not Verner's Law applied, and these grammatical alternations further support Verner's Law and its correlation with the place of the accent in the proto-language.

TABLE 5.13: Verner's Law in grammatical alternations

	'I become'	*'I became'*	*'we became'*	*'became [participle]'*
PIE	*wértō	*(we)wórta	*(we)wr̥təmé	*wr̥tonós
Sanskrit	vártāmi	va-várta	vavr̥timá	vr̥tānáh
	'I turn'	'I have turned'	'we have turned'	'turned'
P-Germ	*werθō	*warθa	*wurðum(i)	*wurðan(a)z
OE	weorþe	warþ	wurdon	worden
OHG	wirdu	ward	wurtum	wortan

Just as expected by Grimm's Law, the Old English forms in the first two columns have /θ/ (spelled <Þ>), where the accent in Proto-Indo-European preceded the original *t* (as illustrated by the Sanskrit forms). However, in the last two columns, Old English does not have the /θ/ expected by Grimm's Law, but the /d/ of Verner's law because the accent came after this medial *t* in Proto-Indo-European, again as shown by the Sanskrit forms. The Old High German forms subsequently underwent other sound changes of their own, but the difference between those with /d/ and those with /t/ has its origin in Verner's Law just as the alternations seen in the Old English cognates. The allomorphic variation which resulted, as for example that seen in the verb paradigm in Table 5.13, illustrates the 'grammatical alternation' that comes from Verner's Law.

So, the Verner's Law cases (as in Tables 5.11, 5.12 and 5.13), which originally appeared to be exceptions to Grimm's Law, turn out also to be explained by regular sound change – by Verner's Law, a conditioned change having to do with the earlier location of the accent.

5.4.4 Indo-European sound laws and regularity of sound change

The laws just considered played an important role in the history of Indo-European studies and as a consequence in the overall history of historical linguistics. Grimm's Law, which was published first (in 1822), was quite general and accounted for the majority of sound correspondences involving the stop series between Germanic and non-Germanic languages. However, as initially formulated, it did appear to have exceptions. When Hermann Grassmann discovered his law (in 1862), a large block of these 'exceptions' was explained, and then Karl Verner through Verner's Law (in 1877) explained most of the remaining exceptions. This success in accounting for what had originally appeared to be exceptions led the Neogrammarians to the confidence that sound change was regular and exceptionless (see Chapter 2). This is one of the most significant conclusions in the history of linguistics.

5.5 Basic Assumptions of the Comparative Method

What textbooks call the 'basic assumptions' of the comparative method might better be viewed as the consequences of how we reconstruct and of our views of sound change. The following four basic assumptions are usually listed.

(1) The proto-language was uniform, with no dialect (or social) variation. Clearly this 'assumption' is counterfactual, since all known languages have regional or social variation, different styles, and so on. It is not so much that the comparative method 'assumes' no variation; rather, it is just that there is nothing built into the comparative method which would allow it to address variation directly. This means that what is reconstructed will not recover the once-spoken proto-language in its entirety. Still, rather than stressing what is missing, we can be happy that the method provides the means for recovering so much of the original language. This assumption of uniformity is a reasonable idealization; it does no more damage to the understanding of the language than, say, modern reference grammars do which concentrate on a language's general structure, typically leaving out consideration of regional, social and stylistic variation. Moreover, dialect differences are not always left out of comparative considerations and reconstructions, since in some cases scholars do reconstruct dialect differences to the proto-language based on differences in daughter languages which are not easily reconciled with a single uniform starting point. This, however, has not been common practice outside of Indo-European studies.

Assumptions (2) and (3) are interrelated, so that it is best to discuss them together.

(2) Language splits are sudden.

(3) After the split-up of the proto-language, there is no subsequent contact among the related languages.

These 'assumptions' are a consequence of the fact that the comparative method addresses directly only material in the related languages which is inherited from the proto-language and has no means of its own for dealing with borrowings, the results of subsequent contact after diversification into related languages. Borrowing and the effects of subsequent language contact are, however, by no means neglected in reconstruction. Rather, we must resort to other techniques which are not formally part of the comparative method for dealing with borrowing and the results of language contact (see Chapters 3, 7 and 12). It is true that the comparative method contains no means for addressing whether the language of some speech community gradually diverged over a long period of time before ultimately distinct but related languages emerged, or whether a sudden division took place with a migration of a part of the community so far away that there was no subsequent contact between the two parts of the original community, resulting in a sharp split and no subsequent contacts between the groups. (Assumptions (2) and (3) are better seen as the consequence of the family-tree model for classifying related languages, dealt with in Chapters 6 and 7, since the tree diagram depicts a parent language splitting up sharply into its daughters.)

(4) Sound change is regular. The assumption of regularity is extremely valuable to the application of the comparative method. Knowing that a sound changes in a regular fashion gives us the confidence to reconstruct what the sound was like in the parent language from which it comes. If a sound could change in unconstrained, unpredictable ways, we would not be able to determine from a given sound in a daughter language what sound or sounds it may have come from in the parent language, or, looking at a particular sound in the parent language, we could not determine what its reflexes in its daughter languages would be. That is, if, for example, an original *p of the proto-language could arbitrarily for no particular reason become f in some words, y in others, q' in others, and so on, in exactly the same phonetic and other linguistic circumstances, then it would not be possible to reconstruct. In such a situation, comparing, say a p of one language with a p of another related language would be of no avail, if the p in each could have come in an unpredictable manner from a number of different sounds.

5.6 How Realistic are Reconstructed Proto-languages?

The success of any given reconstruction depends on the material at hand to work with and the ability of the comparative linguist to figure out what happened in the history of the languages being compared. In cases where the daughter languages preserve clear evidence of what the parent language had, a reconstruction can be very successful, matching closely the actual spoken ancestral language from which the compared daughters descend. However, there are many cases in which all the daughter languages lose or merge formerly contrasting sounds or eliminate earlier alternations through analogy, or lose morphological categories due to changes of various sorts. We cannot recover things about the proto-language via the comparative method if the daughters simply do not preserve evidence of them. In cases where the evidence is severely limited or unclear, we often make mistakes. We make the best inferences we can based on the evidence available and on everything we know about the nature of human languages and linguistic change. We do the best we can with what we have to work with. Often the results are very good; sometimes they are less complete. In general, the longer in the past the proto-language split up, the more linguistic changes will have accumulated and the more difficult it becomes to reconstruct with full success.

A comparison of reconstructed Proto-Romance with attested Latin provides a telling example in this case. We do successfully recover a great deal of the formerly spoken language via the comparative method. However, the modern Romance languages for the most part preserve little of the former noun cases and complex tense–aspect verbal morphology which Latin had. Subsequent changes have obscured this inflectional morphology so much that much of it is not reconstructible by the comparative method.

5.7 Exercises

Exercise 5.1 Aimaran

Consider the following data from the two major branches of the Aimaran language family (Peru and Bolivia). Focus your attention only on the fricatives. What will you reconstruct? How many fricatives do you postulate for Proto-Aimaran? State your evidence.

NOTE: *š* = IPA [ʃ], *č* = IPA [tʃ]; *χ* = voiceless uvular fricative; *C'* = glottalized [ejective] consonants.

	Central Aimara	*Southern Aimara*	*gloss*
1.	saxu	sawu-	'to weave'
2.	sa(wi)	sa(ta)	'to plant'
3.	asa	asa-	'to carry flat things'
4.	usu	usu-	'to become sick'
5.	nasa	nasa	'nose'
6.	aski	hisk^{h}i	'to ask'
7.	muχsa	muχsa	'sweet'
8.	suniqi	sunaqi	'small spring'
9.	šanq'a	sanqa	'to snuffle'
10.	waša	wasa	'silent place'
11.	iši	isi	'dress'
12.	muši	musi	'to take care (of)'
13.	puši	pusi	'four'
14.	išt'a	hist'a-	'to close'
15.	išapa	isapa-	'to hear, listen'

(Cerrón-Palomino 2000: 145–6)

Exercise 5.2 Tulu

Tulu is a Dravidian language (of India) which has several varieties. Consider the following data from two principal varieties. Focus your attention only on the nasals. What will you reconstruct for these? How many nasals do you postulate for Proto-Tulu? State your evidence.

NOTE: j = [y̌], IPA [dʒ]; $n̠$ = IPA [ɳ].

	Shivalli	Sapaliga	gloss
1.	a:n̠ɨ	a:nɨ	'male'
2.	un̠ɨ	a:nɨ	'dine'
3.	man̠n̠ɨ	mannɨ	'soil'
4.	ko:n̠ɛ	ko:nɛ	'room'
5.	e:n̠ɨ	ya:nɨ	'I'
6.	ninɛ	ninɛ	'wick'
7.	ja:nɛ	da:nɛ	'what'
8.	sanɛ	tanɛ	'conceiving'

(Bhat 2001: 11)

Exercise 5.3 Polynesian

The Polynesian languages of the Pacific form a subgroup of the Oceanic branch of the Austronesian family of languages. (1) What are the sound correspondences found in these data? What sound do you reconstruct for the proto-language to represent each sound correspondence set? (2) What sound change or changes have taken place in each of these languages? (3) What is the best reconstruction (proto-form) for 6, 16, 20 and 32? Show how your postulated sound changes apply to each of these to produce the modern forms.

NOTE: <'> = [ʔ].

	Māori	Tongan	Samoan	Rarotongan	Hawai'ian	gloss
1.	tapu	tapu	tapu	tapu	kapu	'forbidden', 'taboo'
2.	pito	pito	pito	pito	piko	'navel'
3.	puhi	puhi	—	pu'i	puhi	'blow'
4.	taha	tafa 'edge'	tafa	ta'a	kaha	'side'
5.	tae 'trash'	ta'e	tae	tae	kae	'excrement'
6.	taŋata	taŋata	taŋata	taŋata	kanaka	'man, person'
7.	tai	tahi	tai	tai	kai	'sea'
8a.	kaha	kafa	'afa	ka'a	'aha	'strong'
8b.	ma:rohi-	malohi	malosi	ma:ro'i	—	'strong'

	Māori	Tongan	Samoan	Rarotongan	Hawai'ian	gloss
9.	karo	kalo	'alo	karo	'alo	'dodge'
10.	aka-	aka	a'a	aka	a'a	'root'
11.	au	'ahu	au	au	au	'gall'
12.	uru	'ulu	ulu	uru	ulu	'head'
	'tip of weapon'				'centre'	
13.	uhi	ufi	ufi	u'i	uhi	'yam'
14.	ahi	afi	afi	a'i	ahi	'fire'
15.	ɸa:	fa:	fa:	'a:	ha:	'four'
16.	ɸeke	feke	fe'e	'eke	he'e	'octopus'
17.	ika	ika	i'a	ika	i'a	'fish'
18.	ihu	ihu	isu	puta-i'u	ihu	'nose'
				'nostril' (puta 'hole')		
19.	hau	hau	sau	'au	hau	'dew'
	'wind' (hauku: 'dew' [-ku: 'showery weather'])					
20.	hika	—	si'a	'ika	hi'a	'firemaking'
21.	hiku	hiku	si'u	'iku	hi'u	'tail'
	'fishtail'					
22.	ake	hake	a'e	ake	a'e	'up'
23.	uru	—	ulu	uru	ulu	'enter'
24.	maŋa	maŋa	maŋa	maŋa	mana	'branch'
25.	mau	ma'u	mau	mau	mau	'constant'
	'fixed'					
26.	mara	—	mala	mara	mala	'fermented
	'marinated'					food'
27.	noho	nofo	nofo	no'o	noho	'sit'
28.	ŋaru	ŋaru	ŋalu	ŋaru	nalu	'wave'
29.	ŋutu	ŋutu	ŋutu	ŋutu	nuku	'mouth'
30.	waka	vaka	va'a	vaka	wa'a	'canoe'
31.	wae	va'e	vae	vae	wae	'leg'
32.	raho	laho	laso	ra'o	laho	'scrotum'
	'testicle'					
33.	rou	lohu	lou	rou	lou	'fruit-
	'long forked stick'					picking
						pole'
34.	roŋo	(loŋo-)	loŋo	roŋo	lono	'hear'
		(loŋo-a:'a 'noise', loŋo-noa 'silence')				
35.	rua	-lua	lua	rua	lua	'two'
		(in compounds)				

Exercise 5.4 Orokolo-Toaripi

Orokolo and Toaripi are two closely related Eleman languages (usually assigned to the Trans-New Guinea grouping, though this is as yet uncertain). Compare the data presented here and reconstruct Proto-Orokolo-Toaripi. (1) List the sound correspondences you find. (2) Give the proto-sounds you reconstruct to represent these. (3) Present the sound changes which you postulate that each language has undergone. (4) If there is any relative chronology involved among these changes, state what it is and the evidence for it. (5) Give your reconstruction of 12, 25 and 35 together with how the individual sound changes apply to these to produce the modern forms.

NOTE: for this problem, consider Orokolo *r* and *l* the same sound. Do not struggle over the difference between *ae* and *ai* in no. 38.

	Toaripi	*Orokolo*	*gloss*
1.	uti	uki	'bone'
2.	ete	eke	'vagina'
3.	tete	keke	'fish scales'
4.	tao	kao	'tooth'
5.	toare	koare	'senior'
6.	tola	kora	'tree'
7.	tolotolo	korokoro	'leaves'
8.	tapare	kapare	'grease'
9.	torea	korea	'theft'
10.	tururu	kurukuru	'thundering'
11.	aite	aire	'after'
12.	kite	kile	'mat'
13.	lauta	laura	'flame tree'
14.	ita	ila	'pig'
15.	puta	pura	'cloth'
16.	uta	ura	'hole'
17.	fi	hi	'cry'
18.	firu	hiru	'portion'
19.	fe	he	'penis'
20.	fere	here	'betel nut'
21.	fapai	hapa	'open'
22.	fave	have	'stone'
23.	forerai	horera	'appear'

	Toaripi	*Orokolo*	*gloss*
24.	furi	huri	'pus'
25.	afutae	ahurae	'ashes'
26.	sisia	hihia	'sour'
27.	siri	hiri	'mildew'
28.	ase	ahe	'sugarcane'
29.	seseroro	heheroro	'thin'
30.	sare	hare	'sun, day'
31.	sarea	harea	'sorcery'
32.	soa	hoa	'time'
33.	sua	hua	'pigeon'
34.	susu	huhu	'plank'
35.	farisa	harita	'arrow'
36.	marisa	marita	'girl'
37.	taisa	kaita	'paddle'
38.	saesa	haita	'dish'
39.	taisa	kaita	'paddle'
40.[=12]	kite	kile	'mat'
41.	kiva	kiva	'care'
42.	koko	koko	'narrow'
43.	ekaka	ekaka	'fish'

Exercise 5.5 *Lencan*

Compare the cognates from the two Lencan languages (both of which
have recently become extinct: Chilanga Lenca was spoken in El Salvador;
Honduran Lenca was spoken in Honduras). Work only with the consonants in this problem (the changes involving the vowels are too complex
to solve with these data alone). (1) Set up the correspondence sets; (2)
reconstruct the sounds of Proto-Lencan; (3) find and list the sound
changes which took place in each language; and (4) determine what the
relative chronology may have been in any cases where more than one
change took place in either individual language, if there is evidence
which shows this.

NOTE: *t'*, *k'* and *ts'* are glottalised consonants. Also, these data do not
provide enough information for you to recover all the consonants of the
proto-language, so that it will be difficult to apply steps 5 and 6 here.

	Honduran Lenca	Chilanga	gloss
1.	pe	pe	'two'
2.	lepa	lepa	'jaguar'
3.	puki	puka	'big'
4.	ta	ta	'cornfield'
5.	tem	tem	'louse'
6.	ke	ke	'stone'
7.	kuma	kumam	'fingernail, claw'
8.	katu	katu	'spider'
9.	waktik	watih	'sandals'
10.	kakma	k'ama	'gourd'
11.	siksik	sisih	'shrimp'
12.	nek	neh	'tooth'
13.	insek	ints'eh	'beak'
14.	taw	t'aw	'house'
15.	tutu	t'ut'u	'flea'
16.	kin	k'in	'road'
17.	kunan	k'ula	'who'
18.	kelkin	k'elkin	'tortilla griddle'
19.	sewe	ts'ewe	'monkey'
20.	saj	ts'aj	'five'
21.	musu	muts'u	'liver'
22.	sak-	ts'ih-	'to wash'
23.	lawa	lawa	'three'
24.	liwa-	liwa-	'to buy'
25.	tal-	tal-	'to drink'
26.	wala	wala	'raccoon'
27.	was	wal	'water'
28.	asa	alah	'head'
29.	wasan	wila	'urine'
30.	wara	wara	'river'
31.	siri	sirih	'star'

	Honduran Lenca	Chilanga	gloss
32.	sili	sili	'iron tree' (tree species)
33.	suri-sur	ʃurih	'squirrel'

[NOTE: *suri-sur* involves reduplications; just compare the *suri-* segment of it]

34.	saj-	ʃej-	'to want'
35.	so	ʃo	'rain'
36.	suna	ʃila	'flower'
37.	soko	ʃoko	'white'
38.	sak	ʃah	'firewood'
39.	wewe	wewe	'baby'
40.	jet-	jete-	'to laugh'
41.	juku	juku	'coyol palm' (palm tree species)
42.	sa	ʃam	'good'

Exercise 5.6 Jicaquean

Jicaque is a family of two languages in Honduras. Jicaque (Jicaque of El Palmar) is extinct; Tol (Jicaque of La Montaña de la Flor) is still spoken by a few hundred people, but has become extinct or nearly so everywhere except in the village of La Montaña de la Flor. Reconstruct Proto-Jicaque; state the sound correspondences which you encounter in the following cognate sets, and reconstruct a proto-sound for each. State the sound changes that have taken place in each language.

HINT: your reconstruction should include the following sounds:

p	t	ts	k	ʔ	i	ɨ	u
p^h	t^h	ts^h	k^h		e		o
p'	t'	ts'	k'			a	
		s					
		l					
m	n						
w		j		h			

What happens to each of the proto-sounds which you reconstruct in initial and in final position in these two languages? Can you make guesses about an appropriate reconstruction and sound changes to account for sounds in medial positions?

NOTE: the correspondences involving affricates and sibilants are quite complex, and you will need to pay special attention to the possibilities for combining some of the initial correspondence sets with some of the medial ones as reflecting the same proto-sound. The consonants *p'*, *t'*, *ts'*, *k'* are glottalized. The accent mark on a vowel (for example *á*) means that it is stressed; this is not relevant to the sound changes. In a few cases, a non-initial *h* does not match well in the two languages; ignore this, since it is due to changes for which you do not have enough evidence in these data. The hyphen (-) before some words, as in 9 (*-rɨk*), means that these occur with some other morpheme before them which is not relevant and so is not presented here.

	Jicaque	*Tol*	*gloss*
1.	pe	pe	'stone'
2.	pit	pis	'meat'
3.	pɨné	pɨné	'big'
4.	pɨga-	pɨʔa-	'jaguar'
5.	pen	pel	'flea'
6.	kamba	kampa	'far, long'
7.	arba-	alpa	'above'
8.	to-bwe	to-pwe	'to burn'
9.	-rɨk	-lɨp	'lip'
10.	kek	kep	'woman'
11.	ik	hip	'you'
12.	huruk	hulup	'grain' (of corn)
13.	huk	hup	'he, that'
14.	nak	nap	'I'
15.	-kuk	-kup	'we'
16.	te	te	'black'
17.	tek	tek	'leg'
18.	tebé	tepé	'he died'
19.	tɨt	tɨt'	'louse'
20.	mandɨ	mantɨ	'vulture'
21.	n-gon	n-kol	'my belly'
22.	harek	halek	'arrow'
23.	mak	mak	'foreigner'
24.	n-abuk	n-ajpʰuk	'my head'
25.	kon	kom	'liver'
26.[=6]	kamba	kampa	'far, long'

	Jicaque	Tol	gloss
27.	pɨrɨk	pɨlɨk	'much'
28.	keré	kelé	'nephew'
29.	mik	mik	'nose'
30.	korok	kolok	'spider'
31.	pʰe	pʰe	'white'
32.	pʰen	pʰel	'arm, shoulder'
33.	-pʰa	-pʰa	'dry'
34.	pʰɨja	pʰɨja	'tobacco'
35.	m-bat	m-pʰats'	'my ear'
36.	lɨbɨ-	lɨpʰɨ	'wind'
37.	pʰɨbɨh	pʰɨpʰɨh	'ashes'
38.	urubana	(j)ulupʰana	'four'
39.	ten	tʰem	'boa constrictor'
40.	tut	tʰutʰ	'spit'
41.	peten	petʰel	'wasp'
42.	kun	kʰul	'fish'
43.	ke-ke	(kʰ)ekʰe	'agouti'

[NOTE: *keke* is a reduplicated form and should be treated as the root *ke-* repeated, rather than as having an intervocalic *-k-*]

44.	kan	kʰan	'bed'
45.	kere	kʰele	'bone'
46.	to-gon-	to-kʰol	'to grind'
47.	kujuh	kʰujuh	'parrot'
48.	pɨt	p'is	'deer'
49.	m-bɨj	m-p'ɨj	'my body'
50.	pɨčá	p'ɨsá	'macaw'
51.	-te	-t'e	'to cut'
52.[=19]	tɨt	tɨt'	'louse'
53.	-tja	-t'ja	'to be late'
54.	mata	mat'a	'two'
55.	kat	ʔas	'blood'
56.	kot	ʔos	'I sit, am'
57.	kaw-	ʔaw-a	'fire'
58.	kona	ʔona	'sour'
59.	kan	ʔan	'zapote' (fruit)
60.[=4]	pɨga-	pɨʔa-	'jaguar'

	Jicaque	Tol	gloss
61.	te-ga	te-ʔa	'to give'
62.	čok	sok'	'tail'
63.	čorin	tsolin	'salt'
64.	ču(h)	tsu	'blue'
65.	čiwiri	-tsiwil-	'to lie'
66.	čigin-	tsikin	'summer'
67.	čoʔ-	tsoʔ-	'to nurse'
68.	čuba	tsupa	'to tie'
69.	nočot	notsots	'fly'
70.	ʃeme	ts^{h}eme	'horn'
71.	ʃijó	ts^{h}ijó	'dog'
72.	ʃe(w)	ts^{h}ew	'scorpion'
73.	čin	ts'il	'hair, root'
74.	-čun	ts'ul	'intestines'
75.	čoron	ts'olol	'oak'
76.	čih	ts'ih-	'caterpillar'
77.	te-neče	te-nets'e	'to sing'
78.	ločak	lots'ak	'sun'
79.	m-bat	m-p^{h}ats'	'my ear'
80.	čot	sots'	'owl'
81.	-čɨ	-sɨ	'water'
82.	čok	sok'	'tail'
83.[=2]	pit	pis	'meat'
84.	-mut	mus	'smoke'
85.	hoč(uruk)	hos-	'his heart'
86.[=50]	pɨčá	p'ɨsá	'macaw'
87.	mon	mol	'cloud'
88.[=25]	kon	kom	'liver'
89.	ma	ma	'land'
90.	wa	wa	'house'
91.	wara	wala	'forehead'
92.	jo	jo	'tree'
93.	he	he	'red'
94.[=22]	harek	halek	'arrow'

(Data from Campbell and Oltrogge 1980)

Exercise 5.7 K'ichean languages

K'ichean is a subgroup of the Mayan family. Compare these cognate forms and set up the sound correspondences; propose the most appropriate reconstruction for the sound in the proto-language for each, and write the sound changes which account for the developments in the daughter languages. Are any instances found in any of the individual languages in which it is necessary to state what the relative chronology of changes was?

NOTE: ɓ = voiced imploded bilabial stop; t', ts', č', k', q', m', w' = glottalized consonants. In Uspanteko, the accent mark over the vowel, as in ò:x 'avocado', indicates falling tone. Although the correspondence set in which Q'eqchi' *h* corresponds to *x* of the other languages is not found in these data before *u*, ignore this – this correspondence occurs in general with no restrictions that have anything to do with *u*.

NOTE: *y* = IPA [j], *š* = IPA [ʃ], *č* = IPA [tʃ] *C'* = glottalized [ejective] consonants.

Kaqchikel	Tz'utujil	K'iche'	Poqomam	Uspanteko	Q'eqchi'	gloss
1. pak	pak	pak	pak	pak	pak	'custard apple'
2. pur	pur	pur	pur	pur	pur	'snail'
3. pim	pim	pim	pim	pim	pim	'thick'
4. toʔ	toʔ	toʔ	toʔ	toʔ	toʔ	'to help'
5. tox	tox	tox	tox	tox	tox	'to pay'
6. kiʔ	kiʔ	kiʔ	kiʔ	kiʔ	kiʔ	'sweet'
7. ka:ʔ	ka:ʔ	ka:ʔ	ka:ʔ	ka:ʔ	ka:ʔ	'quern'(metate)
8. k'el	k'el	k'el	k'el	k'el	(k'el)	'parrot'
9. qa-	qa-	qa-	qa-	qa-	qa-	'our'
10. qul	qul	qul	—	qul	—	'neck'
11. q'o:l	q'ol	q'o:l	q'o:l	q'o:l	q'o:l	'resin, pitch'
12. q'an	q'an	q'an	q'an	q'an	q'an	'yellow'
13. si:p	si:p	si:p	si:p	si:p	si:p	'tick'
14. saq	saq	saq	saq	saq	saq	'white'
15. tsuy	tsuy	tsuh	suh	tsuh	suh	'water gourd'
16. uts	uts	uts	us	uts	us	'good'
17. tsats	tsats	tsats	sas	tsats	sas	'thick'
18. ts'iʔ	ts'iʔ	ts'iʔ	ts'iʔ	ts'iʔ	'ts'iʔ'	'dog'
19. če:ʔ	če:ʔ	če:ʔ	če:ʔ	če:ʔ	če:ʔ	'tree, wood'
20. ču:n	ču:n	ču:n	ču:n	ču:n	ču:n	'lime'
21. č'o:p	č'o:p	č'o:p	č'o:p	č'o:p	č'o:p	'pineapple'
22. xul	xul	xul	xul	xul	xul	'hole, cave'

	Kaqchikel	Tz'utujil	K'iche'	Poqomam	Uspanteko	Q'eqchi'	gloss
23.	winaq	winaq	winaq	winaq	winaq	kwinq	'person'
24.	we:š	we:š	we:š	we:š	—	kwe:š	'trousers'
25.	ya:x	ya:x	ya:x	ya:x	ya:x	ya:x	'genitals, shame'
26.	mu:x	mu:x	mu:x	mu:x	mù:x	mu:h	'shade'
27.	o:x	o:x	o:x	o:x	ò:x	o:h	'avocado'
28.	ča:x	ča:x	ča:x	ča:x	čà:x	ča:h	'ashes'
29.	tu:x	tu:x	tu:x	tu:x	tù:x	tu:h	'steambath'
30.	q'i:x	q'i:x	q'i:x	q'i:x	q'ì:x	(-q'ih)	'day, sun'
31.	ka:x	ka:x	ka:x	ka:x	kà:x	—	'sky'
32.	čax	čax	čax	čax	čax	čax	'pine'
33.	k'ax	k'ax	k'ax	k'ax	k'ax	k'ax	'flour'
34.	k'o:x	k'o:x	k'o:x	k'o:x	k'o:x	k'o:x	'mask'
35.	6a:y	6a:y	6a:h	w'a:h	6a:h	6a:h	'gopher'
36.	6a:q	6a:q	6a:q	w'a:q	6aq	6aq	'bone'
37.	6e:y	6e:y	6e:h	w'e:h	6e:h	6e:h	'road'
38.	si6	si6	si6	sim'	si6	si6	'smoke'
39.	xa6	xa6	xa6	xam'	xa6	ha6	'rain'
40.	xuku:ʔ	xuku:ʔ	xuku:6	xuku:m'	xuku:6	xuku6	'canoe, trough'
41.	a:q'aʔ	a:q'aʔ	a:q'a6	a:q'am'	a:q'a6	(a:q'6)	'night'
42.	xal	xal	xal	xal	xal	hal	'ear of corn'
43.	xe:y	xe:y	xe:h	xe:h	xe:h	he:h	'tail'
44.	č'o:y	č'o:y	č'o:h	č'o:h	č'o:h	č'o:h	'mouse, rat'
45.	k'yaq	k'yaq	k'yaq	k'aq	k'aq	k'aq	'flea'
46.	kyaq	kyaq	kyaq	kaq	kaq	kaq	'red'
47.	(i)kyaq'	(i)kyaq'	kyaq'	kaq'	—	—	'guava'
48.	išk'yaq	šk'yaq	išk'yaq	išk'aq	išk'aq	—	'fingernail'
49.	winaq	winaq	winaq	winaq	winaq	kwinq	'person'
50.	šikin	šikin	šikin	šikin	šikin	(šikn)	'ear'
51.	išoq	išoq	išoq	išoq	—	išq	'woman'
52.	nimaq	nimaq	nimaq	nimaq	nimaq	ninq	'big' (plural)
53.	sanik	sanik	sanik	(sanik)	sanik	sank	'ant'
54.	suʔt	suʔt	suʔt	suʔt	sù:t'	(suʔut)	'cloth, kerchief'
55.	poʔt	poʔt	poʔt	poʔt	pò:t'	poʔot	'blouse'
56.	piʔq	piʔq	piʔq	piʔq	pì:q'	—	'corncob'
57.	atiʔt	atiʔt	atiʔt	atiʔt	atì:t'	atiʔt	'grandmother'
58.	k'ax	k'ax	k'ax	k'ax	k'ax	k'ax	'flour'

Kaqchikel	Tz'utujil	K'iche'	Poqomam	Uspanteko	Q'eqchi'	gloss
59. k'ay	k'ay	k'ah	k'ah	k'ah	k'ah	'bitter'
60. k'ay	k'ay	k'ay	k'ay	k'ay	k'ay	'to sell'
61. mo:y	mo:y	mo:y	mo:y	mo:y	mo:y	'blind' (dark)
62. ča:x	ča:x	ča:x	ča:x	čà:x	ča:h	'ashes'
63. čax	čax	čax	čax	čax	čax	'pine'
64. č'ax	č'ax	č'ax	—	č'ax	č'ax	'to wash'
65. č'ay	č'ay	č'ay	č'ay	—	—	'to hit'

Exercise 5.8 Quechuan

Quechuan is a family of several languages spoken in the Andes region of South America, with varieties found in Columbia, Ecuador, Peru, Bolivia and Argentina.

Compare the cognates from the languages listed here. Set up the correspondence sets; reconstruct the sounds of Proto-Quechuan; find and list the sound changes which took place in each language (variety); determine what the relative chronology may have been in any cases where more than one change took place in an individual language (variety), if there is evidence which shows this. What do you think the inventory of Proto-Quechuan sounds was? (Note that there is some controversy about the historical status of glottalized consonants (p', t', č', k', q') and aspirated consonants (p^h, t^h, č^h, k^h, q^h) in Quechuan. For the purposes of this exercise do not try to reconstruct them, but rather treat those few which occur (in the Cuzco variety) as though they were equal to the plain counterparts.) (NOTE: [ɴ] = uvular nasal; y = IPA [j]; l^y = IPA [lʲ]; n^y = IPA [nʲ].

Ancash	Junín	Cajamarca	Amazonas	Ecuador	Ayacucho	Cuzco	gloss
1. paka-	paka-	paka-	paka-	paka-	paka-	paka-	'begin'
2. apa-	apa-	apa-	apa-	apa-	apa-	apa-	'wash'
3. rapra	lapla	rapra	rapra	—	rapra	raɸra	'leaf, wing'
4. ampa	pampa	pamba	pamba	pamba	pampa	pampa	'plains'
5. tapu-	tapu-	tapu-	tapu-	tapu-	tapu-	tapu-	'ask'
6. wata-	wata-	wata-	wata-	wata-	wata-	wata-	'tie'
7. utka	utka	utka	utka	—	utka	usk^{h}a	'cotton'
8. inti	inti	indi	indi	indi	inti	inti	'sun'

179

	Ancash	Junín	Cajamarca	Amazonas	Ecuador	Ayacucho	Cuzco	gloss
9.	kimsa	kimsa	kimsa	kimsa	kimsa	kimsa	kimsa	'three'
10.	puka	puka	—	puka	puka	puka	puka	'red'
11.	haksa-	saksa-	saksa-	saxsa-	saxsa-	saksa-	saxsa-	'be full, fed up'
12.	kuŋka	kuŋka	kuŋga	kuŋga	kuŋga	kuŋka	kuŋka	neck
13.	qam	am	qam	kam	kaŋ	Xam	qaŋ	'you' (sg.)
14.	qoha	usa	qosa	kusa	kusa	Xosa	qosa	'husband'
15.	waɢa-	waʔa-	waɢa-	waka-	waka-	waXa-	waqa-	'cry'
16.	hoXta	suʔta	soXta	sukta	suxta	soXta	soXta	'six'
17.	heŋɢa	siŋʔa	seŋɢa	siŋga	siŋga	seŋXa	seŋqa	'nose'
18.	tsaki	čaki	čaki	čaki	čaki	čaki	č'aki	'dry'
19.	mutsa-	muča-	muča-	muča-	muča-	muča-	muč'a-	'kiss'
20.	mantsa-	manča-	manča-	manča-	manča-	manča-	manča-	'fear, be afraid'
21.	putska-	pučka-	pučka-	pučka-	puʃka-	pučka-	puska-	'to thread'
22.	e:tsa	ajča	ajča	e:ča	ajča	ajča	ajča	'meat'
23.	čaki	caki	caki	caki	caki	čaki	čaki	'foot'
24.	kača-	ǩaca-	ǩaca-	ǩaca-	ǩaca-	kača-	kača-	'send'
25.	učpa	ucp̌a	ucp̌a	ucp̌a	uʃpa	učpa	uspʰa	'ashes'
26.	kički	kǐcki	kǐcki	kǐcki	kiʃki	kički	k'iski	'narrow'
27.	haru-	salu-	saru-	saru-	saru-	saru-	saru-	'to step on'
28.	hara	sala	sara	sara	sara	sara	sara	'maize, corn'
29.	qaha	asa	qasa	kasa	kasa	Xasa	qasa	'ice'
30.	isqoŋ	isʔuŋ	esqoŋ	iʃkuŋ	iʃkuŋ	isXoŋ	esqoŋ	'nine'
31.	—	ajsa-	ajsa-	e:sa-	ajsa-	ajsa-	ajsa-	'pull'
32.	ʃulʸka	ʃulʸka	ʃuʃka	ʃuĵka	—	sulʸka	sulʸk'a	'feather '
33.	waʃa	waʃa	waʃa	waʃa	waʃa	wasa	wasa	'behind'
34.	iʃke:	iʃkaj	iʃkaj	iʃke:	iʃkaj	iskaj	iskaj	'two'
35.	hatuŋ	hatuŋ	atuŋ	atuŋ	hatuŋ	hatuŋ	hatuŋ	'big'
36.	hutsa	huča	uča	uča	huča	huča	huča	'fault'
37.	humpi	humpi	—	umbi	humbi	humpi	hump'i	'sweat'
38.	laki	lʸaki	ʒaki	ĵaki	ʒaki	lʸaki	lʸaki	pain, trouble
39.	kila	kilʲa	kiʒa	kiĵa	kiʒa	kilʲa	kilʲa	moon

180

	Ancash	Junín	Cajamarca	Amazonas	Ecuador	Ayacucho	Cuzco	gloss
40.	alba	alʲpa	aʃpa	aǰpa	aʒpa	alʲpa	halʲp'a	land
41.	aylu	aylʸu	aj3u	e:ǰu	ay3u	aylʸju	aylʸu	family
42.	rima-	lima-	rima-	rima-	rima-	rima-	rima-	to speak
43.	karu	kalu	karu	karu	karu	karu	karu	far
44.	warmi	walmi	warmi	warmi	warmi	warmi	warmi	woman
45.	waχra	waʔla	waχra	wakra	—	waχra	waχra	horn
46.	nina	nina	nina	nina	nina	nina	nina	'fire'
47.	yana	yana	yana	yana	yana	yana	yana	'black'
48.	wayna	wayna	wayna	wayna	wayna	wayna	wayna	'young man'
49.	aŋya-	aŋya-	aŋya-	aŋya-	aŋya-	aŋya	aŋya-	'to reprove'
50.	nawi	nʸawi	nʸawi	nʸawi	nʸawi	nʸawi	nʸawi	'eye'
51.	wanu-	wanʸu-	wanʸu-	wanʸu-	wanʸu-	wanʸu-	wanʸu-	'to die'
52.	qepa	ipa	qepa	kipa	kipa	χepa	qʰepa	'behind'
53.	weqe	wiʔi	—	wiki	wiki	weχe	weqe	'tear(drop)' (noun)
54.	qeʃpi-	iʃpi-	—	kiʃpi-	kiʃpi-	χeʃpi-	qeʃpi-	'to escape'
55.	qo-	u-	qo-	—	ku-	χo-	qo-	'to give'
56.	qoṇGa-	uŋʔa-	qoŋGa-	kuŋga-	kuŋga-	χoŋχa-	qoŋqa-	'to forget'

Exercise 5.9   Saami (Lapp)

There are ten Saami languages, in northern Scandinavia (Norway, Sweden, and Finland) and adjacent Russia. The Saami language family is a subgroup of Finno-Ugric. Compare the following cognate sets, and focus only on initial consonants. (1) What are the consonantal sound correspondences in word-initial position found in these data? What sound do you reconstruct in the proto-language to represent each of these sound correspondence sets? (2) What sound change or changes have taken place in these consonants in each of these languages? (3) If more than one change is involved in any of these languages, can you determine their relative chronology? What evidence leads you to this conclusion?

NOTE: The cognates are missing for some of the languages in some of the cognate sets. Also, there are insufficient cognate sets to reconstruct the full inventory of Proto-Saami consonants. Double sounds are phonetically geminate or long, for example *aa* = [a:], *kk* = [k:], *ll* = [l:]; *c* = [ts]; *ɜ* = an open mid central vowel.

Lule	*North*	*Ume*	*Inari*	*Kildin*	*gloss*
1. palva	balva	balva	polva	pɜllv	'cloud'
2. pallat	(ballat)	ballat	poollað	pɜlleð	'to fear
3. paauhtjas	baavčas	baaktjas	pooučas	pɜfčas	'sore, pain' (n., adj.)
4. piehtsee	bæcce	biehtsee	peeci	pieʒʒ	'pine'
5. piellee	bælle	bielle	peeli	piell	'half, side'
6. pɔrrɔt	borrat	bɔrrat	puurrað	poorreð	'to eat'
7. paatsooi	boaʒo	bɔɔtsoi	poazuj	poaʒ	'reindeer'
8. tɔllɔ	dolla	tɔlla	tulla	tooll	'fire'
9. tihkkee	dikke	dihkee	tikke	tɨkk	'louse'
10. taktee	dakte	daktee	tæhti	taaxxt	'bone'
11. tahkat	dakkat	dahkat	toohað	tɜggeð	'to do, make'
12. tavvee(n)	davve	divve-	tavve	tavv	'deep'
13. karras	garas	garas	kooras	kɜras	'hard'
14. kaskas	gaskas	gasskas	koska-	kɜssk	'middle'
15. kalmee	galbme	galbmee		kaalm	'grave'
16. kiessee	gæsse	giessee	keesi	kiess	'summer'
17. kiehta	gietta	giahta	kieta	kiidd	'hand'
18. kɔlmɔ	golbma	gulbma	kulma	kollm	'three'
19. kɔɔhtee	goatte	gɔɔhtee	koati	kuedd	'hut'
20. kuokte	guokte	güikte	küehti	kuuxxt	'two'
21. kuollee	guolle	güellee	küeli	kuull	'fish'
22. tsaahkeet	tsakket	tsaahkeet	tsææhið	tsaaggeð	'to push'
23. tsɔɔhkee	tsoakke	tsɔɔhkee	tsoahi	cuegg	'shallow, low'
24. tsiptsoot	tsiktsot		tsiptsið	tipptse	'to squeeze, pinch'
25. tʲoarvve	čoarvi		čuarvi	čuərvv	'horn'
26. tʲoajvve	čoavʲɨ		čuavʲɨ		'belly'
27. tʲahppat	čahppat		čappað		'black'
28. tʲalmme	čalbmi		čalme	čalʲmm	'eye'
29. dakte	dakti		tæhti		'bone'
30. dihkke	dihkki		tikke	tʲihkkʲ	'louse'

	Lule	North	Ume	Inari	Kildin	gloss
31.	diehtet	diehtit		tiettið		'know'
32.	guhkke	guhkki		kukke	kuk^j	'long'
33.	guokta	guokte		kyehti		'two'
34.	lɔdde	loddi		lodde	laan^{j}n^{j}t	'bird'
35.	mɔn	mun		mun	mun	'I'
36.	namma	namma		nomma	nəmm	'name'
37.	niehkke	niehkki		niekki		'nape of neck'
38.	n^{j}almme	n^{j}albmi		n^{j}ælmi	n^{j}aɭ^{j}mm	'mouth'
39.	suovva	suovva		suova	suvv	'smoke'
40.	vaimmo	vaibmu		vaimu	—	'heart'

(Based on data from Lehtiranta 1989, Sammallahti 1998.)

6

Linguistic Classification

Stability in language is synonymous with rigor mortis.

(Ernest Weekley)

6.1 Introduction

How are languages classified and how are family trees established? *Subgrouping*, as the classification of which languages are more closely related to one another in a language family is called, is an important part of historical linguistics, and methods and criteria for subgrouping are the focus of this chapter. Before turning to these methods, however, let us first look briefly at some of the *language families* around the world.

6.2 The World's Language Families

There are some 250 to 300 distinct language families in the world; some indication of where these families are found and how many of them there are in each region is seen in Table 6.1. However, historical

TABLE 6.1: Distribution of language families in the world

Americas:	c. 180+ language families, 2,000+ languages
New Guinea (Papuan):	c. 25+ language families, 750–800 languages
Australia:	26 language families, c. 250 languages
Africa:	c. 20+ families, 2,500+ languages
Europe + Asia:	37 families (18 = isolates)
Europe:	5 surviving families (Indo-European, Uralic and Basque, plus several small Turkic languages and Maltese (Semitic) of Malta in the Mediterranean)

linguistic research has reached an advanced state in only a few of these. For example, Sino-Tibetan (c. 300 languages) is an extremely important family, since its languages are spoken by more people than those of any other language family in the world. Nevertheless, comparative linguistic research in this family is actually quite recent, flourishing only in the last thirty years or so. Its classification has been and continues to be controversial, with many Chinese scholars placing the Hmong-Mien (Miao-Yao) and Tai-Kadai languages also in the family, where most other scholars limit the family to the Chinese and Tibeto-Burman languages. A few of the better-known families, together with an indication of the state of comparative linguistic research in each, are presented in Table 6.2.

TABLE 6.2: Some of the better-known language families

Algonquian (North America, c. 35 languages, very advanced)

Athabaskan (North America, c. 30 languages, relatively good)

Austronesian (c. 800 languages, relatively good, much remains to be done in branches)

Bantu (c. 400 languages, moderate)

Berber (North Africa, c. 35 languages, much needed)

Cariban (South America, c. 60 languages, much needed)

Chadic (Africa, c. 140 languages, much work needed)

Chibchan (Central and South America, c. 20 languages, moderately good)

Cushitic (Africa, c. 40 languages, much needed)

Dravidian (c. 25 languages, moderate)

Hmong-Mien (Miao-Yao; c. 15 languages, much needed)

Indo-European (includes c. 25 Romance languages, many Iranian and Indic languages, c. 85 languages in Europe; the most studied of all language families)

Kartvelian (South Caucasian, 4 languages, advanced)

Maipurean (Arawakan) (South America, 65 languages, much needed)

Mayan (Mexico and Central America, 31 languages, very advanced)

Mon-Khmer (more than 100 languages, much needed)

Munda (India, c. 25 languages, much needed)

North Caucasian (30–35 languages, much needed)

Otomanguean (Mexico and Central America, c. 40 languages, good)

Salishan (North America, 23 languages, good)

Semitic (20–25 languages, moderately good)

Sino-Tibetan (c. 300 languages, much needed)

Siouan (North America, c. 20 languages, good)

Tai (c. 40 languages, moderate)

Tupian (South America, c. 60 languages, much needed)
Turkic (25–35 languages, moderate)
Uralic (northern Eurasia, c. 25 languages, highly advanced)
Uto-Aztecan (c. 35 languages, advanced)

There is also a number of other proposed language families which are accepted by many scholars, but still held to be controversial by some. Some of these are:

> Afro-Asiatic (Africa and the Near East, includes Berber, Chadic, Cushitic, Egyptian and Semitic);
>
> Austro-Asiatic (Southeast Asia and India, includes Munda, Mon-Khmer, Nicobarese) (accepted by most scholars);
>
> Elamite-Dravidian
>
> Pama-Nyungan (Australia, c. 195 languages).

There are also numerous proposed remote relationships which are not widely accepted and are more highly disputed. These are considered in Chapter 13.

6.3 Terminology

Linguistic classification is about the relationships among languages (and language varieties); to see how it works, it is important to understand the terminology used.

Subgrouping is about the internal classification of the languages within language families; it is about the branches of a family tree and about which sister languages are most closely related to one another. The terminology employed in linguistic classifications can be confusing, since the terms are not always used consistently and there is controversy concerning the validity of some of the kinds of entities which some labels are intended to identify. Therefore, it is important to begin by clarifying this terminology. In linguistic classification, we need names for a range of entities which distinguish language groups of greater and lesser relatedness, that is, entities with different degrees of internal diversity (time depth), each more inclusive than the level below it.

Dialect means only a variety (regional or social) of a language, which is mutually intelligible with other dialects of the same language. 'Dialect' is not used in historical linguistics to mean a little-known ('exotic') or minority language, and it is no longer used to refer to a daughter language of a language family, though the word has sometimes been used in these senses.

Language means any distinct linguistic entity (variety) which is mutually unintelligible with other such entities.

A language *family* is a group of genetically related languages, that is, languages which share a linguistic kinship by virtue of having developed from a common ancestor. Many linguistic families are designated with the suffix *-an*, as in, for example, *Algonquian, Austronesian, Indo-European, Sino-Tibetan* and so on. In recent times, many scholars have begun to use the term *genetic unit* to refer to any language family or isolate. An *isolate* is a language which has no known relatives, that is, a family with but a single member. Some of the best-known isolates are Ainu, Basque, Burushaski, Etruscan, Gilyak (Nivkh), Sumerian, Tarascan, Zuni, and several others in the Americas.

Language families can be of different magnitudes; that is, they can involve different time depths, so that some larger-scale families may include smaller-scale families among their members or branches. Unfortunately, however, a number of confusing terms have been utilized in attempts to distinguish more inclusive from less inclusive family groupings.

The term *subgroup* (also called *subfamily, branch*) is relatively straightforward; it is used to refer to a group of languages within a language family which are more closely related to each other than to other languages of that family – that is, a subgroup is a branch of a family. As a proto-language (for example, Proto-Indo-European) diversifies, it develops daughter languages (such as Proto-Germanic, Proto-Celtic and so on, in the case of Indo-European); if a daughter (for instance Proto-Germanic) then subsequently splits up and develops daughter languages of its own (such as English, German and so on), then the descendants (English, German and others, in the case of Germanic) of that daughter language (Proto-Germanic) constitute members of a subgroup (the Germanic languages), and the original daughter language (Proto-Germanic) becomes in effect an intermediate proto-language, a parent of its own immediate descendants (its daughters, English, German and so on), but still at the same time a descendant (daughter) itself of the original proto-language (Proto-Indo-European).

A number of terms have also been used for postulated but undemonstrated higher-order, more inclusive families (proposed but as yet unproven distant genetic relationships); these include *stock, phylum, macrofamily,* and the compounding element '*macro-*' (as in *Macro-Mayan, Macro-Penutian, Macro-Siouan* and the like). These terms have proved confusing and controversial, as might be expected when names are at stake for entities that have been postulated but where agreement is lacking. In order to avoid confusion and controversy, none of these terms should be used. That is, the term *family* is sufficient and clear.

Since the entities called 'stock', 'phylum' and 'macro-' would be bona fide language families if they could be established (demonstrated) on the basis of the linguistic evidence available, and they will not be families if the proposals which they embody fail to hold up, it is much clearer to refer to these proposed but as yet unsubstantiated relationships as 'proposed distant genetic relationships' or 'postulated families'. The question of distant genetic relationships – how to determine whether languages not yet known to be related to one another may be distantly related – is much debated (see Chapter 13).

6.4 How to Draw Family Trees: Subgrouping

Subgrouping is the internal classification of language families to deter-mine which sister languages are most closely related to one another. It is common for a language over time to diversify, that is, to split up into two or more daughter languages (with the consequence that the earlier language ceases to be spoken except as reflected in its descendants) – this means that the original language comes to constitute a proto-language. After the break-up of the original proto-language, a daughter language (for example, Western Romance, which split off from Proto-Romance) may itself subsequently diversify into daughters of its own (Western Romance split up into Spanish, Portuguese, French and others). This gives the first daughter language to branch off (Western Romance in our example) an intermediate position in the family tree – it is a daughter of the original proto-language (Proto-Romance) and it is an ancestor to its own daughters (Western Romance is the parent of Spanish, Portuguese and French). So, the languages which branch off from the intermediate language (Western Romance) belong to the same subgroup (Spanish, Portuguese and French are more immediate daughters of Western Romance, thus belonging to the Western Romance subgroup, which itself belongs to the Romance family). A subgroup, then, is all the daughters which descend from an ancestor (intermediate proto-language) which itself has at least one sister. To say that certain languages belong to the same subgroup means that they share a common parent language which is itself a daughter of a higher-order proto-language, just as English is a descendant of Proto-Germanic (together with its other Germanic sister languages, such as German, Swedish, Icelandic and others) and so is a member of the Germanic subgroup, which in turn is a daughter of (branch of) Proto-Indo-European, together with other subgroups (such as Slavic, Italic, Celtic, Indo-Iranian and so on, which have their own later daughter languages). Also, after the break-up of the original proto-language, a daughter language may remain unified; such a language which branches off directly from the proto-language and does not later split up into other languages constitutes a subgroup (branch) of the family all by itself, a subgroup with only a single member. The goal of subgrouping is to determine which languages belong to intermediate parents. The purpose of subgrouping is to determine the family tree for genetically related languages. An example of a family tree has already been seen in Chapter 5 in Figure 5.1 for the Proto-Romance family tree. Since examples from the Indo-European and Uralic families are cited frequently in this book, and because so much historical linguistic work has been done on these, their family trees are presented in Figures 6.1 and 6.2. The Austronesian family tree is also presented, in Figure 6.3. Frequent examples from Mayan languages are also cited here; the Mayan family tree is given in Figure 6.4.

The particular family trees presented here for Indo-European (Figure 6.1) and Uralic (Figure 6.2) are representative, but far from universally agreed upon. In both families, there is general agreement about the major lower-level subgroups (subfamilies), where the evidence is fairly clear. However, there is disagreement about the higher-order branches. In both families, the evidence for the higher branches, those closer to the proto-language, is limited and often unclear. The most common tree given traditionally for Indo-European usually presents some ten separate subgroups branching directly from Proto-Indo-European with little intermediate branching for higher-order subgroups. The Indo-European family tree presented in Figure 6.1 incorporates some recent hypotheses about higher-order branching, but this is still inconclusive. The position of Albanian, in particular, is unclear. Other ancient Indo-European languages should also be represented, for example, Phrygian, Thracian, Illyrian, Messapic and Venetic, though where they should appear in the tree is less clear. For more details about the internal branchings in the Romance subgroup, see Figure 5.1 in Chapter 5. (For discussion of the classification of Indo-European, see Garrett 1999, Jasanoff 2003, Mallory and Adams 1997: 550–6, and Ringe, Warnow and Taylor 2002.)

The Uralic tree given in Figure 6.2 represents a more traditional classification of the family, though recent opinion is divided. Some find little support for the branching classification with its higher-order intermediate subgroups (see Häkkinen 1984, 2001: 169–71, Salminen 2001). Others are sympathetic to the problems pointed out due to the limited evidence for higher-order internal branches, but nevertheless see sufficient evidence to support much of the branching classification (see Sammallahti 1988, 1998: 119–22). There is fairly general agreement

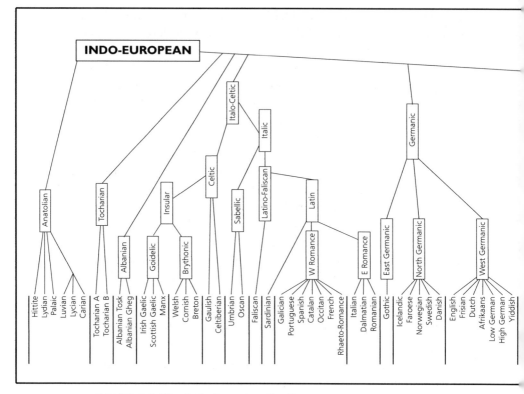

FIGURE 6.1: The Indo-European family tree (above and opposite)

that the former Volgaic branch (not given here), which would group Mari and Mordvin more closely together, should be abandoned. Salminen (2001) would prefer to drop not just this branch, but most of the others, leaving several groups diverging directly from the proto-language with very little intermediate branching in any of these. (For discussion, see Abondolo 1998, Häkkinen 1984, 2001, Janhunen 2001, Salminen 2001, Sammallahti 1988, 1998: 119–22.)

The Austronesian family tree is given in Figure 6.3. It provides another example of a family tree and the subgrouping which it represents (after Ross, Pawley and Osmond 1998: 6). In this figure, note that the names in italics indicate groups of languages which have no exclusively shared common ancestor. Thus, for example, *Formosan languages* refers to a collections of languages all descended from Proto-Austronesian (along with Proto-Malayo-Polynesian), but there is not assumed to be any 'Proto-Formosan'.

The only generally accepted criterion for subgrouping is *shared innovation*. A shared innovation is a linguistic change which shows a

190

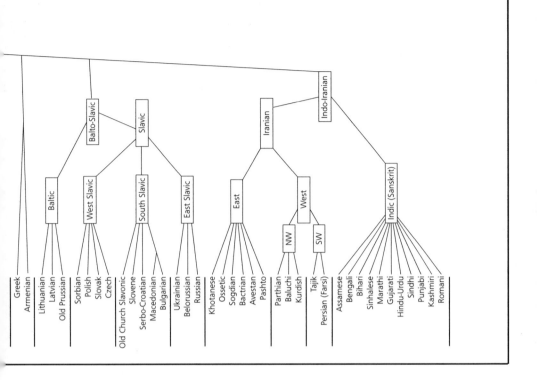

departure (innovation) from some trait of the proto-language and is shared by a subset of the daughter languages. It is assumed that a shared innovation is the result of a change which took place in a single daughter language which then subsequently diversified into daughters of its own, each of which inherits the results of the change. Thus the innovation is shared by the descendants of this intermediate parent but is not shared by languages in other subgroups of the family, since they do not descend from the intermediate parent that underwent the change which the more closely related languages share through inheritance from their more immediate parent. The fact that they share the innovation means that they contain evidence which suggests that they were formerly a unified language which underwent the change and then subsequently split up, leaving evidence of this change in its daughters.

The classification of the Mayan languages will serve as a guided exercise to illustrate how subgrouping is done, and we will examine how shared innovations among these languages determine their subgrouping. Let us look first at the classification which has been established, given

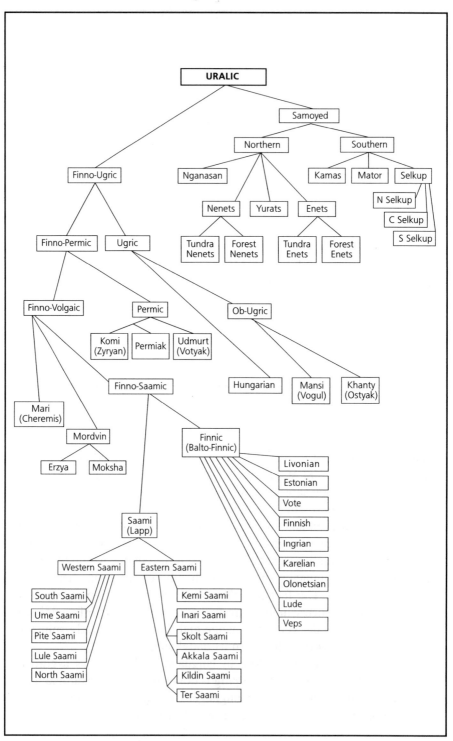

FIGURE 6.2: The Uralic family tree

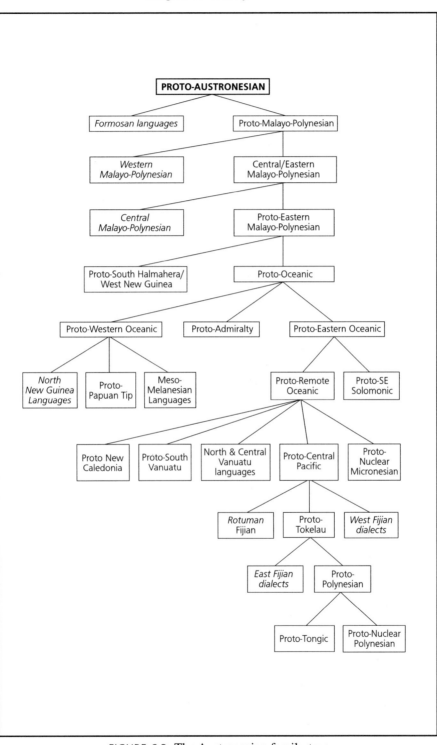

FIGURE 6.3: The Austronesian family tree

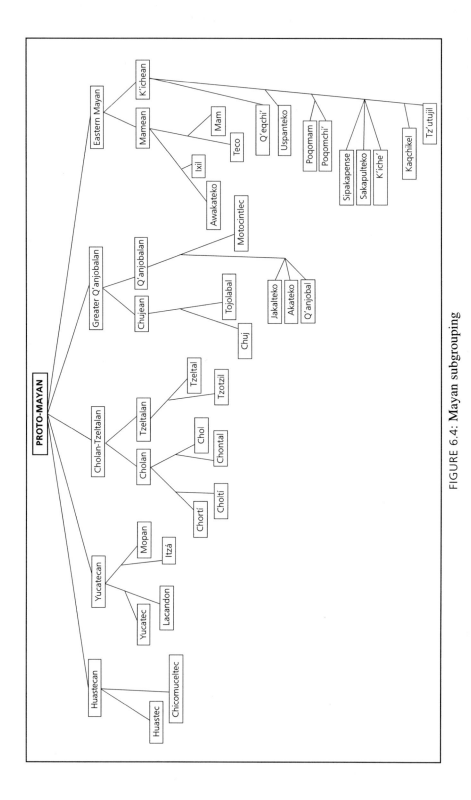

FIGURE 6.4: Mayan subgrouping

in the family tree in Figure 6.4, and then we will consider some of the shared innovations upon which the subgrouping is based.

Given that there are thirty-one Mayan languages and each has undergone several sound changes, we consider only a subset of the many shared innovations to give an idea of how subgroups are established. The following is a list of the major sound changes which are innovations shared among some but not others of the languages of the family. These form the basis for subgrouping the Mayan languages.

(1) *w > Ø / #__ (before *u, o, i, a*) (for example, **winaq* > Huastec *inik* 'person')

(2) *ŋ > w / #__, h /__# (**ŋe:h* > Huastec *we:w* 'tail', **o:ŋ* > Huastec *uh* 'avocado')

(3) **ts, **t̯ > t; *ts', *t̯' > t' (The *t̯* represents a fronted "*t̯*", perhaps palatalized, in traditional Mayan reconstructions.) (**tse?-* > Huastec *te?-* 'laugh')

(4) **-h > -y (final *h* became *y*) (**6a:h* > Kaqchikel *6a:y* 'gopher')

(5) **-6 > -? / VCV__# (in polysyllabic forms final imploded *b* became a glottal stop) (Kaqchikel *xuna:?* 'year' <**xun + ha:6* 'one year')

(6) **h > ? (**ha?* > Mam *?a?* 'water',

(7) **r > t (**ri:x* > Mam *ti:x* 'old man')

(8) **t > č (**tap* > Mam *čap* 'crab')

(9) **č > č̣ (alveopalatal affricate > laminal retroflex affricate) (**č'am* > Mam *č̣'am* 'sour')

(10) **-t > -č (word-final *t* changed to *č*) (**naxt* > Yucatec *ná:č* 'far')

(11) **e: > i, *o: > u (long mid vowels raised to high vowels) (**so:ts'* > Chol *suts'* 'bat')

(12) **ŋ > x̣ (velar nasal > a kind of velar fricative) (**ŋa:h* > K'iche' *xa:h* 'house')

(13) **t̯ > ć (a fronted *t* [dental or palatalized] changed to *ć* [a prepalatal affricate]) (**t̯e:?* > Mam *tse:?*, K'iche' **če:?* 'tree')

(14) **CV?VC > CV?C (**xo?oq* > K'iche' *xo?q* 'corn husk, maize leaf')

(15) *ć > č (the prepalatal affricates became palato-alveolar) (**t̯e:?* > **će:?* > K'iche' **če:?* 'tree')

(16) **q > k, *q' > k' (the uvular stops became velars) (**saq* > Huastec *θak*, Yucatec *sak*, Chol *sak* 'white')

(17) **ŋ > n (**ŋe:h* > Chol *neh* 'tail')

(18) **ts > s (**tsuh* > Q'eqchi' *suh* 'bottlegourd')

(Note that innovations in morphology and syntax are just as important as phonological innovations. Examples involving sound change are utilized here only because it takes less space to describe them than changes in other areas of the grammar usually do.)

Let us begin by looking at the lower-level groupings (the languages most closely related) for ease of illustration. In the Huastecan subgroup, Huastec and Chicomuceltec share the changes (1), (2) and (3). Other Mayan languages did not undergo these changes. We interpret this to mean that Huastec and Chicomuceltec belong together as members of a single subgroup: while Proto-Huastecan was still a unified language, it underwent these sound changes (and others not presented here). After having undergone these changes, Proto-Huastecan split up into its two daughter languages, Huastec and Chicomuceltec. As a consequence of this shared history, when we examine cognates, we see in both Huastec and Chicomuceltec that the cognates show the results of these sound changes, shared innovations, not shared by the cognates in the other Mayan languages. Looking backwards, it is because they share these innovations that we postulate that there was an earlier unified Proto-Huastecan language which underwent these changes before it diversified into the two daughter languages of this branch of the family.

Kaqchikel and Tz'utujil share the two innovations (4) and (5), which show that these two languages are more closely related to one another than to the others, since none of the others has evidence of these changes. Here we assume that there was a unified language which underwent the two changes and then later split up into Kaqchikel and Tz'utujil, accounting for why these two languages share the results of these changes. The alternative would require us to assume that these two languages are not closely related but just happened independently to undergo changes (4) and (5). Such a coincidence is not likely.

The four Mamean languages, Ixil, Awakateko, Mam and Teco, share a series of innovations, (6) through (9) (and others not mentioned here); these include a chain shift in which Proto-Mayan (PM) *r* became *t* (7), while *t* in turn became *č* (8), and *č* in turn changed to Mamean *č* (9) (a chain shift mentioned in Chapter 2).

The four Yucatecan languages (Yucatec, Lacandon, Mopan and Itzá) share innovation (10) (final *-t* > *-č*), among others.

The Cholan languages, but no others, share change (11) (raising of long mid vowels, *e*: > *i*, *o*: > *u*).

At higher, more inclusive levels of the classification, all the languages of the K'ichean and Mamean groups share the innovations (12) through (14), showing that they all descend from a common parent language,

Proto-Eastern Mayan, which had itself branched off from Proto-Mayan.

We proceed in this fashion (not all the evidence is presented here) until we have worked out the classification of all the Mayan languages and subgroups, both lower-level and higher-order ones, and it is on this basis that we draw the family tree presented in Figure 6.4.

It might be asked, why would just a list of shared similarities not be enough to distinguish more closely related languages from more distantly related ones within a language family? Because not just any similarity provides reliable evidence of closer affinity. For example, it is important to keep in mind that *shared retentions* are of practically no value for sub-grouping. A shared retention is merely something that different daughter languages inherit unchanged from the proto-language regardless of whether the daughters belong to the same subgroup or not. For example, Huastec, Mam and Motocintlec (which, as seen in Figure 6.4, belong to separate branches of the family) retain the vowel-length contrast, but this is not evidence that these three necessarily belong to a single sub-group of Mayan, sharing a period of common history, not shared by the other languages of the family. Rather, since Proto-Mayan had con-trastive vowel length, the fact that Huastec, Mam and Motocintlec share this trait means only that these three still retain unchanged some-thing that Proto-Mayan had, and they could retain this inherited trait regardless of whether they belonged together to a single subgroup or to separate subgroups each of which independently retained this feature of the proto-language. Shared retentions just do not reveal which languages share a period of common history *after* the break-up of the proto-language.

Although shared innovation is the only generally accepted criterion for subgrouping, not all shared innovations are of equal value for show-ing closer kinship. Some shared innovations represent sound changes that are so natural and happen so frequently cross-linguistically that they may easily take place independently in different branches of a language family and thus have nothing to do with a more recent common history. For example, in Mayan, change (16) (*$*q > k$, $*q' > k'$*) took place in all the languages of the Huastecan, Yucatecan and Cholan-Tzeltalan branches, as well as in some of the Greater Q'anjobalan languages. However, since uvular stops (q and q') are rarer in languages in general than velars and are more difficult to produce than velars (k and k'), and since they easily and frequently change to velars, the fact that change (16) is shared by languages of these branches does not neces-sarily mean that a single change took place in some more immediate ancestor of these languages before they split up; it is just as likely that the uvulars changed to velars independently in different languages within the family. Change (17) (*η > n) took place in the Yucatecan, Cholan-Tzeltalan and some of the Greater Q'anjobalan languages, but velar nasals (η) can easily become alveolar nasals (n), a change frequently found in the world's languages. In these two cases (changes (16) and (17)), it is assumed that these branches of Mayan independently underwent these very common sound changes, and that they therefore provide no strong evidence for subgrouping. They merely represent independent, convergent innovations. Obviously, such changes are not of as much value for subgrouping as other less expected changes are.

A very telling example of this sort is the loss of the vowel-length contrast through the merger of long vowels with their short counterparts in Cholan and in some dialects of Kaqchikel. This is perfectly understandable, since the loss of vowel length is a very common change which languages seem easily to undergo. In this case, it would be ludicrous to imagine that Chol and the Kaqchikel dialects without the length contrast formed one branch of the family while the other Kaqchikel dialects which maintain the contrast belong to a totally distinct branch. Clearly, the seemingly shared innovation of loss of vowel length came about independently in the two instances. The very natural, very frequent changes are candidates for convergent development (innovations shared due to independent change rather than to inherited results from a single change in the immediate parent), changes such as nasalization of vowels before nasal consonants, intervocalic voicing, final devoicing, palatalization before *i* or *j* and so on.

Finally, some sound changes can be borrowed among related languages, and this can complicate the subgrouping picture. For example, Q'eqchi', Poqomam and Poqomchi' share change (18) (*ts > s); however, documents from the sixteenth and seventeenth centuries reveal that this change took place long after these three were independent languages and that the change is borrowed, diffused across language boundaries (see Chapters 3 and 12). Naturally, if the change is borrowed from one language to another after they had become separate languages, this does not reflect a time of common history when a single language underwent a change and then subsequently split up, leaving evidence of the change in its daughter languages. Therefore, borrowed changes, which may appear to be shared innovations, are also not evidence of subgrouping.

While shared innovation as the only reliable criterion for subgrouping is clear, it must be kept in mind that the subgrouping can be only as successful as the reconstruction upon which it is based. That is, what constitutes an innovation depends crucially on what is reconstructed, and if the reconstruction is wrong, there is a strong possibility that the subgrouping which depends on it will be wrong as well. Let's consider an example illustrated by Nootkan (a family of three languages, Makah, Nitinat and Nootka, spoken in the Northwest Coast area of North America). Consider the sound correspondences presented in Table 6.3. (See Haas 1969b; some of the Nootkan correspondences and changes were seen in Chapter 5.)

TABLE 6.3: Some Nootkan sound correspondences

	Makah	*Nitinat*	*Nootka*	*Proto-Nootkan*
(1)	q'	ʕ	ʕ	*q'
(2)	χ	χ	ħ	*χ
(3)	b	b	m	*m
(4)	d	d	n	*n

Let us begin with what is considered the correct reconstruction and subgrouping before considering the consequences of erroneous alternatives. Proto-Nootkan is reconstructed with *q' for (1), *χ (voiceless uvular fricative) for (2), *m for (3) and *n for (4); Nitinat and Nootka are subgrouped together, with Makah as a separate branch of the family first. This interpretation is based on the fact that Nitinat and Nootka share, for example, the innovation in (1) in which glottalized uvular stops (q') changed to pharyngeal ʕ. While Makah and Nitinat seem to share the innovation (in (3) and (4)) that the Proto-Nootkan nasals (represented by *m and *n here) became corresponding voiced oral stops (b and d, respectively), this change came about through diffusion in the linguistic area after Makah and Nitinat had separated. Nitinat and Makah belong to the area of the Northwest Coast of North America where several languages lack nasal consonants (see Chapters 2 and 12). In (2), since only Nootka changed (*χ > ħ), Makah and Nitinat share only the retention of χ, not evidence for subgrouping. However, suppose now that for (2) we were to reconstruct (erroneously) *ħ (pharyngeal fricative) for Proto-Nootkan; this would presuppose the change of *ħ to χ in Makah and Nitinat, and this would be a shared innovation, evidence to support subgrouping them together and Nootka apart. As this shows, subgrouping is very much at the mercy of how accurate the reconstruction upon which it is based is. In this case, if we did not recognize that the change from nasals to corresponding voiced stops in (3) and (4), *m > b and *n > d, was due to borrowing and we reconstructed erroneously *b and *d instead, with the assumption that Nootka changed these to nasals, nothing would follow for subgrouping, since Nootka alone would change and Makah and Nitinat would only share a retention.

The Mayan subgrouping, considered above, provides a final example, though it is simplified here in that we will consider only one of many sound correspondences together with the changes and the reconstruction based on it. In the Mayan family, the lower-level subgroups are well established; these include Huastecan, Yucatecan, Cholan-Tzeltalan, Greater Q'anjobalan, K'ichean and Mamean. Some of these are grouped together in higher-order, more inclusive branches of the family; we must ask what the evidence for these larger subgroupings is and whether it is accurate. Consider the following sound correspondence (encountered earlier, in Chapter 5):

> Huastecan *h* : Yucatecan *n* : Cholan-Tzeltalan *n* : Q'anjobalan *ŋ* : K'ichean *x* : Mamean *x*

The generally accepted reconstruction in this case is Proto-Mayan *$*ŋ$ (where it is assumed that Huastecan independently changed *$*ŋ > h$, change (3) in the list above), and so we will leave it out of the rest of the discussion). K'ichean and Mamean share the change of *$*ŋ > x$ (change (12) above; *x* then later changed to *x* in Mamean and in most of the K'ichean languages), and this shared innovation (together with others mentioned above) supports subgrouping K'ichean and Mamean together; the group is usually called Eastern Mayan. In this reconstruction for the correspondence set that Proto-Mayan *$*ŋ$ is based on, Yucatecan, Cholan-Tzeltalan and Q'anjobalan each retain the nasal (where it is assumed that the change of *$ŋ > n$ is so natural and easy that Yucatecan and Cholan-Tzeltalan probably underwent it independently), and since this is a shared retention (if viewed this way), nothing follows for whether or not these three groups may have a closer kinship or not. However, K'ichean and Mamean share the innovation *$*ŋ > x$, which is grounds for subgrouping them together. Suppose hypothetically now that this reconstruction were wrong and that Proto-Mayan actually had *$*x$ (although this is highly unlikely). In this case, K'ichean and Mamean would share not an innovation but merely a retention, and nothing would follow from this for their position within the family. However, Yucatecan, Cholan-Tzeltalan and Greater Q'anjobalan would all share an innovation to a nasal (*$*x > ŋ$, then later $ŋ > n$ in Yucatecan and Cholan-Tzeltalan), and this would be evidence for classifying Yucatecan, Cholan-Tzeltalan and Greater Q'anjobalan as members of the same subgroup. That is, if the reconstruction of *$*ŋ$ is wrong, then the subgrouping based on the shared innovations which depart from this reconstruction is also not founded; if the alternative reconstruction with *x is wrong (which is almost certainly the case), then any subgrouping which presupposes it must also be wrong (unless other shared innovations can be found which do support it).

6.5 Glottochronology (Lexicostatistics)

Not all methods of classification that have been proposed are reliable. Glottochronology is a well-known one which is still sometimes used but which has been rejected by most historical linguists. In what follows, it is discussed in some detail, not because it merits such attention, but because it has proven particularly misleading and it is important to understand why it should be avoided. It is sometimes likened to [14]C ('carbon 14') dating in archaeology. Given the attention it has received (and continues to receive in some quarters), it is important to understand why it does not work for subgrouping, or for any other purpose, for that matter.

Though the names *glottochronology* and *lexicostatistics* are usually used interchangeably, some make a distinction; *glottochronology* is defined as a method with the goal of assigning a date to the split-up of some language into daughter languages, whereas *lexicostatistics* is given the definition of the statistical manipulation of lexical material for historical inferences (not necessarily associated with dates). Lexicostatistics in this sense is broader. However, in actual practice, this distinction is almost never made; both names are used interchangeably.

6.5.1 Basic assumptions

There are four basic assumptions of glottochronology, all of which have been challenged. We will look at each in turn and consider some of the criticisms that have been raised concerning them.

(1) *Basic vocabulary*. The first assumption is that there exists a *basic* or *core vocabulary* which is universal and relatively culture-free, and thus is less subject to replacement than other kinds of vocabulary. The Swadesh 100-word list of basic vocabulary is:

1. I	7. who	13. big	19. fish
2. you	8. not	14. long	20. bird
3. we	9. all	15. small	21. dog
4. this	10. many	16. woman	22. louse
5. that	11. one	17. man	23. tree
6. what	12. two	18. person	24. seed

25. leaf	44. tongue	63. swim	82. fire
26. root	45. claw	64. fly	83. ash
27. bark	46. foot	65. walk	84. burn
28. skin	47. knee	66. come	85. path
29. flesh	48. hand	67. lie	86. mountain
30. blood	49. belly	68. sit	87. red
31. bone	50. neck	69. stand	88. green
32. egg	51. breast	70. give	89. yellow
33. grease	52. heart	71. say	90. white
34. horn	53. liver	72. sun	91. black
35. tail	54. drink	73. moon	92. night
36. feather	55. eat	74. star	93. hot
37. hair	56. bite	75. water	94. cold
38. head	57. see	76. rain	95. full
39. ear	58. hear	77. stone	96. good
40. eye	59. know	78. sand	97. new
41. nose	60. sleep	79. earth	98. round
42. mouth	61. die	80. cloud	99. dry
43. tooth	62. kill	81. smoke	100. name

To apply glottochronology, lists of the most natural, most neutral translations of each of these 100 semantic concepts are assembled and compared in two or more related languages – or at least languages thought to be related. The forms which are phonetically similar in the compared lists receive a check mark (tick) to indicate probable cognates; and, as will be seen below, the date when these languages separated from one another is calculated based on the number of these checked/ ticked 'cognates' that they share. Some scholars argue that the method should be constrained to require that only forms known from historical linguistic research to be real cognates be counted, rather than mere 'look-alikes', as in the more common practice.

(2) *Constant rate of retention through time.* The second assumption is that the *rate of retention* of items of core vocabulary is relatively constant through time, that a language will retain about 86 per cent of the words of the 100-word list each 1,000 years (the figure is 80.5 per cent, rounded to 81 per cent retention for the 200-word list, formerly used but found not to be sufficiently culture-free and therefore replaced by the 100-word list).

(3) *Constant rate of loss cross-linguistically.* The third assumption is related to the second; it claims that the *rate of loss* of basic vocabulary is approximately the same for all languages. It is assumed that languages everywhere lose about 14 per cent of the 100-word list, that is, that some

fourteen words from the 100-word list will be replaced (thus some eighty-six of the basic 100 words will be retained) each 1,000-year period throughout their history.

(4) *Calculation of the date of divergence.* The fourth assumption is that when the number of cognates in the basic vocabulary list shared by related languages is known, the number of centuries since the languages split from an earlier ancestor can be computed. The time depth is computed with the formula

$$t = \frac{\log C}{2 \log r}$$

where *t* is 'time depth' in millennia (1,000-year periods), *C* is 'percentage of cognates' and *r* is 'the constant' (the percentage of cognates assumed to remain after 1,000 years, that is, 86 per cent for the 100-word list). *Log* means 'logarithm of'.

6.5.2 Historical background

Glottochronology was invented in the 1950s by Morris Swadesh, an American linguist, who began by trying to determine whether there were broad trends involving vocabulary change within particular language families. He was surprised to discover, so he reported, that not only were there constant trends within particular language families, but that the rate of change turned out to be the same across languages, regardless of their family affiliations. This claim constitutes one of the basic assumptions of the method, and it has been vigorously criticized (see below). Swadesh began with a basic vocabulary list of 500 words, but this was soon reduced to 205, then to 200, and finally to the 100-word list. In developing glottochronology, he examined thirteen test cases – languages with long attested histories where vocabulary change could be checked against written evidence. In these 'test cases', he compared modern versions of English, German and Swedish (Germanic languages) with older attested stages of each language (for example, Modern English with Old English). Catalan, French, Italian, Portuguese, Romanian and Spanish (Romance languages) were compared with Latin. Athenian Greek and Cypriotic Greek were compared with Classical Greek; Coptic was compared with Middle Egyptian (its ancestor); and modern Mandarin Chinese was compared with Ancient Chinese. However, only two of these thirteen (Coptic and Mandarin) are non-Indo-European languages, and this has raised doubts about the method. From later tests with control cases involving Kannada, Japanese, Arabic, Georgian, Armenian and Sardinian, the claim of a constant rate of retention has been challenged (see below).

6.5.3 Criticisms

6.5.3.1 Problems with the assumption of basic vocabulary

There are serious problems with the assumption of a universal, culture-free basic vocabulary. One is that many of the items are not culture-free, but rather are borrowed for cultural reasons in a number of languages. Examples of borrowed terms for items on the 100-word list are found for each item in some language somewhere; only a few revealing examples are mentioned here. In several Mayan languages, (18) *winaq* 'person' was replaced by a loanword, *kriftian* (or something similar), from Spanish *cristiano* 'Christian', colloquially 'person, living soul'. It is thought that in the early colonial period, Spanish contrasted Christianized Indians (the *cristianos*) with pagans. When ultimately all had been 'pacified' (converted), by default all were then called *kriftian* 'person', resulting in the elimination from the vocabulary of former *winaq* 'person'. In the case of (21) 'dog', while native peoples of Central America had dogs before the coming of the Spanish, their dog was small, hairless and barkless, and served as a food item. The big, hairy, noisy dogs which arrived with Europeans were not easily equated with the native dogs, and hence many groups borrowed the foreign name for 'dog' and eventually came no longer to have a native term for 'dog'. Thus, for example, 'dog' in Pipil (Uto-Aztecan) is *pe:lu*, borrowed from Spanish *perro* 'dog' (Pipil has no *r*). The word for (52) 'heart' is widely borrowed in a number of Mayan languages from Totonac (a non-Mayan language of Mexico); this presumably has to do with the importance of 'heart' in native religion (for example, human sacrifice by cutting out the heart was practised). Forms for (72) 'sun' and (73) 'moon' are widely borrowed among many languages of south-east Asia due to their central role in religion and cosmology. Words for (100) 'name' are also often borrowed. In fact, if we just look at the English glosses among the items of the 100-word list, we see borrowings for (18) 'person' (from French) (28) 'skin' (from Scandinavian), (32) 'egg' (from Scandinavian), (33) 'grease' (from French) and (86) 'mountain' (from French), among others. Borrowing is a serious problem for the assumption that there is a relatively culture-free basic vocabulary.

Another problem is that glottochronology assumes that there will be a direct, one-to-one matching between each numbered notion in the 100-word list and a word of each language. However, this is very often not the case. For many of the items on the list, languages often have more than one neutral equivalent. For example, for (1) 'I', many languages of south-east Asia have several forms all meaning 'I' whose use depends on the relative status of the person spoken to. Similarly, (2) 'you' even more frequently than 'I' has multiple forms, depending on social status and degree of intimacy (for example, the familiar versus polite pronouns, Spanish *tu* and *usted*, German *du* and *Sie*, French *tu* and *vous*, Finnish *sinä* and *te*, K'iche' *at* and *la:l*, to mention just a few), where one form is not more basic than the other. For (3) 'we', many languages have distinct forms for 'inclusive' versus 'exclusive' first person plural pronouns. For (8), some languages have no single form for 'not', but rather have conjugated negative verbs with several forms (compare Finnish *en* 'I don't', *et* 'you don't', *ei* 'he/she/it doesn't', *emme* 'we don't', *ette* 'you [plural] don't', *eivät* 'they don't'). For (9) 'all', some languages have different terms depending on whether the meaning is 'all' = 'each member of a group' or 'all' = 'the entire amount'. Navajo and its close sister languages have no unique word for (75) 'water'; rather, they have several different words for 'stagnant water in a pool', 'rain water', 'drinking water' and so on. Some Slavic languages have no unique word for (80) 'cloud', but rather one word for dark storm clouds (as Russian *tuča*) and a separate word for light clouds (as Russian *oblako*). For (84) 'burn', many languages have more than one equivalent; for example, Spanish *arder* 'burn' (intransitive) and *quemar* 'burn (transitive), or several K'ichean (Mayan) languages -*k'at* 'burn' (accidental) and -*por* 'burn' (purposeful). For (93) 'hot', several K'ichean languages have two equally common forms which are equivalent: *k'atan* 'hot' (of weather, water, a room and so on) and *meq'en* 'hot' (of food, drinks, fire and so on). The same is true for (94) 'cold': *te:w* 'cold' (of weather, wind, people, ice and so on) and *xoron* 'cold' (of food, water and so on). K'ichean languages often have as many as seven different terms for 'to eat'; for example, -*waʔ* 'eat (bread-like things)', -*tix* 'eat (meat)' and -*loʔ* 'eat (fruit-like things)' are equally common and none is more neutral or basic than another. Similar examples can be cited for many of the other words in the list.

Not only do many of the items from the 100-word list have more than one natural, neutral equivalent in many languages, but some have no equivalent at all – or better said, in a number of cases, some languages make no distinction between two separate items on the list. For example, (17) 'man' and (18) 'person' are homonymous in many languages. Many languages do not distinguish (27) 'bark' from (28) 'skin' or (36) 'feather' from (37) 'hair', where 'bark' is just 'tree skin', and 'feather' is just 'bird hair'. Some Latin American Indian languages do not distinguish (26) 'root' from (37) 'hair', where 'root' is equivalent to 'tree hair'. More generally, work on colour universals has shown that, while all languages have an equivalent (more or less) for (90) 'white' (or light) and (91) 'black' (or dark) and most have a term for (87) 'red', it is not at all uncommon for languages to lack basic colour terms for (88) 'green' and (89) 'yellow' (Berlin and Kay 1969).

In instances where a language has more than one equivalent per item on the basic vocabulary list or where the same term covers more than one item on the list, the results can be skewed. For example, two languages will appear less closely related than in fact they are if both have, for example, two equivalents for 'hot', but the one meaning 'hot, of weather' turns up checked/ticked on one language's list and the one meaning 'hot, of food' gets checked/ticked on a related language's list. Similarly, if related languages make no distinction between 'feather' and 'hair', then the same word will turn up twice, as the equivalent to these two separate items in the list, making the languages seem to share more and therefore appear to be more closely related than would be the case if only distinct items were compared. Such skewing is a serious problem for the method.

Some 'basic vocabulary' appears to change rather easily for cultural reasons, for example, terms for (38) 'head' in various languages. Proto-Indo-European *kaput-* 'head' gave Proto-Germanic *haubidam/*haubudam* (hence Old English *hēafod* > *head*) and Proto-Romance *kaput*. However, several Germanic and Romance languages no longer have cognates of these terms as the basic form referring to the human head. For example, German *Kopf* 'head' originally meant 'bowl'; the cognate from *kaput* is *haupt*, which now means basically only 'main', 'chief', as in *Hauptbahnhof* 'main/central train station'. French *tête* and Italian *testa* both meant originally 'pot'; the French cognate from Latin *kaput* is *chef*, but this means now 'main, principal, chief', not a human head. The Italian cognate *capo* now means 'top, chief, leader'. Pipil (Uto-Aztecan) *tsuntekumat* 'head' comes from *tsun-* 'top, hair (in compound words only)' + *tekumat* 'bottle gourd', and has replaced Proto-Nahua *$k^w\bar{a}yi$-* for 'head'. It is a problem for the method that some items on the list seem to be replaced more frequently and more easily than others.

Finally, it has been pointed out that taboo has resulted in the replacement of considerable vocabulary, particularly in some languages in Australia, New Guinea and the Americas, where words similar to the names of recently deceased relatives are avoided and substitutions or circumlocutions are used instead. Some of these result in permanent vocabulary replacement. Other kinds of taboo replacement of items in the basic vocabulary list are also very frequent. For example, in dialects of K'iche' and Tz'utujil (Mayan languages), (20) *ts'ikin* 'bird' has been replaced by *čikop* (originally 'small animal') due to taboo. In Latin American Spanish, *pájaro* 'bird' has come to mean 'male genitals' and is obscene; for that reason, many Spanish speakers avoid it and substitute *pajarito* 'small bird' or something else instead. Because Spanish is the dominant national language where Mayan languages are spoken, speakers of some Mayan languages have transferred the obscene associated with 'bird' in Spanish to the term for 'bird' in their native language and for that reason replaced the vocabulary item. Another example is (32) 'egg'; Spanish *huevo* 'egg' also means 'testicle' and is obscene, and for that reason many in rural Mexico substitute *blanquillo* (literally 'little white thing') for 'egg', replacing *huevo* in this meaning.

Facts such as these show that there is no universal, culture-free vocabulary for which a one-to-one translation equivalent exists in all languages. Still, stubborn proponents of glottochronology would respond to this criticism that something must account for the portion of the vocabulary which is replaced and it may be borrowing, taboo and so on which bring about that loss.

6.5.3.2 *Problems with assumptions (2) and (3)*

Since the assumption of a constant rate of retention through time and of a constant rate of loss cross-linguistically are related, criticisms of these two assumptions are considered together.

First, a quick check based on common sense would call these assumptions into question. There are good reasons why sound change might be regular, based on what is known about the structure and limitations of human speech-organ physiology and perception; however, there is nothing inherent in the nature of vocabulary (or in the organization of the lexicon) which would lead us to suspect any sort of regular pattern to lexical change, certainly not that basic vocabulary should be replaced everywhere at the same rate. The study of additional test cases after Swadesh developed the method shows that this doubt based on intuition about vocabulary change is well founded, that there really is no constant rate of loss or retention across languages or through time. Icelandic has retained 97.3 per cent, English 67.8 per cent, Faroese over 90 per cent, Georgian and Armenian about 95 per cent each during the time that these languages have had written attestations. The large difference between Icelandic's 97.3 per cent and English's 67.8 per cent lends little confidence to the claim of an expected 86 per cent, regardless of what the range of error (standard deviation) permitted by the statistical calculation may be. That is, these tests show that the rate is neither constant across time nor the same for all languages.

With respect to the claim of a constant loss through time of 14 per cent for each 1,000-year period, written documentation exists for more than one 1,000-year period for extremely few languages; in Swadesh's thirteen test-case languages, attestations for more than one or two 1,000-year chunks of time are available only for the Coptic and Mandarin cases (the interpretation of which is much less secure). Some scholars argue that it is possible that circumstances were so different in the more remote past that vocabulary loss and retention may have behaved differently in earlier 1,000-year chunks of time from later 1,000-year periods. While this is highly unlikely, without written documentation it is not possible to eliminate the possibility entirely, and it will not do just to assert the constant rate far into the past on the basis of no good evidence.

6.5.3.3 *Problems in calculating dates of separation*

Since the split-ups of language families (or subgroups) are usually not sudden, in principle the notion of attaching a precise date to such gradual diversifications seems overly unrealistic – it is difficult to date a language split. Also, subsequent contact among the sister languages after a split is common; but, as commonly applied, the method makes no effort to distinguish loans that result from such contact from directly inherited cognates. For example, in French and Italian the word for 'head' (Italian *testa*, French *tête* [from earlier *test(a)*]) is similar because French borrowed this form from Italian, which itself had shifted *testa* 'pot' to mean 'head'. That is, in calculating how long ago Italian and French separated from one another, the date is skewed towards a more recent break-up because of this basic vocabulary item which is shared due to contact after they split up.

It is also telling that this basic assumption about being able to calculate the date of separation has been vigorously challenged; or better said, the statistical model upon which glottochronology is based has been severely criticized, although others defend it or try to refine it. The most generous thing that can be said about the mathematical model upon which it is based is that it is controversial.

6.5.4 Purported uses of glottochronology

The principal use to which glottochronology has been put is that of subgrouping language families. It is sometimes thought that glotto-chronological calculations of splits provide a fast and easy means for arriving at the internal classification of a language family with no need to undertake the more difficult and time-consuming determination of subgrouping based on shared innovations. However, since glottochron-ology is unreliable and is discounted by most historical linguists, it should not be thought of as a substitute for the traditional means of subgrouping. It is simply not reliable for this purpose.

On the other hand, some have found glottochronology a useful starting point in beginning to classify large families, such as Austronesian, with a great number of languages (c. 800). Since it would be difficult at the outset to compare all the languages of large families with each other to determine shared innovations among them all, some suggest that a preliminary application of glottochronology can give an idea of the more promising hypotheses which can then later be checked by tradi-tional means. However, it should be recalled that glottochronology used in this way does not find or demonstrate subgrouping relationships, but merely points to directions where other sorts of research may prove fruitful. The other research is still necessary before the groupings can be believed, and such preliminary classifications based on glottochronology may well have to be seriously revised or abandoned.

Some suggest that while the dates offered by glottochronology are not reliable, they nonetheless provide a relative chronology which more or less corresponds with what we know in many actual cases. That is, some scholars who reject glottochronology are still willing to entertain the results as a rough guide to relatively old or relatively young relation-ships. In the absence of other information which can help to establish linguistic dates, this might seem helpful to some. Still, it must be remembered that many glottochronological dates are known to be inaccurate.

Finally, some have thought that glottochronology might help to establish distant genetic relationships among languages. However, glottochronology cannot find or demonstrate remote relationships; rather, in the application of the method, forms which are phonetically similar in the languages being compared are checked/ticked as possible cognates and then, based on the number counted, a date is calculated for when the languages split up. That is, the method does not find or test distant genetic relationships, but rather just assumes relationship and proceeds to attach a date. This is illegitimate for research on possible remote linguistic relationships.

Glottochronology has given linguistics a bad reputation with some other prehistorians. For example, many archaeologists were initially very happy to embrace its dates, and they frequently proposed interpretations of the prehistory of different peoples and areas which relied on glottochronological dates and attempted to correlate them with other sources of information on prehistory. However, as archaeologists came to find out about the problems of the method and the unreliability of the dates, some felt deceived and some came to believe that linguistics had nothing to offer them. This is unfortunate, for though glottochronology proved misleading, other areas of historical linguistics have an important role to play in the study of prehistory in general (as shown in Chapter 15).

In summary, glottochronology is not accurate; all its basic assumptions have been severely criticized. It should not be accepted; it should be rejected. (For references and discussion, see Campbell 1977: 62–5.) For subgrouping, only shared innovations prove reliable, if the cautions about independently occurring changes and possibly inaccurate reconstructions are kept in mind. The best-defined subgroups are those which are based on a number of shared innovations of the type which are not likely to happen independently or to be diffused across language boundaries.

6.6 Exercises

Return to your reconstructions of Proto-Polynesian (Exercise 5.3), Proto-K'ichean (Exercise 5.7), Proto-Quechuan (Exercise 5.8), and Proto-Saami (Exercise 5.9), and based on your reconstruction and the sound changes that you postulated for each language, attempt to establish the subgrouping in these language families. These subgrouping exercises may prove difficult, depending on what you reconstructed and on the number and kind of sound changes which you postulated in each of these reconstruction exercises.

7

Models of Linguistic Change

It is now an axiom of scientific philology that the real life of language
is in many respects more clearly seen and better studied in dialects and
colloquial forms of speech than in highly developed literary languages.

(Henry Sweet 1900: 79)

7.1 Introduction

When textbooks on historical linguistics talk about 'models of change',
they invariably mean the traditional 'family-tree' model and the 'wave
theory', and the conflict that is assumed to exist between them. These are
described in this chapter and the conflict between them is reconciled. In
particular, the contrasting (but actually complementary) approaches taken
by dialectologists and traditional Neogrammarians are examined and clar-
ified, sociolinguistic approaches to language change are brought into the
picture, and the related notion of 'lexical diffusion' is put in perspective.

7.2 The Family-tree Model

The family tree (sometimes called *Stammbaum*, its German name) is
the traditional model of language diversification. The family-tree model
attempts to show how languages diversify and how language families
are classified (as described in Chapter 6). A family-tree diagram's purpose
is to show how languages which belong to the same language family are
related to one another. *Linguistic diversification* refers to how a single
ancestor language (a proto-language) develops dialects which in time
through the accumulation of changes become distinct languages (sister
languages to one another, daughter languages of the proto-language), and

how through continued linguistic change these daughter languages can diversify and split up into daughters of their own (members of a subgroup of the family). The family-tree diagram represents this diversification, being a classification of the languages of a family and the degree of relatedness among the various languages.

The family-tree model is often associated with August Schleicher, prominent in the history of Indo-European linguistics and teacher of several founders of Neogrammarianism, as well as of well-known opponents to Neogrammarian thinking (for example, see Schleicher 1861–2). This model is typically linked in the literature with the development of the comparative method and eventually with the Neogrammarian notion of regularity of sound change. At the heart of the conflict over models are two of the basic assumptions of the comparative method (discussed in Chapter 5), that sound change is regular (the Neogrammarian hypothesis) and that there is no subsequent contact among the sister languages after the break-up of the proto-language.

The Neogrammarian slogan, *sound laws suffer no exceptions* (declared virtually as doctrine in the so-called 'Neogrammarian manifesto', in the foreword to Hermann Osthoff and Karl Brugmann (1878), written mostly by Brugmann), became an important cornerstone of reconstruction by the comparative method (as explained in Chapter 5). There is nothing inherently hostile to language contact and borrowing in the comparative method or the regularity of sound change; it is just that there is no provision in the comparative method for dealing directly with borrowings. For this, it is necessary to resort to considerations that are not properly part of the comparative method itself (see Chapter 3). Nevertheless, this neglect of language contact in the comparative method is the source of dispute about which models are assumed most appropriate for dealing with kinds of changes and kinds of relationships among languages. Clearly, genetic relationship, the only thing represented in family-tree diagrams, is not the only sort of relationship that exists among languages – for example, languages do also borrow from one another.

7.3 The Challenge from Dialectology and the 'Wave Theory'

Some scholars, many of them dialectologists, did not accept the Neogrammarian position that sound change is regular and exceptionless, but rather opposed this and the family-tree model. The slogan associated with opponents of the Neogrammarian position is *each word has its own history* ('*chaque mot a son histoire*'). (This slogan is often attributed to Jules Gilliéron, author of the *Atlas linguistique de la France* (1902–10), the dialect atlas of France (see Gilliéron 1921; Gilliéron and Roques 1912), although it should be credited to Hugo Schuchardt, a contemporary of the Neogrammarian founders, of whose claims he was critical.) The alternative to the family-tree model which was put forward was the 'wave theory'. The wave theory is usually attributed to Johannes Schmidt (1872), though it, too, was actually developed slightly earlier by Hugo Schuchardt (in 1868 and 1870; this history is documented in Alvar 1967: 82-5) – Schuchardt and Schmidt were both students of Schleicher, as were several of the leading Neogrammarians. The 'wave theory' was intended to deal with changes due to contact among languages and dialects. According to Schmidt's wave model, linguistic changes spread outward concentrically like waves, which become progressively weaker with the distance from their central point. Since later changes may not cover the same area, there may be no sharp boundaries between neighbouring dialects or languages; rather, the greater the distance between them, the fewer linguistic traits dialects or languages may share. The dialectologists' slogan, that every word has its own history, reflects this thinking – a word's history might be the result of various influences from various directions, and these might be quite different from those involved in another word's history, hence each word has its own (potentially quite different) history. It is easy to see that this model would reduce historical linguistics to etymology, since etymology is the study of the idiosyncratic particular properties in the history of individual words.

The dialectologists believed that their findings contradicted the regularity hypothesis of the Neogrammarians. To see what is meant by this, let us consider a much-cited example: the French dialects of Normandy. Latin *k* became *ʃ* in Standard French (before *a* and front vowels, as for example Latin *cantāre* > French *chanter* 'to sing'), seemingly a regular sound change. However, in pockets in Normandy, as seen in Map 7.1, a handful of words appear to be exceptions to this change, maintaining *k* (though the majority of words with original *k* in the appropriate phonetic environments did undergo the change to *ʃ* in this area). The exceptional words which retain *k* at least in part of this region are:

chaîne < catēna 'chain'
chambre < camera 'room'
champ < campus 'field'
Chandeleur 'Candlemas (ecclesiastical)' < candēla 'candle'
chandelle < candēla 'candle'
chanson < cantiō(n-) 'song'
chanter < cantāre 'to sing'
chat < cattu(s) 'cat'

These are spelled here in Standard French orthography and shown with the Latin roots from which they come. Their geographical distributions at the time when the French dialect atlas was prepared are seen in Map 7.1. (Compare Lepelley 1971: 63, 93, 362; Palmer 1972: 272–3.)

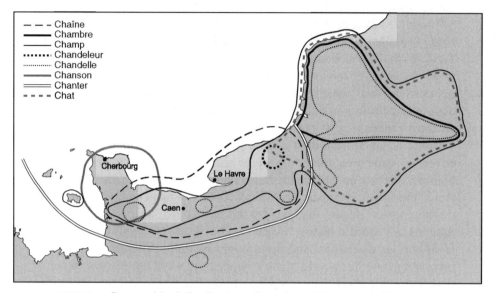

MAP 7.1: Geographical distribution of words which retained /k/ in areas of Normandy (redrawn after Palmer 1972: 273)

Dialectologists took this as evidence that the Neogrammarian idea of exceptionless sound change must be just wrong. A dialectologist might say that each of these words has its own history. For example, 'homey' words characteristic of rural life such as 'cat' and 'field' might more successfully resist the wave of change which brought with it the $k > ʃ$ change which spread outwards from the prestige centre in Paris. On the other hand, words for things like 'candle' and 'to sing', associated with the Church where more prestigious pronunciations were favoured and aided by the Parisian pronunciations of priests assigned to the local parishes, did undergo the $k > ʃ$ change in much of this region, retaining k only in very small pockets. This is seen to explain why the areas where 'candle' and 'to sing' still preserve the k pronunciation are much smaller than those of 'cat' and 'field' with k – the words just had different histories.

However, there are two important things to notice about this case. First, we can identify these words as exceptions only if we recognize the sound change of $k > ʃ$ – without acknowledging the sound change, it

214

would be impossible to recognize these few words in Normandy as exceptions. While these words are exceptions to strict exceptionlessness of sound change, we cannot explain their individual histories, that they are exceptions, without reference to the sound change. Second, it is possible that a situation like this one can tell us something more about how some sound changes take place – in this case apparently through the spread of the Parisian prestige norm (with *ʃ*,) to more remote areas. This sort of change is sometimes called *dialect borrowing*. Most importantly, this example shows that neither model is sufficient to explain all of linguistic change and all the sorts of relationships that can exist between dialects or related languages. Without accepting the sound change, we would not be able to recognize these dialect forms as exceptions, and without the information from dialectology, our knowledge of how some changes are transmitted would be incomplete. Clearly, both are needed. This being the case, it will pay us to look a bit more closely at some basic aspects of dialectology. Other aspects of the explanation of change are deferred until Chapter 11.

7.4 Dialectology (Linguistic Geography, Dialect Geography)

Dialectology deals with regional variation in a language. Some concepts of dialectology that need to be understood are the following.

Isogloss: a line on a map which represents the geographical boundary (limit) of regional linguistic variants. By extension, the term 'isogloss' also refers to the dialect features themselves, an extension of the original sense of the word from dealing with a line on a map to reference to the actual linguistic phenomena themselves. For example, in the USA the *greasy/greazy* isogloss is a line roughly corresponding to the Mason–Dixon line which separates the North Midlands from the South Midlands; it runs across the middle of the country until it dives down across south-eastern Kansas, western Oklahoma and Texas (see Map 7.2). North of the line, *greasy* is pronounced with *s*; south of the line it is pronounced with *z*. Another isogloss has to do with a contrast versus lack of contrast in the vowels in such word pairs as *pin/pen* and *tin/ten*. In these words, [ɪ] and [ɛ] before nasals contrast in other dialects, but in the South Midlands and Southern dialect areas there is no contrast – these vowels have merged before nasals in these dialects. This explains how country-music songs, many of whose writers and singers are from the dialect areas which lack the contrast, can rhyme words such as *win* and *end*, both phonetically [ɪ̃n] (*end* also loses the final consonant [nd > n]), as in the well-known song, 'Heartaches by the Number', where the last line of the refrain goes: 'I've got heartaches by the number for a love that I can't *win*, but the day that I stop countin' is the day my world will *end*.'

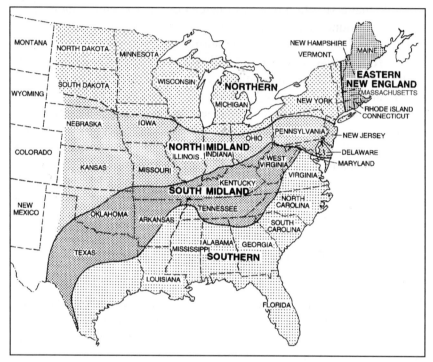

MAP 7.2: Some major dialect areas in the USA

Bundle of isoglosses: several isoglosses whose extent coincides at the same geographical boundary; such bundling of isoglosses is taken to constitute the boundary of a dialect (or dialect area). The two examples of isoglosses just mentioned happen to bundle, both along the Mason–Dixon line (with *greasy* and the *pin/pen* contrast north of the line (for example, in the North Midlands dialect area); with *greazy* and lack of the vowel contrast south of the line (for example, in the South Midlands dialect area) (see Map 7.2).

Focal area: zone of prestige from which innovations spread outwards.

Relic area (*residual area*): an area (usually small) which preserves older forms that have not undergone the innovations that the surrounding areas have; relic areas are often regions of difficult access for cultural, political or geographical reasons, and thus resistant to the spread of prestige variants from elsewhere. The area of Normandy which retained *k* in certain words shown in Map 7.1 is a relic area.

216

Lect: some scholars feel the need for a more open-ended term which signifies any linguistic variety, whether defined by its geographical distribution or by its use by people from different social classes, castes, ages, genders and so on. *Lect* is intended to cover all such varieties (geographical dialect, sociolect, idiolect – the language characteristic of a single individual – and so on).

Mutual intelligibility: when speakers of different linguistic entities can understand one another. This is the principal criterion for distinguishing dialects of a single language from distinct languages (which may or may not be closely related). Entities which are totally incomprehensible to speakers of other entities clearly are mutually unintelligible, and for linguists they therefore belong to separate languages. However, the criterion of mutual intelligibility is often not so straightforward. For example, there are cases of non-reciprocal intelligibility (for instance, Portuguese speakers understand Spanish reasonably well, while many Spanish speakers do not understand Portuguese well at all) and of non-immediate intelligibility, where upon first exposure understanding is limited, but after a time intelligibility grows. There are many studies in the sociolinguistic and dialectological literature of cases of various sorts having to do with how to determine to which language various dialects belong, often having to do with the relationship of regional varieties to some standard or *superordinate* language or to their position within a dialect chain. We do not have the space to get into the details of this here, though these various relationships among varieties are relevant to linguistic change.

Language: the definition of 'language' is not strictly a linguistic enterprise, but sometimes is determined more by political or social factors. For this reason, Max Weinreich's definition of language is very frequently reported: *a language is a dialect which has an army and a navy*. This emphasizes that the definition of a 'language' is not merely a linguistic matter. For example, while speakers of Norwegian and Swedish have little difficulty understanding one another (the languages are mutually intelligible), these are considered separate languages for political reasons. On the other hand, Chinese has several so-called 'dialects' which are so different one from another that their speakers do not easily understand each other's language. By the criterion of mutual intelligibility, linguists would consider these separate languages; however, official policy in China regards these as representing the same language.

Although the literature on the history of linguistics often disposes us to think that dialectology played an important role in the making of the wave theory, giving us the slogan 'every word has its own history', in

fact the study of dialects also significantly influenced the Neogrammarians and the origin of their slogan, that 'sound laws suffer no exceptions'.
The Neogrammarian founders were impressed by Winteler's (1876)
study of the Kerenzen dialect of Swiss German, in which he presented
phonological statements as processes (following the ancient rules for
Sanskrit of Pānini, an important Hindu grammarian from around the
fifth century BC, which Winteler studied in his linguistic training). This
'regularity' which Winteler saw in the dialect's (synchronic) rules – for
example, in Kerenzen every *n* became *ŋ* before *k* and *g* – inspired the
Neogrammarian founders to have confidence in the exceptionlessness
of sound changes (Weinreich et al. 1968: 115). Of course, as we saw,
Gilliéron (1921), who opposed regularity, also based his objections on
the study of dialects, arguing against the Neogrammarians with the
other slogan, 'every word has its own history'. Ironically, both these
famous orientations to historical linguistics were influenced significantly
by dialect studies.

The conflict between the Neogrammarians' 'exceptionless sound
change' and the dialectologists' 'every word has its own history' is
implicated in more recent controversies over how sound change is transmitted. This controversy will be considered presently, but first it will
be helpful to have in mind the general framework which has most
influenced thinking in this area, that of Weinreich, Labov and Herzog
(1968).

7.5 A Framework for Investigating the Causes of Linguistic Change

The framework presented by Weinreich et al. (1968) has been very
influential in historical linguistic thought concerning 'why' and 'how'
linguistic changes take place. They asked a number of questions, which
they also called 'problems', which must be answered (or 'solved') by
any theory which hopes to explain language change. These are:

(1) *The constraints problem*: what are the general constraints on
change that determine possible and impossible changes and directions
of change? For example, among the constraints on change, Weinreich
et al. (1968: 100) postulate that 'no language will assume a form in
violation of such formal principles as are . . . universal in human languages'. The constraints problem is a central issue in linguistic change
for many scholars; it takes the form of a search for the kinds of linguistic
change that will *not* take place. The irreversibility of mergers (see
Chapter 2) is a good example of such a constraint.

(2) *The transition problem*: how (or by what route or routes) does language change? What intermediate stages or processes does a language go through to get from a state before the change began to the state after the change has taken place? For example, a much-debated question is whether certain kinds of changes must be seen as gradual or abrupt.

(3) *The embedding problem*: how is a given language change embedded in the surrounding system of linguistic and social relations? How does the greater environment in which the change takes place influence the change? That is, the parts of a language are tightly interwoven, often in complex interlocking relationships, so that a change in one part of the grammar may impact on (or be constrained by) other parts of the grammar (see Chapter 11). Also, language change takes place in a social environment, where differences in language may be given positive or negative sociolinguistic status, and this sociolinguistic environment plays a very important role in change.

(4) *The evaluation problem*: how do speakers of the language (members of a speech community) evaluate a given change, and what is the effect of their evaluation on the change? What are the effects of the change on the language's overall structure? (How does the system change without damage to its function of serving communication?)

(5) *The actuation problem*: why does a given linguistic change occur at the particular time and place that it does? How do changes begin and proceed? What starts a change and what carries it along? The actuation question is the most central, since the other questions relate to it; and if we succeed in answering it, we will be able to explain linguistic change (see Chapter 11).

7.6 Sociolinguistics and Language Change

Changes typically begin with variation, with alternative ways of saying the same thing entering the language. Variation is the specific subject matter of sociolinguistics, and while sociolinguists are interested in many other things in addition to linguistic change, sociolinguistics is extremely relevant to understanding how and why languages change. Sociolinguistic concerns underlie several of the questions in Weinreich et al.'s framework (just considered). Sociolinguistics deals with systematic co-variation of linguistic structure with social structure, especially with the variation in language which is conditioned by social differences. The most important dimensions which can condition variation have to do with social attributes of the sender (speaker), the receiver (hearer) and the setting (context). Variation in a language can be conditioned by such social characteristics of the speaker as age, gender, social status, ethnic identity, religion, occupation, self-identification with a location, and in fact almost any important social trait. Let's consider just a couple of examples of some of these to get a flavour of what is involved. Grammars of Classical Nahuatl report that where Aztec men pronounced *w*, women spoke the same words with *v*. This is linguistic variation conditioned by the gender of the speaker. Since Proto-Uto-Aztecan had **w* in these words, it is necessary to conclude that the *w/v* variation in Classical Nahuatl is due to a linguistic change which women adopted, **w > v*, but men did not. An example reflecting the social status of the speaker is the variation in the Hindi of Khalapur village in India (in Uttar Pradesh) where in words with a stressed vowel in the next syllable, the higher castes contrast /ʊ/ and /ə/, but the lower castes have only /ə/ both in words with /ʊ/ and those with /ə/ in the speech of the higher castes (as seen in, for example, higher caste *dʊtə́i* / low caste *dətə́i* 'blanket'). Here, it appears that there has been a sound change in which ʊ and ə have merged with ə (ʊ, ə > ə) in the language of the low-caste speakers, affecting the language of only a portion of the population, leading to the variation in speech characteristic of the different castes. Similar examples could be presented for the various other social attributes of speakers. Similarly, social attributes of hearers can condition linguistic variation. This sort of variation is often indicative of changes in progress in a speech community, and this makes the study of such variation and its implications for understanding linguistic change in general extremely important.

Sociolinguistic investigations of change have been of two types: *apparent-time* and *real-time* studies. In apparent-time research, by far the more common, a *variable* (a linguistic trait subject to social or stylistic variation) is investigated at one particular point in time. To the extent that the variation correlates with age, it is assumed that a change in progress is under way and that the variant most characteristic of older speakers' speech represents the earlier stage and the variant more typical of younger speakers' speech shows what it is changing to. The age-gradient distribution shows the change in progress. An example of this sort is the ongoing merger of diphthongs /iə/ (as in *ear, cheer*) and /ɛə/ (as in *air, chair*) in New Zealand English, where in general older speakers maintain the contrast more, most younger speakers merge the two to /iə/, hence jokes based on the homophony of 'beer' and 'bear', for example (see Maclagan and Gordon 1996). Real-time studies compare samples of language from different times; for example, a comparison of recordings from fifty years ago with comparable samples of speech today can reveal changes (see Labov 1994 for discussion of several examples).

Some general claims about linguistic change which have been made based on large-scale sociolinguistic investigations in urban settings are:

1. Linguistic changes originate in the intermediate social classes (the upper working class or lower middle class), not the highest or the lowest classes.
2. The innovators of change are usually people with the highest local status, who play a central role in the speech community.
3. These innovators have the highest density of social interactions within their communication networks and they have the highest proportions of contacts outside the local neighbourhood, as well.
4. Women lead most linguistic changes (women accept and help to propagate the linguistic changes earlier than men do).
5. Different ethnic groups who newly enter a speech community participate in changes in progress only to the extent that they begin to gain local rights and privileges in jobs and housing, and access to or acceptance in the society. (See Labov 1994, 2001.)

Several of these claims are currently being challenged or refined – for example, there is a range of opinion concerning whether (3) holds up, even in the urban settings for which it is designed. Some of these claims may be appropriate only to modern settings; it is important to determine to what extent these and other claims may be true of changes which take place in languages spoken in societies and social settings with very different social organizations, subsistence patterns and economic practices, less nucleated settlements, and so on.

A number of influential historical linguists (for example, Henning Andersen, Eugenio Coseriu, James Milroy) hold that speakers change, and not languages, making all linguistic change social change, rather than language change per se. Some go so far as to deny any language-internal motivation (arising from the structural aspects of the language itself) for language change, but most historical linguists disagree with this, since there is strong evidence that the explanation of some aspects of linguistic change requires appeal to non-social factors. For example, how could the approach which views linguistic change as merely a kind of social change explain why certain changes (for example, intervocalic voicing of stops) recur in language after language, despite the vastly different social settings in which these different languages are used? The explanation of linguistic change is not found solely in conscious change by speakers for social purposes, rather only rarely so. Internal factors are also important; both internal and external factors are important (see Chapter 11).

Different conceptions of linguistic change are often closely linked with the stand taken on the *actuation problem* (mentioned above). For example, James Milroy (1992: 10) stresses network theory's emphasis on language *maintenance*: 'In order to account for differential patterns of change at particular times and places [that is, to solve the actuation problem], we need first to take account of those factors that tend to maintain language states and resist change'. Strong network ties are seen as norm-enforcement mechanisms, a model for maintenance of local language norms against encroaching change from outside the network. How can the actuation problem, the question about how changes get started in the first place, be approached with a model based solely on norm maintenance, that is on resistance to change but not on change itself? In Milroy's view, linguistic change takes place in strong-tie networks only to the extent that they fail at their primary mission of maintaining the network norms and resisting change from outside. If the social network can only resist but not initiate change, with all change entering from without, how could network theory contribute to solving the actuation problem? The origins of these changes in the broader community from where they flow into the strong-tie networks appear to be more relevant to the actuation problem and generally to understanding how and why languages change.

7.7 The Issue of Lexical Diffusion

For the Neogrammarians, the three primary mechanisms of change were regular sound change, analogy and borrowing. Regularity for them meant that every instance of a sound changes mechanically, irrespective of particular words in which it is found, that is, that it affects every word in which the sound occurs in the same phonetic environment. Cases where a change does not affect all words in the same way at the same time were not seen to be the result of regular sound change, but as due to analogy or to dialect borrowing, as in the case of the variable result of the $*k > \int$ change in different words in Normandy (see above, Map 7.1) due to the differential impact of dialect borrowing from the Parisian prestige variety. This, in essence, constitutes an attempt to answer the transition question, of how change is implemented. The concept of *lexical diffusion*, used primarily by William Wang and his associates (Wang 1969; see Labov 1994: 421–543 for an extensive survey and evaluation), challenges Neogrammarian regularity. They see sound change as being implemented not by mechanically affecting every instance of a sound regardless of the particular words in which instances of the sound are found (as in the Neogrammarian position), but rather as change affecting the sound in certain words and then diffusing gradually to other words in the lexicon. Fully regular sound changes, in this view, are those in which the change diffuses across the lexicon until it reaches all words. This is like 'dialect borrowing', but with some words borrowing from others in the same dialect. It constitutes a different outlook on the transition problem. It should be kept in mind, however, that in spite of strong claims that lexical diffusion is a more basic mechanism by which change is transmitted than Neogrammarian regularity, very few cases of lexical diffusion have actually been reported, and most of these are doubtful.

While several cases have been analysed as lexical diffusion, most mainstream historical linguists have not been convinced. They see these cases as being better explained as the results of dialect borrowing, analogy and erroneous analysis. On closer scrutiny, most of these cases prove not to be real instances of lexical diffusion but to be more reliably explained by other means. Often it turns out that the phonetic conditioning environments are quite complex – important phonetic environments were missed in several of the cases for which lexical diffusion was claimed. Detailed studies of the same cases by people aware of the claims for lexical diffusion have found sounds behaving regularly in change in these environments and no evidence of lexical conditioning. When the environments are understood, Neogrammarian regularity is what was behind the changes and not lexical diffusion after all. In the examples from the history of Chinese, which had been influential support for lexical diffusion, it turns out that the extent of borrowing from literary Chinese into the varieties of Chinese studied was vastly more extensive than originally thought. That is, like the Normandy case (in Map 7.1), they amounted to just dialect borrowing, which proponents of lexical diffusion later called 'intimate borrowing'; these cases were a misreading of the influence of stylistic choices, language contact and sociolinguistic conditions in general. (See Labov 1994: 444–71.)

With this background, consider again the irregularities so commonly pointed out in the dialect atlases of various languages and the assumed hostility of dialect atlas data to the Neogrammarian regularity hypothesis. The collectors of the data did not take into account the fact that commonly the data collected from local dialects was the result of long interaction between local dialect forms and the dominant prestige or standard language, as in the case of the French forms recorded in Normandy. These atlas forms did not come to us recorded with tags identifying which words represent an uninterrupted inheritance from an original form versus which were replaced due to influence from an external source. Also, the methods involved in collecting the data for the atlases were not sufficiently sensitive to different styles and socially conditioned variation and were not geared to looking for complex phonetic conditioning environments. It is little wonder, then, that with dialect atlas evidence alone we seem to see support for the slogan 'each word has its own history'; but with more detailed information on social interaction of different varieties/dialects and on phonetic conditioning factors, we find the Neogrammarian regularity more firmly supported. The irregularities seem to develop not internally to a system, but through interaction or interference among systems (Labov 1994: 474). The Neogrammarians with their 'dialect borrowing' account were right all along! In fact, evidence of regular, phonetically conditioned sound change (and not lexical diffusion) in dialect geography turns out to be strong in the cases which have been investigated in detail (Labov 1994: 501).

Labov has attempted to reconcile the mostly regular changes with the few which seem to involve sound changes which affect some lexical items but not others. He notes that 'earlier stages of change are quite immune to such irregular lexical reactions [as implied in lexical diffusion]; and even in a late stage, the unreflecting use of the vernacular preserves that regularity' (Labov 1994: 453). This he calls 'change from below', below the level of awareness. Only in later stages of a change do speakers become aware of the change and give it sociolinguistic value (positive or negative), and this often involves the social importance of words. Change of this sort is what Labov calls 'change from above'. For him, lexical diffusion can involve only the later stages and change from above, the same changes which are often characterized by dialect mixture and analogical change, by a higher degree of social awareness or of borrowing from another system (Labov 1994: 542–3).

In summary, sound change is regular within its own system, though dialect borrowing and various influences from outside the system can result in changes which are less like regular exceptionless sound change. Consequently, to explain change we need both 'sound laws suffer no exceptions' and 'every word has its own history' – they address different things, both of which are important for the full picture of linguistic change.

Some of the topics of this chapter are considered further in relation to the explanation of linguistic change, treated in Chapter 11.

8

Internal Reconstruction

Language is the armoury of the human mind, and at once contains the trophies of its past and the weapons of its future conquests.

(Samuel Taylor Coleridge)

8.1 Introduction

Internal reconstruction is like the comparative method but applied to a single language. It is a technique for inferring aspects of the history of a language from what we see in that language alone. Lying behind internal reconstruction is the fact that when a language undergoes changes, traces of the changes are often left behind in the language's structure, as allomorphic variants or irregularities of some sort. The things that are compared in internal reconstruction, which correspond to the cognates of the comparative method, are the forms in the language which have more than one phonological shape in different circumstances, that is, the different allomorphs of a given morpheme, such as those found in alternations in paradigms, derivations, stylistic variants and the like. Internal reconstruction is frequently applied in the following situations where it can recover valuable information: (1) to isolates (languages without known relatives); (2) to reconstructed proto-languages; and (3) to individual languages to arrive at an earlier stage to which the comparative method can then be applied to compare this with related languages in the family. In this chapter, we will learn how to apply internal reconstruction, and we will take its uses and limitations into account.

8.2 Internal Reconstruction Illustrated

Lying behind internal reconstruction is the assumption that the variants (allomorphs) of a morpheme are not all original, but that at some time

225

in the past each morpheme had but one form (shape) and that the variants known today have come about as the result of changes that the language has undergone in its past. We internally reconstruct by postulating an earlier single form together with the changes – usually conditioned sound changes – which we believe to have produced the various shapes of the morpheme that we recognize in its alternants. The language reconstructed by internal reconstruction bears the prefix *pre-* (as opposed to the *proto-* of comparative-method reconstructions). For example, we would call the results of an internal reconstruction of English *Pre-English*. (Note, though, that *pre-* is sometimes used in historical linguistics where it has nothing to do with internal reconstruction; for example, it is possible to read about the 'Pre-Greeks' where what is intended is the Greeks before they appear in recorded history, or about 'Pre-English' which is not reconstructed but refers to a stage of English assumed to have existed before the earliest Old English texts but after the break-up of West Germanic.)

The steps followed in internal reconstruction, broadly speaking, consist of the following:

Step 1: Identify alternations, that is, forms which have more than one phonological shape (different allomorphs) in paradigms, derivations, different styles and so on.

Step 2: Postulate a single, non-alternating original form.

Step 3: Postulate the changes (usually conditioned sound changes) which must have taken place to produce the alternating forms. (Where relevant, determine the relative chronology – the sequence in which these changes took place.) As in the comparative method, we use all the information at our disposal concerning directionality of change and how natural or likely (or unexpected and unlikely) the changes we postulate are in order to evaluate the reconstruction and the changes we propose.

Step 4: Check the results to make certain that the changes we postulated do not imply changes for other forms that they do not in fact undergo; that is, we must guard against proposing changes which might seem to work for certain morphemes but which, if allowed to take place, would produce non-existent forms of other morphemes. We must also check to make certain that the postulated reconstructions are typologically plausible and do not imply things that are impossible or highly unlikely in human languages.

In actual practice, these steps are typically applied almost simultaneously and with little attempt to distinguish one step from the other. The best way to gain an understanding of internal reconstruction is through examples of its application, and several follow.

8.2.1 First example

Let us begin with a rather easy example from Tojolabal (Mayan). Compare the following words and notice the variants for the morpheme that means 'I':

(1) h-man	I buy	man	to buy
(2) h-lap	I dress	lap	to dress
(3) h-k'an	I want	k'an	to want
(4) k-il	I see	il	to see
(5) k-u?	I drink	u?	to drink
(6) k-al	I say	al	to say

In step 1, we identify *h*- and *k*- as alternants of the morpheme meaning 'I'; *h*- is the variant which occurs before consonants, and *k*- is the form which appears before vowels. In step 2, we attempt to postulate the original form of the morpheme for 'I' in Pre-Tojolabal. Three hypotheses suggest themselves: (1) **h-*(which would presuppose a change to *k*- before vowels to derive the other form of the morpheme, the *k* allomorph); (2) **k*- (with a change **k*- > *h*-before consonants to account for the *h*-variant); or (3) possibly some third thing (which would change into *h*-before consonants and into *k*-before vowels). The third alternative would require two independent changes (and thus would go against the criterion of economy, discussed in Chapter 5), whereas hypotheses (1) and (2) would each need only one change; therefore we abandon (3) under the assumption that it is less likely that two independent changes took place than it is that only one did. There is no particular phonetic motivation for *h*- to change into *k*- before vowels, as presupposed by hypothesis (1) (and if we had more data, we would see that there are plenty of words with initial *h*- before a vowel, for example, *ha?* 'water', *hune* 'one', *hi?* 'unripe ear of maize', etc.). However, a change of *k-to h-* before consonants is not phonetically unusual, a dissimilation encountered in other languages (and if we had more data, we would see there are no consonant clusters in Tojolabal with initial *k*-; the general directionality of *k* > *h* and not *h* > *k* was seen in Chapter 5). Therefore, we assume that hypothesis (2) with **k*- is more plausible. In step 3, we postulate that the **k*- which we reconstruct for 'I' in Pre-Tojolabal undergoes the change **k-to h-* before consonants and that this accounts for the *h*- variant of this morpheme. So, for example, we would reconstruct *k-man* 'I buy', and then the change of *k-* to *h-* before consonants would give modern *h-man*; for 'I see', however, we reconstruct **k-il*, and since this *k-* 'I' is before a vowel, it does not change, leaving modern Tojolabal with *k-il*. This reconstruction and the derivation of the modern forms are seen in Table 8.1.

TABLE 8.1: Internal reconstruction and derivation of Tojolabal *k-*

	'I buy'	*'I see'*
Pre-Tojolabal:	*k-man	*k-il
Change k > h /__C:	hman	—
Modern Tojolabal:	hman	kil

8.2.2 Second example

In Nahuatl (Uto-Aztecan), a large number of morphemes have two variant shapes, one with an initial *i* and one without, of the sort illustrated in 'foot', with its two allomorphs, *ikʃi* when without prefixes and *kʃi* when it occurs with prefixes (as in *ikʃi* -foot', but *no-kʃi* 'my foot'). In internal reconstruction, we must reconstruct a single form as original and attempt to account for the variants which occur by postulating changes which will derive them from the single reconstructed form. In this case, the two most likely choices are: (1) to reconstruct **ikʃi* together with some rule to delete the initial *i* in order to provide for the *kʃi* variant, as in *no-kʃi* 'my foot'; (2) to reconstruct **kʃi* and posit some rule to insert the initial *i* in appropriate contexts to give *ikʃi*. Since in Nahuatl there are numerous forms with initial *i* which do not lose this vowel with prefixes (for example, *n-ihti* 'my stomach' – the change of *no-* to *n-* before vowels is a general trait of the language, that is, $o > \emptyset$ / n_+V), it turns out to be impossible to write a rule which assumes the *i* of *ikʃi* was originally present but got lost due to the presence of the prefix (**no-ikʃi* > *no-kʃi* 'my foot'). This would wrongly predict, in step 4, that the non-alternating forms such as *ihti* should also lose their initial *i* (*no-ihti* > *no-hti*), but this does not happen (there is no ✘*no-hti* 'my stomach'; rather, the initial *i* is preserved in the form with the possessive prefix, *n-ihti*). (The notation ✘ is used here for 'non-occurring', 'erroneous' or 'ungrammatical' forms). The second hypothesis, however, encounters no such problem. We get the right results if we assume that the initial *i* was not originally present in the morpheme for 'foot' and reconstruct the words **kʃi* 'foot' and **no-kʃi* 'my foot', with *i* added to the first later by a rule of initial epenthesis, **kʃi* > *ikʃi* 'foot'. In looking at the phonological pattern of the language, we find that there are no initial consonant clusters and we therefore assume that a change added *i* to the beginning of words which formerly began in a consonant cluster:

Epenthesis rule: Ø > i / #__CC

Thus we reconstruct the forms and apply the epenthesis rule to produce the modern forms as shown in Table 8.2.

TABLE 8.2: Internal reconstruction and derivation of Nahuatl roots with initial *i*

	'foot'	*'my foot'*	*'stomach'*	*'my stomach'*
Pre-Nahuatl:	*kʃi	*no-kʃi	*ihti	*no-ihti
Epenthesis:	ikʃi		—	—
Vowel-loss				
(*o* > Ø / *n*__+V):	—	—	—	n-ihti
Modern Nahuatl:	ikʃi	no-kʃi	ihti	n-ihti

8.3 Relative Chronology

Sometimes in internal reconstruction when more than one change can apply to a particular form it is necessary to pay attention to the order in which the changes took place in the forms in question. The identification of the sequence (temporal order) of different changes in a language is called *relative chronology* (seen also in Chapters 2, 3 and 5). When more than one change is involved in the reconstruction, sometimes they can each affect a form, and in such situations it may be necessary to figure out which change or changes took place earlier and which later. There is no hard-and-fast procedure for working out the relative chronology of the changes. However, the criterion of *predictability* is the most useful – determining a chronological sequence of changes which, when applied in order to the words of that language, does not produce any non-occurring forms. This is illustrated in the next example.

8.3.1 Third example: Finnish

Consider the forms in Table 8.3. They provide a straightforward illustration of relative chronology (compare the discussion of this example in section 2.7 of Chapter 2).

TABLE 8.3: Finnish internal reconstruction

Essive singular		Nominative singular	
1. onne-na	'as happiness'	onni	'happiness'
2. sukse-na	'as (a) ski'	suksi	'ski'
3. vete-nä	'as water'	vesi	'water'
4. käte-nä	'as (a) hand'	käsi	'hand'
5. tuoli-na	'as (a) chair'	tuoli	'chair'

(NOTE: /ä/ = [æ]. The *na / nä* alternation is the result of vowel harmony in Finnish and is of no relevance to the discussion here.)

In these data, we note the alternants (allomorphs) of each root: *onne- / onni, sukse-/ suksi, vete-/ vesi,* amd *käte-/ käsi.* In internal reconstruction, we must postulate some unique, single form for each root in Pre-Finnish together with the changes we believe took place to produce the modern alternant forms of each root. We postulate that in 1–4 the stem-final vowel *e* must have been original and the forms with final *i* (those in the nominative singular case) are derived by the change of final *e* to *i*:

Rule 1: e > i /__#.

This is clearer in 1 and 2:

Pre-Finnish:	*onne-na	*onne	*sukse-na	*sukse
Rule 1:	—	onni	—	suksi
Modern Finnish:	onnena	onni	suksena	suksi

A conceivable alternative solution in which *i* would become *e* when not final (Rule X: *i > e /__+ C* (or something similar)) is impossible, since by Rule X, 5 *tuoli-na* should become *✗tuole-na*, but that does not happen. If we postulate for Pre-Finnish **tuoli-na* and **tuoli*, then Rule 1 simply does not apply to them, since there is no *e* in these forms to which it could apply. (Ultimately, *tuoli* 'chair' is a loanword in Finnish, but this does not change the results as far as this example is concerned.)

Rule 1, then, accounts for the *e-/ i* alternation in the forms in 1 and 2 (and indirectly for the lack of alternation in 5), but for 3 and 4 an additional rule is required:

Rule 2: t > s /__ i.

Both Rule 1 and Rule 2 apply to the forms in 3 and 4. With Rule 1 and Rule 2 in the right sequence – Rule 1 as the first change, followed later in time by the change in Rule 2 – we can account for modern *vesi* and *käsi*, as shown in Table 8.4:

TABLE 8.4: Derivation showing Finnish relative chronology

Pre-Finnish:	*vete-nä	*vete	*käte-nä	*käte
Rule 1:	—	veti	—	käti
Rule 2:	—	vesi	—	käsi
Modern Finnish:	vetenä	vesi	käte-nä	käsi

However, if we were to imagine that perhaps the changes had taken place in the reverse order, Rule 2 earlier and then Rule 1 later, we would get the wrong results, as seen in the hypothetical derivation in Table 8.5.

TABLE 8.5: Hypothetical derivation of Finnish with the wrong relative chronology

Pre-Finnish:	*vete-nä	*vete	*käte-nä	*käte
Rule 2:	—	—	—	—
Rule 1:	—	veti	—	käti
Modern Finnish:	vetenä	✗veti	käte-nä	✗käti

That is, in this hypothetical application of the changes in reverse order (in Step 4), we end up with the erroneous ✗*veti* 'water' and ✗*käti* 'hand'. Rule 2 cannot create the *s* in these words until after Rule 1 creates a final *i*, since Rule 2 requires an *i* after the *t* for it to become *s* (and in these words the *i* comes into existence only with the prior application of Rule 1). In this example, then, we conclude that the relative chronology was that Rule 1 (*e > i /__#*) took place first (**vete > veti*, **käte > käte > käti*) and then later in time the change in Rule 2 (*t > s /__i*) took place *veti > vesi*, *käti > käsi*).

8.3.2 Fourth example: Classical Greek

In Classical Greek paradigms, we find alternative forms of morphemes such as:

genes-si 'race, family (dative plural)'
gene-os 'race, family (genitive singular)'

Here we see two variants (allomorphs) of the root: *gene-* when followed

231

by a vowel-initial suffix (as in *gene-os*, with the 'genitive singular' *-os*), and *genes-* when followed by a consonant-initial suffix (as with 'dative plural' *-si* in *genes-si*). (In later developments, *geneos* changed to end up as *genūs* in major dialects, but that does not affect the story here.) Since there is no compelling phonetic motivation for a language to insert precisely an *s* before consonants (not *gene-si* > *genes-si*), we assume that the original form had the root-final *s* and that this *s* was lost between vowels, represented in Rule 1:

Rule 1 (Deletion of intervocalic *s*): s > Ø / V__V

The reconstruction and the result of this change are seen in the historical derivation presented in Table 8.6. However, in a different set of forms in Classical Greek, we encounter morphemes with different variants

TABLE 8.6: Derivation showing loss of intervocalic *s* in Classical Greek

	'dative plural'	*'genitive singular'*
Pre-Greek:	*genes-si	*genes-os
Rule 1 (Deletion of intervocalic *s*):	—	geneos
Classical Greek	genessi	geneos

(allomorphs) in which *t* and *s* alternate, where *s* is found intervocalically, as in:

ambros-ia 'food of the gods' (that is, 'immortality')/*ambrotos* 'immortal'
pos-is 'drink, beverage/*potēs* 'a drinking, a drink'

In this instance, we might first attempt to reconstruct internally by choosing the variant with *s* as original with a rule to show how it changed to *t* under certain circumstances; or vice versa, we might assume that the original forms are to be reconstructed with *t* with a rule to change this original *t* to *s* in appropriate contexts. The sound change of *s* to *t* before various vowels is extremely rare, and therefore, based on the known directionality of change, the reconstruction which presupposes **s* is unlikely. However, the change of *t* to *s* before *i* is found in many languages around the world, and in these data we see that the alternant with *s* is always before *i*, which leads us to reconstruct **t* as original and to postulate Rule 2:

Rule 2: t > s /__i

232

The reconstruction of these forms and the application of this change to them are illustrated by the historical derivation shown in Table 8.7.

TABLE 8.7: Derivation showing *t* to *s* before *i* in Classical Greek

	'immortality'	'immortal'	'drink'	'drinking'
Pre-Greek:	ambrot-ia	ambrot-os	pot-is	potēs
Rule 2 (*t* to *s* before *i*):	ambrosia	—	posis	—
Greek:	ambrosia	ambrotos	posis	potēs

Now that we have postulated two changes which affect Pre-Greek, Rules 1 and 2, the question of relative chronology comes up: which change took place earlier, which later? If we assume that the relative chronology was that first the change in Rule 2 took place and then later the change of Rule 1 occurred, we end up with the wrong result for forms such as *ambrosia* and *posis*, as shown in the hypothetical historical derivation of Table 8.8. Since ✗*ambroia* and ✗*pois* are erroneous,

TABLE 8.8: Hypothetical derivation showing wrong chronological order in Classical Greek

Pre-Greek:	*ambrot-ia	*pot-is	*genes-os	*genes-si
Rule 2 (*t* to *s* before *i*):	ambrosia	posis	—	—
Rule 1 (Deletion of intervocalic *s*):	ambroia	pois	geneos	—
Erroneous Greek:	✗ambroia	✗pois	geneos	genessi

the relative chronology must be that first the change of Rule 1 (s > Ø / V__V) took place and then sometime later, after the change in which intervocalic *s* was deleted had run its course, Rule 2 (t > s /__i) created some new forms with intervocalic *s*, the result of the change *t* > *s*/__*i*, as seen in the correct historical derivation in Table 8.9.

TABLE 8.9: Derivation showing the correct chronological order in Classical Greek

Pre-Greek:	*ambrot-ia	*pot-is	*genes-os	*genes-si
Rule 1 (Deletion of intervocalic *s*):	—	—	geneos	—
Rule 2 (*t* to *s* before *i*):	ambrosia	posis	—	—
Greek:	ambrosia	posis	geneos	genessi

Often, if comparative evidence from related languages is available, we can check the accuracy of our internal reconstructions. In the case of Greek *geneos* 'race, family (genitive singular)', which we postulated to be from Pre-Greek **genes-os*, the presence of an original **-s-* which we reconstructed for the Pre-Greek form is confirmed by cognates in some of Greek's sister languages, as in Sanskrit *jánas-as* and Latin *gener-is* (both 'genitive singular'), which show the *-s-* that we reconstructed in Pre-Greek **genes-* (in Latin the *-r-* of *gener-is* is due to the rhotacism of an earlier intervocalic *-s-* – *genesis* > *generis*).

8.3.3 Fifth example

Let us look at one more example, also from Classical Greek. Consider first the following forms:

Nominative singular	Genitive singular	
(1) ait^{h}íops	ait^{h}íopos	'Ethiopian'
(2) kló:ps	klo:pós	'thief'
(3) p^{h}léps	p^{h}lebós	'vein'
(4) p^{h}úlaks	p^{h}úlakos	'watchman'
(5) aíks	aigós	'goat'
(6) sálpiŋks	sálpiŋgos	'trumpet'
(7) t^{h}ɛ́:s	t^{h}ɛ:tós	'serf'
(8) elpís	elpídos	'hope'
(9) órni:s	órni:t^{h}os	'bird'
(10) kórus	kórut^{h}os	'helmet'
(11) hrí:s	hri:nós	'nose'
(12) delp^{h}í:s	delp^{h}í:nos	'dolphin'

Throughout these data, we see the non-alternating suffixes *-s* 'nominative singular' and *-os* 'genitive singular'; since they do not alternate, the best that we can do is tentatively reconstruct these to Pre-Greek as **s* and **os*, respectively. In (1), (2) and (4), we also see no alternations in the roots, only the non-alternating morphemes, *ait^{h}íop* 'Ethiopian', *klo:p-* 'thief' and *p^{h}úlak-* 'watchman', presumably from Pre-Greek **ait^{h}íop-*, **klo:p-* and **p^{h}úlak-*, respectively. However, in the other forms, we see alternations: (3) *p^{h}lep-/p^{h}leb-*, (5) *aik-/aig-*, (6) *sálpiŋk-/sálpiŋg-*, (7) *t^{h}ɛ:-/t^{h}ɛ:t-*, (8) *elpí-/elpíd-*, (9) *órni:-/órni:t^h-*, (10) *kóru-/kórut^h-*, (11) *hri:-/hri:n-* and (12) *delp^{h}í:-/delp^{h}í:n-*. These each require us to reconstruct a single original form in internal reconstruction and to postulate changes which derive the variant forms. In the case of (3) *p^{h}lep-/p^{h}leb-*, two hypotheses suggest themselves: Hypothesis I:

reconstruct for (2) $*p^hlep-$ and assume the p^hleb- allomorph is the result of intervocalic voicing, since it is found with *-os* in $p^hleb-ós$. Let's call this Rule A:

Rule A (intervocalic voicing): $p > b / V\_\_V$

TABLE 8.10: Derivation for Hypothesis I for Classical Greek 'vein'

	'nominative singular'	*'genitive singular'*
Pre-Greek	$* p^hlép-s$	$*p^hlep-ós$
Rule A ($p > b/V\_\_V$):	—	$p^hleb-ós$
Classical Greek	$p^hléps$	$p^hlebós$

This hypothesis would give us the derivation in Table 8.10. Hypothesis I would be fine if it only had to account for the alternation in $p^hléps/$ $p^hlebós$. The sound change postulated in Rule A would account for the *p/b* alternation in this form, but it makes the further prediction that Pre-Greek $*ait^híop-os$'Ethiopian (genitive singular)' should have become $ait^híobos$ by the intervocalic voicing of Rule A. However, this is wrong; ✗$ait^híobos$ does not occur – the correct form is $ait^híopos$. This means that we must abandon (or at least seriously modify) Hypothesis I. Let us now look at Hypothesis II.

Hypothesis II: reconstruct $*p^hleb-$ for (3) and assume that the p^hlep- allomorph is the result of devoicing before *s*, since it is found with *-s* in p^hlep-s (nominative singular). Let's call this Rule B:

Rule B (devoicing before *s*): $b > p/\_\_s$ (also $g > k$ and $d > t$, as in examples below)

TABLE 8.11: Derivation for Hypothesis II for Classical Greek 'vein'

	'nominative singular'	*'genitive singular'*
Pre-Greek	$*p^hléb-s$	$*p^hleb-ós$
Rule B ($b > p /\_\_s$):	$p^hléps$	—
Classical Greek	$p^hléps$	$p^hlebós$

This hypothesis would give the derivation in Table 8.11. Hypothesis II accounts for the *p/b* alternation in $p^hléps/p^hlebós$, but does not erroneously predict in (1) that Pre-Greek $*ait^híop-os$ 'Ethiopian (genitive singular)' should become ✗$ait^híobos$ (as the intervocalic voicing of Rule A in Hypothesis I does). Rather, in Hypothesis II we postulate Pre-Greek $*ait^híop-s$ and $*ait^híop-os$, and since these words have no *b*, nothing will change in Rule (B), which affects only forms with *b* (such as $p^h leb\acute{o}s / p^h l\acute{e}ps$), as illustrated in Table 8.12.

TABLE 8.12: Derivation of *ait^hop*- 'Ethiopian' in Hypothesis II

	'nominative singular'	*'genitive singular'*
Pre-Greek	*$ait^h\acute{\imath}op$-s	*$ait^h\acute{\imath}op$-os
Rule B (b > p /__s):	—	—
Classical Greek	$ait^h\acute{\imath}ops$	*$ait^h\acute{\imath}opos$

Thus, Hypothesis II makes correct predictions, while Hypothesis I makes erroneous predictions; therefore Hypothesis II is accepted and Hypothesis I rejected. Since the forms in (2) follow the same pattern, we reconstruct *$klo{:}p$- 'thief' for its root (*$klo{:}p$-s 'nominative singular' and *$klo{:}p$-ós 'genitive singular').

Turning now to the alternants in the forms in (5) for 'goat', *aík-/aig-*, we follow the pattern in Hypothesis II further, reconstructing Pre-Greek *aig-* 'goat' and applying Rule B (devoicing before *s*) to derive the *aík-* variant found in *aík-s* 'nominative singular'. That is, we reconstruct *aig-s* 'goat (nominative singular)' which becomes *aiks* by Rule B, and *aig-ós* 'goat (genitive singular)' which remains *aigós*, since no changes apply to it. The two variants of the root in (6), *sálpiŋk-/sálpiŋg-* 'trumpet', follow the same pattern, and we therefore reconstruct *sálpiŋg-s* 'nominative singular' and *sálpiŋg-os* 'genitive singular' in this case.

If we continue to follow the pattern in Hypothesis II, given $t^h\varepsilon{:}t$-ós 'serf (genitive singular)' in (7), we would reconstruct Pre-Greek *$t^h\varepsilon{:}t$-ós and we would expect the nominative singular to be ✗$t^h\varepsilon{:}t$-s; however, the actually occurring nominative singular form is $t^h\varepsilon{:}s$. Similarly in (8), from *elpíd-os* '(genitive singular)' we would expect the nominative singular to be the non-occurring ✗*elpits*, that is, a Pre-Greek form *elpid-s* to which Rule B (devoicing before *s*) applied would give ✗*elpits*. However, we do not get *elpits*, but rather *elpís*. Similarly, from *órni:t^h-os* in (9), *kórut^h-os* in (10), *hri:n-ós* in (11) and *delp^{h}í:n-os* in (12) we would expect the corresponding nominative singular forms to be ✗*órni:t^h-s*, ✗*kórut^h-s*, ✗*hri:n-s* and ✗*delp^{h}í:n-s*, respectively, not the actually occurring *órni:s*, *kórus*, *hrí:s* and *delp^{h}í:s*. Unlike the forms in (1–6) whose roots end in labials (*p* or *b*) or velars (*k* or *g*), what the forms in (7–12) have in common is that their root-final consonant is an alveolar (*t*, *d*, *t^h*, *n*) in the genitive singular forms, which is missing from the nominative singulars. It would not be possible, starting with the nominative singular forms which lack these root-final consonants, to write a plausible account to predict just which consonant would be added in each instance to derive the genitive singular forms. Therefore, we reconstruct for Pre-Greek roots the forms reflected in the genitive singulars (as we did for the forms in (1–6) in Hypothesis II), and then derive the nominative singular variants by postulating Rule C, deletion of alveolars before *s*:

Rule C (alveolar deletion before *s*): t, d, t^h, n > Ø /__s

Note that in this case we cannot tell whether Rule B took place before Rule C or whether the historical events happened in the reverse order, since in either sequence we obtain correct results. In the order Rule B followed by Rule C, reconstructed *elpid-s* would first be devoiced by Rule B, giving *elpits*, and then the *t* would be lost by Rule C (alveolar loss before *s*), giving the correct form *elpís* (that is, *elpid-s* > by Rule B *elpits* > by Rule C *elpís*). In the order Rule C followed by Rule B, reconstructed *elpid-s* would become *elpís* by Rule C, in which the final alveolar (*d* in this case) is lost before the -*s* of the nominative singular; Rule B would then not apply to this form, since there would no longer be a *d* which could be made voiceless (*t*) by this rule (that is, *elpid-s* > by Rule C *elpís*; Rule B not applicable; result: Classical Greek *elpís*).

The derivation of the nominative singular forms from the postulated Pre-Greek internal reconstruction to Classical Greek is illustrated in Table 8.13.

TABLE 8.13: Internal reconstruction of Classical Greek 'nominative singular' forms

	Pre-Greek	Rule B (devoicing)	Rule C (alveolar loss before *s*)	Classical Greek *form*
(1)	*ait^{h}íop-s	—	—	ait^{h}íops
(2)	*klṓp-s	—	—	klṓps
(3)	*p^{h}léb-s	p^{h}lép-s	—	p^{h}léps
(4)	*p^{h}úlak-s	—	—	p^{h}úlaks
(5)	*aíg-s	aík-s	—	aík-s
(6)	*sälpiŋg-s	sälpiŋk-s	—	sälpiŋks
(7)	*t^{h}ḗt-s	—	t^{h}ḗs	t^{h}ḗs
(8)	*elpíd-s	elpíts	elpís	elpís
(9)	*órnīt^h-s	—	órnīs	órnīs
(10)	*kórut^h-s	—	kórus	kórus
(11)	*hrín-s	—	hrís	hrís
(12)	*delp^{h}ín-s	—	delp^{h}ís	delp^{h}ís

8.4   The Limitations of Internal Reconstruction

In attempting to apply the method of internal reconstruction, we need to keep in mind the circumstances in which we can expect more reliable results and those where it is of limited or no value for recovering a language's history. Let us examine some of these limitations.

(1) The strongest limitation is that, while internal reconstruction is often able to recover conditioned changes, *internal reconstruction cannot recover unconditioned changes*. For example, in the unconditioned merger of **e*, **o*, **a* to *a* in Sanskrit (seen in Chapter 2), these original vowels ended up as *a*. If we attempt to reconstruct internally the Pre-Sanskrit forms of *dánta* 'tooth' or *dva* 'two', we find no alternations in these vowels which would provide clues to the fact that *danta* originally had **e* (Proto-Indo-European **dent*, compare Latin *dent-*) but that *dva-* had **o* (Proto-Indo-European **dwo*, compare Latin *duo-*). It is simply impossible to recover via internal reconstruction the unconditioned change which these Sanskrit vowels underwent: if *a* is all we ever see, there is no basis in Sanskrit itself for seeing anything else in the past of the *a* which occurs in these words.

(2) The method may be reliable if later changes have not eliminated (or rendered unrecognizable) the context or contexts which condition the change that we would like to recover as reflected in alternations in the language. We have seen several examples of this in the cases discussed in this chapter. However, *internal reconstruction can be difficult or impossible if later changes have severely altered the contexts which conditioned the variants that we attempt to reconstruct*. For example, some splits are impossible to recover due to subsequent changes, as illustrated by the case of voiced fricatives in English. We observe in English such forms as *breath/breathe* ([brɛθ]/[brið]), *bath/bathe* ([bæθ]/[beið]), *wreath/wreathe* ([[riθ]/[rið]) which suggest an alternation between θ and ð (voiceless and voiced dental fricative). Because we can identify alternations, we would like to be able to reconstruct a single original form, but since in these forms both alternants can occur in exactly the same phonetic environment, we have no basis for reconstruction. From other sources of information, however, we know that the voiced fricatives in Old English were allophones of the voiceless fricatives in intervocalic position. Remnants of this rule are seen in such forms as *mouths* (with [ð], compare *mouth* with [θ]) and *paths* (with [ð], compare *path* with [θ]), and so on. The problem is that, due to later sound changes which eliminated certain vowels, these voiced fricatives are no longer intervocalic: these later changes have so altered the context which conditioned the change to voicing of fricatives between vowels

that, in spite of the alternations we find which propel us to attempt to reconstruct, we are unable to do so with any reliability in this case. Moreover, later loanwords have also made the original context which conditioned the alternation no longer clearly visible. For example, in looking at *mother*, *rather* and *either* (each with intervocalic [ð]), we might be tempted to see evidence of the former intervocalic voicing (θ > ð/ V__V); however, later loanwords such as *lethal, ether, method, mathematics* and so on, with intervocalic [θ], obscure the former intervocalic voicing beyond recognition, since, after the borrowings entered the language, [θ] and [ð] are both found between vowels, and the former complementary distribution with only [ð] intervocalically and [θ] elsewhere no longer holds. In short, subsequent sound changes and borrowings have rendered the conditioning of the former intervocalic voicing of fricatives in English unrecognizable, making internal reconstruction in this case unsuccessful.

Another example (already considered in a different context in Chapter 2) which illustrates this point is that of such singular–plural alternations as seen in *mouse/mice* and *goose/geese*. Given the alternations, we would like to be able to apply internal reconstruction, but the context which originally produced these variant forms is now totally gone, due to subsequent changes. Though today such plurals are irregular, they came about in a relatively straightforward way. In most Germanic languages (except Gothic), back vowels were fronted (underwent 'umlaut') when followed by a front vowel or glide (semivowel) in the next syllable, and the plural suffix originally contained a front vowel, as in Proto-Germanic *mu:s* 'mouse'/*mu:s-iz* 'mice' and *go:s* 'goose'/*go:s-iz* 'geese'. In the plural, the root vowels were fronted in Pre-English times: *mu:s-i* > *my:s-i* and *go:s-i* > *gø:s-i*. Two later changes took place: this final vowel was lost, and the front rounded vowels *y* and *ø* became unrounded to *i* and *e* respectively, merging with *i* and *e* from other sources. These changes produced the alternations, *mi:s* and *ge:s* as the plurals, but *mu:s* and *go:s* as the singulars. Finally, all these forms underwent the Great Vowel Shift, giving Modern English /maus/ 'mouse', /mais/ 'mice', /gus/ 'goose' and /gis/ 'geese' (see Chapter 2). This sequence of changes is represented in Table 8.14.

However, since the environment for umlaut was lost in subsequent changes which deleted the-*i* which had caused the umlauting, we are unable to recover this history through internal reconstruction, even though the alternations seen in these singular–plural pairs provoke us to imagine that some historical explanation which we cannot recover by this method alone lies behind these different forms of the same root.

Finally, while the examples presented in this chapter deal with sound changes, it is important to mention that internal reconstruction of morphology and aspects of syntax is also possible in favourable circumstances.

TABLE 8.14: Historical derivation of 'mouse', 'mice', 'goose', 'geese'

	'mouse'	*'mice'*	*'goose'*	*'geese'*
Proto-Germanic:	*mu:s	*mu:s-iz	*go:s	*go:s-iz
Early Pre-English:	mu:s	mu:s-i	go:s	go:s-i
Umlaut:	—	my:s-i	—	gø:s-i
Loss of -*i*:	—	my:s	—	gø:s
Unrounding:	—	mi:s	—	ge:s
Great Vowel Shift:	maus	mais	gus	gis
Modern English:	/maus/	/mais/	/gus/	/gis/

8.5 Internal Reconstruction and the Comparative Method

Sometimes it is suggested that internal reconstruction should be under-taken first and the comparative method applied afterwards. In this view, internal reconstruction would help us to see beyond the effects of many recent changes so that we would have access to an earlier stage of the language for use in the comparative method when sister languages are compared with one another. This is often the case. Usually, both internal reconstruction and the comparative method lead in the same direction. However, in reality there is no rigid principle about which method is to be applied first – they can be applied in either order. Often, reconstruction by the comparative method reveals alternations which the proto-language underwent, and it is perfectly legitimate to apply internal reconstruction to these proto-alternations in order to reach even further back in time, to a pre-proto-language. In this event, the sequence would be the com-parative method first, followed by internal reconstruction, or perhaps first internal reconstruction to the individual languages, then the com-parative method to related languages, and then internal reconstruction again to the reconstructed proto-language. In any event, it is important to check, when internal reconstruction is applied before the comparative method, that it does not factor out alternations which were present in the proto-language.

A case from Balto-Finnic will illustrate the point. Finnish had alternations such as *jalka* 'leg (nominative singular)'/*jalan* 'leg (genitive singular)'. This has been internally reconstructed as **jalka* / **jalka-n*, under the assumption that **k* was lost in non-initial closed syllables (in this case in the genitive form, the syllable is closed by *n*, causing the change). (Some postulate that **k* in closed syllables first changed to γ and then later was lost (**k* > γ > Ø), and this view is no doubt aided by the fact that there are older written materials which document that this is precisely what happened in the history of these words.) If the comparative method is applied after internal reconstruction, then the forms utilized by the comparative method will be Pre-Finnish **jalka* and **jalka-n*, and evidence of the alternation will have been factored out. However, if we turn to sister languages of Finnish in the Balto-Finnic subgroup, we find the following forms: Estonian *jalg* [*jalk*] 'leg (nominative singular)' and *jala* 'leg (genitive singular)'. Estonian underwent two additional changes which Finnish did not, loss of final vowels in certain contexts (*jalka* > [*jalk*] 'nominative singular') and loss of final *-n* (*jalan* > *jala* 'genitive singular'). An internal reconstruction of Estonian results in **jalka* 'leg (nominative singular)' and **jalka(X)* 'leg (genitive singular)', where from other forms it is known that the alternation normally takes place in closed syllables and therefore something now missing, signalled here by *X*, is posited as formerly having closed the syllable and causing the alternation. Finally, North Saami, a related language, has the forms *juolʲke* 'leg (nominative singular)'/*juolʲge* 'leg (genitive singular)', where Saami, too, has lost final *-n* in an independent change, and internal reconstruction gives **juolʲke* 'leg (nominative singular)' / **juolʲke(X)* 'leg (genitive singular)'. Notice now that if we compare only the results of internal reconstruction in these three sister languages, we have no access to the alternation, as seen in Table 8.15. However, if the comparative method is applied before internal reconstruction, the alternation is revealed to have been part of the proto-language, as seen in Table 8.16. The moral is clear: internal reconstruction can help by offering forms to be compared in the comparative method which see past the disruptions of many recent changes; nevertheless, caution should be exercised so that alternations which should legitimately be reconstructed to the proto-language by the comparative method are not factored out by previous internal reconstruction and then lost sight of. (See Anttila 1968, 1989: 274.)

TABLE 8.15: Comparison of Balto-Finnic 'leg' forms after internal
reconstruction

	nominative singular	*genitive singular*
Pre-Finnish	*jalka	*jalka-n
Pre-Estonian	*jalka	*jalka(X)
Pre-Saami	*juolke	*juolke(X)
Proto-Balto-Finnic	**jalka	**jalka-n

TABLE 8.16: Comparison of Balto-Finnic 'leg' forms before internal
reconstruction

	nominative singular	*genitive singular*
Finnish	jalka	jala-n
Estonian	jalg [jalk]	jala
Saami	juolke	juolge
Proto-Balto-Finnic	*jalka	*jalɣa-n

8.6 Exercises

Exercise 8.1 German internal reconstruction

Compare the following German words; find the variants of forms of the
roots (do not be concerned with the forms of the suffixes), and apply
internal reconstruction to these. Reconstruct a single original form for
the morphemes which have alternate forms, and postulate the changes
which you think took place to produce the modern variants. Present
your reasoning; why did you choose this solution? (Hint: the criterion
of predictability is important in this case.) (German traditional orthography is given in parentheses after the forms, which are presented in
phonemic transcription. The 'e' of the final syllable in these forms is
phonetically closer to [ə] in most dialects, though this is not a relevant
fact for solving this problem.)

1. ty:p (Typ)	'type'	ty:pen (Typen)	'types'
2. to:t (tot)	'dead'	to:te (Tote)	'dead people'
3. lak (Lack)	'varnish'	lake (Lacke)	'kinds of varnish'
4. tawp (taub)	'deaf'	tawbe (Taube)	'deaf people'
5. to:t (Tod)	'death'	to:de (Tode)	'deaths'
6. ta:k (Tag)	'day'	ta:ge (Tage)	'days'

Exercise 8.2 *Kaqchikel internal reconstruction*

Kaqchikel is a Mayan language of Guatemala. Compare the following words; find the forms which have variants; apply internal reconstruction to these forms. Reconstruct a single original form for the morphemes which have alternate forms, and postulate the changes that you think must have taken place to produce these variants. Present your reasoning; why did you choose this solution and reject other possible hypotheses? (Note that -*ir* is the inchoative suffix, meaning 'to become/turn into', and-*isax* is the causative suffix.)

1. nax	'far'	naxt-ir-isax	'to distance (to make it become far)'
2. čox	'straight'	čoxm-ir	'to become straight'
		čoxm-il	'straightness'
3. war	'sleep'	wart-isax	'to put to sleep (to cause to sleep)'
4. ax	'ear of corn'	axn-i	'of corn' (*i* 'adjective suffix')

Exercise 8.3 *Sanskrit internal reconstruction*

Compare the following forms from Sanskrit. Identify the variants of the various roots and attempt to reconstruct a Pre-Sanskrit form for each root. Note that the reconstructions for the forms in 10–16 are not straightforward and may require some creative thinking on your part. What change do you think took place to produce these forms? Why did you choose this particular analysis and not some other?

NOTE: *j* = [ǰ], IPA [dʒ]; consonants with dots underneath are retroflex.)

	Nominative		*Instrumental*	
1.	šarat	'autumn'	šarad-a	'by autumn'
2.	sampat	'wealth'	sampad-a	'by wealth'
3.	vipat	'calamity'	vipad-a	'by calamity'
4.	marut	'wind'	marut-a	'by wind'
5.	sarit	'river'	sarit-a	'by river'
6.	jagat	'world'	jagat-a	'by world'

	Nominative		*Ablative*	
7.	suhṛt	'friend'	suhṛd-ā	'from friend'
8.	sukṛt	'good deed'	sukṛt-ā	'from good deed'
9.	sat	'being'	sat-ā	'from being'
10.	bhiṣak	'physician'	bhiṣaj-ā	'from physician'
11.	ṛtvik	'priest'	ṛtvij-ā	'from priest'

12. yuk	'yoke'	yuj-ā	'from yoke'
13. srak	'garland'	sraj-ā	'from garland'
14. rāṭ	'king'	rāj-ā	'from king'
15. iṭ	'worship'	ij-ā	'from worship'
16. sṛṭ	'creation'	sṛj-ā	'from creation'

(Bhat 2001: 33, 91, 94)

Exercise 8.4 *Internal reconstruction of Finnish vowels*

Compare the following words; what happens when the *i* 'plural' or *i* 'past tense' morphemes are added to these roots? State what the variants (allomorphs) of the roots are; apply internal reconstruction to these forms. Reconstruct a single original form for each root morpheme and postulate the changes which you think must have taken place to produce these variants. Present your reasoning; why did you choose this solution and reject other possible hypotheses?

NOTE: double vowels, such as *aa, yy,* and so on, are phonetically long vowels ([a:], [y:], etc. Finnish *ä* = IPA [æ], *ö* = [ø].

HINT: Native Finnish words do not have (surface) *oo, ee,* or *öö* [øø]; rather, Finnish has *uo, ie,* and *yö* [yø] where long mid vowels would be expected. The correct answer for words containing these diphthongs does NOT involve the first vowel being lost when *i* is added (that is, NOT *suo + i > soi* by loss of *u*).

1. saa	'gets'	sai	'got'
2. maa	'land'	mai-	'lands'
3. puu	'tree'	pui-	'trees'
4. luu	'bone'	lui-	'bones'
5. pii	'tooth (of rake)'	pii-	'teeth'
6. pää	'head'	päi-	'heads'
7. pyy	'wood grouse'	pyi-	'wood grouses'
8. täi	'louse'	täi-	'lice'
9. suo	'grants'	soi	'granted'
10. suo	'swamp'	soi-	'swamps'
11. luo	'creates'	loi-	'created'
12. syö	'eats'	söi	'ate'
13. lyö	'hits'	löi	'hit'
14. tie	'road'	tei-	'roads'
15. vie	'takes'	vei	'took'
16. talo	'house'	taloi-	'houses'

17. hillo	'jam'	hilloi-	'jams'
18. halu	'desire'	halui-	'desires'
19. hylly	'shelf'	hyllyi-	'shelves'
20. nukke	'doll'	nukkei-	'dolls'
21. tekö	'deed'	teköi-	'deeds'
22. sata	'hundred'	satoi-	'hundreds'
23. pala	'piece'	paloi-	'pieces'
24. hella	'stove'('cooker')	helloi-	'stoves' ('cookers')
25. hilkka	'hood'	hilkkoi-	'hoods'
26. hiha	'sleeve'	hihoi-	'sleeves'
27. sota	'war'	sotei-	'wars' (soti- in Modern Finnish)
28. pora	'drill'	porei-	'drills' (pori- in Modern Finnish)
29. muna	'egg'	munei-	'eggs' (muni- in Modern Finnish)
30. rulla	'roll'	rullei-	'rolls' (rulli- in Modern Finnish)
31. tupa	'cabin'	tupei-	'cabins' (tupi- in Modern Finnish)
32. jyvä	'grain'	jyvei-	'grains' (jyvi- in Modern Finnish)
33. hätä	'distress'	hätei-	'distresses' (häti- in Modern Finnish)
34. mökä	'hullabaloo'	mökei-	'hullabaloos' (möki- in Modern Finnish)

Exercise 8.5 Nahuatl internal reconstruction

Nahuatl is a Uto-Aztecan language, spoken by over 1,000,000 people in Mexico; it was the language of the Aztecs and the Toltecs. Compare the following words. Find the forms which have variants; apply internal reconstruction to these forms. Reconstruct a single original form for the morphemes which have alternate shapes, and postulate the changes which you think must have taken place to produce these variants. Can you establish a relative chronology for any of these changes? Present your reasoning; why did you choose this solution and reject other possible hypotheses? (NOTE: *tl* is a single consonant, a voiceless lateral affricate; k^w is a labialized velar stop and is a single segment.) Note that the morpheme which has the allomorphs *-tl, -tli, -li* is traditionally called the 'absolute'; it has no other function than to indicate a noun root which has no other prefixes or suffixes.

1a	tepos-tli	'axe'		13a	ikʃi-tl	'foot'
1b	no-tepos	'my axe'		13b	no-kʃi	'my foot'
1c	tepos-tlān	'place of axes'		14a	ikni-tl	'fellow'
2a	kak-tli	'shoe, sandal'		14b	no-kni	'my fellow'
2b	no-kak	'my shoe, sandal'		15a	isti-tl	'fingernail'
3a	teʃ-tli	'flour'		15b	no-sti	'my fingernail'
3b	no-teʃ	'my flour'		16a	ihti-tl	'stomach'
4a	mis-tli	'cougar'		16b	n-ihti	'my stomach'
4b	mis-tlān	'place of cougars'		17a	īʃte-tl	'eye'
5a	kal-li	'house'		17b	n-īʃte	'my eye'
5b	no-kal	'my house'		18a	ihwi-tl	'feather'
6a	tlāl-li	'land'		18b	n-ihwi	'my feather'
6b	no-tlāl	'my land'		19a	itskʷin-tli	'little dog'
7a	čīmal-li	'tortilla griddle'		19b	n-itskʷin	'my little dog'
7b	no-čīmal	'my tortilla griddle'		20a	ička-tl	'cotton'
7c	čīmal-lān	'place of tortilla griddles'	20b	no-čka	'my cotton'
8a	mīl-li	'cornfield'		21a	okič-tli	'male, man'
8b	no-mīl	'my cornfield'		21b	n-okič	'my husband'
8c	mīl-lān	'place of cornfields'		22a	kaʃi-tl	'bowl'
9a	āma-tl	'paper, fig tree'		22b	no-kaʃ	'my bowl'
9b	n-āma	'my paper, fig tree'		23a	kʷawi-tl	'tree, wood'
9c	āma-tlān	'place of paper, fig trees'	23b	no-kʷaw	'my tree, wood'
10a	e-tl	'bean'		24a	māyi-tl	'hand'
10b	n-e	'my bean'		24b	no-māy	'my hand'
10c	e-tlān	'place of beans'		25a	ʃāmi-tl	'brick'
11a	siwā-tl	'woman'		25b	no-ʃān	'my brick'
11b	no-siwā	'my wife'		26a	pāmi-tl	'flag'
11c	siwā-tlān	'place of women'		26b	no-pān	'my flag'
12a	ol-li	'rubber'		27a	kōmi-tl	'jug'
12b	n-ol	'my rubber'		27b	no-kōn	'my jug'
12c	ol-lān	'place of rubber'				

Exercise 8.6 Indonesian internal reconstruction

Identify the morphemes which have more than one variant in the following data from Indonesian (an Austronesian language). Apply internal reconstruction to these forms; reconstruct a single original form for each of the roots and for the prefix, and postulate the changes you think must have taken place to produce these variants. Can you establish a relative chronology for any of these changes? Provide sample derivations which show your reconstruction and how the changes apply to it for both the simple and the prefixed forms in 2, 12, 13, 15 and 19. (The prefix in the second column has a range of functions, among them, it places focus on the agent ('doer') of a verb, derives transitive or causative verbs, and derives verbs from nouns.)

HINT: relative chronology is important to the solution of this problem. (/ɲ/ = palatal nasal.)

	simple form	prefixed form	gloss
1.	lempar	məlempar	'throw'
2.	rasa	mərasa	'feel'
3.	wakil	məwakil-	'represent'
4.	yakin	məyakin-	'convince'
5.	masak	məmasak	'cook'
6.	nikah	mənikah	'marry'
7.	ŋačo	məŋačo	'chat'
8.	ɲaɲi	məɲaɲi	'sing'
9.	hituŋ	məŋhituŋ	'count'
10.	gambar	məŋgambar	'draw a picture'
11.	kirim	məɲirim	'send'
12.	dəŋar	məndəŋar	'hear'
13.	tulis	mənulis	'write'
14.	bantu	məmbantu	'help'
15.	pukul	məmukul	'hit'
16.	ǰahit	məɲǰahit	'sew'
17.	čatat	məɲčatat	'note down'
18.	ambil	məŋambil	'take'
19.	isi	məŋisi	'fill up'
20.	undaŋ	məŋundaŋ	'invite'

Exercise 8.7 Tol (Jicaque) internal reconstruction

Jicaque (called Tol by its speakers) is spoken in Honduras. State the variants (allomorphs) of the roots and of the possessive pronominal prefixes; apply internal reconstruction to these forms. Reconstruct a single original form for each root morpheme and write the changes which you think must have taken place to produce these variants. Present your reasoning; why did you choose this solution and reject other possible hypotheses? (HINT: the original form of the possessive pronouns was: *n- 'my', *hi- 'your', *hu- 'his'; original *n+h > n.) Note that what is structurally a labialized *w* is realized phonetically as [w^i], but is written as *w^w* in this problem.

	my	*your*	*his*	*Meaning of the noun root*
1.	mbata	peta	pota	'duck'
2.	mbapaj	pepaj	popaj	'father'
3.	ndaʔ	teʔ	toʔ	'man's brother'
4.	ndarap	terap	torap	'woman's younger sister'
5.	ŋk^{h}an	k^{h}en	k^{h}on	'bed'
6.	nlara	lera	lora	'mouth'
7.	nts^{h}am	ts^{h}em	ts^{h}om	'foot'
8.	mbe	hepe	p^{w}e	'rock, stone'
9.	mbep	hepep	p^{w}ep	'fingernail'
10.	mberam	heperam	p^{w}eram	'tongue'
11.	mp^{h}el	hep^{h}el	p^{hw}el	'arm'
12.	ŋgerew	hekerew	k^{w}erew	'cousin'
13.	ŋk^{h}ere	hek^{h}ere	k^{hw}ere	'bone'
14.	ŋgiwaj	hikiwaj	k^{w}iwaj	'woman's brother'
15.	nǰič	hičič	č^{w}ič	'tendon'
16.	nǰipe	hičipe	č^{w}ipe	'paired sibling'
17.	mbomam	p^{j}omam	hopomam	'chokecherry'
18.	mp^{h}ok	p^{hj}ok	hop^{h}ok	'cheek'
19.	ŋgol	k^{h}ol	hokol	'belly'
20.	nts'ul	ts$^{'j}$ul	huts'ul	'intestines'
21.	mp^{h}ɨja	p^{hj}eja	hɨp^{h}ɨja	'tobacco'
22.	mp'ɨs	p$^{'j}$es	hɨp'ɨs	'deer'
23.	ndɨm	t^{j}em	hɨtɨm	'heel'
24.	mbasas	wesas	wosas	'woman's sister-in-law'
25.	mbis	hiwis	w^{w}is [w^{i}is]	'tooth'
26.	mbin	hiwin	w^{w}in [w^{i}in]	'toad'
27.	mbojum	w^{j}ojum	howojum	'husband'
28.	namas	mes	mos	'hand'
29.	nemen	hemen	m^{w}en	'neck'
30.	nimik	himik	m^{w}ik	'nose'
31.	nɨmɨnɨ	m^{j}enɨ	hɨmɨnɨ	'yam'
32.	namap	hemap	homap	'aunt'
33.	nasunu	hesunu	hosunu	'chest'

Exercise 8.8 Samoan internal reconstruction

Compare words in the two columns. Identify the morphemes which have more than one variant. Reconstruct a single original form for all the morphemes here, and postulate the changes you think must have taken place to produce these forms. Can you establish a relative chronology for any of these changes? Why did you choose this solution and reject other possible hypotheses?

NOTE: many roots will have two allomorphs; the suffix also has more than one variant in several of the cases.

HINT: think 'predictability' and exploit gaps in the inventory of the consonants that can occur as the last consonant in these words.

1.	alofa	'love'	alofaŋia	'loved'
2.	taŋo	'grasp'	taŋofia	'grasped'
3.	fua	'measure'	fuatia	'measure'
4.	au	'reach'	aulia	'reached'
5.	faitau	'read'	faitaulia	'read'
6.	ʔai	'eat'	ʔaia	'eaten'
7.	ula	'smoke'	ulafia	'smoked'
8.	na	'hide'	natia	'hidden'
9.	fau	'bind'	fausia	'bound'
10.	ʔata	'laugh'	ʔataŋia	'laughed'
11.	inu	'drink'	inumia	'drunk'
12.	taofi	'hold'	taofia	'held'
13.	mu	'burn'	muina	'burned'
14.	tuʔu	'put'	tuʔuina	'put'
15.	faŋa	'feed'	faŋaina	'fed'
16.	sauni	'prepare'	saunia	'prepared'
17.	siʔi	'raise'	siʔitia	'raised'
18.	pisi	'splash'	pisia	'splashed'
19.	ao	'gather'	aofia	'gathered'
20.	ilo	'perceive'	iloa	'perceived'
21.	ʔave	'take'	ʔavea	'taken'
22.	oso	'jump'	osofia	'jumped'
23.	ʔino	'hate'	ʔinosia	'hated'
24.	filo	'mix'	filoŋia	'mixed'
25.	fasioti	'kill'	fasiotia	'killed'
26.	utu	'fill'	utufia	'filled'
27.	ufi	'cover'	ufitia	'covered'
28.	ʔai	'eat'	ʔaiina	'eaten' (cf. 6)
29.	afio	'come in'	afioina	'(has) come in'
30.	laʔa	'step over'	laʔasia	'stepped over'
31.	manaʔo	'want'	manaʔomia	'wanted'
32.	mataʔu	'destroy'	mataʔutia	'destroyed'
33.	milo	'twist'	milosia	'twisted'

| 34. taŋi | 'cry' | taŋisia | 'cried' |
| 35. vavae | 'divide' | vavaeina | 'divided' |

Exercise 8.9 Chulupí internal reconstruction

Chulupí (also called Nivaklé) is a Matacoan language of northern Argentina and Paraguay. Compare the forms in the two columns; identify the morphemes which have more than one phonological shape (variant). Attempt to reconstruct a unique form for each of these words in Pre-Chulupí, and state the changes which have taken place, according to your analysis, in the transition from Pre-Chulupí to modern Chulupí. Is there any relative chronology involved in the changes you postulate? If so, state what it is and show sample derivations of at least four word pairs (for example both words of 12, 14, 18, and 20).

NOTE: /kl/ is a single segment, both phonemically and phonetically – the velar closure and the lateral articulation are released simultaneously as a single sound; /ɑ/ is a back low vowel, and contrasts with /a/, a cental low vowel; ł = voiceless *l*; *C'* = glottalized [ejective] consonants. The plural suffixes, in the second column, have several different forms, but do not attempt to reconstruct them.

Set I

1. axutsax	'hawk'	axutsx-as	'hawks'
2. fatsux	'centipede'	fatsx-us	'centipedes'
3. snomax	'ash'	snomx-as	'ashes'
4. łasex	'seed'	łasx-ey	'seeds'
5. kutsxanax	'thief'	kutsxanx-as	'thieves'
6. ipɑset	'my lip'	ipɑst-es	'my lips'
7. nas-uk	'guayacán (tree)'	nas-k-uy	'guayacans'
8. faʔay-uk	'algarrobo (acacia tree)'	faʔay-k-uy	'algarrobos'
9. axay-uk	'mistol (tree)'	axay-k-uy	'mistols '

Set II

10. inkɑʔp	'year'	inkap-es	'years'
11. łuʔp	'nest'	łup-is	'nests'
12. k'utxaʔn	'thorn'	k'utxan-is	'thorns'
13. łsaʔt	'vein'	łsat-ay	'veins'
14. tisuʔx	'quebracho (tree)'	tisx-uy	'quebrachos'
15. k'utsaʔx	'old man'	k'utsx-as	'old men'

Set III

16. towɑk	'river'	towx-ay	'rivers'
17. finok	'tobacco'	finx-ay	'tobaccos'
18. ituʔk	'my arm'	itx-uy	'my arms'
19. tsanuʔk	'duraznillo (tree)'	tsanx-uy	'duraznillos'

20. namač	'axe'	namx-ay	'axes'
21. klišaʔklayič	'mute person'	klišaʔklayx-es	'mute persons'
22. sateč	'head'	satx-es	'heads'

Set IV

23. asakts-uk	'bola verde (tree)'	asakts-uk-uy	'bola verde trees'
24. yikts-uk	'palo borracho (tree)'	yikts-uk-uy	'palo borracho trees'
25.[= 10] inkɑʔp	'year'	inkɑp-es	'years'

9

Semantic Change and
Lexical Change

They that dally [= converse idly] nicely [= foolishly] with words may
quickly make them wanton [= unmanageable].

(Shakespeare, *Twelfth Night* III, 1)

9.1 Introduction

Changes in meaning and vocabulary excite people. Non-linguists are
fascinated by why *bloody* and *bugger* are obscene in Britain and not in
America – the words don't even mean the same thing in the two
places – and why *pissed* means 'angry' in the USA but 'drunk' in the UK,
and why *pissed* is so much less obscene and more tolerated than it was
a generation ago in both countries. People want to know how words such
as *ditz, dork, dweeb, geek, nerd, twit, wimp, wuss* and *yutz* get added to
the language so fast and why their meanings seem to change so rapidly,
and whatever happened to the *groovy* of late 1960s love songs, anyway?
Some find a certain delight (some would say a twisted satisfaction) in
the seeming irony in the semantic history of *to bless*, from Old English
blēdsian (earlier *blōdsian*), which originally meant 'to mark with blood'
in an act of consecration in pagan sacrifice. With umlaut in mind, it is
easy to see the connection between *blood* and the *blēd-* part of *blēdsian*
(just think *to bleed* to see the connection more clearly). Some are
charmed (perhaps perversely so) by a favourite example of handbooks,
the story behind *cretin*. English *cretin* is borrowed from French *crétin*
'stupid', which comes, to the surprise and delight of etymology-lovers,
ultimately from Latin *christiānum* 'Christian'. In Romance languages,

252

the term for 'Christian' was used also for 'human being' to distinguish people from beasts; the semantic shift which gives the modern sense of *cretin* 'a stupid person' apparently came about in Swiss French dialects especially in reference to a class of dwarves and physically deformed idiots in certain valleys of the Alps, used euphemistically to mean that even these beings were human, and from this came the semantic shift from 'Christian' to 'idiot'. Those who learn other languages often ask how true cognates can come to have such different meanings in related languages, as in the English–German cognates *town/Zaun* 'fence', *timber/Zimmer* 'room', *bone/Bein* 'leg', *write/reissen* 'to tear, rip'. They ask why a seemingly innocent French word such as *baiser*, which the dictionary says means 'to kiss', has changed its meaning to 'to copulate' with no warning to save the unsuspecting language learner from embarrassment. Vocabulary change can be a matter of alarm and deep emotional concern. This is evidenced by the creation of language academies and the appointment of language commissions to protect the purity of languages such as French and Spanish, and as seen, for example, in letters to the press in Canada, Britain, New Zealand and South Africa which denounce on the one hand the invidious creeping encroachment of Americanisms in vocabulary and on the other hand decry the degeneration of young people's all-too-limited vocabulary into nothing but slang (so they claim), holding up writers of famous literature as models of how we all should talk in order to be considered proper human beings who uphold our moral and linguistic obligations to the language. This chapter is about what linguists think about changes in meaning and in vocabulary, the topic which non-linguists find both exciting and alarming.

In linguistics (also in anthropology, philosophy and psychology), there are many approaches to semantics, the study of meaning. Unfortunately, these various theoretical approaches to semantics and the traditional historical linguistic treatments of change in meaning have typically had little in common, though clearly we would be in a better position to explain semantic change if we could base our understanding of change in meaning on a solid theory of semantics. Some recent approaches do attempt, with limited success, to reconcile the differences. Given the importance of semantic change, this chapter presents both a traditional classification of kinds of semantic changes and some more recent thinking concerning regularities and general tendencies in meaning change. Semantic change deals with change in meaning, understood to be a change in the concepts associated with a word, and has nothing to do with change in the phonetic form of the word. However, there are also aspects of lexical change which do not fall under this definition of semantic change, and we will look into them as well. Note that some aspects of semantic change and vocabulary change have already come up in previous chapters, under analogy in Chapter 4 and calques (semantic borrowing) in Chapter 3; we will consider grammaticalization in Chapter 10.

9.2 Traditional Considerations

Work in semantic change has been almost exclusively concerned with lexical semantics (change in the meaning of individual words), and that is the focus in this chapter. Semantic change is mostly concerned with the meaning of individual lexical items, whereas much of semantic theory involves logical relations among items in longer strings. There are various classifications of types of semantic change, and there is nothing special about the classification presented here. Some of the categories overlap with others, and some are defined only vaguely, meaning that some instances of semantic change will fit more than one type while others may fit none comfortably. It is probably best to consider this classification as offering a sort of broad scheme for organizing kinds of semantic change, but with no pretensions of being particularly complete or adequate, only (it is hoped) useful.

9.2.1 Widening (generalization, extension, broadening)

In semantic changes involving widening, the range of meanings of a word increases so that the word can be used in more contexts than were appropriate for it before the change. Changes from more concrete to more abstract meanings fit here.

(1) *Dog*. English *dog* first appeared with the more specific meaning of 'a (specific) powerful breed of dog', which generalized to include all breeds or races of dogs.

(2) *Salary*. Latin *salārium* was a soldier's allotment of salt (based on Latin *sal* 'salt'), which then came to mean a soldier's wages in general, and then finally, as in English, wages in general, not just a soldier's pay.

(3) *Cupboard*. In Middle English times, *cupboard* meant 'a table ("board") upon which cups and other vessels were placed, a piece of furniture to display plates, a sideboard', whose meaning then became 'a closet or cabinet with shelves for keeping cups and dishes', and finally in America it changed to mean any 'small storage cabinet'. In parts of Canada, *cupboard* has been extended to mean also what others call a 'wardrobe' or 'clothes closet'. Spanish *armario* 'cupboard' was borrowed from Latin in the Middle Ages where it had to do with 'arms',

'weapons', and meant 'armoury'; later its meaning widened to include present-day 'clothes closet, cupboard'. French *armoire* 'wardrobe, locker, cabinet' (also borrowed into English form French) has the same history.

(4) Spanish *caballero*, originally 'rider, horseman', expanded to include also 'gentleman, man of upper society' (since only men of means could afford to be riders of horses).

(5) Spanish *estar* 'to be' (especially 'to be in a location') < Latin *stāre* 'to stand'.

(6) Spanish *pájaro* 'bird' < Latin *passer* 'sparrow'.

(7) Finnish *raha* 'money' originally meant 'a fur-bearing animal' and its 'pelt'. The skins were an important means of exchange in the past, and *raha* came to mean 'skin used as medium of exchange'; when new means of exchange took the place of the old ones, *raha* shifted its meaning to 'money', its only meaning today (Ravila 1966: 105).

9.2.2 Narrowing (specialization, restriction)

In semantic narrowing, the range of meanings is decreased so that a word can be used appropriately only in fewer contexts than it could before the change. Changes of more abstract meanings to more concrete ones fit this category.

(1) *Meat* originally meant 'food' in general (as in the King James translation of the Bible) and later narrowed its meaning to 'meat' ('food of flesh'); this original meaning is behind compounds such as *sweet-meat* 'candy'. (Compare the Swedish cognate *mat* 'food'.)

(2) *Hound* 'a species of dog (long-eared hunting dog which follows its prey by scent)' comes from Old English *hund* 'dog' in general.

(3) *Wife* meant 'woman' in Old English times (as in the original sense of *midwife*, literally a 'with-woman'). It narrowed to mean 'woman of humble rank or of low employment, especially one selling commodities of various sorts'. The former meaning is preserved in *old wives' tales* and the second in *fishwife*. Finally it shifted to 'married woman, spouse'.

(4) *Deer* narrowed its sense from Old English *dēor* 'animal' (compare the German cognate *Tier* 'animal').

(5) *Fowl* 'bird (especially edible or domestic)' has narrowed its sense from Old English *fugol* which meant 'bird' in general (compare the German cognate *Vogel* 'bird').

(6) *Girl*, which meant 'child or young person of either sex' in Middle English times, narrowed its referent in Modern English to 'a female child, young woman'.

(7) *Starve* 'to suffer or perish from hunger' is from Old English

steorfan 'to die'. (Compare the German cognate *sterben* 'to die').

(8) French *soldat* 'soldier' comes from *solder* 'to pay' and thus meant 'a paid person', a narrowing from 'any paid person' to 'someone in the military'.

(9) French *drapeau* 'flag' meant first 'the piece of cloth fastened to a staff' (derived from *drap* 'cloth, sheet'; compare English *drape*, borrowed from French).

(10) Spanish *rezar* 'to pray' < Old Spanish *rezar* 'to recite, say aloud' (from Latin *recitāre* 'to recite, say aloud', the source from which *recite* in English is borrowed).

As will be seen in Chapter 10, many examples of grammaticalization involve semantic narrowing, from a broader lexical meaning to a narrower grammatical function.

9.2.3 Metaphor

Definitions of 'metaphor' (from Greek *metaphorā* 'transference') vary and are often vague; that is, it is often difficult to determine whether a given instance fits the definition or not. Metaphor involves understanding or experiencing one kind of thing in terms of another kind of thing thought somehow to be similar in some way. Metaphor in semantic change involves extensions in the meaning of a word that suggest a semantic similarity or connection between the new sense and the original one. Metaphor is considered a major factor in semantic change. It has been likened to analogy where one thing is conceptualized in terms of another, with a leap across semantic domains. The semantic change of *grasp* 'seize' to 'understand', thus can be seen as such a leap across semantic domains, from the physical domain ('seizing') to the mental domain ('comprehension') (see Traugott and Dasher 2002: 28). A much-repeated example is English *bead*, now meaning 'small piece of (decorative) material pierced for threading on a line', which comes from Middle English *bede* 'prayer, prayer bead', which in Old English was *bed*, *beode* 'prayer' (compare the German equivalent *Gebet* 'prayer'). The semantic shift from 'prayer' to 'bead' came about through the metaphoric extension from the 'prayer', which was kept track of by the rosary bead, to the rosary bead itself, and then eventually to any 'bead', even including 'beads' of water. Frequently mentioned examples of metaphoric extensions involve expressions for 'to kill': *dispose of, do someone in, liquidate, terminate, take care of, eliminate* and others. In slang, there are many metaphoric changes for 'drunk' based on forms whose original meaning is associated with being 'damaged' in some way: *blasted, blitzed, bombed, hammered, obliterated, ripped, shredded, smashed, tattered, wasted* and many more. Another area of metaphor for 'drunk' involves being saturated with liquid: *pissed, sauced, sloshed, soaked.*

Other examples are:

(1) French *feuille* 'leaf, sheet of paper' < 'leaf (of plant)'; Spanish *hoja* 'leaf, sheet of paper' < 'leaf' (both from Latin *folia* 'leaves, plural of *folium* 'leaf').

(2) French *entendre* 'to hear' comes by metaphor from original 'to understand' (compare the Spanish cognate *entender* 'to understand').

(3) Spanish *sierra* 'saw' was applied by metaphor to 'mountain range'; now there is *sierra* 'saw' and *sierra* 'mountain range'.

(4) Spanish *pierna* 'leg' < Latin *perna* 'ham'.

(5) *root* (of plant) > 'root of plant, root of word, root in algebra, source'.

(6) French *fermer* 'to close' originally meant 'to fix, make firm or fast'. Spanish *firmar* 'to sign (with one's signature)' has the same source.

(7) Latin *captāre* 'to catch, to try to seize, to trap' became in French *chasser* 'to hunt, to chase, to drive away, to cause a hurried departure' (the source from which English *chase* is borrowed, which means both 'to go after, try to catch' and 'to drive (away)').

(8) French *chapeau* 'hat, bonnet' originally meant 'garland'.

(9) English *stud* 'good-looking, sexy man' of slang origin, derived by metaphor from *stud* 'a male animal (especially a horse) used for breeding'.

(10) English *chill* 'to relax, calm down' of slang origin came about by metaphoric extension of the original meaning of *chill* 'to cool'.

9.2.4 Metonymy

Metonymy (from Greek *metōnomia* 'transformation of the name') is a change in the meaning of a word so that it comes to include additional senses which were not originally present but which are closely associated with the word's original meaning, although the conceptual association between the old and new meanings may lack precision. Metonymy tra-ditionally was held to be an important factor in semantic change, though less important than metaphor. Metonymy might be thought to be con-ceptual shifts within the same semantic domain (Traugott and Dasher 2002: 28–29). That is, metonymic changes typically involve some con-tiguity in the real (non-linguistic) world. They involve shift in meaning from one thing to another that is present in the context (though being present may be a conceptual judgement call not necessarily immediately apparent to us before the change takes place). For example, English *tea* means, in addition to the drink, 'the evening meal' in many English-speaking locations. A much-repeated example is English *cheek* 'fleshy side of the face below the eye'; Old English *cēace* meant 'jaw, jawbone', which over time shifted to the sense of Modern English *cheek*.

Traugott and Dasher (2002) give metonymy a more important role in semantic change than is traditionally the case. They do not believe that metaphor and metonymy in principle exclude each other, since easily understood metaphors can also be seen as typical associations – in some instances the notion of a leap across semantic domains (metaphor) and change within the same domain (metonymy) may not be clear or even relevant. Traugott and Dasher believe that it must be possible for the target (the semantic concept after the change) and/or the source (before the change) of a potential metaphor to be understood or conceptualized metonymically for metaphor to be possible (p. 29).

Some examples of metonymy are:

(1) French *jument* 'mare' < 'pack horse'.

(2) Spanish *cadera* 'hip' < 'buttocks' < ultimately Latin *cathedra* 'armchair'. (Compare the French cognate *chaise* 'chair', from earlier *chaire*, from the same Latin source.)

(3) Spanish *mejilla* 'cheek' < Latin *maxilla* 'jaw'.

(4) Spanish *plata* 'silver' has been extended to mean also 'money'.

(5) Spanish *acera* 'sidewalk' < Old Spanish *façera* 'façade, front of buildings on street or square'.

(6) Spanish *timbre* 'bell (as a telephone bell or doorbell), postage stamp' originally meant 'drum'; by metonymy this extended to include a 'clapperless bell' (struck on the outside with a hammer), then 'the sound made by this sort of bell', and then 'the sonorous quality of any instrument or of the voice', then 'tone' (of a sound); from the round shape of a bell, it also extended to mean 'helmet-shaped', then 'the crest of a helmet', 'the crest in heraldry' (the ornament placed above the shield), and from this the meaning was extended to include 'the official mark stamped on papers', to 'the mark stamped by the post office upon letters', and finally to 'postage stamp'. (French *timbre* 'tone, postage stamp' has the same history of semantic changes; English *timbre* 'the distinctive quality of a sound' is borrowed from French.)

(7) French *sevrer* 'to wean' comes from Latin *sēparāre* 'to part, divide, separate' (that is, from 'to separate' in general to 'to separate from the mother's breast'). (English to *sever* 'to separate (by force, by cutting or tearing)' was borrowed from French *sevrer* before the semantic shift to 'to wean' had taken place.)

(8) English *flake* 'irresponsible person' of slang origin is by metonymy from the original meaning of *flake* 'a small, loose, flat bit' – 'flaking' is usually considered an unfortunate thing to happen to most things.

A common sort of metonymy, sometimes thought to be connected with *clipping* or *ellipsis* (see Section 9.4.9), is the use of the name of the place for a product characteristic of it, as in French *champagne* 'champagne', from the name of the region, *Champagne*. (For other examples, see section 9.4.3 below.)

9.2.5 Synecdoche

Synecdoche (from Greek *sunekdokhé* 'inclusion'), often considered a kind of metonymy, involves a part-to-whole relationship, where a term with more comprehensive meaning is used to refer to a less comprehensive meaning or vice versa; that is, a part (or quality) is used to refer to the whole, or the whole is used to refer to part, for example *hand*, which was extended to include also 'hired hand, employed worker'. Some common examples found in various languages are 'tongue' > 'language', 'sun' > 'day', 'moon' > 'month'.

(1) Spanish *boda* 'wedding' comes from Latin *vōta* 'marriage vows', where the term for part of the whole, namely the 'vows', came to signal the whole, in this case the 'wedding'.

(2) German *Bein* 'leg' originally meant 'bone' (cognate with English *bone*).

(3) French *tableau* 'picture, panel, board' < Latin *tabula* 'board' (compare English *table*, a loanword ultimately from this same source).

A special kind of synecdoche is *displacement* (also called *ellipsis*), where one word absorbs part or all of the meaning of another word with which it is linked in a phrasal constituent (usually Adjective–Noun), for example, *contact(s)* from *contact lens(es)* and *a capital* from *a capital city*, where the notion of 'city' has been absorbed into the word *capital* (English *capital* is a loan from French). (Some see this also as a kind of syntactic change.)

(1) French *succès* 'success' comes from *succès favorable* 'favourable issue, event' (derived from *succéder* 'to follow, transpire'; compare Latin *successus* 'advance, result', derived from *succēdere* 'to follow, undergo, replace'). (French is the source of borrowed *success* in English.)

(2) French *journal* 'newspaper' is a displacement from *papier journal* 'daily paper' (*papier* 'paper' + *journal* 'daily'). In English, *a daily* (from *daily paper*) has the same meaning and has developed in the same way.

(3) Spanish *hermano* 'brother' < Latin *frāter germānus* 'brother of the

259

same parent', where *germānus* 'of the same parent' was used in the sense of 'true, authentic' and eventually displaced the expected form from Latin *frāter* 'brother'.

(4) *sexual intercourse > intercourse.*

(5) French *foie* 'liver' and Spanish *higado* 'liver' < Latin *iecur ficatum* 'fig-stuffed liver' by ellipsis so that only the reflex of *ficatum* 'fig-stuffed' remains in the meaning 'liver'.

(6) Finnish *yskä* 'cough' comes from original *yskä tauti*, literally 'chest sickness', *yskä* 'breast, lap' + *tauti* 'sickness', where *yskä* now no longer has the connotation of 'breast, chest' (Ravila 1966: 106).

(7) An often-cited example is *private soldier > private*, where *private* after the change came to mean 'ordinary/regular soldier' (contrasted with 'officer'), taking on the meaning of the whole phrase.

9.2.6 Degeneration (pejoration)

In degeneration (often called *pejoration*), the sense of a word takes on a less positive, more negative evaluation in the minds of the users of the language – an increasingly negative value judgement. A famous, oft-cited example is English *knave* 'a rogue', from Old English *cnafa* 'a youth, child', which was extended to mean 'servant' and then ultimately to the modern sense of *knave* 'rogue, disreputable fellow' (compare the German cognate *Knabe* 'boy, lad'). Examples of the degeneration of terms for women are well known and are often cited as examples in works dealing with social issues. For example, in colloquial German, *Weib* means 'ill-tempered woman' though in Standard German it just means 'woman' (the English cognate *wife* also formerly meant 'woman'). A great many of the terms for women which initially were neutral (or at least not so negative) degenerated so that today they are quite negative in connotation:

> *spinster* 'unmarried older woman' < 'one who spins'.
> *mistress* < originally from a borrowing from Old French *maistresse* 'a woman who rules or has control'; earlier in English it meant 'a woman who employs others in her service, a woman who has the care of or authority over servants or attendants'.
> *madam* 'the female head of a house of prostitution' < 'a title of courtesy used as a polite form of address to a woman' (from *Madame*, originally borrowed from Old French *ma dame* 'my lady').
> Italian *putta* and Spanish *puta* 'whore' earlier meant just 'girl' (compare Old Italian *putta* 'girl', *putto* 'boy'; Latin *putus* 'boy', *puta* 'girl').

Spanish *ramera* 'prostitute' earlier meant 'innkeeper's wife, female innkeeper'.

Some other examples of degeneration are:

(1) English *silly* 'foolish, stupid' comes from Middle English *sely* 'happy, innocent, pitiable', from Old English *sǽlig* 'blessed, blissful' (compare the German cognate *selig* 'blissful, happy').

(2) English *churl* 'a rude, ill-bred person' is from Old English *ceorl* 'man, man without rank, lowest rank of freemen', which became 'serf, tenant farmer' in Middle English, later 'countryman, peasant, rustic', then debased to 'base fellow, villain', and finally it came to have the modern sense of 'rude, ill-bred fellow' (compare the German cognate *Kerl* 'guy, chap, fellow').

(3) English *villain* 'criminal, scoundrel' was borrowed from French *villein* 'person of the villa/farm/homestead, serf, farm worker', and in Middle English meant 'low-born, base-minded rustic, a man of ignoble ideas or instincts', but later came to mean 'unprincipled or depraved scoundrel' and 'a man naturally disposed to criminal activities'.

(4) Spanish *siniestro* 'sinister' < Old Spanish *siniestro* 'left' (from Latin *sinister* 'left', the source of the loanword *sinister* in English).

(5) English *dilettante* did not originally have a negative connotation, but meant 'devoted amateur, one with love of a subject'; it shifted its meaning to 'a dabbler, amateur who lacks the understanding of professionals', and then to 'one with superficial interest in an area of knowledge'. *Amateur* is similar, originally a lover of the topic (a French loan into English, from Latin *ama-tor* 'lover, one who loves'), then it acquired the meaning of 'a non-professional who engages in an activity for pleasure', and eventually was extended also so that now it includes the meaning of 'an incompetent person'.

(6) English *disease* 'illness' formerly meant 'discomfort' (*dis-* + *ease*, like *un-easy* today).

9.2.7 Elevation (amelioration)

Semantic changes of elevation involve shifts in the sense of a word in the direction towards a more positive value in the minds of the users of the language – an increasingly positive value judgement.

(1) *pretty* < Old English *prættig* 'crafty, sly'.

(2) *fond* < past participle of Middle English *fonnen* 'to be foolish, silly'.

(3) English *knight* 'mounted warrior serving a king', 'lesser nobility (below baronet)' comes from Old English *cniht* 'boy, servant', which

shifted to 'servant', then 'military servant', and finally to the modern senses of 'warrior in service of the king' and 'lesser nobility'. (Compare the German cognate *Knecht* 'servant, farm hand'.)

(4) Spanish *caballo* 'horse' < Latin *caballus* 'nag, workhorse'.

(5) Spanish *calle* 'street' < Latin *calle* '(cattle-)path'.

(6) Spanish *casa* 'house' < Latin *casa* 'hut, cottage'.

(7) Spanish *corte* 'court' < Latin *cohortem*, *cortem* 'farmyard, enclosure', which came to mean 'division of a Roman military camp', which was extended to include 'body of troops (belonging to that division)' to 'imperial guard' and then further to 'palace' (see English *court*, a loan from Old French *court*, Modern French *cour* 'court (legal, royal), courtship' with the same Latin origin as the Spanish forms).

(8) The *villa* of the Middle Ages meant 'farm, homestead', but was elevated in French *ville* to 'city, town', Spanish *villa* 'village, town, country house' (compare Italian *villa* 'country house').

(9) English *dude* 'guy, person' (slang in origin) was in 1883 a word of ridicule for 'a man who affects an exaggerated fastidiousness in dress, speech and deportment, concerned with what is aesthetically considered "good form", a dandy'.

(10) English *nice* originally meant 'foolish, stupid, senseless', borrowed from Old French *ni(s)ce* 'foolish, stupid' (from Latin *nescius* 'ignorant, unaware'; compare Spanish *necio* 'foolish, imprudent', from the same Latin source).

9.2.8 Taboo replacement and avoidance of obscenity

Much is written about semantic changes and changes in vocabulary which involve responses to taboo and obscenity, and euphemism in general, though many of these changes might better be treated merely as examples of degeneration and metaphor and so on. In the sorts of semantic changes considered so far, focus is on changes in the meaning of words whose phonetic form mostly remains unaltered. There are cases of lexical replacement where a meaning remains but the phonetic realization of it is changed in some way, usually by substituting some other lexical item which had other denotations of its own before the change. Thus, lexical replacements involve more than meaning shifts, although change in the meaning may also be involved. Changes involving taboo and obscenity are prime examples of this sort. For instance, in English, *ass* 'long-eared animal related to a horse' has essentially been replaced in America by *donkey* (or *burro*) because it is considered too close for comfort to obscene *ass* 'derriere, arse'; *cock* 'adult male chicken' is replaced by *rooster* due to discomfort from the obscene associations of *cock* with 'penis'. In dialects of English where *bloody* is obscene, what is generally called a *bloody nose* in North America becomes *blood nose* or *bleeding nose* in order to avoid the taboo word. The following two examples were mentioned in Chapter 6.

(1) Spanish *huevo* 'egg' came to mean both 'egg' and 'testicle', but because of the obscene associations of 'testicle', in colloquial Mexican Spanish *huevo* as 'egg' was avoided and replaced by *blanquillo* 'egg', originally 'small white thing' (*blanco* 'white' + -*illo* 'diminutive').

(2) Latin American Spanish *pájaro* 'bird' came to be associated obscenely also with 'penis', and for this reason *pajarito* is usually substituted for 'bird', from *pájaro* 'bird' + -*ito* 'diminutive'. This taboo avoidance is carried even further in Kaqchikel and K'iche' (Mayan languages of Guatemala), where in many dialects the native term *ts'ikin* 'bird' has become taboo due to influence from Spanish *pájaro* 'penis, bird' (Spanish is the politically dominant language of the region), and therefore has been replaced by *čikop* '(small) animal'. Thus the meaning of *čikop* has been extended to include both '(small) animal' and 'bird', while that of *ts'ikin* has been restricted now to only or predominantly 'penis', with the meaning 'bird' either eliminated or now very recessive.

Changes involving *euphemism*, the replacement of words regarded as unpleasant, are part of this discussion. Favoured examples involve the many euphemistic replacements of words meaning 'toilet'. Terms for 'toilet' frequently come to be considered indelicate, and substitutions lacking the distressing sentiments are made. The room where indoor toilets were installed was called *water closet* (abbreviated WC) in Britain; this was soon replaced by *toilet*, originally a loan from French *toilette* 'small cloth' (diminutive of *toile* 'cloth, towel') which in English originally meant 'a wrapper for clothes, a night-dress bag', then 'a cloth or towel thrown over the shoulders during hairdressing', then 'a cloth cover for a dressing table', then 'articles used in dressing', 'furniture of the toilet' 'toilet-table', 'toilet service', and then 'the table upon which these articles are placed', 'the action or process of dressing', 'a dressing room with bathing facilities', and finally 'toilet/WC/bathroom'. Other euphemistic replacements include *lavatory, bathroom, restroom, commode, loo, john* and many others.

Spanish *embarazada* 'pregnant' (originally meaning 'encumbered') has essentially replaced earlier *preñada* 'pregnant'. (English *embarrass* also earlier meant 'to encumber, impede, hamper [movements, actions]', a borrowing from French *embarrasser* 'to block, to obstruct'.)

Not only can words be replaced or lost due to avoidance of obscenities and taboo, but also they are often changed phonetically to give more euphemistic outcomes, one source of new vocabulary. English has many such 'deflected' forms, for example: *blasted, darn, dang, dadnabbit, fudge, gadzooks, gosh, jeez, shucks, zounds* and many others. Varieties of Spanish have *pucha, puchis, púchica, futa* and the like as euphemistic replacements for *puta* 'whore' (very obscene); *chin* in Mexican Spanish replaces the very obscene *chingar* 'to have sexual intercourse (crudely)'. Examples of this sort are found in many languages. (Other cases of avoidance of taboo and obscenity are also seen in the discussion of *avoidance of homophony*, Chapter 11.)

9.2.9 Hyperbole

Hyperbole (*exaggeration*, from Greek *hyperbolē* 'excess') involves shifts in meaning due to exaggeration by overstatement.

(1) English *terribly, horribly, awfully* and other similar words today mean little more than 'very' (a generic intensifier of the adjective which they modify); by overstatement they have come to have no real connection with their origins, *terror, horror, awe* and so on.

(2) German *sehr* 'very' < 'sorely'.

(3) German *quälen* 'to torment, torture' < Proto-Germanic *k^waljan* 'to kill' (compare the English cognate *quell*, from Old English *cwellan* 'to kill, slay').

(4) English slang *lame* 'stupid, awkward, socially inept', from the original meaning 'crippled, having an impaired limb'.

9.2.10 Litotes

Litotes (*understatement*, from Greek *litótēs* 'smoothness, plainness') is exaggeration by understatement (such as 'of no small importance' when 'very important' is meant). In many languages, examples of litotes are found involving verbs meaning 'to kill'. For example, English *kill* originally meant 'to strike, beat, hit, knock'. If you were to say *hit* but intend it to mean 'kill', this would be an understatement.

(1) French *meurtre* 'murder, homicide' comes via litotes from 'bruise', still seen in the etymologically related verb *meurtrir* 'to bruise' (compare the Spanish cognate *moretón* 'bruise, black-and-blue spot').

(2) French *poison* 'poison' originally meant 'potion, draught' (English *poison* was borrowed from French after this semantic shift).

(3) English *bereaved, bereft* 'deprived by death' < 'robbed' (Old English *be-* + *rēafian* 'to rob, plunder, spoil').

(4) English slang *inhale* 'to eat something fast' < 'to breathe in, draw in by breathing'.

9.2.11 Semantic shift due to contact

Though it is not generally found in traditional classifications of semantic change, examples of semantic shift due to language contact are occasionally pointed out in work on the history of specific languages. The following are a few examples.

(1) In K'iche' (Mayan), *kye:x* originally meant 'deer'; however, with the introduction of horses with European contact, *kye:x* came to mean 'horse'. Eventually, to distinguish 'deer' from 'horse', the term for 'deer' became *k'iče' kye:x*, literally 'forest horse'. (NOTE: *y* = IPA [j], [kje:χ].)

(2) In Lake Miwok (in California, of the Miwok-Costanoan family), with the introduction of European guns, the word *kó:no*, which originally meant 'bow', shifted to include 'gun'; the 'gun' meaning then extended so fully that 'bow' is now *hintí:l kó:no*, literally 'old-time gun' (*hintí:l* is a borrowing from Spanish *gentil* 'pagan', originally used to refer to unchristianized Indians) (Callaghan and Gamble 1997: 112). (See also calques, in Chapter 3 (3.7.7).)

9.2.12 Summary of traditional classification

As is easy to see, the categories of semantic change in this classification are not necessarily distinct from one another; rather, some of them overlap and intersect. For this reason, some scholars consider 'narrowing' and 'widening' to be the principal kinds of semantic change, with others as mere subtypes of these two. Some emphasize the tendency for change to be in the direction from *concrete* to *abstract* (see below). Instances of overlapping and intersection are easily found in the examples listed here. For example, a semantic change could involve widening, degeneration and metonymy all at once, as in instances where terms for male and female genitals have taken on negative meanings for a man or woman of negative character, though often obscene (as in the meanings of English *prick* as 'penis' and 'miscreant male'). Another case is Yiddish *schmuck* 'penis, fool, stupid person', which originally meant 'jewel' (compare German *Schmuck* 'jewel, ornament'), but shifted to mean 'penis' (roughly analogous to the English jocular expression *the family jewels* to refer to the same general thing), then, as in the previous example, was extended further to 'fool, stupid person' (and along the way lost the original meaning of 'jewel'). *Schmuck* has been borrowed into English, primarily with the meaning of 'miscreant male'.

9.3 Attempts to Explain Semantic Change

Such general classifications of semantic change seem to offer little in the way of explaining how and why these changes take place in the ways they do. Nevertheless, many scholars have called for a search for regularities and explanations in semantic change, and some general tendencies have been discussed and some generalizations proposed. It is important to see what general understanding they may offer. The more traditional classifications of kinds of semantic change are generally thought to be useful for showing what sorts of changes might occur, but some of the generalizations that have been based on them amount to little more than a repetition in different form of the classification on which they are based. Others point out that semantic change and lexical change will not be explained in a vacuum, but will require appeal to and coordination with analogy, syntax (especially in the form of grammaticalization; see Chapter 10), discourse analysis, pragmatics and social history. Because sociocultural historical facts are often relevant, some insist that it is useless to seek generalizations to explain semantic change, although most would admit that some general statements about how and why meanings change may be possible even if not all semantic changes are regular or predictable.

Earlier work on semantic change was not totally without attempts at generalization. A general mechanism of semantic change was believed to be the associative patterns of human thought, and thus traditional approaches to meaning change typically had a psychological-cognitive orientation, though social context and pragmatic factors were emphasized by others. All of these factors play a role in more recent work on semantic change.

In the past, it was rarely asked how semantic change might come about, what pathways it might follow, and how it was to be explained, but many now recognize that semantic change must go through a stage of *polysemy*, where a word has more than one meaning. Thus in a historical shift a word might expand its sphere of reference to take on additional readings, becoming polysemous. Alternatively in a semantic change, a polysemous form may lose one (or more) of its meanings. A view which some have of semantic change combines both these situations: the word starts out with an original meaning, then acquires additional, multiple meanings, and then the original sense is lost, leaving only the newer meaning. Schematically this can be represented in three stages, beginning with form *a* which has meaning '*A*':

Stage 1:   a 'A'

Stage 2:   a 'A', 'B'   ('A' > 'A', 'B')
Stage 3:   a 'B'   ('A', 'B' > 'B')

Some examples will be helpful.

(1) English *timber*, German *Zimmer* 'room'. In Stage 1, form *a* = Germanic **tem-ram*, meaning *A* = 'building' (originally from Proto-Indo-European **dem-rom*; compare Latin *dom-us* 'house' and Old English *timrian* 'to build'). In Stage 2, English *a* = *timber*, *A* = 'building', *B* = 'material for building', 'wood which supplies building material'. Similarly in Stage 2, German *a* = *Zimmer*, *A* = 'building', *B* = 'room'. In Stage 3, English *a* = *timber*, *B* = 'material for building', 'wood which supplies building material' (meaning *A* 'building' was lost). In Stage 3, German *a* = *Zimmer*, *B* = 'room' (meaning *A* 'building' was lost).

(2) English *write*. In Stage 1, *write* meant 'to cut, score' (compare the German cognate *reissen* 'to tear, split'). In Stage 2, the meaning was extended to include both 'to cut, scratch' and 'to write'; the connection is through runic writing, which was carved or scratched on wood and stone (compare Old Icelandic *ríta* 'to scratch, to write'). This stage is attested in Old English *wrītan* 'to write', 'to cut'. Stage 3 is illustrated by modern English *write* meaning 'to write' only, where the sense of 'to cut' or 'to scratch' has been lost.

(3) Spanish *alcalde* 'mayor', when first borrowed from Arabic *qāḍī* meant 'judge (in Islamic law)' ('*A*'), but was later broadened to mean 'an official who is magistrate and mayor' ('*B*', added with '*A*'), and then eventually the term was restricted in meaning to only 'mayor' (only '*B*', since '*A*' was lost).

This view recognizes (at least implicitly, and often explicitly) an intervening stage of polysemy as necessary in semantic changes. Others do not emphasize this view so much; rather, they recognize that lexical items typically have a core meaning (or group of related core concepts) but also various less central, more peripheral senses when used in a variety of discourse contexts, and they see semantic change as a less central sense becoming more central and the original core concept receding to be more peripheral, often being lost altogether. Still others see meaning as a network or semantic map where items within a semantic domain and from other domains are related by various overlappings in the polysemous choice which each lexical item has. Semantic change in this view follows paths of connections in the network, selecting and emphasizing different senses which the items have in different contexts. These are not really different approaches, but rather just more realistic versions of the view that holds that polysemy is a necessary intermediate step in semantic change.

Most linguists, past and present, have looked to structural (linguistic) and psychological factors as a primary cause of semantic change; however, historical factors outside of language have also been considered important causes of semantic change. Changes in technology, society, politics, religion and in fact all spheres of human life can lead to semantic shifts. Thus, for example, *pen* originally meant 'feather, quill' (a loan from Old French *penne* 'feather, writing quill'; compare Latin *penna* 'feather'), but as times changed and other instruments for writing came into use, the thing referred to by the word *pen* today is not remotely connected with 'feathers'. As guns replaced older hunting implements and weapons, terms meaning 'bow' (or 'arrow') shifted to mean 'gun' in many languages. Thus in the Lake Miwok (a Miwok-Costanoan language of California) example mentioned above, *kó:no* 'gun' originally meant 'bow'. The word for 'blowgun' in K'iche' (Mayan), * uɓ*, shifted its meaning to include 'shotgun'. In the wake of automobiles and aeroplanes, *fly* and *drive* have taken on new meanings. There are countless such examples, of words whose meanings have changed due to sociocultural and technological change in the world around us, and several of the examples presented here in the classification of kinds of semantic changes are of this sort. For example, changes in religion and society are behind the shift from *blēdsian* 'to mark with blood in an act of consecration in pagan sacrifice' to modern *to bless*; and, as 'pelts' were replaced as a medium of exchange, Finnish *raha* shifted its meaning from 'pelt' to 'money'. In the historical events that brought English-speaking settlers to America, Australia, New Zealand, South Africa and so on, new plants and animals were encountered and sometimes native English words which originally referred to very different species were utilized for these new species, leading to semantic shifts in the meaning of these words. Thus, for example, *magpie* and *robin* refer to totally different species of birds in North America, in the UK and in Australia and New Zealand. *Magpie* in Europe is *Pica caudata* (of the family of *Corvidae*); the American magpie is *Pica pica hudsonia*; and the New Zealand and Australian magpie is *Gymnorhina tibicen* (of the *Cracticidae* family). *Robin* in England is of the genus *Erithacus*; in North America *robin* refers to *Turdus migratorius*; the New Zealand robin is *Petroica australis* (of the family *Muscicapidae*). The American *possum* (or *opossum*) (*Didelphis virginiana*) and Australian *possum* (*Trichosurus vulpecula*, and other species) are very different animals. Many Spanish words have undergone semantic changes as the result of similar historical events; for example, *gorrión* means a 'sparrow' in Spain, but shifted its meaning to 'hummingbird' in Central America; *tejón* means 'badger' in Spain, but 'coati-mundi' in Mexico; *león* refers to 'lion' in Spain, but has shifted to 'cougar, mountain lion' in many areas of Latin America; similarly, *tigre*, originally 'tiger', means 'jaguar' in much of Latin America. It is this sort of shift in meaning which makes it so difficult to generalize about semantic change. Since changes in society and technology are for the most part unpredictable, their affects on semantic change are also not predictable.

More recent work concentrates on the general directionality observed for some kinds of semantic changes, and attempts based on these are being made to elaborate a more explanatory approach, one which might predict possible and impossible changes or directions of change. Eve Sweetser's and Elizabeth Closs Traugott's work in this area has been the most influential (see Sweetser 1990, Traugott 1989, Traugott and Dasher 2002, Traugott and Heine 1991, and Traugott and König 1991; see also Hopper and Traugott 1993: 68–93). Some general claims about semantic change which have been formulated are the following.

1. Semantically related words often undergo parallel semantic shifts. For example, various words which meant 'rapidly' in Old English and Middle English shifted their meaning to 'immediately', as with Old English *swifte* 'rapidly' and *georne* 'rapidly, eagerly', both of which changed the meaning to 'immediately' in about 1300 (Traugott and Dasher 2002: 67).

2. Phonetic similarity (especially cases of phonetic identity, homophony) can lead to shifts which leave the phonetically similar forms semantically more similar (sometimes identical). Note the confusion and lack of contrast in many English dialects for such sets of related words as *lie/lay* and *sit/set*.

3. Spatial/locative words may develop temporal senses: *before*, *after*, *behind*. Also, spatial terms often develop from body-part terms, as in *ahead of*, *in the back of*, *at the foot of*.

4. Some common semantic shifts typically (though not absolutely always) go in one direction and not the other; cases which recur and are found in numerous languages include the following.

(1) Words having to do with the sense of touch may typically develop meanings involving the sense of taste: *sharp*, *crisp*, *hot* ('spicy').

(2) Words involving the sense of taste may develop extended senses involving emotions in general: *bitter*, *sour*, *sweet*.

(3) Obligation > possibility/probability – more precisely, *root* senses of modals, also called *deontic* senses, by which is meant real-world forces, such as obligation, permission and ability, typically develop

epistemic meanings (where epistemic means 'speaker's assessment' and denotes necessity, probability and possibility involving reasoning). For example, in the history of *may*, the meaning was first physical ability (*Jane may come* = 'Jane is able to come'); then the sense of social permission developed ('Jane is allowed to come'); finally the epistemic, logical possibility sense came about ('it is perhaps the case that Jane will come'). The history of *must* is similar: first, *Bess must sing* had the root meaning 'it is a requirement that Bess sing'); second, an epistemic sense was added, 'that Bess must sing is a reasoned conclusion based on the evidence that her father and mother and brothers and sisters all sing, so it is likely that she, too, sings'. In these examples, the root senses are original and the epistemic senses developed later.

(4) Propositional > textual – things with propositional meanings tend to develop textual and later expressive meanings. For example, *while* in modern English means (1) 'a period of time' (propositional, a specific temporal situation), (2) 'during the time that' and (3) 'although' (textual, connecting clauses); however, *while* comes from Old English *þa hwīle þe* [that.Accusative while/time.Accusative Subordinate.particle] 'at the time that', which had only the propositional sense, not the later textual one. This phrase was reduced by late Old English times to *wile*, a simple conjunction (Traugott and König 1991: 85).

(5) 'see' > 'know, understand'.

(6) 'hear' > 'understand', 'obey'.

(7) Physical-action verbs (especially with hands) > mental-state verbs, speech-act verbs. For example, verbs such as 'grasp', 'capture', 'get a hold on', 'get', 'catch on to' very commonly come to mean 'understand'; thus, *feel* goes from 'touch, feel with hands' to 'feel, think, have sympathy or pity for'; Spanish *captar*, originally 'capture, seize', added the sense 'to understand'; Finnish *käsittää* 'to comprehend' is derived from *käsi* 'hand'; Spanish *pensar* 'to think' comes from Latin *pēnsāre* 'to weigh'. English *fret* 'worry, be distressed' formerly meant 'to eat, gnaw' (compare the German cognate *fressen* 'to eat, devour, consume (of animals, or rudely of people)').

(8) Mental-state verbs > speech-act verbs (*observe* 'to perceive, witness' > 'to state, remark').

(9) 'man' > 'husband' (German *Mann* 'man, husband' < 'man').

(10) 'woman' > 'wife'.

(11) 'body' > 'person' (compare *somebody*).

(12) 'finger' > 'hand'.

(13) 'left(-handed, left side)' > 'devious, evil, foreboding' (English *sinister*, ultimately from Latin *sinister* 'left').

(14) 'know' > 'find out', 'taste' (compare Spanish *saber* 'to know, to taste, to find out' < Latin *sapere* 'to know').

(15) animal names > inanimate objects. For example, Spanish *gato* 'jack (for raising cars)' < *gato* 'cat'; in Central American Spanish *mico* 'jack'< *mico* 'monkey'; Spanish *grúa* '(construction) crane' < Old Spanish *grúa* 'crane' (bird) (compare Modern Spanish *grulla*, *grúa* 'crane (bird)' (compare English *crane* '(bird) crane', 'building crane').

Traugott speaks of broad explanatory tendencies:

1. Meanings based on the external situation > meanings based on the internal situation (evaluative/perceptual/cognitive). This would cover, for example, the cases called degeneration and elevation, which involve value judgements on the part of the users of the language. It would also include many of the examples from (5–7) above.
2. Meanings based on external or internal situations > meanings based on textual or (meta)linguistic situations. This would include many instances from (4), (7) and (8) above.
3. Meanings tend to become increasingly based on speakers' subjective beliefs/states/attitudes towards the proposition. Instances of (1), (2) and especially (3) above illustrate the change of meaning involving increase in subjective reaction. Many metonymic semantic changes fall under this. (See Traugott 1989.)

It is frequently claimed that semantic shifts typically go from more *concrete* to more *abstract*. For example, there are many semantic changes which extend body-part notions to more abstract meanings, but not the other way around, as with German *Haupt* originally meaning only 'head' (body part, concrete), which was later extended to mean 'main' or 'principal', as in *Hauptstadt* 'capital' (*Haupt* 'head' + *Stadt* 'town, city'), *Hauptbahnhof* 'central station' ((*Haupt* 'head' + *Bahnhof* 'railway station'), and then later *Haupt* lost its primary original meaning of 'head' in most contexts. While this is an interesting and important claim, a number of the traditional classes of semantic change, for example narrowing in particular, often involve change towards more concreteness, and therefore the claim needs to be understood as only a broad general tendency which can easily have exceptions.

In their recent explanatory treatment of semantic change, Traugott and Dasher (2002) emphasize the typical direction of certain kinds of semantic change. They identify 'regular' tendencies in semantic change, that is changes that are encountered frequently across languages and also repeatedly within single languages. They propose an 'Invited

Inferencing Theory of Semantic Change'. Polysemy is central in this theory, and it typically arises out of the pragmatic forces of *invited inferences* and *subjectification*. *Invited inferences* arise in the pragmatic use of language in given contexts. For example, *as long as* and *so long as* formerly had only spatial and temporal meanings, as in *King Alfred's long ships were almost twice **as long as** the other ships* (spatial) and *Squeeze the medication through a linen cloth onto the eye **as long as** he needs* (temporal). But such temporal sentences could invite the inference that *as/so long as* might also mean conditional ('provided that'), 'squeeze the medication on the eye for the length of time that he needs it' or 'if/on the condition that he still needs it'. Later, in some contexts the conditional sense became the only one possible, as in *He told the jury that it is proper for police to question a juvenile without a parent present **so long as** they made a reasonable effort to notify the parent.* In *subjectification*, speakers come to develop meanings for words 'that encode or externalize their perspectives and attitudes as constrained by the communicative world of the speech event, rather than by the so-called "real-world" characteristics of the event or situation referred to' (Traugott and Dasher 2002: 30). For example, an increase in subjectivity is seen in semantic changes involving *indeed*: first as *in dede* 'in action', then 'certainly, in actuality'; second, *indeed* changed to include 'in truth' (subjective, reflecting speaker's attitude) in its meaning; third, *indeed* changed to add 'what's more', 'adding to that' (a discourse marker). Another example is the verb *promise*. Its original sense was as 'a directive imposing obligation on oneself as speaker', as in *I promise to do my best*. Semantic change added later the sense 'speaker's high degree of certainty' (more subjective, internalizing the speaker's perspective/attitude), as in *She promises to be an outstanding student*.

9.4 Other Kinds of Lexical Change – New Words

There are many kinds of lexical change that are not limited to semantic change. Several sources of new vocabulary have already come up in the treatment of various kinds of analogy, borrowing and the semantic changes. We will not bring these up again here, but will concentrate on other sources of *neologisms* (new words in a language), presenting a more or less traditional classification of kinds of lexical change together with examples. Abundant examples involving the more productive sources of neologisms are found especially in slang, advertising and political discourse.

9.4.1 Creations from nothing *(root creations)*

Creations of new words from nothing, out of thin air, are rare, but putative examples exist. Examples that are often cited of this include:

1. *blurb* coined by Gelett Burgess (American humorist) in 1907.
2. *gas* coined by Dutch chemist J. B. van Helmont in 1632, inspired by Greek *khāos* 'chaos', where the letter *g* of Dutch is pronounced [x], corresponding to the pronunciation of the Greek letter *χ*, the first of the word for 'chaos'.
3. *paraffin* invented by Reichenbach in 1830, based on Latin *parum* 'too little, barely' + *affīnis* 'having affinity'.

It might be objected that in most cases of this sort, the creation isn't really fully out of 'nothing'; for example, *gas* has Greek 'chaos' lying in some way behind it; the creation of *paraffin* utilized pieces from Latin. Probably better examples of creations from nothing could be found in certain slang terms (*zilch*, *bonking*) and product names (see below).

A related source of new words is *literary coinage*, new words created by (or at least attributed to) authors and famous people.

1. *blatant* < Edmund Spenser (between 1590 and 1596).
2. *boojum* < Lewis Carroll.
3. *chortle* < Lewis Carroll (a blend of *chuckle* + *snort*).
4. *pandemonium* 'the abode of all the demons, the capital of Hell', from John Milton's *Paradise Lost*, 1667 (the pieces from which this was created are Greek).
5. *yahoo* < Jonathan Swift's *Gulliver's Travels*, the name created for an imaginary race of brutes with human form.

9.4.2 From personal names

From names of individuals we have examples such as:

1. *guillotine* borrowed from French *guillotin*, named after the French physician Joseph-Ignace Guillotin, who suggested that the instrument be used in executions in 1789.
2. *macadam (road)* named after John Loudon McAdam (1756–1836) for the kind of road he invented and the kind of material used in it.
3. *sandwich* said to be named after John Montagu, the 4th Earl of Sandwich (1718–92), who spent twenty-four hours gambling with no other food than slices of cold meat between slices of toast.
4. *volt* named after Alessandro Volta, Italian scientist and physician (1745–1827).

There are also words which originate from names of groups of people:

gothic from the Goths (Germanic tribes);

to gyp 'to cheat, swindle' from 'Gypsy' (today considered improper, racist);

to jew (a price down) from 'Jew' (now avoided because of its negative stereotype of an ethnic group);

vandal, vandalize from the Vandals (another Germanic tribe);

welch, welsh 'to cheat by avoiding payment of bets', said to be from 'Welsh'.

9.4.3 From place names

1. *canary* < Canary Islands.
2. *currant* ultimately from *Corinth*, a loan from Old French *raisins de Corauntz* (Modern French *raisins de Corinthe*) 'raisins of Corinth'.
3. *denim* ultimately from French *serge de Nîmes* 'serge (a woollen fabric) of Nîmes' (a manufacturing town in southern France).
4. *jeans* < Genoa (for a twilled cotton cloth associated with Genoa).
5. *peach* < Persia. English *peach* is a loan from French *pêche* which derives from Latin *malum persicum* 'Persian apple'; 'Persia' as the source of words for 'peach' is more visible in German *Pfirsich* and Finnish *persikka*.
6. *sherry* < Jerez (a place in Spain associated with this fortified Spanish wine).
7. *spa* < Spa (place in Belgium celebrated for the curative properties of its mineral water).
8. *tangerine* < Tangier, Morocco.
9. *turkey* < Turkey (shortened from *turkeycock, turkeyhen*, originally a guinea-fowl imported through Turkey, later applied erroneously to the bird of American origin).

9.4.4 From brand (trade) names

1. *coke, cola* (drink), *coca-cola* < Coca-Cola.
2. *frig, frigidaire* < Frigidaire (in the USA).
3. *jello* (jelly crystals, a gelatin dessert in North America) < Jell-O.
4. *kleenex* (tissue) < Kleenex.
5. *levis, levi jeans* < Levi Strauss.
6. *xerox* < Xerox.
7. *hoover* (vacuum cleaner) < Hoover.

9.4.5 Acronyms

Acronyms are words derived from the initial letters or syllables of each of the successive parts of a compound term or word: *ASAP* < 'as soon as possible'; *beemer* < 'BMW automobile'; *Benelux* < Belgium–Netherlands –Luxembourg; *BS* < 'bullshit'; *CD* < 'compact disc'; *CIA* < 'Central Intelligence Agency'; *DJ* < 'disc jockey'; *emcee* < 'master of cere-monies'; *Gestapo* < from German *Geheime Staatspolizei* 'secret state's police', borrowed into English; *MD* < 'medical doctor'; *MP* < 'military police', *MP* < 'member of parliament'; *OJ* < slang for 'orange juice'; *PDQ* 'fast' < 'pretty damned quick'; *radar* 'radio direction and ranging'; *RAM* < 'random access memory'; *ROM* < 'read-only memory'; *scuba* (diving) < 'self-contained underwater breathing apparatus'; *SNAG* < 'sensitive new-age guy'; *TMJ* 'temporomandibular-joint disorder'; *UK*; *USA*; *VCR* < 'video cassette recorder'; *yuppie* < 'young urban profes-sional'; and many more.

Some forms are turned into acronym-like words even though they do not originate as such; these usually involve sequences of letters from principal syllables in the word, for example: *TV* < television; *PJs* < pyjamas.

9.4.6 Compounding

Compounds are words (or better said, lexical items) formed from pieces or units that are (or were) themselves distinct words. Compounding is a productive process in English and many other languages. A number of examples of compounds that are relatively new in English include the following: *all-nighter* (*to pull an all-nighter* 'to stay up all night long, usually to study for exams'); *bad(-)ass*; *bag lady*; *boombox*; *brain-dead* 'stupid, unable to think'; *cashflow*; *couch potato* 'lazy person, someone who just lies around'; *downmarket* 'less expensive, less sophisticated'; *downside*; *glass ceiling* 'hypothetical barrier which allows a goal to be viewed but denies access to it'; *-head* (as in *airhead, butthead, deadhead, dickhead, doughhead*); *knee-jerk* (adjective); *mad cow disease*; *melt-down*; *motormouth*; *-person* (as in *busperson, chairperson, clergyperson, minutepersons*); *red-eye* 'cheap whisky', *red-eye* 'early-morning or late-night flight'; *scumbucket* 'despicable person'; *shareware*; *slamdunk*; *stargaze*; *studmuffin* 'a muscular or attractive male'; *tummytuck*; *under-handed*; and so on.

In the case of older compounds, later changes often make the original components of the compound no longer recognizable, for example:

1. *elbow* < Proto-Germanic **alinō* 'forearm' + **bugōn* 'bend, bow' (compare Old English *eln* 'forearm, cubit').
2. *gamut* < *gamma*, the name of the Greek letter *gamma*, introduced in the Middle Ages to represent a note on the musical scale one note lower than *A*, which began the scale, + *ut*, the first of a series of six syllables used to name the six notes of a hexachord.
3. *gossip* < Old English *godsībb* (*God* + *sib* 'related') 'one who has contracted spiritual affinity with another by agreeing to act as sponsor at a baptism', which came to mean 'family acquaintance, friend' and 'a woman's female friends invited to be present at a birth', and to 'someone, usually a woman, of light and trifling character' to 'the conversation of such a person', 'idle talk'.
4. German *Elend* 'misery, miserable' < Old High German *elilenti* 'sojourn in a foreign land, exile' (compare Gothic *alja-* 'other' + *land* 'land').

In others, the source of the compounding is only partially perceived today: *cobweb* < Middle English *coppe* 'spider' + *web; nickname* < *an* + *eke* 'additional' + *name; werewolf* < Old English *wer* 'man' (cognate with Latin *vir* 'man') + *wolf*.

9.4.7 Other productive word-formation and derivation devices

In addition to compounding, new words are derived more or less productively through the employment of various derivational affixes in word-formation processes. Others involve what have been called 'neo-classical' compounds (involving elements from Greek or Latin (such as *auto-*, *trans-*, *bio-* and so on). A few examples illustrating these processes are: *auto-* (*autopilot, auto-suggestion*); *-belt* (*banana belt, bible belt, cow belt*); *mega-* (*mega-sound, mega-show, mega-event*); *micro-* (*microenvironment, microbiotic, microcapsule, microprocessor, microsurgery*); *mini-* (*minibike, minicomputer, minimart, miniskirt, mini-series*); *pan-* (*pandemic, pan-galactic, pan-national*); *pre-* and *post-* (*pre-packaged, pre-washed, post-colonialist, post-structuralism*); *pseudo-* (*pseudo-friend, pseudo-psychological, pseudo-scholar, pseudo-Western*); *trans-* (*transmigration, transnationals, transpacific*); *ultra-* (*ultraliberal, ultramodern, ultraradical, ultrashort*); *-ism/-ist* (*racist, sexism, fattist, neologism*) among many others. Some of these overlap with blends, such as *bio-*: *biodegradable, biodiversity, biosphere*; and *eco-* (< *ecology, ecological*): *ecotourism, eco-friendly, ecofreak*.

9.4.8 Amalgamation

Amalgamations are forms which formerly were composed of more than one free-standing word (which occurred together in some phrase), which as a result of the change get bound together in a single word. For example, English *nevertheless* and *already* are now single words, but come from the amalgamation of separate words, of *never + the + less* and *all + ready*. English has many words of this sort in whose background lies the amalgamation of earlier separate words into a single lexical item. Amalgamation is often considered a kind of analogy. (Similarly, cases of blending and contamination are sometimes treated as kinds of lexical change, as discussed in Chapter 4 on analogy.) We can see amalgamation under way in the frequent (mis)spellings of *alright* for *all right* (probably influenced by analogy with *already*), *alot* for *a lot* meaning 'many, much', and *no-one* for *no one*.

(1) Some examples of amalgamations in English are: *almost < all most, alone < all one, altogether < all together, always < all ways, however < how ever, without < with out*.

(2) English *don < do on, doff < do off*.

(3) Spanish *usted* 'you (formal, polite)' *< vuestra merced* 'your grace'.

(4) Spanish *también* 'also' *< tan bene* 'as well', *todavía* 'still, yet' *< tota via* 'all way(s)'.

(5) Latin *dē mānē* (*dē* 'of' + *manus* 'good (ablative)'), meaning 'in good time', is behind amalgamated forms meaning 'morning, tomorrow' in some of the Romance languages, for example French *demain* 'tomorrow' and Italian *domani* 'morning, tomorrow'. Later, French underwent further amalgamations: *en demain* ('in' + 'tomorrow') *> l'endemain* (*l(e)* 'the' + *endemain*) *> le lendemain* 'tomorrow, the next day'.

(6) Latin *hodie* 'today' should have ended up in French as *hui*, but this was further amalgamated, first to *jour d'hui* (from *jour* 'day' + *d(e)* 'of' + *hui* 'today') and then on to *aujourd'hui* 'today, nowadays' (from *au* 'to the' + *jour d'hui* – even *au* is an amalgam of *a* 'to' + *le* 'the').

(7) Spanish *hidalgo* 'noble', Old Spanish *fijodalgo*, comes from *fijo* 'son' (Latin *filiu-*, compare Modern Spanish *hijo* 'son') + *d(e)* 'of' + *algo* 'something/wealth'.

(8) French *avec* 'with' comes from Latin *apud* 'with, by, beside' + *hoc* 'this, it', literally 'with/by this'.

(9) Spanish *nosotros* 'we' comes from *nos otros* 'we others', *vosotros* 'you (familiar plural)' from *vos otros* 'you others'.

(10) English *wannabe(e)* of slang origin ('someone who tries to be accepted by a group, adopting its appearance and manners') *< want to be*.

Note that many of the cases today called *grammaticalization* (see Chapter 10) are instances of amalgamation, where formerly independent words are amalgamated with the result that one becomes a grammatical affix.

(11) For example, in Spanish and other Romance languages, forms of the verb *haber* 'have' (from Latin *habēre*) were amalgamated with infinitives to give the 'future' and 'conditional' morphological constructions of today, for example *cantar he > cantar-hé > cantaré* 'I will sing' (*he* 'first person singular' of *haber*), *cantar has > cantar-has > cantarás* 'you will sing' (*has* 'second person singular' of *haber*); *cantar habías > cantarías* 'you would sing' (*habías* 'you had').

(12) In another example, *mente* 'in mind' (from the ablative of Latin *mens* 'mind') was grammaticalized in Romance languages as an adverbial clitic (in Spanish) or suffix (in French). From *absoluta mente* 'in absolute mind' we get Spanish *absolutamente* and French *absolument* 'absolutely'. (For discussion and other examples, see Chapter 10.)

9.4.9 Clipping (compression, shortening, ellipsis)

Often, new words or new forms of old words come from 'clipping', that is, from shortening longer words. The several examples from English which follow show this process: *ad* < advertisement, *bike* < bicycle, *bus* < Latin *omnibus* 'for everyone' (*-bus* dative plural case ending – this is a much-cited example), *condo* < condominium, *decaf* < decaffeinated coffee, *dis(s)* (*dissing*) < 'to be disrespectful towards someone', *fan* < fanatic, *gym* < gymnasium, *jock* ('athlete') < jockstrap, *limo* < limousine, *math/maths* < mathematics, *mod* < modern, *nuke* (*nukes, to nuke*) < nuclear weapons, *a perm, to perm* < permanent wave, *perp* < perpetrator, *phone* < telephone, *pro* < professional, *psycho* < psychotic, *pub* < public house, *rad* < radical, *schizo* [skɪtso] < schizophrenic, *stats* < statistics, *sub* < substitute ('a substitute, to substitute'), *telly* < television, *veg, to veg out* < vegetate. Popular on restaurant menus (in North America) is *shrooms*, a clipped form of *mushrooms*; it remains to be seen whether it will survive.

9.4.10 Expressive creations

Onomatopoeia is another source of new words, creations with only sounds in nature as a model, thought to be the source of words such as *buzz*, *gag* and so on. Interjections (ejaculations) are another source, exemplified by *ah*, *oh*, *wow*, *pow*, *whew*, *shush* and many others. Some expressive words seem to develop out of nothing, as for example *bodacious* 'remarkable, fabulous' and *humongous* (also spelled *humungous*) 'very large'. In most cases such as these, blending is involved, and while the origin of these two words is uncertain, it is possible that *bodacious* is connected in some way to *bold* and *audacious*, and that *humongous* perhaps involves *huge* in some way.

9.4.11 Obsolescence and loss of vocabulary

Those who work on lexical change are interested not only in the adoption of new vocabulary, but also in the question of why vocabulary items become archaic and sometimes disappear altogether from a language. While the use of particular words can fade for a number of social and stylistic reasons, the primary cause is the disappearance in common talk of a word because of the disappearance in society of the thing it refers to – that is, historical changes in society can lead to vocabulary loss as well as to semantic shifts (mentioned above). For example, there was a large range of vocabulary involving falconry, armour, feudal society and other institutions and technologies of the Middle Ages which in effect has become totally forgotten, as these things faded from modern life. Replacement of one word by another for the same meaning is another frequent means by which vocabulary is lost. A few examples of older words now essentially lost to modern English vocabulary are the following (though some are occasionally resurrected for special purposes in fantasy literature and games reflecting medieval themes):

dorbel: a dull-witted pedant, a foolish pretender to learning; from Nicholas Dorbellus, a fifteenth-century professor of scholastic philosophy at Poitiers and follower of Duns Scotus, whose name gave us *dunce*.

dousabell: a common name in sixteenth-century poetry for a sweetheart, especially an unsophisticated country girl < French *douce et belle* 'sweet and beautiful'.

fribbler: a trifler; one who professes rapture for a woman yet dreads her consent.

jarkman: he that can write and read, and sometimes speak, Latin and uses these skills to make counterfeit licences, which they call *gybes*, and sets to seals, in their language falsified documents called *jarks*; sixteenth-century slang for an educated beggar able to forge passes, licences, etc. *Jark* was rogues' cant for a seal, whence also a licence of the Bethlehem Hospital ('Bedlam') to beg.

kelchyn: a fine paid by one guilty of manslaughter, generally to the kindred of the person killed.

kexy: dry, brittle, withered.

mulligrubs: a twisting of the guts, so called from the symptomatic fever attending it.

palliard: a vagabond who slept on the straw in barns, hence a dissolute rascal, a lecher, a debauchee < French *paille* 'straw'.

parnel: a punk, a slut; the diminutive of Italian *petronalla*; a priest's mistress.

rogitate: to ask frequently.

thural: of or pertaining to incense.

towrus: among hunters a roebuck eager for copulation is said to 'go to his towrus'.

tyromancy: divining by the coagulation of cheese.

wittol: a husband who knows of and endures his wife's unfaithfulness; a contented cuckold; from *woodwale*, a bird whose nest is invaded by the cuckoo, and so has the offspring of another palmed off on it for its own.

yelve: dung-fork; garden-fork; to use a garden fork.

9.5 Exercises

Exercise 9.1

Attempt to find examples of your own of new vocabulary items which represent some of the categories of lexical and semantic change discussed in this chapter. Try to name or identify the categories involved. You can do this by listening for words that you think are new in the speech of your friends and family or by asking others if they can think of any examples. Slang is a fertile area for new vocabulary and semantic shifts.

Exercise 9.2 Lexical change

The *Longman Register of New Words* for 1990 (see Ayto 1990) lists, among hundreds of others, the following new English words which were first recorded after 1988. Can you determine where these come from, that is, how they came about? What processes of vocabulary creation, semantic change or other kinds of linguistic changes do you think lie behind these new words? (You may have to look some of these up, or ask your friends who might know what they mean.)

barbify; bimboy; birth-mother; bonk-happy; dweeb; geeky; karaoke; motormouth; sicko; soundbite

Exercise 9.3 Semantic change

Look up the following words in a dictionary which provides basic etymologies for words. (*The Oxford English Dictionary* is generally recognized as the primary authority in this area and is recommended here, although a number of other dictionaries also provide useful etymological information.) Determine what change in meaning has taken place in each word. State which type of semantic change is involved (from among the types defined in this chapter).

For example, if you were to see *villain* in the list, you would look it up and find out that it originally meant 'person of the villa/farm' but has changed its meaning to 'criminal, scoundrel', and you would state that this is an example of *degeneration* (or *pejoration*).

corpse; crafty; disease; fame; journey; officious; science; starve; thing; vulgar

Exercise 9.4

In the following examples of semantic change, identify the kind of semantic change involved (widening, narrowing, metonymy and so on).

1. Spanish *cosa* 'thing' < Latin *causa* 'matter, cause, question'.
2. Spanish *dinero* 'money' < Latin *dēnāriu* 'coin (of a particular denomination)'.
3. Spanish *pariente* 'relative' < Old Spanish *pariente* 'parent'.
4. Spanish *segar* 'to reap (to cut grain, grass with a scythe)' < Latin *secāre* 'to cut'.
5. Old Spanish *cuñado* 'relation by marriage' shifted to 'brother-in-law' in Modern Spanish. (This Spanish word comes ultimately from Latin *cognātus* 'blood-relation'.)
6. Mexican Spanish *muchacha*, formerly only 'girl', now has a primary meaning 'maid, servant woman' in some contexts.
7. Modern Spanish *siesta* 'afternoon nap (rest period during the heat of the day)' < Old Spanish *siesta* 'midday heat' (ultimately from Latin *sexta (hōra)* 'sixth (hour)').
8. English *gay* 'homosexual' is the result of a recent semantic shift, where the original sense, 'cheerful, lively', has become secondary; the shift to the 'homosexual' sense perhaps came through other senses, 'given to social pleasures, licentious', which the word had.
9. English *to spill* formerly meant (from c. 1300 to 1600) 'to destroy by depriving of life, to put to death, to slay, to kill'.
10. French *cuisse* 'thigh' < Latin *coxa* 'hip' (Spanish *cojo* 'lame, crippled' is thought also to be from Latin *coxa* 'hip').
11. Spanish *cadera* 'hip' < Latin *cathedra* (from Greek) 'seat'.

12. Spanish *ciruela* 'plum' < Latin *prūna cēreola* 'waxy plum' (*prūna* 'plum' + *cēreola* 'of wax').

13. French *viande* 'meat' formerly meant 'food' in general. (This change parallels English *meat* which originally meant 'food'.)

14. Spanish *depender* 'to depend' < Latin *dēpendere* 'to hang'.

15. English *lousy* 'worthless, bad' < 'infested with lice'.

10

⸺

Syntactic Change

⸺

Our speech hath its infirmities and defects, as all things else have. Most
of the occasions of the world's troubles are grammatical.

(Montaigne, Essays II, xii)

10.1 Introduction

The study of syntactic change is currently an extremely active area of
historical linguistics. Nevertheless, there has been no generally recognized approach to the treatment of syntactic change, such as there is
for sound change. While there were some excellent studies in historical
syntax in the nineteenth century and many in the last twenty years or so,
syntactic change was very often not represented (or present only super-
ficially) in the textbooks on historical syntax. The approach followed in
this book is that of Harris and Campbell (1995) (on which this chapter
relies heavily). In this chapter, we learn about the mechanisms of syntactic change – reanalysis, extension and borrowing – and the common
pathways that grammatical changes take; that is, we are interested in
the more commonly occurring kinds of syntactic changes found in the
world's languages. Grammaticalization, an approach currently of much
interest, is also considered together with its limitations. Finally, the
possibilities for syntactic reconstruction are described and defended.

10.2 Mechanisms of Syntactic Change

There are only three *mechanisms* of syntactic change: *reanalysis, extension* and *borrowing*. Let us consider these mechanisms in turn, first with
a brief characterization of each, followed by additional examples.

10.2.1 Reanalysis

Reanalysis changes the underlying structure of a syntactic construction, but does not modify surface manifestation. The *underlying structure* includes (1) constituency, (2) hierarchical structure, (3) grammatical categories, (4) grammatical relations and (5) cohesion. We will come to examples illustrating changes in several of these shortly. *Surface manifestation* includes (1) morphological marking (for example, morphological case, agreement, gender) and (2) word order.

An important axiom of reanalysis is: *reanalysis depends on the possibility of more than one analysis of a given construction.* The following example from English exemplifies both reanalysis and this axiom. A new construction with a 'future' auxiliary (seen here in (2)) was derived through reanalysis from the construction in (1) which has a main verb (a verb of motion with a purposive sense):

(1) *Hermione is going to marry Ron.*
    Structure: Hermione is going ᵥₑᵣᵦ ᴏꜰ ᴍᴏᴛɪᴏɴ to marry Ron
The purposive *be going (to)* was reanalysed as a 'future auxiliary':
(2) *Hermione is going to marry Ron.*
    Structure: Hermione is going ꜰᴜᴛᴜʀᴇ ᴀᴜxɪʟɪᴀʀʏ to marry Ron

In the reanalysis which produced (2), the surface manifestation remained unchanged – (1) and (2) are identical in form, but are not the same in internal structure or meaning, which changed in the reanalysis. In this case, (1) came to be interpreted as having more than one possible grammatical analysis – it underwent reanalysis, yielding (2) with its different structural analysis. For another example, in Finnish, a new postposition (seen here in (2)) was derived through reanalysis from what was formerly an ordinary noun root with a locative case (as in (1)):

(1) *miehe-n rinna-lla*
    man-Genitive chest-Adessive ('Adessive' is a locative case)
    'on the man's chest'   (Original)
(2) *miehe-n rinna-lla*
    man-Genitive Postposition-Adessive
    'beside the man'   (Reanalysed)

In this case there is nothing ambiguous or opaque at all about (1), and in fact it is still fully grammatical in the language. However, it came to be interpreted as having more than one possible analysis, as a regular noun in locative case (as in (1)), but also as a postposition (as in (2)). This new postposition in Finnish is quite parallel to the development of the preposition *abreast of* in English, which comes historically from a-'on' + *breast*. Such developments are common in English and other languages, as seen in English *beside* < *by* + *side*, *behind* < *by* + *hind*, and so on. In this instance, an original construction with an ordinary lexical noun in a locative case, as in (1), was the basis of the reanalysis which produced the new construction with the postposition, as in (2). Notice, however, that (1) and (2) are the same except for their internal analysis; that is, though a reanalysis took place to produce (2), the sur- face manifestation remained unchanged – (1) and (2) are identical in form, but not in their internal structure.

10.2.2 Extension

Extension results in changes in surface manifestation, but does not involve immediate modification of underlying structure. This can be seen in the reanalysis mentioned above in which a new future auxiliary came from 'be going to'. After this reanalysis took place, there was a subsequent extension so that *be going to* as a future auxiliary could appear with new verbs that were not possible earlier. Before it could occur only with verbs which could be the complements in the purposive and motion verb constructions, for example, *I am going to eat* (as in, *going there to eat* or *going in order to eat*). However, the new con- struction was extended so that it could occur with complement verbs which were not possible in the former sense of a verb of motion, for example, *It is going to rain on the muggles*, *Ron is going to like Hermione, Hermione is going to go to Hogwarts*.

10.2.2.1 *First example: change in some Finnish subordinate clauses*

Finnish subordinate clauses provide an example which underwent first reanalysis and then extension. Old Finnish had sentences of the form illustrated in (3):

(3) näen miehe-m tule-va-m
     (NOTE: orthographic *ä* is phonetically [æ])
     I.see man-Accusative.Singular come-Participle-Accusative.Singular
     'I see the man who is coming'

Here, the noun *miehe-m* 'man' is the direct object of the verb *näen* 'I see', and the participle *tule-va-m* 'coming/who comes' modifies this noun ('man') and agrees with it in case and number (both take the 'accusative singular' suffix *-m*). Later, Finnish underwent a sound change in which final *-m* > *-n*, and as a result the accusative singular *-n* (formerly *-m*) and genitive singular -*n* became homophonous, both -*n*. After this sound change, the resulting form, shown in (4), was seen as having two possible interpretations, in (4a) and (4b). (Acc = Accusative, Part = Participle, Pl = Plural, Sg = Singular):

(4)   näen miehe-n tule-van
(4a) I.see man-Acc.Sg come-Part
(4b) I.see man-Gen.Sg come-Part
      'I see the man who is coming'

This led to a change in which the older interpretation in (4a) was eventually eliminated and this subordinate clause construction was reanalysed as (4b). That is, *miehe-n* was reinterpreted not as the direct object (in accusative case) of the verb *näen* 'I see' as it had originally been in Old Finnish (as in the example in (3)), but as the subject (in genitive case) of the participle *tule-van* (as in (4b)). (The change is somewhat like starting with the equivalent of *I saw the man coming* and changing it to *I saw the man's coming*.) At this stage there is still no visible difference in the surface manifestation ((4a) of older Finnish and (4b) of modern Finnish are in form the same, though different in analysis).

The next phase was the *extension* of the reanalysed structure to other instances where the surface manifestation was visibly changed, as seen in the comparison of Old Finnish (5) with modern Finnish (6):

(5)   näin venee-t purjehti-va-t
      I.saw boat-Acc.Pl sail-Part.Acc.Pl
      'I saw the boats that sail'

(6)   näin vene-i-den purjehti-van
      I.saw boat-Pl-Gen sail-Part
      'I saw the boats that sail'

In Old Finnish, sentence (5), with *venee-t* in the 'accusative plural', did not permit a second interpretation, as (4) did, where the 'accusative singular' had the same form as the 'genitive singular'; however, the reanalysis (from accusative to genitive) that began with the homophonous singular form was extended to include the plurals, so that in modern Finnish *venee-t* 'accusative plural' is no longer possible in this construction (as it was in (5) in Old Finnish), but was replaced through extension by *vene-i-den* 'genitive plural', as in (6). Where formerly the singular had two possible interpretations, accusative singular direct object of the main verb or genitive singular subject of the participle, after the change had been extended to the plural making it also genitive, the original (accusative) interpretation was no longer available. The shift from *veneet* 'accusative plural' to *veneiden* 'genitive plural' made the change very evident, now visible in the surface manifestation.

10.2.2.2 Second example: Spanish reflexive to passive

A second example which shows both reanalysis and extension involves changes in the reflexive in Old Spanish. Old Spanish had only the reflexive as in (7), with none of the other functions that the Spanish reflexive later came to have:

(7)   Yo no vestí a Juanito; Juanito *se* vistió
      I no dressed Object Johnny; Johnny *Reflexive* dressed
      'I didn't dress Johnny; Johnny dressed *himself*'

A reanalysis of the reflexive took place in which *se* could also be interpreted as a passive. In the first stage of this change, certain transitive verbs with *se* and a human subject came to have multiple interpretations as either a reflexive of volitional/consentive action, or as a passive, as illustrated in (8) and (9) (REFL = reflexive):

(8)   El rico se entierra en la iglesia
      the rich REFL bury in the church
      (8a) 'The rich person has himself interred/buried in the
           church' (volitional reflexive; literally:
           'the rich person inters himself in the church')
      (8b) 'The rich person gets buried/is buried in the church'
           (*passive*)

(9)   Cum esto se vençen moros del campo
      with this REFL they.conquer Moors of.the countryside
      (9a) 'Therefore Moors of the countryside give themselves up
           for conquered' (*consentive*; literally: 'with this Moors of
           the countryside conquer themselves')
      (9b) 'Therefore Moors of the countryside get conquered/are
           conquered' (*passive*)

In (8) and (9), different interpretations are possible, either reflexive or passive; the surface manifestation is unaltered in the new, reanalysed passive interpretation of these sentences. Also, the original reflexive construction (as in (7)) remains grammatical in Spanish. In the next step, the passive interpretation of the former reflexive *se* was extended to include not just human subjects, but also non-animate subjects, where no reflexive interpretation was possible, as in (10) and (11):

(10) Los vino-s que en esta ciudad se vende-n . . .

the wine-Pl that in this city REFL sell-3rd.Pers.Pl
'The wines that are sold in this city . . .'

(11) Cautiváron-se quasi dos mil persona-s
they.captured-REFL almost two thousand person-Plural
'Almost two thousand persons were captured'

These sentences are now clearly passive and not reflexive; in (10) the 'wines' cannot 'sell themselves', and in (11) the 'two thousand persons' are not 'capturing themselves'.

10.2.3 Syntactic borrowing

Syntactic borrowing is much more frequent and important than some scholars have thought in the past, though others have gone to the other extreme of assuming that everything not otherwise readily explained in a language's grammar is due to borrowing. It is important to avoid such excesses but also to recognize the proper role of syntactic borrowing in syntactic change. The following is a straightforward example of syntactic borrowing. Pipil (a Uto-Aztecan language of El Salvador) borrowed the comparative construction, *mas . . . ke*, from Spanish, as in (12):

(12) ne siwa:t *mas* galá:na *ke* taha
the woman more pretty than you
'That woman is prettier than you are'

Compare the Spanish equivalent in (12'):

(12') esa mujer es *más* linda *que* tú (/mas . . . ke/)
that woman is more pretty than you

Pipil had several different comparative expressions before its contact with Spanish, but these have been eliminated, replaced by this borrowed comparative construction.

Another case involves the extensive borrowing of grammatical elements and constructions among the Australian aboriginal languages of Arnhem Land, in particular among Ritharngu, Ngandi, Nunggubuyu and Warndarang. This includes the direct borrowing of case affixes (for example, for ergative markers, instrumental, ablative, genitive-dative-purposive, comitative), number affix, noun-class affixes (with discourse functions of reference and anaphora), diminutive affix, derivational verbal affixes, negative affix, postpositions and the inchoative verbaliser, among others (Heath 1978). (For several more examples of syntactic borrowing and discussion, see Harris and Campbell 1995: 120–50.)

10.3 *Generative Approaches*

Most work on historical syntax since 1960 has taken the perspective of Generative Grammar (or its descendants). Generative linguists generally associate syntactic change with child language acquisition, seeing syntactic change as part of what happens in the transition of grammars from one generation to the next. In this view, child language learners hear the output of adults around them and on the basis of these data they must construct their own grammar. The grammar which the children acquire reproduces the output which they hear from the adults' grammar more or less accurately, but it does not necessarily coincide with the internal structure of adults' grammar. After learning an optimal grammar as children, adults may later add rules to their grammars which make them no longer optimal. Children of the next generation, hearing the output of this non-optimal adult grammar, restructure it as they construct their own internal grammars, making it more optimal.

We can illustrate this approach with a somewhat hypothetical example, but one that figured in early generative work on syntactic change (cf. Klima 1964). Suppose that an earlier generation of English speakers had learned a grammar with the rule that pronouns, including *who*, require an object case marking (*me, him, whom*) when they occur as the object of a verb (*Harry saw him/me, Whom did Harry see?*) or a preposition (*to him, to me, to whom*). Let us call this Grammar₁, informally characterized as in Table 10.1 (Pro = Pronoun, Prep = Preposition, Pers = Personal.).

TABLE 10.1: Derivation of *whom* in Grammar₁

Underlying:	*saw who* [Verb + Pro] _{Verb Phrase}	*to who* [Prep + Pro] _{Prepositional Phrase}
Rule 1 : (Case-marking)	*saw whom* [Verb + Pro-Case] Verb Phrase	*to whom* Prep + Pro-Case] Prepositional Phrase
Result:	*saw whom*	*to whom*

(A later rule which fronts question words such as *who(m)* gives, for example, *Whom did Harry see?*)

Now suppose that later in life, as adults, speakers of Grammar₁ changed their grammar by adding a rule which deletes the case marking with *whom*; let's call this Grammar₁', characterized informally as in Table 10.2.

TABLE 10.2: Derivation of *who(m)* in Grammar₁'

Underlying:	*saw who*	*to who*
	[Verb + Pro] _{Verb Phrase}	[Prep + Pro] _{Prepositional Phrase}
Rule 1:	*saw whom*	*to whom*
(Case-marking)	[Verb + Pro-Case]	[Prep + Pro-Case]
	Verb Phrase	Prepositional Phrase
Rule 2:	*saw who*	*to who*
(Delete Case from *whom*)		
Result:	*saw who*	*to who*

The next generation of children learning the language would hear only *who* as the output of the adult grammar, Grammar ₁', and therefore for their own grammar would simply learn *who* in all contexts, having no need for Rule 2 of adult Grammar₁'. That is, the adults' non-optimal Grammar₁' would have two rules, Rule 1 to add object case marking (*whom*) to pronoun objects of verbs and prepositions, and Rule 2 to convert *whom* into *who* (deletion of the object case marking for *who*). The children learning the language, hearing only the output *who*, would not learn Rule 2, but would simply learn to use *who* in all contexts. They thus construct their grammar with simpler internal structure. They have no Rule 2 to eliminate case marking from *who*, and their Rule 1 is modified to apply only to personal pronouns (*me, him, us*, etc.) but to leave *who* out. Let us call these children's grammar Grammar₂, which can be characterized informally as in Table 10.3.

TABLE 10.3: Derivation of *who* in Grammar₂

Underlying:	*saw who*	*to who*
	[Verb + Pro] _{Verb Phrase}	[Prep + Pro] _{Prepositional Phrase}
Rule 1:	[Verb + PersPro-Case]	[Prep + PersPro-Case]
	Verb Phrase	Prepositional Phrase

(Case-marking): (Not applicable with *who*: *saw who, to who*; but *saw him, to him*)

Result:	*saw who*	*to who*

(A later rule which fronts question words gives, for example, *Who did Harry see?*)

The children's grammar (Grammar$_2$) achieves the same output as the adult grammar (Grammar$_{1'}$) but is now more optimal again.

David Lightfoot's (1979, 1991) work has been very influential and is considered a major representative of later generative views. His scenario for the explanation of syntactic change is that grammatical complexity builds up gradually in a language (through minor changes of little importance) until eventually a sudden catastrophic and far-reaching restructuring of the grammar takes place which eliminates this complexity that made the language's grammar difficult for children to learn. One criticism of this view is that there is no reliable means of distinguishing the catastrophic changes (which overhaul grammars that become too complex, Lightfoot's major interest) from the gradually accumulating less significant changes. Another criticism is that catastrophic changes of this sort are extremely rare in the attested history of most languages. A central feature of Lightfoot's (1979) treatment is the claim that syntactic change (and syntax in general) is autonomous, meaning that syntactic change takes place independently of semantic relations, pragmatic considerations, discourse functions or sociolinguistic considerations. For Lightfoot, syntactic changes operate independently of considerations of meaning and use. This claim has been much criticized because syntactic rules and changes do not operate independently of meaning, use, pragmatics, sociolinguistic value judgements, foreign-language influences and so on.

Central to the generative view of language change is the notion that linguistic change in general, and therefore also syntactic change, takes place in the language acquisition process and in the transition of grammars from one generation to the next. Many cases of syntactic changes would seem to conform to this view, though others seem at odds with it. This approach assumes that many of the kinds of changes are the results of the child language learners just getting it wrong, making mistakes. For example, this view claims for the change in the Finnish participle construction (sentences (3–6) above) that in language acquisition children incorrectly assumed that sentence (4) was to be analysed as containing the genitive singular because they incorrectly perceived what was (formerly) the accusative singular (in (4)) and then they carried through with this assumption (by extension) by imposing their new and erroneous genitive interpretation on sentences with the plurals (as in (6)) as well, which were not ambiguous at all, as the singulars had been (where the suffix *-n* might be seen as either 'accusative singular' or 'genitive singular'), resulting in a restructuring of the grammar. However, this view is simply not available for many kinds of syntactic change where after the change the original construction still remains grammatical and unchanged alongside the innovative construction that the change is based on; the development of the new Finnish postposition (above) is such a case. In such changes, the original construction remains but in effect gains additional interpretations, that is, multiple analyses. In the development of the new Finnish postposition ((1) and (2) above), the source construction (in (1)) and the new postpositional construction based on it (in (2)) both survive; the same is true of the changes involving the Spanish reflexive (in (7) above) and the new passive construction derived from it (in (10–11)). In these changes, there is nothing which requires the assumption that the child language learner got it wrong which resulted in the grammar with a different construction (a new and different analysis of the old construction) which eliminates the original interpretation of the construction from the grammar. In these examples, there is nothing that requires child language acquisition to be the driving force behind the changes. Adult speakers could just as easily initiate the new analyses alongside the pre-existing ones. If these changes did begin with adults, their results would be part of the language which the next generation would hear around them, and consequently the children would simply learn these new, additional constructions together with any others that happen to be around as part of the grammar which they acquire. The argument that the language acquisition process need not be seen as the crucial locus of syntactic change challenges assumptions of the generative approach to syntactic change.

10.4   Grammaticalization

Grammaticalization is a topic of extensive current interest. The famous French Indo-Europeanist Antoine Meillet (1912: 132) introduced the term 'grammaticalization' with the sense of 'the attribution of a grammatical character to a formerly independent word', where an independent word with independent meaning may develop into an auxiliary word and, if the process continues, it ends up as a grammatical marker or bound grammatical morpheme. Jerzy Kuryłowicz's (1965: 52) much-cited definition is: 'Grammaticalization consists in the increase of the range of a morpheme advancing from a lexical to a grammatical or from a less grammatical to a more grammatical status'. This process is often characterized by a concurrent 'weakening' of both the meaning and the phonetic form of the word involved. In grammaticalization, two related processes are the typical objects of investigations: (1) changes of the lexical-item-to-grammatical-morpheme sort, which can involve phono-logical reduction and exhibit change from independent word to clitic or affix; and less commonly (2) the discourse-structure-to-morphosyn-tactic-marking sort, the fixing of discourse strategies in syntactic and morphological structure (Traugott and Heine 1991: 2). In both kinds, grammaticalization is typically associated with *semantic bleaching* and *phonological reduction* (to which we return below). Thus, Heine and Reh (1984: 15) define grammaticalization as 'an evolution whereby linguistic units lose in semantic complexity, pragmatic significance, syntactic freedom, and phonetic substance'.

A frequently cited example is English *will*, which originally meant 'want', as its German cognate, *will* '(he/she) wants', still does. We can see remnants of the former 'want' meaning in such things as *have the will* [= desire], *if you will* [= if you want to] and *good will* [= wishes, desires]. English *will* became semantically bleached (lost its sense of 'want') and was grammaticalized as a 'future' marker. Grammaticalized forms are also often associated with 'phonetic erosion' (reduction of fuller forms to phonologically shorter ones). In this example, grammat-icalized *will* 'future' can also be reduced in form, as in contractions such as *I'll, she'll, my dog'll do it*, and so on. Meillet presented a parallel example in Greek of the grammaticalization of a verb 'to want' as a future marker, though its history is more complex than the change in English and is coupled with the loss of infinitives in Greek. Modern Greek *θa* 'future marker' began life as the Classical Greek main verb *thélei* 'want'. Greek lost its original infinitive construction and replaced it with a subordinate clause construction: *thélō hina gráphō* 'I want to write' [literally 'I want that I write'], *thélei hina gráphei* 'he/she wants to write' ['he/she wants that he/she writes']. Though *thélei* continued as a main verb meaning 'want', it also came to mean 'will' (future), so that *thélō hina gráphō*, for example, could mean either 'I want to write' or 'I will write'. Later, the 'future' became restricted to the 'third person' form only, /θeli/ (from *thélei*), and eventually the combination of /θeli hina/ changed to /θa/, going through the steps: /θeli hina/ > /θeli na/ > /θe na/ > /θa na/ > /θa/, giving Modern Greek /θa ɣráfo/ 'I will write' (Joseph 1990). Another example is the frequent grammaticalization of lexical 'go' to 'future', as with English *(be) going to* which originally referred only to the verb of motion, but then acquired a sense of 'future'/'future intention', which can be reduced phonologically to *gonna* in spoken language.

10.4.1 Examples of typical grammaticalization changes

It may be helpful to mention some of the sorts of grammaticalization changes, and the pathways they typically take, that are seen to recur with some frequency in languages around the world.

(1) Auxiliary < main verb (as in English *will* 'future auxiliary' < 'want').

(2) Case suffixes < postpositions (as in Estonian *–ga* (/-ka/) 'comitative case' suffix < *kanssa* 'with' postposition).

(3) Between < 'centre', 'middle'.

(3) Case marking < serial verbs.

(4) Causatives < causal verb ('make', 'have', 'get', 'cause', 'force') + Clause with another verb.

(5) Classifiers (numeral and noun) < concrete nouns ('man', 'woman', 'child', 'animal', 'tree', etc.)

(6) Complementizer/subordinate conjunction < 'say'; demonstrative, relative clause markers.

(7) Coordinate conjunction ('and') < 'with'.

(8) Copula ('to be') < positional verbs 'stand', 'sit', or 'give', 'exist' (Spanish *estar* 'to be' < Latin *stāre* 'to stand'; varieties of Quechua *tiya-* 'to be' < **tiya-* 'to sit'). Note that Spanish *ser* 'to be' comes from a blending of Latin *sedēre* 'to sit' and *esse* 'to be' (*essere* in Vulgar Latin) 'to be'.

(9) Dative case marker < 'give'.

(10) Definite article < demonstrative pronoun.

(11) Direct object case markers < locatives, prepositions (for example, a dative marker has become an accusative marker in Spanish, Kwa, Bemba and others; compare Spanish *Harry vio a Ron* [Harry saw **OBJECT.MARKER** Ron] 'Harry saw Ron' with *Harry lo dio a Ron* [Harry it gave **TO** Ron] 'Harry gave it to Ron').

(12) Dual < 'two'.

(13) Durative, habitual, iterative < 'stay'; durative aspect < 'remain, stay, keep, sit'.

(14) Existential/presentational constructions < 'have', 'be' (often with no inflection or only third person present inflection allowed), or < locative pronoun (Spanish *hay* 'there is/are' < *haber* 'to have'; French *il y a* < *y* 'there' + *a* 'has'; English *there is/are*).

(15) Future < 'want', 'have', 'go', 'come' (English *will* 'future auxiliary' < 'want'); adverbs ('quickly', 'tomorrow', 'then', 'afterwards').

(16) Grammatical gender < noun (masculine < 'man, male, boy'; feminine < 'woman, female, girl').

(17) Habitual < 'to live', 'stay', 'go', 'sit', 'use'; continuous.

(18) Hortative < 'come', 'go', 'leave' ('abandon').

(19) Impersonal/agentless verb forms: the following constructions are interrelated in many languages and changes frequently go from one to another among these, though directionality is not strongly determined in most cases: reflexive ~ reciprocal ~ spontaneous/automatically occurring ~ potential ~ honorific ~ plural ~ detransitivizing constructions ~ middle/medio-passive/pseudo-passive ~ passive ~ defocusing ~ non-agent topicalization ~ impersonal verb ~ first person plural imperative/hortatory ~ causative ~ transitive (for example, 'Mr. Weasley had/got his car stolen') ~ stative/resultative ~ perfect ~ ergative. A directionality is frequently attested in which reflexive > reciprocal > passive > impersonal (where reflexive > passive, or reflexive > impersonal are possible and occur with frequency).

(20) Indefinite article < 'one'(English *a(n)* comes from 'one').

(22) Indefinite pronoun < 'person', 'man', 'body', 'thing'; 'one'; 'you'; 'they' (as with English *somebody, anybody* which incorporate 'body').

(23) Infinitive < 'to', 'for' (purpose).

(24) Locative constructions < body-part terms (compare English *at the head of, at the foot of*, etc.).

(25) Negative < negative intensifiers (for example, French *ne pas,* originally 'not a step' where *pas* was a negative intensifier much like English *not a bit* is today; similar changes are attested in many languages).

(26) Negative < 'leave', 'abandon', 'lack'.

(27) Quotative < 'say'.

(28) Obligation < 'need', 'necessity', 'owe' (for example, English *ought (to)* from Old English *āhte*, past tense of *āgan* 'to owe').

(29) Obligation < copula (for example, *you are to go to the doctor tomorrow*).

(30) Passive < 'get', 'obtain', 'receive'; 'they'.

(31) Perfect(ive) < 'finish', 'complete', 'have/possess', 'end'.

(32) Preposition/postpositions < verb (preposition < VO; postposition < OV).

(33) Progressive < locative + non-finite verb (English, for example, *is hunting < is a-hunting < is on hunting*; Pennsylvania German, Cologne German *ist am Schreiben* [is on.the to.write] 'is writing').

(34) Progressive/habitual < durative verbs ('keep'), 'do', copula, positional verb.

(35) Reflexive pronoun < some body-part noun ('body, head, belly, person') + possessive; 'reciprocal' < 'body'.

(36) Relative pronouns < *wh*-question words/interrogative pronouns (compare English relative pronouns *who, which* with question words *who?, which?*).

(37) Relative clause markers < demonstratives.

(38) Third person pronoun < demonstrative, 'man', 'person'.

(39) *Wh*-questions < cleft or pseudo cleft (equivalents to 'what did she do?' < 'what is it that she did?'

(40) Yes–no question < 'or'; negation.

These are just a few of the many. Also, these are not the only paths by which many of these elements can develop. (For actual examples of these and others, see especially Heine and Kuteva 2002, also Harris and Campbell 1995, and Hopper and Traugott 1993.)

10.4.2   The status of grammaticalization

Some argue that grammaticalization has no independent status of its own, that there is nothing special or unique about it, that it merely involves other kinds of linguistic changes which are well understood and not inherently connected with grammaticalization: sound change, semantic change and reanalysis. It is important to understand the basis for this challenge to grammaticalization.

Most scholars agree that grammaticalization is not a mechanism of change in its own right, but relies on the other mechanisms, primarily on reanalysis, but also sometimes on extension and borrowing. There are, however, many reanalyses which do not involve grammaticalization, for example those involving word-order changes, affixes becoming independent words (which is rare, but a number of examples are known from various languages), changes from one syntactic structure to another, and so on – that is, any reanalysis which does not involve lexical items shifting towards having a more grammatical status or discourse structure becoming more fixed morphosyntactically.

That grammaticalization is often associated with 'semantic bleaching' (also called *fading, weakening*) should perhaps not be seen so much as a special attribute of grammaticalization as just regular semantic change in action (see Chapter 9). Semantic bleaching in grammaticalization can hardly be seen as very remarkable, since it is essentially part of the definition of grammaticalization, a shift from more lexical meaning to more grammatical content. The types of semantic change involved in grammaticalization are primarily narrowing, sometimes coupled with metaphor, metonymy, and others (see Chapter 9). The emphasis on semantic loss or weakening is perhaps unwarranted, however, since in the process of grammaticalization forms also take on new meanings, such as 'future' in the case of *will* and *gonna*, and it is not necessarily the case that any lexical meaning is lost, since often the source of the grammaticalization remains in the language with its former meaning alongside the new grammaticalized form, as *be going to* as the original meaning of directional verb has in English alongside the new 'future' meaning acquired in the grammaticalization. The semantic bleaching (the semantic change) in grammaticalization can in no way be considered independent of semantic change in general.

The phonological reduction ('erosion' of form) which many associate with grammaticalization is also best not seen as unique to grammaticalization, but as normal phonological change. Phonological reduction processes apply to items of the appropriate phonological character generally in a language, not just to certain items which happen to be involved in processes of grammaticalization. Reduction often follows grammaticalization because it is at that stage that the conditions favourable to changes of phonological reduction first come about, for example where the forms which get reduced no longer have an independent lexical meaning and hence come to be in relatively unstressed positions.

In short, grammaticalizations involve reanalysis, but reanalysis is a much more powerful mechanism of change and is by no means limited to nor coextensive with grammaticalization. Sound change and semantic change apply to all sorts of things in addition to grammaticalizations. For this reason, many find grammaticalization derivative, perhaps an interesting intersection of these various sorts of change, but with no special explanatory status of its own. (For general treatments of grammaticalization, see C. Lehmann 1995, Hopper and Traugott 1993, and Traugott and Heine 1991; for critiques of grammaticalization as an explanatory theory, see the articles in Campbell 2001.)

10.5 Syntactic Reconstruction

Opinions are sharply divided concerning whether syntax is reconstructible by the comparative method. Nevertheless, the evidence available for comparison is often sufficient for successful reconstruction of many aspects of the syntax of a proto-language. To understand why there has been doubt about reconstruction of syntax and to see the real potential which we have for successful reconstruction in this area, we need to look at some of the obstacles to such reconstruction that are sometimes mentioned and to ways of surmounting the difficulties which they raise. Following this, we will consider some beneficial things which can help in syntactic reconstruction.

10.5.1   Reanalysis as an obstacle to reconstruction

Instances of traditional analogy sometimes pose obstacles in phonological and lexical reconstruction. Reanalysis in syntactic change is like analogy, and cases of reanalysis can make syntactic reconstruction difficult. However, in instances where analogy changes the form in one language so that it does not fit those of the related languages with which it is compared, we seek an explanation for the non-fitting form, and often we find the analogical reformation which caused the form to deviate, as in the following cognate set from Germanic:

English	German	Gothic	Old Norse	
adder	*natter*	*nadr-*	*naðra*	'adder'/'snake'

The weight of the evidence in German, Gothic and Old Norse suggests an initial *n-* in the proto-form, and this bids us seek an explanation for why no reflex of this *n-* is seen in the English cognate. In seeking an explanation, we eventually discover that the pattern of the English indefinite article with *a* before words beginning in a consonant (as *a plum*) and *an* before vowel-initial words (*an apple*) suggests analogical reinterpretation, from *a #nadder* to *an #adder* (compare Old English *næddre* 'snake'). In a situation such as this one, the analogical change is not devastating to lexical reconstruction, and it is precisely the comparative method and the evidence from the other languages which helps us to unravel the complication. We reconstruct initial *n-* and posit an analogical change to account for the deviance of the English cognate.

Using the same procedure, in many instances where one of the languages being compared has undergone reanalysis in some particular construction, we can discover the reanalysis and explain it so that it no longer prevents us from reconstructing the syntactic pattern in question. Earlier in this chapter, we saw the example in which a Finnish participle construction was reanalysed so that the noun that had originally been an accusative direct object of the main verb (as in (3) and (5)) came to be interpreted as the genitive subject of the participle (as in (4b) and (6)). If we compare cognate constructions among the Balto-Finnic languages, which include Finnish and its close relatives, we soon discover that Finnish stands out as not fitting the pattern of the other languages, as seen in the following examples:

(13a) *Finnish*: näin häne-n tule-van   [genitive]
                I.saw he-Gen come-Part
                'I saw him coming/that he comes'

(13b) *Estonian*: nägin te-da tule-va-t   [accusative]
                I.saw he-Acc come-Part-Acc
                'I saw him coming/that he comes'

(13c) *Vote*:   näin me:s-sä tulə-va-a te:tä mö   [accusative]
                I.saw man.Acc come-Part-Acc street along
                'I saw a man coming/who comes along the street'
      Compare *Finnish*: näin miehe-n tule-van tietä pitkin
                    [genitive]
                    I.saw man-Gen come-Part road along
                    (same meaning)

(13d) *North*   son oia'dna boc'cu-i-d vuol'-ga-m [accusative]
       Saami: he see reindeer-Pl-Acc leave-Past.Part-Acc
                'he sees that the reindeer have left'
      Compare *Finnish*: hän näkee poro-j-en lähte-neen
                    [genitive]
                    he sees reindeer-Pl-Gen leave-Past.Part

The cognate constructions in Balto-Finnic languages, except for Finnish, present the noun phrase which plays the role of the subject of the subordinate clause syntactically as a direct object in accusative case of the main verb, not as a genitive subject of the participle, as in Finnish. The difference in Finnish demands an explanation. In seeking an explanation, we soon discover that the accusative singular and genitive singular cases are both signalled by -*n*, allowing for multiple interpretations. Given this and the difference between Finnish and the other languages with respect to this construction, we encounter little difficulty in determining that Finnish has undergone a reanalysis and does not reflect the original form. We reconstruct the construction as reflected in the other Balto-Finnic languages, with the noun phrase as accusative object of the main verb, and we write out the changes of reanalysis and extension that have caused Finnish to depart from this structure.

10.5.2 Borrowing as an obstacle to syntactic reconstruction

Just as borrowing can complicate lexical reconstruction, it can be a serious obstacle to syntactic reconstruction as well. However, the techniques for identifying borrowing (in Chapter 3) can often help to identify syntactic borrowing and thus get beyond this obstacle. For example, a comparison of the words for 'mother' across Finno-Ugric languages reveals reflexes of **ema* 'mother' in most of them; however, Finnish has *äiti* 'mother' instead, and this difference turns out to be the result of borrowing. Closer investigation reveals that Finnish did indeed borrow this word from Germanic 'mother' (Gothic *aiþei* [ɛθī] Old High German *eidī*, Proto-Germanic **aiθī*). Since it is borrowed, it is not a legitimate witness of what the form in the proto-language may have been; to determine that, we rely rather on the information available from the other languages which did not replace the original cognate word through borrowing. In syntactic reconstruction, we do the same thing. For example, in most varieties of Finnish, verbal constructions involving obligation require the subject to be in the genitive case and the verb to be in a third person singular form (that is, the verb does not agree with this genitive subject), as in the following example from Standard Finnish (Gen = genitive, Sg = Singular, Nom = nominative, Pl = Plural, Part = Participle):

(14a) minu-n täyty-y mennä
I-Gen must-3rd.Person.Present to.go
'I must go'
(14b) minu-n pitä-ä mennä
I-Gen must-3rd.Sg.Present to.go

However, Western Finnish lacks this obligation construction; rather, it has borrowed its construction from neighbouring Swedish, now with a subject in nominative case and with the verb agreeing in person with this subject, as in the following examples:

Western Finnish:
(14c) mä täydy-n mennä
I.Nom must-I to.go
'I must go'
(14d) mä pidä-n mennä
I.Nom must-I to.go
'I must go'

When we compare the many regional varieties of Finnish (in (15–16)),

Western Finnish (illustrated in (14c–d)), with its nominative subjects and verb agreement, stands out as inconsistent with the others, which take genitive subjects and no verb agreement. This is illustrated here with an example from just two of the many dialects, Vermland (in Sweden) and Koprina (Inkeri, former Soviet Union):

Vermland:
(15a) nii-j-en ois pitän-nä lahata oamuśe-lla
   these-Pl-Gen would.have must-Past.Part to.slaughter
    morning-on
   'they should have slaughtered in the morning'
   Compare *Standard Finnish*:
(15b) nii-den olisi pitä-nyt lahdata aamu-lla
   these-Pl.Gen would.have must-Past.Part to.slaughter
    morning-on
   Inkeri (Koprina):
(16a) sulhaśe-n pit^j antaa kolme ruplaa pojil viinarahaa
   bridegroom-Gen had to.give three roubles boys.to
    wine.money.of
   'The bridegroom had (was supposed) to give three roubles
    of drinking money to the boys'
   Compare *Standard Finnish*:
(16b) sulhase-n piti antaa pojille kolme ruplaa viinarahaa
   bridegroom-Gen had to.give three roubles boys.to
    wine.money.of

Given that all other varieties of Finnish have the genitive subject and non-agreeing third person verb form in verbal obligation constructions, we reconstruct this pattern and we explain the Western Finnish one with nominative subjects and verbs that agree in person with their subjects as a later change due to borrowing from the Swedish model. The evidence from other varieties shows that Western Finnish is inconsistent, and further research reveals that it is due to borrowing. Therefore, in spite of the borrowing in this case, we are able successfully to reconstruct the older stage of the language, with genitive subjects and non-agreeing verbs, based on the weight of the comparative evidence from the other varieties compared.

 In summary, there are many obstacles to reconstruction of syntax, but they are largely the same sort that we encounter in phonological and lexical reconstruction, and often it is possible to see beyond the obstacles. Let us turn now to some considerations which prove beneficial in efforts to reconstruct syntax.

10.5.3 Morphological reconstruction as clues to syntactic reconstruction

Morphology and syntax are so interrelated that to the extent that morphology can be reconstructed, many aspects of the proto-syntax in many cases will automatically become clear. The techniques used for lexical reconstruction (Chapter 5), based on the sequence of sound correspondences in cognate words, can frequently be used to reconstruct polymorphemic words. Morphological analysis of these reconstructed proto-words provides the proto-morphology free, so to speak. An example of this sort is seen in Table 10.4, where some polymorphemic cognate words for the paradigm for the verb 'to read' in Balto-Finnic are compared. With just these few compared words, we see indications of such aspects of Proto-Balto-Finnic morphosyntax as tenses and aspects, passive, embedded clauses with the third infinitive, and the participle (which is also used in relative clauses). This is enough to illustrate how the technique of reconstructing the proto-morphology can help us to obtain aspects of the proto-syntax.

TABLE 10.4: Balto-Finnic comparative verbal morphology

	Finnish	*Vote*	*Estonian*	*Proto-Balto-Finnic*
1.	luen	lugən	loen	*luɣe-n
	\<center\>'I read (indicative)'\</center\>			
2.	olen lukenut	ələn lukənnu	olen lugenud	*ole-n luke-nut
	'I have read' (first person perfect indicative)			
3.	luettiin	lugəti:	loeti [loetti]	*luɣe-ttiin
	'(it) was read' (past passive)			
4.	lukemaan	lukəma:	lugema [lukema]	*luke-ma-han
	'third infinitive'			
5.	lukeva	lukəva	lugev [lukev]	*luke-vaʔ
	'reading' (present active participle, basis of relative clauses)			

The 'third infinitive' is an infinitival form (formerly nominal) used especially with verbs of motion.

While in some situations this technique can recover a considerable amount of the proto-syntax, it works less well where the cognate grammatical morphemes have undergone functional or positional shifts or have been lost due to other changes in the languages. Successful reconstruction here, as with phonological and lexical reconstruction, depends on the nature of the evidence preserved in the languages being compared. For example, when we compare the modern Romance languages, we are able to recover much less of the original morphology because so much has been lost in the various languages. This being the case, the technique of morphological reconstruction which worked well for aspects of Proto-Balto-Finnic syntax provides less for Proto-Romance syntax.

10.5.4 Directionality

Just as knowing the characteristic direction of change in various sound changes provides clues to the best reconstruction in phonology, the directionality of a number of grammatical changes is also known, and this provides clues for the best grammatical reconstruction. An example of this is the fact that postpositions frequently become attached to roots and lose their independent status, becoming case suffixes; however, case suffixes hardly ever become independent postpositions. With the directionality Postposition > Case in mind, consider the comparisons of forms meaning 'with' in Table 10.5, where Postp = Postposition; Com = Comitative case ('with'). In this example, given the known directionality of Postposition > Case, it is incumbent upon us to reconstruct the postposition as original and to postulate that the comitative case endings which are the cognates in Veps and Estonian are due to a grammatical change, 'postposition' > 'comitative' case or clitic.

TABLE 10.5: Comparison of Balto-Finnic 'with' forms

Finnish	Karelian	Veps	Estonian	Vote	Livonian	Proto-Balto-Finnic
kanssa	kanssa	-ka	-ga [-ka]	ka:sa	ka:zu	*kans(s)a?
(Postp)	(Postp)	(Com)	(Com clitic)	(Postp)	(Postp)	(Postp)

10.5.5 Archaisms

An *archaism* (also often called *relic*) is something characteristic of the language of the past, a vestige, which survives chiefly in specialized uses. Archaisms are in some way exceptional or marginal to the language in which they are found. They are most commonly preserved in certain kinds of language such as in proverbs, folk poetry, folk ballads, legal documents, prayers and religious texts, very formal genres or stylistic variants, and so on. A straightforward example is English *pease* for 'pea', an archaism preserved in the nursery rhyme 'Pease porridge hot, pease porridge cold, pease porridge in the pot nine days old'; it reflects the older *pease* before it was changed by analogical back formation to *pea* (mentioned in Chapter 4). As examples of archaisms in English more relevant to historical grammar, we might mention the verb forms with the *-eth* third person and *-st* second person agreement markers and the auxiliary forms *hath, hast, art, doth* (*doeth*), and the archaic second singular pronoun forms, *thou, thee, thy, thine*. These are all archaic and no longer productive. Some examples of these are:

> Hell **hath** *no fury like a woman scorned.* (Proverb)
> *What therefore God* **hath** *joined together, let not man put asunder.* (Marriage ceremony, Biblical, from Matthew 19:6.)
> *The lady* **doth** *protest too much, methinks.* (*Hamlet*)
> *O Romeo, Romeo!* **wherefore art thou***?* (*Romeo and Juliet*)

Several of these are illustrated in the 23rd Psalm, oft repeated in litera-ture, poetry and song:

> *The Lord is my shepherd . . . He* **maketh** *me to lie down in green pastures; he* **leadeth** *me beside the still waters. He* **restoreth** *my soul; he* **leadeth** *me in the paths of righteousness . . . for* **thou art** *with me;* **thy** *rod and* **thy** *staff they comfort me.* **Thou preparest** *a table . . .* **thou anointest** *my head . . . my cup* **runneth** *over.*

As exceptions, archaisms have somehow been bypassed or exempted from the general changes which the language has undergone. Grammat-ical archaisms are favoured in syntactic reconstruction – some scholars believe them to be the single most useful source of evidence. Naturally, if we can tell what is archaic – by definition 'old' – it affords us extremely valuable information for historical reconstruction.

A difficulty with using archaisms (relics) for reconstruction is that it can be difficult to tell whether we are dealing with a legitimate archaism or something that is exceptional for other reasons but is not old. Another difficulty comes from the frequent situation in which we easily identify exceptions, but where the archaism provides too little information for reliable reconstruction.

Let us look at a slightly more complicated example. As we saw above, Proto-Balto-Finnic had a participle construction in which the logical subject of the participial verb was originally a direct object (in accusative case, as in (3) and (5)) of the main verb, but this was reanalysed in Finnish so that the noun phrase came to be interpreted as the subject (in genitive case) of the participle (as in (4b) and (6)). This reanalysis was made possible by the homophony of the accusative and genitive singular case endings, both *-n*. Finnish archaisms preserve evidence of the construction before the change with the accusative. For example, in folk poems there are instances of relics such as (17a) (Acc = 'accusative', Pass = 'passive', Pl = 'plural', Part = 'participle', Gen = 'genitive'):

(17a) kuul-tihin kala-t kute-van, lohenpursto-t loiskutta-van
      hear-Past.Pass fish-Acc.Pl spawn-Part salmon.tail-Acc.Pl
      splash-Part
    'the fish were heard spawning, salmon-tails splashing'

Instead of the accusative plural of 'fish' (*kala-t*) and 'salmon-tails' (*lohenpursto-t*), modern Standard Finnish has the genitive plural, as in (17b):

(17b) kuul-tiin kalo-j-en kute-van, lohenpursto-j-en loiskutta-van
      hear-Past.Pass fish-Pl.Gen spawn-Part salmon.tail-Pl.Gen
      splash-Part

The relic contained in this folk poem provides additional support for the reconstruction above with the accusative pattern which was securely established on the basis of comparative evidence from the related languages. However, if other supporting evidence from related languages were not available, this archaism alone would be insufficient for a reliable reconstruction. We would not be certain whether this was in fact an archaism (and thus evidence of a former state of the language) or perhaps just some exception to the normal pattern for expressive or poetic purposes.

10.5.6 What can be successfully reconstructed

Another way of appreciating the possibilities for successful syntactic reconstruction is by evaluating the results of attempts to reconstruct the syntax of language families. The application of the comparative method to languages of the Uralic family reveals a proto-language with the following grammatical features. There were three contrasting grammatical numbers, 'dual' (*-kə(-)), 'plural' (*-t and *-j) and 'singular' (Ø). Direct objects of finite verbs were marked by the 'accusative' case (*-m), but the objects of an imperative verb bore no accusative marker. Case and definiteness were related; the genitive and accusative cases implied definiteness, while indefinite nouns took no marking (that is, in form they were not distinct from the nominative case). The 'genitive' case marked not only the possessor but also served to signal an adjective attribute before its head noun. Proto-Uralic verb tenses included: *-j 'past', *-mə 'past (perfect)', *-pA 'present' and *-śA 'past' ('A' denotes vowel harmony with the attached root). There was a negative verb, *e-*. Sentences minimally had a nominal subject and a predicate (verbal or nominal); the subject could be signalled by personal pronominal suffixes attached to the predicate. The predicate agreed with its subject (in person and number); there was no other agreement. The predicate of embedded clauses was in form a verbal noun, where personal possessive pronominal suffixes were used to signal its subject. The role of the embedded clause in the overall sentence was shown by case markings on the verbal noun (a nominalization) which was the core of the embedded clause. Proto-Uralic had no overt conjunctions or relative pronouns; embedded verbal nouns, nominalizations, were the only means of showing subordination. In brief, the application of the comparative method to the reconstruction of Proto-Uralic morphosyntax has proven quite successful and this case shows that, at least in some instances, we are capable of syntactic reconstruction (Janhunen 1982; Campbell 1990a).

In summary, there are many obstacles to successful syntactic reconstruction, but many of these are like the obstacles encountered in phonological and lexical reconstruction, and in many instances, using normal historical linguistic techniques (recognition of borrowing, analogy and so on), we can get beyond the obstacles through the weight of the comparative evidence from related languages. Reliance on the known directionality of many grammatical changes helps, and reconstructed morphology and syntactic archaisms can provide very valuable information. In short, while syntactic reconstruction can be very difficult, it is clearly possible.

10.6 Exercises

Exercise 10.1 Syntactic change in Panare

Consider the following from Panare (a Cariban language of Venezuela). (NOTE: *y* = IPA [j], *ñ* = IPA [ɲ], *č* = IPA [tʃ].) The basic word order is verb first and subject final.) When the subject is 'I' or 'you', no copula (form of the verb 'to be') is required in the present tense, as in:

(1) maestro yu
    teacher   I
    'I am a teacher'

(2) maestro amən
    teacher   you
    'You are a teacher'

However, with a third-person subject, a copula is obligatory. With an inanimate subject, the copula is *mən*, as in (3):

(3) e?čipen mən manko
    fruit   mən mango
    'Mango is a fruit'

For this exercise, such examples with inanimate subjects are not so relevant. However, with an animate subject, the copula is either *kəh* or *nəh*, with a difference in meaning. Sentences (4) and (5) show that sentences with third-person subjects but with no copula are ungrammatical (here /✗/ means ungrammatical):

(4) ✗maestro e?ñapa
    teacher   Panare

(5) ✗e?čipen manko
    fruit   mango

Sentences (6) (7) and (8) illustrate the *kəh* and *nəh* copulas and their difference:

(6) maestro *kəh* e?ñapa
    teacher *kəh* Panare
    'This Panare here is a teacher'

(7) e?čipen *mən* manko
    fruit   *mən* mango
    'Mango is a fruit'

(8) maestro *nəh* e?ñapa
    teacher *nəh* Panare
    'That Panare there is a teacher'

Now consider some demonstratives. The demonstratives *məh* 'this person whom I can see now' and *kən* 'that person whom I can't see now' at first glance appear to behave straightforwardly, as in (9) and (10):

(9) maestro *kəh* <u>məh</u>
    teacher *kəh* this.guy
    'This guy is a teacher here'

(10) maestro *nəh* <u>kəh</u>
     teacher *nəh* that.guy
     'That guy is a teacher
                     there'

But consider the additional Panare copular sentences in (11) through (14) (note here that /y/ changes to /č/ after /h/, so that *yu* 'I' in this example is *ču* in this context):

(11) maestro *nəh* məh
     teacher *nəh* this.guy
     'This guy was a teacher'

(12) maestro *nəh* ču
     teacher *nəh* I
     'I was a teacher'

(13) maestro *nəh* amən
     teacher *nəh* you
     'You were a teacher'

(14) maestro *kəh* kən
     teacher *kəh* that.guy
     'That guy is being a
     teacher right now'(that
     is, he is off somewhere
     performing his teaching
     duties at this very
     moment)

Though originally not possible, notice also that *kəh* and *nəh* now can also occur with ordinary verbs, as in (15) through (18) (the question mark indicates a sentence which sounds very strange to native speakers):

(15) əʔ púmanəpəh *kəh* Toman   (16)   ? əʔ púmanəpəh *nəh* Toman
     be-falling   *kəh* Thomas   be-falling   *nəh* Thomas
     'Tom is falling'   'Tom is falling (but I can't
                                      see him)'

(17) yɨupúmən   *kəh* Toman   (18) yɨupúmən   *nəh* Toman
     fall   *kəh* Thomas   fall   *nəh* Thomas
     'Tom is going to fall!'   'Tom is going to fall one day'
                                     or 'Tom fell'

State the syntactic changes which have affected *kəh* and *nəh*. Explain the historical development of these items as best you can using the terms and mechanisms presented in this chapter.

(Based on Gildea 1993, exercise prepared by Verónica Grondona.)

Exercise 10.2 Syntactic change in Estonian

Compare the sentences in this exercise, which represent different stages of Estonian (a Finno-Ugric language); explain what changed and identify the kinds of changes or the mechanisms involved.

Stage I: Estonian had two alternative constructions for subordinate clauses involving the complements of speech-act and mental-state main verbs, illustrated in (1) and (2) (Gen = 'genitive', Nom = 'nominative', Part = 'participle', Pres = 'present indicative'):

(1) sai   kuulda,   et   seal   üks   mees   ela-b
     got   to.hear   that   there   one.Nom   man.Nom   live-3rd.Pres
     'he/she came to hear that a man lives there'

(2) sai   kuulda   seal   ühe   mehe   ela-vat
     got   to.hear   there   one.Gen   man.Gen   live-Part
     (same meaning as (1))

Stage II: (1) and (2) remain possible, but the construction in (3) also became possible (note that 'participle' became 'indirect'):

(3) sai   kuulda,   (et)   seal   üks   mees   ela-vat
     got   to.hear   (that)   there   one.Nom   man.Nom   live-Indirect
     (3a) 'he/she came to hear that they say a man lives there'/
     (3b) 'he/she came to hear that reportedly a man lives there'

Stage III: (1), (2) and (3) are all possible now, but forms formerly found only in subordinate clauses, as in (3), came to be found also in main clauses, as in (4):

(4) ta   tege-vat   töö-d
     he.Nom   do-Indirect   work-Partitive
     'They say he is working' / 'Reportedly he is working'

Exercise 10.3 The development of perfect auxiliaries in Spanish

In the following, the stages in the development of perfect auxiliaries in Spanish from its Latin origins are described and illustrated. On the basis of this information, compare the stages and attempt to determine the changes which took place and to identify the kinds of changes or the mechanisms involved. (Fem = 'feminine', Masc = 'masculine', Part = 'participle', Pl = 'plural', PPP = 'past passive participle').

Stage I: Latin used expressions with 'past passive participle' (PPP) in combination with the verbs *tenēre* 'hold', *habēre* 'keep, hold' and others meaning 'hold, possess, own', to represent something as ready or kept in a completed condition, as in (1):

(1) Metuō enim nē   ibi   vos   habeam   fatigā-tō-s (Late Latin)
     fear.I   truly   lest   there   you   have.I   fatigue-PPP.Masc-Pl
     'I fear that I have you tired'/'that I have tired you'/'that you
       are tired'

This construction with 'past passive participle' was quite limited in its occurrence in Classical Latin, but became associated with 'perfect' aspect in combination with the development of *habēre* as an auxiliary. Originally this construction had *habēre* 'keep, hold, have' (a main verb) with the 'past passive participle' form as an adjective which modified the direct object (both the logical and surface object) of this main verb (*habēre*), which agreed in number and gender with this object as its head, as in (2):

(2) [habeō]   [litter-ā-s   scrip-t-ā-s]
     have.I   letter-Fem-Pl.Acc   write-PPP-Fem-Pl.Acc
     'I have written letters' = 'I have letters which are written'

Stage II: In Old Spanish, *haber* (spelled *aver* in Old Spanish, from Latin *habēre* 'to have, hold') in such constructions began to lose its possessive meaning and to consolidate the auxiliary function, resulting in compound tenses, but still with agreement in gender and number between the participle and the direct object until the mid-sixteenth century, as illustrated in (3) (where the *-o-s* 'masculine plural' of *hechos* 'made' agrees with the *-o-s* 'masculine plural' of *enemigos* 'enemies'):

(3) Los   *había* . . . *he-ch-o-s*   enemig-*o-s*   de estotros
    Them had   make-Past.Part-Masc-Pl enemy-Masc-Pl of these.
                                                                             others
    'He had made enemies of these others' (from Hernán Cortés)

Stage III: Gradually, the *haber* + PPP construction changed, eliminating the requirement that 'past passive participle' must agree in number and gender with the noun which it modified, losing its passive sense, with the verb *haber* becoming the 'perfect auxiliary', and Modern Spanish no longer permits agreement between the participle and the object, as in (4):

(4) Hemos   escri-to   cart-a-s
    have.we   write-Past.Part letter-Fem-Pl
    'We have written letters'

The adjectival participle source with number and gender agreement still survives in other contexts (but not in the perfect construction with forms of the verb *haber*), for example:

(5) Tenemos cart-a-s   escri-t-a-s   en   tint-a   roj-a
    have.we   letter-Fem-Pl write-Past.Part-Fem-Pl in   ink-Fem.Sg red-Fem.Sg
    'We have letters written in red ink'.

In the series of changes described here, the meaning is no longer 'X possesses that which has been done', but 'X has done', and is accompanied by the structural change of *haber* from main verb to an auxiliary.

Stage IV: Additional changes in connection with the new 'perfect' construction also came about. First, the verb *ser* 'to be' had formerly also been an auxiliary used with certain intransitive verbs (especially verbs of motion) (as in (6a) and (7a)), but this was replaced by the auxiliary *haber*, as seen in the Modern Spanish equivalents in (6b) and (7b):

(6a) Old Spanish   ella   *es*   naci-d-*a*
                       she   is   born-Past.Part-Fem
(6b) Modern Spanish   ella   ha   naci-d-o
                       she   has   born-Past.Part
                     'she has been born'

(7a) Old Spanish   ellos   *son*   i-d-*o-s*
                       they   are   go-Past.Part-Masc-Pl
(7b) Modern Spanish   ellos   *han*   i-d-*o*
                       they   have   go-Past.Part
                     'they have gone' (Lapesa 1981: 212)

Second, the word order changed, placing the participle closer to the auxiliary, for example from the equivalent of 'I have a letter written' (as in (2)) to 'I have written a letter' (as in (4)).

Exercise 10.4 *Finding examples of grammaticalization*

The following are some of the most common pathways of grammaticalization (that is, lexical sources which often become grammatical morphemes as a result of grammaticalization changes). Attempt to find examples from English (or from other languages you may be familiar with) which might illustrate these processes. (A few which are extremely common around the world are also included even though English alone may not offer examples.) As an example, for 'go to' > Future, you might list English 'going to' > Future as in 'Hermione is going to marry Ron.'

(1) Allative ('to') > complementizer (for example, marker of infinitives)
(2) 'come' > future
(3) Copula ('to be') > obligation (such as 'must', 'should')
(4) Demonstrative pronoun (such as 'this', 'that') > definite article (such as 'the')
(5) 'get' > passive
(6) 'have' (possession) > obligation
(7) 'have' (possession) > perfect or completive aspect
(8) 'keep' ('hold', 'grasp') > continuous
(9) 'keep' > possession ('have')
(10) 'man' > indefinite pronoun
(11) 'need' > obligation
(12) 'one' > indefinite pronoun, indefinite article
(13) 'owe' > obligation
(14) 'say' > quotative
(15) 'say' > conditional
(16) 'want' > future
(17) Wh-question word (such as 'what?', 'which?', 'who') > relative pronoun, relative clause marker.

11

―

Explaining Linguistic Change

―

These phonetic changes [in Grimm's Law] have, it is true, been brought about by the influence of climate, food, laziness or the reverse, analogy, and fashion; but we are still ignorant of the relative power of these causes, and the precise manner in which they affect the phonology of a language.

(Sayce 1874: 16)

11.1 Introduction

This chapter is concerned with the explanation of linguistic change or, perhaps better said, with attempts that linguists have made towards explaining why languages change as they do. The explanation of linguistic change is a topic of much debate and considerable disagreement. In this chapter, we try to cut through the disagreements to see how linguists have attempted to explain linguistic change and to see whether the different kinds of explanations that are proposed provide a foundation for understanding why languages change. Until the early 1970s, it was common to find statements in historical linguistic works to the effect that we should be concerned with 'how' languages change, but that the question of 'why' languages change could not be answered and therefore should be avoided. For example, from Joos (1958: v) we read: 'If the facts have been fully stated, it is perverse or childish to demand an explanation into the bargain' (intended perhaps more of descriptive linguistics); in Lehmann's introduction to historical linguistics, we are told: 'A linguist establishes the facts of change, leaving its explanation to the anthropologist' (1962: 200, in a discussion of semantic change). What is behind the comment about leaving explanation to the anthropologist is the once widely shared notion that the reasons for linguistic

312

change were like those for change in fashion – in one year new cars might have fins and in another not, or the hemlines of women's dresses might be higher one year and lower in another. So, the driving force behind language change was held to be cultural, to do with social choices and thus outside of the structure of language itself and hence not primarily even a linguist's concern. However, not everyone had such a pessimistic view, and many causal factors in linguistic change had been identified and discussed earlier, and in the last few decades much has been done to consolidate what we know about the causes of linguistic change. In this chapter, the term *causal factors* is used to designate both factors which always bring about change and those which create circumstances which are known to facilitate change but the change is not always obligatory when the factors are present. Much current research is directed at revealing the factors which help to explain language change.

In this chapter, we examine some of the better-known efforts in the direction of explaining linguistic change. We begin with a brief look at some of the earlier and less successful claims about why languages change, the ones we can safely eliminate from any theory of linguistic change.

11.2 Early Theories

Almost anything affecting humans and their language has at one time or another been assumed to be behind some change in language. Some of these today seem hilarious – for example, nearly all the 'causes' given by Sayce in the quote at the head of this chapter – some socially or morally disturbing, but fortunately some seem pointed, if only vaguely, in the right direction.

Climatic or *geographical determinism* was thought by some to lie behind some linguistic changes. A revealing example is the claim that the consonantal changes of Grimm's Law were due to life in the Alps, where all that running up and down mountains caused huffing and puffing which led to the voiceless stops becoming fricatives (the changes $*p > f$, $*t > \theta$, $*k > h$). Since examples of the same change are known in languages not found in mountainous regions and many other languages found in mountains are known where changes of this sort have not taken place, the suggested cause is neither necessary (given the existence of such changes in non-mountain languages) nor sufficient (given the lack of change in other mountain languages). In any case, the Alps were not the homeland of Proto-Germanic speakers. In another case, even from as distinguished a linguist as Henry Sweet (1900: 32) we read:

> The influence of climate may be seen in the frequency with which (a) is rounded in the direction of (o) in the northern languages of Europe – as in English *stone* from Old English *stān* – as compared with the southern languages, in which it is generally preserved; this rounding of (a) is doubtless the result of unwillingness to open the mouth widely in the chilly and foggy air of the North.

We now know that geographical determinism plays no significant role in language change.

Some spoke of '*racial*' and *anatomical determination*. One example of this is the notion that Germanic tribes had a greater build-up of earwax (for reasons left unaddressed) which somehow impeded their hearing, resulting in the series of consonantal changes in Grimm's Law. Whatever else we might say of this theory, it at least has the advantage of being specific enough that it could perhaps be tested – we assume that the results of any such test would be a negative correlation, that earwax in those with Germanic genes is not a significant factor for bringing about change in the languages which they speak. More insidious are claims of language change due to physical attributes assumed to be associated with different races. A most obvious example attributes phonetic traits encountered in some African languages – such as implosives, clicks or labiovelar sounds – to changes that must have taken place to produce such sounds in the first place, which, according to those making these claims, are due to the anatomical structure of the lips of black Africans. Needless to say, this assumed correlation has proven totally devoid of foundation – change in African languages is in character just like that in languages elsewhere, and 'race' (i.e. human genetics) plays no role.

Etiquette, social conventions and *cultural traits*. Many have speculated concerning cultural motivations for certain linguistic changes. For example, Wilhelm Wundt (a famous psychologist and linguist, writing in 1900) believed that the reason why Iroquoian languages have no labial consonants is because according to Iroquoian etiquette, so he reported, it is improper to close the mouth while speaking. Apparently the only evidence for this principle of Iroquoian etiquette was the fact that the Iroquoian languages lack labials. The same absence of labial consonants from Aleut, Tlingit and some African languages has at times been attributed to labrets (plugs, discs inserted in holes cut into the lips, an important part of personal adornment and ornamentation in some societies). However plausible this idea might seem to some, it has the disadvantage of not being testable. If a group is found who lack labials, who also do not use labrets, it could be claimed that at some former time they did use the lip devices and this led to the loss of labial consonants and then sometime subsequently they just stopped utilizing labrets. Or, if a language possessing labial consonants were found among a group which did wear labrets, it might be claimed that the lip-ornament fashion must not yet have been in vogue long enough to lead to the loss of labials. That is, again, the proposed account for the loss of labials due to the wearing of labrets is neither a sufficient nor a necessary explanation.

Indolence. A particularly common assumption, especially among lay people, is that language change is the result of laziness – young people or particular social groups who are seen to be changing their speech in ways disapproved of are assumed to be just too slovenly to pronounce correctly, or to produce the full or distinct grammatical forms, and so on.

Ease and *simplification.* A common assumption has been that language speakers tend towards 'ease of articulation', which leads to language change. 'Simplification' became an important part of the generative linguists' approach to linguistic theory and consequently also to their views of linguistic change. We will need to look at this in more detail as we explore plausible explanations for why languages change.

Foreign influence (substratum) – borrowing. Languages do change through borrowing, indisputably, though often language contact has been exaggerated and abused in attempts to explain particular changes. Any change whose cause is otherwise not understood, or any exception to otherwise general accounts, was often attributed to influence from other languages, often in spite of no evidence in the neighbouring languages that might support such a view. For more practical views of the role of borrowing in linguistic change, see Chapters 3 and 12.

Desire to be distinct and *social climbing.* It is sometimes proposed that groups of people changed their language on purpose to distinguish themselves from other groups. Sociolinguistic study shows that group identity is a very important factor in many changes, but it is not achieved in quite such a simple-minded way as formerly conceived of. A more pervasive notion was that members of lower classes purposefully changed their speech by imitating the elite of society in order to improve their own social standing, and that as a consequence the upper class changed its language in order to maintain its distance from the masses – that is, the idea of the social-climbing masses in hot linguistic pursuit of society's fleeing elite. Sociolinguistic study of change, however, reveals that the more typical pattern is for the middle classes to initiate linguistic change and for the highest and lowest classes of society to change only later, if at all (see Labov 1994, 2001; see section 7.6 of Chapter 7).

External historical events. It is sometimes asserted that particular historical events are the cause of certain linguistic changes. A typical example is the proposed correlation between certain linguistic changes and the expansion of the Roman Empire. Jespersen correlates the Black Death and the wars and social disruption of the later Middle Ages which coincided in England and France with rapid linguistic change. Romance linguistics has had a tradition of more tolerance for explanations of linguistic changes involving external history; however, external history has not been accorded as much attention in the Germanic historical linguistics tradition, which has had the strongest influence on general historical linguistics of today. Perhaps there should be more tolerance for it, but also appeal to external historical factors should not be abused – there are many examples in past scholarship of assumed external causes presented without evidence of causal connections between the linguistic change and the external history asserted to be involved.

11.3 Internal and External Causes

Recent literature on linguistic change often distinguishes *internal* and *external* causes of change. The internal causes are based on what human speech production and perception is and is not capable of – that is, the internal causes are determined for the most part by the physical realities of human biology, by limitations on control of the speech organs and on what we humans are able to distinguish with our hearing or are able to process with our cognitive make-up. Thus, *internal* causes include physical and psychological factors. An example of a *physical* factor, involving the physiology of human speech organs, is seen in the typical sound change which voices stops between vowels (let us symbolize this as VpV > VbV). This change is in some sense explained by the limitations of human muscle control, which tends to maintain the vibration of the vocal cords (the voicing, which is inherent in vowels) across the intervening consonant. That is, it is much easier to allow the vocal cords to continue to vibrate right through the V-p-V sequence (resulting in *VbV*) than it is to have the vocal cords vibrating for the first vowel, then to break off the voicing for the stop, and then to start up the vibration of the vocal cords once again for the second vowel (to produce *VpV*). *Psychological* or *cognitive* explanations involve the perception, processing and learning of language. For example, the change in which nasalized vowels are lowered (let us symbolize this as $\tilde{\imath} > \tilde{\varepsilon}$), found so frequently in languages with contrastive nasalized vowels, is explained by the fact that, with nasalization, vowel height tends to be perceived as lower. Thus [$\tilde{\varepsilon}$] tends to be perceived as [æ̃], for example, and this perception leads to changes in what speakers think the basic vowel is. This is illustrated, for example, by changes in French nasalized vowels:

ẽ > ã (in the eleventh century), as in *pendre* > [pãdr(e)] 'to hang'
ĩ > ẽ (in the thirteenth century), as in *voisin* > [vwa'zẽ] 'neighbour'
ỹ > œ̃ (thirteenth century), as in [brỹ] (spelled *brun*) > [brœ̃] 'brown'.

External causes of change involve factors that are largely outside the structure of language itself and outside the human organism. They include such things as expressive uses of language, positive and negative social evaluations (prestige, stigma), the effects of literacy, prescriptive grammar, educational policies, political decree, language planning, language contact and so on. The following are a few examples of changes which illustrate external motivation.

(1) Finnish changed *ð* to *d* (for example, *veðen* > *veden* 'water (genitive singular)') due to spelling pronunciation based on the Swedish reading model which dominated in Finland and was imposed in Finnish schools.

(2) Teotepeque Pipil (of El Salvador) changed *s* to *r* (voiceless retroflex fricative became a trilled 'r') because local Spanish has *s* as a highly stigmatized variant of its *r*. In this case, Spanish is the dominant national language and sociolinguistic attitudes about variant pronunciations of its /r/ have been transferred to this variant of Pipil, the minority language, leading to a change in its native phoneme which originally in Pipil had nothing to do with different pronunciations of /r/ – native Pipil has no 'r' sound of any sort.

11.4 Interaction of Causal Factors

Change in one part of a language may have consequences for other parts. There is a trade-off between the phonological needs and the semantic needs of a language. A change in sound may have deleterious effects on aspects of the meaning side of language, and a change in meaning/function can have consequences for the sound system. At the crux of much debate concerning the explanation of linguistic change is thinking about the outcome of cases where a change in one side of a language has consequences for another side of the language. To understand the sort of causal factors that have been proposed and the debate over explanation of linguistic change, it will be helpful to begin with some examples which illustrate what is debated, and then to return to the debated explanations themselves afterwards with the examples as a basis for understanding the claims. Let us begin with well-known (putative) examples of morphological conditioning of sound change.

11.4.1 Classical Greek loss of intervocalic *s*

In a well-known change in Classical Greek, *s* was lost between vowels (s > Ø / V__V) except in certain 'future' and 'aorist' forms. In this case, loss of *s* by regular sound change would have destroyed the phonological form of the 'future' morpheme. One view of this set of circumstances is that the sound change was blocked, prevented from happening in just those cases where the meaning distinction between 'future' and 'present' would have been lost, and that is why intervocalic *s* was not lost in those 'future' forms. Changes such as this are called *morphologically conditioned* sound changes. Note, however, that the *s* of the 'future' was freely lost in verbs ending in a nasal or a liquid, where the future/present distinction could be signalled formally by the *e* which these future stems take. Compare the following two sets of verbs, where Set I retains *s* in the 'future' and Set II – *l*-stem or *n*-stem verbs with *e* in the future stem – loses the *s*:

Set I:

páu-ō	'I stop, cease'	páu-s-ō	'I will stop, cease'
lú-ō	'I loosen'	lū-s-ō	'I will loosen'

Set II:

stéllō	'I send'	steléō [< *stele-s-ō]	'I will send'
mén-ō	'I remain'	mené-ō [< *mene-s-ō]	'I will remain'

It is said in this case that the need of the meaning side of language to be able to distinguish 'future' from 'present' prevented the sound change from occurring in Set I verbs where the 'future' would have been lost, but the sound change was allowed freely to delete intervocalic *s* even of the 'future' in Set II verbs where the contrast could be signalled by other means. With the verb stems ending in a nasal or a liquid, in Set II, where the distinction between 'present' and 'future' could still be signalled by the presence of the *e* of 'future' stems, the *s* of 'future' was freely lost (compare Anttila 1989: 99).

Another view of this example relies on analogy. Its supporters point to Greek verb roots which end in consonants (other than liquids and nasals) where the *s* of 'future' was not threatened, since it came after a consonant and was thus not between vowels, as for example *trép-s-ō* 'I will turn' (compare *trép-ō* 'I turn'). They argue that forms such as *lū̆sō* actually did at one time lose the intervocalic *s* which marked the 'future', but that later in time, the *s* of 'future' was restored to them under analogy with the *s* 'future' found with verbs such as *trép-s-ō* whose roots ended in a consonant: (*lúso* > *lúo* (by sound change), then > *lúso* (by analogy)).

The first view, favouring morphological conditioning (the blocking of the sound change in just those cases where it would have negative effects on important meaning distinctions), sees *prevention* for functional reasons (to maintain important meaning distinctions) as the explanation behind this example. Supporters of the second view, which favours analogical restoration after the initial loss by regular sound change, see post-operative *therapy* as the explanation, the fixing-up after the fact of the negative consequences of sound change for meaning distinctions by other means. We will soon turn to a more direct consideration of the notions of prevention, therapy, compensation and multiple causation; however, for now let us look further at some additional examples first.

11.4.2 Estonian loss of final -*n*

A change in Estonian, similar to that in Classical Greek, is also well known in the linguistic literature (Anttila 1989: 79, 100). The Northern Estonian and Southern Estonian dialects are quite different from one another. In all of Estonian, final *n* was lost; however, in Northern Estonian the -*n* of 'first person singular' verb forms was exempted from this otherwise regular sound change, while in Southern Estonian the change took place without restrictions, as illustrated in Table 11.1. Loss of both *ʔ* and *n* in Northern Estonian would have left the 'first person singular' and 'imperative' forms indistinct; prevention of loss of final *n* in the 'first person singular' forms maintained the distinction. In Southern Estonian, where *ʔ* was not lost, these verb forms remained distinct and so final *n* could freely be lost in 'first person singular' verb forms as well without distress to the meaning difference.

TABLE 11.1: Estonian verb forms after certain sound changes

Northern Estonian	Southern Estonian	Proto-Balto-Finnic	
kannan	kanna	*kanna-n	'I carry'
kanna	kanna?	*kanna-?	'Carry!'

Those who favour analogical restoration after the regular sound change must rely in this case on variation in an early stage of the change in which final *n* was lost when the next word began with a consonant or when there was no following word, but -*n* was not yet lost when the next word began with a vowel. They would say that, based on the instances of final *n* before a following vowel, -*n* was restored also before a following consonant (that is, in all instances) where it served to signal the 'first person' in Northern Estonian, but that -*n* was later lost completely in all contexts in Southern Estonian (including also before following vowel-initial words) and in non-first person contexts in Northern Estonian (that is, lost now also before an initial vowel of a following word).

11.4.3 Estonian compensation for lost final -*n*

The loss of final *n* in Estonian was not blocked in all instances where its loss would have resulted in the loss of meaning distinctions. For example, the 'accusative singular' suffix was also -*n*, but this was entirely lost in the sound change which deleted final -*n*. Rather than the sound change being 'prevented' from damaging the accusative's ability to be signalled, the change applied also to the final -*n* of the accusative singular; however, the damage to the meaning side of the language was *compensated* for by other means in the language. In many nouns, the nominative and accusative forms could still be distinguished by other means in the absence of the -*n* 'accusative singular'. Final vowels in certain contexts were deleted by an earlier sound change, and many roots underwent what is called consonant gradation, essentially a change in stops in closed syllables (syllables that terminate in a consonant). Thus, for example, the 'nominative' and 'accusative' for a noun such as *kand* [kant] 'heel' could still be signalled in spite of the lost *n*: *kand* (< **kanta*) 'nominative singular', *kanna* (< **kanna-n* < **kanta-n*) 'accusative singular' (where the difference between *nt* and *nn*, and the presence or absence of the root-final *a*, signal the distinction between nominative and accusative which formerly was indicated by Ø 'nominative singular' versus -*n* 'accusative singular'). However, in nouns such as *kala* 'fish', consonant gradation (which did not apply to *l*) and final-vowel loss (which applied in other contexts, but not this one) could not compensate for the lost -*n* of 'accusative' to signal the difference: *kala* (<**kala*) 'nominative', *kala* (<**kala-n*) 'accusative'. However, a different sort of therapy came to be called upon to fix up the negative consequences of the sound change, namely in instances such as *kala* 'nominative' / *kala* 'accusative' , where nothing in the phonological form functions to distinguish the two, the particle *ära* 'up' could be used in partial compensation for the lost 'accusative', as in *söön kala ära* 'I eat the fish (up)'.

11.4.4 Compensation in Caribbean Spanish

Standard Spanish freely allows independent pronouns optionally to be absent, since the bound pronominal suffixes on verbs are sufficient to indicate the subject of the verb (for example, *ando* 'I walk', *andas* 'you walk', *andamos* 'we walk', and so on), and in connected discourse the independent pronouns are usually absent except when used for emphasis. However, in numerous studies of varieties of Caribbean Spanish, it has been observed that there is a much higher frequency of occurrence of the independent pronouns *tú* 'you (familiar)', *usted* 'you (formal)', *él* 'he' and *ella* 'she' than in other varieties of Spanish, and internally within these varieties these subject pronouns are much more frequent than the other subject pronouns (than *yo* 'I', *nosotros* 'we', *ustedes* 'you (plural)' and *ellos* 'they'). This is explained as therapeutic compensation in the wake of disruptive sound changes. In these varieties of Spanish, final *s* is changed to *h* and further to Ø with extreme frequency (approaching 100 per cent of occurrences for some speakers in colloquial contexts). This means that verb forms which are quite distinct in Standard Spanish, such as *andas* 'you walk' versus *anda* 'he/she walks', fail to be distinct if the final *s* is not realized. The loss of this distinction is compensated for through the more rigid use of the independent pronouns, especially *tú* 'you (familiar)', precisely where they are needed to help maintain the formal difference in verbs, now *tú anda* 'you walk' versus *él anda* 'he walks' in the colloquial language. This greater use of *tú* to compensate for the lost *-s* pronominal suffix parallels the change in French, where French once worked like modern Standard Spanish, with *vas* 'you go' versus *va* 'he/she goes', but as a result of sound changes which affected final consonants in French, the *-s* of the 'you' forms was completely lost and in French today the independent pronouns are obligatory, /ty va/ 'you go' (spelled *tu vas*) versus /il va/ 'he goes'. That is, the use of independent pronouns was made obligatory to compensate for the meaning contrast that would otherwise be lost with the loss of the final *-s* of second person.

11.4.5 Saami (Lapp) compensation for lost final *-n*

Saami (Finno-Ugric) also lost final *-n* in a change which was quite independent of Estonian's loss of final *-n*. However, as in Estonian, this

Saami loss also affected certain grammatical cases – the 'genitive singular' suffix -*n* was lost. As in Estonian, consonant gradation in closed syllables could compensate for the loss in some instances. Since the former -*n* 'genitive singular' constituted a consonant and therefore closed syllables, pairs formerly distinguished primarily by Ø 'nominative' versus -*n* 'genitive' could still be distinguished after the loss of final -*n* by non-gradated consonants in the stem in the nominative form and gradated consonants in the genitive form, as in Northern Saami *jokkâ* 'river (nominative singular)' : *jogâ* 'river (genitive singular)'. However, such compensation was not available for all nouns, since many contained no stops and so originally underwent no consonant gradation. In such cases, Saami underwent a therapeutic change whereby the consonant gradation pattern was extended to these consonants which earlier had not been subject to gradation, as seen here in the change from Proto-Saami to Northern Saami:

*kōlē > guolle 'fish (nominative singular)'
*kōlē-n > guole 'fish's (genitive singular)'.

Consonant gradation was extended to consonants, such as *l*, which formerly had not undergone gradation, to signal the difference between 'nominative' and 'accusative' (Korhonen 1981: 148).

11.4.6 Avoidance of pernicious homophony

Discussions of explanation of change in the linguistic literature often involve the concept of avoidance of homophony and refer to examples attributed to it. Therefore, *avoidance of homophony* will be the final example before we concentrate more directly on notions of how linguistic change may be explained.

While scholars opposed to functional explanations in linguistic changes have never been friends of avoidance of pernicious homophony as an explanation of certain changes, instances of such avoidance are nevertheless well documented. Avoidance of homophony can take several forms.

Lexical replacement and loss. The best-known cases involve lexical replacement or loss. A famous example comes from France, where in Gascony reflexes of Latin *gallus* 'rooster' (commonly *gal* in southern France) were replaced in exactly those dialects found within the area where a sound change took place in which original *ll* changed to *t*, where *gal* 'rooster' (from *gallus*) would have become *gat*, leaving *gat* 'rooster' homophonous with *gat* 'cat'. This homophony was avoided by the replacement of 'rooster' with other forms which formerly meant 'pheasant' (*faisan*) or 'vicar' (*vicaire*), and this allowed 'cat' and 'rooster' to be signalled by phonetically distinct forms. Without appeal to avoidance of homophony, it would be difficult to explain why it is precisely and only in the area where the sound change would have left 'rooster' and 'cat' homophonous that this lexical replacement has taken place (Gilliéron 1921; Gilliéron and Roques 1912 as seen in Map 11.1.). It will be helpful to look at a few other examples attributed to the avoidance of homophony.

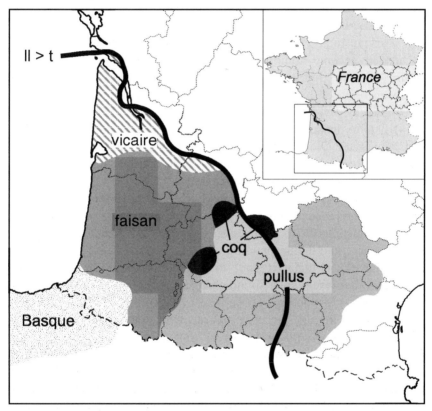

MAP 11.1: Distribution of the names for 'rooster' in the southwest of France (redrawn after Irali 2001: 27)

(1) A much-cited example involves the fact that English had two words, *quean* 'low woman' and *queen*, but the former has disappeared nearly everywhere because of homophonic clash after Middle English [ɛː] (of *quean*) and [eː] (of *queen*) merged, especially in East Midlands and Southeast English dialects. Interestingly, in the southwestern area, the two vowel sounds remained distinct and both words, *quean* and *queen*,

still survive there, where there is no homophonic clash between them, but survive nowhere where they would have become homophonous (Menner 1936: 222–3).

(2) In Standard German, *Fliege* [fli:gə] 'fly' and *Flöhe* [flø:ə] 'fleas' are phonetically distinct, but in certain German dialects the two would have become homophonous through regular sound changes (loss of intervocalic *g* and changes in the vowels). In this case, *Fliege* for 'fly' was replaced by *Mücke*, which had originally meant 'gnat, mosquito', as it still does in Standard German (Bach 1969: 168).

(3) In southern French dialects, reflexes of the Latin word *serrāre* 'to saw' survive today only in a few scattered areas. It has disappeared because it became homophonous with the French reflexes of Latin *serāre* 'to close'. In these areas where *ser(r)āre* 'to saw' disappeared, it has been replaced by words which come from Latin *sectāre* 'to cut', *secāre* 'to cut, divide', *resecāre* 'to cut back, curtail' (Palmer 1972: 331).

(4) Due to the sound change in which initial *h* was lost before other consonants, the Old English word *hrūm* 'soot', homophonous after the change with *rūm* 'room', was simply dropped from the language, and *soot* now exclusively carries that meaning.

Prevention. Avoidance of homophony can also sometimes block otherwise regular sound changes from taking place in certain forms. For example, in some German dialects, regular sound changes (the loss of intervocalic *g* and the unrounding of *ü*) would have left *liegen* [li:gən] 'to lie (down)' and *lügen* [ly:gən] 'to lie (tell falsehoods)' homophonous, but these otherwise regular sound changes were blocked in these words to preserve the distinction between these two common words (Öhmann 1934). Not all linguists accept proposals which call upon prevention as a way of dealing with problems of impending homophony. In this German example, some would argue that it is not that the changes were blocked and prevented from taking place in these words so much as that the changes took place and the sounds were later restored to these words by analogy based on related verb forms in which these sounds appear. (See Anttila 1989: 182 for other examples.)

Deflection. Another way by which some languages have avoided certain uncomfortable homophonies is through irregular or spontaneous changes in one or more of the homophonous forms, the result of which maintains a distinction between the forms that clash. A simple example that illustrates how such deflection can come about is seen in the euphemistic *fudge!* as an expletive to avoid the stronger obscene expletive which begins with the same sounds but ends with a different consonant. A change of this sort involving the homophonous *quean/queen* pair of words took place in some locations. In some northern English dialects, an initial *wh* [ʍ] was substituted for the *qu* [kw] of *quean* (but not of *queen*), and both words survive; the homophonic conflict is avoided through this special, sporadic change. The Middle English form for 'rabbit', variously spelled as *cony*, *coney* or *cunny*, was considered too close in pronunciation to a phonetically similar obscenity for comfort and so was changed by deflection to *bunny*.

11.4.7 Loss (neglect)

As is well known, many cases of homophony are not prevented, deflected or replaced; in these, the sound changes create homophonous forms that remain in the language – we see this in English in such sets of words as *sun/son*, *eye/I*, *rock* (stone)/*rock* (move back and forth), *to/too/two* and so on. An example from German illustrates a change in which neither blocking nor direct therapy was exercised, and as a consequence a portion of the grammar was just lost. Old and Middle High German marked some objects as partitives (only partially, not fully affected) by means of the genitive case, as Middle High German:

Ich will im mîn-es brôt-es geben
I want to.him my-Genitive bread-Genitive to.give
'I want to give him some of my bread'   (Ebert 1978: 52).

The loss of this partitive construction is attributed to phonological changes which affected inflectional endings. Due to phonological merger, in neuter adjectives the former *-es* 'genitive' (of which *mînes* is an instance) and *-ez* 'nominative/accusative' were no longer distinguishable in many contexts. The old *-es* ('genitive') with partitive interpretation was seen, as a result, as 'accusative' with full direct object interpretation in these instances. The outcome was that the partitive object construction was simply lost from German as a result of the phonological merger which left the genitive and accusative undifferentiated – neither prevention nor compensation occurred to rescue it.

As the discussion of these examples (several of them well known in the literature) shows, a broad view of language will be required in order to explain linguistic change, a view which must include internal factors, external factors, the structure of the language as a whole and how different parts of the language interact with one another, the communicative and social functions of the language, the role of the individual, the role of society/the speech community, and more – that is, the complex interaction and competition among a large number of factors. Let us look at some views of what it means to 'explain' linguistic change, with the examples just considered as background for the discussion.

11.5 Explanation and Prediction

The recognition of a large number of interacting and competing causal factors in language change means that at present we are unable fully to predict linguistic change. Some scholars conclude from this that it is impossible to explain linguistic change, since they equate 'explain' with 'predict', as required in some approaches to the philosophy of science. These scholars believe that the need to postulate competing principles and multiple causes renders law-like explanations of the sort sought in physics and chemistry impossible in historical linguistics. Others are more optimistic, believing that the current unpredictability may ultimately be overcome through research to identify causal factors and to understand the complex ways in which these factors interact. This more optimistic approach hopes for prediction (for law-like explanations) in the future, to the extent that they may be possible. On the other hand, some scholars recognize that absolute predictability may not be an appropriate requirement, since evolution by natural selection in biology is almost universally recognized as scientifically legitimate explanation, though it does not 'predict' the evolutionary changes that it explains.

In the view held by many historical linguists, the overall outcome of changes is usually (though not always) in the direction of maintaining or achieving the language's functional needs (a loose but hopefully useful notion about languages being able to serve the communicative needs of speech communities). These functional needs may be served in some cases by preventing or deflecting certain changes in order to avoid their detrimental effects on the language, or by permitting the disruptive changes to take place but then following them with subsequent compensatory (therapeutic) changes which rectify the situation. Of course, not all historical linguists agree with all of this; some insist that 'languages do not practise prophylaxis [no prevention or blocking], only therapy' (first said by Hermann Paul in the late nineteenth century, and reasserted more recently by linguists such as Paul Kiparsky (1982: 190), William Labov (1994) and David Lightfoot (1979: 123)) – that is, they accept the compensatory changes, therapy after a change has had negative consequences, but reject the interpretations which involve prevention and deflection in the examples considered above.

From the point of view of scholars who insist on predictability for explanation, it might be objected that appeal to such things in the examples above as prevention (prophylaxis, to head off the ill effects of some changes) and compensation (therapy, to fix things up after deleterious changes) cannot predict when such changes will take place, what exact form they may take, or when they may fail to occur even though the appropriate condition may have been present. It is important to distinguish what is impossible to predict (for example, that a change will occur, which change will occur, when a change will occur, and so on) from what is possible to predict (the nature of the changes that do occur, the conditions under which they can occur, what changes cannot occur).

Certain predictions may in fact already be possible, though these are not necessarily the mechanistic causal or deterministic kind known from physics or astronomy which some scholars would insist on for any explanation in any field to be considered valid. For example, to use an analogy (from Wright 1976), given certain circumstances, we may be able to determine in an objective manner that a rabbit will flee from a pursuing dog and that the paths which the rabbit follows are indeed appropriate for attempting to escape the dog, but we may not be able to predict the particular escape route which it will follow. Similarly, given certain conditions, we may be able to predict that a language (or more accurately, its speakers) may resort to one of a variety of alternative means for resolving the conflicting consequences of changes, though we may not be able to predict the particular 'escape route' that will be taken, be it prevention of sound change (as claimed in the morphological-conditioning view of the Greek in 11.4.1 and first Estonian example in 11.4.2 and for some of the cases of avoidance of homophony in 11.4.6), or compensation (as in the Saami example in 11.4.5, the second Estonian case in 11.4.3, and in Caribbean Spanish in 11.4.4 above), or deflection (as in some of the instances of homophony avoidance in 11.4.6). That is, there are different kinds or degrees of prediction: weak prediction (something is likely to happen), strong prediction (something will happen, though when and where is unclear), and absolute prediction (something will happen at a specifiable time and place) (Aitchison 1987: 12). We may be able to obtain some degree of predictability without needing to insist on the strongest absolute sort of prediction.

That more than one cause is frequently involved in a particular change also makes prediction difficult. Change within complex systems (languages, living organisms, societies) involves many factors which are interrelated in complex ways. Given that multiple causes frequently operate simultaneously in complex ways to bring about particular linguistic changes, to explain linguistic change, we must investigate the multiple causes and how they jointly operate in some cases and compete in others to determine the outcome of linguistic change.

Because we do not yet understand fully the complex interactions among the causal factors, we cannot predict all outcomes. The internal causal factors (mentioned above) rely on the limitations and resources of human speech production and perception, physical explanations of change stemming from the physiology of human speech organs, and cognitive explanations involving the perception, processing or learning of language. These internal explanations are largely responsible for the natural, regular, universal aspects of language and language change. However, even well-understood internal causal factors can compete in their interactions in ways which make prediction difficult and for the present out of reach. Consider another analogy, that of a car smashed against a tree, where the following conditions obtain: it is dark and foggy (poor visibility), the road is narrow and covered with ice (poor driving conditions), the driver is intoxicated and suffers from several physical disabilities (driver impaired), and the car was in poor operating condition (worn tyres, bad brakes, loose steering), the driver was exceeding the speed limit and not watching the road at the time of the accident (poor judgement), and finally, the tree happened to be situated at just the spot where the vehicle left the road (chance). In such a situation, it would not be possible to determine a unique cause (or even a joint interaction of causes) of the accident with sufficient precision to allow us to predict the crash. Linguistic changes are often like this crash, where competing or overlapping causal factors may be at play, but precise prediction of whether a change will take place (will the car in fact crash?) or when and how a change (a crash) will be realized is not fully possible. Still, it would be foolish to dismiss the probable or potential contributing causal factors as irrelevant to the event (a car crash, a linguistic change). From the study of many other crashes, we may be certain that each of these is capable of contributing to car accidents.

At this stage of our understanding, we cannot ignore any potential causal factor, such as prevention or therapy in the examples above, and thus cut off inquiry before we arrive at a fuller picture of how and why changes occur. It will only be through further extensive investigation of the interaction of the various overlapping and competing factors that are suspected of being involved in linguistic changes that we will come to be able to explain linguistic change more fully.

Moreover, even if mechanistic (internal) explanations were more readily available for linguistic change, that would not necessarily invalidate other sorts of explanations. There are different kinds of legitimate explanation. Consider one more analogy (from Wright 1976: 44). To answer the question 'why did the window break?' with 'because John slammed it' is a completely adequate answer/explanation, even if shock waves and molecular structure may lie behind the breaking at some other level of interpretation. There are contexts in which an answer of 'because of a certain causal factor x' is correct and adequate, even if there may be deeper, more mechanistic causal things which one could mention. For example, consider the constraint 'no language will assume a form in violation of such formal principles as are postulated to be universal in human languages' (Weinreich et al. 1968: 100) (mentioned already in Chapter 7). That languages cannot undergo changes which would violate universals is an adequate explanation in certain contexts of inquiry even if we discover the aspects of human physiology and cognition (mechanistic, internal factors) which explain the universals themselves. The existence of the underlying internal explanation of universals at some level does not invalidate explanations such as 'because languages do not undergo changes which would violate universals' at some other level. Even if we may ultimately come to understand more fully the aspects of human cognition which underlie avoidance of homophony or therapeutic compensation in the wake of other disruptive changes, and the like, at another level these factors remain potentially valid in explanations for the changes which they deal with.

12

Areal Linguistics

Life is a foreign language: all men mispronounce it.
(Christopher Morley)

12.1 Introduction

Areal linguistics, related to borrowing (Chapter 3), is concerned with the diffusion of structural features across language boundaries within a geographical area. This chapter defines areal linguistics, surveys the features of a few of the better-known linguistic areas of the world, and then addresses issues concerning how areally diffused features are identified, how linguistic areas are established, and what impact areal linguistics has on other aspects of historical linguistics – its implications for subgrouping, reconstruction and proposals of distant genetic relationship. Areal linguistics is very important because the goal of historical linguistics is to determine the full history of languages, to find out what really happened. The full history includes understanding both inherited traits (traits shared in genetically related languages because they come from a common parent language) and diffused features (traits shared because of borrowing and convergence among neighbouring languages). This is important in many ways. For example, in order to reconstruct proto-languages accurately or to determine family relationships, it is necessary to distinguish material which is borrowed from that which is inherited from a common ancestor.

12.2 Defining the Concept

The term *linguistic area* refers to a geographical area in which, due to borrowing and language contact, languages of a region come to share certain structural features – not only borrowed words, but also shared elements of phonological, morphological or syntactic structure. Linguistic areas are also referred to at times by the terms *Sprachbund, diffusion area, adstratum relationship* and *convergence area.* The central feature of a linguistic area is the existence of structural similarities shared among languages of a geographical area (where usually some of the languages are genetically unrelated or at least are not all close relatives). It is assumed that the reason why the languages of the area share these traits is because at least some of them are borrowed.

The studies of linguistic areas that have been undertaken are of two sorts. The more common approach, called *circumstantialist*, mostly just lists similarities found in the languages of a geographical area, allowing the list of shared traits to suggest diffusion. In this approach, firm evidence that the shared traits actually are due to diffusion is typically not required. Circumstantialist areal linguistics has been criticized, since it does not eliminate chance, universals, and possibly undetected genetic relationships as alternative possible explanations for shared traits. The other approach, called *historicist*, attempts to find concrete evidence showing that the shared traits are diffused (borrowed). The historicist approach is preferred because it is more rigorous and reliable, although the lack of clear evidence in many cases makes it necessary to fall back on the less reliable circumstantialist approach (Campbell 1985a).

While some linguistic areas are reasonably well established, more investigation is required for nearly all of them. Some other linguistic areas amount to barely more than preliminary hypotheses. Linguistic areas are often defined, surprisingly, by a rather small number of shared linguistic traits.

12.3 Examples of Linguistic Areas

A good way to get a solid feel for linguistic areas and how they are defined is to look at some of the better-known ones. In what follows, some are presented with the more important of the generally accepted defining traits shared by the languages of each linguistic area.

12.3.1 The Balkans

The languages of the Balkans linguistic area are Greek, Albanian, Serbo-Croatian, Bulgarian, Macedonian and Romanian (to which some scholars also add Romani [the language of the Gypsies] and Turkish). Some salient traits of the Balkans linguistic area are:

(1) A central vowel /ɨ/ (or /ə/) (not present in Greek or Macedonian).

(2) Syncretism of dative and genitive (dative and genitive cases have merged in form and function); this is illustrated by Romanian *fetei* 'to the girl' or 'girl's' (compare *fată* 'girl'; *ă* represents a short or reduced *a*), as in *am data o carte fetei* 'I gave the letter to the girl' and *frate fetei* 'the girl's brother'.

(3) Postposed articles (not in Greek); for example, Bulgarian *mɔʒ-ət* 'the man'/ *mɔʒ* 'man'.

(4) Periphrastic future (futures signalled by an auxiliary verb corresponding to 'want' or 'have'; not in Bulgarian or Macedonian), as in Romanian *voi fuma* 'I will smoke' (literally 'I want smoke') and *am a cínta* 'I will sing' (literally 'I have sing').

(5) Periphrastic perfect (with an auxiliary verb corresponding to 'have').

(6) Absence of infinitives (instead, the languages have constructions such as 'I want that I go' for 'I want to go'); for example, 'give me something to drink' has the form corresponding to 'give me that I drink', as in: Romanian *dă-mi să beau*, Bulgarian *daj mi da pija*, Tosk Albanian *a-më të pi*, Greek *dós mu na pjó*.

(7) Use of a personal pronoun copy of animate objects so that the object is doubly marked, as illustrated by Romanian *i-am scris lui Ion* 'I wrote to John', literally 'to.him-I wrote him John', and Greek *ton vlépo ton jáni* 'I see John', literally 'him.Acc I see the/him.Acc John' (Joseph 1992; Sandfeld 1930).

12.3.2 South Asia (Indian subcontinent)

This area is composed of languages belonging to the Indo-Aryan, Dravidian, Munda and Tibeto-Burman families. Some traits shared among different languages of the area are:

(1) Retroflex consonants, particularly retroflex stops.

(2) Absence of prefixes (accept in Munda).

(3) Presence of a 'dative-subject construction' (that is, dative-experiencer, as in Hindi *mujhe maaluum thaa* I knew it' [*mujhe* 'to me' + know + Past], *mujhe pasand hai* 'I like it' [to.me + like + Past]).

(4) Subject–Object–Verb (SOV) basic word order, including postpositions.

(5) Absence of a verb 'to have'.

(6) The 'conjunctive or absolutive participle' (tendency for subordinate clauses to have non-finite verb forms and for them to be preposed; for example, relative clauses precede their heads).

(7) Morphological causatives.

(8) So-called 'explicator compound verbs' (where a special auxiliary from a limited set is said to complete the sense of the immediately preceding main verb, and the two verbs together refer to a single event, as in, for example Hindi *kho baiṭhnaa* 'to lose' ['lose' + 'sit'], *le jaanaa* 'to take away' ['take' + 'go']).

(9) Sound symbolic (phonesthetic) forms based on reduplication, often with *k* suffixed (for example in Kota, a Dravidian language: *kad-kadk* '[heart or mind] beats fast with guilt or worry'; *a:nk-a:nk* 'to be very strong [of man, bullock], very beautiful [of woman]').

Some of these proposed areal features are not limited to the Indian subcontinent, but can be found in neighbouring languages (for example, SOV basic word order is found throughout much of Eurasia and northern Africa) and in languages in many other parts of the world, while some of the other traits are not necessarily independent of one another (for example, languages with SOV basic word order tend also to have non-finite subordinate clauses (as in (6)), especially relative clauses, and not to have prefixes). (Compare Emeneau 1980.)

12.3.3 Mesoamerica

The language families and isolates which make up the Mesoamerican linguistic area are: Nahua (branch of Uto-Aztecan), Mixe-Zoquean, Mayan, Xinkan, Otomanguean, Totonacan, Tarascan, Cuitlatec, Tequistlatecan and Huave. Five areal traits are shared by nearly all Mesoamerican languages, but not by neighbouring languages beyond this area, and these are considered particularly diagnostic of the linguistic area. They are:

(1) Nominal possession of the type *his-dog the man* 'the man's dog', as illustrated by Pipil (Uto-Aztecan): *i-pe:lu ne ta:kat*, literally 'his-dog the man'.

(2) Relational nouns (locative expressions composed of noun roots and possessive pronominal affixes), of the form, for example, *my-head* for 'on me', as in Tz'utujil (Mayan): *(č)r-i:x* 'behind it, in back of it', composed of *č-* 'at, in', *r-* 'his/her/its' and *-i:x* 'back', contrasted with *č-w-i:x* 'behind me', literally 'at-my-back'.

(3) Vigesimal numeral systems based on combinations of twenty, such as that of Chol (Mayan): *hun-k'al* '20' (1x20), *čaʔ-k'al* '40' (2x20), *uʃ-k'al* '60' (3x20), *hoʔ-k'al* '100' (5x20), *hun-bahk'* '400' (*1-bahk'*), *čaʔ-bahk'* '800' (2x400) and so on.

(4) Non-verb-final basic word order (no SOV languages) – although

Mesoamerica is surrounded by languages both to the north and south which have SOV (Subject–Object–Verb) word order, languages within the linguistic area have VOS, VSO or SVO basic order.

(5) A large number of loan translation compounds (calques) are shared by the Mesoamerican languages; these include examples such as 'boa' = 'deer-snake', 'egg' = 'bird-stone/bone', 'lime' = 'stone(-ash)', 'knee' = 'leg-head' and 'wrist' = 'hand-neck' (mentioned also in 3.7.7. of Chapter 3). Since these five traits are shared almost unanimously throughout the languages of Mesoamerica but are found almost not at all in neighbouring languages outside of Mesoamerica, they are considered strong evidence in support of the validity of Mesoamerica as a linguistic area.

Additionally, a large number of other features are shared among several Mesoamerican languages, but are not found in all the languages of the area, while other traits shared among the Mesoamerican languages are found also in languages beyond the borders of the area. Some widely distributed phonological phenomena of these sorts are:

(1) Devoicing of final sonorant consonants (*l, r, w, y*) (K'ichean, Nahuatl, Pipil, Xinkan, Totonac, Tepehua, Tarascan and Sierra Popoluca), as for example in Nahuatl /no-mi:l/ [no-mi:l̥] 'my cornfield'.

(2) Voicing of obstruents after nasals (most Otomanguean languages, Tarascan, Mixe-Zoquean, Huave, Xinkan), as in Copainalá Zoque /n-tɨk/ [ndɨk] 'my house'.

(3) Predictable stress; most Mesoamerican languages have predictable stress (contrastive stress is rare in the area). Some of the languages share the rule which places the stress on the vowel before the last (rightmost) consonant of the word (V→V́/__C(V)#) (Oluta Popoluca, Totontepec Mixe, Xinkan and many Mayan languages (by default in these Mayan languages, where stress falls on final syllables, but roots do not end in vowels)).

(4) Inalienable possession of body parts and kinship terms (in almost all Mesoamerican languages, but this feature is characteristic of many languages throughout the Americas).

(5) Numeral classifiers (many Mayan languages, plus Tarascan, Totonac, Nahuatl and so on), as in Tzeltal (Mayan) *oʃ-tehk teʔ* [three plant-thing wood] 'three trees', *oʃ-k'as teʔ* [three broken-thing wood] 'three chunks of firewood'.

(6a) Noun-incorporation, a construction where a general nominal object can become part of the verb, is found in some Mayan languages (Yucatec, Mam), Nahua and Totonac. An example is Nahuatl *ni-tlaʃkal-čiwa* [I-tortilla(s)-make] 'I make tortillas'.

(6b) Body-part incorporation (Nahuatl, Totonac, Mixe-Zoquean,

Tlapanec, Tarascan), a sort of noun-incorporation where specific forms for body parts can be incorporated in the verb, usually as instrumentals, though sometimes also as direct objects, as for example in Pipil (Uto-Aztecan): *tan-kwa* [tooth-eat] 'bite', *ikʃi-ahsi* [foot-arrive] 'to reach, overtake', *mu-yaka-pitsa* [Reflexive-nose-blow] 'to blow one's nose'. This type of construction is found also in various languages elsewhere in the Americas.

(7) Directional morphemes ('away from' or 'towards') incorporated into the verb (Mayan, Nahua, Tequistlatec, Tarascan, some Otomanguean languages, Totonac), as in Kaqchikel (Mayan) *y-e-ɓe-n-kamisax* [Aspect-them-thither-I-kill] 'I'm going there to kill them'.

(8) An inclusive–exclusive contrast in the pronoun system (Chol, Mam, Akateko, Jakalteko, Chocho, Popoloca, Ixcatec, Otomí, Mixtec, Trique, Chatino, Yatzachi Zapotec, Tlapanec, Huave, several Mixe-Zoquean languages), as, for example, in Chol (Mayan) *honon la* 'we (inclusive)', *honon lohon* 'we (exclusive)'.

(9a) 'Zero' copula (no form of the verb 'to be'). An overt copula is lacking from most Mesoamerican languages in equational constructions, as in K'iche' (Mayan) *saq le xah* [white the house] 'the house is white'. This feature is also found widely elsewhere in the Americas and beyond.

(9b) A pronominal copular construction (Mayan, Nahua, Chocho, Chinantec, Mazatec, Otomí, several Mixe-Zoquean languages). Copular sentences with pronominal subjects are formed with pronominal affixes attached directly to the complement, as in Q'eqchi' (Mayan) *iʃq-at* [woman-you] 'you are a woman', *kwinq-in* [man-I] 'I am a man'; Pipil *ti-siwa:t* [you-woman] 'you are a woman' (Campbell, Kaufman and Smith-Stark 1986).

12.3.4 The Northwest Coast of North America

As traditionally defined, the Northwest Coast linguistic area includes Tlingit, Eyak, the Athabaskan languages of the region, Haida, Tsimshian, Wakashan, Chimakuan, Salishan, Alsea, Coosan, Kalapuyan, Takelma and Lower Chinook. This is the best-known of North American linguistic areas. The languages of this area are characterized by elaborate systems of consonants, which include series of glottalized stops and affricates, labiovelars, multiple laterals (*l*, *ɬ*, *tl*, *tl'*) and uvular stops in contrast to velars. The labial consonant series typically contains fewer consonants than those for other points of articulation (labials are completely lacking in Tlingit and Tillamook and are quite limited in Eyak and most Athabaskan languages); in contrast, the uvular series is especially rich in most of these languages. The vowel systems are limited, with only three vowels (*i, a, o*, or *i, a, u*) in several of the languages, and only four vowels in others. Several of the languages have pharyngeals (ʕ, ħ), and most have glottalized resonants and continuants. Shared morphological traits include extensive use of suffixes; nearly complete absence of prefixes; reduplication processes (often of several sorts, signalling various grammatical functions, for example iteration, continuative, progressive, plural, collective and so on); numeral classifiers; alienable/ inalienable oppositions in nouns; pronominal plural; nominal plural (distributive plural is optional); verbal reduplication signifying distribution, repetition and so on; suffixation of tense–aspect markers in verbs; evidential markers in the verb; and locative–directional markers in the verb; plus masculine/feminine gender (shown in demonstratives and articles); visibility/invisibility opposition in demonstratives; and nominal and verbal reduplication signalling the diminutive. Aspect is relatively more important than tense (and aspect includes at least a momentaneous/durative dichotomy). All but Tlingit have passive-like constructions. The negative appears as the first element in a clause regardless of the usual word order. Northwest Coast languages also have lexically paired singular and plural verb stems (that is, an entirely different lexical root may be required with a plural subject from the root used with a singular subject).

Some other traits shared by a smaller number of Northwest Coast languages include:

(1) A widely diffused sound change of **k > č*, which affected Wakashan, Salishan, Chimakuan and some other Northwest Coast languages.

(2) Tones (or pitch-accent contrasts), found in a number of the languages (Tlingit, Haida, Bella Bella, Upriver Halkomelem, Quileute, Kalapuyan and Takelma).

(3) Ergative alignment in several of the languages (where the subject of intransitive verbs and the object of transitives have similar morphosyntactic marking, while the subject of transitive verbs is marked differently) (Tlingit, Haida, Tsimshian, some Salishan languages, Sahaptin, Chinookan, Coosan).

(4) 'Lexical suffixes', found in a number of the languages (Wakashan and Salishan); lexical suffixes designate such familiar objects (which are ordinarily signalled with full lexical roots in most other languages) as body parts, geographical features, cultural artifacts and some abstract notions. Wakashan, for example, has some 300 of these.

(5) In the grammar of these languages, one finds a severely limited

role for a contrast between nouns and verbs as distinct categories (some assert the total lack of a noun–verb distinction for some of the languages).

The sub-area of the Northwest which lacks primary nasals includes the languages Twana and Lushootseed (Salishan languages), Quileute (Chimakuan) and Nitinat and Makah (Nootkan, of the broader Wakashan family). The last two, for example, have changed their original *$m > b$, *$\dot{m} > b'$, *$n > d$ and *$\dot{n} > d'$ due to areal pressure, but closely related Nootka has retained the original nasals (Haas 1969b; Campbell 1997a: 333–4). (Mentioned also in Table 5.7 in Chapter 5.)

12.3.5 The Baltic

The Baltic linguistic area is defined somewhat differently by different scholars. It includes at least (Balto-)Finnic languages (especially Estonian and Livonian) and Baltic languages (Indo-European), and usually also Baltic German. Some have included all of the following (and others) in their treatment of the Baltic linguistic area: Old Prussian (now extinct), Lithuanian, Latvian (Baltic, branch of Indo-European); the ten Saami (Lapp) languages, Finnish, Estonian, Livonian, Vote, Veps, Karelian and others (of the (Balto-)Finnic branch of Finno-Ugric); High German, Low German, Baltic German, Yiddish (West Germanic); Danish, Swedish, Norwegian (North Germanic); Russian, Belorussian, Ukranian, Polish, Kashubian (Slavic); Romani (Indo-Aryan, branch of Indo-European); and Karaim (Turkic).

The Baltic area is defined by several shared features, some of which are:

(1) First-syllable stress.

(2) Palatalization of consonants.

(3) Tonal contrasts.

(4) Partitive case/partitive constructions (to signal partially affected objects, equivalent to, for example, 'I ate (some) apple', found in Finnic, Lithuanian, Latvian, Russian, Polish, etc.

(5) Nominative objects in a number of constructions which lack overt subjects (Finnic, Baltic, North Russian).

(6) Evidential mood ('John works hard [it is said/it is inferred]': Estonian, Livonian, Latvian, Lithuanian.)

(7) Prepositional verbs (as German *aus-gehen* [out-to.go] 'to go out': German, Livonian, Estonian, Baltic and others.

(8) Subject-Verb-Object (SVO) basic word order.

(9) Agreement of adjectives in number with the nouns which they modify (all languages of the area except Saami languages and Karaim);

they also agree in case in all except the Scandinavian languages (which have lost case distinctions for adjectives); they also agree in gender in Baltic, Slavic, Scandinavian, and German, Yiddish, and some others.

(For a more complete list of traits which have been attributed to this linguistic area, see Zeps 1962, Dahl and Koptjevskaja-Tamm 2001, and especially Koptjevskaja-Tamm and Bernhard Wälchli 2001.)

12.3.6 Ethiopia

Languages of the Ethiopian linguistic area include: Cushitic (Beja, Awngi, Afar, Sidamo, Somali, etc.), Ethiopian Semitic (Ge'ez, Tigre, Tigrinya, Amharic, etc.), Omotic (Wellamo [Wolaytta], Kefa, Janjero [Yemsa], etc.), Anyuak, Gumuz and others. Among the traits they share are the following:

(1) SOV basic word order, including postpositions.

(2) Subordinate clause preceding main clause.

(3) Gerund (non-finite verb in subordinate clauses, often inflected for person and gender).

(4) A 'quoting' construction (a direct quotation followed by some form of 'to say').

(5) Compound verbs (consisting of a noun-like 'preverb' and a semantically empty auxiliary verb).

(6) Negative copula.

(7) Plurals of nouns are not used after numbers.

(8) Gender distinction in second and third person pronouns.

(9) Reduplicated intensives.

(10) Different present tense marker for main and subordinate clauses.

(11) The form equivalent to the feminine singular is used for plural concord (feminine singular adjective, verb or pronoun is used to agree with a plural noun).

(12) A singulative construction (the simplest noun may be a collective or plural and it requires an affix to make a singular).

(13) Shared phonological traits such as f but no p, palatalization, glottalized consonants, gemination, presence of pharyngeal fricatives ($\hbar$ and Ω).

(Ferguson 1976; cf. Tosco 2000; see also Thomason 2001: 111–13.)

12.4 How to Determine Linguistic Areas

On what basis is it decided that something constitutes a linguistic area? Scholars have at times utilized the following considerations and criteria: the number of traits shared by languages in a geographical area, bundling of the shared traits in some significant way (for example, clustering at roughly the same geographical boundaries), and the weight of different areal traits (some are counted differently from others on the assumption that some provide stronger evidence than others of areal affiliation).

With respect to the number of areal traits necessary to justify a linguistic area, in general the rule is: the more, the merrier – that is, linguistic areas in which many diffused traits are shared among the languages are generally considered more strongly established; however, some argue that even one shared trait is enough to define a weak linguistic area (Campbell 1985a). Regardless of debate over some arbitrary minimum number of defining traits, it is clear that some areas are more securely established because they contain many shared traits, whereas other areas may be weaker because their languages share fewer areal traits. In the linguistic areas considered above, we see considerable variation in the number and kind of traits they share which define them.

With respect to the relatively greater weight or importance attributed to some traits than to others for defining linguistic areas, the borrowed word order patterns in the Ethiopian linguistic area provide an instructive example. Ethiopian Semitic languages exhibit a number of areal traits diffused from neighbouring Cushitic languages. Several of these individual traits, however, are interconnected due to the borrowing of the SOV (Subject–Object–Verb) basic word order patterns of Cushitic languages into the formerly VSO Ethiopian Semitic languages. Typologically, the orders Noun–Postposition, Verb–Auxiliary, Relative Clause–Head Noun and Adjective–Noun are all correlated and they tend to co-occur with SOV order cross-linguistically. If the expected correlations among these constructions are not taken into account, we might be tempted to count each one as a separate shared areal trait. Their presence in Ethiopian Semitic languages might seem to reflect several different diffused traits (SOV counted as one, Noun–Postposition as another, and so on), and they could be taken as several independent pieces of evidence defining a linguistic area. However, from the perspective of expected word order co-occurrences, these word order arrangements may not be independent traits, but may be viewed as the result of the diffusion of a single complex feature, the overall SOV word order type with its various expected coordinated orderings of typologically interrelated constructions. However, even though the borrowing of SOV basic word order type may count only as a single diffused areal trait, many scholars would still rank it as counting for far more than some other individual traits based on the knowledge of how difficult it is for a language to change so much of its basic word order by diffusion.

With respect to the criterion of the bundling of areal traits, some scholars had thought that such clustering at the boundaries of a linguistic area might be necessary for defining linguistic areas correctly. However, this is not correct. Linguistic areas are similar to traditional dialects in this regard (see Chapter 7). Often, one trait may spread out and extend across a greater territory than another trait, whose territory may be more limited, so that their boundaries do not coincide ('bundle'). This is the most typical pattern, where languages within the core of an area may share a number of features, but the geographical extent of the individual traits may vary considerably one from another. However, in a situation where the traits do coincide at a clear boundary, rare though this may be, the definition of a linguistic area which matches their boundary is relatively secure. As seen earlier, several of the traits in the Mesoamerican linguistic area do have the same boundary, but in many other areas, the core areal traits do not have the same boundaries, offering no clearly identifiable outer border of the linguistic area in question.

In the end, what is important is to try to answer the question, 'what happened?' If we succeed in determining what changes have taken place, and how, when and where they took place, we will have provided the information upon which linguistic areas depend. If we succeed in finding out what happened, we will know which changes are due to borrowing and which to other factors, and we will know how the changes are distributed in languages involved. The geographical patterning characteristic of linguistic areas will be a natural consequence of this fuller historical account. In the end, areal linguistics is not distinct from borrowing; rather, it depends on an understanding of the patterns of borrowing. Therefore, a full account of the linguistic changes in the languages involved, including in particular contact-induced changes, is a sufficient goal, even if in the end the definition of a linguistic area based on these traits is not entirely clear. It is the borrowed traits that tell us about linguistic areas; linguistic areas are not necessary to understand these traits themselves and to answer the question of what really happened.

12.5 Implications of Areal Linguistics for Linguistic Reconstruction and Subgrouping

Areal diffusion can have important implications for reconstruction and for subgrouping within known language families (see Chapter 6). Nootkan provides a good example which illustrates this. The sound correspondences upon which Nootkan subgrouping is based are given in Table 12.1 (some of which have been seen in other chapters). Nitinat

TABLE 12.1: Nootkan sound correspondences

	Makah	Nitinat	Nootka	Proto-Nootkan
(1)	b	b	m	*m
(2)	b'	b'	m̓	*m̓
(3)	d	d	n	*n
(4)	d'	d'	n̓	*n̓
(5)	q'	ʕ	ʕ	*q'
(6)	q'ʷ	ʕ	ʕ	*q'ʷ
(7)	χʷ	χʷ	ħ	*χʷ
(8)	χ	χ	ħ	*χ

(Haas 1969b)

and Makah appear to share the innovation which changed nasals to corresponding voiced stops (in (1–4)), while Nitinat and Nootka appear to share the change of the glottalized uvulars to pharyngeals (in (5) and (6)). Makah and Nitinat also share the retention of uvular fricatives, which Nootka has changed to a pharyngeal (in (7) and (8)); however, shared retentions are not valid evidence for subgrouping (see Chapter 6). That is, one innovation (denasalization) suggests a subgrouping of Makah–Nitinat, with Nootka as more distantly related, while the other innovation (pharyngealization) suggests Nitinat–Nootka, with Makah less closely related. This seeming impasse is solved when we take into account the fact that the absence of nasals is an areal feature shared by several other languages of the area; it diffused into both Makah and Nitinat under areal pressure and is thus not solid evidence of a shared common development before the languages separated, but rather diffused after these languages split up. The innovation shared by Nitinat and Nootka of glottalized uvulars changing to pharyngeals (in (5) and (6)) is real evidence of subgrouping – a true (non-diffused) shared innovation. So, Nitinat and Nootka together constitute one branch of the family, Makah the other branch. Moreover, with respect to areal implications for reconstruction, if we did not know about the areal diffusion in this case, we might be tempted to reconstruct the voiced stops in Proto-Nootkan and postulate a change of these to nasals in Nootka (for (1–4)), getting it wrong in this case. Thus, recognition of areal linguistic traits can be important for how we classify (subgroup) and how we reconstruct. (See also 3.7.2 in Chapter 3, Table 5.7 in Chapter 5, and Table 6.3 in Chapter 6.)

12.6 Areal Linguistics and Proposals of Distant Genetic Relationship

Unfortunately, it is not uncommon to find cases of similarities among languages which are in reality due to areal diffusion but which are mistakenly taken to be evidence of a possible distant family relationship among the languages in question. One example will be sufficient to illustrate this. The Mosan hypothesis proposes a genetic connection between the Salishan, Wakashan and Chimakuan language families of the Northwest Coast of North America. Several scholars had noted structural similarities among these languages and a number accepted Mosan as a genetic grouping, though today this hypothesis has for the most part been abandoned. A big part of why the Mosan hypothesis was not found convincing has to do with the fact that much of the evidence originally presented in its favour turns out to be widely borrowed traits of the Northwest Coast linguistic area. For example, Morris Swadesh (1953) presented sixteen shared structural similarities in support of the proposed Mosan genetic grouping, but most of these features turn out to be traits of the linguistic area (others of Swadesh's traits are typologically expected correlations with other traits and are widely found in languages throughout the world, not just in putative 'Mosan' languages. Typologically commonplace traits are also not good evidence of genetic relationship, since they can easily develop independently in languages.)

For illustration's sake, we look at just a few of the putative 'Mosan' features which Swadesh presented which turn out to be Northwest Coast areal traits (identified above in the discussion of the Northwest Coast linguistic area):

(1) 'Extensive use of suffixes.'

(2) 'Nearly complete absence of functioning prefixes in Chimakuan and Wakashan, minor role in comparison to the suffixes in Salish.' (Notice that typologically it is quite common for suffixing languages to lack prefixes.)

(3) 'Extensive use of stem reduplication, including initial reduplication . . . and . . . full stem reduplication.'

(4) 'Aspect, including at least the dichotomy of momentaneous and durative.'

(5) 'Tense is an optional category.'

(6) 'Distributive plural is an optional category. This is very different from the European kind of plurality.'

(7) 'Dichotomy of non-feminine versus feminine gender shown in demonstratives and articles.'

(8) 'Numeral classifier notions, shown by suffixes.'

342

(9) 'Two alternate stems for number' (lexically paired distinct singular and plural verb stems).

(10) 'Lexical suffixes (sometimes called field suffixes), referring to body parts and other space references.'

(11) 'Predicative use of nouns.'

(12) 'Demonstrative distinctions such as the present versus absent, or visible versus invisible.'

As is clear, these traits which Swadesh listed as evidence for the Mosan hypothesis of remote linguistic relationship are better explained as the results of borrowing within the Northwest Coast linguistic area (see Campbell 1997a for details).

From this example, it is easy to see why the identification of areal traits is so important in historical linguistics. In this case, failure to recognize the areal borrowings led to an erroneous proposal of genetic relationship among neighbouring language families. (The methods for investigating distant genetic relationship are treated in detail in Chapter 13.)

13

Distant Genetic Relationship

De Laet [1643], speaking of Hugo Grotius' methods: If you are willing to change letters, to transpose syllables, to add and subtract, you will nowhere find anything that cannot be forced into this or that similarity; but to consider this as evidence for the origin of peoples – this is truly not proved as far as I am concerned.

(Metcalf 1974: 241)

13.1 Introduction

A topic of great current interest in historical linguistics is that of distant genetic relationships, and both the methods and the hypothesized distant family relationships have been much debated. Postulated remote relationships such as Amerind, Nostratic and Proto-World have been featured in newspapers, magazines and television documentaries, and yet these same proposals have been rejected by most mainstream historical linguistics. How is one to know what to believe? How can claims about very remote linguistic relationships be evaluated? This chapter addresses these questions by surveying the various methodological principles, criteria and rules of thumb that are considered important in proposals of distant genetic relationship. The goal is to prepare you to be able to see past the controversies by explaining the methods and their limitations. Armed with these, you should be able to evaluate proposals of remote linguistic affinity for yourself.

Two outlooks can be distinguished, or stages in research on potential distant genetic relationships, each with its own practices. The first is like a scouting expedition. In it, the intention is to call attention to a possible but as yet untested connection between languages not known to be related to one another. In this approach, a wide net is often cast in

order to haul in as much potential evidence as possible. The second outlook comes into play typically when the intention is to test a proposal
that has already been made. In it, those forms considered initially as
possible evidence are submitted to more careful scrutiny. Unfortunately,
the more laissez-faire setting-up type hypotheses of the first approach
are not always distinguished from the more cautious hypothesis-testing
type of the second. Both orientations are valid. Nevertheless, long-range
proposals which have not been evaluated carefully are not considered
acceptable or established. As Antoine Meillet, a famous Indo-Europeanist
well known for his common-sense discussions of historical linguistic
methods, cautioned, excessive zeal for long-range relationships can lead
to methodological excesses: 'The difficulty of the task of trying to make
every language fit into a genetic classification has led certain eminent
linguists to deprive the principle of such classification of its precision
and its rigour or to apply it in an imprecise manner' (1948 [1914]: 78).
The comparative method has always been the basic tool for establishing
genetic relationships, though it is necessary to discuss a number of
particular aspects of how it is applied in work on distant genetic relationships and to address approaches which have sometimes been advocated
as competitors of the comparative method.

In order to give an idea of what is at issue, the following is a list of
some of the better-known hypotheses which would group together
languages which are not yet known to be related. None of the proposed
genetic relationships in this list has been demonstrated yet, even though
some are repeated frequently, for example in encyclopaedias and textbooks. Many other unconfirmed proposals of distant genetic relationship
(not listed here) have also been made.

Altaic (proposed grouping of Turkic, Tungusic, Manchu and
   Mongolian, to which some proposals also add Ainu, Japanese,
   Korean and others)
Amerind (Joseph Greenberg's proposal which would lump all the 180
   or so Native American language families except Eskimo-Aleut and
   so-called Na-Dene into one large group)
Austric (Austro-Asiatic with Austronesian)
Austro-Tai (Japanese–Austro-Thai)
Basque–Caucasian, Basque–Sino-Tibetan–Na-Dene
Dene-Sino–Tibetan (Athabaskan [or Na-Dene] and Sino-Tibetan
Dravidian–Japanese
Dravidian–Uralic
Eskimo and Indo-European

Eskimo–Uralic

Eurasiatic (Greenberg's grouping of Indo-European, Uralic, Eskimo-Aleut, Ainu and several other otherwise unaffiliated languages)

Hokan (in various versions which group many American Indian families and isolates)

Indo-European and Afroasiatic

Indo-European and Semitic

Indo-Pacific (Greenberg's grouping of all the non-Austronesian languages of the Pacific, including all Papuan families, Tasmanian, and the languages of the Andaman Islands)

Indo-Uralic (Indo-European and Uralic)

Japanese–Altaic

Japanese–Austronesian

Khoisan (the African families with clicks, except the Bantu languages which borrowed clicks; now considered more likely an areal grouping than a genetic one)

Macro-Siouan (Siouan, Iroquoian, Caddoan, sometimes also Yuchi)

Maya-Chipayan (Mayan, Uru-Chipayan of Bolivia)

Na-Dene (Eyak-Athabaskan, Tlinglit, Haida – the position of Haida is highly disputed)

Niger-Kordofanian (Niger-Congo) (Africa, Greenberg's grouping which includes Mande, Kru, Kwa, Benue-Congo [of which Bantu is a branch], Gur, Adamawa-Ubangi, Kordofanian, and others)

Nilo-Saharan (large number of African families; Greenberg's grouping which contains most of the African languages not otherwise classified as belonging to one of the other three groupings)

Nostratic (various versions; the best-known groups Indo-European, Uralic, Altaic, Kartvelian, Dravidian and Afroasiatic, though some add also Chuckchi-Kamchatkan, Eskimo-Aleut, Sumerian and Gilyak (Nivkh))

Penutian (in various versions which group a number of American Indian families and isolates)

Proto-Australian (all twenty-six or so of the Australian families)

Proto-World (Global Etymologies)

Ural-Altaic (Uralic and 'Altaic')

Ural-Altaic and Eskimo-Aleut

Yukagir-Uralic

(Compare the less controversial classifications in Table 6.2, Chapter 6.)

Let us look now at the methods and criteria that have been used in research on distant genetic relationships. (These are treated in more detail in Campbell 1997a: 206–59 and Campbell (2003), upon which this chapter is based.)

13.2 Lexical Comparison

Throughout history, word comparisons have been employed as evidence of family relationship, but, given a small collection of likely-looking potential cognates, how can we determine whether they are really the residue of common origin and not the workings of pure chance or some other factor? It turns out that lexical comparisons by themselves are seldom convincing without additional support from other criteria. Because lexical comparisons have typically played the major role in hypothesized distant genetic relationships, we begin by considering the role of basic vocabulary and lexically based approaches.

13.2.1 Basic vocabulary

Most scholars insist that basic vocabulary should be part of the supporting evidence presented in favour of any distant family relationship. Basic vocabulary is usually not defined rigorously but is understood generally to include terms for body parts, close kinship, frequently encountered aspects of the natural world (mountain, river, cloud and the like) and low numbers. Basic vocabulary is in general resistant to borrowing, and so, similarities found in comparisons involving basic vocabulary items are unlikely to be due to diffusion and hence stand a better chance of being evidence of distant genetic relationships, of being inherited from a common ancestor, than other kinds of vocabulary. Of course, basic vocabulary can also be borrowed – though less frequently – so that its role as a safeguard against borrowing is not foolproof (see examples below).

13.2.2 Glottochronology

Glottochronology (discussed in Chapter 6), which depends on basic, relatively culture-free vocabulary, has been rejected by most linguists, since all its basic assumptions have been challenged. Therefore, it warrants little discussion here. Suffice it to repeat that it does not find or test distant genetic relationships, but rather it *assumes* that the languages compared are related and merely proceeds to attach a date based on the number of core-vocabulary words that are considered similar among the languages compared. This, then, is no method for determining whether languages are related.

Glottochronology's focus on vocabulary replacement does draw attention indirectly to a serious problem concerning lexical evidence in long-range relationships. Related languages which separated long ago may have undergone so much vocabulary replacement that insufficient shared original vocabulary will remain for an ancient shared linguistic kinship to be detected. This constitutes a serious problem for detecting really ancient relationships.

13.2.3 Multilateral (or mass) comparison

The best-known of the approaches which rely on inspectional resemblances among lexical items is that advocated by Joseph Greenberg, called 'multilateral (or mass) comparison'. It is based on 'looking at ... many languages across a few words' rather than 'at a few languages across many words' (Greenberg 1987: 23). The lexical similarities determined by superficial visual inspection which are shared 'across many languages' alone are taken as evidence of genetic relationship. This approach stops where others begin, at the assembling of lexical similarities. These inspectional resemblances must be investigated to determine why they are similar, whether the similarity is due to inheritance from a common ancestor (the result of a distant genetic relationship) or to borrowing, accident, onomatopoeia, sound symbolism, nursery formations and the various things which we will consider in this chapter. Since multilateral comparison does not do this, its results are controversial and rejected by most mainstream historical linguists.

In short, no technique which relies on inspectional similarities in vocabulary alone has proven adequate for establishing distant family relationships.

13.3 Sound Correspondences

It is important to emphasize the value and utility of sound correspondences in the investigation of linguistic relationships. Nearly all scholars consider regular sound correspondences strong evidence of genetic affinity. While sound correspondences are fundamental to most approaches to determining language families, they can be misused, and it is important to understand how this can be.

First, it is systematic correspondences which are crucial, not mere similarities; correspondences do not necessarily involve similar sounds. The sounds which are equated in proposals of remote relationship are typically very similar, often identical, although such identities are not so frequent among the daughter languages of well-established non-controversial older language families. The sound changes that lead to such non-identical correspondences often result in cognate words being so changed that their cognacy is not apparent. These true but non-obvious cognates are missed by methods, such as multilateral comparison, which seek only inspectional resemblances. They miss such well-known true cognates as French *cinq*/Russian *p^{j}at^j*/Armenian *hing*/English *five* (all derived by straightforward changes from original Indo-European *penk^{w}e-* 'five'), French *bœuf*/English *cow* (from Proto-Indo-European *g^{w}ou-*), French /nu/ (spelled *nous*) 'we, us'/English *us* (both ultimately from Proto-Indo-European *nos-*; English from Germanic *uns* <*n̥s*); the words in these cognate sets are not visually similar to each other, but they exhibit regular correspondences among the cognates.

There are a number of ways in which the criterion of sound correspondences can be misapplied. Sometimes regularly corresponding sounds may also be found in loanwords. For example, it is known from Grimm's Law that real French–English cognates should exhibit the correspondence *p* : *f*, as in *père/father, pied/foot, pour/for* (mentioned in Chapter 5). However, French and English appear to exhibit also the correspondence *p* : *p* in cases where English has borrowed from French or Latin, as in *paternel/paternal, piédestal/pedestal, per/per*. Since English has many such loans, examples illustrating this bogus *p* : *p* sound correspondence are not hard to find. In comparing languages not yet known to be related, we must use caution in interpreting sound correspondences to avoid the problem of apparent correspondences found in undetected loans. Generally, sound correspondences found in basic vocabulary warrant the confidence that the correspondences are probably legitimate, since, as mentioned above, terms for basic vocabulary are borrowed only infrequently. However, even here we have to be careful, since items of basic vocabulary can also be borrowed, though more rarely. For example, Finnish *äiti* 'mother' and *tytär* 'daughter' are borrowed from Indo-European languages; if these loans were not recognised, one would suspect a sound correspondence of *t* : *d* involving the medial consonant of *äiti* (compare Old High German *eidī*) and the initial consonant of *tytär* (compare Germanic *duhtēr*) based on these basic vocabulary items (found also in other loans).

Some non-genuine sound correspondences can also come from accidentally similar lexical items among languages. Languages share a certain amount of similar vocabulary by sheer accident. A few examples that show this are: Proto-Je *niw* 'new'/English *new*; Kaqchikel dialects *mes* 'mess, disorder, garbage'/English *mess*; Jaqaru *aska* 'ask'/English *ask*; Māori *kuri* 'dog'/English *cur*; Lake Miwok *hóllu* 'hollow'/English *hollow*; Gbaya *be* 'to be'/English *be*; Seri *kiʔ*/French *qui* (/ki/) 'who?'; Yana *t'inii-* 'small'/English *tiny, teeny*; and the famous handbook examples of Persian *bad*/English *bad*, and Malay *mata* 'eye'/Modern Greek *mati* 'eye'.

Other cases of unreal sound correspondences may turn up if one permits wide semantic latitude in proposed cognates, so that phonetically similar but semantically disparate forms are equated. For example, if we were to compare Pipil (Uto-Aztecan) and Finnish (Uralic) words such as Pipil *teki* 'to cut' : Finnish *teki* 'made', *te:n* 'mouth' : *teen* 'of the tea', *tukat* 'spider' : *tukat* 'hairs', *tila:n* 'pulled' : *tilaan* 'into the space', *tu:lin* 'cattails, reeds' : *tuulin* 'by the wind', and so on, we note a recurrence of a *t* : *t* correspondence. However, the phonetic correspondence in these words is due to sheer accident, since it is always possible to find phonetically similar words among languages if their meanings are ignored. With too much semantic liberty among compared forms, it is easy to come up with spurious correspondences such as the Pipil–Finnish *t* : *t*. Unfortunately, wide semantic latitude is frequently a problem in proposals of remote relationship. Additional non-inherited phonetic similarities crop up when onomatopoetic, sound-symbolic and nursery forms are compared. A set of proposed cognates involving a combination of loans, chance enhanced by semantic latitude, onomatopoeia and such factors may exhibit false sound correspondences. For this reason, some proposed remote relationships which purportedly are based on regular sound correspondences nevertheless fail to be convincing.

Most linguists find sound correspondences strong evidence, but many neither insist on them solely nor trust them fully. Most are happier when additional evidence from comparative morphology and grammar also supports the hypothesis.

13.4 Grammatical Evidence

Scholars throughout linguistic history have considered morphological evidence important for establishing language families. Many favour 'shared aberrancy' (talked about sometimes as 'submerged features', 'morphological peculiarities', 'arbitrary' associations'), as illustrated, for example, by the corresponding irregularities in forms of the verb 'to be' in branches of Indo-European in Table 13.1; Pers = person, Pl = plural, Sg = singular; OCS = Old Church Slavonic). For example, the Algonquian–Ritwan hypothesis, which groups Wiyot and Yurok (two languages of California) with the Algonquian family, was controversial, but morphological evidence such as that in the following comparison of Proto-Central Algonquian (PCA) and Wiyot helped to prove the relationship to everyone's satisfaction:

PCA   **ne* + **ehkw-* = **netehkw* 'my louse'
Wiyot   *du* + *híkw* = *dutíkw* 'my louse' (Teeter 1964: 1029).

TABLE 13.1: Forms of the verb 'to be' in some Indo-European languages

	3rd Pers Sg	*3rd Pers Pl*	*1st Pers Sg*
Hittite	estsi	asantsi	—
Sanskrit	ásti	sánti	asmi
Greek	estí	eisí	eimí
Latin	est	sunt	sum
OCS	jestı	sãntı	jesmı
Gothic	ist	sind	im

In Proto-Central Algonquian, a -*t*- is inserted between a possessive pronominal prefix and a vowel-initial root, while in Wiyot a -*t*- is inserted between possessive prefixes and a root beginning in *hV* (with the loss of the *h* in this process). Sapir (1913) had proposed that Wiyot (and also Yurok) of California were related to the Algonquian family; this proposed relationship was controversial, but evidence increased, including that presented here, which ultimately demonstrated the validity of the hypothesis to the satisfaction of all.

There is no phonetic (or other natural) reason for why a language would add a *t* in this environment (between vowels or between a vowel and *h*), and this is so unusual that it is not likely to be shared by borrowing or by accident. Inheritance from a common ancestor which had this peculiarity is more likely, and this is confirmed by other evidence shared by these languages. Another often-repeated example is the agreement between English *good/better/best* and German *gut/besser/best*, said to be 'obviously of enormous probative value' for showing that languages are related (Greenberg 1987: 30).

Morphological correspondences of the 'shared aberrancy'/'submerged features' type, just like sound correspondences, are generally thought to be an important source of evidence for distant genetic relationships. Nevertheless, caution is necessary here as well. There are impressive cases of apparent idiosyncratic grammatical correspondences which in fact have non-genetic explanations. Since some languages do share some seemingly submerged features by accident, caution is necessary in the interpretation of morphological evidence. Clearly, then, the strongest hypotheses of relationship are those which have evidence of several sorts, recurrent sound correspondences in basic vocabulary and multiple examples of grammatical evidence of the sort just discussed.

13.5 Borrowing

Diffusion is a source of non-genetic similarity among languages. It can complicate evidence for remote relationships. Too often, scholars err in not eliminating loans from consideration as possible evidence of wider relationship. An example which was presented as evidence of the controversial 'Chibchan–Paezan' genetic grouping (involving several South American language families) illustrates this problem. For the proposed cognate set meaning 'axe', forms from only four of the many languages were cited, two of which are loanwords: Cuitlatec *navaxo* 'knife', borrowed from Spanish *navajo* 'knife, razor', and Tunebo *baxi-ta* 'machete', from Spanish *machete* (in Tunebo [x] alternates with [ʃ]; nasal consonants do not occur before oral vowels; the vowels of the Tunebo form are expected substitutes for Spanish *e*) (Greenberg (1987: 108). Clearly, because two of the four pieces of evidence are borrowings, the putative 'axe' cognate is not good evidence for the hypothesis. Among compared forms cited as support for the controversial Nostratic hypothesis (which would join Indo-European, Uralic, so-called Altaic, Kartvelian, and for some scholars also Dravidian and Afroasiatic into one large superfamily; see Kaiser and Shevoroshkin 1988), some involve known loanwords (for example, those for 'practise witchcraft'), and others have been claimed to involve loans, for example those for 'vessel', 'honey', 'birch', 'bird-cherry', 'poplar', 'conifer' and so on (see Campbell 1998, 1999).

Since it is not always possible to recognize loanwords without extensive research, it is frequently suggested (as mentioned above) that the problem of borrowing can be made less severe by sticking to basic vocabulary and avoiding words with cultural content. By this rule of thumb, the Nostratic forms which have been questioned as possible loans would all be set aside. While this is good practice, it must be remembered (as mentioned above and shown in Chapter 3) that even basic vocabulary can sometimes be borrowed. Finnish borrowed from its Baltic and Germanic neighbours various terms for basic kinship and body parts, for example 'mother', 'daughter', 'sister', 'tooth', 'navel', 'neck', 'thigh', 'fur' and so on. English has borrowed from French or Latin the basic vocabulary items 'stomach', 'face', 'vein', 'artery', 'intestine', 'mountain', 'navel', 'pain', 'penis', 'person', 'river', 'round', 'saliva' and 'testicle'. The problem of loans and potential loans is very serious for distant genetic relationships.

13.6 Semantic Constraints

It is dangerous to present phonetically similar forms with different meanings as potential evidence of remote genetic relationship under the assumption that semantic shifts have taken place. Of course meaning can shift, as seen in Chapter 10 (for example, Albanian *motër* 'sister', from Indo-European 'mother'), but in hypotheses of remote relationship the assumed semantic shifts cannot be documented, and the greater the semantic latitude permitted in compared forms, the easier it is to find phonetically similar forms which have no historical connection (as in the Pipil–Finnish examples above). When semantically non-equivalent forms are compared, the possibility that chance accounts for the phonetic similarity is greatly increased (cf. Ringe 1992). Within families where the languages are known to be related, etymologies are still not accepted unless an explicit account of any assumed semantic changes can be provided. The advice often given is to count only exact semantic equivalences. The problem of excessive semantic permissiveness is one of the most common and most serious in long-range proposals. The following are a few of the many examples from various proposals of long-range relationships, presented just for illustration's sake (only the glosses of the various forms compared are cited). Among evidence cited for Nostratic, we find 'lip/mushroom/soft outgrowth', 'grow up/become/tree/be', 'crust/rough/scab' (see Kaiser and Shevoroshkin 1988). In the proposed global etymology for 'finger, one' (in the Proto-World hypothesis, the claim that all the world's languages are related), we find all the following: 'one/five/ten/once/only/first/single/fingernail/finger/toe/hand/palm of hand/arm/foot/paw/guy/thing/to show/to point/in hand/middle finger' (Ruhlen 1994: 322–3). In forms from the Amerind hypothesis (which proposes that most of the languages of the Americas are related), we find semantic equations such as the following: 'excrement/night/grass', 'body/belly/heart/skin/meat/be greasy/fat/deer', 'child/copulate/son/girl/boy/tender/bear/small', 'field/devil/bad/underneath/bottom' (Greenberg 1987). It is for reasons like this that each of these proposals of more remote linguistic relationship is highly disputed.

13.7 Onomatopoeia

Onomatopoetic words imitate the real-world sound associated with the meaning of the word, such as *bow-wow* for the noise that dogs make when barking, *cockadoodledoo* for roosters' crowing, and so on. Sometimes the connection to the sounds in nature is strong enough to inhibit onomatopoetic words from undergoing otherwise regular sound changes. For example, English *peep*/pip/, from earlier *pīpen*, would have become /paip/ by regular sound change (via the Great Vowel Shift; see Chapter 2) if not for the influence of onomatopoeia (Anttila 1989: 86). Onomatopoetic forms may be similar in different languages because they have independently approximated the sounds of nature, not because they share any common history. Examples involving onomatopoeia must be eliminated from proposals of distant genetic relationship. A way to reduce the sound-imitative factor is to omit from consideration words which cross-linguistically are often imitative in form, for example, words meaning 'blow', 'breathe', 'suck', 'laugh', 'cough', 'sneeze', 'break/cut/chop/split', 'cricket', 'crow' (and many bird names in general), 'frog/toad', 'lungs', 'baby/infant', 'beat/hit/pound', 'call/shout', 'choke', 'cry', 'drip/drop', 'hiccough', 'kiss', 'shoot', 'snore', 'spit' and 'whistle', among others. Unfortunately, examples of ono-matopoetic words are found very frequently in proposals of distant genetic relationships.

13.8 Nursery Forms

It is generally recognized that nursery words (the 'mama–nana–papa–dada–caca' sort of words) should be avoided in considerations of potential linguistic relationships, since they typically share a high degree of cross-linguistic similarity which is not due to common ancestry. Nevertheless, examples of nursery words are frequent in evidence put forward for distant genetic relationship proposals. The forms involved are typically 'mother', 'father', 'grandmother', 'grandfather' and often 'brother', 'sister' (especially elder siblings), 'aunt' and 'uncle', and have shapes like *mama, nana, papa, baba, tata, dada*, where nasals are found more in terms for females, and stops for males, but not exclusively so. Jakobson explained the cross-linguistic non-genetic similarity among nursery forms which enter adult vocabulary. In his view, the sucking activities of a child are accompanied by a nasal sound, which can be made while nursing, then the nasal sound first associated with nursing is reproduced to show a desire to eat or impatience for missing food or the absent nurse/mother. Since the mother dispenses the food, most of the infant's longings are addressed to her, and the nasal form is turned into a parental term. Then comes a transitional period when *papa* means whichever parent is present while *mama* signals a request for need-fulfilment, and eventually the nasal–mother, oral–father association becomes established (1962 [1960]: 542–3). This helps to explain frequent spontaneous symbolic, affective developments, seen when inherited *mother* in English is juxtaposed to *ma, mama, mamma, mammy, mommy, mom, mummy, mum,* and *father* is compared with *pa, papa, pappy, pop, poppy, da, dad, dada, daddy.* Such nursery words do not provide reliable support for distant genetic proposals.

13.9 Short Forms and Unmatched Segments

How long proposed cognates are and the number of matched sounds (segments) within them are important, since the greater the number of matching segments in a proposed cognate set, the less likely it is that accident accounts for the similarity. Monosyllabic words (composed of a single consonant and vowel) may be true cognates, but they are so short that their similarity to forms in other languages could also easily be due to chance. Likewise, if only one or two sounds of longer forms are matched (and other sounds are left unmatched), then chance remains a strong candidate for the explanation of the similarity. Such comparisons will not be persuasive; the whole word must be accounted for. (See Ringe 1999.)

13.10 Chance Similarities

Chance (accident) is another possible explanation of similarities among compared languages, and it needs to be avoided in questions of deep family relationships. Conventional wisdom holds that 5–6 per cent of the vocabulary of any two compared languages may be accidentally similar. Also, phoneme frequency within a language plays a role in how often one should expect chance matchings involving particular sounds to come up in comparisons of words from that language with ones from other languages; for example, about 15 per cent of English basic vocabulary begins with *s*, while only about 7.5 per cent begins with *w*; thus, given the greater number of initial *s* words in English, one must expect a higher possible number of chance matchings for *s* than for *w* when English is compared with other languages. The potential for accidental matching increases dramatically when one leaves the realm of basic vocabulary, or when one increases the pool of words from which potential cognates are sought or when one permits the semantics of compared forms to vary even slightly (Ringe 1992: 5).

Cases of non-cognate words which are similar in related languages are well known, for example French *feu* 'fire' and German *Feuer* 'fire'

(French *feu* < Latin *focus* 'hearth, fireplace' [-k- > -g- > -Ø-; o > ø]; German *Feuer* < Proto-Indo-European **pūr* 'fire', Proto-Germanic **fūr-i*; compare Old English *fȳr*). As is well known, these cannot be cognates, since French *f* comes from Proto-Indo-European **bh*, while German *f* comes from Proto-Indo-European **p* (by Grimm's Law). The phonetic similarity which these basic nouns share is due to the accidental convergence resulting from sound changes that they have undergone, not to inheritance from any common word in the proto-language. That originally distinct forms in different languages can become similar due to sound changes is not surprising, since even within a single language originally distinct forms can converge, for example, English *son/sun*, *eye/I* and *lie/lie* (Proto-Germanic **ligjan* 'to lie, lay'/**leugan* 'to tell a lie').

13.11 Sound–Meaning Isomorphism

A generally accepted principle (advocated by Meillet) permits only comparisons which involve both sound and meaning together. Similarities in sound alone (for example, the presence of tonal systems in compared languages) or in meaning alone (for example, grammatical gender in the languages compared) are not reliable, since they often develop independently of genetic relationship, due to diffusion, accident and typological tendencies (see Greenberg 1963).

13.12 Only Linguistic Evidence

Another valid principle permits only linguistic information, with no non-linguistic considerations, as evidence of distant genetic relationship. As Gabelentz (1891: 157) put it, 'the only sure means for recognizing a [genetic] relationship lies in the languages themselves.' (See also Greenberg 1963.) Shared cultural traits, mythology, folklore, technologies and gene pools must be eliminated from arguments for linguistic relationship. The wisdom of this principle becomes clear when we take into account the many strange proposals based on non-linguistic evidence. For example, some earlier African classifications proposed that Ari (Omotic) belongs to either Nilo-Saharan or Sudanic 'because the Ari people are Negroes', that Moru and Madi belong to Sudanic because they are located in central Africa, or that Fula is Hamitic because its speakers herd cattle, are Moslems, and are tall and Caucasoid (Fleming 1987: 207). Clearly, language affinities can be independent of cultural and biological connections.

13.13 Erroneous Morphological Analysis

Where compared words are analysed as being composed of more than one morpheme, it is necessary to show that the segmented morphemes (roots and affixes) in fact exist in the grammatical system. Unfortunately, unmotivated morphological segmentation is found very frequently in proposals of remote relationship. Often, a morpheme boundary is inserted in forms where none is justified, as for example the arbitrarily segmented Tunebo 'machete' as *baxi-ta* (a loanword from Spanish *machete*, as mentioned above, which contains no morpheme boundary but rather is a single morpheme). This false morphological segmentation makes the form appear more similar to the other forms cited as putative cognates, Cabecar *bak* and Andaqui *boxo-(ka)* 'axe' (Greenberg 1987: 108).

Undetected morpheme divisions are also a frequent problem. An example of this, taken from the Amerind hypothesis (which attempts to unite most of the language families and isolates of the Americas in one very large genetic grouping), compares Tzotzil *ti?il* 'hole' with Lake Miwok *talok*[h] 'hole', Atakapa *tol* 'anus', Totonac *tan* 'buttocks' and Takelma *telkan* 'buttocks' (Greenberg 1987: 152); however, the Tzotzil form is *ti?-il*, from *ti?* 'mouth' + *-il* 'indefinite possessive suffix', meaning 'edge, border, outskirts, lips, mouth', but not 'hole'. The appropriate comparison *ti?* bears no particular resemblance to the other forms in this comparison set.

13.14 Non-cognates

Another problem is the frequent comparison of words which are not cognates within their own family with words from other languages as evidence of distant genetic relationship. Often, unrelated words from related languages are joined together in the belief that they might be cognates and then are compared further with forms from other language families as evidence for even more distant relationships. However, if the words are not even cognates within their own family, any further comparison with forms from languages outside the family is untrustworthy. Examples from the Maya–Chipayan hypothesis (Olson 1964, 1965) illustrate this difficulty. Tzotzil *ay(in)* 'to be born' (actually from Proto-Mayan *ar-* 'there is/are', Proto-Tzotzilan *ay-an* 'to live, to be born') is not cognate with the *ya?* (*yah*) 'pain' of the other Mayan languages listed in this set (< Proto-Mayan *yah* 'pain, hurt'), though its inclusion makes Mayan comparisons seem more like Chipaya *ay(in)* 'to hurt'. (*y* = [j] in these examples.) Yucatec Maya *čal(tun)* 'extended (rock)' is compared to non-cognate *č'en* 'rock, cave' in some other Mayan languages;

357

the true Yucatec cognate is *č'eʔen* 'well' (and 'cave of water') (< Proto-Mayan **k'eʔn* 'rock, cave'). Yucatec *čal-tun* means 'cistern, deposit of water, porous cliff where there is water' (from *čal* 'sweat, liquid' + *tun* 'stone' compare Proto-Mayan **to:ŋ* 'stone'). The non-cognate *čaltun* suggests greater similarity to Chipaya *cara* 'rock (flat, long)' with which the set is compared than the **ƙ'eʔn* cognates do (Campbell 1993b). (*č* = [tʃ] in these examples; *c* = retroflex affricate.)

13.14.1 Words of limited distribution

Often in proposals of distant genetic relationship, an isolated word from some language with no known cognates in other languages of its family is compared to forms in languages from other families. However, a word which has cognates in its own family stands a better chance of perhaps having an even more remote connection with words of languages that may be distantly related than an isolated word which has no known cognates in other languages in its family and hence offers no prima facie evidence of potential older age. Inspectionally resemblant lexical sets of this sort are not convincing. Meillet's principle for established families is just as important – even more so – when considering proposals of distant genetic relationship, where the languages are not yet known to be related:

> When an initial 'proto language' is to be reconstructed, the number of witnesses which a word has should be taken into account. An agreement of two languages . . . risks being fortuitous. But, if the agreement extends to three, four or five very distinct languages [of the same family], chance becomes less probable. (Meillet 1966: 38, Rankin's 1992: 331 translation)

13.14.2 Neglect of known history

It is not uncommon in proposals of distant genetic relationship to encounter forms from one language which exhibit similarities to forms in another language where the similarity is known to be due to recent changes in the individual history of one of the languages. In such cases, when the known history of the languages is brought back into the picture, the similarity disintegrates. An example of this sort is seen in the set of lexical comparisons labelled 'dance' in the Amerind hypothesis which compares Koasati (a Muskogean language) *bit* 'dance' with Mayan forms for 'dance' or 'sing': K'iche' *bis* (actually *b'i:ʃ* 'sing'),

Huastec *bisom* and so on (Greenberg 1987: 148). However, Koasati *b* comes from Proto-Muskogean $*k^w$; the Muskogean root was $*k^w it$- 'to press down', where 'dance' is a semantic shift in Koasati alone, apparently first applied to stomp dances (Kimball 1992: 456). Only by neglecting the known history of Koasati (that $b < *k^w$, and the original meaning was not 'dance') could the Koasati form be seen as similar to Mayan.

13.15 Spurious Forms

Another problem is that of non-existent 'data', that is, difficulties that have to do with the 'bookkeeping' and 'scribal' errors which result in spurious forms being compared. For example, among the forms presented as evidence for the Mayan–Mixe-Zoquean hypothesis (Brown and Witkowski 1979), Mixe-Zoquean words meaning 'shell' were compared with K'iche' (Mayan) *sak'*, said to mean 'lobster', but which actually means 'grasshopper' – a mistranslation of the Spanish gloss *langosta* found in a K'iche'–Spanish dictionary, which in Guatemala means 'grasshopper', though it means 'lobster' in other varieties of Spanish. While a 'shell'–'lobster' comparison is a semantic stretch, it is not as fully implausible as the comparison of 'shell'–'grasshopper'; which makes no sense. Errors of this sort can be very serious. Such a case is that of the words given as Quapaw in the Amerind hypothesis (Greenberg 1987) where in fact none is from the Quapaw language, but rather all are from Biloxi and Ofo (other Siouan languages, not closely related to Quapaw; see Rankin 1992: 342). Skewed forms also often enter proposals due to philological mishandling of the sources. For example, in the Amerind evidence, the <v> and <e> of the Creek source of the data was systematically mistransliterated as *u* and *e*, although these represent /a/ and /i/ respectively. Thus <vne> 'I' is presented as *une* rather than the accurate *ani* (Kimball 1992: 448). Spurious forms skew the comparisons.

13.16 Methodological Wrap-up

Given the confusion that certain claims regarding proposed distant genetic relationships have caused, the methodological principles and procedures involved in the investigation of possible distant genetic relationships are extremely important. Principal among these are reliance on regular sound correspondences in basic vocabulary and patterned grammatical (morphological) evidence involving 'shared aberrancy' or 'submerged features', with careful attention to eliminating other possible explanations for similarities noted in compared material (for example, borrowing, onomatopoeia, accident, nursery forms and so on). Research on possible distant genetic relationships which does not heed the methodological recommendations and cautions of this chapter will probably remain inconclusive. On the other hand, investigations informed by and guided by the principles and criteria surveyed here stand a good chance of advancing understanding, by either further supporting or denying proposed family connections.

Many proposals of distant genetic relationship have not stood up well when the evidence presented for them has been subjected to the methodological considerations surveyed in this chapter. This fact might seem to cast a doubt on the likelihood of demonstrating new as yet unproven relationships. However, we can take encouragement from the number of success stories of previously unknown or disputed relationships which subsequently have come to be demonstrated since the beginning of the twentieth century which satisfy the methodological recommendations seen in this chapter. A few examples are: Hittite and the other Anatolian languages demonstrated to be Indo-European; the Uto-Aztecan family demonstrated to the satisfaction of all; the Otomanguean family proven, and then later the proof that Tlapanec belongs to Otomanguean (not to 'Hokan' as previously believed); Algic demonstrated to the satisfaction of all (that Yurok and Wiyot of California and the Algonquian family belong to a more inclusive family); Miwokan and Costanoan proven to be related, members of the more inclusive Miwok-Costanoan family; Rama shown to be Chibchan; Sino-Tibetan established. Indeed, in recent years numerous new families have been recognized and the membership of others has been extended to include additional languages in Papua New Guinea, southeast Asia, Australia and Latin America. Future demonstrations of linguistic relatedness can be expected if proper methodological procedures are followed.

14

Philology: The Role of Written Records

Philologists, who chase
A panting syllable through time and space
Start it at home, and hunt it in the dark,
To Gaul, to Greece, and into Noah's Ark.

(William Cowper [1731–1800], *Retirement*, 691)

14.1 Introduction

Philology has to do primarily with the use of written attestations of earlier stages of languages, and with how the information from written forms of a language can be used to determine aspects of that language's history. The investigation of written records has always been important in historical linguistics. This chapter deals with philology and the methods for extracting historical linguistic information from written sources.

14.2 Philology

Philology is understood in different ways. Sometimes philology is taken to be merely the study of some classical or older language – in this sense, we see university departments and professional journals dedicated to Classical philology, English philology, Germanic philology, Nordic philology, Romance philology and so on. Sometimes philology is understood to mean historical linguistics as practised in the nineteenth century, since what is today called historical linguistics was often referred to earlier as 'philology', as in 'Indo-European philology'. In another sense of the word, philology is understood as the scholarly activity which attempts to get systematic information about a language from written records. One aim of philology in this sense is to get historical information from documents in order to learn about the culture and history of the people behind the text; another aim is to examine and interpret older written attestations with the goal of obtaining information about the history of the language (or languages) in which the documents are written. This aim is the most common in historical linguistics today, and it is in this sense that the term *philology* is used in this book.

In the use of philology for historical linguistic purposes, we are concerned with what linguistic information can be obtained from written documents, with how we can get it, and with what we can make of the information once we have it. The philological investigation of older written attestations can contribute in several ways, for example, by documenting sound changes, distinguishing inherited from borrowed material, dating changes and borrowings, and helping to understand the development and change in writing systems and orthographic conventions. Results of these studies can have implications for claims about scribal practice, subgrouping classification, causes of changes, the reconstruction of a proto-language, borrowed changes and rules, the identification of extinct languages, and for the historical interpretation of many changes within the languages investigated in this way.

14.3 Examples of What Philology Can Contribute

The following examples illustrate some of the kinds of information that can be retrieved through philological investigations and the implications which it can have for historical linguistic understanding of the languages involved. Since examples of this sort abound for Indo-European and ancient Near Eastern languages, to show the general applicability of philological notions, the cases selected for illustration here are taken from the rich written attestations in various Mayan languages since the 1500s and from Mayan hieroglyphic writing. This makes the exercise more interesting, since it is often believed, erroneously, that Native American languages lack old written sources and that therefore little can be gained from philological investigation of them.

14.3.1 First example

Proto-Mayan contrasted *x (velar fricative) and *h (glottal fricative), as several of the thirty-one Mayan languages still do; however, in Yucatec

Maya these both merged to h (*x, *$h > h$). Nevertheless, colonial sources show that the contrast survived until after European contact. For example, in the Motul Dictionary from c. 1590, the two sounds were distinguished as 'loud H' (< *x) and 'simple H' (< *h); some example dictionary entries which illustrate the contrast are seen in Table 14.1.

TABLE 14.1: Contrastive h and x in Classical Yucatec Maya

under 'simple H' ([h])	*under 'loud H'* ([x])
halab- [*halaɓ*-] 'thing said or sent'	halab- [Proto-Mayan *xal- 'to weave'] 'weaving stick'
hel- [Proto-Mayan *hil] 'rest'	hel [Proto-Mayan *xel] 'succeed, exchange'
haa [Proto-Mayan *$ha\textipa{P}$] 'water'	haa [$xa\textipa{P}$] 'to scrape, file'

This example shows that through philological investigation we can sometimes recover information about sound changes in the language under investigation, in this case about a merger in Yucatec Maya, and information about the relative date when the change took place; in this case the merger of $x, h > h$ was sometime after the Motul Dictionary was written in c. 1590. (The orthography of this and following examples is based on that of Spanish at the time when the documents were written.)

14.3.2 Second example

Huastec, another Mayan language, has contrastive k^w (labialized velar stop) and $k^w{}'$ (glottalized labialized velar stop), though no other Mayan language has these sounds. Based on the correspondence sets of Huastec k^w : others k, and Huastec $k^w{}'$: others k', some had thought that Proto-Mayan must be reconstructed with *k^w and *$k^w{}'$. However, written attestations from the eighteenth century show that the labialized velars in Huastec are the results of a recent change. In words which originally had a velar stop (k or k') followed by a back rounded vowel (u or o) followed by a glide (w, j, h or $\textipa{P}$) followed by a vowel, the velars were labialized and the rounded vowel together with the glide was lost:

$$\begin{Bmatrix} k \\ k' \end{Bmatrix} \begin{Bmatrix} u \\ o \end{Bmatrix} \begin{Bmatrix} w \\ j \\ h \\ \textipa{P} \end{Bmatrix} V > \begin{Bmatrix} k^w \\ k^w{}' \end{Bmatrix} V$$

Some examples are seen in Table 14.2. The notation < . . . > is used to enclose written attestations, to symbolize that the material is presented precisely as found in the source.

TABLE 14.2: The origin of Huastec labialized velars

Colonial Huastec	Modern Huastec
<cuyx> [kuwi(:)ʃ] 'vulture'	kʷiːʃ 'vulture'
<coyen> [kojen] 'mass'	kʷen 'piled together'
<cohuych> [kowi(:)č] 'tamale'	kʷiːč 'tamale'

This philological evidence shows that Huastec k^w and $k^{w'}$ are the results of a later sound change and therefore do not belong in separate correspondence sets which would require reconstructing these sounds to Proto-Mayan. This case shows how philological information can be relevant both to the reconstruction of proto-languages and to determining the source of certain sounds and what sound changes brought them about. It also reveals something about when the change took place, in this case some time after these eighteenth-century sources were written.

14.3.3 Third example

Poqomam, Poqomchi' and Q'eqchi', three neighbouring Mayan languages, have all undergone the sound change *ts > s. Some scholars had thought that this shared innovation (see Chapter 6) was evidence that the three should be grouped together in a subgroup of languages more closely related to one another than to other languages of the family. Other evidence, however, shows that while Poqomam and Poqomchi' are very closely related, Q'eqchi' is considerably more distant. Philological evidence shows that the change *ts > s is not in fact a shared innovation reflecting a change in some immediate ancestor of the three languages at a time before they split up. Rather, the earliest written attestations in these languages reveal that the change was under way but not completed until after European contact and that the change diffused later through these three languages. For example, the Zúñiga Poqomchi' dictionary (from c. 1608) has entries such as *vatz* [w-ats], *vaz* [w-as] 'elder brother' (modern Poqomchi' *w-as* 'my older brother', Proto-Mayan *ats* 'elder brother'), *azeh* [as-ex], *atzeh* [ats-ex] 'to treat as a brother, to take an older brother' – 'some say it with *tz* atzeh, and others with only *z*, azeh; say it as you please. Most say azeh, with *z*, and some with *tz*.' Some other examples are:

tzeel, zeel	'laugh' (Proto-Mayan *tseʔ-)
tzab, zab	'addition, balancing weight'
tzinuh, zinuh	'oak'
tzub, zub	'the profit from what is sold'.

The Morán Poqomam dictionary (c. 1720) has examples such as:

azvez, atzvez	'elder brother' (Proto-Mayan *ats, modern Poqomam *as-wes*)
ah zeel, ah tzeel	'one who laughs' (Proto-Mayan *tseʔ-)
alaz, alaatz	'descendants'
ah itz	'witch, sorcerer' (modern Poqomam *ax is*, Proto-Mayan *its* 'evil').

Other sources show that this change was complete in Poqomchi' and Poqomam shortly after these were written, but that it diffused to Q'eqchi' only later. For example, the Morales Q'eqchi' grammar (1741) shows most forms with <tz> ([ts]):

tzum	'companion' (modern Q'eqchi' *sum*)
tzuc	'gnat' (modern Q'eqchi' *suq*)
tzimaj	'bow, arrow' (modern Q'eqchi' *simax*).

Only a very few of the words cited then show the beginnings of the change, for example:

tzununk, sununk 'smell' (modern Q'eqchi' *sunu:nk*)

The philological evidence in this example shows that the change *ts > s in these three languages took place after European contact and spread later among these already independent languages. This means that this change is not support for subgrouping these languages together as more closely related. This case shows how philological evidence can be relevant for subgrouping, as well as for determining the date when changes took place.

14.3.4 Fourth example

Philological information which can be derived from Mayan hieroglyphic writing helps to identify the language in which the older hieroglyphic texts (c. AD 250–900) were written as Cholan, and that it had already undergone such distinctive Cholan sound changes as *k > č. For example, some Mayan glyphic signs represent rebuses (depictions of one thing to represent another thing that sounds like it, such as a picture of an 'eye' to represent 'I' in English). A depiction of a small snake was used rebus-style in Classic Maya glyphic texts to represent 'from' (as in expressions of time, 'it was so much time since/from . . .'). This symbol was used because in Cholan 'snake' is *čan*, while 'from' is *čaʔan* – and it is hard to draw a picture of 'from'. This shows that the language of the writing system must be identified as Cholan, since among the Mayan languages only Cholan has *čaʔ an* 'from', and because in Cholan *čan* 'snake' and *čaʔ an* 'from' are similar enough to provide the basis for a rebus. This would not be the case in other languages of the family. For example, in Yucatec Maya, whose speakers acquired knowledge of the hieroglyphic writing much later, 'snake' is *kà:n*, reflecting Proto-Mayan **ka:n* 'snake'. Since the rebus works only with identical initial consonants, a form with *k*, as in Yucatec, could not have provided the basis for a rebus to signal a word which began with *č*, whereas Cholan *čan* 'snake' with *č* could stand in for *čaʔan* 'from', because of the **k >* *č* change in Cholan (**ka:n > čan* 'snake'). This helps to identify the language as Cholan, but furthermore shows that the change **k > č* had to have taken place already by the time the hieroglyphic texts were written (where the dates when the texts were written are clearly established by Mayan calendric dates in these texts).

Another example involves the hieroglyphic spelling of the name of *Chac* the 'rain god', which in Cholan is *čahk*, from Proto-Mayan **kah(o)q* 'thunder, rainstorm'. Some Mayan glyphic signs were syllabic, representing CV (consonant + vowel); Mayan monosyllabic roots of CVC shape could be spelled with two CV signs, where the vowel of the second was 'silent'. *Chac* was spelled with the syllabic signs /ča/ + /ki/. Since the /ča/ sign never substituted for /ka/ – for example, was never used to spell the Yucatec cognate *kawak* 'a calendric day name' (where both Cholan *čahk* and Yucatec *kawak* are from Proto-Mayan **kah(o)q* 'storm, thunder') – the sound change of **k* to *č* had already taken place before this name came to be written with these syllabic signs, the change found in Cholan.

These brief examples from Mayan hieroglyphic writing show how the philological investigation of these written records contributes by showing which language the hieroglyphic script was written in, and that the change **k > č* took place at a time before the texts were written. (For other examples from Mayan hieroglyphic writing, see Campbell 1984 and Justeson et al. 1985.)

The examples cited in this section show that findings from philological investigation can have implications for, among other things, (1) documenting former contrasts now lost and sound changes that have taken place, (2) refining and clarifying the reconstructions of proto-phonology, (3) distinguishing borrowed changes from legitimate shared innovations and clarifying evidence for subgrouping, (4) identifying ancient, sometimes extinct, languages, and deciphering writing systems, and (5) establishing the relative age of changes. In effect, if the right kind of information is preserved in the written sources, philology can contribute insight and understanding to most areas of linguistic change.

14.4 The Role of Writing

The relationship of writing (of early written traditions) to the comparative method is sometimes misrepresented but needs to be understood. As Mary Haas pointed out,

> Since the existence of written languages ... was of great strategic importance in the development of our knowledge of Indo-European, some scholars came to believe that the historical and comparative study of languages was impossible without written records of earlier stages of the same or related languages. (1969a: 20)

This belief persisted in spite of the fact that the comparative study of unwritten, so-called 'exotic' languages has had a long and successful history. Leonard Bloomfield resolved to disprove once and for all the assertion that a proto-language could not be reconstructed successfully in the absence of written records from earlier stages of the language. Bloomfield's (1925, 1928) famous proof of the applicability of the comparative method in unwritten languages (presented in Chapter 5) was based on the assumption that sound change is regular so that different sound correspondence sets among Algonquian languages which could not be explained away required different proto-sounds to be reconstructed. His decision to reconstruct *çk for one sound correspondence set, even though it contained sounds found in other correspondence sets but corresponding to different sounds in the different daughter languages, was confirmed by the discovery of Swampy Cree which contained distinct sounds as the reflexes in each of the sound correspondences (see Chapter 5 for details). Bloomfield's proof of the applicability of the comparative method to unwritten languages is seen as a major contribution to historical linguistics. It means that while we are happy to have the testimony of written records for earlier periods when we can get it, it is by no means necessary to comparative reconstruction. Moreover, it must be recalled that written records have to be interpreted – one of the things done in philology – and they are only as valuable and reliable as our ability to determine the phonetic and phonemic system underlying them.

Hittite illustrates this point. While Hittite has radically revised our understanding of Indo-European phonology, it was written in an imprecise cuneiform syllabary on clay tablets from 1650 to 1200 BC, and some aspects of its phonetic interpretation are still in dispute. For example, it is not clear whether Hittite had four or five vowels. The interpretation of some vowels in certain positions is also unclear. They may be just empty ('dummy') vowels as a consequence of how the syllabary was used as a graphic system or they may actually have been present. For example, for things spelled with <i> as in <išpant-> 'to libate', we do not know whether the *i* was really present phonetically or was just an artifact of the spelling conventions in the syllabary (/išpant-/ or /špant-/); for <epta> 'he took', we do not know whether it was one or two syllables in length (/epta/ or /ept/); and, more dramatically, for <išparzašta> 'you/he escaped', we do not know whether it was two, three or four syllables long. Clearly, then, Hittite writing provides much useful information, but it also has limitations for the historical interpretation of the language.

In part, the prejudice in favour of old written traditions is a hold-over from a pre-Neogrammarian stage of comparative linguistics when language change was thought to take place in discrete stages of first progress and then decay. The languages of so-called 'savage' people were thought to be 'primitive' relics which had not yet evolved (progressed, through processes of compounding and amalgamation) to the state of greater perfection which in this view older written Indo-European languages, in particular Sanskrit, had attained; modern languages were typically viewed as just decayed reflections (due to analogy and sound changes, which were assumed to be operative only in this later phase) of their more perfect ancestors. Thus, the old written languages, thought to be more perfect, were allotted a special status. In the Neogrammarian movement, comparative linguistics adopted the position that language change did not take place in discrete stages of either progress or decay, but rather languages undergo the same kinds of changes (sound change and analogy) at all times throughout their histories. With this reorientation, written language was accorded less of a special status and attention turned more towards spoken language, in particular to dialects, and attention to dialectology promoted the development of phonetics, techniques for recording forms of spoken language (see Chapter 7). Thus, speaking of the principle that sound laws are without exception, Berthold Delbrück affirmed in his influential Neogrammarian introduction to linguistics:

This natural constitution of language is not manifested in the cultivated tongues, but in the dialects of the people. The guiding principles for linguistic research should accordingly be deduced not from obsolete written languages of antiquity, but chiefly from the living popular dialects of the present day. (1882 [1880]: 61)

In short, the existence of an old written tradition with older texts is by no means necessary for the comparative method to be applicable, and in any case, the written records for historical linguistic interests are only as valuable as our ability to interpret them and to determine accurately the phonetic and structural properties of the language which they represent.

The comparative method has been applied successfully over and over again to languages lacking any significant written tradition, and each success story further confirms its applicability to such languages. For example, what we know of Finno-Ugric through the comparative method in some ways rivals our knowledge of Proto-Indo-European, and yet none of the Finno-Ugric languages except Hungarian has a long written tradition. The detailed knowledge we have of the histories of language families such as Austronesian, Bantu, Mayan and many others is impressive indeed, but writing has played no significant role in working out these histories. Old written records can be very helpful, but much can be achieved also without them.

14.5 Getting Historical Linguistic Information for Written Sources

The techniques employed and the sorts of information which one can expect to obtain from written records vary greatly from case to case, depending on the circumstances. For example, how we investigate texts written in a logographic writing system (where signs represent whole words) will differ markedly from how we treat syllabaries (with symbols based on syllables, usually representing consonant + vowel) or alphabetic scripts. However, in general, philology will use anything which provides information helpful for interpreting the phonetic, phonemic and grammatical contents of the language which the written records represent so that this information can be put to use in unravelling further the history of the language involved.

Very often, what information we can derive for interpreting the structure of the language at the time when the texts were written and extrapolating from that for the understanding of the history of the language is a matter of luck, of what happens to show up in the sources available. In the best cases, we may have descriptions or commentaries about the pronunciation at the time, and these can be immensely helpful. In most situations, however, we are not so fortunate as to have worthwhile, readily interpretable phonetic descriptions from the past. Other valuable sources of phonetic information include rhymes, metre, occasional spellings, transliterations of forms from other languages whose phonology is better known, aid from translations from texts known in other languages, and clues from related languages and dialects. Let us consider some of these briefly.

14.5.1 Rhymes and the testimony of poetry

For example, the word 'night' was spelled variously <niht>, <ny3t>, <nyght> and <nicht> in Middle English texts (see also Scots English <nicht> /nixt/). For various reasons, it is assumed that the consonant before the final *t* represented in these various spellings (especially by <gh> and <3>) of the word for 'night' and others like it was /x/, a voiceless velar fricative, even though the sound is gone from Modern English /nait/ 'night'. Some of the evidence for it representing /x/ in Middle English comes from the fact that in Middle English poetic texts, words with <gh> and <3>, with the postulated /x/, rhyme only with other words spelled in this way and never with words which contain the same vowel but lack a spelling of the /x/. For example, Chaucer rhymes *knight* with *wight* 'strong' but not with *white* (Lass 1992: 30).

14.5.2 Occasional spellings

An indirect source of knowledge about changing pronunciation is the variant spellings which sometime provide clues concerning what was changing and when the change took place. In the history of English, in the 1600s spelling conventions were starting to regularize, as printers increasingly used uniform spelling, but standard spelling was far from fixed. Occasional spellings (not the more expected ones) from the period show change in pronunciation. For example, variants such as *ceme/came*, *credyll/cradel* 'cradle' and *teke/take* show that former /a/ had changed to something closer to modern /e(i)/. Examples such as *symed/semed* 'seemed' and *stypylle/stepel* 'steeple' reflect the /e:/ > /i:/ of the Great Vowel Shift. Spellings of *marcy/mercy* 'mercy', *sarten/certein* 'certain', *parson/persoun* 'person', and so on, show that /er/ changed to /ar/ in the pronunciation of the writer of these forms. (This change was fairly general, though sociolinguistically conditioned, and it was ultimately reversed, but left such doublets in English as *clerk/clark, person/parson, vermin/varmint* and *university/varsity*.)

14.5.3 Interpretation from material from foreign languages

For example, the principal source of information on Gothic is Bishop Wulfila's (AD 311–82) translation of the Bible, part of which has survived, whose orthography was based on that of Greek at the time when Wulfila wrote. The spellings with <ai> and <au> are interpreted as representing /ɛ/ and /ɔ/ respectively, based on the value of <ai> and <au> in Greek spelling at the time. This interpretation is supported by the Gothic spellings of foreign names and words known to have had *e(:)* and *o(:)* in the source languages, for example: *Aílisabaíþ* 'Elizabeth', *Nazaraíþ* 'Nazareth', *praúfetus* 'prophet', *Gaúmaúrra* 'Gomorrah', *Naúbaímbaír* 'November'. This gives greater confidence in the interpretation of the phonetic value of Gothic <ai> and <au> (Krause 1968: 67).

14.5.4 Clues from related languages

In the case of texts in languages which are less well known, sometimes clues to the interpretation of the writing can be obtained from related languages. For example, in the case of Middle English <gh>/<3> (above), although 'night' in Modern English has no /x/, we can be relatively more assured of our /x/ interpretation of the phonetic value based on the fact that English's closest relatives have /x/ in cognate words, as in German *Nacht* [naxt] 'night' and similar forms in Dutch and Frisian (Lass 1992: 30).

An example which shows how both translated texts and clues from related languages can help comes from Chicomuceltec, an extinct Mayan language, reasonably closely related to Huastec. Very little is known directly about Chicomuceltec, just very limited word lists (no more than 500 words) and one text from before it became extinct. The text is a *Confesionario* from 1775 with about ten lines in Chicomuceltec corresponding to the adjacent Spanish text. The orthography is based on Spanish, and by referring to the translated Spanish text for possible meanings and to corresponding Huastec forms, it is possible to work out much of the contents of the text, as seen in the following example line:

Chicomuceltec: ixcataton tan Domingo?
Spanish: Has trabajado los Domingos?

The Spanish line means 'have you worked on Sundays?' and leads us to believe that the Chicomuceltec version has the same meaning. In the Spanish orthography at the time, <x> represented [ʃ] (Spanish /ʃ/ changed to a velar fricative [x] later and is spelled today primarily with <j>). In comparing Huastec material, we postulate for Chicomuceltec that *ixca-* [iʃka-] is 'you past' (containing within it -*a*- 'you singular') + *t'ohn-* 'work', *tan* 'in' and the Spanish loanword *Domingo* 'Sunday'. Without access to related Huastec forms and corresponding translation of the same text in Spanish, we would have no basis for segmenting the morphemes or guessing what this line means. Without reference to Huastec forms, we would not be able to recover the word 'to work' or to postulate that it contained a glottalized *t'* as in the Huastec cognate, since the glottalized stops are not distinguished from plain ones in the Spanish-based orthography of the Chicomuceltec text. Together, the corresponding translation in a better-known language (Spanish in this case) and comparison with closely related languages (Huastec) provide for a fairly successful philological interpretation of this text in an otherwise very poorly known language (Campbell 1988: 202–7).

There are also many potential pitfalls and sources of error in attempts to interpret older written sources, and it is important to keep in mind the many ways in which well-meaning interpretations can go astray. Sometimes the writing system just underrepresents the contrasts that existed in the language at the time it was written, and so information is simply not available for a full interpretation. In the Chicomuceltec example, this is illustrated by the lack of distinction in the Spanish-based orthography between /t/ and /t'/ in the language. In early attestations of other Native American languages, contrastive tones, glottal stops and long vowels, for example, are simply not represented at all in the documents. Other problems can come from the difficulty of interpreting variations in the writing, from cases where different dialects with different features are represented, and from the tendency for writing systems to preserve representations of features which have been lost in the spoken language long after the language has changed (witness the <gh> in Modern English *night*). The needs of poetic form (especially metre) may distort the written language, for example under poetic licence using word orders not normally found in the spoken language. Old texts which are translations of other texts, such as the Bible in Gothic based on Greek, or in English based on translations from Latin versions, often lead to grammatical distortions, loan translations or calques, and so on which were not actually part of the language.

In summary, in many cases, exercising appropriate caution, we can obtain much information from older written attestations of value to the historical interpretation of languages. This is an important source of historical linguistic information, useful in the arsenal of tools which the historical linguist uses to recover the history of languages.

14.6 Exercises

Exercise 14.1 Philological analysis of Latin Appendix Probi

The *Appendix Probi* ('Appendix of Probus') was compiled in 3rd–4th century AD. It lists 227 Latin words in what the scribe considered both 'correct' and 'incorrect' form. It was devised to aid scribes with the orthography, but the forms listed also illustrate some phonological and analogical changes that were taking place or had already taken place in spoken Latin language at that time. Compare the following examples from the list and attempt to formulate the changes that they appear to reflect. These examples are of the form *X non Y*, that is *X not Y*, where the scribe considers the 'X' form 'correct' and the 'Y' form 'incorrect', as in *masculus non masclus*, meaning '*masculus* ['male'] not *masclus*', that is, more precisely, 'write *masculus*; do not write *masclus*'. For this exercise, assume that the forms on the left of *non* represent conservative and thus older pronunciations and that the forms on the right of *non* ('Y') correspond to later pronunciations which result from changes in the language.

HINT: in instances where some forms seem to change in the opposite direction of others, consider the possible role of hypercorrection.

Appendix Probi	*Conventional Classical Latin spelling and gloss*
Set I	
1. masculus non masclus	māsculus 'male, manly'
2. vetulus non veclus	vetulus 'little old, poor old'
3. vitulus non viclus	vitulus 'calf, foal'
4. vernaculus non vernaclus	vernāculus 'native, of home-born slaves'
5. articulus non articlus	articulus 'joint, knuckle, limb'
6. angulus non anglus	angulus 'angle, corner'
7. oculus non oclus	oculus 'eye'
8. tabula non tabla	tabula 'board, plank'
9. calida non calda	calida 'warm, hot'
10. frigida non frigda	frīgida 'cold'
11. viridis non virdis	viridis 'green'

Set II
12. vacua [vakua] non vaqua   vacua 'empty, void'
    [vakwa]
13. equs [ekwus] non ecus [ekus] equus 'horse'
14. coqus [kokwus] non cocus   coquus 'cook'
    [kokus]
15. rivus [rīwus] non rius [rius] rīvus 'stream, brook'
16. avus [awus] non aus   avus 'grandfather'
17. flavus [flāwus] non flaus   flāvus 'yellow, golden'
    [flāus]

Set III
18. passim non passi   passim 'here and there,
                                  at random'
19. pridem non pride   prīdem 'long ago, long'
20. olim non oli   ōlim 'once, at the time, at times'
21. idem non ide   īdem, idem 'the same, likewise'
22. numquam non numqua   numquam 'never'
23. triclinium non triclinu   trīclīnium 'dining-couch, dining
                                  room'

Set IVa (the more common direction of change)
24. ansa non asa   ānsa 'handle'
25. mensa non mesa   mēnsa 'table, meal'
26. Capsensis non Capsessis   Capsensis 'from Capsitanus'

Set IVb (occasional examples)
27. Hercules non Herculens   Herculēs
28. occasio non occansio   occāsiō 'opportunity,
                                  convenient time'

Set Va (the more common direction of change)
29. vinea non vinia   vīnea 'vineyard'
30. cavea non cavia   cavea 'cage, coop, hive'
31. lancea non lancia   lancea 'lance, spear'
32. balteus non baltius   balteus 'belt, girdle, sword-belt'
33. cochlea non coclia   coclea, cochlea 'snail'

Set Vb (occasional examples)
34. ostium non osteum   ōstium 'door, entrance'
35. noxius non noxeus   noxius 'harmful'
36. alium non aleum   ālium 'garlic'

Set VI

37. vapulo non baplo   vāpulō 'be beaten, flogged'
38. alveus non albeus   alveus 'hollow, trough, bathtub'
39. tolerabilis non toleravilis   tolerābilis 'bearable, tolerable'

Set VII The more common direction of change was <x> [ks] becoming <s> [s]. In light of this, how would you explain the following:

40. miles non milex   mīles 'soldier'
41. aries non ariex   ariēs 'ram'
42. poples non poplex   poplēs 'knee'
43. locuples non locuplex   locuplēs 'rich, reliable'

(From Baehrens 1922.)

Exercise 14.2 Greek philological comparison

The short text in line (1) is from Mycenaean Greek (before 1200 BC), given in the conventional transliteration for the Linear B syllabary. Roots for the words in this text are compared in line (2) with Attic Greek (Classical Greek from Athens, end of the fifth century BC), and then in line (3) with Modern Greek. Each is given with its phonetic equivalents, well understood from a variety of sources of information. Compare the Greek from these three different times and attempt to specify sound changes that can be detected in these data. What other historical information can you draw from this example? Note that FOOTSTOOL is represented by an ideogram, where the sign signals the whole word and it is not spelled out in the syllabary. Inst = Dative-Instrumental. 'Octopus' is literally 'many-foot' (*polu-/poly-* 'many' + *pod-* 'foot'). The word for 'griffin' (glossed as 'phoenix' in Modern Greek) also means 'palm tree'. This text means 'One footstool inlaid in ivory with a man and a horse and an octopus and a griffin/palm tree.'

(1) Linear B (c. 1400 BC):

Ta-ra-nu	a-ja-me-no	e-re-pa-te-jo	a-to-ro-qo	i-qo-qe	po-ru-po-de-qe	po-ni-ke-qe FOOTSTOOL 1
[tʰrâ:nus	aia:ménos	elepʰanteío:i	antʰró:kʷo:i	híkkʷo:ti-kʷe	polupódei-kʷe	pʰoiní:kei-kʷe X]
stool.Nom	inlaid.Nom	ivory.Inst	man.Inst	horse.Inst-and	octopus.Inst-and	griffin.Inst-and X

(2) Attic Greek (c. 400 BC):

θρανίον   ελεφάντινο-   'άνθρωπο-   ἱππο-   πολύποδ-   φοίνικ-
[tʰra:níon   elepʰántino-   ántʰro:po-   híppo-   polýpod-   pʰoíni:k-]

(3) Modern Greek (c. 2000 AD):

θρανίο	ελεφάντινο-	ανθρωπο-	ιππο-	πολύποδ-	φίνιξ
[θraní̇o	elefá(n)dino-	ánθropo-	íppo-	polī̇pod-	fínix]
'desk, form'	'made of ivory'	'man'	'horse'	'polyp, polypod'	'phoenix/
			(in 'horsepower')		palm tree'

(From Horrocks 1997: 4–5.)

Exercise 14.3 Spanish philological interpretation

The epic poem, *Cantar de Mio Cid*, is one of the oldest texts in Spanish, from about 1140 AD. A fragment of the poem is given here and compared with the modern equivalent in Latin American Spanish (as, for example, spoken in Mexico or Central America). Each line is given with broad phonetic equivalents. Compare the two versions. What lexical changes do you note? What other changes have taken place in this variety of modern Spanish? Assume for present purposes that any non-lexical, non-grammatical phonetic difference between the two versions represents a general change even if only one example appears in these data. What conclusions can you draw about the history of some of these changes?

NOTE: ñ = palatal nasal, IPA [ɲ]; [s̪] = dental 's' (which in modern Peninsular Spanish became [θ]); [s̺] = apical post-alveolar 's'. OBJ = marker of human specific object; REFL = reflexive.

Original from Cantar de Mio Cid:

(1) Nós çercamos   el   escaño por curiar   nuestro señor,
    [nos s̺erkamos̺   el   es̺kaño por kuriar   nuestro s̺eñor]
    We surrounded the   bench   for to.guard   our   lord,

(2) fasta do despertó mio Cid, el   que Valencia gañó;
    [fas̺ta do des̺pertó mio s̺id el   ke   valens̺ia gañó]
    until where awoke my   Cid   he   who Valencia won

(3) levantós   del   escaño   e   fos   poral león;
    [levantó-s̺   del   es̺kaño e   fo-s̺   por-al león]
    got.up-REFL from.the bench and went-REFL for.the lion;

(4) el   león premió la   cabeça, a   mio Cid esperó,
    [el   león premió la   kabes̪a   a   mio s̺id es̺peró]
    the lion lowered the   head,   for my   Cid waited

(5) dexósle   prender   al   cuello, e   a   la   red   le   metió.
[deʃó-ṣ-le   prender   al   kuelʲo   e   a   la   red   le   metió]
allowed-REFL-him   to.take   to.the   neck   and   to   the   net   it   put

Modern equivalent:

(1) Nosotros   rodeamos   el   escaño   para custodiar   a   nuestro   señor,
[nosotros   rodeamos   el   eskaño   para kustodiar   a   nuestro   señor]
We   surrounded the bench   for   to.guard   OBJ   our   lord,

(2) hasta   que   se   despertó   mi   Cid,   el   que   ganó   Valencia;
[asta   ke   se   despertó   mi   sid   el   ke   ganó   balensia
until   that   REFL   awoke   my   Cid   he   who   won   Valencia;

(3) se levantó   del   escaño y   se   fue   por   el   león;
[se lebantó   del   eskaño i   se   fue   por   el   león]
REFL got.up   from.the bench   and REFL went   for   the   lion;

(4) el   león   bajó   la   cabeza, esperó   a   mio   Cid,
[el   león   baxó   la   kabesa, esperó   a   mi   sid]
the   lion   lowered   the   head,   waited   for   my   Cid

(5) se le   dejó   coger por   el   cuello y   meter-lo   en   la   jaula.
[se le   dexó   koxer por   el   kueyo i   meterlo   en   la   xaula]
REFL   him allowed to.take by   the neck   and put-it   in   the cage

'We surrounded the bench to guard our lord,
until my Cid awoke, he who conquered Valencia;
he got up from the bench and he went for the lion;
the lion lowered its head, waited for my Cid;
it allowed him to take it by the neck and put it in the cage.'

(Additional notes: *nosotros* < *nos* 'we' + *otros* 'others'; *do* = modern *donde* 'where'.)

15

Linguistic Prehistory

Language, too, has marvels of her own, which she unveils to the inquiring glance of the patient student. There are chronicles below her surface, there are sermons in every word.

(Max Müller 1866: 12–13)

15.1 Introduction

Linguistic prehistory has been associated with a number of names in the literature: linguistic palaeontology, linguistic archaeology, applied historical linguistics and so on. It has a long (and sometimes chequered) history, though in recent years it has again come into focus. Broadly speaking, linguistic prehistory uses historical linguistic findings for cultural and historical inferences. Linguistic prehistory correlates information from historical linguistics with information from archaeology, ethnohistory, history, ethnographic analogy, human biology and other sources of information on a people's past in order to obtain a clearer, more complete picture of the past. Thus, the comparative method, linguistic homeland and migration theory, cultural inventories from reconstructed vocabularies of proto-languages, loanwords, place names, classification of languages, internal reconstruction, dialect distributions and the like can all provide valuable historical information useful to linguistic prehistory. How these methods can contribute to a fuller picture of prehistory is the focus of this chapter. What linguistic prehistory is all about is illustrated by a few well-known and informative cases. At the same time, it is also important to be aware of the limitations of linguistic prehistory and of the possible pitfalls and problems which can be encountered by attempts to correlate historical linguistic information with the findings in other fields. This is the subject of the last section of this chapter.

378

15.2 Indo-European Linguistic Prehistory

To get started, it is helpful to look briefly at some of the findings and claims about the prehistory of Indo-European-speaking peoples as reflected in linguistic evidence. This is an instructive case study.

By the mid-1800s, comparative Indo-European linguistics had advanced sufficiently that it was possible to say how the Indo-European languages had diversified and to make reasonably informed hypotheses about the material culture and social structure of the Proto-Indo-Europeans (the speakers of Proto-Indo-European) and about their homeland – all based solely on linguistic findings and interpretations (see Kuhn 1845, Pictet 1859–1863 and Schrader 1883 [1890]). However, crucial archaeological and other information was not yet available at that time, and the first archaeological data that did become available seemed to clash with the most probable linguistic interpretations. For example, according to an early hypothesis based on linguistic evidence, the Indo-European homeland (the place where Proto-Indo-European was originally spoken, from where Indo-European languages diversified and spread out, ultimately to their current locations) was located in the steppes to the north of the Black Sea; however, it was objected that no likely archaeological culture was known from this area at that time. In fact, supportive archaeological evidence did not appear until some 100 years later, with Marija Gimbutas' (1963) work on the Kurgan culture of the Pontic and Volga steppes. The correlation between Proto-Indo-European and the Kurgan archaeological culture now has much support, though there is also much debate (see Mallory 1989). In Gimbutas' view, the expansion of Kurgan culture corresponds in time and area with the expansion of Indo-European languages outwards from this homeland, and correlates with the arrival in these areas of such typically Indo-European things as horses, wheeled vehicles, double-headed axes, small villages, pastoral economy and patriarchal society.

Reconstruction by the comparative method has provided a fairly clear view of important aspects of Proto-Indo-European culture, including valuable information on the original homeland, social structure, kinship, subsistence, economy, law, religion, environment, technology and ideology. As Calvert Watkins observed,

When we have reconstructed a proto language, we have also necessarily established the existence of a prehistoric society . . . the contents of the Indo-European lexicon provide a remarkably clear view of the whole culture of an otherwise unknown prehistoric society . . . Archaeology, archaeological evidence, is limited to material artifacts alone.

The reconstruction of vocabulary can offer a fuller, more interesting view of a prehistoric people than archeology precisely because it includes nonmaterial culture. (1969: 1,498)

Aspects of Proto-Indo-European's cultural inventory can be recovered from the reconstructed vocabulary of Proto-Indo-European, as seen in the list below, which is based upon Mallory and Adams (1997) and Watkins (2000). The traditional Indo-Europeanist notation used here requires some explanation.

Most specialists in Indo-European recognize three sounds traditionally labelled laryngeals, but their phonetic values are disputed. They are represented conventionally as: $*h_1$ ('neutral', perhaps /h/ or /ʔ/); $*h_2$ ('a-colouring', perhaps /x/ or /ħ/); and $*h_3$ ('o-colouring', perhaps /ʕ/). Undisputed consonantal reflexes of these survive only in Hittite and the other Anatolian languages. The laryngeals are gone from all the other Indo-European languages, but not without a trace. The evidence of their earlier presence is seen primarily in their effect on vowels in these languages, changing the quality of both preceding and following vowels, and lengthening any vowel preceding them. In addition a number of languages provide other bits of evidence for the reconstruction of the Proto-Indo-European laryngeals. In Greek and Armenian initial laryngeals before consonants leave a trace in a prothetic vowel. In the earliest Indo-Iranian a hiatus (a break between vowels so they do not occur in the same syllable) is sometimes preserved which arises from the loss of an intervocalic laryngeal. In Balto-Slavic and Germanic certain accentual and intonational phenomena can point to the former presence of laryngeals.

Indo-Europeanists normally reconstruct three distinct series of velars: the palatovelars ($*\hat{k}, \hat{g}, \hat{g}^h$), the plain velars ($*k, *g, g^h$) and the labiovelars ($*k^w, *g^w, *g^{wh}$). This reconstruction has not gone unchallenged, for until recently, it was generally believed that no single language preserved distinct reflexes of all three series. However, it has now been shown that the Anatolian language Luvian has in fact kept the reflexes of all three series apart, requiring all three to be reconstructed for Proto-Indo-European.

The position of the accent in Proto-Indo-European is reconstructible for many lexical items. However, in many forms the accent could move depending on its morphology (its paradigm), and in many cases the crucial testimony from the limited number of branches which preserve direct or indirect traces of the Proto-Indo-European accent (Balto-Slavic, Indo-Iranian, Greek, Germanic and Anatolian) is missing. For these reasons no indication of the accent has been given in the following reconstructions.

Verbal roots are cited with an inserted *e* vowel (the so-called *e*-grade), which should in principle appear in certain morphological categories. Most nouns are cited in a stem-form without case endings. (The exceptions are neuter nouns, which are cited in the nominative–accusative form, and those nouns for which a stem cannot be reconstructed with certainty. These are cited as mere roots.)

(I thank Michael Weiss for his very considerable help with these Indo-European forms and with this section generally.) The reconstructed cultural lexicon of Proto-Indo-European includes the following:

15.2.1. Agriculture

'grain'
  *yewo- 'a grain, particularly barley'
  *grh_xnom (younger than *yewo-, perhaps meaning 'ripened grain', which replaced *yewo- in most of the west and centre of the IE world and competes with it in Iranian)

CROP

'fruit'
  *seso (occurred on the margins of IE world if derived from the root *seh_1 -'sow'; the reconstruction could be *$sesh_1o$- or *sh_1eso-)
'barley'
  *$\hat{g}^hrV(s)d(h)$ (a very problematic reconstruction)
  *b^haros (confined to the northwest of the IE world)
'wheat'
  *puh_xro-
  *ga/ond^h- (southern and eastern peripheries of the IE world)
'rye'
  *rug^hi (confined to the northwest of the IE world)
'ear of grain, chaff'
  *h_2ekos (from *$h_2e\hat{k}$- 'point, sharp')

LAND

'field'
  *$h_2e\hat{g}ro$ (probably derived from *$h_2e\hat{g}$- 'to drive', hence originally 'pasture'; Vedic *ájra*- still just means 'plain')
  *$h_2erh_3u/*h_2erh_3uo$ - (derived from *h_2erh_3- 'to plough', at least late PIE in the west and centre of the IE world)
'piece of land/garden'
  *$\hat{k}eh_2po$-/eh_2-

381

'enclosure/garden'

*$g^h orto$- (connection with the root *$\hat{g}^h er$- 'take' uncertain)

TECHNOLOGY

Field preparation and planting

'to plough'

*$h_2 erh_3$-

'plough'

*$h_2 erh_3 trom$ (widespread derivative of *$h_2 erh_3$-)

'ploughshare'

*$wog^{wh} ni$- (at least west and centre of the IE world)

'furrow'

*$le/oiseh_2$- (west and centre of the IE world)

'harrow'

*$h_x oketeh_2$-

'hoe'

*mat- (root only)

'sow'

*seh_1-

HARVESTING

'harvest'

*$(s)kerp$-

'mow'

*$h_2 meh_1$-

'sickle'

*$srpo$-/eh_2-

GRAIN PROCESSING

'thresh'

*$peis$- (earlier meaning 'stamp, crush')

*$wers$- (earlier meaning perhaps 'sweep')

'winnow'

*$neik$- (at least late PIE)

'grind'

*$melh_2$- (agreement in various European subgroups on the agri-
cultural sense of 'grind')

*$g^h rend(h)$- 'grind' (a somewhat problematic reconstruction;
younger than *$melh_2$-; west and centre of the IE world)

'quern'

*$g^w réh_2 won$- ~ *$g^w erh_2 nu$- 'quern' (from suffixed form of
*$g^w erh_2$- 'heavy')

15.2.2 Domestic animals and animal husbandry

'livestock'

pek̂u ('moveable wealth' > 'wealth')

'herdsman'

westor- (though not widely attested, the distribution (Anatolian and Iranian) suggests great antiquity in IE probably derived from the following)

'graze'

wes-

'guard, protect'

peh₂- (to describe the herdsman's activities)

'larger domestic animal'

steuro-

'pig'

sū- or *suhₓ-*

'boar'

h₁epero- (at least west and centre of the IE world)

'piglet'

pork̂o-

'sheep'

h₂owi-

'ram/fleece'

moiso-

'ewe'

h₂owikeh₂-

'lamb/kid'

h₁er- (root only)

'lamb'

h₂egʷno- (at least the west and centre of the IE world; some prefer the reconstruction h₂egʷʰno-)

wr̥(hₓ)en- (centre and east of the IE world)

'goat'

h₂eiĝ- (centre and east of the IE world)

gʰaido- (northwest region)

'he-goat'

bʰuĝo- (also male animal of various kinds, stag, ram)

kapro-

h₂eĝo- (centre and east of the IE world)

'bovine'

gʷou-

'bull'

    uksen-

    tauro- (possibly also 'aurochs')

  'cow'

    wakeh₂-

  'cowherd'

    $*g^wouk^wolh_1o$- (at least west and centre of the IE world, based on $*g^wou$- 'cow' + $*k^wolh_1o$- 'one who turns, moves' from $*k^welh_1$- 'turn, move around')

DAIRY PRODUCTION

  'to milk'

    $*h_2mel\hat{g}$-

  'milk'

    g(a)lakt

  'coagulated' milk'

    $*d^hed^hh_1i$ (at least centre and east of the IE world)

  'curds'

    $*tuh_xro/i$- (at least centre and east of the IE world)

  'whey'

    $*ksih_xrom$ (centre and east of the IE world)

  'buttermilk'

    tenklom ~ tnklom (from *temk-* 'congeal')

  'butter'

    $*h_3eng^wn$ (from $*h_3eng^w$- 'anoint')

  'rich in milk'

    $*pipih_xusih_2$- (at least centre and east of the IE world; a feminine perf. ptc. of the root $*peih_x$- 'swell')

  'dog'

    $*\hat{k}(u)won$-

  'horse'

    $*h_1e\hat{k}wo$-

15.2.3 Foods

  'salt'

    sal-

  'honey'

    melit (also $*melit-ih_2$- 'honey bee')

  'mead'

    $*med^hu$

'beer'

> *h₂elut- or *alut- (northwest of the IE world with an outlier in eastern Iranian; at least late IE in date)

'wine'

> *wihₓVno- ~*woihₓno- ~ wihₓnom (related to words for wine in non-Indo-European Georgian and West Semitic; the ultimate relationship between these forms is unclear)

'apple'

> *h₂ebVl-
>> (late PIE?)
> *meh₂lom (or any seed- or pit-bearing fruit)

'cherry'

> kṛnes- ~ *kṛnom 'cornel cherry'

'fruit /berry'

> *h₂ogeh₂-
> *hₓoiweh₂- (at least west and centre of the IE world)

'blackberry, mulberry'

> *morom

'bean'

> *bʰabʰeh₂- (at least west and centre of the IE world, with variant *bʰa-un in Germanic)

'porridge'

> *pḷt- ~ polto- (late IE of the west and centre?)

'broth'

> *yuhₓ- 'broth'

15.2.4 Economy and commerce

'exchange'

> *mei- (extended form *meit-'to change, go, move'; with derivatives referring to the exchange of goods and services within a society as regulated by custom or law)

'to sell'

> *perh₂- (at least of late IE status)

'to buy'

> *wes-

'purchase'

> *wVs-no- (derived from the above)

'payment, prize'

> *h₂elgʷʰo-/eh₂- (derived from *h₂elgʷʰ- 'to earn, be worth')

'gift'

    deh₃rom (derived from *deh₃-* 'give')

'apportion, get a share'

    bʰag-

'wealth'

    h₃ep-

15.2.5 Legal terms

'law'

    dʰeh₁ti- 'thing laid down or done, law, deed' (derived from *dʰeh₁-* 'to set, put')

    yewos 'religious law, ritual, norm'

'plead a case'

    (h₁)argʷ-

'guilty'

    h₁sont- (literally 'being' the present participle of the verb *h₁es-* 'be')

'penalty'

    kʷoineh₂- (derived from *kʷei-* 'to pay, atone, compensate')

'make whole'

    serk- (legal expression 'to pay for damages')

15.2.6 Transport

'yoke'

    yugom (derived from *yeug-* 'to yoke')

'wagon'

    we/og̑ʰno- (derived from *weg̑ʰ-* 'to go, transport in a vehicle')

'wheel'

    h₂wr̥g- (root only; reflexes in Hittite and Tocharian suggest antiquity, derived from *h₂werg-* 'turn')

    roteh₂- (derived from *ret-* 'to run, roll'; old PIE word for 'wheel', derivatives came to mean 'wagon' or 'war-chariot' in a number of eastern subgroups)

    kʷekʷlom (probably from the root *kʷelh₁-*)

'axle'

    h₂ek̑s-

'shaft' (of a cart or wagon)

    h₂/₃eih₁os ~ *h₂/₃(e)ih₁so-*

'pole/peg'

  d^hur- 'pivot of door or gate, axle of a chariot, harness, means of harnessing a horse to a cart, pole, yoke, peg of axle'

'reins'

  $h_2ensiyo$-/eh_2- (the equivalence in form and meaning in Greek and Irish is evidence of PIE antiquity)

'boat'

  neh_2us derived from the verb *neh_2*- 'float'

  h_xold^hu- '(dugout) canoe, trough' (probably late PIE)

'row'

  h_1erh_1-

15.2.7 Technology (other tools and implements)

'craftsman'

  d^hab^hro- (from *d^hab^h*- 'to fit together')

'craft'

  kerdos

'metal'

  $h_2ey(o)s$ (often specialized as 'copper' or 'bronze')

'gold'

  h_2eusom

'silver'

  $h_2erĝntom$ 'white (metal), silver' (based on *$h_2erĝ$*- 'white')

TOOLS

'axe'

  $(h_1)ad^hes$- or *h_1od^hes*-?

'spit'

  g^weru (presence in Avestan, Celtic and Italic strongly suggests it was once widespread in PIE)

'auger'

  $terh_1trom$ (derived from *$terh_1$*- 'to rub, turn')

'awl'

  h_xoleh_2-

'whetstone'

  $ĉoh_xno$- ~ *$ĉoh_xini$*- ((limited distribution, from PIE *$ĉeh_x(i)$* 'sharpen, hone', which is widespread)

'net'

  h_1ekt-

15.2.8 House and building(s)

'to build'
    demh₂-
'carpenter'
    tetk̂⁻on- (derived from *tek̂-* 'create')
'house'
    dom-
    domh₂o- (both derived from *demh₂-* 'build')
'hearth'
    h₂eh_xseh₂-
'door'
    dʰwor-
'doorjamb'
    h₂enh_xt(e)h₂
'roof'
    (s)tegos (derived from *(s)teg-* 'cover')
    h₁rebʰ- 'cover with a roof'
'room'
    ket- (root only)
'beam/plank'
    bhelh₂ĝ- (at least west and centre of the IE world)
    k̥lh₂ro- (late IE)
'dwelling'
    wǎstu (not related to *h₂wes-* 'spend the night')
    treb- (west and centre of the IE world)
HOUSEHOLD
  'cauldron'
    kʷeru-
  'dish'
    potr̥
  'plate'
    tek̂steh₂- (an Iranian-Italic match)
  'cup'
    peh₃tlom (derived from *peh₃(i)-* 'to drink')
  'bed'
    *legʰos ~ *logʰo-* (derived from *legʰ-* 'to lie, lay')

15.2.9 Clothing and textiles

'wool'
    h₂wl̥h₁neh₂-

'comb'

> *kes- (early meaning probably 'put in order')
>
> *kars- (the meaning 'comb (wool)' is found only in European languages)

'spin'

> *sneh$_1$- 'twist fibres together to form thread; occupy oneself with thread'
>
> *spenh$_1$- (earlier meaning 'stretch'; the specialization of 'working with thread' must be at least late IE)

'braid'

> *pleк̂-

'plait'

> *resg-

'twist'

> *weih$_x$-

'weave'

> *h$_x$eu-
>
> *web^h- 'weave' (in later PIE)
>
> *tek(s)-

'sew'

> *syeuh$_x$-

'fasten'

> *(s)ner- 'fasten with thread or cord' (a late PIE word at least)

'thread'

> *deк̂- (root only; probably the oldest which can be reconstructed whose meaning subsumes 'thread')

'sinew'

> *g^{wh}ih$_x$slo-

'wear'

> *wes-

'skin bag'

> *b^{h}olĝ^{h}i- (derived from *b^{h}elĝ^h- 'to swell')

15.2.10 Warfare and fortification

'war-band'

> *koryo- ~ koro- (at least from the west and centre of the IE world)

'hold/conquer'

> *seĝ^h-

'citadel'

> *pelh$_x$- (of the centre and east of the IE world, at least)

'hillfort'
>   *$b^hr̥ĝ^h$- (derived from *$b^herĝ^h$- 'high')

'fort'
>   *$wriyo$-/eh_2-

'booty'
>   *$soru$ (particularly men, cattle and sheep)

'sword'
>   *$h_{2/3}n̥si$-

'spear'
>   *$ĝ^hais$-o-

'spear-point'
>   *$k̂el(h_x)$- (root only)

15.2.11 Social structure and social interaction

'master'
>   *$poti$-

'housemaster'
>   *$dems$-$pot(i)$-

'household/village'
>   *$k̂oimo$- (west and centre of the IE world)

'member of a household'
>   *$k̂eiwo$-

'group'
>   *$wik̂$- (a settlement unit composed of a number of extended families which was later extended to the complex of buildings they occupied and, later still, to the socio-political unit; derived from PIE *$weik̂$- 'to settle')

'groupmaster'
>   *$wik̂$-$pot(i)$- (at least of the centre and east of the IE world)

'family'
>   *$ĝenh_1os$ (derived from *$ĝenh_1$- 'to give birth, beget')

'people'
>   *$teuteh_2$-

'member of one's group'
>   *$(h_1)aro$- ~ *$(h_1)aryo$- 'self-designation of the Indo-Iranians' (perhaps derived from *$(h_1)ar$- 'to fit')

'dear'
>   *$prih_xo$- (in west of IE world 'free'; from *$preih_x$- 'delight')

'king'
>   *$h_3rēĝs$ (derived from *$h_3reĝ$- 'to move in a straight line' with derivatives meaning 'to direct in a straight line, lead, rule')

'rule'

> *welh$_x$- (earlier meaning 'be strong')
>
> *med- 'to apply the appropriate measures' (sometimes special-
> ized in medical sense)

'free'

> *h$_1$leud^{h}ero- 'free born' (derived from *h$_1$leud^h- 'to mount up,
> grow')

'stranger, guest/host'

> *g^{h}osti- 'someone with whom one has reciprocal duties of hospi-
> tality' (an outsider could be considered both guest and poten-
> tial foe)

'servant'

> *h$_2$entb^{h}i-k^{w}olh$_1$o- (compound, *h$_2$entb^{h}i- 'on either side, around'
> + *k^{w}olh$_1$o- from *k^{w}elh$_1$- 'turn, move round in a circle')

'dowry'

> *h$_2$wedmno- (west and centre of the IE world)

'one's own custom'

> *swed^h- 'custom, characteristic, individuality' (connected in par-
> ticular to reciprocal and contractual relationships, including
> poet–patron relations and other gift exchanges; from *swe-
> 'third person pronoun and reflexive', appearing in various
> forms referring to the social group as an entity)

'fame'

> *k̂lewos- (literally 'what is heard' derived from *k̂leu- 'to hear')

'poet/seer'

> *weh$_2$t- (as 'poet' confined to west of the IE world (Greek and
> Indo-Iranian provide evidence of a pie *wekwos tetk^on-
> 'fashion speech')

15.2.12 Religion and beliefs

'holy'

> *ish$_1$ro-
>
> *sakro- (derived from *sak- 'to sanctify')
>
> *k̂wen(to)-
>
> *noib^{h}o-

DIVINITIES

'god'

> *deiwo- (derivative of *dyeu- 'daylight sky god of daylight sky',
> itself a derivative of a root *dei- 'shine')

'sky-father' nom

dyeusph₂tḗr VOC., *dyeu-ph₂ter* 'o father Jove' (cf. Jupiter, Zeus) (compound of *dyeu-* 'Jove, god of the daylight sky, head of the Indo-European pantheon' + *ph₂ter* 'father')

PRAYER

'pray'

prek̂-

meldʰ-

gʷʰedʰ-

'speak solemnly'

h₁wegʷʰ-

'call/invoke'

ĝʰeuh_x- (perhaps English *god* < *ĝʰu-to-* from 'that which is invoked', but derivation from *ĝʰu-to-* 'libated' from *ĝʰeu-* 'libate, pour' is also possible)

'priest, seer/poet'

kowh_xei-

CULT PRACTICE

'worship'

h_xiaĝ-

'consecrate'

weik- (earlier meaning perhaps 'to separate')

'handle reverently'

sep-

'libate'

spend-

*ĝʰeu- *ĝʰeu-mn* 'libation'

'sacrificial meal'

dapnom (derived from *dap-* 'to apportion (in exchange)')

'meal'

tolko/eh₂- (at least late PIE)

'sacred grove'

nemos (west and centre of the IE world)

'sacred enclosure'

werbʰ- (attestation in Anatolian, Tocharian and probably Italic suggests antiquity)

SUPERNATURAL

'magical glory'

keudos

'sorcery'

(h₁)alu-

'phantom'

 dʰrougʰo- (from *dʰreugʰ-* 'deceive')

'dragon'

 dr̥ḱont- (from *derḱ-* 'see', from the dangerous, potentially lethal, gaze of dragons)

The implications of Indo-European linguistic research were seldom ignored by archaeologists working in the area; they frequently took linguistic hypotheses into account in framing their own research. Archaeology and linguistics have contributed reciprocally in famous cases of Old World ancient history where, for example, archaeology brought forth the tablets and documents of such places as Boğaz-köy (in modern Turkey), Knossos (on Crete), Tel El Amarna (in Egypt) and so on, and then scholars with linguistic skills deciphered and translated them, pushing back the recorded history of this part of the world by several millennia. Such decipherments also contributed to the picture of which languages were spoken, when and where they were spoken, and how they are classified. For example, the picture of the Indo-European family was radically revised by the addition of the languages of the Anatolian branch (in which Hittite is of major importance), which came to light through these discoveries and decipherments. Successful interaction to the mutual benefit of both archaeology and linguistics is perhaps not surprising for cultures with ancient writing systems, which provide written documentation of ancient history. However, linguistic prehistory is able to contribute significantly to cases which lack writing, and indeed it has contributed much to the interpretation of the prehistory of many other regions of the world.

15.3 The Methods of Linguistic Prehistory

Virtually any aspect of linguistics which renders information with historical content or implications for historical interpretations can be valuable in linguistic prehistory. Let's consider some of these and see how they work in specific examples.

15.3.1 The cultural inventory of reconstructed vocabulary

As we saw in the Indo-European case study (above), much information about the culture and society of the speakers of a proto-language can be recovered from the reconstructed vocabulary. Here we look at a few other cases, where the cultural inventory of the reconstructed vocabulary has been investigated. In these cases, only the glosses of the items that have been reconstructed in these proto-languages are given. (For the actual forms and details of the studies, see the references cited after each case.)

15.3.1.1 Proto-Finno-Ugric and Proto-Uralic culture

Uralic is a language family of about forty-five languages spoken across northern Eurasia. It includes the various Samoyed languages, Saamic (Lapp) languages, Finnish, Estonian, Hungarian and many others (see Map 15.1 and Figure 6.2: The Uralic family tree, in Chapter 6). Studies have dealt with both older Proto-Uralic culture and younger Proto-Finno-Ugric culture based on the reconstructed vocabulary, though these are difficult (perhaps impossible) to separate based on the evidence. We look at each, in turn.

15.3.1.1.1 Proto-Uralic culture

Kaisa Häkkinen (2001) finds in the vocabulary reflecting Proto-Uralic culture thirty-one animal and animal-related terms, seventeen terms for transport, traffic and motion, five for water and water systems, nine hunting and fishing terms, six for buildings, constructions and equipment, two for foodstuffs and four for dishes and food preparation, sixteen for family and personal relationships, twenty-two for tools, work and work implements, and two for clothing. Analysis of the cultural inventory of reconstructed Proto-Uralic vocabulary (based on Sammallahti's 1988 rigorously constrained reconstructions) reveals aspects of the life of a Stone Age hunting and gathering people. Bearers of Proto-Uralic culture knew and presumably utilized the following things which reflect their culture:

> *Hunting, fishing and food terms:* bow, arrow, bowstring, knife; egg, fish, berry, bird-cherry (?), hare, to pursue/hunt, track.
> *Other tools, implements, clothing and technology:* needle, belt, glue birch-bark, drill, cord/rope, handle, (lodge)pole, bark/leather, enclosure/fence, metal, to braid, shaft, to cook.
> *Travel and transport:* ski, to row, fathom, cross-rail (in boat).
> *Climate and environment:* snow, lake, river, wave, summer/thaw, water.
> *Commerce:* to give/sell.
> (Cf. Sammallahti 1988, Janhunen 1981.)

From such evidence Péter Hajdú (1975: 51–9) concluded that the Proto-Uralic people were engaged in hunting and fishing, with close connections to water. Their food was mostly fish and game. They travelled

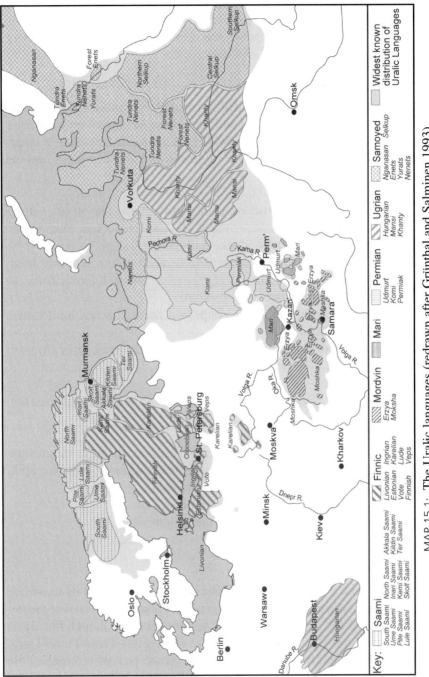

MAP 15.1: The Uralic languages (redrawn after Grünthal and Salminen 1993)

Key:

Saami
South Saami
Ume Saami
Pite Saami
Lule Saami
North Saami
Inari Saami
Kemi Saami
Skolt Saami
Akkala Saami
Kildin Saami
Ter Saami

Finnic
Livonian
Estonian
Vote
Finnish
Ingrian
Karelian
Lude
Veps

Mordvin
Erzya
Moksha

Mari

Permian
Udmurt
Komi
Permiak

Ugrian
Hungarian
Mansi
Khanty

Samoyed
Nganasan
Enets
Yurats
Nenets
Selkup

Widest known distribution of Uralic Languages

in boats, on skis and in sleighs (slays). Hajdú doubts they were involved in reindeer breeding, since reindeer breeding is fairly recent, but believes, rather, that wild reindeer was 'one of the most important prizes for the hunter' (Hajdú 1975: 54; see also various papers in Fogelberg 1999; Campbell 1997b).

15.3.1.1.2 Proto-Finno-Ugric culture

The reconstructed Proto-Finno-Ugric vocabulary is more extensive than that of its parent, Proto-Uralic, and provides a somewhat better picture of the cultural inventory of the speakers of the proto-language. It inherited all that was in Proto-Uralic culture (listed above) plus it had the following:

> *Fishing*: spawn, net, to fish with a net, gill/mouth, raft/loft (?), netting needle, ide (fish species), tench (fish species), fish skin/scales, crossrail (in boat), loon, duck, wall/dam.
>
> *Hunting and animal foods*: spear, drive, track/trace, to skin/flay, horn, marrow, (domestic) animal (?), grouse, tallow, hunting party, to catch, to shoot/hit, to rut, goose/bird.
>
> *Plant and other foods*: broth/soup, two berry species, honey, bee, butter, mushroom.
>
> *Technology* (tools and implements): birch-bark vessel, knife, rope, to grind, pole, (soft) metal, gold (?), to sew, knife, pot, rope, needle, net.
>
> *Building and household items*: canopy, bed, house/hut, scoop, pot, shelter, hut/house, board, to cook, pole.
>
> *Clothing*: sleeve, glove, to sew.
>
> *Climate and environment*: ice crust, frost, ice, to melt, sleigh/slay/ sled, to snow, ski, winter, summer, autumn, bog, to sink, lake/flood, flood soak, downriver, stream.
>
> *Social structure and society*: lord, orphan.
>
> *Religion and beliefs*: soul, spirit, ghost, idol/village.
>
> *Commerce*: to buy, value/price/worth, to give/sell.
>
> (Cf. Sammallahti 1988.)

There is no evidence of agriculture in Proto-Uralic and its existence in Proto-Finno-Ugric culture is also generally doubted. Reasonably widespread terms for 'wheat' and 'grain' are encountered, though mostly as diffused loanwords. Hajdú (1975: 57) believes that Proto-Finno-Ugric speakers did not know agriculture based on the lack of reconstructible names for implements and processes connected with agriculture; for example, no word for 'sowing', 'reaping', 'scythe', 'hoe', and so on can be traced to Proto-Finno-Ugric (Fogelberg 1999; Campbell 1997b.) He believes that 'pig' and probably also 'sheep' were known through contact with Indo-European neighbours, but that pig breeding began only later. In the realm of religion, Hajdú thinks that ancestor worship and gods in natural phenomena were typical (Hajdú 1975: 58). He finds animism suggested by cognates for: (1) 'evil spirit', 'lord (of underworld)', 'giant' (with compounds found in disease names), and (2) 'spirit, fall into a trance', though not all of these are fully accepted as cognates. (Cf. Campbell 1997b.)

15.3.1.2 *Proto-Mayan culture*

Mayan is a family of thirty-one languages, argued to have begun to separate at around 2200 BC. Both the linguistic and the non-linguistic prehistory of Mayan-speaking peoples has been intensively investigated, perhaps because of the romantic appeal of Classic Maya civilization. The cultural inventory reflected in the reconstructed vocabulary of Proto-Mayan includes the following:

Maize complex: maize, corncob, ear of corn, roasting ear, atole (a corn drink), to sow, to harvest, to grind, metate (grindstone for corn), to roast (grains), flour, lime (used to leach corn kernel).

Other cultivated plants/food plants: avocado, chili pepper, sapodilla, custard apple, sweet manioc, squash, sweet potato, bean, achiote (bixa, a food-colouring condiment), century plant, cotton, tobacco, cigar.

Animals: dog, jaguar, opossum, mouse, gopher, armadillo, cougar, squirrel, deer, weasel, coyote, skunk, fox, bird, crow, vulture, hummingbird, owl, bat, hawk, flea, bee, honey, fly, gnat, ant, louse, spider, tick, butterfly, bumblebee/wasp, scorpion, toad, fish, worm, snake, snail, crab, alligator, monkey, quetzal.

Trees and other plants: nettle, vine, willow, oak, cypress, pine, palm, silk-cotton tree (ceiba).

Religion and ritual: god/holy, writing, paper, evil spirit/witch, priest, sing/dance, drum/music, rattle, tobacco (used ritually).

Social structure: lord, slave/tribute.

Implements (and other technology): water gourd, trough/canoe, bench, cord, mat, road, house, home, whetstone, axe, toy, hammock, sandals, trousers, to sew, spindle.

Economy and commerce: to pay, to lose, to sell, poor, market, town (Campbell and Kaufman 1985; Kaufman 1976).

15.3.1.3 Proto-Mixe-Zoquean culture

Mixe-Zoquean is a family of some twenty languages spoken in southern Mexico in the region across the Isthmus of Tehuantepec. It is assumed to have been unified until about 1500 BC, and is considered to be of great cultural significance in the region, since it is argued that bearers of the Olmec archaeological culture (the earliest civilization in the region) were speakers of Mixe-Zoquean languages (see below). The reconstructed vocabulary reveals the following cultural inventory:

Maize complex: corn field, to clear land, to sow, to harvest, seed, maize, to grind corn, leached corn, corncob, corn gruel, to grind grains, to shell corn, lime (used to soften kernels of corn for grinding).

Other cultivated plants (and food plants): chili pepper, bean, tomato, sweet potato, manioc, a tuber (species); chokecherry, custard apple, avocado, sapote, coyol palm, guava, cacao.

Animals and procurement of animal resources: deer, rabbit, coatimundi, honey, bee; fish, crab, to fish with a hook, to fish with a net, canoe.

Religion and ritual: holy, incense, knife/axe (used in sacrifice), to write, to count/divine/adore, to dance, to play music, ceremony, year, twenty, bundle of 400, tobacco, cigar, to smoke tobacco (tobacco was used ceremonially).

Commerce: to sell, to pay, to cost, to buy.

Technology: to spin thread, agave fibre, to twist rope/thread, hammock, cord, water gourd, gourd dish, ladder, house, house pole, adobe wall, rubber, ring, arrow, bed, to plane wood, sandals; remedy-liquor (Campbell and Kaufman 1976; Justeson et al. 1985).

15.3.1.4 Cautions about reconstructed vocabulary

Textbooks are fond of repeating warnings about anachronistic reconstructions, which can complicate cultural interpretation based on the reconstructed vocabulary. For example, Bloomfield, in his reconstruction of Proto-Central Algonquian, found cognates which seemed to support reconstructions for a couple of items which were unknown before contact with Europeans, for example 'whisky'. It turns out that the different languages had created names based on the same compound, 'fire'+ 'water' (for example, Cree *iskote:w-a:poy*, composed of *iskote:w* 'fire' + *a:poy* 'water, liquid'), and this 'firewater' compound found in each of the languages looked like a valid cognate set to support the reconstruction, though it is due either to independent parallel development or to diffusion of a loan translation (calque) among these languages. We have no secure guarantees against such anachronisms entering our cultural interpretations of the past based on reconstructed vocabulary, although we rely on clues from our knowledge of what things were introduced by Europeans and on the criterion which we will see directly (below) that the age of analyzable terms (ones with multiple morphemes) is not as secure as that of unanalyzable terms (those composed of but a single morpheme). In actual cases, this problem comes up rarely; that is, it is not as serious as it might at first appear to be.

15.3.2 Linguistic homeland and linguistic migration theory

A question which has been of great interest in the study of many language families, and especially of Indo-European, is that of the geographical location of the speakers of the proto-language. Two different techniques have been utilized in attempts to determine where speakers of proto-languages lived, that is, where the linguistic 'homeland' (*Urheimat*) of the family was located. We consider each in turn.

15.3.2.1 Homeland clues in the reconstructed vocabulary

The first technique seeks geographical and ecological clues from the reconstructed vocabulary which are relevant to the location of where the proto-language was spoken, especially clues from reconstructed terms for plants and animals. In this approach, attempts are made to find out what the prehistoric geographical distributions were of plants and animals for which we can successfully reconstruct terms in the proto-language, and then these are plotted on a map. The area where the greatest number of these reconstructible plants' and animals' ranges intersect is taken to be the probable homeland of the language family. We will see how this works in the examples considered below.

For the prehistoric geographical distributions of the plants and animals involved, the information which palaeobotany, biology or other fields can provide is relied on. Due to climatic changes and other factors during the last few thousand years, the range of plants and animals is often not the same today as it was in former times. For example, earlier it was argued, based on the reconstruction of *$bhera\hat{g}$- (*$bherh_1\hat{g}$-) 'birch', that the Proto-Indo-European homeland lay north of the 'birch line' (where birches grow) which today runs roughly from Bordeaux (France) to Bucharest (Romania). However, this interpretation failed; the birch has shifted its habitat significantly over time and formerly extended considerably to the south, and furthermore it has always been present in the Caucasus region (Friedrich 1970: 30). That is, to locate the birch's distribution during Proto-Indo-European times, we must rely on the results of palynology (the study of ancient pollens). While the case of the birch's earlier distribution is clear, this can make matters difficult, since palynological information may not yet be available for some of the regions in question. Also, in many cases we may have only the roughest of estimates concerning the time when the proto-language was spoken. It is difficult to correlate the distribution of ancient plants based on palynology and of languages without some idea of the period of time at which their respective distributions are being correlated (Friedrich 1970).

15.3.2.2 Linguistic migration theory

The other technique for getting at linguistic homelands – called *linguistic migration theory* – looks at the classification (subgrouping) of the family and the geographical distribution of the languages, and, relying on a model of maximum diversity and minimal moves, hypothesizes the most likely location of the original homeland. The underlying assumption is that when a language family splits up, it is more likely for the various daughter languages to stay close to where they started out and it is less likely for them to move very far or very frequently. Therefore, turning this process around, if we look at today's geographical distribution of related languages, we can hypothesize how they got to where they are now and where they came from. This procedure deals not with just the geographical spread of the languages of the family, but rather with the distribution of members of subgroups within the family. The highest branches on a family tree (the earliest splits in the family) reflect the greatest age, and therefore the area with the greatest linguistic diversity – that is, with the most representatives of the higher-order subgroups – is likely to be the homeland. This is sometimes called the *centre of gravity* model (after Sapir 1949: 455). Lower-level branches (those which break up later) are also important, because they may allow us to postulate the direction of later migration or spread of members of the family. In this model, we attempt to determine the minimum number of moves which would be required to reverse these migrations or spreads to bring the languages back to the centre of gravity of their closest relatives within their individual subgroups, and then to move the various different subgroups back to the location from which their later distribution can be accounted for with the fewest moves. In this way, by combining the location of maximum diversity and the minimum moves to get languages back to the location of the greatest diversity of their nearest relatives, we hypothesize the location of the homeland.

Let's consider some of the better-known cases in which these two techniques have been employed in order to get a feel for how they work.

15.3.2.3 Proto-Indo-European homeland

There is a very large literature on the question of the Proto-Indo-European homeland (see Mallory 1989, Mallory and Adams 1997: 290–9). While there are a number of competing hypotheses, most mainstream historical linguists favour the view which places the Proto-Indo-European homeland somewhere in the Pontic steppes-Caspian region. The evidence for this comes from a linguistic migration theory, interpretation of geographical and ecological clues in the reconstructed vocabulary of the proto-language, loans and the location of their neighbours from whom they borrowed, and attempted correlations with archaeology (though the archaeological interpretations are subject to dispute).

Proto-Indo-European tree names have been at the centre of some homeland considerations, and Proto-Indo-European *bhāĝo- (*bheh₂ĝo-) 'beech' has been given much weight. It was thought that beech did not grow to the east of a line running from Königsberg (in East Prussia) to Odessa (in the Crimea). This would seem to place constraints on the location of the Proto-Indo-European homeland, locating it essentially in Europe. However, there are various difficulties with this. There are doubts about the original meaning of the word; the cognates do not all refer to the same tree; Greek *phēgós* means 'oak' and the Slavic forms mean some sort of 'elder', as for example Russian *buziná* 'elder(berry)'; and no reflexes are known from Asiatic Indo-European languages. If *bhāĝo- did not originally mean 'beech', then arguments based on the distribution of beeches in Proto-Indo-European times would not be relevant. There are phonological problems in that the sounds in the putative cognates for 'beech' in some branches of the family do not correspond as they should. Finally, two species of beech are involved and the eastern or Caucasian beech was (and still is) present in the Caucasus and extended to the east. Therefore, many Indo-European groups would have been familiar with it, not just those of Europe west of the infamous Königsberg–Odessa line (Friedrich 1970: 106–15). The problem with the arguments for the homeland based on this distribution of 'birch' was mentioned already above (15.3.2.1); the current distribution of birches is not the same as it was in Proto-Indo-European times and this nullifies the original argument.

Another important participant in the discussion has been Proto-Indo-European *loĝs- 'salmon', which was formerly thought to have a limited distribution, involving rivers which flowed into the Baltic Sea – this was seen as indicating a Northern European homeland. However, the original meaning of the word appears to include not only 'salmon' but species of salmon-like trout which are found in a very wide distribution which includes also the Pontic steppes and Caspian region, the current best candidate for the homeland (Mallory 1989: 160–1).

The centre of gravity model, when applied to Indo-European, also suggests this area. (For details of other hypotheses for the Indo-European homeland, see Mallory and Adams 1997: 290–9.)

15.3.2.4 *Proto-Algonquian homeland*

Frank Siebert (1967) found some twenty Proto-Algonquian terms for plants and animals whose distributions overlap in southern Ontario; these animal terms are included among the various ones reconstructed for Proto-Algonquian: golden eagle, pileated woodpecker, oldsquaw, common raven, quail, ruffed grouse, kingfisher, common loon, nighthawk, sawbill duck, seal, raccoon, lynx, squirrel, flying squirrel, moose, porcupine, skunk, fox, bear, woodchuck (groundhog), buffalo (bison), caribou, buck, fawn, beaver, muskrat, weasel, mink, white spruce, tamarack (larch), white ash, conifer–evergreen tree, elm, alder, basswood (linden), sugar maple, beech, willow, quaking aspen; black bass, lake trout, northern pike and brown bullhead. From this he concluded that the original homeland lay between Lake Huron and Georgian Bay and the middle course of the Ottawa River, bounded by Lake Nipissing and the northern shore of Lake Ontario. Dean Snow (1976) reconsidered the Proto-Algonquian homeland focusing on only the names of species whose ranges were most sharply defined; these included five tree names and six animal terms. This resulted in a broader homeland than Siebert had defined, a homeland defined most clearly by the overlap in the territories of the 'beech' and 'tamarack' – the Great Lakes lowlands east of Lake Superior, the St Lawrence valley, New England and Maritime Canada. This was bounded on the west by the Niagara Falls in order to accommodate the reconstructed word for 'harbour seal'. This constitutes a large hunting and trapping zone for nomadic bands. (Considerations mentioned below give a different picture of the Proto-Algonquian homeland.)

15.3.2.5 *Proto-Uto-Aztecan homeland*

For the Uto-Aztecan family, the results are interesting but not so definitive. Early work on the Proto-Uto-Aztecan homeland had suggested the region between the Gila River and the northern mountains of north-west Mexico, though later work showed that not all the items upon which this conclusion was based could actually be reconstructed in Proto-Uto-Aztecan. Terms which can be reliably reconstructed include, among others, 'pine', 'reed/cane' and 'prickly pear cactus', upon which considerable attention has been focused. Based on nine certain reconstructions and eighteen less secure but likely reconstructed terms, the Proto-Uto-Aztecan homeland was interpreted to be in 'a mixed woodland/grassland setting, in proximity to montane forests', and this fits a region across south-eastern California, Arizona and north-western Mexico (see Map 15.2) (Fowler 1983).

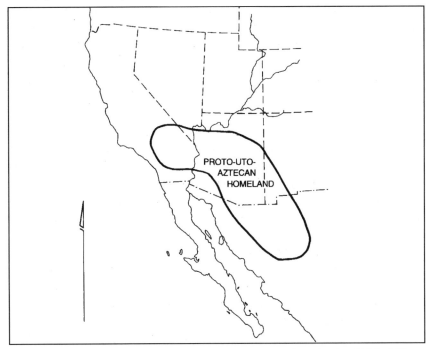

MAP 15.2: The Uto-Aztecan homeland (redrawn after Fowler 1983: 233)

The results for the Proto-Numic homeland, however, are much more precise. Numic is a subgroup of Uto-Aztecan (to which Shoshoni, Ute and Comanche belong, as well as several others from southern California to Oregon and across the Great Basin into the Great Plains). Catherine Fowler (1972: 119) found that

> The homeland area for Proto-Numic ... must have been diverse in elevation, allowing for stands of pine and pinyon, but also for such mid- to low-altitude forms as cottonwood, oaks, chia, cholla and tortoises; two, the homeland area was probably in or near desert zones capable of supporting prickly pear, chia, lycium, ephedra, cholla, tortoise, ... three, based on the presence of proto-forms for cane, crane, heron, mud-hen, tule [reeds], cattail and fish, the area probably contained marshes or some other substantial water sources.

She concludes that the Proto-Numic homeland was in Southern California slightly west of Death Valley.

15.3.2.6 *Proto-Salishan homeland*

Salishan is a family of twenty-three languages spoken on the north-west coast of North America and into the interior as far as Montana and Idaho. From more than 140 reconstructed plant and animal terms in Proto-Salishan, most of which occur throughout the area and thus are of less value in localizing the homeland, M. Dale Kinkade (1991: 143) has determined that some 'two dozen represent species found only on the coast, and hence suggest a coastal, rather than an interior, homeland for the Salish'. These terms include 'harbour seal', 'whale', 'cormorant', 'band-tailed pigeon', 'seagull' (two terms), 'flounder', 'perch', 'smelt' (two terms), 'barnacle', 'horse clam', 'littleneck clam', 'cockle', 'oyster', 'sea cucumber', 'sea urchin', 'red elderberry', 'bracken fern', 'bracken root', 'sword fern', 'wood fern', 'red huckleberry' (two terms), 'salal' (a plant), 'salmonberry' (two terms), 'seaweed', 'red cedar' and 'yew' (Kinkade 1991: 144). Several of these strongly suggest a coastal origin, but not all are equally good as evidence. The terms for 'band-tailed pigeon', 'oyster', 'barnacle', 'sea urchin' and 'flounder' would be supportive, but 'similar forms occur widely throughout the area in several non-Salishan languages and may in the long run turn out to be loanwords; for example, "sea cucumber" and "seaweed" were probably borrowed from neighbouring Wakashan languages' (Kinkade 1991: 147). Proto-Salishan speakers, with their coastal homeland, 'must also have had access to mountains, in particular the Cascade Mountains, because they had names for mountain goats and hoary marmots, both of which are found only at higher elevations' (Kinkade 1991: 147). Based on the distribution of 'bobcats' (not far up the Fraser River) and 'porcupines' and 'lynx' (which did not extend past southern Puget Sound) – for which Proto-Salishan terms are reconstructible – the homeland is further pinpointed:

> extend[ing] from the Fraser River southward at least to the Skagit River and possibly as far south as the Stillaguamish or Skykomish rivers . . . From west to east, their territory would have extended from the Strait of Georgia and Admiralty Inlet to the Cascade Mountains. An arm of the family probably extended up the Fraser River through the Fraser Canyon. (Kinkade 1991: 148)

15.3.2.7 Uralic and Finno-Ugric homeland

Much research has been done on the Proto-Uralic and the Proto-Finno-Ugric homelands, and their identification is on firmer footing than that of Proto-Indo-European (Mallory 2001: 345). These homeland studies often did not distinguish between Proto-Uralic and Proto-Finno-Ugric (a daughter of Proto-Uralic), and many scholars place the homeland of both in the same location. Information from linguistics, archaeology, human genetics and other areas of knowledge has been correlated, generally interpreted in more or less consistent ways, but in hypotheses that differ in their details. For example, the Uralic peoples today have no common culture and are genetically diverse – all Uralic-speaking peoples have received cultural and genetic traits from several directions, in several cases sharing more with non-Uralic neighbours than with other Uralic groups.

Study of the Finno-Ugric homeland has an ample history, though earlier proposals assigning the homeland to central Asia, southern Europe and the like, have now few supporters. The main candidates differ from one another mainly according to the size assumed for the area of the original homeland. They include: (1) the region of the middle course of the Volga River and its tributaries; (2) the region of the northern Urals on both sides of the mountains; (3) the central and southern Urals on both sides; (4) rather eastward on the Asian side of the Urals; (5) rather westward on the European side; (6) the broad area between the Urals and the Baltic Sea. There is actually considerable agreement in these views, since the areas represented are near one another and partially overlapping (Korhonen 1984 and Suhonen 1999; see Map 15.1).

Plant and animal terms have been presented as supporting evidence for hypothesis (1), which is widely held, that the homeland was in the region of the Middle Volga. In view (4), also widely held, the homeland would have been further east and north, between the Urals and the Volga–Kama–Pechora area or on both sides of the Ural Mountains. Supporters of candidate (6) believe that the Proto-Uralic population, at least in its final phases and perhaps also the Proto-Finno-Ugric population, may have occupied a wide area from the Urals to the Baltic Sea, based on the notion that hunting and fishing groups need to exploit wide territories for their subsistence. Ethnographic analogies from subarctic peoples of both the Old and New Worlds have been called upon for supporting evidence, with examples of some reindeer and caribou hunters who travel over 1,000 kilometres twice yearly as they follow the migrating herds of deer (Sammallahti 1984, Mallory 2001). Mikko Korhonen (1984: 63) was of the opinion that while hunting societies typically exploit wide ranges, the proto-language could not have remained unified for long if the speakers were spread from the Ural Mountains to the Baltic. For Korhonen, such a picture could be true, if at all, only briefly at the very end of the unified Finno-Ugric period – the earlier homeland would need to be sought in a smaller area. Pekka Sammallahti (1984: 153), on the other hand, points out that a journey from Lake Ladoga (in the Baltic region) to the Urals (c. 1,200 km) is no longer than from one extreme of Saami territory to the other (c. 1,500 km), and he therefore supposes that a Proto-Uralic or Proto-Finno-Ugric population could have lived in the area between Finland and the Urals and still have maintained a relative linguistic unity (see also Mallory 2001). Hajdú argues that fishing kept the Finno-Ugric people to relatively fixed bases, that 'their manner of life offers no reason for extending their homeland as far as the Baltic' (1975: 38). In any event, most scholars assume that the relative homogeneity of the family was broken up by the introduction of Neolithic techniques and agriculture from areas south of the Proto-Uralic and Proto-Finno-Ugric homeland, that the onset of farming and cattle herding – factors con- tributing to sedentarism – probably contributed to diversification of the family. Sammallahti points to the uniformity of practically all the paleolithic cultures between the Baltic Sea and the Ural Mountains, which might suggest a linguistic unity, with all the languages of the area perhaps members of a single language family. As long as there were no surplus-producing cultures anywhere nearby, communication among groups was confined to a common ecological (and perhaps cultural) zone, and unity may have been maintained over wide areas by marriage patterns in which spouses as well as linguistic innovations moved from one community to another. However, with the emergence of surplus-producing cultures to the south of the Uralic area, communication was reoriented from latitudinal change to longitudinal change. Longitudinal communication (and weaker latitudinal exchange) caused the ultimate disintegration of the Proto-Uralic area into a series of areas with their own identity and with relatively little interaction, genetic or linguistic, with others. (See also Carpelan 2001.)

Paavo Ravila (1949), employing the techniques of linguistic migra- tion theory, noticed that the Finno-Ugric speaking groups are spread geographically today in a way that reflects their linguistic relationships (degree of relatedness), as though the modern situation was created by movements of these groups to settle in the economically most favourable sections of their former overall territory. Indeed, the region around the middle course of the Volga River with its Oka and Kama tributaries appears to be a Finno-Ugric centre of gravity; speakers of Mordvin, Mari (Cheremis) and Udmurt (Votyak) live in this region as neighbours, though they represent diverse branches of the family.

Proto-Finno-Ugric vocabulary offers clues for delimiting the homeland; some plant and animal names and some culture words have been considered relevant. The words for 'honey bee' (*mekʃi*) and 'honey' (*meti*) have been emphasized. These were borrowed into Proto-Finno-Ugric from Indo-European. The area where such contact could have taken place is thought to be the region of the middle course of the Volga River, where apiculture was practiced from early times. The honey bee was unknown in Siberia, Turkestan, Central Asia, Mongolia and most of the rest of Asia, but was found in eastern Europe west of the Urals. This area of bee-keeping is often considered one of the clues to the Proto-Finno-Ugric homeland, though this is not without controversy. That the terms refer to wild bees and honey collecting are not ruled out as possibilities (Häkkinen 2001: 176).

There are a sizeable number of reconstructed Proto-Finno-Ugric plant names, but most of these are found in a wide area and are thus not very helpful in limiting the homeland. However, reconstructed tree names have been vigorously discussed in this regard along with five principal trees that have played a role: 'spruce' [Picea obovata], 'Siberian pine' [Pinus sibirica], 'Siberian fir' [Abies sibirica], 'Siberian larch' [Larix sibirica] and 'brittle willow' [Salix fragilis]/'elm' [Ulmus] (outside the Balto-Finnic subgroup the cognates mean 'elm' [Ulmus], compare Finnish *salava* 'willow' and Hungarian *szil* 'elm'). According to Hajdú (1969, 1975), the Finno-Ugric homeland could be located only in an area where all these trees were found at the appropriate time. The only place which fits temporally and geographically is from the Middle Urals toward the north, including the lower and middle course of the Ob and the headwaters of the Pechora river in the area of the northern Urals. Not everyone, however, accepts this interpretation.

Other sorts of vocabulary have also been part of the picture. Cognates for 'hedgehog' have also been taken as evidence for the Finno-Ugric homeland (compare Estonian *siil*, archaic Hungarian *szül-* [syl-] (cf. *sün-* [ʃyn-]); hedgehogs are not found east of the Urals, but do extend as far north as the 61º latitude. A word that has given rise to much speculation is 'metal', with cognates in nearly all Uralic languages meaning 'copper, iron, ore, or metal' (reconstructed as *wäśkä* for Proto-Uralic, seen in Finnish *vaski* 'copper, Hungarian *vas* 'iron', Nenets *veś* 'iron, money', etc.). Since Uralic dates to the Stone Age, such an ancient term for metal is interesting; some suggest the presence of copper trading or cold working of crude copper, but not metallurgy. A metal term of similar shape is also found in various Indo-European (for example, Tocharian A *wäs* 'gold'), and and other languages, so that it may be an old widely borrowed word (Joki 1973: 339–40). It has also been argued that the lack of old terms for 'sea' ('ocean') in Finno-Ugric languages points to a landlocked original homeland (for example, Finnish *meri* 'sea' is a loanword from Baltic Indo-European). There are, however, abundant freshwater terms in the Finno-Ugric vocabulary. Of course, arguments from negative evidence can never be fully persuasive, although this one has been popular. Salminen (2001) believes the reconstructed plant and animal names are not specific enough in their distribution to a conclusion of anything more than that the homeland was far from the sea, in the deep forests rather than in a tundra or steppe environment, though he sees the distribution of the languages as better support for locating the homeland, in the traditional area between the Volga River and the Ural Mountains.

Evidence for the original homeland has also been sought in contacts with other languages. Finno-Ugric has a significant layer of loans from Proto-Indo-European, and also from Indo-Iranian. If we knew the location of Proto-Iranian, perhaps it would help us locate more precisely the Proto-Finno-Ugric homeland. Some scholars argue for even older Indo-European loans in Uralic, though this is controversial, and some others imagine that the loans were all younger but spread across the Finno-Ugric area by diffusion. That is, the testimony of loans is helpful, but apparently not conclusive. Nevertheless, on strong evidence, most scholars believe Proto-Finno-Ugric and Proto-Indo-European were neighbours. (See Joki 1973, Campbell 1997b, Häkkinen 2001, Koivulehto 2001, Sammallahti 2001.)

15.3.2.8 Cautions concerning linguistic homelands migration theory

In linguistic migration theory, the homeland of a language family is inferred to be in the area represented by the greatest diversity (largest number of subgroups) for which the minimum number of moves (migrations) would be required to bring the speakers of the diverse languages back to one place. On the whole, the inferences afforded by this method are strong, and few documented cases fail to conform. In principle, however, it is not difficult to imagine rather straightforward situations in which linguistic migration theory would fail to produce reliable results. For example, suppose a language family with a number of subgroups had once been found in one particular geographical area, but something forced all their speakers to abandon that area, say a volcanic eruption, a drought, an epidemic or the onslaught of powerful aggressors. In such a case, it is possible that many of the migrating speakers of the different subgroups could end up bunched relatively closely together in a new area, particularly if driven until they encountered some serious obstacle such as insurmountable mountains, an ocean, inhospitable lands without sufficient subsistence resources, or other peoples who prevented entry into their territory. It is also possible that, rather than being driven, several groups speaking languages of the same family might independently be attracted to the same area (or nearby areas), for example to take advantage of better resources available there, to forge alliances with other groups of the area, and so on. In such scenarios, it is in principle possible that we might find that the greatest linguistic diversity would in fact not be in the original homeland, but in the new area where the groups come to be concentrated. Another problem for linguistic migration theory would be the possible situation in which all the languages of a family in the former area of greatest diversity were lost with no trace (where the speakers were annihilated by war or pestilence or whatever), or where the inhabitants remained but their languages were replaced by some other unrelated language or languages. In such a situation, what may appear to be a language family's area of greatest diversity today may not have been that in former times.

The fact that such counter-examples could exist means that the conclusions which we draw from linguistic migration theory can never be absolute, but rather remain inferences, warranted by the evidence but not proven. In our attempts to understand the past, we accept that migration theory has a stronger probability of being correct than any random guess we might make which is not based on these principles. That is, all else being equal, in the absence of other information to help us answer the question, our inference about original homeland based on linguistic migration theory has a better chance of being right than anything else we have to go on.

There are similar problems in relying on clues from reconstructed vocabulary for determining the most likely location of the homeland. One is that groups may migrate to geographical zones where certain flora or fauna of the homeland area are no longer found and as a result lose the words which refer to those items. In such a case, those languages lack the sort of evidence upon which we typically rely to infer the homeland. It is possible that in some cases so many languages have left and as a result lost the relevant vocabulary that these items could not be reconstructed in the proto-language and therefore the evidence for inferring the homeland would be inadequate. To take a specific example, Goddard (1994: 207) finds the terms which Siebert reconstructed 'consistent with the homeland of Proto-Algonquians being somewhere immediately west of Lake Superior' (see above), but points out the circularity of the method. Words for 'harbour seal' would typically only survive in languages in areas where harbour seals are found, leaving out languages (and hence regions) to the west which lacked a cognate for this word. In fact, Goddard concluded that the Proto-Algonquians were located more to the west based on other information, especially the distribution of the languages and the nature of the innovations which they share.

Another problem has to do with instances where the original word is not lost, but its meaning has shifted. Sometimes in such cases it is not sufficiently clear what the proto-meaning may have been to be able to make inferences about the geographical location of its speakers. For example, as mentioned, tree names have played an extremely important role in identifying the Proto-Indo-European and the Proto-Finno-Ugric homelands. If we know what tree names the proto-language had and if we can figure out the geographical distribution of these trees during the time when the proto-language was spoken, we can narrow the homeland down to an area where the distributions of all the trees known in the proto-language intersect. However, semantic shift in some of the tree names to accommodate the fact that the original tree is not found in the new areas to which some groups have migrated, or a shift in the name to accommodate new kinds of trees found in the new areas, severely complicates this sort of research. For example, in Proto-Finno-Ugric, the tree name **sala-* is reconstructed on very solid evidence from across the family; however, as mentioned earlier, this means 'willow' in Finnish and its closer relatives but 'elm' in Hungarian and its closer relatives. That is, we cannot be certain what the testimony of **sala-* is for the location of the homeland of Proto-Finno-Ugric, since the distribution of 'elms' and of 'willows' is quite distinct, but presumably one of these is not the original sense, but rather was acquired as the languages moved out of the territory where the original tree name was known. To take an Indo-European example, even **bherəĝ-* (**bherh₁ĝ-*) 'birch', which is one of the best supported of Proto-Indo-European tree names, shifted its meaning to 'ash' in Latin and to 'fir, pine, larch' in Albanian, and is absent in Greek (Friedrich 1970: 29–30; Mallory 1989: 161).

Semantic shifts need not always be a serious problem; in fact, in some cases they can provide us with additional evidence of homeland and migrations away from it. For Proto-Algonquian, a term for 'woodland caribou' is reconstructed based on abundant evidence across many of the branches of the family. This term has shifted its meaning in a few of the languages whose speakers have moved south of the caribou's range. It has come to mean 'bighorn sheep' in the Arapahoan branch and 'deer' in some Eastern Algonquian languages. Because the reconstruction with the meaning 'caribou' is secure on other grounds (distribution across branches of the family), the instances where it has shifted meaning to something else are additional evidence that Arapahoan and those Eastern Algonquian languages involved have moved away from the homeland area where the woodland caribou was found (Goddard 1994).

A problem of a different sort with linguistic homeland models is that they typically imagine a proto-language spoken in a rather restricted region from where groups spread out or migrated to fill up more territory later on. When we go through the exercise of reversing these movements or spreads to the assumed homelands of the various proto-languages, we often find that huge blank areas are left between homelands. The linguistic models seem to imply that these areas were simply not occupied at the time, but typically archaeology finds evidence of human occupation both in the homeland areas and throughout the zones left blank in the linguistic homeland interpretations. These conflicting results need to be accounted for. One possibility is that we have fully misunderstood the nature of how the languages expanded and the territory of the homelands in some cases, though we would like to be able to maintain some faith in these methods. Another possibility is that we do correctly recover the homelands for the most part with our techniques, and that the evidence of human presence in the areas left blank represents languages which have become extinct or been replaced.

15.3.3 Borrowing

Loanwords by their very definition provide evidence of contacts among peoples speaking different languages. The semantic content of loanwords often reveals a great deal about the kinds of contacts that took place and thus about the social relationships among different peoples. The following examples reveal something of the nature and range of historical information that can be retrieved from loanwords in different situations.

A rather straightforward example which illustrates the point about loanwords contributing historical information involves wine-making terms in German, most of which are borrowed from Latin, for example German *Wein* 'wine'< Latin *vīnum*, *Most* 'new wine, must' < *mustum*, *Kelter* 'wine-press' < *calcātūra* 'stamping with the feet' and so on. On the basis of these loans, the inference is drawn that very probably German-speaking people acquired knowledge of viticulture and wine production from the Romans (compare Polenz 1977: 23).

Another similar example comes from Xinkan (in south-eastern Guatemala) which borrowed most of its terms for cultivated plants from Mayan languages, leading to the inference that Xinkan speakers were not agriculturalists until their contact with Mayan groups and that they acquired knowledge of agriculture from their Mayan neighbours. Xinkan also borrowed several terms of a commercial nature from Cholan-Tzeltalan (a subgroup of Mayan), including 'to buy', 'to sell' and 'market', which suggests commercial contact between the two groups.

15.3.3.1 Turkic loans in Hungarian

Hungarian contains many loans, perhaps up to 35 per cent of the vocabulary, and the earliest stratum of these is from Turkic ('Chuvash-type'), many of them borrowed before the arrival of the Hungarians in present-day Hungary. The Turkic loans in Hungarian involve chiefly cattle breeding, agriculture, social organisation, technology and implements, dress and religion. These demonstrate that there was extensive contact with Chuvash-type Turkic and that this led to important economic and social changes. Even the name of 'Hungary' appears to be a Turkish loan (see below) (Róna-Tas 1988; Hajdú 1975).

15.3.3.2 The Olmec–Mixe-Zoquean hypothesis

The Olmec civilization was the earliest in Mesoamerica (c. 1200–400 BC) and it had a huge impact on the languages and cultures of the region. Based primarily on loanwords, the Olmecs have been identified as a Mixe-Zoquean-speaking people. The geographical distribution of Olmec archaeological sites and the Mixe-Zoquean languages (spoken across the narrowest part of Mexico and in adjacent areas) coincides to a large degree, which initially suggested the hypothesis that if speakers of Mixe-Zoquean were there during Olmec times, perhaps the Olmecs spoke a Mixe-Zoquean language. This hypothesis is strongly supported by the many loanwords from Mixe-Zoquean languages found far and wide among other languages of the Mesoamerican area. Several of these loans are of significant cultural content, including many terms for things which are diagnostic of the Mesoamerican culture area. Therefore, Mixe-Zoquean speakers had to be involved in a culture important enough to contribute on an extensive scale to others during Olmec times when the culture area was being formed. Examples of

Mixe-Zoquean borrowings into the various other languages of the area include the following.

Cultivated plants: 'cacao', 'gourd', 'small squash', 'pumpkin', 'tomato', 'bean', 'sweet potato', as well as 'guava', 'papaya', 'sweet manioc' and others.

Terms in the maize complex (maize was at the centre of Mesoamerican cultures): 'to grind corn', 'nixtamal (leached corn for grinding)', 'tortilla', 'corn dough' and others.

Ritual and calendric terms: 'incense', 'to count, divine' (into Q'eqchi and Poqomchi' 'twenty-year period', 'twenty', into Yucatec 'calendar priest', into K'iche' and Kaqchikel 'calendar'), 'day names in various calendars of the region', 'sacrifice/axe', 'woven mat' (which functioned as 'throne' for rulers), 'paper' and so on.

Other terms: 'turkey', 'salt', 'pot', 'tortilla griddle', 'ripe', 'fog/cloud', 'child/infant' (a central motif in Olmec art), 'iguana', 'rabbit', 'opossum', among others. Based on these loans, it is concluded that the Olmecs spoke a Mixe-Zoquean language.
(Campbell and Kaufman 1976.)

This example shows how loanwords can contribute to hypotheses about the ethnolinguistic identity of past cultures.

15.3.3.3 *Cautions about interpreting loans*

Some cautions are necessary, too, in the cultural interpretation of loanwords, since some loans may not come immediately from the original donor language but via some intermediate language which borrowed the form first. For example, in the case of English *coyote*, which is borrowed from Spanish *coyote*, which originally borrowed the word from Nahuatl *koyō-tl* 'coyote', it would be wrong to propose a direct cultural contact between English and Nahuatl based on the fact that English has a word which is ultimately Nahuatl in origin. (English has several other loans which have this history, borrowed from Spanish, but being originally from Nahuatl, for example *avocado*, *chilli*, *chocolate*, *tomato* and so on.) Also, some loans come about in spite of very limited contact between speakers of the respective languages, for instance English *yak* from Tibetan *gyag* 'yak'.

15.3.4 'Wörter und Sachen'

Wörter und Sachen means 'words and things' in German and has to do with historical cultural inferences that can be made from the investigation of words. For example, one *Wörter und Sachen* technique is based on the 'analyzability of words'. It is assumed that words which can be analyzed into transparent parts (multiple morphemes) tend to be more recently created in their language than words which have no internal analysis. This technique gives a rough relative chronology for different sorts of vocabulary, but more importantly, it is assumed that cultural items named by analyzable terms were also acquired more recently by the speakers of the language and those expressed by unanalyzable words represent older items and institutions. For example, by this technique, we would reason that *skyscraper* – analyzable into the pieces *sky* and *scraper* – is a newer term in the language and hence a more recent acquisition in the culture than *house* or *barn*, which, since they are unanalyzable today, must be older in the language and in the associated culture. As Edward Sapir said, 'we know, for instance, that the objects and offices denoted in English by the words *bow*, *arrow*, *spear*, *wheel*, *plough*, *king*, and *knight*, belong to a far more remote past than those indicated by such words as *railroad*, *insulator*, *battleship*, *submarine*, *percolator*, *capitalist*, and *attorney-general*' (1949: 434–5).

Of course, this kind of inference does not always work out. Sometimes languages borrow names from other languages which result in unanalyzable terms coming into the language to represent newly acquired cultural items. For example, in English, *palace* is unanalyzable (monomorphemic), but is a loan (from Old French *palais*) and yet is younger than *house* and *barn* (compare Old English *hūs* 'house' and *bere-ern* 'barley-storeroom'). Sometimes older unanalyzable names for things are replaced for various reasons by later names which are analyzable. For example, replacement of names of things due to taboo and euphemism can result in older items and institutions coming to have analyzable names, for example, older *toilet* which is replaced later by analyzable *restroom*, or *bathroom* in North America.

Another *Wörter und Sachen* technique involves deriving historical information from cultural items whose names have visibly undergone a change in meaning. Sapir (1949: 439) cites *spinster* 'unmarried female of somewhat advanced age' as an example, since it comes originally from 'one who spins', which suggests that the specialized meaning of 'spinster' is the result of a change and that 'the art of spinning was known at an early time and that it was in the hands of the women'. The age of the form is further suggested by the fact that the suffix *-ster* for someone who does something is no longer a productive one (seen frozen in such names as *Baxter*, originally 'baker' *Webster*, 'weaver'). To be completely reliable, this technique requires fairly explicit comparative evidence from related languages.

As in the *spinster* example, another technique infers that vocabulary items which have morphological forms which are no longer productive refer to things that are older in the culture. Thus, *ox* and *calf* must be reasonably old cultural items in English, since they both have non-productive plural forms which new nouns entering the language today would not have, *oxen* with the archaic *-en* plural and *calves* with the *f/v* alternation. Such irregularities 'are practically always indicative of the great age of the words that illustrate them and, generally speaking, of the associated concepts'. Sapir cites the example in Nootka (Northwest Coast of North America) of *ħaʔwiḷ* 'chief' and *qo:ḷ* 'slave' having the irregular, non-productive plural forms *ħaʔwi:ħ* 'chiefs' and *qaqo:ḷ* 'slaves', from which we infer a relatively remote antiquity for an office of chief, the institution of slavery, and some degree of social stratification (Sapir 1949: 441).

Another *Wörter und Sachen* strategy has already been encountered in the investigation of the cultural inventory revealed in the reconstructed vocabulary of a proto-language. Related to this is the assumption that cultural items which are represented by terms which have cognates widely spread across the languages in the language family are older in the associated cultures than terms which lack such a wider distribution among the related languages.

15.3.5 Toponyms (place names)

Linguistic aspects of place names very often permit historical inferences about languages and the people who spoke them. A much-cited example is that of place names in England whose distribution and linguistic content reflect aspects of history. For example, English place names which end in *-caster*, *-cester* and *-chester* reflect Latin *castra* 'camp' (originally 'military posts') borrowed into Old English as *ceaster*, as in *Lancaster*, *Gloucester*, *Chester*, *Dorchester*, *Winchester* and so on. These provide information on the history of Roman occupation in England. The area with heavy settlement from Scandinavia during Old English times (called the 'Danelaw', north and east of a line running roughly from Chester to London) has over 2,000 place names of Scandinavian origin (see Map 15.3), and these reflect the invasion and impact of Scandinavians in the history of England. The names of Scandinavian origin are recognized from linguistic elements of Scandinavian origin such as *-by*, from Old Norse *by* 'settlement' ('village, town'), as in *Busby, Derby, Grimsby, Kirby, Rugby*; *-thorp*, from Old Norse *þorp* 'village', as in *Gunthorpe, Scunthorpe, Winthorp*; *-waite /-thwaite*, from Old Norse *þveit* 'clearing', as in *Curthwaite, Linthwaite, Mickelthwaite*,

415

Seathwaite. This distribution is seen in Map 15.3. In the region south of
the Danelaw, names with analyzable Anglo-Saxon (Old English) elements predominate, for example Old English-*hām* 'home' (used also in
the sense of 'town, village', as in *hamlet*), seen in places with -*ham*, as
in *Birmingham, Buckingham, Chatham, Durham, Nottingham*, etc.; and
tūn 'enclosure, village, farmstead', seen in the -*ton* of *Arlington, Burton,
Kensington, Southampton*, and so on.

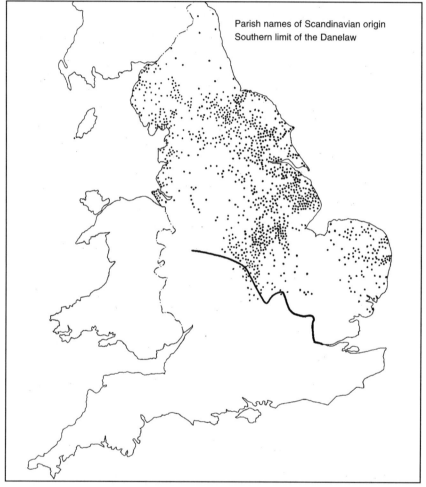

Parish names of Scandinavian origin
Southern limit of the Danelaw

MAP 15.3: Distribution of place names of Scandinavian origin in England
(redrawn after Wakelin 1988: 24)

The evidence from place-name etymology shows that although today
Xinkan speakers are relegated to a very small area near the coast in
southeastern Guatemala, in former times Xinkan territory was much

larger. This is demonstrated by place names found in the region which have an etymology in Xinkan but not in any other language. A few examples, with their probable Xinkan sources, are:

Ayampuc: *ay-* 'place of' + *ampuk* 'snake' (Ayampuc is on a snake-like ridge)
Ipala: *ipal'a* 'bath' (the volcano of Ipala has a crater lake)
Sanarate: *san-* 'in, at' + *aratak* 'century plant'
Sansare and *Sansur*: *san-* 'in, at' + *sar-* 'flats, coast'.

It is interesting in this case that J. Eric S. Thompson, the famous Mayan archaeologist and explorer, concluded from place names ending in *-agua*, *-ahua*, *-gua* and *-hua* that there had been what he called an '*Agua* people' in the region, a non-Mayan people who were displaced by invading lowland Maya (Chortí speakers) (1970: 98–9). On closer inspection, however, many of Thompson's *-agua* place names appear to be based on Xinkan *sawɨ* 'town, to dwell'. Some of the place names involved are: Xagua, Jagua, Anchagua, Sasagua, Eraxagua (*ɨra-* 'big'), Conchagua, Comasahua and Manzaragua. When Spanish speakers began to record these names, since Spanish had no equivalent of the Xinkan retroflex laminal fricative /ʂ/ (which varies with /ʃ/ in some varieties), Spanish speakers rendered it as <s>, <x> (/ʃ/ in Guatemalan Spanish) or <r>. Later, ʃ changed to /x/ (velar fricative), spelled <j> in Standard Spanish. Thus, these place names appear to contain reasonable renditions of Xinkan *sawɨ* 'town'; Thompson's *Agua* people appear to have been Xinkan speakers.

An often-mentioned but less reliable approach to obtaining information from place names is the same as the *Wörter und Sachen* technique involving the analyzability of vocabulary terms, where it is assumed that names which are not analyzable are older and that toponyms which can be analyzed into component morphemes are younger. Sapir (1949: 436) explains the logic of this: 'the longer a country has been occupied, the more do the names of its topographical features and villages tend to become purely conventional and to lose what descriptive meaning they originally possessed'. From this we infer that the place names *London*, *Paris* and *York*, which are otherwise meaningless today, are older than those with more transparent analyses such as *New York*, *St Louis*, *New Orleans* and *Buffalo*. Though these older place names are unanalyzable, they may once have exhibited a more descriptive meaning or clearer linguistic analysis which was obscured by changes over time (which confirm Sapir's point), as in the case of *London* < Latin *Londinium*, based on a Celtic root *lond-* 'wild, bold'; *Paris* < *Parisii* (the name of a Gallic tribe); *York* < *Jor-vik* (a Scandinavian name containing *vik* 'small bay').

15.3.6 Onomastics (peoples' names)

Often, valuable information for linguistic prehistory can be recovered from names for peoples. For instance, there is evidence of early cultural contact in the ethnonyms for 'Russia' and 'Russian'. As is well known, English *Russian*, German *Russe* and similar names in other European languages derive from the early Scandinavians, a dominant force, in the Novgorod region of Russia, as is reflected in the Finnish word *Ruotsi* 'Sweden, Swedish', a loan from Old Swedish *$*r\bar{o}p(r)s$-* 'inhabitant of Roslagen' (in Sweden just north of Stockholm, associated with the Vikings), which was also borrowed into Old Russian as *rusĭ* 'Russia' – the Viking source for these terms for 'Russia' and 'Russian' in these European languages. Finnish *Venäjä* 'Russia', *Venä-läinen* 'Russian' (*-läi-nen* '-ite'; compare dialectal *Venät*) and Estonian *vene* (dialectal *vend*) 'Russian' tell a different story. The source of these names is actually an old loan from Germanic *$*vene\eth$, reflected by Old English *Winedas*, Old High German *Winidā* and Old Norse *Vindr*, names which refer to the 'Wendish' (also called 'Sorbians'), speakers of a Slavic language who lived on the south coast of the Baltic sea. The Hungarian ethnonym is revealing, reflected in German *Ungarn*, Russian *wengry*, English *Hungarian/Hungary* and Hungarian *Ugry* (< *Ogry*). These apparently reflect the tribal confederation of the *Onogurs* and the close contact between Hungarians and the Onogur-Bulgar Turks. It is by this Turkic tribal name, *on-ogur*, which means 'ten-arrows', that the Hungarians came to be known.

15.4 Limitations and Cautions

So far, we have considered only the various historical linguistic sources of information and how they might be applied to contribute to greater understanding of prehistory. All these things reflect historical events and connections. However, we need also to consider potential problems and limitations that we may encounter in attempting to recover the past of a people through historical linguistic evidence.

Very often, a principal criterion for determining ethnic identity is the language which a group speaks, and anthropologists and linguists often use language as the most important marker of ethnicity. However, it is well understood that language, culture and human genetics need not coincide and frequently do not. There are many cases where a single culture involves speakers of various languages, where a single language involves diverse cultures, and where human population genetics does not correspond in a straightforward fashion to either cultural identity or linguistic identity. The genetic make-up of speakers of Indo-European languages varies considerably; there is a large difference between speakers of the Indo-European languages in northern India and those of Iceland. Similarly, Finno-Ugric languages are spoken by the western Caucasian Finns and the eastern mongoloid Ostyaks and Voguls. Multi-cultural language groups and multilingual cultural groups (societies) exist, both with or without a relatively fluid gene pool. Language is often a symbol of identity, but it is not the only such symbol, and difference in language does not necessarily mean difference in ethnicity. Ethnic identity can be based on various things other than language, for example shared cultural tradition (heritage), kinship or perceived genealogy, religion, territory, national origin, even ideology, values and social class.

All this notwithstanding, most of the correlations between linguistics and other sources of information in linguistic prehistory assume a more or less clearly identifiable correlation between language and culture (and sometimes also human biology) through time. This raises important questions which call for caution in research in linguistic prehistory. To what extent do groups with a shared cultural tradition and a common language tend to coincide? To what extent does the correlation, when it does exist, tend to last? Unfortunately, on the whole, cultural change and linguistic change are very different in nature. In particular, it is much easier for a group to change its material culture substantially in a relatively short period of time, but a language's structure changes much more slowly. This means that a lack of correlation between language and non-linguistic culture can develop relatively easily.

It is important to acknowledge this problem, but it does not defeat the overall enterprise of linguistic prehistory. Some scholars seem to fear that, if linguistic identity and ethnic identity do not coincide through history, then we can say nothing about prehistory from linguistic data. However, this is short-sighted. We have many sorts of information from 'language history' that tell us about the past: place names, information on contacts from borrowings, cultural inventory from reconstructed proto-languages, and evidence of language spread or migration. This remains historical information regardless of whether there was continuity in the linguistic-ethnic identity. This could be turned around. We cannot always know from material culture whether the language remained constant, whether new genes filtered into the population, whether a trait of material culture spread across ethnic and language boundaries or spread with the expansion of its bearers into territory formerly associated with other cultural and linguistic groups. The whole point of research in prehistory is to take as much evidence from as many lines as possible to try to answer questions such as these. Knowing that speakers of Proto-Indo-European had horses, cows, wagons, tribal kings and so on is historical information regardless of whether we know their precise ethnic and genetic identity, who their present-day lineal descendants are, and so on, and it would be foolish to ignore such information when trying to come to grips with a fuller picture of prehistory.

Attempts to correlate language with material culture may be complicated by the fact that a single cultural tradition may not be continuous in time, since it may change radically through contact with other cultures. Language, too, can change and even be replaced due to contact with other languages. Thus, how successful can we be when we look at the cultures and languages which we know about today and attempt to project back in time to the human groups with whom each may have been associated in the past? We cannot always know, and for that reason it is very important that the lines of evidence be investigated independently before correlations are attempted. However, when independently established sources of evidence point to the same sorts of conclusions, we can be happier about the plausibility of the conclusions which we reach about prehistory. Linguistic prehistory has an important role to play in prehistory in general.

Bibliography

Abondolo, Daniel, 'Introduction', in Daniel Abondolo (ed.), *The Uralic Languages* (London: Blackwell, 1998), pp. 1–42.

Aitchison, Jean, 'The language lifegame: prediction, explanation and linguistic change', in Willem Koopman, Frederike van der Leek, Olga Fischer and Roger Eaton (eds), *Explanation and Linguistic Change* (Amsterdam: John Benjamins, 1987), pp. 11–32.

Aitchison, Jean, *Language Change: Progress or Decay?*, 3rd edn, Cambridge Approaches to Linguistics Series (Cambridge: Cambridge University Press, 2001 [1st edn London: Fortuna, 1981]).

Alvar, Manuel, *Lingüística románica*, reworked and heavily annotated; originally by Iorgu Iordan (Madrid: Ediciones Alcalá, 1967).

Anderson, James M., *Structural Aspects of Language Change* (London: Longman, 1973).

Anttila, Raimo, 'The relation between internal reconstruction and the comparative method', *Ural-Altaischer Jahrbücher* 40 (1968), 159–73.

Anttila, Raimo, *An Introduction to Historical and Comparative Linguistics* (New York: Macmillan, 1972 [2nd edn: Current Issues in Linguistic Theory, 4, Amsterdam: John Benjamins, 1989]).

Arlotto, Anthony, *Introduction to Historical Linguistics* (Boston: Houghton Mifflin, 1972 [reprinted: Washington, DC: University Press of America, 1981]).

Ayto, John, *The Longman Register of New Words*, vol. 2 (Harlow: Longman, 1990).

Bach, Adolph, *Deutsche Mundartforschung*, 3rd edn (Heidelberg: Carl Winter, 1969).

Baehrens, W. A., *Sprachlicher Kommentar zur vulgärlateinischen Appendix Probi* (Halle an der Saale: Max Niemeyer, 1922). (Reprinted, Groningen: Bouma's Boekhuis, 1967.)

Beekes, Robert S. P., *Comparative Indo-European Linguistics: An Introduction* (Amsterdam: John Benjamins, 1995).

421

Berlin, Brent and Paul Kay, *Basic Color Terms: Their Universality and Evolution* (Berkeley: University of California Press, 1969).

Bhat, D. N. S., *Sound Change* (Delhi: Motilal Banarsidass Publishers, 2001).

Bloch, Oscar and Walther von Wartburg, *Dictionnaire étymologique de la langue française*, 5th edn (Paris: Presses Universitaires de France, 1968).

Bloomfield, Leonard, 'On the sound system of Central Algonquian', *Language* 1 (1925), 130–56.

Bloomfield, Leonard, 'A note on sound-change', *Language* 4 (1928), 99–100.

Bloomfield, Leonard, *Language* (New York: Holt, Rinehart and Winston, 1933).

Brown, Cecil H. and Stanley R. Witkowski, 'Aspects of the phonological history of Mayan-Zoquean', *International Journal of American Linguistics* 45 (1979), 34–47.

Brown, Herbert A., 'A comparative dictionary of Orokolo Gulf of Papua', (Pacific Linguistics, C-84) (Canberra: Pacific Linguistics, 1986).

Bynon, Theodora, *Historical Linguistics* (Cambridge: Cambridge University Press, 1977).

Callaghan, Catherine A. and Geoffrey Gamble, 'Borrowing', in Ives Goddard (ed.), *Handbook of North American Indians*, vol. 17 (Washington, DC: Smithsonian Institution, 1997), pp. 111–16.

Campbell, Lyle, 'Distant genetic relationships and the Maya-Chipaya hypothesis', *Anthropological Linguistics* 15:3 (1973), 113–35. (Reprinted: *Special Issue: A Retrospective of the Journal of Anthropological Linguistics: Selected Papers, 1959–1985. Anthropological Linguistics* 35:1–4 (1993), 66–89.)

Campbell, Lyle, 'Language contact and sound change', in William M. Christie Jr (ed.), *Current Progress on Historical Linguistics: Proceedings of the Second International Conference on Historical Linguistics* (Amsterdam: North Holland, 1976), pp. 111–94.

Campbell, Lyle, *Quichean Linguistic Prehistory*, University of California Publications in Linguistics, 81 (Berkeley and Los Angeles: University of California Press, 1977).

Campbell, Lyle, 'Quichean prehistory: linguistic contributions', in Nora C. England (ed.), *Papers in Mayan Linguistics* (Columbia, MO: Department of Anthropology, University of Missouri, 1978), pp. 25–54.

Campbell, Lyle, 'The implications of Mayan historical linguistics for glyphic research', in John Justeson and Lyle Campbell (eds), *Phoneticism in Mayan Hieroglyphic Writing*, Institute for Mesoamerican Studies, pub. 9 (Albany: State University of New York Press, 1984), pp. 1–16.

Campbell, Lyle, 'Areal linguistics and its implications for historical linguistic theory', in Jacek Fisiak (ed.), *Proceedings of the Sixth International Conference of Historical Linguistics* (Amsterdam: John Benjamins, 1985a), pp. 25–48.

Bibliography

Campbell, Lyle, *The Pipil Language of El Salvador* (Berlin: Mouton de Gruyter, 1985b).

Campbell, Lyle, *The Linguistics of Southeast Chiapas*, Papers of the New World Archaeological Foundation, 51 (Provo, UT: The New World Archaeological Foundation, 1988).

Campbell, Lyle, 'Syntactic reconstruction and Finno-Ugric', in Henning Andersen and Konrad Koerner (eds), *Historical Linguistics 1987* (Amsterdam: John Benjamins, 1990a), pp. 51–94.

Campbell, Lyle, 'Philological studies and Mayan languages', in Jacek Fisiak (ed.), *Historical Linguistics and Philology* (Berlin: Mouton de Gruyter, 1990b), pp. 87–105.

Campbell, Lyle, 'Some grammaticalization changes in Estonian', in Elizabeth C. Traugott and Bernd Heine (eds), *Approaches to Grammaticalization, vol. I: Theoretical and Methodological Issues* (Amsterdam: John Benjamins, 1991), pp. 285–99.

Campbell, Lyle, 'On proposed universals of grammatical borrowing', in Henk Aertsen and Robert Jeffers (eds), *Historical Linguistics 1989: Papers from the 9th International Conference on Historical Linguistics* (Amsterdam: John Benjamins, 1993a), pp. 91–109.

Campbell, Lyle, 'Linguistic reconstruction and unwritten languages', in R. E. Asher and J. M. Y. Simpson (eds), *Encyclopedia of Language and Linguistics* (London: Pergamon Press, 1994), pp. 3,475–80.

Campbell, Lyle, 'On sound change and challenges to regularity', in Mark Durie and Malcolm Ross (eds), *The Comparative Method Reviewed: Regularity and Irregularity in Language Change* (Oxford: Oxford University Press, 1996), pp. 72–89.

Campbell, Lyle, *American Indian Languages: The Historical Linguistics of Native America* (Oxford: Oxford University Press, 1997a).

Campbell, Lyle, 'On the linguistic prehistory of Finno-Ugric', in Raymond Hickey and Stanisław Puppel (eds), *Language History and Linguistic Modelling: A Festschrift for Jacek Fisiak on his 60th Birthday* (Berlin: Mouton de Gruyter, 1997b), pp. 829–61.

Campbell, Lyle, 'Nostratic: a personal assessment', in Brian Joseph and Joe Salmons (eds), *Nostratic: Sifting the Evidence and Status* (Amsterdam: John Benjamins, 1998), pp. 107–52.

Campbell, Lyle, 'Nostratic and linguistic palaeontology in methodological perspective', in Colin Renfrew and Daniel Nettle (eds), *Nostratic: Evaluating a Linguistic Macrofamily* (Cambridge: The McDonald Institute for Archaeological Research, 1999), pp. 179–230.

Campbell, Lyle (ed.), *Grammaticalization: a critical assessment.* Special issue of *Language Sciences*, vol. 23, 2–3 (2001).

Campbell, Lyle, 'How to show languages are related: methods for distant genetic relationship', in Brian D. Joseph and Richard D. Janda (eds), *Handbook of Historical Linguistics* (Oxford: Blackwell, 2003), pp. 262–82.

423

Campbell, Lyle, Vit Bubenik and Leslie Saxon, 'Word order universals: refinements and clarifications', *Canadian Journal of Linguistics* 33 (1988), 209–30.

Campbell, Lyle and Terrence Kaufman, 'A linguistic look at the Olmecs', *American Antiquity* 41 (1976), 80–9.

Campbell, Lyle and Terrence Kaufman, 'Mayan linguistics: where are we now?', *Annual Review of Anthropology* 14 (1985), 187–98.

Campbell, Lyle, Terrence Kaufman and Thomas Smith-Stark, 'Mesoamerica as a linguistic area', *Language* 62 (1986), 530–70.

Campbell, Lyle and Ronald Langacker, 'Proto-Aztecan vowels' parts 1–3, *International Journal of American Linguistics* 44:2 (1978), 85–102, 44:3 (1978), 197–210, 44:4 (1978), 262–79.

Campbell, Lyle and David Oltrogge, 'Proto-Tol (Jicaque)', *International Journal of American Linguistics* 46 (1980), 205–23.

Campbell, Lyle and Jon Ringen, 'Teleology and the explanation of sound change', in Wolfgang U. Dressler, Oskar E. Pfeiffer and John R. Rennison (eds), *Phonologica* (Innsbruck: Innsbrucker Beiträge zur Sprachwissenschaft, 1981), pp. 57–68.

Canfield, Lincoln D., *Spanish Pronunciation in the Americas* (Chicago: University of Chicago Press, 1982).

Carpelan, Christian, 'Late palaeolithic and Mesolithic settlement of the European north – possible linguistic implications', in Christian Carpelan, Asko Parpola and Petteri Koskikallio (eds), *Early Contacts between Uralic and Indo-European: Linguistics and Archaeological Considerations* (Mémoires de la Société Finno-Ougrienne, 242) (Helsinki: Finno-Ugrian Society, 2001), pp. 37–53.

Cerrón-Palomino, Rodolfo, *Lingüística quechua*, Biblioteca de la tradición oral andina, 8 (Cuzco: Centro de Estudios Rurales Andinos 'Bartolomé de las Casas', 1987).

Cerrón-Palomino, Rodolfo, *Lingüística aimara.* (Cuzco: Centro de Estudios Regionales Aninos 'Bartolomé de Las Casas', 2000).

Collinge, N. E., *The Laws of Indo-European* (Amsterdam: John Benjamins, 1985).

Corominas, Joan, *Diccionario crítico etimológico de la lengua castellana*, 4 vols (Madrid: Gredos, 1974).

Corominas, Joan and José Pascual, *Diccionario crítico etimológico castellano e hispanico*, 6 vols (Madrid: Gredos, 1980).

Cortelazzo, Manlio and Paolo Zolli, *Dizionario etimologico della lingua italiana* (Bologna: Zanichelli, 1979–88).

Croft, William, *Explaining Language Change: An Evolutionary Approach* (Harlow: Longman, 2000).

Crowley, Terry, *An Introduction to Historical Linguistics*, 3rd edn (Auckland: Oxford University Press, 1997).

Dahl, Östen and Maria Koptjevskaja-Tamm (eds), *The Circum-Baltic Languages: Typology and Contact* (Amsterdam: John Benjamins, 2001).

Darmesteter, Arsène, *A Historical French Grammar* (London: Macmillan, 1922).

Dauzat, Albert, *La Géographie linguistique*, 9 cartes (Paris: Flammarion, 1822).

Delbrück, Berthold, *Introduction to the Study of Language: A Critical Survey of the History and Methods of Comparative Philology of the Indo-European Languages* (1882), English trans. of *Einleitung in das Sprachstudium: Ein Beitrag zur Methodik der vergleichenden Sprachforschung* (Leipzig: Breitkopf & Härtel, 1880).

Ebert, Robert Peter, *Historische Syntax des Deutschen* (Stuttgart: Sammlung Metzler, 1978).

Emeneau, Murray B., *Language and Linguistic Area: Essays by Murray B. Emeneau*, selected and introduced by Anwar S. Dil (Stanford: Stanford University Press, 1980).

Ferguson, Charles, 'The Ethiopian language area', in M. L. Bender, J. D. Bowen, R. L. Cooper and C. A. Ferguson (eds), *Language in Ethiopia* (Oxford: Oxford University Press, 1976), pp. 63–76.

Fisher, John H. and Diane Bornstein, *In form of speche is chaunge: Readings in the History of the English Language* (Englewood Cliffs, NJ: Prentice-Hall, 1974).

Fleischman, Suzanne, 'The Romance languages', in William Bright (ed.), *International Encyclopedia of Linguistics*, 4 vols (Oxford: Oxford University Press, 1992), vol. 3, pp. 337–43.

Fleming, Harold C., 'Towards a definitive classification of the world's languages' (Review of *A Guide to the World's Languages* by Merritt Ruhlen), *Diachronica* 4 (1987), 159–223.

Fogelberg, Paul (ed.), *Pohjan poluilla: Suomalaisten juuret nykytutkimuksen mukaan [On Paths of the North: The Roots of the Finns according to Current Research]*', Bildrag till kännedom av Finlands natur och folk, 153 (Helsinki: Finnish Society of Science and Letters, 1999).

Fowler, Catherine S., 'Some ecological clues to Proto-Numic homelands', in D. D. Fowler (ed.), *Great Basin Cultural Ecology: A Symposium*, Desert Research Institute publications in the social sciences, 8 (Reno: University of Nevada, 1972), pp. 105–21.

Fowler, Catherine S., 'Some lexical clues to Uto-Aztecan prehistory', *International Journal of American Linguistics* 49 (1983), 224–57.

Friedrich, Paul, *Proto-Indo-European Trees: The Arboreal System of a Prehistoric People* (Chicago: University of Chicago Press, 1970).

Gabelentz, Georg von der, *Die Sprachwissenschaft: ihre Aufgaben, Methoden, und bisherigen Ergebnisse* (Leipzig: T. O. Weigel Nachfolger, 1891).

Garrett, Andrew, 'A new model of Indo-European subgrouping and dispersal', in Steve S. Chang, Lily Liaw and Josef Ruppenhofer (eds), *Proceedings of* the *Twenty-fifth Annual Meeting of the Berkeley Linguistics Society* (Berkeley: Berkeley Linguistics Society, 1999), pp. 146–56.

Gildea, Spike, 'The development of tense markers from demonstrative pronouns in Panare (Cariban)', *Studies in Language* 17 (1993), 53–73.

Gilliéron, Jules, *Pathologie et thérapeutique verbales* (Paris: Champion, 1921).

Gilliéron, Jules and Mario Roques, *Étude de géographie linguistique* (Paris: Champion, 1912).

Gimbutas, Marija, 'The Indo-Europeans: archaeological problems', *American Anthropologist* 65 (1963), 815–36.

Goddard, Ives, 'The West-to-East cline in Algonquian dialectology', in William Cowan (ed.), *Actes du vingt-cinquième congrès des algonquinistes* (Ottawa: Carleton University, 1994), pp. 187–211.

Goodman, Morris, 'Some questions on the classification of African languages', *International Journal of American Linguistics* 36 (1970), 117–22.

Greenberg, Joseph H., *Languages of Africa*, Publications of the Research Center in Anthropology, Folklore, and Linguistics, no. 25 (Bloomington: Indiana University Press, 1963).

Greenberg, Joseph H., *Language in the Americas* (Stanford: Stanford University Press, 1987).

Grimm, Jakob and Wilhelm Grimm, *Deutsches Wörterbuch* (Leipzig: Hirzel, 1854).

Grünthal, Riho and Tapani Salminen (eds), *Geographical Distribution of the Uralic Languages* [map] (Helsinki: Finno-Ugrian Society, 1993).

Haas, Mary R., *The Prehistory of Languages* (The Hague: Mouton, 1969a).

Haas, Mary R., 'Internal reconstruction of the Nootka-Nitinat pronominal suffixes', *International Journal of American Linguistics* 35 (1969b), 108–24.

Hajdú, Péter, 'Finnougrische Urheimatforschung', *Ural-Altaische Jahrbücher* 41 (1969), 252–64.

Hajdú, Péter, *Finno-Ugric Languages and Peoples* (London: André Deutsch, 1975).

Häkkinen, Kaisa, 'Wäre es schon an der Zeit, den Stammbaum zu fallen? Theorien über die gegenseitigen Verwandtschaftsbeziehungen der finnisch-ugrischen Sprachen', *Ural-Altaische Jahrbücher* 4 (1984), 1–4.

Häkkinen, Kaisa, 'Prehistoric Finno-Ugric culture in the light of historical lexicology', in Christian Carpelan, Asko Parpola and Petteri Koskikallio (eds), *Early Contacts between Uralic and Indo-European: Linguistics and Archaeological Considerations* (Mémoires de la Société Finno-Ougrienne, 242) (Helsinki: Finno-Ugrian Society 2001), pp. 169–86.

Harris, Alice C. and Lyle Campbell, *Historical Syntax in Cross-linguistic Perspective* (Cambridge: Cambridge University Press, 1995).

Heath, Jeffrey, *Linguistic Diffusion in Arnhem Land*, Australian aboriginal studies research and regional studies, no. 13 (Canberra: Australian Institute of Aboriginal Studies, 1978).

Heine, Bernd and Mechthild Reh, *Grammaticalization and Reanalysis in African Languages* (Hamburg: Buske, 1984).

Heine, Bernd and Tania Kuteva, *World Lexicon of Grammaticalization* (Cambridge: Cambridge University Press, 2002).

Hock, Hans Henrich, *Principles of Historical Linguistics* (Berlin: Mouton de Gruyter, 1986).

Hock, Hans Henrich and Brian D. Joseph, *Language History, Language Change, and Language Relationship: An Introduction to Historical and Comparative Linguistics* (Berlin: Walter de Gruyter, 1996).

Hogg, Richard M., 'Phonology and morphology', in Richard M. Hogg (ed.), *The Cambridge History of the English Language*, vol. 1, *The Beginnings to 1066* (Cambridge: Cambridge University Press, 1992), pp. 67–167.

Holloway, Charles E., *Dialect Death: The Case of Brule Spanish*, Studies in bilingualism, 13 (Amsterdam: John Benjamins, 1997).

Hopper, Paul J. and Elizabeth Closs Traugott, *Grammaticalization* (Cambridge: Cambridge University Press, 1993).

Horrocks, Geoffrey, *Greek: A History of the Language and its Speakers* (London: Longman, 1997).

Ihalainen, Ossi, 'The dialects of England since 1776', in Robert Burchfield (ed.), *The Cambridge History of the English Language*, vol. 5: *English in Britain and Overseas: Origins and Development* (Cambridge: Cambridge University Press, 1994), pp.197–274.

Ilari, Rodolfo, *Lingüística Românica*, 3rd edn (São Paulo:Editora Ática, 2001).

Jakobson, Roman, 'Why "mama" and "papa"?', in Bernard Kaplan and Seymour Wapner (eds), *Perspectives in Psychological Theory* (New York: International Universities Press, 1960), pp. 21–9. (Reprinted: *Roman Jakobson: Selected Writings*, vol. 1, *Phonological Studies* (The Hague: Mouton, 1962), pp. 538–45.)

Janhunen, Juha, 'Uralilaisen kantakielen sanastosta [On the vocabulary of the Uralic proto-language]', *Journal de la Société Finno-Ougrienne* 77 (1981), 219–74.

Janhunen, Juha, 'On the structure of Proto-Uralic', *Finno-Ugrische Forschungen* 44 (1982), 23–42.

Janhunen, Juha, 'On the paradigms of Uralic comparative studies', *Finno-Ugrische Forschungen* 56 (2001), 29–41.

Janson, Tore, *Speak: A Short History of Languages* (Oxford: Oxford University Press, 2002).

Jasanoff, Jay H., *Hittite and the Indo-European Verb* (Oxford: Oxford University Press, 2003).

Jeffers, Robert J. and Ilse Lehiste, *Principles and Methods for Historical Linguistics* (Cambridge, MA: MIT Press, 1979).

Jespersen, Otto, *Language, its Nature, Development, and Origin* (New York: W. W. Norton & Co., 1964).

Joki, Aulis J., *Uralier und Indogermanen*, Suomalais-ugrilaisen Seuran toimituksia, 151 (Helsinki: Suomalais-ugrilaisen Seura, 1973).

Joos, Martin, 'Preface', in idem (ed.), *Readings in Linguistics: The Development of Descriptive Linguistics in America since 1925*, 2nd edn (New York: American Council of Learned Societies, 1958), pp. v–vii.

Joseph, Brian, *Morphology and Universals in Syntactic Change: Evidence from Medieval and Modern Greek* (New York: Garland Publishers, 1990).

Joseph, Brian, 'Balkan languages', in William Bright (ed.), *International Encyclopedia of Linguistics*, 4 vols (Oxford: Oxford University Press, 1992), vol. 1, pp. 153–5.

Joseph, Brian D. and Richard D. Janda (eds), *The Handbook of Historical Linguistics* (Oxford: Blackwell, 2003).

Justeson, John S., William Norman, Lyle Campbell and Terrence Kaufman, *The Foreign Impact on Lowland Mayan Languages and Script*, Middle American Research Institute, publication 53 (New Orleans: Tulane University, 1985).

Kacirk, Jeffrey, *Forgotten English* (Rohnert Park, CA: Pomegranate Communications, 1999).

Kaiser, Mark and Vitaly Shevoroshkin, 'Nostratic', *Annual Review of Anthropology* 17 (1988), 309–30.

Kaufman, Terrence, 'Archaeological and linguistic correlations in Mayaland and associated areas of Meso-America', *World Archaeology* 8 (1976), 101–18.

Kettunen, Lauri, *Suomen murteet II: Murrealueet* [*Finnish Dialects II: Dialect Areas*] (Helsinki: Suomalaisen Kirjallisuuden Seura, 1930).

Kettunen, Lauri, *Suomen murteet III: Murrekartasto* [*Finnish Dialects III: Dialect Atlas*], 3rd 'abridged' edn, (Helsinki: Suomalaisen Kirjallisuuden Seura, 1969).

Kimball, Geoffrey, 'A critique of Muskogean, "Gulf", and Yukian material in *Language in the Americas*', *International Journal of American Linguistics* 58 (1992), 447–501.

King, Robert, *Generative Grammar and Historical Linguistics* (Englewood Cliffs, NJ: Prentice-Hall, 1969).

Kinkade, M. Dale, 'Prehistory of the native languages of the Northwest Coast', in *The North Pacific to 1600*, 2 vols (Portland: The Oregon Historical Society Press, 1991), vol. 1, pp. 137–58.

Kiparsky, Paul, *Explanation in Phonology* (Dordrecht: Foris, 1982).

Klima, Edward, 'Relatedness between grammatical systems', *Language* 40 (1964), 1–20.

Kluge, Friedrich, *Etymologisches Wörterbuch der deutschen Sprache*, 24th edn [1st edn 1883] (Berlin: de Gruyter, 2002).

Koch, Harold, 'Pama-Nyungan reflexes in the Arandic languages', in Darrell Tryon and Michael Walsh (eds), *Boundary Rider: Essays in Honour of*

Geoffrey O'Grady, Pacific Linguistics C-136 (Canberra: Research School of Pacific Studies, Australian National University, 1997), pp. 271–301.

Koivulehto, Jorma, 'The earliest contacts between Indo-European and Uralic speakers in the light of lexical loans', in Christian Carpelan, Asko Parpola and Petteri Koskikallio (eds), *Early Contacts between Uralic and Indo-European: Linguistics and Archaeological Considerations* (Mémoires de la Société Finno-Ougrienne, 242) (Helsinki: Finno-Ugrian Society, 2001), pp. 235–63.

Koptjevskaja-Tamm, Maria and Bernhard Wälchli, 'The Circum-Baltic languages: an areal-typological approach', in Östen Dahl and Maria Koptjevskaja-Tamm (eds), *The Circum-Baltic Languages: Typology and Contact* (Amsterdam: John Benjamins, 2001), pp. 615-761.

Korhonen, Mikko, *Johdatus Lapin kielen historiaan* [*Introduction to the History of the Lapp Language*] (Helsinki: Suomalaisen Kirjallisuuden Seura, 1981).

Korhonen, Mikko, 'Suomalaisten suomalais-ugrilainen tausta historiallis-vertailevan kielitieteen valossa [The Finno-Ugric background of the Finns in the light of comparative-historical linguistics]', in Jarl Gallén (ed.), *Suomen väestön esihistorialliset juuret*, Bidrag till kännedom av Finlands natur och folk, Utgivna av Finska Vetenskaps-Societeten, 131 (Helsinki: Finska Vetenskaps-Societeten, 1984), pp. 55–71.

Krause, Wolfgang, *Handbuch des Gotischen*, 3rd edn (Munich: Beck, 1968).

Kuhn, Franz Felix Adalbert, *Zur ältesten Geschichte der indogermanischen Völker* (Berlin: Berliner Real-Gymnasium, 1845).

Kuryłowicz, Jerzy, 'Zur Vorgeschichte des germanischen Verbalsystems', in *Beiträge zur Sprachwissenschaft, Volkskunde und Literaturforschung: Wolfgang Steinitz zum 60. Geburtstag* (Berlin: Akademie-Verlag, 1965), pp. 242–7.

Labov, William (ed.), *Locating Language in Time and Space* (New York: Academic Press, 1980).

Labov, William, *Principles of Linguistic Change: Internal Factors* (Oxford: Blackwell, 1994, 2001).

Lapesa, Rafael, *Historia de la lengua española*, 9th edn (Madrid: Gredos, 1981).

Lass, Roger, *On Explaining Language Change* (Cambridge: Cambridge University Press, 1980).

Lass, Roger, 'Phonology and morphology', in Norman Blake (ed.), *The Cambridge History of the English Language*, vol. 2, *1066–1476* (Cambridge: Cambridge University Press, 1992), pp. 23–155.

Lehiste, Ilse, *Lectures on Language Contact* (Cambridge, MA: MIT Press, 1988).

Lehmann, Christian, *Thoughts on Grammaticalization* (Munich: Lincom Europa, 1995).

Lehmann, Winfred P., *Historical Linguistics: An Introduction* (New York: Holt, 1962).

Lehtiranta, Juhani, *Yhteissaamelainen sanasto* [*Common Saami Vocabulary*] (Mémoires de la Société Finno-Ougrienne, 200) (Helsinki: Finno-Ugrian Society, 1989).

Lepelley, René, *Le parler normand du Val de Saire* (Caen: Musée de Normandie, 1971).

Lightfoot, David, *Principles of Diachronic Syntax* (Cambridge: Cambridge University Press, 1979).

Lightfoot, David, *How to Set Parameters: Arguments from Language Change* (Cambridge, MA: MIT Press, 1991).

Lord, Robert, *Comparative Linguistics*, 2nd edn (London: English Universities Press, 1974).

Maclagan, Margaret A. and Elizabeth Gordon, 'Out of the AIR and into the EAR: another view of the New Zealand diphthong merger', *Language Variation and Change* 8 (1996), 125–47.

Mallory, J. P., *In Search of the Indo-Europeans: Language, Archaeology, and Myth* (London: Thames and Hudson, 1989).

Mallory, J. P., 'Uralics and Indo-Europeans: problems of time and space', in Christian Carpelan, Asko Parpola and Petteri Koskikallio (eds), *Early Contacts Between Uralic and Indo-European: Linguistics and Archaeological Considerations* (Mémoires de la Société Finno-Ougrienne, 242) (Helsinki: Finno-Ugrian Society, 2001), pp. 345–66.

Mallory, J. P. and D.Q. Adams (eds), *Encyclopedia of Indo-European Culture* (London: Fitzroy Dearborn, 1997).

Martinet, André, *Économie des changements phonétiques: traité de phonologie diachronique*, 3rd edn [1st edn 1955] (Berne: A. Francke, 1970).

Masica, Colin P., *The Indo-Aryan Languages* (Cambridge: Cambridge University Press, 1991).

Meillet, Antoine, 'L'évolution des formes grammaticales', *Scientia* 12:26 (Milan, 1912). (Reprinted: *Linguistique historique et linguistique générale* (Paris: Champion, 1948), pp. 130–48.)

Meillet, Antoine, 'Le problème de la parenté des langues', *Scientia* 15:35 (1914). (Reprinted: *Linguistique historique et linguistique générale* (Paris: Champion, 1948), pp. 76–102.)

Meillet, Antoine, *Linguistique historique et linguistique générale*, Société Linguistique de Paris, Collection Linguistique, 8 (Paris: Champion, 1948).

Meillet, Antoine, *The Comparative Method in Historical Linguistics* (trans. of *La Méthode comparative en linguistique historique*, 1925, reissued 1966) (Paris: Champion, 1967).

Menner, Robert, 'The conflict of homonyms in English', *Language* 12 (1936), 229–44.

Metcalf, George J., 'The Indo-European hypothesis in the sixteenth and seventeenth centuries', in Dell Hymes (ed.), *Studies in the History of Linguistics: Traditions and Paradigms* (Bloomington: Indiana University Press, 1974), pp. 233–57.

Bibliography

Meyer-Lübke, Wilhelm, *Romanisches Etymologisches Wörterbuch*, 5th edn (Heidelberg: Winter, 1972).

Milroy, James, *Linguistic Variation and Change: On the Historical Sociolinguistics of English* (Oxford: Blackwell, 1992).

Müller, Max, *Lectures on the Science of Language* (New York: Charles Scribner and Company, 1866).

Munro, Pamela, *Slang U* (New York: Harmony Books, 1989).

Mutaka, Ngessimo N., *An Introduction to African Linguistics* (Munich: Lincom Europa, 2000).

Newman, Paul, 'Comparative linguistics', in Bernd Heine and Derek Nurse, *African Languages: An Introduction* (Cambridge: Cambridge University Press, 2000), pp. 259–71.

Öhmann, Emil, 'Über Homonymie und Homonyme im Deutschen', *Suomalaisen Tiedeakatemian Toimituksia*, series B, 32 (1934), 1–143.

Olson, Ronald D., 'Mayan affinities with Chipaya of Bolivia I: Correspondences', *International Journal of American Linguistics* 30 (1964), 313–24.

Olson, Ronald D., 'Mayan affinities with Chipaya of Bolivia II: Cognates', *International Journal of American Linguistics* 31 (1965), 29–38.

Osthoff, Hermann and Karl Brugmann, *Morphologische Untersuchungen auf dem Gebiete der indogermanischen Sprachen* (Leipzig: S. Hirzel, 1878).

Oxford English Dictionary, 2nd edn [1st edn 1971] (Oxford: Oxford University Press, 1989).

Palmer, Leonard R., *Descriptive and Comparative Linguistics: A Critical Introduction* (London: Faber & Faber, 1972).

Paul, Hermann, *Prinzipien der Sprachgeschichte*, 5th edn [1st edn 1880] (Tübingen: Max Niemeyer, 1920).

Penny, Ralph, *A History of the Spanish Language* (Cambridge: Cambridge University Press, 1991).

Pictet, Adolphe, *Les Origines indo-européennes, ou, les Aryas primitifs: Essai de paléontologie linguistique* (Paris: J. Cherbuliez, 1859–1863).

Pierce, Joe E., 'The validity of genetic linguistics', *Linguistics* 13 (1965), 25–33.

Pinker, Steven, *The Language Instinct* (New York: W. Morrow & Co., 1994).

Polenz, Peter von, *Geschichte der deutschen Sprache* (Berlin: Walter de Gruyter, 1977).

Rankin, Robert L., 'Review of *Language in the Americas*, by Joseph H. Greenberg', *International Journal of American Linguistics* 58 (1992), 324–51.

Ravila, Paavo, 'Suomen suku ja suomen kansa [The Finnish stock and the Finnish people]', *Suomen historian käsikirja I [Handbook of the History of Finnish I]* (Porvoo: Werner Söderström, 1949).

Ravila, Paavo, *Johtadus kielihistoriaan [Introduction to Language History]* (Helsinki: Suomalaisen Kirjallisuuden Seura, 1966).

Rédei, Károly, *Uralisches etymologisches Wörterbuch* (7 fascicles) (Budapést: Akadémiai Kiadó, 1986–8).

Resnik, Melvyn C., *Introducción a la historia de la lengua española* (Washington, DC: Georgetown University Press, 1981).

Ringe, Donald A. Jr, 'On calculating the factor of chance in language comparison', *Transactions of the American Philosophical Society* 82:1 (1992), 1–110.

Ringe, Donald A. Jr, 'How hard is it to match CVC-roots?', *Transactions of the Philological Society* 97 (1999), 213–44.

Ringe, Donald Jr, Tandy Warnow and Ann Taylor, 'Indo-European computational cladistics', *Transactions of the Philological Society* 100 (2002), 59–129.

Róna-Tas, András, 'Turkic influence on the Uralic languages', in Denis Sinor (ed.), *The Uralic Languages: Description, History, and Foreign Influences* (Leiden: Brill, 1988), pp. 742–80.

Ross, Malcolm D., Andrew Pawley and Meredith Osmond (eds), *The Lexicon of Proto Oceanic: The Culture and Environment of Ancestral Oceanic Society*, 1: *Material Culture* (Pacific Linguistics, C-152) (Canberra: Pacific Linguistics, 1998).

Ruhlen, Merritt, *On the Origin of Languages: Studies in Linguistic Taxonomy* (Stanford: Stanford University Press, 1994).

Salminen, Tapani, 'The rise of the Finno-Ugric language family', in Christian Carpelan, Asko Parpola and Petteri Koskikallio (eds), *Early Contacts between Uralic and Indo-European: Linguistic and Archaeological Considerations* (Mémoires de la Société Finno-Ougrienne, 242) (Helsinki: Finno-Ugrian Society, 2001), pp. 385–96.

Sammallahti, Pekka, 'Saamelaisten esihistoriallinen tausta kielitieteen valossa [The prehistorical background of the Saami in the light of linguistics]', in Jarl Gallén (ed.), *Suomen väestön esihistorialliset juuret*, Bidrag till kännedom av Finlands natur och folk, Utgivna av Finska Vetenskaps-Societeten, 131 (Helsinki: Finska Vetenskaps-Societeten, 1984), pp. 137–56.

Sammallahti, Pekka, 'Historical phonology of the Uralic languages: with special reference to Samoyed, Ugric, and Permic', in Denis Sinor (ed.), *The Uralic Languages: Description, History, and Foreign Influences* (Leiden: Brill, 1988), pp. 478–554.

Sammallahti, Pekka, *The Saami Languages: An Introduction* (Karasjohka: Davvi Girji, 1998).

Sammallahti, Pekka, 'The Indo-European loanwords in Saami', in Christian Carpelan, Asko Parpola and Petteri Koskikallio (eds), *Early Contacts between Uralic and Indo-European: Linguistic and Archaeological Considerations* (Mémoires de la Société Finno-Ougrienne, 242) (Helsinki: Finno-Ugrian Society, 2001), pp. 397–415.

Sandfeld, Kristian, *Linguistique balkanique: problèmes et résultats* (Paris: Champion, 1930).

Bibliography

Sapir, Edward, 'Wiyot and Yurok, Algonkin languages of California', *American Anthropologist* 15 (1913), 617–46.

Sapir, Edward, 'The Hokan affinity of Subtiaba in Nicaragua', *American Anthropologist* 27 (1925), 402–35, 491–527.

Sapir, Edward, 'The concept of phonetic law as tested in primitive languages by Leonard Bloomfield', in S. Rice (ed.), *Methods in Social Science: A Case Book* (Chicago: University of Chicago Press, 1931), pp. 297–306. (Reprinted in David G. Mandelbaum (ed.), *Selected Writings of Edward Sapir in Language, Culture, and Personality* (Berkeley: University of California Press, 1949), pp. 73–82.)

Sapir, Edward, 'Time perspective in aboriginal American culture: a study in method', in David G. Mandelbaum (ed.), *Selected Writings of Edward Sapir in Language, Culture, and Personality* (Berkeley: University of California Press, 1949), pp. 389–467. (Original ed. Department of Mines, Geological survey, Memoir no. 90) (Ottawa: Government Printing Bureau, 1916).)

Sayce, Archibald Henry, *The Principles of Comparative Philology* (London: Trübner, 1874).

Schleicher, August, *Compendium der vergleichenden Grammatik der indogermanischen Sprachen: Kurzer Abriss einer Laut- und Formenlehre der indogermanischen Ursprache* (Weimar: Hermann Böhlau, 1861–2).

Schmidt, Johannes, *Die Verwandtschaftsverhältnisse der indogermanischen Sprachen* (Weimar: Böhlau, 1872).

Schrader, Otto, *Sprachvergleichung und Urgeschichte: Linguistisch-historische Beiträge zur Erforschung des indogermanischen Altertums* (Jena: Costenoble, 1883). (English translation: *Prehistoric Antiquities of the Aryan peoples: A Manual of Comparative Philology and the Earliest Culture* (London: C. Griffin and Company, 1890).

Schuchardt, Hugo, *Vokalismus*, vol. 3 (Leipzig: Teubner, 1868).

Siebert, Frank T. Jr, 'The original home of the Proto-Algonquian people', Contributions to Anthropology: Linguistics 1, *National Museum of Canada Bulletin* 214 (1967), 13–47.

Snow, Dean R., 'The archaeological implications of the Proto-Algonquian Urheimat', in William Cowan (ed.), *Papers of the Seventh Algonquian Conference* (Ottawa: Carleton University, 1976), pp. 339–46.

Spaulding, Robert K., *How Spanish Grew* (Berkeley: University of California Press, 1965).

Suhonen, Seppo, 'Uralilainen alkukoti [The Uralic homeland]', in Paul Fogelberg (ed), *Pohjan poluilla: Suomalaisten juuret nykytutkimuksen mukaan [On Paths of the North: The Roots of the Finns according to Current Research]*, Bildrag till kännedom av Finlands natur och folk, 153 (Helsinki: Finnish Society of Science and Letters, 1999), pp. 240-4.

Swadesh, Morris, 'Diffusional cumulation and archaic residue as historical explanation', *Southwestern Journal of Anthropology* 7 (1951), 1–21.

Swadesh, Morris, 'Mosan I: a problem of remote common origin', *International Journal of American Linguistics* 19 (1953), 26–44.

Swadesh, Morris, 'Perspectives and problems of Amerindian comparative linguistics', *Word* 10 (1954), 306–32.

Sweet, Henry, *The History of Language* (London: J. M. Dent & Co., 1900).

Sweetser, Eve, *From Etymology to Pragmatics: Metaphorical and Cultural Aspects of Semantic Structure* (Cambridge: Cambridge University Press, 1990).

Teeter, Karl V., 'Algonquian languages and genetic relationship', in Horace G. Lunt (ed.), *Proceedings of the 9th International Congress of Linguists* (The Hague: Mouton, 1964), pp. 1,026–33.

Thomason, Sarah G., *Language Contact: An Introduction* (Edinburgh: Edinburgh University Press, 2001).

Thomason, Sarah Grey and Terrence Kaufman, *Language Contact, Creolization, and Genetic Linguistics* (Berkeley: University of California Press, 1988).

Thompson, J. Eric S., *Maya History and Religion* (Norman: University of Oklahoma Press, 1970).

Tosco, Mauro, 'Is there an "Ethiopian Language Area"?' *Anthropological Linguistics* 42 (2000), 329–65.

Trask, R. L., *Historical Linguistics* (London: Arnold, 1996).

Traugott, Elizabeth Closs, 'On the rise of epistemic meanings in English: an example of subjectification in semantic change', *Language* 65 (1989), 31–55.

Traugott, Elizabeth Closs and Richard B. Dasher, *Regularity in Semantic Change* (Cambridge: Cambridge University Press, 2002).

Traugott, Elizabeth Closs and Bernd Heine, 'Introduction', in Elizabeth Closs Traugott and Bernd Heine (eds), *Approaches to Grammaticalization*, Typological studies in language, 19 (Amsterdam: John Benjamins, 1991), pp. 1–14.

Traugott, Elizabeth Closs and Ekkehard König, 'The semantics-pragmatics of grammaticalization revisited', in Elizabeth Closs Traugott and Bernd Heine (eds), *Approaches to Grammaticalization* (Amsterdam: John Benjamins, 1991), vol. 1, pp. 189–218.

Vendryes, Joseph, *Le langage: introduction linguistique à l'histoire* (Paris: La Renaissance du Livre [re-edition 1968]).

Wakelin, Martyn, *The Archaeology of English* (Totowa, NJ: Barnes & Noble, 1988).

Wang, William, 'Competing sound changes as a cause of residue', *Language* 45 (1969), 9–25.

Watkins, Calvert, 'Indo-European and the Indo-Europeans', *American Heritage Dictionary* (Boston, MA: Houghton Mifflin, 1969), pp. 1,496–502.

Watkins, Calvert, *The American Heritage Dictionary of Indo-European Roots* (Boston, MA: Houghton Mifflin Co., 1985, 2nd edn, 2000).

Watkins, Calvert, 'Etymologies, equations, and comparanda: types and values, and criteria for judgement', in Philip Baldi (ed.), *Linguistic Change and Reconstruction Methodology* (Berlin: Mouton de Gruyter, 1990), pp. 289–303.

Weinreich, Uriel, *Languages in Contact: Findings and Problems*, Publications of the Linguistic Circle of New York, 1 (New York, 1953). (9th printing, The Hague: Mouton.)

Weinreich, Uriel, William Labov and Marvin Herzog, 'Empirical foundations for a theory of language change', in Winfred P. Lehmann and Yakov Malkiel (eds), *Directions for Historical Linguistics* (Austin: University of Texas Press, 1968), pp. 95–195.

Wells, J.C., *Accents of English I: An Introduction* (Cambridge: Cambridge University Press, 1982).

Wessén, Elias, *Språkhistoria I: ljudlära och ordböjningslära* (Stockholm: Almqvist & Wiksell, 1969).

Winteler, J., *Die Kerenzer Mundart des Kantons Glarus in ihren Grundzügen dargestellt* (Leipzig: Winter, 1876).

Wright, Larry, *Teleological Explanation* (Berkeley: University of California Press, 1976).

Wundt, Wilhelm, *Völkerpsychologie. Eine Untersuchung der Entwicklungsgesetze von Sprache, Mythus und Sitte*, vol. 1, *Die Sprache* (Leipzig: W. Engelmann, 1900).

Zeps, Valdis, *Latvian and Finnic Linguistic Convergence*, Uralic and Altaic Series, 9 (Bloomington: Indiana University Press, 1962).

Zvelebil, Kamil V., *Dravidian Linguistics: An Introduction* (Pondicherry: Pondicherry Institute of Linguistics, 1990).

Language Index

Adamawa-Ubangi, 346
Afar, 338
Afrikaans, 40, 71, 73, 84, 190
Afroasiatic (*also* Afro-Asiatic), 186, 346, 352
Ainu, 187, 345–6
Akateko, 76, 99–101, 194, 335
Akkala Saami, 192, 395
Albanian, 189–90, 331–2, 353, 410
Aleut, 314
Algonquian, 74, 185, 187, 350–1, 367, 411
Algonquian-Ritwan, 350
Alsea, 335
Altaic, 345–6, 352
Amazonas Quechua, 179–81
Amerind, 344–5, 353, 357–8
Amharic, 338
Amoy, 63–4
Anatolian, 147, 190, 383, 392–3
Ancash Quechua, 179–81
Andaman Islands languages, 346
Andaqui, 357
Anglo-Saxon *see* Old English
Anyuak, 338
Apache, 68–9
Arabic, 63–5, 68, 71, 81, 89–90, 117, 203, 267
Arandic, 37
Arapahoan, 411
Arawakan *see* Maipurean
Arawak-Taino, 90
Ari, 356
Armenian, 77, 191, 203, 207, 349
Assamese, 191
Atakapa, 357
Athabaskan, 185, 335, 345
Austric, 345
Austro-Asiatic, 186, 345
Austronesian, 168, 185, 187,189–90, 209, 345–6, 369
Austro-Tai, 345

Avestan, 27, 191, 387
Awakateko, 80, 194, 196
Awngi, 338
Ayacucho Quechua, 179–81
Aymara, 79, 167
Aymaran, 196

Bactrian, 191
Balkan Romance, 124
Baltic, 63, 65, 72, 168, 191, 337–8, 352
Baltic German, 337
Balto-Finnic, 45, 59–61, 192, 241–2, 298–9, 302–3, 337, 407; *see also* Finnic
Balto-Slavic, 191
Baluchi, 191
Bantu, 32, 117, 185, 346, 369
Basque, 63, 184, 187, 345
Basque–Caucasian, 345
Basque–Sino-Tibetan–Na-Dene, 345
Beja, 338
Bella Bella, 336
Belorussian, 191, 337
Bemba, 294
Bengali, 191
Benue-Congo, 346
Berber, 185–6
Bihari, 191
Biloxi, 359
Breton, 70, 190
Brule Spanish, 57–61
Brythonic, 190
Bulgarian, 191, 331–2
Burushaski, 187

Cabecar, 357
Caddoan, 346
Cajamarca Quechua, 179–81
Carib, 90
Cariban, 64, 185, 306
Carian, 190

Catalan, 124, 190, 203
Celtiberian, 190
Celtic, 89, 190, 387, 417
Central Algonquian, 140–1
Central/Eastern Malayo-Polynesian, 193
Central Malayo-Polynesian, 193
Chadic, 185
Chatino, 335
Cheremis *see* Mari
Chibchan, 185–6
Chibchan-Paezan, 352
Chicomuceltec, 194–6, 371–2
Chilanga Lenca, 171–3
Chimakuan, 335–7, 342
Chinantec, 335
Chinese, 63–4, 84, 185, 203, 207, 217, 223
Chinookan, 336
Chinook Jargon, 83
Chipaya, 358
Chiricahua Apache, 68–9
Chocho, 335
Chol, 66, 70, 72, 76–8, 100–2, 142–3, 194–5, 198, 333, 335
Cholan, 42, 70, 77, 194, 196, 198, 365–6
Cholan-Tzeltalan, 194, 199–200, 412
Choltí, 100, 194
Chontal, 194
Chortí, 194, 317
Chuckchi–Kamchatkan, 346
Chuj, 80, 142–3, 194
Chujean, 194
Chulupí, 250–1
Chuvash, 412
Classical Greek (Athenian Greek, Attic Greek) *see* Greek
Comanche, 403
Coosan, 335–6
Copainalá Zoque, 334
Coptic, 203, 207
Cornish, 190
Cree, 141, 147, 367, 398
Creek, 79, 359
Cuitlatec, 333, 352
Cushitic, 185–6, 338–9
Cuzco Quechua, 45, 179–81
Cypriotic Arabic, 78
Cypriotic Greek, 78, 203
Czech, 78, 84, 191

Dalmatian, 124, 190
Danish, 105, 124, 190, 337
Dene–Sino-Tibetan, 345
Dravidian, 34, 44–5, 68, 70, 80, 167, 185, 332–3, 346, 352
Dravidian–Japanese, 345
Dravidian–Uralic, 345
Dutch, 63, 83, 118, 124, 190, 273, 371

Early Modern English, 7–8, 11–12, 14–15, 105

Eastern Algonian, 411
Eastern Mayan, 194
Eastern Romance, 124, 190
Eastern Saami, 192
East Fijian dialects, 193
East Germanic, 36, 190
East Iranian, 191
East Slavic, 191
Ecuador Quechua, 179–81
Egyptian, 186, 203, 312
Elamite-Dravidian, 186
Enets, 192, 395
English, 4–15, 17, 19, 21–5, 28–30, 32–4, 36–43, 50–3, 63, 66, 68, 72–5, 79, 82–5, 90–1, 104–11, 113–21, 124–5, 127–8, 130, 139, 156–62, 187, 190, 203, 207, 220, 226, 238–40, 252–65, 267–70, 274, 275, 279–82, 284–5, 288–90, 293–5, 298, 303–4, 311, 313–14, 323–5, 349–52, 354–5, 366, 370–2, 413–16, 418; *see also* Old English, Middle English
Erzya Mordvin, 192, 395
Eskimo, 345
Eskimo-Aleut, 345–6
Eskimo–Uralic, 346
Estonian, 34, 59–61, 192, 241–2, 294, 299, 302–3, 308–9, 319–22, 327, 337, 395, 407, 418
Ethiopian Semitic, 338
Etruscan, 187
Eurasiatic, 346
Eyak, 335
Eyak-Athabaskan (*same as* Athabaskan), 346

Faliscan, 190
Faroese, 190, 207
Farsi *see* Persian
Finnic (Balto-Finnic), 45, 59–61, 192, 241–2, 298–9, 302–3, 337, 395, 407
Finnish, 29, 31–2, 36, 42–5, 47, 59–61, 63, 66–8, 72, 74–5, 79, 81, 83, 105, 114, 119–21, 147–54, 192, 204, 229–31, 241–2, 244–5, 260, 268, 270, 273–4, 284–7, 292, 298–305, 317, 337, 349–50, 352–3, 395, 407, 410, 418
Finno-Saami, 192
Finno-Ugric, 34, 65, 72, 148–54, 181, 192, 300, 308, 321, 337, 369, 395, 405–8, 419
Finno-Volgaic, 192
Flemish, 190
Forest Enets, 192
Forest Nenets, 192
Formosan languages, 190, 193
Fox, 141
French, 4–6, 8, 26, 29–30, 33, 35–7, 42–4, 63–5, 67, 71–3, 74, 79, 81–4, 89, 116, 118–19, 124–5, 127, 130–9, 188, 190, 203–4, 208, 213–15, 222, 252–3,

256–64, 274, 277–82, 294–5, 317,
    322–4, 349, 352, 356
Frisian, 40, 124, 190, 371
Fula, 356

Galician, 124, 190
Gallo-Romance, 124
Gaulish, 190
Gbaya, 350
Ge'ez, 338
Georgian, 203, 207, 385
German, 7, 9, 17, 30, 33, 36, 39–42, 63, 71,
    75, 78, 81–4, 107, 115, 117, 120, 124,
    159, 187, 190, 203–4, 218, 241, 253,
    256, 259–61, 264–5, 267, 270–1, 273,
    275–6, 295, 298, 316, 324–5, 337–8,
    351, 356, 371, 411–13, 418
Germanic, 7, 30, 38–40, 49–51, 63–6, 72–5,
    89, 104, 112, 156–64, 187–8, 190, 203,
    206, 239, 267, 275, 298, 300, 314, 349,
    351–2, 385, 418
Gheg (Albanian), 190
Gilyak, (Nivkh), 187, 346
Goidelic, 190
Gothic, 21, 39, 65, 75, 156–63, 190, 239, 276,
    298, 300, 351, 371–2
Greater Q'anjobalan, 194, 197, 199–200
Greek, 4–6, 21, 30–1, 34–7, 38–40, 64, 75,
    78–9, 81, 107, 112, 117, 156–63, 191,
    203, 226, 231–7, 256–7, 264, 273, 276,
    281, 293, 318–19, 327, 331–2, 350–1,
    371–2, 375–6, 387, 391, 401, 410
Gujarati, 38, 191
Gumuz, 338
Gur, 346

Haida, 335–6, 346
Halkomelem, 336
Hamitic, 323
Hamito-Semitic, 356
Hanti *see* Ostyak
Hawai'ian, 84, 168–9
Hebrew, 84
Hindi-Urdu, 38, 191, 220, 332–3
Hittite, 147, 190, 351, 368, 393
Hmong-Mien, 185
Hokan, 346
Honduran Lenca, 171–3
Huastec, 71, 76, 100–1, 139–40, 194–7, 359,
    363–4
Huastecan, 194, 199–200
Huave, 333, 335
Hungarian, 63, 147–54, 192, 369, 395, 407,
    409, 410, 412, 418

Ibero-Romance, 124
Icelandic, 124, 188, 190, 207
Illyrian, 189
Inari Saami, 182–3, 192, 395
Indic, 185, 191

Indo-Aryan (*see* Indic), 38, 77, 80, 332, 337
Indo-European, 21, 30, 49, 72, 75, 109, 147,
    155–64, 166, 184–5, 187–91, 337, 340,
    345–6, 349, 351–3, 362, 367–8, 379–93,
    397, 399–402, 407–8, 410, 419;
    see also Proto-Indo-European
Indo-Iranian, 188, 191, 391, 408
Indo-Pacific, 346
Indo-Uralic, 346
Indonesian, 64, 246–7
Ingrian, Inkeri, 192, 301, 395
Insular Celtic, 190
Iranian, 185, 191, 381, 388
Irish *see* Old Irish, Irish Gaelic
Irish Gaelic, 190
Iroquoian, 314, 346
Italian, 28, 30, 43, 64–5, 72, 85, 106, 116, 119,
    121, 124–5, 127, 131–3, 135–9, 190,
    203, 206, 208, 260, 277
Italic, 4, 28, 188, 190, 387–8, 392
Italo-Celtic, 190
Italo-Dalmatian, 124
Itzá, 87, 194, 196
Ixcatec, 335
Ixil, 80, 194, 196

Jakalteko, 71, 80, 101, 142–3, 194, 335
Janjero, 338
Japanese, 63–4, 85, 91–9, 203, 345
Japanese–Altaic, 346
Japanese–Austronesian, 346
Japanese–Austro-Thai, 345
Jaqaru, 345
Jicaque, 173–6, 247–8
Jicaquean, 173
Junín Quechua, 179–81

Kalapuyan, 335–6
Kamas, 192
Kannada, 45, 203
Kaqchikel, 41, 70, 80, 127–8, 141–2, 177–9,
    194–6, 198, 243, 263, 335, 349, 413
Karaim, 337
Karelian, 192, 303, 337, 352, 395
Kartvelian, 185, 346, 352
Kashmiri, 191
Kashubian, 337
Kefa, 338
Kemi Saami, 192, 395
Khanty (Ostyak), 192, 395, 420
Khoe, 73, 77
Khoisan, 77, 346
Khotanese, 191
K'iche', 32, 72, 76, 79–80, 99–102, 139–42,
    177–9, 194–5, 204, 206, 263, 265, 268,
    335, 358–9, 413
K'ichean, 79–80, 141–3, 177–9, 194, 199–200,
    205, 334
Kikuyu, 32
Kildin Saami, 182–3, 192, 395

Koasati, 358–9
Komi (Zyrian), 149–50, 192, 395
Kordofanian, 346
Korean, 65, 345
Kota, 332
Kru, 346
Kurdish, 191
Kwa, 294, 346

Lacandon, 194, 196
Lake Miwok, 265, 268, 350, 357
Lapp *see* Saami
Latin, 5–6, 8, 18, 21, 25–6, 28–30, 33–7, 39,
    41–5, 48–51, 63–4, 72, 75–6, 81–3, 89,
    109–13, 116, 118–19, 123, 125, 136,
    138, 156–60, 162, 167, 190, 203, 206,
    213, 234, 238, 254–62, 267–8, 270–1,
    276–9, 281–2, 294, 309, 324, 349,
    351–2, 356, 372–5, 410–11, 415, 417
Latino-Faliscan, 190
Latvian, 191, 337
Lencan, 171–3
Lithuanian, 27, 65, 157, 191, 337
Livonian, 192, 303, 337, 395
Lower Chinook, 335
Low German, 190, 337
Lude, 192, 395
Lule Saami, 182–3, 192, 395
Lushootseed, 337
Luvian, 190
Lycian, 190
Lydian, 190

Macedonian, 191, 331–2
Macro-Siouan, 346
Madi, 356
Maipurean (Arawakan), 185
Makah, 78, 146, 198–9, 337, 341
Malay, 63–4, 350
Malayalam, 80
Maltese, 184
Mam, 52, 80, 100–1, 140, 142–3, 194–6, 334
Mamean, 52, 79, 194, 196–7, 199–200
Manchu, 345
Mandarin (*see* Chinese), 203, 207
Mande, 346
Mandigo, 63
Mansi (Vogul), 192, 395, 419
Manx, 190
Māori, 26, 85–9, 168–9, 350
Marathi, 80, 191
Mari (Cheremis), 190, 192, 194, 395, 407
Matacoan, 250
Mator, 192
Maya-Chipayan, 346, 357
Mayan, 32, 40, 42, 44, 52, 66, 68, 70–1, 73–4,
    76, 79–80, 99–102, 112, 127, 139–43,
    177, 185, 189, 191, 194–200, 204–7,
    227, 243, 263, 265, 268, 333–5, 346,
    357–9, 362–5, 369, 371, 397, 412, 417

Mayan-Mixe-Zoquean, 359
Mazatec, 335
Menomini, 141
Meso-Melanesian Languages, 193
Messapic, 189
Miao-Yao *see* Hmong-Mien
Middle Egyptian, 203
Middle English, 8–9, 13, 46, 52, 82, 111, 115,
    117, 121, 254–6, 261, 269, 276, 323,
    325, 370–1
Middle High German, 42, 325
Middle Indo-Aryan, 38
Miwok-Costanoan, 265, 268
Mixean, 73, 145
Mixe-Zoquean, 66, 69, 73, 99, 145, 333–5,
    359, 398, 412–13
Mixtec, 335
Moksha Mordvin, 192, 395
Mongolian, 345
Mon-Khmer, 185–6
Mopan, 100–1, 194, 196
Mordvin, 190, 192, 395, 407
Moru, 356
Mosan, 342–3
Motocintlec, 72, 76–7, 100–2, 140, 194, 197
Munda, 185–6, 332
Muskogean, 79, 358–9

Na-Dene, 345–6
Nahuatl, Nahua, 24–5, 35, 63, 69–70, 73, 83,
    90, 106, 115, 220, 228–9, 245–6, 332–5,
    413
Navajo, 205
Nenets, 192, 395, 407
Nez Perce, 73
Ngandi, 288
Nganasan, 192, 395
Nicobarese, 186
Niger-Congo, 346
Niger-Kordofanian, 346; *see also* Niger-Congo
Nilo-Saharan, 346, 356
Nitinat, 78, 146, 198–9, 337, 341
Nivaklé *see* Chulupí
Nivkh *see* Gilyak
Nootka, 78, 145–6, 198–9, 337, 341, 415
Nootkan, 145–6, 198–9, 341
North and Central Vanuatu languages, 193
North Caucasian, 185
Northern Samoyed, 192
North Germanic, 39, 190, 337
North New Guinea languages, 193
North Saami, 182–3, 192, 241, 299, 322, 395
Northwest Iranian, 191
Norwegian, 190, 217, 337
Nostratic, 345–6, 352–3
Numic, 403
Nunggubuyu, 288
Nyamwezi, 32

Ob-Ugric, 192

Oceanic, 168, 193
Occitan, 124, 190
Ofo, 359
Ojibwa, 141
Old Church Slavonic (OCS), 27, 191, 350–1
Old English, 4, 7–10, 21, 27, 29, 34, 36,
      39–41, 46, 52–3, 63, 81, 104–5, 107,
      109–10, 115–17, 121, 155–60, 162–4,
      203, 226, 238, 252, 255–6, 258, 260–1,
      264, 267, 269–70, 276, 298, 314, 324,
      356, 414–16, 418
Old Finnish, 285–6
Old French, 4–5, 8, 30, 32, 35, 37, 63, 67, 72,
      82, 106, 116–17, 125, 130, 260, 262,
      268, 274, 414
Old High German (OHG), 21, 39, 65, 157,
      159–60, 162–4, 276, 300, 325, 349,
      418
Old Icelandic (*see* Old Norse), 267
Old Irish, 38
Old Norse, 38, 40, 46, 267, 298, 415, 418
Old Prussian, 191, 337
Old Russian, 24, 67, 418
Old Spanish, 76, 115, 120, 287, 309–10, 256,
      258, 261, 271, 277, 281
Old Swedish, 118, 418
Oluta Popoluca, 334
Omotic, 338, 356
Orokolo, 170–1
Orokolo-Toaripi, 170
Oscan, 190
Ossetic, 77, 191
Ostyak *see* Khanty
Ostyak Samoyed *see* Selkup
Otomanguean, 185, 333–4
Otomí, 335

Palaic, 190
Pali, 53–5
Pama-Nyungan, 37, 186
Panare, 306–8
Papuan families, 346
Parthian, 191
Pashto, 191
Peninsular Spanish *see* Spanish
Pennsylvania German, 294
Penutian, 346
Permiak, 192, 395
Permic, Permian, 192, 395
Persian (Farsi), 191, 350
Phrygian, 189
Pipil, 19, 45, 106, 204, 206, 288, 317, 333–5,
      350, 353
Pite Saami, 192, 395
Plains Cree, 141
Polish, 191, 337
Polynesian, 168
Popoloca, 335
Poqomam, 80, 141–2, 177–9, 194, 198, 364–5
Poqomchi', 80, 112, 194, 198, 364–5, 413

Portuguese, 4, 116, 124–5, 127, 131–6, 139,
      188, 190, 203, 217
Pre-Germanic, 30, 110
Proto-Admiralty, 193
Proto-Aimaran, 167
Proto-Algonquian, 402, 410
Proto-Australian, 346
Proto-Austronesian, 193
Proto-Balto-Finnic, 59–61, 242, 302–4, 319
Proto-Bantu, 77
Proto-Celtic, 38, 187
Proto-Central Algonquian, 141, 350, 398
Proto-Central Pacific, 193
Proto-Dravidian, 44, 72
Proto-Eastern Malayo-Polynesian, 193
Proto-Eastern Mayan, 196
Proto-Eastern Oceanic, 193
Proto-Finno-Ugric, 47, 148, 154, 394, 396–7,
      405–8, 410
Proto-Germanic, 21, 23, 28, 38–9, 46, 49–50,
      65, 74–5, 110, 112, 123–4, 187–8, 206,
      239–40, 264, 276, 300, 313, 356
Proto-Huastecan, 196
Proto-Indo-European (PIE), 21, 28–30, 36, 39,
      43, 49, 72–3, 109, 112, 147, 156–64,
      187–9, 206, 238, 267, 349, 356, 368,
      369, 379–93, 399, 401, 405, 408, 410,
      420
Proto-Iranian, 408
Proto-Je, 349
Proto-Jicaque, 173
Proto-K'ichean, 112, 142–3, 210
Proto-Lencan, 171
Proto-Malayo-Polynesian, 190, 193
Proto-Mayan, 70, 76, 112, 139–40, 143, 194,
      196–7, 200, 357–8, 363–4, 366, 397
Proto-Mixe-Zoquean, 73, 145, 398
Proto-Muskogean, 359
Proto-Nahua, 19, 106, 206
Proto-New Caledonia, 193
Proto-Nootkan, 78, 146, 199, 341
Proto-Nuclear Micronesian, 193
Proto-Nuclear Polynesian, 193
Proto-Numic, 403–4
Proto-Oceanic, 193
Proto-Papuan Tip, 193
Proto-Polynesian, 193, 210
Proto-Quechuan, 179, 210
Proto-Remote Oceanic, 193
Proto-Romance, 42, 123–5, 131, 138, 146–7,
      167, 188, 189, 206, 303
Proto-Saami, 181, 210, 322
Proto-Salishan, 404
Proto-Scandinavian, 38, 46, 75
Proto-SE Solomonic, 193
Proto-Slavic, 55–6
Proto-South Halmahera/West New Guinea, 193
Proto-South Vanuatu, 193
Proto-Tokelau, 193
Proto-Tongic, 193

Proto-Tulu, 168
Proto-Tzotzilan, 357
Proto-Uralic, 306, 394, 396, 405–8
Proto-Uto-Aztecan, 69, 220, 402–3
Proto-Western Oceanic, 193
Proto-World, 345–6, 353
Punjabi, 191

Q'anjobal, 76, 80, 99–101, 194
Q'anjobalan, 76, 194, 200
Q'eqchi', 44, 76, 80, 100–2, 112, 141–2,
    177–9, 194–5, 198, 335, 364–5, 413
Quapaw, 359
Quechua (Quechuan), 45, 63, 79, 90, 115,
    179–81, 294
Quileute, 336–7

Rarotongan, 168–9
Rhaeto-Romance, 124, 190
Ritharngu, 288
Romance, 4, 30, 42, 50, 72, 118–19, 123–8,
    130–9, 146–7, 167, 185, 189, 203, 252,
    277–8, 303, 316
Romani, 191, 331, 337
Romanian, 124, 190, 203, 331–2
Rotuman Fijian, 193
Russian, 24, 56, 64–5, 82, 85, 112, 191, 205,
    337, 349, 401, 418

Saami (Lapp), 79, 181–3, 192, 241–2, 299,
    321–2, 327, 395, 406
Sabellic, 190
Sahaptian, 73
Sahaptin, 336
Sakapulteko, 194
Salishan, 185, 335–7, 342, 404
Samoan, 168–9, 248–50
Samoyed, 192, 395
San, 77
Sanskrit, 21, 26, 27, 30, 43, 51, 53–5, 63–4,
    72, 156–64, 191, 218, 234, 238, 243–4,
    351, 368
Sapaliga Tulu, 34–5, 56–7, 168
Sardinian, 124, 190, 203
Sayula Popoluca, 66, 68, 99
Scandinavian, 33, 38, 40, 63, 85, 204, 338,
    415–16, 418
Scots English, 5, 370
Scottish Gaelic, 190
Selkup, 192, 395
Semitic, 184–6, 338, 346, 385
Serbo-Croatian, 191, 331
Seri, 350
Setswana, 117
Shivalli Tulu, 34–5, 168
Shoshoni, 403
Sidamo, 338
Sierra Popoluca, 334
Sindhi, 191
Sinhalese, 191

Sino-Tibetan, 185, 187, 345
Siouan, 185, 346, 359
Sipakapense, 194
Skolt Saami, 192, 395
Slavic, 42, 112, 181, 188, 191, 337–8, 401, 418
Slovak, 191
Slovene, 191
Sogdian, 191
Somali, 338
Sorbian, 191, 418
Sotho, 77
South Caucasian see Kartvelian
South Dravidian, 44
Southern Samoyed, 192
South Saami, 192, 395
South Slavic, 191
Spanish, 4, 17–20, 26, 28–30, 33–7, 39, 41–5,
    48, 50, 57–61, 63–73, 75, 81, 83–5,
    89–90, 99, 105, 107–9, 111–12, 114–16,
    119–21, 124–5, 127, 131–7, 139, 188,
    190, 203–7, 217, 254–65, 267–71,
    277–8, 281–2, 287–8, 292, 294, 309–10,
    317, 321, 327, 352, 357, 359, 371–2
Sudanic, 356
Sumerian, 187, 346
Swahili, 117
Swampy Cree, 141, 147, 367
Swedish, 28, 33, 46, 59, 67, 79, 81–2, 85, 118,
    124, 188, 190, 203, 217, 255, 301, 317,
    337, 418

Tai, 185
Tai-Kadai, 185
Taino, 64, 90
Tajik, 191
Takelma, 335–6, 357
Tamil, 64, 80
Tarascan, 187, 334–5
Tasmanian, 346
Tatar, 65
Tavgi see Ngansan
Teco, 98, 194, 196
Telugu, 80
Temne, 63
Tepehua, 334
Tequistlatec, Tequistlatecan, 333, 335
Ter Saami, 192, 395
Thracian, 189
Tibetan, 413
Tibeto-Burman, 185, 332
Tigre, 338
Tigrinya, 338
Tillamook, 335
Tlapanec, 335
Tlingit, 335–6, 346
Toaripi, 170–1
Tocharian, 190, 392, 408
Tocharian A, 190
Tocharian B, 190
Tojolabal, 72, 76, 101, 194, 227–8

Tol (Jicaque), 173–6, 247–8
Tongan, 168–9
Tosk Albanian, 190, 332
Totonac, Totonacan, 69, 204, 333–5, 357
Totontepec Mixe, 334
Trique, 335
Tsimshian, 335–6
Tulu, 34, 56–7, 80, 167–8
Tundra Enets, 192, 395
Tundra Nenets, 192, 395
Tunebo, 352, 357
Tungusic, 345
Tupian, 186
Tupi-Guarani, 90
Turkic, 63, 65, 184, 185, 337, 345, 412, 418
Turkish, 79, 331
Twana, 337
Tzeltal, 76, 99–102, 107, 139–40, 194, 334
Tzeltalan (*also* Tzotzilan), 194
Tzotzil, 68, 71, 76, 78, 99–102, 112, 194, 357
Tz'utujil, 80, 141, 177–9, 194, 196, 333

Udmurt (Votyak), 65, 147–54, 192, 395, 407
Ugric, Ugrian, 192, 395
Ukrainian, 191, 337
Umbrian, 190
Ume Saami, 182–3, 192, 395
Upriver Halkomelem, 336
Ural-Altaic, 346
Uralic, 184, 186, 189, 192, 305, 345–6, 350, 352, 405–8
Uru-Chipayan, 346
Uspanteko, 80, 141–2, 177–9, 194
Ute, 403
Uto-Aztecan, 19, 24, 45, 70, 182–3, 186, 204, 228, 245, 288, 333–5, 350, 402–3

Venetic, 189
Veps, 192, 303, 337, 395
Vogul *see* Mansi
Volgaic, 189–90, 358

Vote, 192, 299, 302–3, 337, 395
Votyak *see* Udmurt
Vulgar Latin, 29, 33, 42, 123, 294

Wakashan, 335–7, 342, 404
Warndarang, 288
Wellamo, 338
Welsh, 190
Wendish *see* Sorbian
Western Malayo-Polynesian, 193
Western Romance, 33, 41, 124, 131–3, 188, 190
Western Saami, 192
West Fijian dialects, 193
West Germanic, 39, 190, 226, 337
West Iranian, 191
West Semitic, 385
West Slavic, 191
Wiyot, 350–1
Wolaytta *see* Wellamo

Xhosa, 77
Xinkan, 74, 80, 333–4, 412, 417

Yana, 350
Yemsa *see* Janjero
Yenisei Samoyed *see* Enets
Yiddish, 85, 190, 265, 337–8
Yucatec (Maya), 70, 139–40, 142–3, 194–6, 334, 358, 362–3, 413
Yucatecan, 73, 194, 196–7, 199–200
Yuchi, 346
Yukagir-Uralic, 346
Yurats, 192, 395
Yurok, 350

Zapotec, 335
Zoquean, 145
Zulu, 73, 77
Zuni, 187
Zyrian *see* Komi

Name Index

Name Index

Abondolo, Daniell, 190
Adams, D. Q., xviii, 189, 401
Aitchison, Jean, 327
Alvar, Manuel, 213
Andersen, Henning, 221
Anttila, Raimo, 65, 69, 82, 103, 109, 241, 318–19, 324, 354
Arlotto, Anthony, 38, 103

Bach, Adolph, 324
Baehrens, W. A., 375
Beekes, Robert S. P., 40, 107
Berlin, Brent, 205
Bloomfield, Leonard, 140–1, 147, 367, 398
Brown, Cecil H., 359
Brugmann, Karl, 17–18, 212
Burgess, Gelett, 273

Callaghan, Catherine A., 74, 265
Campbell, Lyle, 32, 77–80, 90, 140, 176, 210,
    283, 288, 296, 306, 335, 337, 343, 347,
    352, 358, 366, 396–9, 408
Cantinflas, Mario Moreno, 119
Carroll, Lewis, 273
Carpelan, Christian, 406
Caxton, William, 14–15
Chaucer, Geoffrey, 1, 13, 370
Cicero, 112–13
Collinge, N. E., 32
Corominas, Joan, 90
Coseriu, Eugenio, 221

Dahl, Osten, 338
Darmesteter, Arsène, 43
Dasher, Richard, B., 269, 271–2
Delbrück, Berthold, 17, 368–9

Ebert, Robert Peter, 325
Emeneau, Murray B., 333

Ferguson, Charles, 338
Fleischman, Suzanne, 124
Fleming, Harold C., 356
Fogelberg, Paul, 396–7
Fowler, Catherine, 403
Friedrich, Paul, 399, 401, 410

Gamble, Geoffrey, 74, 265
Garret, Andrew, 189
Gildea, Spike, 309
Gilliéron, Jules, 213, 218, 323
Gimbutas, Marija, 379
Goddard, Ives, 410–11
Gordon, Elizabeth, 220
Grassmann, Hermann, 161, 164
Greenberg, Joseph, 348, 351–3, 356–7, 359
Grimm, Jakob, 3, 16, 62; see also Grimm's
    Law
Grimm, Wilhelm, 3
Guillotin, Joseph-Ignace, 273
Grondona, Verónica, 308

Haas, Mary R., 69, 198, 337, 341, 367
Hajdú, Péter, 394, 396–7, 406–7, 412
Häkkinen, Kaisa, 189–90, 407–8
Harris, Alice C., 283, 288, 296
Heath, Jeffrey, 288
Heine, Bernd, 269, 286–7, 293
Helmont, J. B. van, 273
Herzog, Marvin, 218
Hock, Hans Henrich, 5, 82
Hogg, Richard M., 40
Holloway, Charles E., 57
Hopper, Paul J., 269, 296–7
Horrocks, Geoffrey, 376
Jakobson, Roman, 354–5
Janhunen, Juha, 190, 306, 394
Jasanoff, Jay H., 189

Jespersen, Otto, 105, 316
Joki, Aulis J., 408
Joos, Martin, 312
Joseph, Brian D., 5, 82, 293, 352
Justeson, John S., 70, 73, 366, 398

Kaiser, Mark, 352–3
Kaufman, Terrence, 82, 335, 398
Kay, Paul, 205
Kimball, Geoffrey, 359
Kinkade, M. Dale, 404
Kiparsky, Paul, 326
Klima, Edward, 289
Koch, Harold, 37
Koivulehto, Jorma, 408
König, Ekkehard, 269–70
Koptjevskaja-Tamm, Maria, 338
Korhonen, Mikko, 322, 405–6
Krause, Wolfgang, 75, 370
Kuhn, Franz Feliz Adalbert, 379
Kuryłwicz, Jerzy, 292
Kuteva, Tania, 296

Labov, William, 218–24, 315, 326
Lapesa, Rafael, 90
Lass, Roger, 14, 370–1
Lehmann, Christian, 297
Lehmann, Winfred P., 312
Lepelley, René, 214
Leskien, August, 17
Lightfoot, David, 291, 326
Luther, Martin, 108

McAdam, John Loudon, 273
Maclagan, Margaret A., 220
Mallory, J. P., xviii, 189, 379–80, 401–2, 405,
    410
Martinet, André, 48
Meillet, Antoine, 292, 345, 356, 358
Menner, Robert, 324
Milroy, James, 221–2
Milton, John, 273
Müller, Max, 378
Mutaka, Ngessimo, 32

Nash, Ogden, 3

Öhmann, Emil, 324
Olson, Ronald D., 357
Oltrogge, David, 176
Osmond, Meredith, 190
Osthoff, Hermann, 17–18, 212

Palmer, Leonard R., 115, 214, 324
Pāṇini, 218
Paul, Hermann, 17, 113, 120, 326
Pawley, Andrew, 190
Pictet, Adolphe, 379
Pinker, Stephen, 5
Polenz, Peter von, 108, 412

Rankin, Robert L., 359
Ravila, Paavo, 114, 255, 260, 406
Reh, Mechthild, 293
Resnik, Melvyn C., 90
Ringe, Donald A. Jr., 189, 353, 355
Róna-Tas, András, 412
Ross, Malcolm, 190
Roques, Mario, 213, 323
Ruhlen, Merritt, 353

Salminen, Tapani, 189–90, 395, 408
Sammallahti, Pekka, 189–90, 394, 396, 405–6, 408
Sandfeld, Kristian, 332
Sandwich, the 4th Earl of (John Montagu), 273
Sapir, Edward, 69, 400, 414–15, 417
Sayce, Archibald Henry, 312
Schleicher, August, 213
Schmidt, Johannes, 213
Schrader, Otto, 379
Schuchardt, Hugo, 213
Shakespeare, William, 11–12, 103, 118, 252
Shevoroshkin, Vitaly, 352–3
Siebert, Frank, 402, 410
Smith-Stark, Thomas, 82, 335
Snow, Dean, 402
Spaulding, Robert K., 90
Spenser, Edmund, 273
Suhonen, Seppo, 405
Swadesh, Morris, 201, 203, 207, 342
Sweet, Henry, 211, 313
Sweetser, Eve, 269

Swift, Jonathan, 273

Taylor, Ann, 189
Teeter, Karl V., 351
Thomason, Sarah G., 338
Thompson, J. Eric S., 417
Tosco, Mauro, 338
Traugott, Elizabeth Closs, 269–72, 293, 296–7

Vendryes, Joseph, 68
Verner, Karl, 162–4; *see also* Verner's Law
Volta, Alessandro, 273

Wächli, Bernard, 338
Wakelin, Martyn, 416
Wang, William, 222
Warnow, Tandy, 189
Watkins, Calvert, xvii, 380
Weekley, Ernest, 184
Weinreich, Max, 217
Weinreich, Uriel, 78, 218–19, 329
Weiss, Michael, 381
Wessén, Elias, 28, 33, 38, 46, 118
Winteler, J., 218
Witkowski, Stanley R., 359
Wright, Larry, 327, 329
Wulfila (Bishop), 371
Wundt, Wilhelm, 314

Zeps, Valdis, 338
Zvelebil, Kamil V., 44, 72

Subject Index

accident *see* chance similarities
accommodation, 66–8
acronyms, 275
actuation problem, 219, 222
adaptation, 66
adstratum *see* linguistic area
affrication, 45
allophonic changes *see* non-phonemic changes
amalgamation, 6, 117, 277–8, 368
amelioration *see* elevation
analogical extension, 108–9
analogical levelling, 106–8
analogical models, 111–13
analogical restoration, 318–19
analogy, 6, 103–21, 166, 254, 266, 272, 277, 298–9, 318–19, 368

anaptyxis, 36
aphaeresis, 34–5
apocope, 33–4
apparent-time studies, 220
Appendix Probi, 373–5
archaeology, 209, 339, 378–9, 393, 401, 406, 411
archaisms, 303–5
areal linguistics, 77–9, 330–43
assimilation, 28–30, 37

back formation, 116–17, 304
Balkans linguistic area, 331–2
Baltic linguistic area, 79, 337–8
basic vocabulary, 126, 128, 201–7, 347–9, 352, 355, 359

bilingualism, 62, 67
blending, 118–20, 277, 279
borrowing, 6, 8–9, 62–102, 104, 106, 126–7,
    165, 198–9, 204, 212–15, 222–4, 239,
    272, 300–1, 310–43, 347, 349–50, 352,
    360, 362, 404, 407–8, 411–13, 419
branch *see* subgroup
breaking, 40
broadening *see* widening
bundle of isoglosses, 216

calques, 81–2, 254, 334, 372, 398
Caucasus linguistic area, 77
chain shift, 49–52, 196
chance similarities, 127–8, 331, 348–50,
    355–6, 360
Classics Maya civilization, 70, 76, 366
classification, 122–4, 132, 184–210, 340–1,
    362–5, 400
clipping, 6, 278–9
cognate, 50, 72–3, 126–8, 138, 142, 146–8,
    202–3, 253, 302, 349–50, 355–8, 401,
    407
cognate sets, 126–8, 134–6, 148, 352
cohesion, 284
comparative method, 18, 122–83, 212, 225,
    240–2, 305, 345, 367–9, 378–9
compensation, 319–22, 326–7
compensatory lengthening, 37–8
compounding, 275–6, 368
compression *see* clipping
conditioned merger *see* primary split
conditioned sound change, 18, 20, 26–7,
    137–8, 160, 164, 226, 238
consonant gradation, 320–2
constraints problem, 218–19
contamination *see* blending
convergence area *see* linguistic area
correspondence set *see* sound correspondence

Dahl's Law, 32
daughter languages, 123–4, 129, 166
deaffrication, 45
deflection, 264, 324–5
degemination, 45
degeneration, 260–5, 271
deletion, 33–5
diachronic linguistics, 4
dialect, 186, 211, 217, 223–4, 340, 378
dialect atlas, 212–16, 223
dialect borrowing, 223–4
dialect geography *see* dialectology
dialectology, 211–18, 368
diffused sound changes, 80, 198, 362, 364–5
diffusion, 77–80, 330–43, 347, 356, 398
diffusion area *see* linguistic area
diphthongization, 40, 42
directionality of borrowing, 69–74
directionality of sound changes, 132–3, 151–5,
    226–7, 232

displacement, 259
dissimilation, 30–2, 36–7, 161
distant genetic relationships, 112, 187–8, 209,
    227, 330, 342–3, 344–60
donor language, 62
drag chain *see* pull chain

economy, 133–6, 151–3, 155, 227
elevation, 261–2, 271
ellipsis *see* clipping, displacement
embedding problem, 219
emphatic foreignization, 82
epenthesis, 35–7, 228–9
Ethiopian linguistic area, 338
Ethnic identity *see* ethnicity
Ethnicity, 418–20
ethnographic analogy, 378, 405–6
ethnohistory, 378, 420
etymology, 5–6, 213, 252–3, 281, 353
euphemism, 262–4, 324, 414
evaluation problem, 219
excrescence, 36–7
expressive creations, 278–9; *see also*
    onomatopoeia
extension, 283, 384–8, 286, 299; *see also*
    widening
external causes of change, 221, 316–17

fading *see* semantic bleaching
family-tree model, 123–4, 166, 188–9,
    211–13
final devoicing, 41
focal area, 216
folk etymology, 72, 114–16
fricativization *see* spirantization

gemination, 44–5
generative approaches, 289–92
genetic relationship, 212, 331; *see also*
    language family
genetic unit, 187
glottochronology, 200–10, 347–8
grammatical alternation, 163–4; *see also*
    Verner's Law
grammatical change, 7–10, 283–311; *see also*
    syntactic change
grammatical correspondences, 350–1
grammaticalization, 283, 254, 256, 266, 278,
    292–7, 311
Grassmann's Law, 30–1, 155, 161, 164
Great Vowel Shift, 8–9, 23, 42–3, 51–2,
    239–40, 354, 370
Grimm's Law, 48–51, 112, 155–64, 313–14,
    349, 356

haplology, 40
hispanisms, 63, 71, 75–6, 99–102
history of linguistics, 2, 217–18
homeland *see* linguistic homeland
homophony, 269, 304, 322–5

hyperbole, 264
hypercorrection, 82, 113–14

immediate models, 111–13
Indian linguistic area *see* South Asian linguistic area
interference (phonetic interference), 66–7
internal causes of change, 221, 316, 328
internal reconstruction, 225–51, 378
isogloss, 215–16
isolate, 187, 225

Junggrammatiker *see* Neogrammarians

Kurgan culture, 379

laísmo, 105–6
language (definition of), 186, 217
language acquisition, 289–92
language contact, 62–102, 165, 208, 212–13, 223, 291, 315, 330–43
language family, 122–4, 184–94
lect, 217
lengthening, 45; *see also* compensatory lengthening
lenition, 44
lexical change, 7, 9, 118, 252–4, 272–80
lexical conditioning *see* lexical diffusion
lexical diffusion, 222–4
lexical reconstruction, 298, 302
lexical replacement, 7, 128, 322–4, 347–8
lexicostatistics *see* glottochronology
linguistic area, 330–43
linguistic geography *see* dialectology
linguistic homeland, 378, 399–411
linguistic migration theory, 378, 399–411
linguistic palaeontology *see* linguistic prehistory
linguistic prehistory, 122, 209, 378–419
literary coinage, 273
litotes, 264–5
loan *see* loanword
loan translation *see* calque
loanword, 62–77, 116–17, 128, 130, 204, 239, 378, 401, 404, 407–8, 411–13
logographic writing system, 369
loss, 325–6
luxury loan, 64

macro-family (macro-), 187–8
majority-wins principle, 131–3, 135
markedness, 47
mass comparison *see* multilateral comparison
Mayan hieroglyphics, 362, 365–6
maximum differentiation, 47–8
maximum diversity, 400, 408–9
mechanisms of syntactic change, 283–8
merger, 20–5, 75–6, 79, 166, 198, 325, 363
Mesoamerica (culture area), 412–13

Mesoamerican linguistic area, 81–2, 333–5, 340, 412–13
metanalysis, 117–18; *see also* reanalysis
metaphor, 291, 256–7, 262
metathesis, 39
metonymy, 257–9, 265, 271, 291
metre, 370, 372
models of linguistic change, 211–23
monophthongization, 42–3
morphological change, 7–9, 284–5, 302–3
morphological conditioning, 318–20, 327
morphological reconstruction, 302–3
multilateral comparison, 348–9
multiple causation, 319, 326–9
mutual intelligibility, 217

narrowing, 255–6, 265, 297
nasal assimilation, 41
nasalization, 44, 131, 189, 316–17
naturalness, 47, 129, 145
natural selection, 326
neoclassical compound, 276
Neogrammarians, 17–18, 103, 120, 164, 211–14, 218, 222–3, 368
neologism, 272–9
network theory, 222
non-immediate models, 111
non-phonemic changes, 19–20
Northwest Coast linguistic area, 42, 78, 80, 146, 198, 335–7, 340–2
nursery forms, 348, 354–5, 360

obscenity (avoidance of), 262–4
obsolescence (of vocabulary), 279–80
occasional spellings, 370–1
Olmec civilization, 398, 412–13
onomastics, 418
onomatopoeia, 78, 278, 348, 350, 353–4, 360
orthographic changes, 8, 10, 362

palatalization, 24, 41–2, 55, 67, 110, 153, 198
paragoge, 37
parent language *see* Proto-language
pejoration *see* degeneration
philology, 4, 8, 361–77
phonemic change, 18–19, 20–7
phonemic change *see* sound change
phonetic change *see* sound change
phonological change *see* sound change
phonological accommodation, 66
phonological change *see* sound change
phonological reduction, 292, 297
phonologicalization *see* secondary split
phylum, 187–8
place names *see* toponyms
polysemy, 266
popular etymology *see* folk etymology
pre-language, 226
pre-Proto-language, 240

prevention (of change), 319–20, 324, 326–7
primary split, 25
proportional analogy, 104–8
prothesis, 35
Proto-Algonquian homeland, 402, 410–11
Proto-Finno-Ugric culture, 396–7
Proto-Finno-Ugric homeland, 405–8
Proto-Indo-European language *see*
    Indo-European
Proto-Indo-European culture, 379–93
Proto-Indo-European homeland, 379, 399–402,
    408
Proto-language, 122–7, 129, 131, 136, 139–40,
    143–7, 165–6, 189, 191, 225, 240
Proto-Mayan culture, 397
Proto-Mixe-Zoquean culture, 398
Proto-Numic homeland, 403–4
Proto-Salishan homeland, 404
Proto-Uralic culture, 394–6
Proto-Uralic homeland, 405–8
Proto-Uto-Aztecan homeland, 402–4
pull chain, 47–52
push chain, 47–52

rate of loss, 202, 207–8
rate of retention, 202–3, 207
real-time studies, 220
reanalysis, 117–18, 283–8, 296–9, 304
recipient language, 62
reconstructed vocabulary, 378–94, 396–412
reconstruction, 74–7, 124–83, 198–200,
    297–306, 330, 340–1, 362, 367, 419
reflex, 126, 132–3, 135, 141
regularity principle, 17–18, 109–10, 137, 141,
    155–64, 166, 207, 212–15, 218, 222–4,
    324, 367–8
regular sound change, 17–18, 30, 32, 36, 39,
    320, 324
relative chronology, 46–7, 56, 76, 170–1, 181,
    226, 229–37, 246–7, 249–50
relic area, 216
relics *see* archaisms
residual area *see* relic area
restructuring, 291
retrograde formation *see* back formation
rhotacism, 38–9, 110–11, 234
root creation, 273
runic alphabet, 10

secondary split, 25–6
semantic bleaching, 293, 296–7
semantic borrowing *see* calques
semantic change, 6, 13–14, 252–72, 280–1,
    293, 296–7, 353, 410, 414
semantic loans *see* calques
semantic shift *see* semantic change
shared aberrancy, 350–2, 359
shared innovation, 190–1, 194–200, 208, 341,
    364
shared retention, 197, 199, 341

shift (sound), 19, 79
shortening, 45–6; *see also* clipping
simplification, 315
sister language, 123–4
sociolinguistics, 217, 219–22, 291, 315, 317,
    370
sound change, 6, 8–9, 16–61, 69, 103, 109–11,
    129–46, 150–64, 177, 194–200, 212–15,
    218, 222–4, 226–39, 285, 296–7,
    316–18, 320–5, 327, 349, 356, 362–8
sound correspondence, 72, 126–47, 150–5,
    168, 170–1, 173, 177, 179, 181, 341,
    348–50, 359, 367
sound laws *see* sound change
sound symbolism (affective symbolism,
    expressive symbolism), 77–8, 348,
    350
South Asian linguistic area, 77, 332–3
specialization *see* narrowing
spelling pronunciation, 68, 317
spirantization (fricativization), 45
split, 22–6, 238–9
sporadic sound change, 6, 9, 27, 30, 32, 39
Sprachbund *see* linguistic area
spurious forms, 359
Stammbaum *see* family-tree model
stock, 187
strengthening, 44
Sturtevant's paradox, 109
subfamily *see* subgroup
subgroup, subgrouping, 131–2, 184, 186–200,
    208, 330, 340–1, 362, 364–5, 367,
    400
submerged features *see* shared aberrancy
substratum, 315; *see* areal linguistics
surface manifestation, 284
Swadesh list, 201–7
syllabaries, 369
symmetry, 47, 144, 155
synchronic linguistics, 4
syncope, 33, 36, 46
synecdoche, 259–60
syntactic blends, 120
syntactic borrowing, 288, 300–1
syntactic change (grammatical change), 7–9,
    283–331
syntactic reconstruction, 297–306

taboo, taboo replacement (taboo avoidance), 6,
    206, 262–4, 414
therapy (therapeutic change), 319–21, 326
theories of language change, 313–29
toponyms, 415–18
transition problem, 219, 223
typology, 134, 145–6, 155, 226

umlaut, 22–3, 30, 46, 75, 107, 109, 239–40,
    252
unconditioned sound changes, 18–20, 23, 26,
    238

universals, 134, 328–9, 331

variable, 220
variation, 219–20
Verner's law, 110, 155, 162–4
vocabulary change *see* lexical change
vocabulary loss, 5, 9, 279–80, 322–3
voicing, 41, 235

wave theory, 211–15
weakening *see* lenition, semantic
    bleaching
widening, 254–5, 265
word order changes, 284, 296
Wörter und Sachen, 413–15, 417
writing systems, 362, 369, 372, 393
written records, 361–77, 393